LENIN

D1387564

BLOOMSBURY READER

Discover books by Ronald Clark published by
Bloomsbury Reader at
www.bloomsbury.com/RonaldClark

LENIN
The Man Behind the Mask

RONALD CLARK

BLOOMSBURY READER
LONDON · NEW DELHI · NEW YORK · SYDNEY

This electronic edition published in 2012 by Bloomsbury Reader

Bloomsbury Reader is a division of Bloomsbury Publishing Plc,

50 Bedford Square, London WC1B 3DP

ISBN: 978 1 4482 0090 0
eISBN: 978 1 4482 0222 5

Visit www.bloomsburyreader.com to find out more about our authors and their books
You will find extracts, author interviews, author events and you can sign up for
newsletters to be the first to hear about our latest releases and special offers

Printed and bound by CPI Group (UK) Ltd, Croydon, CR0 4YY

Contents

Lenin: The Man Behind the Mask

Ronald W. Clark's widely praised major biographies include lives of Einstein, Bertrand Russell and Sigmund Freud. Born in London in 1916, he served as a War Correspondent with the Canadian Army in the Second World War, landing in Normandy on D-Day, and later covered the Nuremberg and other war crimes trials in Germany.

He wrote extensively on scientists and the impact of science on contemporary life, and displayed an ability to describe scientific work excitingly but accurately. His books include the well-known *The Birth of The Bomb* (1961), the first detailed account of the European work that led to the nuclear age, and its sequel, *The Rise of the Boffins* (1962), dealing with other aspects of science and war. These were followed by his biography of *Tizard* (1965), a life of Sir Henry Tizard, scientist and government adviser during the Second World War.

Ronald Clark then took as his subjects, makers of modern thought: *The Huxleys* (1968), a history of the Huxley family: *J. B. S: The Life and Work of J. B. S. Haldane* (1968); *Einstein: The Life and Times* (1973); *The Life of Bertrand Russell* (1975); *Freud: The Man and the Cause* (1980); and *The Survival of Charles Darwin: A Biography of a Man and an Idea* (1985). He was also a distinguished historian of mountaineering and wrote extensively on the subject.

Ronald W. Clark completed the text of *Lenin: The Man Behind the Mask* shortly before his death in 1987.

Acknowledgements

Responsibility for the facts in *Lenin: The Man Behind the Mark*, and for the opinions expressed in it, is entirely the author's expect where the reverse is made clear. He is nevertheless extremely grateful for the help and advice of many Russian experts in Britain, the United States and Canada, and would like to thank the following in particular: for having read separate chapters of the book in draft, Professor John Erickson, the University of Edinburgh; Professor John Keep, the University of Toronto; Professor Lionel Kochan, the University of Warwick; Professor Alec Nove, the University of Glasgow; Dr S. A. Smith, the University of Essex; Dr A. L. Tait, the University of Birmingham; Professor Robert Thurston, the University of Texas at El Paso; Professor Z. A. B. Zeman, the University of Oxford; and for reading the entire manuscript in draft, Orlando Figes of Trinity College, Cambridge.

The author wishes to thank the Clerk of the Records, House of Lords Record Office and the Trustees of the Beaverbrook Foundation for permission to quote from the Lloyd George Papers; the Cumbria Record Office, Carlisle, for granting access to Sir Esmé Howard's Papers; and the Houghton Library, Harvard University, for permission to quote from its archives.

For the use of copyright material the author wishes to thank Lawrence & Wishart for permission to quote from their English translations of Lenin's *Collected Works* and the writings of this wife, Krupskaya; Allen & Unwin for extracts from *Not By Politics Alone* edited by Tamara Deutscher; Mouton & Co. for extracts from *The Trotsky Papers* edited by Jan M. Meijer; the University of Michigan Press for extracts from Nikolai Valentinov's *The Early Years of Lenin*; the Oxford University Press for extracts from Valentinov's *Encounters with Lenin*; Peter Janson-Smith for extracts from Isaac Deutscher's *Lenin's Childhood*; Methuen & Co. for extracts from *Memoirs of a British Agent* by R. H. Bruce Lockhart; Chapman & Hall for extracts from *The Letters of Lenin* edited by Elizabeth Hill and Doris Mudie; Doubleday for extracts from Trosky's *The Young Lenin*; Harrap for extracts from Trostsky's *On Lenin*; the Columbia University Press for extracts from *The October Revolution* by Roy Medvedev; Henry Holt for extracts from I.N., Steinberg's *In the Workshop of the Revolution*; Cambridge University Press for extracts from Thomas H. Rigby's *Lenin's Government: Sovnarkom 1917–1922*; the Beaverbrook Foundation for extracts from David Lloyd George's *War Memoirs*; and Madame Marguerite Bonnet of the Trostsky Estate for quotations from Trotsky's writings.

Among the library staffs who have been helpful are those of London University's School of Slavonic and East European Studies; the Marx Memorial Library, London; the British Library (formerly the British Museum Library); and the London Library. The staff of Elgin Public Library, a few miles from Ramsay MacDonald's birthplace at Lossie-mouth, was particularly helpful in obtaining material not easily available elsewhere. Valuable assistance was also given by Hazel Orme far beyond her responsibilities as copy editor.

The Mansell Collection, the David King Collection and the picture libraries of the Novosti Press Agency, and of the Society for Cultural Relations with the USSR have been helpful in tracking down specific illustrations.

RWC
9 March 1987

Apprenticeship

1

The Boy from the Volga

From the Novyi Venets or New Summit and the Staryi
Venets or Old Summit, each rising some 400 feet above the
central stretches of the River Volga, in 1870 it was possible to
look down on a peaceful landscape dominated by the town of
Simbirsk. Its 30,000 inhabitants were served by no railway; only
poor roads linked it with the rest of Russia or even with the port
of Astrakhan at the mouth of the Volga more than 600 miles to
the south. Apple and cherry orchards covered much of the
rolling country that stretched across the immensities of Russia,
and at night there could be heard the song of numerous night-
ingales. Here, in surroundings that had changed little over the
centuries, Vladimir Ilyich Ulyanov, later known to the world as
Lenin, was born in April 1870–10 April by the Julian calendar
then used in Russia, 22 April by the Gregorian calendar of
Europe which was twelve days ahead in the nineteenth century,
then thirteen days ahead until 1 February 1918 when Russian

dating was brought into line with Western usage.[*]

On 16 April the boy was baptized in the local church of St Nicholas, his parents being described as 'collegiate councillor Ilya Nikolayevich Ulyanov and his lawful wife Maria Alexandrovna of the Orthodox Faith.' His first name, often used in the affectionate form 'Volodya', was taken from the saint who had converted Russia in the tenth century to the Eastern Orthodox Church, while 'vladi-mir' means 'rule the world'.

Lenin's background was by no means totally plebeian, a fact often obscured in twentieth-century Russia. It is true that his father was the son of a shoemaker with Kalmuck blood, a Mongolian ancestry that may have accounted for Lenin's slanted eyes and high cheekbones, but Ilya Nikolayevich had, nevertheless, attended Kazan University, some 150 miles up the Volga from Simbirsk. Here he was supported by Nikolay Lobayechevsky, the pioneer of non-Euclidean geometry, and later, for his work as a Government inspector, was brought formally into the ranks of the nobility with a civilian rank the equivalent of major-general. His wife, Maria Alexandrovna Blank, Lenin's mother, was the daughter of a doctor from a wealthy and cultured family in Lübeck, northern Germany; thus Lenin, the prototype revolutionary, had to admit to a grandfather who had been a serf-owning landlord. But it was

---

[*] The Julian calendar, used in Russia until 1 February 1918, is given from Lenin's birth until 1900, from 1905 to 1907 and from 1917 to 1 February 1918. The Gregorian calendar is used for the periods of Lenin's life in Europe – from 1900 to 1905 and from 1908 to 1917. In a few cases, notably at the times of the two Revolutions in 1917 and of the events leading to the treaty of Brest-Litovsk in March 1918, both dates are given to avoid confusion, the date in brackets being that of the Gregorian calendar.

not only this bourgeois background that Lenin inherited from his mother. 'No sooner had I come to know [his mother] than I discovered the secret of Vladimir Ilyich's charm,' a friend was later to say.

Lenin's parents had much in common, notably a respect for hard work, but in many ways they differed considerably. Ilya Nikolayevich was a practising member of the Russian Orthodox Church; his wife Maria sometimes accompanied him to services but did so more out of duty than conviction, being of a basically sceptical nature. Quite as important was the difference in emphasis between the father's dedication to the spread of education in general, and the mother's dedication to the care and education of her own children. Both were to affect Lenin's upbringing, the first by pushing his father some way up the professional ladder, the second by ensuring that at school he was regularly at the top of his form and that he was subsequently able to romp through his professional studies in less time than most young men.

Details of Lenin's comfortable if not wealthy middle-class background are not easy to come by, and for reasons which are highlighted in more than one study of his early days. 'Accurate and complete information about [his] ancestry', it has been pointed out, 'has been systematically suppressed or overlooked [in Russia] because it does not fit into the carefully projected official image of the founder of Bolshevism – because it would reveal that Lenin did not come "from the people" or from a low social origin.' Lenin himself never attempted to fudge the facts or conceal that as an exile in 1900, after asking to visit his wife, also in exile, permission was granted 'to Vladimir Ilyich Lenin, nobleman by birth'.

Attempts to trace the Ulyanov family tree further back towards its roots have brought suggestions that Lenin had

Jewish blood; some attention has focused on his maternal grandfather, Dr Aleksandr Dmitriyevich Blank, who has been described as a converted Odessa Jew. This has been denied by other researchers, but no evidence to settle the question has come from the Russian archives, voluminous as they are on the background to Lenin's life, which in itself can be considered suspicious. The idea of a Jewish root somewhere below Lenin's family tree was later nourished by those holding anti-Jewish or anti-revolutionary views, and with the geographical and ethnographic circumstances of his forebears such a possibility would be difficult to disprove. However, the idea would not have been given such weight but for the rise of the Nazis who found it useful when elaborated by Hermann Fest in his *Bolshevismus und Judentum: Das jüdische Element in der Führerschaft des Bolshevismus* (Berlin; Leipzig, 1934).

What remains undoubted is the intellectual quality of Lenin's parents, particularly of his father for whom in 1854 Lobayechevsky secured a post as teacher of physics and mathematics in the Dvoriansky Institut, an institute for the nobility in Penza. It was here that Ilya Nikolayevich met Maria Blank whom he married in 1863. Soon afterwards he left the Penza Institute for the Gymnasium at Nizhni Novgorod (renamed Gorky in 1932). There followed six years of academic life which he then abandoned to become an inspector of schools.

Ulyanov's territory as inspector was the *guberniya* (province) of Simbirsk and he and his wife moved to its main town of the same name in the autumn of 1869. Their first child, Anna, had been born in 1864; their first son, Aleksandr, also known as 'Sasha', two years later. A second daughter, Olga, was born in 1868 and died the same year. Maria was again pregnant when the family moved to Simbirsk where Vladimir was born in 1870, to be followed by a second Olga in 1871, Nikolay, born and died in 1873, Dmitri in 1874, and Maria, also known as 'Manyasha', in 1878.

The empty steppes among which the children were brought up, and through which flowed the mile-wide Volga, lay some 650 miles from Moscow and nearly 1,500 miles to the south-east of St Petersburg, the centre of revolutionary emotion during the nineteenth century and the capital of Russia until after the Revolution of 1917. Yet the area had not escaped the upheavals that from the start of recorded history had regularly drenched the country in blood.

In 1671 a major battle was fought in Simbirsk, the revolutionary Don Cossack, Stenka Razin, defeated, 800 of his followers hanged, and Razin handed over to the Tsar by more conservative colleagues for execution in Moscow. Repercussions from revolutions and attempted revolutions continued to reach as far as the Volga – from the days of Emilian Pugachev, who called himself Tsar Peter III and was executed in 1775, to the early years of the nineteenth century, which in 1825 witnessed the failure of the Decembrists to seize power. The abolition of serfdom in 1861 followed the humiliations of Russia in the Crimean War but failed to assuage general discontent constantly bubbling beneath the surface; the second half of the nineteenth century saw the rise to fame of at least three pre-Marxian revolutionaries under whose influence Lenin was to grow up: Mikhail Aleksandrovich Bakunin (1814–76), Aleksandr Ivanovich Herzen (1812–70) and Nikolay Gavrilovich Chernyshevsky (1828–89). During Lenin's early years, two of his later comrades also marched into history: Vera Ivanovna Zasulich, who in 1878 fired at and wounded the chief of the St Petersburg police, but was acquitted by a jury and then protected from rearrest by the crowd; and Georgy Valentinovich Plekhanov, an early exponent of philosophical Marxism, who in 1876 addressed workers and students in the Kazan square, St Petersburg, at what became one of the first workers' demonstrations in Russia. Seven years later Plekhanov, Vera Zasulich and Pavel Borisovich Akselrod, a carpenter who was twice forced to leave Russia because of his political views, and who had been converted to Marxism by his working experiences, founded the Liberation of Labour Group outside Russia, one of the first bodies with which Lenin was to become associated. He was also an editor of Lenin's *Iskra (The Spark)*. Plekhanov, who emigrated from Russia in 1880, quickly became a leading theoretician of the Marxist movement. During the early years of the twentieth century his view of Lenin varied between extreme support and extreme opposition. He criticized terrorism, derided many of the policies that Lenin advocated as he created what became the Bolshevik Party, and strongly denounced Lenin's determined opposition to the war that broke out in 1914.

The complex relationships that these attitudes produced were all subsidiary to Lenin's overwhelming and dedicated support for a revolution in Russia and the spread of Marxism throughout the world, aims to whose success he devoted his life; however bitter the arguments with Plekhanov, or with other supporters of drastic change in Russia, his conviction of the overriding need for revolution was continually seeping into him by a process of intellectual osmosis. The later claim by his sister Maria was true: 'His entire life was one of revolutionary struggle and his private life was part of that struggle, part of his labour on behalf of the cause of the proletariat.'

The family move to Simbirsk in 1869 had repercussions on all the Ulyanovs. The town's standing is left in no doubt by the description given by I. A. Goncharov in his novel *The Precipice* (1870). Looking over the city, he wrote, one saw

'. . . various kinds of houses – little houses, little huts bunched close together, houses scattered along the hills and the edges of ravines with balconies, sun-blinds, belvederes, annexes, superstructures, with Venetian windows, pigeon-houses, small wooden boxes for starlings, and courtyards overgrown with grass. There were alleys winding their way between fences, empty streets without houses carrying the inscription "Moscow Street", "Astrakhan Street" and "Saratov Street", with bazaars where heaps of bast were piled up, salted and dried fish, vats of tar and *kalatch* [a kind of fancy bread], the gaping gates of inns with the far-spreading smell of manure. *Over the city lay the torpidity of peace, the calm on land* which is found at sea, the calm of the generous rural and urban Russian life. Everything is colour-ful, green, and everything is silent. The dust from wheels passing by forms a pattern along the streets; in the shade of the fence a goat and chickens are resting. Dogs, rolled up in groups of three or four, lie in ill-assorted heaps on every farmstead. Here and there someone sticks his head out of a window, looks around, gaping in both directions, spits, and disappears. On the deserted street one can hear two or three talk among themselves for a whole *verst*, the voices resound and ring out in the emptiness as do the steps on the wooden pavement. Below the city the Volga flows as if in deep thought, overgrown with small islands, bushes, dotted with banks. In the distance the sandy mountain sides turned yellow, and on them the forest showed up blue; the seagulls, smoothly flapping their wings, sank down to the water hardly touching it, and rose upwards again in circles; high above the gardens a kite drifted slowly.'

In 1888, Goncharov added:

'The outward appearance of my home town represented nothing else but a picture of slumber and stagnation. Thus one wants to fall asleep, looking at this caim, at the sleepy windows with lowered blinds, at the sleepy physiognomy of the people sitting in the houses or chancing to be in the street. We don't have anything to do, all of these people think, yawning and looking lazily at you.'

All his life Lenin fought against the lethargy of Simbirsk and the apathy epitomized in Goncharov's Oblomov, a character created as the personification of apathy. In his early fifties, speaking to the All-Russian Congress of Metal Workers, Lenin cited Oblomov as a warning to the new Russia he was helping to create, as a man who

'lay on his bed all the time and made up plans. Many years have passed. Russia has undergone three revolutions, and yet the Oblomovs remain . . . for Oblomov is not only a land-owner or a peasant, he is also an *intellectual;* he is not only an *intellectual,* but a worker and a Communist as well . . . The old Oblomov has remained [with us], and we must wash him, cleanse him, shake him and thrash him, in order to get some sense [out of him].'

One reason for Lenin's semi-obsessional interest in Oblomov was that in his youth he had been taken by his father with other young men from Simbirsk on a tour of the places described in *The Precipice,* a day's walk which made a lasting impression on him. This was to be expected since Lenin reacted strongly to external influences, and just as in the physicist's world every action produces a reaction, so in Lenin's mind circumstances tended to produce a natural opposition. Thus it seems likely that the slumbering atmosphere of Simbirsk towards the end of the nineteenth century played its part in encouraging the enthusiasm for change and revolution which so vigorously prodded his desire to mould a new world from the old.

The Ulyanovs' first house in Simbirsk was small, but following Lenin's birth, and the promotion of his father, who had started on his progress in the civil service, the family moved to a larger home, no. 46 on what was then Moscow Street and is now Lenin Street. While no. 46 was not comparable to the more wealthy Simbirsk houses, it had ten or eleven rooms and a garden. Lenin's room was next to Aleksandr's room at one end of the house while Anna's and that of the three younger children were along the other staircase. To one side of the courtyard there was a small building, once used as a kitchen but converted into a workshop and laboratory, and a smaller building which the Ulyanovs rented out. The garden contained poplars, elms and fruit trees as well as strawberries and raspberries.

This little domestic empire was serviced by an odd-job man, a cook, the cook's daughter, and a nurse, Varvara Grigor'evna Sarabatova who worked for the Ulyanovs for nearly twenty years and brought up three of their children, including Lenin, of whom she said: 'These other children are good – they are gold – but my Voloden is a diamond.' It was probably their nurse whose relatives were killed fighting the Bulgarians when Lenin was aged seven and whom he remembers as commenting: 'Russian blood is flowing in vain because of some alien and accursed Bulgarians. What good are they to us, we have more than enough trouble ourselves.'

Ulyanov's promotion in 1874 from inspector to director of the *guberniya*'s primary schools meant that he was even more frequently absent from home carrying out his duties. Eventually awarded the Order of St Vladimir and raised to the rank of Actual State Councillor, he formally wore a blue gold-embroidered uniform, and was properly addressed as 'Your Excellency'. But for his wife there were long days with only the children for company. According to Anna, her mother

'very painfully felt the change from the lively Nizhnyi Novgorod to this wretched and dull provincial hole, to the poor housing, less civilized conditions, but above all, to the complete loneliness . . . She would tell us later how sad the first years at Simbirsk were for her. Her only friend was the midwife Ilina, who lived in the same house and assisted at the delivery of all the younger children.'

In this atmosphere Lenin grew up a normal healthy lad, stout enough in his early years to earn the nickname of 'Kubyshkin' meaning bellied jug and, according to his sister, frequendy tumbling down and knocking his head. He outgrew the tendency and became a boisterous boy who would end games with his toys by breaking them. Until the age of five he was taught at home by Maria Ulyanova who encouraged her children to produce their own handwritten news sheet. Later there were 'French only' and 'German only' days with instruction from their mother, who spoke both languages fluently. From the age of five Lenin's education was taken over by a tutor who came daily to the house, a practice which lasted for four years until in August 1879 he began attending the local Gymnasium. The head was Fyodor Kerensky, father of Aleksandr Kerensky, who as head of the Provisional Government some three decades later struggled with Lenin for control of revolutionary Russia.

It was a closely knit family in which Lenin was brought up. All the children helped their mother, especially when their father was absent on his travels, and acquaintances long remembered how they would all lay the table at mealtimes with Aleksandr, the eldest son, having the task of carrying in the samovar. It was Aleksandr who exercised the greatest influence over Vladimir. While he had a natural bent for literature and history, science dominated Aleksandr's thoughts and he was constantly carrying out chemical experiments, often helped by his younger brother. Much of his pocket money was used to buy test tubes or chemicals, and even before he left school, with a gold medal for being top of the class, he was determined to become a scientist.

According to Anna Ulyanova, Aleksandr not only had a profound influence on the young Lenin's maturing mind but even helped restrain a naturally quick temper. 'At first,' she wrote, 'Vladimir imitated his brother and then started consciously to curb his quick temper, and when he grew up we never, or almost never, observed any signs of it in him.' The two boys occupied adjoining rooms, worked together in the family garden, often played chess, walked on the banks of the Volga and swam in its tributary, the Sviyaga.

Aleksandr easily came to influence not only Lenin's attitude to work but also his social attitudes. These were suggested in the elder brother's essay on 'Qualities a Person Must Have to Be Useful to Society and the State', an essay in which he demanded honesty, love for work, a firm character and intelligence and knowledge.

Whether by following the example of Aleksandr, or by drawing on the virtues with which he had been born, Lenin made a definite mark as a youngster in a family which, while decidedly progressive, never veered openly towards the extremes which led to revolutionary enthusiasm. Ilya Ulyanov was almost the prototype of those who supported evolutionary rather than revolutionary change. Even this, however, tended to set him and his family apart from the mainstream of Simbirsk society so that his professional accolades and honours do not seem to have been acknowledged among his fellow citizens as they might otherwise have been. Ulyanov himself probably did not worry greatly about this, but it is doubtful if his observant son Vladimir missed neighbours' instinctive reactions to the family.

The boy's appearance and character have both been described in some detail by Aleksandr Naumov, who shared Lenin's desk at the Gymnasium. 'Rather short, but fairly powerfully built,' Naumov has written of his colleague, who invariably won the gold medal for being top of the class while Naumov won the silver for being runner-up. He continued:

'with slightly hunched-up shoulders and a large head, slightly compressed at the sides, Vladimir Ulyanov had irregular and, I would say, unhandsome features: small ears, prominent cheekbones, a short, wide, slightly squashed nose, and, in addition, a large mouth with yellow, widely-spaced teeth. With no eyebrows on his freckled face, Ulyanov had longish, blond, soft and slightly curly hair which he combed straight back. But all these irregularities were redeemed by his high forehead, under which burned two fierce little brown eyes. His ungainly appearance was easily forgotten in conversation under the effect of these

14

small but unusual eyes which sparkled with extraordinary intelligence and energy . . .

'At school Ulyanov differed considerably from all of us, his comrades. Neither in the lower forms nor later did he take part in the childish and youthful games and pranks, always keeping to himself, busy either with his studies or some written work. Even when walking between classes, Ulyanov kept to his books, reading as he walked up and down past the windows. The only thing which he liked as a distraction was playing chess, a game in which he usually came out victorious, even when playing against several opponents . . .'

All agree that Vladimir Ulyanov was gifted, keen, possessed with insatiable, scholarly curiosity and an extraordinary capacity for work. According to one investigator of his youth he was:

'a walking encyclopaedia, extremely useful to his comrades and the pride of his teachers.

'As soon as he appeared in the form Ulyanov was immediately surrounded by schoolmates who asked him for a translation or for the solution of a problem. He helped everybody willingly, but it seemed to me at that time that he nevertheless resented those who tried to live and do their schoolwork at the expense of another's labour and intellect.

'Ulyanov had an even and rather gay temperament, but he was extremely secretive and cool in his relations with comrades; he had no friends. He said "you" to everybody [instead of the "thou" common amongst schoolmates in Russia] and I do not remember a single time when he would unbend and allow himself to be intimately outspoken with me. On the whole, he commanded respect and displayed businesslike authority to his comrades, but one couldn't say that he was liked, rather that he was esteemed, and although everyone in the form realized his intellectual and scholarly superiority over all of us, it is only fair to point out that Ulyanov never flaunted it.'

Lenin continued to progress as well at the Gymnasium as he had under his mother's instruction. He worked hard and methodically and his sister remembered how he would copy out French irregular verbs so carefully that they looked on the page as if printed. It appears that Anna Ulyanova did not 'remember with advantages' since Lenin's teachers seem to have been equally impressed by his work. 'A very gifted and reliable student' went the report from one. 'He is very success-ful in all of his subjects. His conduct is exemplary.' And, the following year: 'He is very attentive in class and diligent. His conduct is excellent.'

One reason for Lenin's success as a youngster was the method-ical way in which he tackled problems, a characteristic contrasting strongly with the view of the born revolutionary as being, typically, rather unorganized. When set the task of writing an essay, he would first draw up a rough outline and write its headings down the side of a sheet of paper. During the following days, he would jot in notes of sources, possible refer-ences and quotations on the other side. Only when this was finished would he incorporate the work on the left and right sides of the paper into a final draft.

At school all seemed set for a prosperous life during which he would diligently climb the ladder of a suitable profession. His elder brother Aleksandr successfully entered St Petersburg University, studied science and sent back to the family regular newsletters which were read aloud at the evening meal and whose sober character is shown by one which went: 'I am sending father the brochure "Mathematical Sophisms" which he wanted very much. I believe it might be very useful to Vladimir if he studies them on his own. Did he receive the German translation I sent him?'

Two events now directed Lenin on to other paths, events without which the Russian Revolution of 1917 would certainly have taken a different course. The first was the death of his father from a brain haemorrhage in January 1886 at the early age of fifty-five. A few months earlier Ilya Ulyanov had learned to his dismay that he was to be compulsorily retired. He believed, possibly with good cause, that one reason was the progressive line he had taken since coming to Simbirsk; in fourteen years he had helped found more than 400 new secondary schools, but the Tsar's Government was now less inclined to promote the spread of education. Although Ulyanov took the news badly it is not certain that disappointment was the prime cause of his death, but on 13 January he fell ill without warning, lay down on a sofa in his study, and was dead before the afternoon was over. There followed an elaborate funeral but he had left his family almost penniless and his widow was forced to apply immediately for a pension. When approved the amount was so small that she had to let part of the family home.

The most significant result of Ilya Ulyanov's death was that Lenin lost his religious faith, thus enabling him to embrace easily any of the revolutionary beliefs which were struggling for ascendancy in the Russia of the 1880s. As with almost all details of his youth, there is not merely disagreement but contradiction about

17

when agnosticism took over; even Lenin and his wife Krupskaya later gave different dates.

Lenin is reported to have said that he had been an atheist since the age of sixteen. Friends subsequently provided an array of colourful detail, one even claiming that he tore a cross from his neck and threw it on the ground. The story certainly suggests an attitude which was to be significant in the years ahead even though Lenin's religious feelings could never have been described as devout. His father's death was followed, in the next year, by a second, more shocking calamity.

On 1 March 1887 – according to the Julian calendar – his elder brother, Aleksandr, was arrested in St Petersburg and charged with plotting to assassinate the Tsar, Aleksandr III, with a bomb he had concealed in a medical encyclopaedia. Their sister Anna had been visiting Aleksandr when the police arrived at his rooms and she too was arrested, together with other members of what was soon discovered to be a long-planned plot. These events were to be of paramount significance since they affected Lenin's future and therefore that of the world. However, they were by no means exceptional in the situation that had been developing in Russia since the middle 1850s.

The first revolutionary group to form in that country during the nineteenth century was that of the Decembrists (founded soon after the Napoleonic wars and recruited largely from aristocratic officers), whose attempt to seize power in 1825 failed totally. Five of the leaders were hanged, some were imprisoned and others were banished to Siberia. It was only after Russia's defeat in the Crimean War and the accession of a reformist tsar, Aleksandr II, that new revolutionary ideas began to flourish, many of them covered by Populism, an agrarian socialist group with an anarchistic flavour which included a wide variety of social and political aims supported to differing degrees by the threat of violence.

Prominent in the movement were two groups bearing the same title of Zemlya i Volya (Land and Freedom). The first, founded in 1862, included certain followers of Chernyshevsky, whose writings were so greatly to influence Lenin, and Herzen. The second Land and Freedom group was founded in 1876. Government repression and the relative ineffectiveness of the second group's agitation, mainly among the peasants, brought about a split in 1879 when advocates of terrorist tactics formed Narodnaya Volya (People's Freedom). Some of its members assassinated Aleksandr II on 1 March 1881 and the party was disbanded soon afterwards by the police although isolated groups continued to exist. Other Populists who emphasized propaganda and agitation among industrial workers as well as peasants set up another group, which turned towards Marxism and whose leaders, Plekhanov, Akselrod and Vera Zasulich, formed the Liberation of Labour group in 1883. At first it was all but isolated from the small clandestine groups of workers and radical intellectuals in Russia, but in the 1890s this began to change.

In 1887 Lenin, like most alert young men of the time, was aware of the discontent below the surface of Russian life, but there is no indication that he was yet drawn to, let alone personally involved in, the developing revolutionary movement. For at least some time, literature successfully competed with politics for his interest. He would read and reread Turgenev even during the months when he lived in the same room with Aleksandr.

He was certainly surprised in 1887 not only by the assassination plot in which his brother was to have played a leading part but by his own ignorance of his brother's line of thought. When, for instance, Aleksandr was asked 'Why did you not try to escape abroad?', it apparently having been known that the police had been on his track, he is claimed to have answered: 'I did not want to escape – I would rather die for my country.' This accords with the widely accepted belief that had he petitioned for mercy, a course he would not consider, the sentence would have been a term in prison. Instead, he was sentenced to death.

His mother had hastened to St Petersburg, vainly hoping that by personal intervention with the authorities she might lighten what she still thought would be no more than a long prison sentence. She travelled by horse and by wagon, and she travelled alone since despite various attempts to find a companion for her, no one from Simbirsk would accompany the mother of a terrorist. This was typical of local reaction; even an old schoolteacher who had regularly visited the Ulyanov household to play chess, stopped calling. Lenin was bitter about the treatment of his family by the people of Simbirsk. Their attitude confirmed, if it did not give birth to, Lenin's distrust of the liberal approach to the problems of the times.

In court Aleksandr ruled out any chance of clemency when he said in a speech:

'After studying social and economic sciences, [this] conviction of the abnormality of the existing system strengthened in me and the vague hopes of freedom, equality and fraternity acquired strictly scientific and socialist forms in my mind. I realized that a change in the social system is not only possible but even unavoidable . . . Among the Russian people you can always find a dozen men or so who are so utterly devoted to their ideas and take the misfortunes of their country so much to heart that they do not consider it a sacrifice to die for their cause. There is nothing that can frighten such people.'

The execution of Aleksandr, in the Schlüsselburg Fortress on 8 May together with that of others who had taken part in the conspiracy, caused something of a stir, even in Russia where political offences were dealt with severely. Dmitri Ivanovich Mendeleyev, the chemist who created the periodic table and who had been one of Aleksandr's teachers, is said to have commented: 'These accursed social questions, this needless, I believe, enthusiasm for revolution – how many great talents it is destroying.'

Aleksandr's mother turned grey-haired overnight. Anna, against whom no charges were brought, was released from prison within a few days but only on condition that she went to live at Kokushkino in the province of Kazan, 150 miles up the Volga from Simbirsk where her mother had inherited one-fifth of a family estate, and remained there under police surveillance.

The effect on Lenin of his brother's execution has been described by a school-fellow.

'. . . the evening was so still, as if nature itself wanted to calm and reassure us. I said so to Volodya. After a moment of silence he told me that on 8 May Alexander had been put to death. I was stunned. Droopingly, slouchingly, Volodya sat next to me. Under the rush of thoughts, it was impossible to speak. We sat so for a long time in silence. At last Volodya got up, and, saying nothing, we went towards the town. We walked slowly. I saw Volodya's deep grief but also had the feeling that just then a spirit of firm determination welled up in him . . . Before parting I strongly grasped his hand. He looked into my eyes, responded to the hand-shake, and quickly turned and walked home.'

The significance of these events for the seventeen-year-old Lenin has been percipiently described by that inveterate enemy of Communism, Winston Churchill.

'He was at the age to feel [he had written of Lenin at the time]. His mind was a remarkable instrument. When its light shone it revealed the whole world, its history, its sorrows, its stupidities, its shams, and above all its wrongs. It revealed all facts in its focus – the most unwelcome, the most inspiring – with an equal ray. The intellect was capacious and in some phases superb. It was capable of universal comprehension in a degree rarely reached among men. The execution of the elder brother deflected this broad white light through a prism: and the prism was red.'

Lenin became deeply interested in the beliefs that had led his brother into revolutionary plotting and closely questioned a youth who had been a student with Aleksandr at St Petersburg University and had shared an apartment with him until shortly before his arrest. '[He] questioned me . . . especially about the impression Aleksandr had made on me when he sat in the dock,' the youth later wrote, '. . . but apparently not merely out of simple curiosity. He was especially interested in the revolutionary outlook and orientation of his brother.'

Lenin was apparently dissatisfied with the information he could extract from Aleksandr's friends, but he knew that his brother had had great respect for Chernyshevsky's *What Is To Be Done?*, written during the early 1860s when the author was held

22

in St Petersburg's St Peter and St Paul fortress prison; Lenin had read the book, part novel, part propaganda tract, at the age of fourteen. Now he read it again, more seriously, trying to gather from it the motives that had led Aleksandr along his path to the hangman's noose. Chernyshevsky was no compromiser, a believer in violence and subsequently an exile in Siberia for many years. Much later, when Lenin heard *What Is To Be Done?* criticized, his response was explosive.

'Chernyshevsky's novel . . . fascinated and captivated my brother. It also captivated me. *It ploughed me over again completely* . . . It is useless to read it when your mother's milk has not yet dried on your lips. Chernyshevsky's novel is too complex, too full of thoughts and ideas, in order to be understood and valued at a young age. I myself tried to read it . . . when I was fourteen years old . . . it was a worthless and superficial reading that did not lead to anything. But then, after the execution of my brother, knowing that Chernyshevsky's novel was one of his most favourite works, I began what was a real reading and pored over the book, *not several days, but several weeks.* Only then did I understand its full depth. It is a work which gives one a charge for a whole life.'

He continued to stress the importance of the Chernyshevsky book telling Vaclav Vorovsky:

'Before I came to know the works of Marx, Engels and Plekhanov, only Chernyshevsky wielded a dominating influence over me, and it all began with *What Is To Be Done?* . . . It is Chernyshevsky's great merit that he not only showed that any correctly thinking and truly honest person must be a revolutionary, but also something more important: what a revolutionary should be like, what rules he should follow, how he should approach his goal and what means and methods he should use to achieve it.'

In Siberia, to which he was exiled shortly before the turn of the century, Lenin built up a collection of photographs of revolutionary leaders. But while there were single pictures of Marx and Engels, there were two of Chernyshevsky. And years later, as ruler in the Kremlin, Lenin had a library containing a complete edition of Chernyshevsky's works.

Lenin's grief at his brother's execution, like that of his mother, is not in doubt. What has been debated, and still is, concerns some of its long-term effects. One result, which cannot be disputed, is that from now onwards he became a marked man; the police not unnaturally regarded the brother of a dedicated potential assassin as a suspect character: a man to be watched, reported on, and treated differently from the rest of the population. To one of Lenin's make-up this was an invitation to take the revolutionary road.

Until the traumatic impact of Aleksandr's execution on Lenin's life, however, there had been nothing inevitable about his dedication to revolution and no reason for him to set off along the path that would give him leadership of one-fifth of the world. It is true that, like many thinking men, he had a dislike of the excesses of the Russian autocracy and landowners. Also, he had a natural sympathy for the underdog and a warm humanity that was only slowly cooled and then frozen by the exigencies of gaining and keeping power. His intellect was soon to latch on to what he saw as the attractions of Marxism. And his skill as an organizer who understood the techniques necessary to survive in the revolutionary world of intrigue fitted him for underground work as well as the limbs of a mole fit it for burrowing. But these abilities could have remained latent in the competent young lawyer into which Lenin was quickly to grow. Within a few years a duality developed in Lenin's work and correspondence. Half his time was devoted to his work as a legal apprentice while the other half was spent studying and propagating the methods by which the overthrow of the Government could be achieved.

Yet it is clear that however important Aleksandr's execution may have been in driving Lenin down the road of the revolutionary, none of the motives conventionally thought of as leading to revolt were involved in his case. His early years had been the reverse of deprived and there is no indication that he, or any other member of the Ulyanov family, resented the richer circumstances in which the more prosperous inhabitants of Simbirsk lived.

If it is certain that the execution of Aleksandr brought Lenin under police surveillance, and also that from this time onwards he thought, acted and lived as a dedicated revolutionary, there is doubt about the execution's exact effect on his attitude to terrorism. Throughout almost the whole course of Russian revolutionary activity there had been a division between those who believed that terrorism – epitomized by the assassination of Government officials – was not only justified but essential, and those who believed that killing was counter-productive. The division varied in importance, particularly during the years when Lenin's revolutionary plans were developing, when the revolutionary movement itself was abnormally fissiparous, and when the teachings, written or unwritten, on what was tactically or morally justifiable, became as complex as those of medieval theologians. Any accurate assessment of Lenin's attitude to terror should therefore be qualified by date and circumstance, and even then given with some caution.

What he really felt about terror in 1887 has tended to be as fudged as the social context of his early years. According to Maria, his younger sister, he said, on hearing of his brother's execution, 'No, we shall not take that road.' But Maria was only nine years old at the time; Lenin had barely begun his study of revolution and if the remark was ever made, there is doubt as to whether it specifically referred to violence. However during his trial Aleksandr had said:

'Terror is the sole form of defense that is left to a minority, strong only in spiritual force and in the consciousness of its rightness against the consciousness of the physical force of the majority . . . Among the Russian people there will always be found scores who are so devoted to their ideas that it is no sacrifice for them to die for their cause.'

Yet it is still uncertain whether, without Aleksandr's execution, Lenin would have accepted the need for violence or instead would have thrown in his lot with those who believed that terror should be either avoided or at least kept to a minimum. But it seems likely that his pragmatic view would probably have been that which he voiced in 1901, when he said: 'Basically we have never rejected terrorism, and we cannot reject it. It is a method of warfare which may certainly be used and may even be essential at a definite stage in the battle. But the fact of the matter is that at present . . . such a method of warfare is untimely and inefficient . . .' Trotsky is one who has provided an at least plausible answer to Lenin's reaction. His frequent disagreements with Lenin were interspersed with long periods during which they discussed their own pasts as well as the world's future.

Certainly the evidence suggests that from 1887 onwards he was strongly drawn to terrorism, even though in later years he skated over any connections with Narodnaya Volya who saw individual acts of violence as the best way of achieving their aims. Only later, and only occasionally, was the truth allowed to slip out, as when Lenin's wife wrote in her memoirs that one paragraph in Lenin's *What Is To Be Done?* (which is named after Chernyshevsky's book) represented a piece of autobiography.

> 'Many of [the Social-Democrats] [ran the passage] had begun their revolutionary thinking as adherents of Narodnaya Volya. Nearly all had in their early youth enthusiastically worshipped the terrorist heroes. It required a struggle to abandon the captivating impressions of those heroic traditions, and the struggle was accompanied by the breaking off of personal relations with people who were determined to remain loyal to the Narodnaya Volya and for whom the young Social-Democrats had profound respect.'

Whatever general justification Lenin used for terror during various stages of his life, the justification of assassination of individuals – at some periods as much a way of revolutionary life at the time as the humps on the back of the camel – remained clear to him. After Dmitri S. Sipiagin, the Russian Minister of the Interior, was killed in 1902 by a Socialist Revolutionary, Lenin, then in London, commented: 'A neat job', and later wrote of the killing:

> 'We consider it not only our right, but our sacred duty,

notwithstanding all the repulsion which such means of struggle inspire in us, to answer violence with violence and to pay for the spilled blood of the people with the blood of its oppressors. The crack of the bullet is the only possible means of talking with our ministers, until they learn to understand human speech and listen to the voice of the country.

'We do not need to explain why Sipiagin was executed. His crimes are too notorious, his life was too generally cursed and his death too generally greeted.'

Although in 1887 there were few indications of the ordeals to come, and although Lenin himself was still a model student, there were few in Simbirsk who did not heed the obloquy which his brother's execution created for the Ulyanovs. One of the exceptions was Fyodor Kerensky who, after Lenin had passed out from high school in Simbirsk with flying colours in 1887, gave him a glowing letter of recommendation:

'Quite talented, invariably diligent, prompt and reliable, Ulyanov was first in all his classes, and upon graduation was awarded a gold medal as the most meritorious pupil in achievement, growth and conduct. There is not a single instance on record either in school or outside of it, of Ulyanov's evoking by word or deed any adverse opinion from the authorities and teachers of this school. His parents always watched carefully over the educational and moral progress of Ulyanov, and since 1886, i.e., after the death of his father, the mother alone has devoted all care and labor to the upbringing of her children. The guiding principles of this upbringing were religion and rational discipline. The goodly fruits of Ulyanov's upbringing were obvious in his excellent conduct. Upon closer examination of Ulyanov's home life and character, I could not but observe in him an excessive introversion and lack of sociability even with acquaintances, and outside the school even with fellow students who were the school's pride and joy, in short, an aversion to companionship. The mother of Ulyanov intends to remain with him throughout his stay at the university.'

2

Novice Conspirator

The death of Lenin's father and the execution of his brother were quickly followed not only by the completion of his studies at Simbirsk but by the first of a series of moves which were, over the next few years, to give him a succession of homes up and down the central Volga region. After departure from the town where he had been born he failed to put down deep roots, a circumstance which made it easier for him to bear with the wanderings of an apprentice revolutionary as he grew up.

Soon after Lenin left school his mother sold her house at Simbirsk and moved with her son to the Blank family estate at Kokushkino where Anna was living under police surveillance. She later moved to the Kazan area and subsequently to Moscow after her youngest son, Dmitri, had gone to university there. Her life continued to be peripatetic and her passport, issued only when she had reached the age of sixty, eventually contained forty residential registrations.

By 1887 the Ulyanovs had already spent many summers at

Kokushkino and Lenin had always been fascinated by the journey up the Volga from Simbirsk. It began with a steamboat trip lasting nearly a day, first between flat banks, then between higher ground as the hills closed in and, with sixty-six miles still to go, the sight of the splendid river Kama which flowed into the Volga. He was interested in everything: the mooring and unmooring of the steamboat, the rafts they met, the banks, the waves, the bearded peasants on the quays running after the boat wanting money for tea and vodka, the Tartars in embroidered skull-caps, the Mordvinians and Chuvash in embroidered shirts. Delighted with this part of the journey, Lenin was the noisiest passenger on deck, and his mother would stop him with, 'You must not shout so on the boat!' 'The boat itself shouts,' he would answer. The winter apple orchards of Antonovka appeared when they were approaching Kazan, and soon the city, former capital of a Tartar khanate, came into sight with the sixteenth-century minaret of its cathedral and the seven-storey tower of the Tsarevna Sumbeki. Here they disembarked and, after a night spent with an aunt, began the thirty-mile journey on horses which had been sent for them from Kokushkino.

On the estate it was a peaceful life in a rural environment whose scent of mignonette, stocks, sweet peas, tobacco plant, nasturtiums, phlox, geraniums and hollyhocks Lenin remembered long after political struggle became the centre of his interests.

'We began to dream about our move to Kokushkino [each year] and make preparations for it long in advance [Anna has written]. We thought there was nothing better or more beautiful than Kokushkino, a little country place which is really very picturesque. I think we inherited our love for

Kokushkino, and our joy at seeing it again, from our mother, who had spent her best years there. Naturally, the open spaces, the joys of country life, and the company of our cousins were in themselves very attractive to us. Later on, especially after the agony of our detested, prison-like high schools and the torture of the May examinations, summer at Kokushkino seemed lovely and happy beyond compare.'

For Lenin there was bathing in the river and boat trips; walks in the forest to gather berries and mushrooms; flying of kites, fireworks and picnics. These memories of a childhood more patrician than plebeian, were echoed by other revolutionaries who helped change the old world. To the end of his life Plekhanov recalled the estate of Gudalovka where he had been brought up, and asked his wife to visit it for him after his death. Vera Zasulich, who in 1900 became with Lenin one of the founders of *Iskra,* wrote: 'I did not imagine that I would remember Byakolovo [the estate where she had been brought up] in all my life, that I would never forget a single shrub in the front garden, nor a single one of the old cupboards in the passage, that for many, many years I would dream about the silhouettes of the old trees which I used to see from my balcony.' Such revolutionaries, like Lenin and other members of the privileged classes, were more human than many of the mob would later be allowed to admit.

While living on the Kokushkino estate in the summer of 1887 Lenin enrolled as a law student in the university at Kazan. Here, judged by the few details recorded, he began to emerge for a while as a bit of a dandy, wearing a shirt with a soft collar held together, as was then fashionable, by a cord with tassels on the ends. 'In contrast to the overwhelming majority of the revolutionary intelligentsia, especially those belonging to the *narodnik*

[Populist] orientation, who were indifferent and careless in regard to how they dressed, the clothing of Lenin, this stormy individual, was always in perfect order,' wrote Nikolay Valentinov (Volsky), a revolutionary who broke with Lenin in 1904 after a year's work with him in Geneva, but who left revealing reminiscences of the period. 'He never wore anything expensive, but his clothes were always neat and well-cared for. He never had a spot on his suit and there were no signs of wear on his trousers; he did not wear shoes worn down at the heels (Lenin loved shoes with high, new heels!) and he always had clean boots.' As a student he mended his own clothes, sewing on buttons when necessary, and generally kept up a neatness of appearance very different from his companions.

Lenin's increasing attention to his appearance was accompanied by a growing concern with the conditions in which students lived. In Kazan he joined the illegal Samara-Simbirsk group; became involved in student protests; was arrested in December 1887 for taking part in student demonstrations, and then expelled for his activities.

'He attracted attention by his secretiveness, inattentiveness and indeed rudeness [says an official report]. Two days before the riotous assembly he gave grounds for suspecting that he was meditating some improper behaviour: he spent much time in the common room, talking to the less desirable students, he went home and came back again with some object which the others had asked for, and in general behaved very strangely. And on December 4 he burst into the assembly hall among the leaders, and he and Polyansky were the first to rush shouting into the corridor of the second floor, waving their arms as though to encourage the others . . . In view of the exceptional circumstances of the Ulyanov family, such behaviour by Ulyanov . . . gave reason to believe him fully capable of unlawful and criminal demonstration of all kinds.'

On his arrest he was asked, according to one story: 'Why are you rebelling, young man? You are up against a wall!' The reply, recorded years later: 'A wall, yes, but *a rotten one*. Give it a push, and it will come tumbling down!'

Lenin does not seem to have been accused of anything serious, but the report showed that even by the age of seventeen he was receiving the police attention that lasted for three decades. However justified the authorities may have been by their own lights, their action in enforcing Lenin's expulsion from Kazan University and then formally exiling him to Kokushkino was extraordinarily misguided, since any revolutionary ambitions which he nurtured now had time to mature. Banishment to Kokushkino, moreover, gave ample opportunity for whatever serious study attracted the young man.

Following Aleksandr's execution, he had begun to toy with the ideas that had won over his brother, but now had the opportunity to study them seriously, which would have been at least restricted amid the demands and interests of a university. Thus it is not surprising that from the start of his regular life at Kokushkino, his previous preoccupations with music, litera-ture and chess began to be judged by their relevance first to what could be called political change and then to revolution. And he also began to study Marx's *Das Kapital*. According to his sister Anna he 'surrounded himself with books and spent most of the day poring over them'. He himself has said that never in his later life did he read so much as during the year of his exile from Kazan.

The gradual process of 'politicization' was discouraged as far as possible by his mother. She had unexpectedly lost one son and now exercised as much influence as she could wield to keep her second son from the same dangerous interests. It was almost certainly at her demand that Lenin, who never lost his love and respect for his mother, tried to return to the university five months after he had been expelled. He might have succeeded eventually had it not been for Aleksandr's record: when it was realized that the applicant was the brother of a youth who had been executed, the words: 'Not to be accepted under any circumstances' were entered on the application form.

Lenin's mother reacted strongly to her son being denied the education she had expected for him. 'It is a sheer torment to look at my son', she wrote to the Russian Minister of Education, L. V. Delyanov, 'and to see how fruitlessly pass those years of his life which are most suitable for a higher education. Almost inevitably it must push him even to thoughts of suicide.'

The period between his expulsion from Kazan University in December 1887 and the award to him of a degree by the St Petersburg Board of Education in January 1892, saw the growth of his legal qualifications and also his progressive immersion in the revolutionary movement.

Having passed the first of his law examinations, Lenin worked in Samara for eighteen months as an advocate-in-training, the first of his legal employments. Here he handled ten cases under a lawyer, A. N. Khardin. And here, one must assume, he began to acquire his dislike for the law and lawyers, as shown in a letter he wrote in 1907 to a Social-Democratic Party Member (RSDLP, see p. 80–82) awaiting trial.

'One must rule the advocate with an iron hand and keep him in a state of siege, for this intellectual scum often plays dirty. Announce to him ahead of time: "If you, son of a bitch, allow yourself even the slightest indiscretion or political opportunism . . . then I, the accused, will at once separate myself from you publicly, label you a scoundrel, and state that I reject such a defence."'

During the period of Lenin's professional apprenticeship, Chernyshevsky was among the most influential of those writers moulding his beliefs, and not only through *What Is To Be Done?*.

'Everything that [Chernyshevsky] published in *Sovremennik [The Contemporary]* I read from beginning to end [he said later]. It was through Chernyshevsky that I first became acquainted with philosophical materialism. He was the first to point out to me the role of Hegel in the development of philosophical thought, and from him came the idea and the concept of the dialectical method – after which it was much easier for me to assimilate the dialectic of Marx. I read Chernyshevsky's . . . articles on the peasant question and his notes to the translation of Mill's "Political Economy". Since Chernyshevsky lashed out against bourgeois economic science, this was good preparation for my later transition to Marxism. With *special interest and benefit* I read his surveys of life abroad, which were remarkable for their depth of thought. I read Chernyshevsky "with pencil in hand", taking extensive notes on what I had read and writing summaries . . . After I found out his address, I even wrote him a letter about this, and was very much grieved when I did not receive a reply.'

It was through Chernyshevsky, he went on, that he became interested in economic questions in general and especially in Russian village conditions.

Lenin's existing interest in the writer was stimulated in that there lived in Kazan a member of Narodnaya Volya called Maria Chetvergova. She and Lenin were drawn together by their mutual admiration for Chernyshevsky since he later said: 'I do not know another person with whom one could talk as pleasantly and profitably about Chernyshevsky as with Chetvergova.'

It was probably at this time that Lenin came so strongly under the influence of Marx. When the first volume of *Das Kapital* was published in Russian in 1872 the authorities regarded it as too dull and academic to be subversive. Thus while officially frowned upon, it was not banned, and during the last three decades of the nineteenth century both legal and illegal Marxist groups and publications grew up, the latter distinguished from the former not so much by the principles in which they believed as by the ways in which it was proposed that these principles might be implemented. Just when Lenin first became absorbed in Marxism is uncertain. The evidence is again conflicting. It seems most likely, however, that, in the words of Karl Radek, later one of his loyal supporters, he 'got hold of the first volume of *Das Kapital* which revealed to him the external world', soon after his expulsion from Kazan University. It was certainly in this period that he began to master the book and use it as a tool.

His first contact with Marx, wherever it took place, was followed by continuous, hard study of whatever Marxist material he could obtain. This was not always easy since the censorship kept an eye on anything with subversive leanings and on the discussion of social issues in the legal press. Even mention of Marx's writings could be unwise and Krupskaya has pointed out that as late as 1897, when he wrote 'The Characteristics of Economic Romanticism' for *Novoye Slovo (New Word)* he 'was compelled to avoid using the words "Marx" and "Marxism" and to speak of Marx in a roundabout way so as not to get the journal into trouble'.

One of the touchstones was the attitude to terrorism. But it was not only this distinction that divided those who at the end of the nineteenth century believed in and worked for the overthrow of the Russian autocracy. The relative priorities of revolution and economic reform produced different parties and sub-parties, as did the methods by which these objectives might be achieved. This gave to the atmosphere in which Lenin grew up a complexity requiring him always to describe his aims and working methods in minute detail and with the greatest possible clarity, which led to arguments on detail which have some similarity with the debate of medieval churchmen as to how many angels could dance on the head of a pin. The arguments at times hampered revolutionary progress but also constituted a whetstone on which Lenin was forced to sharpen his considerable dialectical ability. Yet they also hastened the merging in Lenin's mind of the revolutionary tradition of Russia, shaped by the structure of the tsarist state, and the scientific socialism he drank in from Marx.

It was not only the philosophy of revolutionary life in general that Lenin absorbed: from Chernyshevsky he had learned of its difficulties and one passage that he often quoted no doubt supported his morale during the more difficult of the revolutionary days ahead:

'The highroad of History is not the sidewalk of the Nevsky Prospekt: it passes all the way through open fields, dusty and muddy; at times it cuts across marshes or forests. If one shrinks from getting covered with dust and dirtying one's boots, then one should never enter into public activity. This is a salutary occupation if one is really inspired by the idea of the good of mankind, but it is not a particularly cleanly occupation. However, there are different ways of defining moral purity.'

In addition to Marx and Chernyshevsky there was also Petr Nikitich Tkachev, member of a minor noble family who was first arrested for dissident activities in 1861 at the age of twenty-five and who quickly became a potential revolutionary. His beliefs were an amalgam of Jacobinism, classical Populism and Marxism, and demanded revolution as soon as possible with the use of force if necessary. Lenin made comparatively few references to Tkachev in his writings but such as he made were invariably favourable; in his *What Is To Be Done?*, he wrote: 'The attempt to seize power, which was prepared by the preaching of Tkachev, and carried out by means of the "terrifying" terror that did really terrify, had grandeur.'

As Lenin's interest in revolutionary movements grew his mother moved to Alakayevka, the small village near Samara – down the Volga from Simbirsk – where she had bought a 223-acre farmstead and mill with the proceeds from the Simbirsk house and her share in the Kokushkino property which had also now been sold. The permanent country life was not the only inducement. His mother would have liked him to have taken up farming but he was not happy about his relations with the peasants. Nevertheless, the family move was a lucky one for him. The previous year he had joined a Marxist study circle in Kazan and soon after reaching Alakayevka learned that many of its members had been arrested. 'I think that I, too, might easily have been arrested had I remained in Kazan that summer,' he wrote.

If he had been arrested in Kazan, Lenin would have had a longer police record when caught with seditious literature in 1895 and would almost certainly have received a sentence more severe than the three-year banishment to Siberia – of which he made excellent use.

The change from the estate at Kokushkino to the smaller farm at Alakayevka seems to have had little effect on his studies. The village was poor; some of the householders owned neither horse nor cow, suggesting the ultimate in poverty, and most could neither read nor write. Yet the small farm, with its old garden running down to the river, the pond in which one could swim, and the fields in which raspberries could be gathered all helped to make it a splendid summer home.

Lenin occupied his own corner of the garden under the shade of a linden tree, and from 1889 to 1893, his brother Dmitri has said that this became Lenin's regular workroom. Nearby was a horizontal bar set on two posts for gymnastics on which Lenin exercised with energy and passion – on one occasion calling out to Dmitri 'I have balanced myself at last' and then showing him how he had been able to sit on the bar.

On summer evenings the family would sit on the porch of the house in the twilight, when there was no need for the lamps that would attract the mosquitoes. They would drink tea, or milk brought up in a big pitcher from the cellar. Often they would sing, Lenin being the soloist and enjoying especially 'You Have Charming Little Eyes'.

During this period, although Lenin read any revolutionary literature on which he could lay his hands, he kept up with his law books – 'On the assumption that I might soon be permitted to return to the university, I read my university textbooks,' he later wrote – but he also read a great deal of fiction, and became an admirer of the poet N. V. Nekrasov. 'What is more,' he wrote, 'my sister [Anna] and I used to compete to see who could learn the greater number of Nekrasov's poems by heart.'

Yet while he made the most of the spare time available for study, he was by no means a library-bound bookworm. He long remembered the four-day tours he made on his own from Samara, travelling downstream on the Volga for some forty-seven miles, then hauling his boat overland for a mile to the river Usa which flowed roughly parallel to the Volga but in a different direction; and finally, after a boat trip that brought him roughly opposite his starting-point, an overland haul back to the Volga. He never lost his love for the great river and in 1911, at the age of forty-one, he admitted in a letter to his sister Anna's husband, Mark Yelizarov, *'How* I miss the Volga!' The following year he asked his mother, significandy, 'What is spring on the Volga like this year?'

The hearty exercise of taking a boat down one river and up another was typical of the young Lenin, a great outdoor-sports enthusiast. As a boy he was an ardent sled user. He rowed, swam, exercised on the trapeze, and was an expert skater who could cut intricate figures on the ice. When he was living in Cracow, Polish Austria, in his early forties, he encouraged his sister Maria to go skating and added that when he had found himself in a cold place the previous year he had immediately looked for a skating-rink.

As a youth, Lenin enjoyed all the pleasures of a patrician outdoor life, and as an adult revolutionary was quick to defend such an existence.

'I too used to live on a country estate which belonged to my grandfather [he once said]. In a sense, I too am a scion of the landed gentry. This is all many years ago, but I still haven't forgotten the pleasant aspects of life on our estate. I have forgotten neither its lime-trees nor its flowers. So go on, put me to death. I remember with pleasure how I used to loll about in haystacks, although I had not made them, how I used to eat strawberries and raspberries, although I had not planted them, and how I used to drink fresh milk, although I had not milked the cows. I gather from what you've just said . . . that you consider such memories unworthy of a revolutionary. So am I to understand that I too am unworthy to be called a revolutionary?'

During his time in Samara he translated *The Communist Manifesto* (1845) and read Engels's *The Condition of the Working Class in England* (1845). One of his acquaintances, Maria Golubeva-Yasneva, a former member of the terrorist wing of the Populist movement, remembering her contacts with him in Samara, later came to the conclusion 'that the idea of the dictatorship of the proletariat had already occurred to him then. Not without reason did he talk to me so often about the question of the seizure of power (one of the points of our Jacobin programme).'

In May 1890, Lenin's mother finally obtained permission for her son to take his final examinations at a university as an external student, and in September Lenin travelled to St Petersburg to arrange the details. In 1891, he took two sets of examinations in the city, interspersing his journeys between St Petersburg and Samara with attendance at illegal meetings and the continued study of revolutionary literature.

He seems to have been stretching himself and judging by a

letter to Maria from his sister Olga, who was also studying in St Petersburg, his mother knew it.

'I think, darling Mamochka, that you have no reason to worry that he is over-exerting himself,' [wrote Olga on 20 April 1891]. 'Firstly, Volodya is reason personified and secondly, the examinations were very easy. He has already completed two subjects and received a 5 [top marks] in both. He rested on Saturday (the examination was on Friday). He went early in the morning to the River Neva and in the afternoon he visited me and then both of us went walking along the Neva and watched the movement of the ice.'

The following month Olga died of typhoid, an event which brought her mother to St Petersburg. She then returned to Samara with Lenin where he remained until the autumn when he went back to St Petersburg, took his final examinations and passed them all, having crammed a four-year course into eight months. Later in the year he was awarded a first-class degree by the St Petersburg Board of Education and soon afterwards became an assistant barrister at the Samara Circuit Court.

As a budding lawyer Lenin appears to have been involved mainly in defending peasants accused of petty crime. They included a group who had together stolen 300 roubles from a peasant in the same village; several hired hands who tried to steal grain from a barn but were caught red-handed; and a peasant who had committed four minor thefts. But he must have taken a certain political satisfaction from the defence of one client – a tailor sentenced to a year's imprisonment for blasphemy, having, in the words of the indictment, 'cursed the blessed Virgin, the

Mother of God, the Holy Trinity, and also our sovereign Lord the Emperor and his heir-apparent, saying that our Lord the Emperor managed his affairs badly'.

In 1892 Lenin began preparatory work on 'What the "Friends of the People" are: How They Fight the Social Democrats'. This was a defence of Marxist views in which Lenin attacked the Russian agrarian socialists, and an early example of his writings – which have been estimated to total ten million words. It was not finished until 1894 when its three sections were first hectographed and then printed before being illegally distributed. If not yet a fully fledged revolutionary he was by now an enthusiastic Marxist and ready to attack other Marxists who kept their activities within the law.

In October 1893, having become an assistant to the St Petersburg lawyer M. F. Volkenstein, he settled into the city in what he described to his mother as 'a good room, or so it seems; there are no other lodgers and the landlady has a small family; the door between my room and their drawing-room is papered over, so that sounds are faint. The room is clean and light. There is a good entrance. Since, in addition, it is not far from the centre (only some 15 minutes from the library) I am quite satisfied.'

While his professional career began to flourish, Lenin was pushing his political and revolutionary roots deeper. In 1893 he wrote 'On the So-called Question of Markets', a paper whose main points he had already expounded in lectures even though the pamphlet itself was not published until after his death. In Moscow, where his mother had now moved with her other children, he attended a legal meeting on 21 January 1894 at which, according to the police who were reporting it, the defence of Marxist views was 'taken over by a certain Ulyanov (allegedly the brother of the hanged Ulyanov) who then carried out the defence with a complete command of the subject'.

One of the Marxist circles that Lenin joined while in St Petersburg was attended by both men and women, and it was here, in February 1894, at an illegal meeting disguised as a Shrovetide celebration, that he met not only Gleb Krzhizhanovsky, who in 1920 he made chairman of GOELRO (the State Commission for the Electrification of RSFSR) and in 1921 chairman of Gosplan (the State Committee for planning the economy of the country), but also Nadezhda Konstantinovna Krupskaya, who became his wife within four years, remained his personal and political supporter until his death thirty years later, and without whose devotion and dedication Lenin and his Party would have had to clear many additional hurdles in the rise to power. According to Krupskaya, whose evidence on this point can be assumed to be reliable, Lenin's engagement and then marriage to her came after he had been rejected by another young woman who worked in the same school as Krupskaya. She was Apollinaria Yakubova who subsequently married K. M. Takhtarev, the editor of *Rabochaya Mysl (Workers' Thought)* and whose path, with that of her husband, crossed Lenin's in 1902 when he settled in London, where the Takhtarevs had come some time earlier.

Krupskaya, as she was known to everyone throughout Lenin's life, had been born in Poland in 1869. Her father was first a schoolteacher, then a factory inspector. Her mother also taught, and Krupskaya's youth and upbringing were those of a normal middle-class girl. She was brilliant as a student, and following her family's move to Russia took a series of teaching posts in St Petersburg where her parents lived. She was something of a bluestocking and worked for educational good causes. One significant trait showed itself early and was later defined by a former school colleague who says: 'Earlier than any of us, more unyieldingly than any of us, she had defined her views, had set her course. She was one of those who are forever committed, once they have been possessed by their thoughts or feelings.' These thoughts and feelings were revolutionary from her earliest years, and after reading in volume I of Marx's *Das Kapital* that 'The knell of capitalist private property sounds. The expropriators are expropriated', she wrote that her 'heart beat so that it could be heard'.

Before the end of 1894 Krupskaya heard Lenin read to the circle in which they had first met, his 'What the "Friends of the People" are; How They Fight the Social Democrats', on which he had begun work in Samara two years earlier.

'I had already been working for years . . . as a teacher in the Smolensky Sunday Evening Adult School, and was already fairly well acquainted with local working-class life [Krupskaya has written of the group into which she drew Lenin]. Quite a number of the workmen in Vladimir Ilyich's circle were my pupils at the Sunday School . . . In those days the Sunday Evening Adult School was an excellent means for getting a thorough knowledge of the everyday life, the labour conditions, and the mood of the working masses . . . Workers belonging to our organization went to the school in order to observe the people and note who could be brought into the circles or drawn into the movement . . . It was a kind of silent conspiracy. We were actually able to talk about anything in the school, although there was rarely a class without a spy . . . Vladimir Ilyich was interested in the minutest detail describing the conditions and life of the workers. Taking the features separately he

46

endeavoured to grasp the life of the worker as a whole – he tried to find what one could seize upon in order better to approach the worker with revolutionary propaganda . . . Vladimir Ilyich read with the workers from Marx's "Kapital", and explained it to them. The second half of the studies was devoted to the workers' questions about their work and labour conditions. He showed them how their life was linked up with the entire structure of society, and told them in what manner the existing order could be transformed. The combination of theory with practice was the particular feature of Vladimir Ilyich's work in the circles. Gradually other members of our circle also began to use this approach.'

It appears to have been from this time that a casual friendship began to evolve and soon led Lenin to propose marriage. The relationship was complicated and rested, at least in part, on Krupskaya's organizing ability, which from the 1890s onwards she was able increasingly to deploy on Lenin's behalf. Commentators have tended to stress her undoubted ability but it should not obscure the affection that bound Lenin to Krupskaya and which kept him emotionally anchored for the greater part of his life. There was, at the typical age of forty, one exception, that of Inessa Armand, although its importance has been exaggerated in the welter of myth and rumour which has grown around so much of Lenin's activities.

So, too, with myths about Krupskaya's physical appearance. It is true that when imprisoned in St Petersburg in the late 1890s she became known as 'the Fish' on account of her bulging eyes which indicated a tendency to thyroid trouble, but this feature has been over-emphasized; the woman who played such an important part in supporting Lenin was more attractive than she is often painted.

> 'Physically, there was much in her favor [says her latest biographer who has studied a mass of contemporary Russian photographs]. Had she been a princess, involved in stylishly shocking escapades writers probably would not have called her a rare beauty, but might have referred to her arched eyebrows, fine, high cheekbones and firm jaw – all conveying a sense of feminine challenge. They might have mentioned her slightly over-full lips, presuming them sensuous, and her intense eyes, which are not in fact bulging in the photographs taken about this time, including the mug picture the police took. As it was, Krupskaya wanted to look like the opposite of a frivolous princess, while still retaining an air of middle-class respectability. Judging by her pictures, her dress in these years was invariably a dark, long-sleeved affair, with very little shape except for slightly puffed-out shoulders and upper arms and a collar of the same stuff that pretty well covered her throat. Her luxuriant hair, parted a little off the middle, was drawn straight back, both neat and austere. Far from seeming drab to Lenin, it is fair to guess that Krupskaya's conservative style was just right for his taste. Here was a young woman whose obvious disdain for frivolous display bespoke her devotion to more important things, but did not conceal the fact that she was fundamentally good-looking.'

By the time that Lenin met Krupskaya he already had, she later recalled, a wonderful knowledge of Marx. He was also, although still in his early twenties, a useful speaker; a man able as one listener wrote, to drown his audience 'in a torrent of statistics which he used to illustrate his points', but he was not yet the charismatic 'character' of later years. Aleksandr Nikolayevich Potrezov, a follower of the Liberation of Labour group which had been set up in Geneva in 1883 by Plekhanov and Akselrod, has written:

'I met [Lenin] for the first time during the 1894–95 Christmas and New Years holidays, at a meeting in a St Petersburg suburb, in the Okhta quarter. Lenin was only young according to his birth certificate. One could have taken him for at least a 35–40 year old. The face withered, the head almost bald, a thin reddish beard, eyes which observed one from the side, craftily and slightly closed, an unyouthful, coarse voice. A typical merchant from any north Russian province – there was nothing of the "radical" intellectual about him, so many of whom were making contact with the workers in those years just when the workers were beginning to stir. No trace either of the service or noble family from which Lenin came.'

There were other critical reports of Lenin's entry into the revolutionary society of St Petersburg but most of them, like the details of his work there, have been forgotten or obscured. His experiences in the city in the early 1890s were the subject of contradictory reports which only began to be untangled some seventy years later with the publication of Richard Pipes's *Social Democracy and the St Petersburg Labor Movement, 1885–1897* (1963). This was almost to be expected since the natural difficulties of charting the movements of small and usually illegal groups were increased after Lenin's death in 1924 by the efforts of the Communist Party in Russia.

'By minimizing or altogether ignoring the achievements of his colleagues and competitors [Pipes has pointed out], by eliminating or suppressing evidence that might diminish his own attainments, by taking events out of their historical context, the party-controlled historical profession in the Soviet Union has succeeded in distorting virtually beyond resemblance facts bearing on the young Lenin.'

What is certain is that although Lenin as yet lacked the finer points that were later to make him such a magnetic speaker, he went on with his proselytizing work and continued with his revolutionary apprenticeship.

In the autumn of 1894 he read to Petr Struve, a Marxist intellectual who was to move steadily to the right until he became one of Lenin's bitter enemies, a summary of his paper subtitled 'The Reflection of Marxism in Bourgeois Literature'. Struve, the grandson of a famous German astronomer and the son of a governor of the Russian province of Astrakhan, was later to make clear that it was not only on political possibilities that he and Lenin failed to see eye to eye. He was one of the few who subsequently drew attention to Lenin's unattractive characteristics, which were discernible even in youth.

'The impression which Lenin at once made on me – and which remained with me all my life – was an unpleasant one [he recalled forty years after their first meeting]. It was not his brusqueness that was unpleasant. There was something more than an ordinary brusqueness, a kind of mockery, partly deliberate and partly irresistibly organic, breaking through from the inmost depths of his being, in Lenin's way of dealing with those on whom he looked as his adversaries. And in myself he sensed at once an adversary, even though then I stood still fairly near to him. In this he was guided not by reason, but by intuition, by what hunting people call "flair". Later on I had much to do with Plekhanov. He, too, had a brusqueness verging on mockery in dealing with people whom he wanted to strike or to humble. Yet, compared with Lenin, Plekhanov was an aristocrat. The way in which they both treated other people could be described by the untranslatable French expression *"cassant"*. But in Lenin's *"cassant"* there was something intolerably plebeian and at the same time something lifeless and repulsively cold . . . Vera Zasulich, the cleverest and subtlest of all the women I have ever met in my life, felt an antipathy for Lenin verging on physical aversion – their subsequent political quarrel was due not only to theoretical or tactical differences, but to the profound dissimilarity of their natures . . . Truly, in his attitude to his fellow men Lenin breathed coldness, contempt and cruelty. To me it was clear even then that in those unpleasant, even repulsive, qualities of Lenin, lay also the pledge of his power as a politician; he always had in view nothing but his objective towards which he marched, firm and unflinching. Or rather, there always was, before his mental eyes, not one objective, more or less distant, but a whole system, a whole chain of them. *The first link in that chain was power in the narrow circle of his political friends.'*

In April 1895, Lenin's essay on 'The Economic Content of Narodism (Populism) and the Criticism of It in Mr Struve's

Book' was published in the miscellany entitled *Material on the Nature of our Economic Development,* (St Petersburg, 1895). It was a volume in which men such as Lenin, who unreservedly supported Marxism, found it possible to collaborate with others such as Struve who followed Marxism only as far as it advocated keeping within the law. Despite – or arguably because of – this compromise the volume was seized and burned by the authorities for its 'pernicious intention' and only 100 of the 2,000 copies were saved. Shortly afterwards Lenin fell severely ill with pneumonia, but before he had fully recovered he was asked by the St Petersburg Marxists to make contact with the Liberation of Labour Group, which had already set up groups at various places in Western Europe.

He set off later in the month, now aged twenty-five, on a four-month trip which took him to Austria, Switzerland, France and Germany. The journey was the first of many over the next two decades which followed a similar pattern and exemplified Lenin's single-minded dedication to the revolutionary cause. The nub of the tour consisted of making, or consolidating, contacts with suitable groups or parties; he would research into socialist archives; make speeches or lectures, and a constant effort to keep socialist supporters moving along the lines he believed they should follow. As he increased his influence among the revolutionary forces which proliferated in Europe during the last decades of the nineteenth century and the early years of the twentieth, so opposition increased to what were often seen as his extremist policies and the methods he used to forward them. Only a few of these developments, which were to make some of Lenin's engagements in the early 1900s more like battles in a campaign than items in a propaganda tour, were present in 1895.

While he was away, Krupskaya continued her clandestine meetings but also took a post with the accounts section of the state railways for practical reasons she later revealed in a letter to Lenin's sister Maria. 'If money is needed,' wrote Lenin's future wife, 'you can get a job with some railroad, where at least you will be able to work off the necessary number of hours and have no cares; you will be free as a bird; but all this pedagogy, medicine and so on absorbs a person more than it should (for the good of the cause).'

The 1895 journey was Lenin's first outside Russia, and from his reactions, described in long and frequent letters to his mother, two points emerge. One was his surprise, and annoyance, at his lack of mastery of German, and the resolution with which he began to put this right. The second was his response to, and love of, natural scenery, particularly mountains. It was a trait which developed during his life in Switzerland, a country which became his second home for many years. Lenin could always relax in the mountains, and if he never became a mountaineer was soon a mountain walker and scrambler who appears to have tired out most companions. He inquired, moreover, about the prospects for staying in the huts of the Swiss Alpine Club but never followed up the possibilities open to him.

It has been speculated that the development by the British during the mid-nineteenth century of mountain-climbing as a sport distinct from a scientific or geographical occupation can be linked to the atmosphere of sexual repression that permeated so much of Victorian society. Similarly, it can be claimed that Lenin's interest in mountains combined with his obsession for revolution to sublimate any sexual urgings resulting in a life singularly free from hints of scandal. The one exception was his feelings for Inessa Armand, whom he met in middle age, but even here it is difficult not to believe that rumour and hindsight greatly embroidered whatever facts existed.

Lenin's delight in mountain scenery and his consequent attachment to Switzerland played its part in history; had he moved to Scandinavia from Switzerland before early 1917 there would have been no need for the famous 'sealed train' journey across Germany. And had he been able to return to Russia without dealing with the Germans, as Trotsky returned from the USA, then the months leading to his seizure of power in the autumn of 1917 could have been very different.

His first traumatic sight of the Alps came in 1895 near Salzburg, roughly at the same time as he experienced the shock of realizing how little German he knew. As he explained to his mother: 'I ask the guard on the train a question, he answers and I don't understand him. He repeats the [answer] more loudly. I still don't understand, and so he gets angry and goes away.' However, he continued: 'In spite of this disgraceful fiasco, I am not discouraged and continue distorting the German language with some zeal.'

It is clear from letters to his mother that Alpine scenery provided some compensation for his deficiencies in German, and he wrote: 'The scenery here is splendid. I am enjoying it all the time. The Alps began immediately after the little German station I wrote to you from; then came the lakes and I could not tear myself away from the window of the railway carriage.' Most forms of mountain activity also fascinated Lenin. 'Do you ski?' he asked one friend. 'Certainly take it up. It's wonderful in the mountains in winter!'

However, in 1895 work took over, and for some weeks he was involved in a series of meetings with men whose lives were to be closely linked with his during the next few years. First he went to

Geneva to see Potrezov, who took him to a meeting with Plekhanov, then on holiday near Les Diablerets, a resort above the Rhone Valley. Although he was in the comparative safety of Switzerland, Lenin still believed that tsarist police might be following him and took a tortuous route to Les Diablerets, going on foot across the Col des Mosses and through the Ormonts valley. Lenin and Plekhanov, who were to collaborate and disagree at regular intervals despite the basic similarity of their objectives, were men of contrasting characters. The differences were well summed up by Maxim Gorky (the Russian author whose fortunes became increasingly bound up with those of Lenin) who said that those talking of Lenin would say: 'He's one of us all right' but of Plekhanov that his frock coat was too tight for him. Gorky also wrote: 'I have rarely met two people with less in common than G. V. Plekhanov and V. I. Lenin; and this was natural . . . The one was finishing his work of destroying the old world, the other was beginning the construction of a new.' In 1895, Lenin, Potrezov later reported, was 'overawed in the presence of the great theoretician, of the doyen of Marxism' while Plekhanov looked 'not without warm sympathy, at the able practitioner of revolution'.

This would seem to have been a partial view of Plekhanov's reaction and some years later he reported that Lenin made a slightly different impression during this first meeting.

'He all the time tried to convince me that the liberals and democrats belong to the bourgeois species [he told Lenin's later colleague Valentinov]. But I had known this at the time when Lenin did not yet know how to blow his nose in a handkerchief. I also knew something else – about which he had no idea and conception. . . . He did not understand that in Russia there are no political, legal, and cultural forms or any customs and usages which would give her the right to call herself a capitalist country. Those things which bourgeois liberalism must bring to a country and everywhere in Europe has already brought, never occurred to Lenin, and therefore, instead of attracting and enlisting the liberals as allies in the fight against absolutism and the *old, antediluvian order*, he saw in them only the bitterest enemies.'

In 1895, however, there were few outward warnings of the differences which were to divide the two men. From Les Diablerets Lenin travelled back through Switzerland to meet Pavel Akselrod in Zurich. 'I felt then,' Akselrod later said of Lenin, 'that I had to do with the future chief of the Russian Revolution. He was not only an educated Marxist – of these there were very many – but he knew what he wants to do and how it is necessary to do this. He smacked of the Russian land.' They spent a week discussing future possibilities and then Lenin left for Paris where he made contact with Paul Lafargue, Karl Marx's son-in-law. He was probably disappointed with Lafargue since the Frenchman was surprised to hear from Lenin that Marx was read in Russia. 'And they understand it?' he asked. On being told that that was so, he replied: 'You're wrong. They understand nothing. Here in France, after twenty years of socialist propaganda, nobody understands Marx.'

Despite any disappointment with Lafargue, Lenin was much intrigued by the French capital. 'It makes a very pleasant impression–' he informed his mother, 'broad, light streets, many boulevards, and lots of greenery; the people are quite unrestrained in their manners – at first it comes as rather a surprise after one has been accustomed to the sedateness and primness of St Petersburg.'

He carried out research on the Paris Commune of 1871, copying extracts from G. Lefrançais' *Étude sur le mouvement communaliste à Paris en 1871* and then, despite what he described as the very cheap Paris rooms, was off to Berlin. Here he took lodgings near the Tiergarten, bathed every day in the Spree and worked on the Commune in the Prussian Staatsbibliothek. He still found German difficult and in spite of reading Hauptmann's *The Weavers* before seeing it performed, was unable to understand all of the play. He had little taste for normal sightseeing and spent most evenings 'studying the Berlin mores and listening to German speech . . .'he wrote to his mother. 'In general I much prefer wandering around and seeing the evening amusements and pastimes of the people to visiting museums, theatres, shopping centres, etc.'

He continued to sharpen up his political contacts, and a few days before leaving Germany went with a letter of introduction from Plekhanov to visit Wilhelm Liebknecht, the veteran socialist leader who had been a close friend of Marx and Engels.

Lenin arrived back in St Petersburg in September 1895, and was soon working enthusiastically for what became the Union of Struggle for the Liberation of the Working Class. This was formed by the amalgamation of two older organizations and named by Y. O. Martov, the sobriquet usually used by the young revolutionary worker Y. O. Tsederbaum. Martov had served a short prison sentence at the age of eighteen, been barred from university but allowed to live in St Petersburg, had served another short prison sentence and then been barred for two years from St Petersburg or any other university city. He was to form a complex, changing, and at times ambiguous relationship with Lenin. Both men were to criticize the Economists and other would-be revisionists of the pure Marxist faith but the alliance broke down at the Party Congress in 1903 although Martov was ready to welcome attempts to heal the schism.

Their differences hinged on Martov's adoption of a more liberal outlook than Lenin – the 'soft' rather than the 'hard' approach. This became apparent on frequent occasions, none of which would have been crucial to their relationship if considered in isolation but which when seen as a whole reveal the two men as contrasting political animals. During the early months of the First World War Martov supported Lenin in the Zimmerwald peace movement and continued to do so in many of the breaches and controversies that preceded the autumn Revolution of 1917, as well as those that followed it. As one reviewer of Martov's biography has put it: 'Few men knew Lenin's attitudes and methods so well. Few Russian social democrats hated them more. And yet Martov would not break away from Lenin once and for all . . . But if he would not excommunicate the Bolsheviks he was equally unwilling to join them or justify them.'

While Lenin had been making his first acquaintance with potential revolutionaries abroad, conditions in Russia had been changing significantly as a belated capitalist industrialization gathered speed. The railways, often built with foreign capital, were being extended throughout the country; coal and iron mines grew in numbers; industrial development gathered pace. This tended to produce, for the first time in Russia, a working-class population more accessible than the Russian peasantry to revolutionary or pseudo-revolutionary propaganda and ideas. Nicholas II had ascended the throne in 1894 and from the start of his reign found himself facing a more organized opposition, in whose nourishment both Lenin and Martov were to play continuing but differing roles.

In 1895 Lenin had brought a trunk with him to St Petersburg fitted with a double lining and crammed with illegal literature. He had taken easily to clandestine work and Krupskaya later claimed that of all the underground groups working in St Petersburg, his was the best equipped for conspiratorial activities. 'He knew all the through courtyards, and was a skilled hand at giving police-spies the slip,' she wrote. 'He taught us how to write in books with invisible ink, or by the dot method; how to mark secret signs, and thought out all manner of aliases.' Certainly his correspondence shows much evidence of underground work, giving advice about the best method of employing invisible ink and the amount of paste necessary for fixing secret material in the bindings of books. He told Akselrod:

'It is essential to use liquid paste: not more than a teaspoonful of starch to a glass of water (and moreover, potato flour, not the ordinary flour, which is too strong). The ordinary (good) paste is only necessary for the top sheet and for coloured paper, because the paper holds well together under a press, even with the thinnest of pastes. In any case, it is a suitable method and ought to be used.'

However, he was still new to the game and over-confident. Moreover, he was slow in taking to heart any warning that the groups with which he was associated could have been infiltrated by a spy. This was a trait which showed itself again during the next two decades and must be put down to an inability to doubt the honesty of any man whose credentials he had accepted. More than once it led him – and colleagues – to the brink of disaster.

In the autumn of 1895, the St Petersburg Marxists were joined by a local dentist who, unknown to any of the revolutionaries, was working for the authorities. A dangerous situation developed early in December as Lenin prepared copy for the first number of *Raboche Delo (The Workers' Cause)*, including two articles by himself – 'To the Working Men and Women of the Thornton Factory' and 'What Are Our Masters Thinking About?' Informed of the progress being made with the new illegal paper, the police struck at the critical moment, on the night of 8 December, as most members of the board were together. Lenin was caught while in possession of the two incriminating articles, which were about to be typeset for printing; he was arrested and with other members of the group taken to the 'House of Preliminary Detention'. Here, he well knew, he might be kept for two weeks or two years before being tried and sentenced, probably to a term of exile in Siberia.

There was one other significant result of the police swoop apart from Lenin's arrest. A few days later four men who had not been caught up in the police raid, including Martov, met to decide what should be done next. They agreed to give a 'blanket' name to the various Social-Democrat groups working in St Petersburg, settling on the 'Union of Struggle for the Liberation of the Working Class' ['Soyuz bor'by za osvobozhdenya rabochego klassa'] – an organization to which Lenin gave enthusiastic support in the immediate future.

3

A Youth in Exile

Lenin's arrest in December 1895 gave him his first important cachet as a would-be revolutionary. He had previously written short pamphlets, spoken to small groups, and as the brother of an executed potential assassin had been marked down by the authorities as requiring special surveillance. In addition, he had the qualities required for leadership. It was clear to all who crossed his path that Lenin was becoming a formidable intellectual opponent. His experience of political possibilities and of the impact which revolutionary activity could be expected to make on them was small but growing quickly. More important, he had an instinctive understanding of the ways in which political intrigue could be manipulated to his own ends, and immense personal charm. He was incorruptible; absolutely dedicated to the revolutionary cause. These attributes carried him over the worst of barriers which, during the decades following 1895, might have halted his progress. At the end of 1895 the strength of these attributes was yet to be displayed and it is ironic that they were given such a fine chance to develop in the aftermath of his arrest by the tsarist police.

Lenin was interrogated four times during his imprisonment, which lasted from December 1895 until February 1897. He seems to have kept remarkably fit both physically and mentally, perhaps because he followed the regime which he later laid down for his sister Maria, after she and Mark Yelizarov had been arrested in February 1901 for helping to organize the Moscow section of the Social-Democratic Party (RSDLP).

'I particularly recommended translations [to Mark], especially *both ways* – first do a written translation from the foreign language into Russian, then translate it back from Russian into the foreign language [he wrote]. My own experience has taught me that this is the most rational way of learning a language. On the physical side I have strongly recommended him, and I repeat it to you, to do gymnastics every day and rub himself down with a wet towel. In solitary confinement this is absolutely essential . . . I also advise you to arrange your work on the books you have in such a way as to vary it; I remember quite well that a change of reading or work – from translation to reading, from writing to gymnastics, from serious reading to fiction – helps a great deal . . . I remember that after dinner, for recreation in the evening, I read fiction *regelmässig* [regularly], and never enjoyed it anywhere as much as I did in prison. The main thing is never to forget the obligatory daily gymnastics. Force yourself to go through several dozen (no allowances!) movements of all kinds! This is very important.'

To his mother he also described in some detail the benefits of the prison exercises he carried out every day:

'They loosened my joints so that I used to get warm even on the coldest days, when my cell was icy cold, and afterwards one sleeps much better. I can recommend this . . . as well as a fairly easy exercise (though a ridiculous one): fifty prostrations. It is exactly what I used to make myself do – and I was not in the least perturbed that the warder, on peeping through the little window, would wonder in amazement why this man had suddenly grown so pious when he had not once asked to visit the prison church. But [the prisoner] must not do less than fifty prostrations, without stopping, and touch the floor each time without bending the knees – write and tell him this. You know that doctors for the most part only know how to talk about hygiene.'

While he kept himself healthy in the St Petersburg prison Lenin began work on his first major book, *The Development of Capitalism in Russia*. 'I sleep about nine hours a day and see various chapters of my future book in my sleep,' he told Anna. Conditions were almost agreeable, and visitors brought him more than he needed. 'Someone, for instance, brought me a frock coat, waistcoat and travelling rug,' he added. 'All this was immediately "dispatched" to the storeroom as superfluous.' However, he needed pillow-slips and towels, both of which his sister was asked to add to the list of linen he had requested.

Despite the comparatively easy conditions, a good many subjects could not be discussed openly and secret letters were often necessary. Correspondence was brought in with the books that the prisoners were allowed to have, the sign that letters contained words written in some invisible liquid, frequently milk, being underlining of the date on the envelope. 'At six o'clock they brought in hot water for tea and the wardress led the criminals out to the church,' Krupskaya wrote later. 'By this time the "politicals" would have the letters torn into long strips. Then they would make their tea, and as soon as the wardress departed begin to drop the strips into the hot tea. Thus the letters would be "developed".' (In prison it was not advisable to treat these letters by candle flame, and it was Lenin who thought of developing them in hot water.)

'In order not to be discovered while writing with milk, he made little milk "ink-pots" out of bread. These he popped into his mouth immediately he heard a rattle at the grating. "Today I have eaten six ink-pots" ran the postscript to one of his letters.'

In cell 193 of the House of Preliminary Detention, St Petersburg, where Lenin spent his fourteen months before being ordered into exile, he was allowed to receive both money and food parcels from his family, while on Wednesdays and Saturdays Anna brought him books from the libraries of the Academy of Sciences, the university, and the Free Economic Society. The books were important – as they always were in Lenin's life.

'One was struck by his incredible power of concentration and ability to work . . . [was the recollection of one fellow prisoner]. When in the corridors of the jail . . . one would hear the wardens dragging heavy cases full of books, one knew that this load was meant for Lenin's cell . . .

'Whenever I watched Lenin poring over a book, I was always impressed by his ability to separate quickly chaff from grain. His process of reading, as well as of writing, was fast and testified to his habit of mental work, to his ability to concentrate. He seemed to be just scanning the book, and yet he immediately detected its strong and weak points. Reading a book which had passed previously through his hands, you willy-nilly adopted his point of view: the passages underlined by him, his exclamation marks, question marks, his expressive "hm . . . hm . . ." were so suggestive that the trend of his thought became at once obvious to you.'

He continued writing *The Development of Capitalism in Russia* and later commented: 'If I had been in prison longer, I would have finished the book.'

On 29 January 1897, he was sentenced to three years' exile in Siberia, although the place where he was to serve the sentence had not yet been decided. At his mother's request, he was given permission to journey into exile at his own cost and not under police surveillance. Released from prison on 13 February he was allowed to remain in St Petersburg for a few days. Characteristically, he used them to visit, with Martov, other members of the Union of Struggle for the Liberation of the Working Class who, he was shocked to find, were veering away from revolutionary activity towards what he regarded as the less important organization of strikes. At the end of the meeting Lenin and Martov both went to stay at the house of a mutual friend. 'They would not even go to sleep but talked into the morning,' Martov's youngest brother has written. 'This night very likely marked the beginning of the close personal relations between them while in exile; for until their arrest they had been acquainted only for a few months and met mainly on an official footing.' A few days later Lenin began his journey into exile, travelling under unusual conditions since, at his mother's request, he was permitted to break his journey in Moscow. And before leaving St Petersburg he wrote to Krupskaya telling her – in a letter partly written in invisible ink – that he wished to marry her.

In Moscow Lenin overstayed his permitted 'leave' by two days, but on 6 March finally left for Siberia – accompanied for the first part of the journey by his mother, his sisters Maria and Anna, and Mark Yelizarov. His relatives left him at Tula the next day and it was not until a week later that he could write to his mother from Ob station, recording that he had crossed the river Ob in a horse-sleigh:

'The country covered by the West Siberian Railway that I have just travelled throughout its entire length (1,300 versts from Chelyabinsk to Krivoshchokova – three days), is astonishingly monotonous – bare, bleak steppe. No sign of life, no towns, very rarely a village or a patch of forest – and for the rest, all steppe. Snow and sky – and nothing else for the whole three days.'

In Krasnoyarsk where his journey had to be broken, Lenin quickly found two forms of relaxation. One was studying in the Yudin Library, a rich collection of books and journals built up by a Krasnoyarsk merchant, later sold to America and today in the Library of Congress. On the journey, Lenin had struck up a conversation with a revolutionary who had known his sister Anna and also Yudin. He received a letter of introduction, was given the run of the library, which he found contained complete sets of periodicals dating from the end of the eighteenth century, and in Krasnoyarsk often walked the two miles from his quarters and spent the day there working on *The Development of Capitalism in Russia*.

His other relaxation was conversation with four members of

the Union of Struggle who had arrived from St Petersburg – Martov, Krzhizhanovsky, A. A. Veneyev and V. V. Starkov. Before the end of April, he was told by the authorities that he was to serve his exile in Shushenskoye, a town of 1,500 inhabitants on the right bank of the river Yenisei, which he reached after an eight-day steamer journey on the river as far as Minusinsk. A number of other exiles went with him, including Olga Lepeshinskaya whose bunk was next to Lenin's in the nine-berth cabin they shared. She wrote:

'I remember that one day we were both reading. I could not help noticing the speed with which [Lenin] turned the pages of his book. I just managed to read five or six lines and Ilyich was already turning a new page. I listened to the rustle of pages being turned rhythmically. I looked up at the volume in Lenin's hands. It was a book in a foreign language.
 ' "Vladimir Ilyich," I asked, "what are you doing?"
 ' "What do you mean? I am reading . . ."
 ' "Is that how you are reading?" I said. "Are you really reading or are you only scanning the book?"
 ' "Of course, I am reading, and very attentively at that."
 ' "But can one read so quickly?" I asked in astonishment.
 ' "Well, that's how it is. You are right. I do read very fast. But I have to, I have trained myself in fast reading. I simply must read a great deal and that is why I just cannot read slowly . . ." '

In Shushenskoye Lenin found a home in a peasant's house round which there stretched the Siberian plain; steppe and wood and swamp, broken only in the far distance by the snow-covered hills of the Sainskiya range. He spent the rest of his exile there, first on his own, then with Krupskaya who was allowed to join him and whom he married in July 1898. Judging by the letter he wrote to his mother on arrival it was quite a pleasant spot.

'Shu-shu-shu is not a bad village [he said]. True, it lies in a fairly bare place, but there is a wood not far away (about one and a half to two versts) although much of it has been cut down. There is no way of getting to the Yenisei, but the River Shush flows close by the village and there is also a fairly large tributary of the Yenesei not far away (one to one and a half versts) and there I shall be able to bathe. On the horizon lie the Sayan hills or their offshoots. Some of them are all white and the snow on them hardly ever melts, so that there is even something artistic about them and it was not in vain that I composed a poem in Krasnoyarsk: "In Shusha, at the foot of Sayan . . ." Unfortunately I have not composed any more than the first line!'

From the start, Lenin appears to have been little worried by the prospect of exile and his early letters to his mother and sister are remarkably confident. Writing to his mother in mid-April he suggested that Dmitri might come to Shushenskoye:

'We can go shooting together – if only Siberia can manage to make a sportsman out of me, and if he does not find work (and shooting) for himself in places not so far distant . . . Ho, ho! If in three weeks and a bit I have become such a Siberian that I am inviting people from "Russia", what shall I be like in three years?'

By the next month he was settling down to sport, saying that the shooting was not bad.

'Yesterday I travelled about 12 versts to shoot duck and great snipe. There is a lot of game, but without a dog the shooting is difficult, especially for such a poor shot as I. There were even wild goats, and in the mountains and in the taiga (30–40 versts from here, where the local peasants sometimes go shooting) there are squirrel, sable, bear and deer.'

Lenin went out in all weathers, often wearing the heavy bear-skin coat he had inherited from his father and which he took with him to the Kremlin two decades later.

He was a poor shot according to more than one of his companions.

'The amount of game he used to bring back from his expeditions was usually minimal [according to Olga Lepeshinskaya's husband, also in exile]. The birds at which he aimed his deadly weapon nearly always had an opportunity to jeer at the art of this amateur marksman. But this in no way discouraged him. The instinct of a hunter was quite satisfied when he could steal cleverly towards his intended prey perched on a branch of a tree, when he could measure with his "practised" eye the distance between the unfortunate woodcock and the muzzle of his gun, when he could savour with all his being the anticipation of his "perfect" shot, without, however, worrying unduly when his feathery victim, after the "deadly shot" was fired, would soar towards the blue sky and disappear into the brightness of the day instead of toppling head over heels to the ground.

'Perhaps he did not find the main delight in the illusion of shooting exploits; the truth was that he liked nature. And one could clearly see with what enjoyment he marched over the thickets and marshes of Shushenskoye: here he was, hopping from mound to mound on his muscular legs, watching the frightened woodcock flying away right in front of the hunter's nose . . .'

One story, told of him in a variety of ways, seems to typify his attitude. While he was fox-hunting with colleagues, a large fox stopped nearby and made a perfect target. Lenin did not fire. Asked the reason by exasperated friends, he replied: 'Well, he was so beautiful, you know.'

It was not only sport but the chance for strenuous exercise in the open air that Lenin welcomed in exile. A third of a century later Robert Bruce Lockhart, Britain's semi-official envoy to Petrograd* after the Revolution, noted of him: 'In addition to being an ardent cyclist and the father of modern "hiking", that great man was a passionate lover of outdoor life and a sportsman who, if he preferred shooting, did not disdain the angle.' These sporting enthusiasms were remarked upon, more critically, by Winston Churchill who commented that Lenin was 'as mildly amused to stalk a capercailzie as to butcher an Emperor'.

But Lenin devoted as much time to study as to sport, ensuring that his family bought and forwarded to him whatever books he required. When it became too expensive he worked out a scheme with his sister Anna by which she could borrow books on long loan from the Moscow Library and send them on to him. Even with the high postage rates, he discovered that this would be

---

* St Petersburg was renamed Petrograd during the First World War, subsequently becoming Leningrad.

cheaper than buying them.

His method of work has been described by Krzhizhanovsky who managed to spend a few weeks in Shushenskoye:

'At that time he was still living alone. His day, thoughtfully planned to the last minute, consisted of long hours of solid work alternating with regular periods of much needed rest. It was in the mornings that he experienced quite an extraordinary abundance of vitality and energy and he was ready for a bout of wrestling or for a fight, and very often I would fall in with his mood and give him the full satisfaction by pitting my strength against his. Then after a brisk walk, we would begin our work. Special hours were set apart for writing, for the collection of statistical material from available sources, for reading philosophical and economic literature (Russian and foreign) and for relaxation – when we read novels.

'We did receive newspapers but, of course, with a great delay, and in sizeable batches. But Vladimir Ilyich very astutely devised a means of reading them in a systematic manner: he arranged them in such a way that he read one issue a day, taking into consideration the overall delay. This arrangement made him feel that he received the paper regularly, daily, though somewhat late. Whenever I tried to upset this order and maliciously picked out and read aloud news from subsequent issues, he blocked his ears and vehemently defended the advantages of his method.'

Life in Shushenskoye quickly became an almost pleasant mixture of sport and study, and more than one of his fellow exiles has described how Lenin used one as a foil for the other. Olga Lepeshinskaya has recorded of him:

> 'Able to work productively and with great energy, Lenin knew also how to give his much preoccupied mind the rest it needed and how to bring variety into the monotous life of the exile. For Ilyich rest consisted not just in doing nothing, but in giving his muscles the necessary exercise, in loosening every part of his vascular system, in making his heart beat strongly and rhythmically, in forcing his lungs into a more active condition, in a word, in stimulating his nerves and his whole body into the physical state in which one enjoys the mere fact of existence. At rest, Ilyich was as active and lively as he was in the process of most strenuous work.
>
> 'Sometimes I accompanied him in his favourite sport of skating. Our group would scatter over the smooth icy surface of the frozen river. Ilyich, vigorous and full of joy, was there first, calling aggressively: "Hey, who is going for a race?" Our skates would cut into the ice. In front of everybody Ilyich, straining all his willpower and his muscles in order to win at any price, no matter how big the effort.'

In exile there appear to have been few money problems. Lenin's basic allowance from the State of eight roubles a month may not seem much but it was twice the wages of the more poorly paid St Petersburg workers and more than three times the wages which he was soon to pay his hired help in Shushenskoye. The allowance was supplemented with surprisingly little difficulty by payment for his literary activities.

Mail arrived in quantity, if sometimes irregularly, and on one occasion Lenin was happy to report: 'I received a pile of letters to-day from every corner of Russia and Siberia and therefore felt in a holiday mood all day.' His sister Maria regularly received instructions from him as to what he wanted: books on the economics of agriculture in England and France were in demand, as were those dealing with industry, and the works of the scientific writer Andrew Ure and the computer pioneer Charles Babbage. 'Buy them, if the prices are reasonable,' Maria was told. His family in Moscow had little difficulty in sending him additional clothes as he needed them, as well as cartridges and barrel wads for the gun. His mother was asked to send kid gloves and 'smooth black tulle for a mosquito net' for the summer months, as well as socks, suit, and his straw hat if it was still in existence.

Krupskaya joined him in 1898. She had been arrested at a revolutionary meeting, while Lenin was still imprisoned in St Petersburg, and had been sentenced to a term of exile in Siberia. She was to serve it far from Lenin, but the authorities changed the place to Shushenskoye on condition that she married him immediately on her arrival. She was allowed to take her mother, Elizaveta Vasilyevna Krupskaya, with her.

> 'I am already looking for quarters for them [Lenin informed his own mother] – the room next to mine. I am having an amusing competition with a local priest who is also asking the landlord for a room. I protest and insist that they should wait until my "family affairs" are finally settled. I do not know whether I shall succeed in overcoming the competitor. If visitors come in the summer we shall be able to occupy the entire house; (the landlord would then move into the old hut in the yard, and that would be much more convenient than equipping one's own house).'

Krupskaya and her mother arrived at dusk on 6 May 1898, having been delayed because the water on one stretch of the river was too low for their steamer. Lenin was out hunting and was at first disturbed by a neighbour reporting as a practical joke that the signs of newcomers were the result of a drunken neighbour who had broken in and thrown all his books about. 'I found Nadezhda Konstantinovna looking not at all well,' he reported to his mother. 'She will have to look after her health a little better here. But about me, Elizaveta Vasilyevna said: "Gracious! How you have spread!" So you see, you do not need a better report.'

The marriage was delayed first by Krupskaya and her mother having arrived in the period during which marriages could not be solemnized by the Orthodox Church. Next, Lenin found to his surprise that the local priest insisted on the use of a wedding ring. He did not have one, but the situation was saved by another exile, Oscar Engberg, who was learning the jeweller's trade and who, from a five-copeck copper piece, made a thin ring for Krupskaya and a thicker one for Lenin. The authorities were flexible in their interpretation of 'immediately', and Lenin and Krupskaya were eventually married on 10 July. Krupskaya's mother seems to have fitted in with the new and, for her, somewhat strange environment quite as well as her daughter. She was a more than useful helper around the house, who allowed Lenin's wife to give him the maximum literary and secretarial help, and there seems no doubt that he nourished a genuine affection for her. Years later, asked what was the worst punishment for bigamy, his reply of 'Having two mothers-in-law' was not only accepted as a joke but told to Krupskaya's mother without embarrassment.

The three of them settled down to what was, in some ways, an almost idyllic life in Shushenskoye.

'The peasants are particularly clean in their habits [Krupskaya wrote]. The floors [of Lenin's house] are covered with brightly coloured home-spun mats, the walls white-washed and decorated with fir branches. The room used by Vladimir Ilyich, though not large, was spotlessly clean. My mother and I were given the remaining part of the cottage . . .

'For example, Vladimir Ilyich, on his "salary" – a subvention of eight roubles – had a clean room, food, and his laundry and mending done. And this was considered dear! It is true, dinner and supper were rather plain. One week they would kill a sheep and feed Vladimir Ilyich with it from day to day until it was all eaten up. When it was all gone they would buy the meat for another week, and the farm-girl chopped up this supply in the trough where the cattle fodder was prepared. This mincemeat was used for cutlets for Vladimir Ilyich – also for a whole week. But there was plenty of milk for both Vladimir Ilyich and his dog – a fine Gordon setter named Zhenka, whom he taught to fetch and carry, to retrieve and to perform other canine manoeuvres.'

After the arrival of Krupskaya, links with the outside world increased and a regular routine developed. In the mornings they would systematically translate Sidney and Beatrice Webb's *History of Trade Unionism* (1894). In the evenings they worked on *The Development of Capitalism in Russia,* or improving Lenin's German. Yet it seems rather an overstatement to have claimed that 'It was a strange marriage, held together not by love, affection or companionship, but by devotion to the Marxist cause.' Krupskaya was later to criticize the emphasis that reports of their life in Shushenskoye put on their work. 'We were newly-weds, you know', she wrote 'and brought beauty to this exile. If I did not write about this in my memoirs, that does not mean that there was neither poetry nor youthful passion in our life.' But there is no doubt that a joint interest in revolutionary politics helped to cement their relationship. So did similar interests in literature. He had been fond of Turgenev since his youth, and in 1898 a new edition of the novelist's works was published. As soon as he heard the news Lenin asked relatives to send him the new edition, a German dictionary, a German grammar book and the best German translation of Turgenev then available.

There was also chess. Since his youth Lenin had been a keen player and in the evenings, when he had written himself to a standstill, he often carved chessmen from tree bark. To his mother and sister he wrote in March 1898: 'Send me one of our sets of chess. I have found several partners among our friends at Minusinsk and I suddenly remembered the past with great pleasure. I was wrong in thinking that Eastern Siberia was such a wild country where chess would not be needed.' He played matches by correspondence with P. N. Lepeshinsky, in exile in another part of Siberia, although his opponent thought a match worthwhile only if Lenin had handicapped himself by removing one of his own pawns at the start of the game. According to S.J. Bagocki, who played with him a decade and a half later when both men were living outside Cracow, he always played with great concentration and rarely left his opponents' mistakes unpunished. If his position became difficult

'he would become more serious, would stop joking, would think deeply and get out of the difficult situation. Those watching him could gather from his smile that he had already found a way of extricating himself. When he lost he would jovially admit his defeat. He liked to explain where his particular fault lay and gave all due praise to the effective moves of his opponent. I was a much weaker player than V.I. and always derived great satisfaction if I managed to defeat him.'

The ability to suffer defeat equably eventually disappeared and his later friend, Maxim Gorky, was to recall 'When he lost [he] grew angry and even despondent like a child.'

Lenin also gave legal advice to the local inhabitants. This was officially forbidden but the authorities turned a blind eye to it, even after he had helped a worker in one of the local mines win an action against his employer for wrongful dismissal. Shushenskoye lay in a distant part of the empire where the writ of the Tsar was not enforced as rigorously as elsewhere, and perhaps Lenin was lucky in serving his exile during a period when chance had brought comparatively liberal officials to the top; nevertheless, in exile he may well have benefited from his ability in man-management, which was to stand him in such good stead in the years ahead.

With a wife to share his life, he began to change.

'At first [Krupskaya told his mother] Volodya announced that he did not know how to gather mushrooms and did not like it, but now you cannot drag him out of the forest, he gets real "mushroom fever". Next year we intend to have a vegetable garden and Volodya has already agreed to dig the seedbeds. That will be physical exercise for him. Up to now he has been enthusiastic only about his shooting. Right now he is arming himself for the hunt. He shoots grey-hen and we eat them and praise them.'

He also took up fishing, crossing the Yenisei at night, according to Krupskaya, in the hope of catching burbot (a freshwater gadoid food fish). 'The last time,' she told Lenin's mother, 'he came back without so much as a tiddler, and since then there has been no talk of burbot.'

Late in the summer he began to experience trouble with his teeth and in mid-August travelled to Minusinsk hoping for treatment. Unable to find a competent dentist, he applied to the authorities for permission to travel to Krasnoyarsk and, having received it, left Shushenskoye the following month. He was worried about leaving his wife and mother-in-law alone, and before setting out for Krasnoyarsk arranged for a neighbour to sleep in the house, made certain that windows and doors could be properly bolted and taught Krupskaya how to use a revolver.

He spent a fortnight in Krasnoyarsk, seeing the dentist, playing chess with other exiles and buying presents for his neighbours' children. He returned in mid-September to Shushenskoye, found that his dog had missed him but that the two women had come to no harm. Krupskaya had acclimatized particularly well to Siberia as is evident from her letter to Lenin's mother in December when she stated that acquaintances were coming to stay with them for Christmas 'to skate, play chess, sing, argue, etc' and adding: 'It looks as though we shall have a good time.' She seems to have enjoyed the country life as much as Lenin and in March 1899 both of them wrote to his sister Maria saying: 'Spring is in the air. The ice on the river is covered with water all the time and the sparrows in the willow trees are chirping furiously; the bullocks low as they pass up and down the street and the landlady's hen under the stove clucks so loudly in the morning that she wakes everyone up.'

Lenin had soon become reconciled to the restrictions on travel which seem to have been one of the few disadvantages of his sentence.

'At the beginning of my exile, [he wrote] I decided never to touch a map either of European Russia even of Russia; it would mean too much bitterness, as I looked at those various black spots. But it is not so bad now; I have grown patient and can examine maps more calmly. Sometimes we even dream into which of the "spots" it would be interesting to land later on. During the first half of my exile I must have been constantly looking back, now I look forward. Ah well, "qui vivra-verra".'

But there are hints here that despite the comparatively pleasant conditions of exile Lenin was anxious for a move – if only, perhaps, for political reasons. His mother apparently travelled to St Petersburg in 1899 in the hope of gaining permission for him to live nearer the city. She was told, by the chief of police, as recorded by a member of the Simbirsk (now Ulyanovsk) branch of the Central Lenin Museum: 'You can be proud of your offsprings: one has been hanged already and the rope is waiting for the other.'

During the last year of his exile, due to end on 29 January 1900, Lenin carried out a wide variety of literary work and began to lay his plans for the future. In 1899 he completed *The Development of Capitalism in Russia*, saw the first volume of his and Krupskaya's translation of the Webbs' *History of Trade Unionism* through the press and completed with her the translation of the second volume. He threw himself even more ardently into the battle developing between orthodox Marxists and revisionists in whom he found it difficult at this period to see any virtue. One group tended to maintain, under a variety of names and for a variety of reasons, that reform of economic conditions in Russia should take priority over political revolution. The main proponent of this belief, which came to be known as Economism, was Edward Bernstein, a German Jew who had studied under the Webbs and whose *Die Veraussetzungen des Sozialismus und die Aufgaben der Sozialdemokratie (Evolutionary Socialism)* arrived in Shushenskoye in September 1899. 'Its contents', Lenin reported to his mother after he and his wife had begun to work their way through it, 'astound us more and more. Theoretically, it is incredibly weak; . . . Practically, it is opportunism . . . It is indifferent opportunism and possibilism and cowardly opportunism at that.' Bernstein gave priority to higher wages, shorter hours and better factory conditions in contrast to those such as Lenin who put first the purely political battle. In short, Bernstein and those who agreed with him thought it was possible to advance by reform rather than revolution. Lenin responded to what he saw as heresy by reviewing Karl Kautsky's *Bernstein and the Social-Democratic Programme: A Counter-criticism,* and by producing a series of articles dealing not only with Bernstein's ideas but with those of his supporters. As usual, he fought vigorously for his beliefs, using any weapons available and with little regard for the Queensberry Rules.

Such attention to what some might have regarded as comparatively peripheral affairs might have led to a dispersal of effort but it was part of Lenin's genius that while he fought those whom he regarded as backsliders from the sacred cause of revolution, he still continued to concentrate the bulk of his energies on what he regarded as the practical revolutionary possibilities of the not-so-distant future. Thus he transformed his reviews of new political books into a miscellany of articles on other rifts and arguments in the proto-revolutionary movement. The St Petersburg journal *Nacholo (The Beginning)* published a number before it was closed down in June 1899, among them one on 'The World Market and the Agricultural Crisis' written by Alexander Israel Helphand, known as Parvus, who played a complex role later in Lenin's life, including the drama of his wartime involvement with the Germans, and was described by Lenin in his review as 'the gifted German journalist'. In *Nacholo* there also appeared Lenin's review of J. A. Hobson's *The Evolution of Modern Capitalism* (1894), in which he displayed an early sympathy for Britain that continued to show itself even during, and immediately after, the First World War when he saw Britain as irretrievably tarred with the capitalist brush. Reviewing Hobson, he noted what he called 'the special features of English history and of English life' – 'the high development of democracy, the absence of militarism, the enormous strength of the organized trade unions, the growing investment of English capital outside of England, which weakens the antagonism between the English employers and workers, etc'

By the late 1890s, through his polemical articles as well as his pre-exile activities, Lenin had achieved in exile an outstanding position as a Marxist able to expound the cause in terms that the ordinary reader or listener could understand. It was natural, therefore, that although still in exile, he should be drawn towards the Social-Democrats, the name meaning socialists who based their ideas on those of Marx. The Russkaya Sotsial-Demokraticheskaya Rabochaya Party (RSDRP), translated variously as the All-Russian Social-Democratic Workers' Party, (RSDWP), or

All-Russian Social-Democratic Labour Party, (RSDLP), had held its first Congress in Minsk on 1 to 3 March 1898. Only nine people attended, but they formally elected a Central Committee of three and issued a manifesto. Shortly afterwards most of them were arrested. This was only the beginning of some disastrous early days, and a Second Congress which was to have been held in Smolensk the following year failed because most of the delegates were picked up by the police while on their way to it. Yet after these unfortunate beginnings the RSDLP – the initials most usually used to represent it in English – was to grow into the most important of the Russian revolutionary parties, largely owing to Lenin's success in piloting it through its early turbulent days when it was split by almost unceasing rifts over planning and policy. By contrast, its first manifesto, written by Struve, was distinguished from those of other revolutionary groups by its clarity and outspokenness.

By this time Lenin – still in exile – had been invited to edit *Rabochaya Gazeta (Workers' Gazette),* a popular newspaper, which had been adopted as the official organ of the RSDLP. The scheme for the journal fell through and none of the three articles which Lenin wrote for it were published until after his death nearly three decades later. However, in one, entitled 'Our Programme', he outlined the strictness with which he felt that his own interpretation of Marxism should be followed. It was an outline that he adhered to as closely as was possible all his life, and if inflexibility is often a handicap there is little doubt that Lenin's resolute dedication, which he revealed here, helped carry him through the turmoil of later years.

'Marxism [he maintained] was the first to transform social-ism from a utopia into a science, to lay a firm foundation for this science, and to indicate the path that must be followed in further developing and elaborating it in all its parts. It disclosed the nature of modern capitalist economy by explaining how the hire of the labourer, the purchase of labour-power, conceals the enslavement of millions of propertyless people by a handful of capitalists, the owners of the land, factories, mines, and so forth. It showed that all modern capitalist development displays the tendency of large-scale production to eliminate petty production and creates conditions that make a socialist system of society possible and necessary. It taught us how to discern, beneath the pall of rooted customs, political intrigues, abstruse laws, and intricate doctrines – the *class struggle,* the struggle between the propertied classes in all their variety and the propertyless mass, the *proletariat,* which is at the head of all the propertyless. It made clear the real task of a revolutionary socialist party: not to draw up plans for refashioning society, not to preach to the capitalists and their hangers-on about improving the lot of the workers, not to hatch conspiracies, *but to organize the class struggle of the proletariat and to lead this struggle, the ultimate aim of which is the conquest of political power by the proletariat and the organization of a socialist society.'*

It was with the aim of carrying out this 'real task' that Lenin ended his exile on 29 January 1900. The future of the RSDLP, he felt convinced, must depend on the establishment of a journal to be published outside Russia, and he was equally convinced that he was the man to found and run it. He was still forbidden to live in metropolitan cities, in university towns, or in big industrial centres, but his term of exile had not been extended and neither had that of his wife (although under the terms of her

exile Krupskaya was able to travel with him only as far as Ufa).
Lenin planned to travel on to Pskov.

On 19 January 1900, Krupskaya told Lenin's mother that
they were talking of nothing else but the journey from
Shushenskoye.

'We have packed the books in a box and had it weighed –
about 15 poods (a pood equals 36 pounds). We are sending
the books and some of our things by carrier; I don't think
we shall have very many things. Because of the frosts we
wanted to get a sleigh with a hood but we could not find
one in the town and to have one made here is a risky business, it probably would not last as far as Achinsk.'

The couple left Shushenskoye on 10 February together with
Krupskaya's mother, who had made dumplings for the journey.
The first leg of the trip took them to Minusinsk, continued down
the Yenisei and was completed on a horse-drawn cart to Achinsk
where they caught the train to Ufa. Here Lenin had a pleasant
encounter since Maria Chetvergova was now living in the town,
and he made a point of visiting her.

'It was a great pity to have to part [from my husband], just at
a time when "real" work was commencing,' Krupskaya later
wrote. 'But it did not even enter Vladimir Ilyich's head to
remain in Ufa when there was a possibility of getting nearer to
St Petersburg.' He was, moreover, able to return later in the
year and spent the first half of July in the town, meeting not only
Krupskaya but local Social-Democrats.

4

Great Expectations

During the months following the end of his exile Lenin was not only to get near to the capital from which he was legally barred but actually into it for discussions on the 'real task' on which he had planned to embark: the foundation of what was to become the first revolutionary paper to circulate illegally but in some numbers throughout Russia. This was *Iskra*, a publication named after a phrase used by the Decembrists of 1825: 'A spark will start a big blaze.' The allusion had hung on and in 1895 Lenin had written of one tsarist minister's letter to another: 'The minister regards the workers as powder, and knowledge and education as sparks; the minister is convinced that if a spark falls in the powder, the explosion will first of all damage the government.'

It was not only pessimism that in the last years of the nineteenth century made some tsarist ministers fear that Russia was ripe for explosion. The accession in 1894 of a new tsar, Nicholas II, might have coincided with a change in the country's structure like that which had followed the freeing of the serfs. Towards the end of the nineteenth century Russia was acquiring fresh industrial muscle, though often with the help of foreign capital, which on an increasing scale was helping to finance factories and the expanding network of railways to serve them, yet any comparable political moves to prepare the country were frustrated by the attitude of the Tsar himself. Article 1 of the Fundamental Laws of the Empire (published in 1892) had stated: 'The Emperor of all the Russias is an autocratic and unlimited monarch. God himself commands that his supreme power be obeyed out of conscience as well as fear.' This was an injunction that Nicholas intended to follow, and it left little room for conciliation of the revolutionary forces building up beneath the surface in so many parts of Russia. It was these forces for which Lenin was determined to provide an outlet. He did so during the first decade and a half of the twentieth century, but there were two other fields, dominated by the Tsar's beliefs, on which he could make little impression until he came to power in 1917. One was agriculture, where change was persistently diluted; the other was foreign policy in which the Tsar's failure to guide his ministers allowed them to slip into the disastrous Russo-Japanese war of 1904 to 1905.

In 1900 Lenin correctly estimated that the success of his planned revolutionary paper would rest on co-operation with the Liberation of Labour group, and correspondence with its members, including Plekhanov, Akselrod, Potrezov and Vera Zasulich began to occupy a good deal of his time. The meeting between them, which was obviously necessary, would have been held in St Petersburg had that not been considered too dangerous. Instead, Pskov was chosen and here, early in April, Lenin met Martov and Potrezov as well as a number of the legal

Marxists he had been criticizing, and began to make his plans.

In spite of the remaining restrictions on his movements he set out on a lengthy tour. First he went to Moscow, barred to him, and stayed with relatives. Early in March he moved to St Petersburg, again illegally, and there met Vera Zasulich – like Lenin residing there illegally – and discussed the projected paper with her. From St Petersburg he moved on to Pskov where he was placed under surveillance by the police and where he found a job in the official statistical office. In the town he wrote a draft declaration of intent for both *Iskra* and for *Zarya (Dawn)*, a planned bimonthly magazine, and attended a meeting of legal Marxists before moving on to Riga. After talks there with local Social-Democrats, he made another illegal trip to St Petersburg. This time he was unlucky in being arrested and and held for ten days. On his release, and the confiscation by the police of 1,000 roubles, he visited Krupskaya in Ufa once more, breaking his journey at Nizhni Novgorod for more talks about the future of *Iskra*. Next, he travelled to Samara and after a visit to Smolensk left Russia at the end of July.

Lenin was convinced by now that it would be possible to publish the paper he planned, and he had succeeded in drumming up financial support from a number of well-wishers, notably Aleksandra Kalmykova, the wife of an important civil servant, who had provided an initial 1,600 roubles with which Lenin left Russia, was soon supplying more money obtained from her friends, and who, in 1902, was approached by Lenin, apparendy successfully, for a further and larger sum.

At the start of 1900 the important question of where Plekhanov would fit into the proposed publishing arrangements still had to be settled. This was finally decided at meetings held in August 1900 at various places in Switzerland. Their character can be gathered from the tide which Lenin gave to his account of them – 'How *Iskra* was Nearly Extinguished'. The main trouble was that Plekhanov, who had been running a small but not unsuccessful socialist group for almost two decades, considered that he should be in charge of the paper's policy and that Lenin should be little more than a technical assistant. Lenin, on the other hand, saw himself as the main director. The conflict would not have been so important had not the socialist movement in Russia been so riven by differences of approach on policy and tactics. It was natural enough in the circumstances, but it tended to exaggerate minor problems that might otherwise have been overlooked, and demanded compromises of those whose devotion to the cause frequently discouraged compromise.

After one meeting both Lenin and Potrezov felt indignant at their treatment by Plekhanov. Lenin subsequently wrote:

'Had we not felt such love (for Plekhanov), had we behaved toward him in a more circumspect manner, we would not have experienced such a crushing comedown, such a spiritual cold shower – This was a most severe, an injuriously severe, injuriously harsh lesson. Two young comrades "courted" an older comrade because of their great love for him, and, all of a sudden, he injects into this love an atmosphere of intrigue, and makes them feel – not like younger brothers – but like idiots who are being led around by the nose, like pawns that can be moved around with impunity, like ineffectual careerists who must be cowed and quashed. And the enamored youth receives a bitter lesson from the object of his love: to regard all persons without "sentimentality", to keep a stone in his sling . . . Blinded by love, we had actually behaved like slaves.'

Plekhanov later threatened to withdraw from the editorial board altogether, a threat that induced Lenin and Potrezov to agree to his having two votes on it, which they later regretted when they found that he still made every effort to override their opinions. After a period during which it seemed likely that the enterprise would be stillborn, as *Rabochaya Gazeta* had been, it was agreed that Vera Zasulich should sit on the board as representative of the new Marxists abroad, but in practice supporting Plekhanov's point of view. Potrezov represented the legal Marxists. There were also Akselrod, Martov and Lenin himself, the engine behind the enterprise and by far the most successful at exercising control. While divergences were over political tactics, these tended to cloak a more fundamental difference. For the older members of the Party, who had twenty years of exile behind them, *Iskra* and *Zarya* were literary undertakings while for Lenin they were instruments of revolutionary activity.

It was during this period that Lenin sent a revealing letter to Krupskaya:

'In the turmoil here I live rather fairly well, even too much so – and this in spite of special, extraordinary measures for defense against the turmoil! One might almost say that I live in loneliness – and in turmoil nevertheless! I dare say that in any novel situation turmoil is inevitable, unavoidable, and it would be a sin not to murmur thanks to God that I am far from being as nervous as our dear bookseller [Potrezov], falling into black melancholia and momentary prostration under the influence of this turmoil. There is much that is good along with the turmoil.'

The Russia that Lenin set out to transform at the start of the twentieth century, was, in many ways, not so very different from that of the preceding 100 years, a country whose record was liberally spattered with assassinations and the executions of men like his elder brother. Spread over huge distances between the European West and the Asiatic East, it absorbed as a matter of course a degree of violence and an excess of extremes which few European nations would have tolerated, which helps to explain the success of Lenin's progress along the path to power. Its predominantly peasant population, which had begun to be changed only slowly by the spread of industrialization during the last years of the nineteenth century, presented problems with which Europe's ruling classes had never had to cope, and which, moreover, were compounded by the ineptitude of a succession of tsars. The three Aleksandrs, Nicholas I and Nicholas II, ruled by a combination of harsh laws, administrations of terrorist character, and what was at times an alarming failure to judge correctly the results of their actions. Arrests of an almost arbitrary nature, followed by long prison sentences, were commonplace, and between rulers and ruled there yawned a gulf which could be bridged neither by Count Sergei Yuliyevich Witte, briefly Prime Minister after the abortive Revolution which occurred in 1905, nor by his successor, P. A. Stolypin, whose plans for agricultural reform were partially implemented only shortly before his assassination in 1911, and who was remembered not for these but for the harsh measures he employed to deal with the aftermath of 1905.

Lenin's ambition was the creation of a totally different political and social climate as he settled down to achieve his first priority: the creation of a revolutionary publication which could be circulated throughout Russia, a task beset with difficulties political, organizational and financial.

Even if all concerned with running *Iskra* had lived close together, held similar views on the more important political issues, and had similar revolutionary backgrounds, there would have been difficulties in six editors co-ordinating their running of such a publication. But Plekhanov and Akselrod lived in Switzerland, Potrezov elsewhere in Europe, and Vera Zasulich in London while Lenin and Martov can be considered European birds of passage, taking up residence wherever was most convenient. In addition, their methods of operating were very different. On this point Trotsky remembers that Vera Zasulich recalled how she had once said to Lenin: 'George [Plekhanov] is a greyhound. He shakes and shakes the adversary and lets him go; but you are a bulldog: you have a deadly bite.' Lenin had repeated 'deadly bite', obviously with great pleasure.

Among the most important points which had to be decided was where *Iskra* should be published. Plekhanov preferred Switzerland, since he would then have it more surely under his own control. Finally, however, Germany was chosen, as despite the greater chance of police surveillance, printing facilities were better there than in Switzerland. Certainly publication in Germany made Lenin his own master in a way that would have been decidedly more questionable under Plekhanov's watching eye.

From Switzerland, Lenin travelled first to Nuremberg, where he discussed printing problems, then to Munich where early in September he settled down. After a short spell at an inn owned by a Social-Democrat, he found quarters on the outskirts of the city near a park with much greenery and good connections to the city centre by electric tram. There was, in addition, an inexpensive nearby swimming-pool to which he went every day. However, when winter came he wrote to his mother saying:

'It is unpleasant without snow; I get sick of the slush, it is boring and I remember with pleasure our real Russian Winter – the sledges and the clear frosty air. I am spending my first Winter abroad, a Winter which is not like Winter and I cannot say I am pleased, though sometimes there are occasional fine days like those we have in a fine late Autumn. My life goes on as usual and fairly lonely . . . and unfortunately pretty senseless. I hope to begin my studies more systematically, but somehow I cannot manage it. Probably it will be better when the Spring comes and I shall then get "into my stride". Having wandered about Russia and Europe after sitting in Shushenskoye I long for some peaceful bookwork and only the strangeness of living abroad prevents me from settling down to it properly.'

He quickly found himself in touch with Helphand, a born conspirator who was now deeply involved in underground work and who owned in Schwabing (a suburb of Munich) an illegal press with built-in selfdestruction machinery so that if police raided the premises the type could be broken up and the illegality of the material thus concealed. And it was in Munich that Lenin wrote 'The Declaration of the Editorial Board of *Iskra*' which appeared as an offprint in October, two months before *Iskra* itself was finally published.

On 18 October he wrote to Akselrod in Zurich about continuing difficulties of both policy and printing, which were not helped by the distribution across Europe of the members of the editorial board. That the paper was to be printed in Russian in Germany further complicated matters, he emphasized to Akselrod: 'We [Lenin and Potrezov] are both quite well, but very edgy: the main thing is this agonizing uncertainty; these

German rascals keep putting us off daily with "tomorrows". What I could do to them!'

The status that Lenin was acquiring even by this date is shown by a comment of Potrezov:

'Plekhanov was esteemed, Martov was loved, but only Lenin was followed unquestioningly, as the only undisputed leader. For only Lenin embodied . . . a personage of iron will, indomitable energy, combining a fanatical faith in the movement, in the cause, with as great a faith in himself. Louis XIV could say: "I am the state"; so Lenin without unnecessary words invariably felt that he was the party, that he was the will of the movement concentrated into one person. And he acted accordingly . . . '

By 1900 he was also involved in seeing the first number of *Zarya* through the press and was responsible for distribution of it and *Iskra*, both of which were dispatched from a number of separate post offices. 'Each packet', said one colleague, 'went to a different address in Switzerland and in Belgium.' A number of Lenin's helpers in the enterprise were later to rise high in what became the Bolshevik Party, notably Vladimir Dmitriyevich Bonch-Bruyevich. A founder member of the RSDLP, he had emigrated to Switzerland in 1896, became an efficient organizer of revolutionary publications, contributed to *Iskra*, and became both business manager of the Council of People's Commissars and head of Lenin's Chancellery in the Soviet Government set up after the autumn Revolution of 1917.

Lenin remained proud all his life of what he achieved with *Iskra*. In 1917 Krupskaya wrote a brief biography of her husband and said in it: 'there is no need to speak of *Iskra*'s significance.' Lenin evidently disagreed since he added the sentence: *'Iskra* laid the foundation for the Russian Social Democratic Labor Party.'

Certainly the *Iskra* agents, whose records were to be kept so assiduously by Krupskaya, quickly became more than mere distributors. In effect they were soon the equivalent of intelligence teams from whose information it was possible to trace the development of the social-democratic forces throughout Russia. Thus the Iskrovtsky, or *Iskra-men* as they were known, gained an added importance while the paper itself became an increasingly significant factor in the revolutionary movement.

The first issue of *Iskra* appeared on 11 December according to the Julian calendar – Christmas Eve elsewhere in Europe – printed on specially thin paper and in a typeface chosen so that the maximum number of words could be packed on to a page. While this first issue was printed in Leipzig, editorial offices had remained in Munich and early in 1901 printing was moved to Helphand's press in Schwabing. Three of Lenin's articles were included in the first issue: 'The Urgent Tasks of Our Movement', 'The War in China' and 'The Split in the Union of Russian Social Democrats Abroad'. The first copies sent over the frontier near Memel in January 1901 were seized but news of this did not reach Munich until much later.

Money was a problem from the outset, as it was with most of the early RSDLP enterprises. Only in 1902 did help come from the intervention of Maxim Gorky. While on a visit to London in that year, Gorky met the rich Savva Morozov, a Russian whom he persuaded to pledge 2,000 roubles a month to Lenin's supporters, a sum which, for a while, played a key role in keeping *Iskra* in business.

Lenin's predominance among the contributors became openly

clear in 1903 when *Iskra'*s contents were analysed for discussion at the Congress of the RSDLP held in Brussels and London. Plekhanov had contributed twenty-four articles, Potrezov eight, Vera Zasulich six, Akselrod four and Lenin thirty-two. Only Martov had contributed more, with a total of thirtynine. The opening issue sketched out a programme:

> 'Do not merely organize yourselves into mutual aid societies, strike funds and workers' circles. Organize yourselves also as a political party, organize yourselves for a close struggle against autocratic government and against the whole of capitalist society. Without such an organization the proletariat is not capable of rising to a conscious class struggle. Without such an organization the workers' movement is condemned to impotence and the working class will never succeed by means of mere strike funds, circles and mutual aid societies in carrying out the great historical task that is incumbent upon it: to free itself and the whole Russian people from political and economic slavery.'

In addition to writing extensively for *Iskra*, Lenin selected contributors and allocated them subjects. A name he noted down as of possible future use was that of Aleksandra Kollontay, whose *Life of the Finnish Workers* was published in 1903. Kollontay, later to become the only woman in the Government Lenin formed after the Revolution of 1917, was the daughter of a liberal-minded Russian general. Born in 1872, she followed an unsuccessful marriage at the age of twenty-one with a quick move into social work which soon fostered revolutionary ambitions. Her book showed considerable talent and her interest in the RSDLP was equalled by Lenin's conviction of her future value to him. She became a committed Bolshevik and was later an ambassador for Soviet Russia.

In 1903 his attention was soon concentrated on dealing with the skirmishes within the RSDLP, which had preceded publication of *Iskra* and were continued immediately afterwards – as they were to continue throughout much of its history. The verbal violence accompanying the argument was typified by Lenin's report of a meeting he had at the end of December 1900 with Struve. A few hours afterwards he wrote:

'It was a remarkable meeting, "historic" in a way . . . at least it was historic as far as my life is concerned; it summed up, if not a whole epoch, at least a page in a life history, and it determined my conduct and my life's path for a long time to come.

'As the case was first stated by [A.N.] Arsenyev [Potrezov], I understood that the twin [Struve] was coming over to us and wished to take the first steps, but the very opposite turned out to be the case . . .

'The twin revealed himself in a totally new light, as a "politician" of the purest water, a politician in the worst sense of the word, an old fox, and a brazen huckster. He arrived *completely convinced of our impotence.*'

The 'old fox and brazen huckster' were typical examples of the abuse which marked many of Lenin's disputes with his opponents, and which were to have important repercussions. J. P. Nettl, Rosa Luxemburg's biographer, has stressed in his discussion of early twentieth-century Communism that:

'The harshness of his [Lenin's] polemics became settled

Bolshevik practice and Stalin's translation of words into corresponding action, physical violence to complement verbal brutality, was no more than reification, a logical end to the process. No doubt it was a manner of argumentation peculiarly suited to Lenin's personality.'

Plekhanov, always trying to keep the peace among comrades, uttered a word of warning about Lenin's criticisms of Struve. Having agreed that the criticism was entirely justified, he went on:

'You must tone down something. There is no call now for abusing the liberals in general. This is not tactful; we must appeal from the bad to the good liberal – even though we have doubts concerning the existence of such a liberal . . . It should be mentioned repeatedly that those whom you contemptuously certify as liberals, properly speaking, do not deserve to be called liberals, that such liberals are bad ones, but that liberalism in itself deserves great respect. We must regard the liberals as possible allies, but your tone, it must be admitted, is not at all that of an ally. Tone it down, my dear fellow! You are talking like an enemy when you should be talking like an ally (even though only potentially).'

All this was true enough and put a finger on one of the weaknesses in the political campaigns that Lenin was to wage during the coming years.

However, *Iskra* appeared, and Lenin's important step had been successfully taken. It is possibly significant that it was in a letter to Plekhanov in January 1901 that Vladimir Ilyich

Ulyanov first used the name Lenin by which he was to be known to the world. There was a very practical purpose behind the assumption of a different name, which was commonplace among potential revolutionaries: Russian police control required that every traveller had to register with the authorities whenever he or she arrived in a new town, but there was nothing to prevent a person from assuming a new name and the practice naturally made it more difficult for the police to keep track of them. Only later in 1901 did Ulyanov appear publicly as 'Lenin' and another eighteen months passed before the name became generally known and used outside a limited circle. How and why he adopted it is much disputed, but it has been remarked that Plekhanov had already used the sobriquet Volgin, taken from the river beside which Lenin's early years were spent. With that name already in use, Lenin took the next best available and signed himself after the longest of the Siberian rivers, the 2,648-mile Lena, which rises near Lake Baikal and flows north to empty itself through a 150-mile-wide delta into the Laptev Sea.

From now onwards he faced two major problems. One concerned *Iskra* where he found himself responsible not only for the editorial content but for distribution and the multiple other complexities of circulating a prohibited publication throughout Russia. The other dealt with putting the RSDLP on a sound organizational basis and smoothing over the frictions that arose. Both issues are apparent in the scores of letters with which he bombarded his colleagues during the early 1900s, from Munich, London or Geneva. His involvement in a multiplicity of linked tasks is shown by his letter from Munich during January 1901 to Victor P. Nogin, later Chairman of the Moscow Soviet and then Commissar of Commerce and Industry.

'Over here everything now depends on transport, which is eating up a lot of money because this is a new undertaking. I cannot therefore give you any definite reply as regards financial aid for fabricating passports, until it has become clear just how much money is needed for this, and what the chances are that all the other essentials (money apart) are available.'

Later in the year he was stressing another point. 'What is essential though', he wrote in December, 'is that the *[Iskra]* management committee should *without fail* have in view the whole of Russia, and not by any means one district only, because *Iskra*'s whole future depends on whether it will be able to overcome local rule-of-thumb work and district separateness, and become an all-Russia paper *in practice* . . . '

One specific problem was created by the fact that at the turn of the century revolutionaries were already falling into two groups, the older more experienced members and the younger ones, who had as much enthusiasm but less experience. Lenin had told Plekhanov in 1900 that:

'The fact that quite young workers and intellectuals are being drawn into the mass movement, who have almost completely forgotten, or rather have no knowledge of what used to happen in the old days and how, and the absence of organisation of "experienced" revolutionaries – all this makes it necessary to publish pamphlets about rules of behaviour for socialists.'

He himself could be said to have a foot on both camps. This had its advantages but was soon creating its own problems as he pointed out to Plekhanov when criticizing the current Party programme. 'This is not a program for a practical fighting party,' he wrote. 'It is rather a programme for scholars in an elementary course, in which capitalism in general is discussed but not capitalism in Russia.' Eventually a programme to suit everyone was hammered out, but only after much discussion.

For Lenin, 1901 was to be a year not only of argument with his co-editors about policy, but of administrative problems and considerable travel – during which he welcomed Krupskaya back from her exile. After a number of discussions, Lenin, Potrezov, Zasulich, Plekhanov, Akselrod and Martov settled their disagreements. But in the meantime Lenin had thought it necessary to inform Plekhanov: 'If the majority expresses itself in favour – I shall, of course, submit, but only after having washed my hands of it beforehand.'

The second number of *Iskra* appeared in mid-February, printed in Munich as were the next seven issues. In the city, Lenin had witnessed, apparently with some surprise, the annual carnival.

'This is the first time I have seen the last day of a carnival in a foreign country – [he wrote to his mother] processions of people in fancy dress, general buffoonery, showers of confetti (tiny scraps of coloured paper) thrown in your face, paper streamers and so on. People here do know how to make merry publicly, in the streets!'

The following month he was off on a sortie, first to Prague and then to Vienna, to arrange for his application for Krupskaya's passport to be witnessed by a Russian consul. She arrived in Munich in mid-April after first going to Prague where, owing to their attempts to mislead the police, she had expected to find her husband living under the pseudonym of Modraczek. In Munich she at first had little better luck, looking for a Herr Rittmeyer at an address that turned out to be a beer hall. Luckily she was received by a barman whose wife said: 'Ah, it must be Herr Meyer's wife. He is expecting his wife from Siberia. I'll take you to him.'

Krupskaya eventually found him with his sister Anna and Martov. After being slightly put out – 'Couldn't you write and tell me where you were?' she asked her husband – she settled down with him in the suburb of Schwabing, carrying a Bulgarian passport in the name of Frau Maritzen while Lenin used a passport which described him as another Bulgarian, Dr jur Jordan Jourdanoff.

Lenin continued to expand his revolutionary contacts in Munich, meeting Rosa Luxemburg for the first time, and having regular meetings with Karl Kautsky and Helphand, whose press was now printing *Iskra*. Its fourth issue contained 'Where to Begin', a brief outline of Lenin's views on party organization, which were developed in *What Is To Be Done?*

During this period Lenin wrote some of the minor articles in the first person although he left them unsigned.

'At that time, [Trotsky later wrote] one might have perceived a trace of "egocentricity" in this literary form. However, by giving to his literary articles, even the unsigned ones, a specific style, Lenin took full personal responsibility for their political line; evidently he was not quite sure that this line was shared by his close collaborators. Here we had, on a small scale, the persistence, the stubbornness of Lenin: his whole being was geared to one great purpose and he would make use of any circumstance and disregard all formalities in straining towards his goal – this was indeed Lenin the leader.'

During *Iskra's* first three years he is estimated to have written a total of sixty articles. It was a summer of hard work, and Krupskaya told Lenin's mother, 'I am glad for his sake; when he throws himself completely into some task he feels well and strong – that is one of his natural qualities; he is in very good health, there does not seem to be a trace of the catarrh left and no insomnia, either. Every day he takes a cold rub down and we go bathing almost every day, too.'

In Munich, as later in England and Switzerland, they kept up the custom, started in Siberia, of taking a long celebratory walk on Lenin's birthday, a custom they maintained until illness finally struck him down in Moscow in the early 1920s.

In September 1901, they were both off to Switzerland, Lenin to attend the 'unification' conference of the League of Russian Social-Democrats Abroad and, said Krupskaya as she explained to Lenin's mother, 'to have a look at the mountains. I don't know what these mountains are like, I have never seen them, except in pictures.'

Lenin gave his first public speech to Russian Social-Democrats Abroad in Zurich, returned to Munich before the end of October and was soon bemoaning to Plekhanov that he was ill and still 'struggling' with *What Is To Be Done?*, which he describes as 'advancing in a crab-like fashion'. The short book did, in fact, occupy a good deal of his time between May 1901 and February 1902. However, he felt that the administrative jobs on *Iskra* were closing in on him and on 17 December wrote to Akselrod: 'The whole burden of our newspaper now rests on my shoulders; also administrative matters due to delays in transport and the confusion in Russia have become more complex. My pamphlet *[What Is To Be Done?]* is suffering. I am terribly behind.'

Despite the stress and strain, *What Is To Be Done?* was eventually finished and appeared in Stuttgart in mid-March. For some time before its publication Lenin had been criticizing what he saw as aberrations from the pure truth of Marxist theory but in *What Is To Be Done?* he tidied up his criticisms and developed from them the need for a triple struggle, theoretical, political and economic, which would ensure that the RSDLP followed the correct path ahead. Even more important were the sections of the book in which he emphasized that any party with a chance of success would be a centralized party of dedicated men and women, disciplined in a way that no Party members had before been disciplined. Here was a blueprint with which Lenin was to split the RSDLP into two feuding bodies but from which the Bolshevik Party eventually emerged. Its essential was contained in three sentences: 'The organization of the revolutionaries must consist first and foremost of people who make revolutionary activity their profession . . . ', he wrote. 'Such an organization must perforce not be very extensive and must be as secret as possible . . . Give us an organization of revolutionaries, and we will overturn Russia!'

If there was any doubt about what this meant it was removed by what followed. Lenin wrote:

'We are marching in a compact group along a precipitous and difficult path, firmly holding each other by the hand. We are surrounded on all sides by enemies, and we have to advance almost constantly under their fire. We have combined, by a freely adopted decision, for the purpose of fighting the enemy, and not of retreating into the neighbouring marsh, the inhabitants of which, from the very outset, have reproached us with having separated ourselves into an exclusive group and with having chosen the path of struggle instead of the path of conciliation.'

Lenin traced the development of social democracy, concluded that the movement was in its third period, and finished his argument by writing:

'We firmly believe that the fourth period will lead to the consolidation of militant Marxism, that Russian Social-Democracy will emerge from the crisis in the full flower of manhood, that the opportunist rearguard will be replaced by the genuine vanguard of the most revolutionary class.

'In the sense of a call for such a "replacement", and summing up all that has been set forth above, we can give to the question "what is to be done" a short answer: Liquidate the third period.'

An announcement that *What Is To Be Done?* had been published was made in *Iskra* and this no doubt increased the existing worries of the Munich printers that the Russian secret police might encourage the Germans to take action against them – a worry intensified by a new Russo-German agreement on the exchange of political prisoners, a move expected to increase operations against underground organizations. By this time Lenin was already warning his correspondents to take care and to 'bear in mind that communication by wire is very dangerous, for they take copies of telegrams'. The conspiratorial atmosphere is suggested by the plea that the invisible ink used should be more concentrated as 'It is terribly annoying to get a letter and not be able to read it'; and by a request, made soon afterwards, from a colleague that 'a passport and small files be sewn into the soles of a pair of boots and passed on to him'. Code phrases increased: the news that an epidemic had broken out in a specific town or area merely meant that the police had been making many arrests there.

The editorial board of *Iskra* sustained growing fears and before the end of March 1902, a move to either Switzerland or London was being discussed. Plekhanov and Akselrod favoured Switzerland; Lenin preferred London, largely, it appears, because he believed that the paper would be less subject to police harassment than it would be on the Continent. Another factor, although one that he did not put bluntly on record, was that a paper produced in London would be less susceptible to influence from Plekhanov than one produced elsewhere.

These disputes might have crippled the movement's future had it not been for Lenin's ability to cope with the problems so frequently produced by his own attitude. Instead, the movement, which could increasingly be regarded as his own creation, continued in the early years of the century to attract strong characters who were to affect the destiny not only of Lenin but of the whole world. Prominent among them were two men whose lives were to be intimately linked with Lenin's – Lev Davidovich Bronstein, better known as Trotsky, and Josef Vissarionovich Dzhugashvily who entered the wider revolutionary world as Joseph Stalin.

Trotsky was the son of a Jewish landowner in the Ukraine, exiled to Siberia for his dissident activities and nicknamed 'Pen' because of his extensive writings. He had a fluctuating relationship with Lenin, played a crucial role in the Bolshevik seizure of power in 1917, an even more important role in securing victory during the civil war of 1918 to 1921, and was principally responsible for creating the Red Army, which made that victory possible.

Stalin – a Caucasian born near Tiflis in 1875 and banished to Siberia for revolutionary activities after working in a Tiflis seminary – played his most significant role in Russia's destiny after Lenin's death, although from 1917, when he reached Moscow after a further spell in exile, he began to influence the new Bolshevik Government.

The future of neither Trotsky nor Stalin could have been foreseen in 1902 as the editors of *Iskra* argued about where the paper should be printed in future. Lenin's view prevailed and towards the end of March he and Krupskaya left Munich for England. They broke their journey in Cologne to visit the cathedral and on 1 April (14 April according to the Gregorian calendar) arrived in London, Lenin having made notes for a new draft programme for the RSDLP during the journey. They were met by Nikolay Alekseyev, a Russian refugee who had been living in Britain for some time and who now shepherded them through the problems of a city entirely new to them. He was not the only friend who rallied to their help. Another was Apollinaria Yakubova who had been exiled to Siberia where she had met Krupskaya again, had escaped, made her way to England and married Takhtarev, the former editor of *Rabochaya Mysl*. The Takhtarevs helped Lenin and Krupskaya, now travelling as Mr and Mrs Richter, to find two rooms at 30 Holford Square in the Grays Inn Road area of central London. Here they settled down in the house of a Mrs Yeo, a landlady who was mildly allergic to foreigners, was suspicious of Krupskaya's lack of a wedding ring (the makeshift Siberian product having apparently been discarded) and disliked the fact that the

Richters, German as they were considered to be, put up curtains in their room on a Sunday. But Lenin, revealing a lifelong weakness, gave Mrs Yeo's cat a friendly reception, which helped their cause.

Lenin showed great interest in the city, its people, and an environment that was entirely new to him. '[We] at once . . . began to look round at this citadel of capitalism with curiosity, Plekhanov and the editorial conflicts for the moment forgotten,' Krupskaya remembered. He acclimatized well, and although he never became reconciled to the swift changes in the English weather, appears to have adapted himself equably to a totally new environment. Judging by Krupskaya's comments, it was only the food that worried them. 'We found,' she said, 'that all those "ox-tails", skates fried in fat, and indigestible cakes were not made for Russian stomachs.'

During this first period in London Lenin spent much of his time in what was then an area favoured by Jewish immigrants and on 21 March 1903 addressed a meeting at the New Alexandra Hall in Whitechapel under the auspices of the Jewish branch of the Social-Democratic Federation. Although his Jewish ancestry has always remained in dispute, Lenin's views on Jewry were decided if complicated. Always taking a strong line against anti-Semitism, he was an almost equally fervid anti-Zionist, once writing that Zionism appeared to be a greater enemy to social democracy than anti-Semitism.

In London he attended any left-wing meetings to which he could gain access. He appears to have been distinctly unimpressed by them, but did his best to improve matters. Hence on 29 November 1902 he lectured in Whitechapel, speaking in Russian on the programme and tactics of revolution, and later discussed sentence by sentence with the members of a study group started by Alekseyev, the draft programme which had been printed in *Iskra*.

When he was not attending political meetings he explored the equivalent of London's contemporary Green Belt, which in the nineteenth century ringed London far more tightly than it does today, and in September was writing to his mother: 'Nadya and I have often been out locally in search of "real countryside" and have found it.'

Soon afterwards he was joined in London by Trotsky. After escaping from Siberia he had made his way to England. Trotsky later wrote:

'A cab that I engaged because I saw others doing so took me to an address jotted down on a scrap of paper, my destination. This was Vladimir Ilyich's home. Before this (it must have been in Zurich) I had been taught to knock at a door in a certain definite way. As far as I remember, Nadezda Constantinovna opened the door for me; I had fetched her out of bed with my knocking, as one can imagine. It was early in the morning, and any sensible man, more familiar with the ordinary conventions of life, would have waited an hour or two at the station, instead of knocking at strange doors at dawn. But I was still completely under the influence of my flight from Vercholensk [where he had been in exile]. I had already roused Akselrod's household in Zurich in the same way, only not at dawn, but in the middle of the night.

'Vladimir Ilyich was still in bed, and he greeted me with justifiable surprise. Under such conditions our first meeting and our first conversation took place.'

Pen was given tea and an improvised breakfast in the kitchen-dining room and handed over to Krupskaya latest details of the RSDLP organization in various parts of Russia.

The following day he was taken on one of his first conducted tours of London, during which Lenin pointed out the sights with such comments as: 'That's *their* famous Westminster [Abbey].' ' "Their",' Trotsky later explained, 'meant not, of course, the one belonging to the English, but to the enemy.' On one occasion Lenin led him into a socialist church where Trotsky remembered the congregation singing what he recalled as 'Almighty God, put an end to all kings and all rich men'. As they left the building, Lenin turned to him saying: 'The English proletariat has in itself many revolutionary and socialist elements but they are all mixed up with conservatism, with religion and prejudices; and there seems to be no way in which these elements can come to the top.'

But Lenin's main task in London was to arrange for the printing of *Iskra*. It was Alekseyev who solved the problem. Martov had written to him early in the year suggesting that he, Martov, should contact Harry Quelch, the editor of the British Social-Democratic Party's *Justice*, a journal printed in cramped quarters at 37a Clerkenwell Green. The house had been connected with a variety of revolutionary or socialist movements and used for Chartist demonstrations some sixty years earlier. Members of the General Council of the First International had spoken there, and the printing press set up on the premises had later been used to produce pamphlets by Marx, Engels, Liebknecht and August Bebel. Quelch agreed to print *Iskra* and Lenin found the atmosphere friendly although space was cramped. A corner was boarded off at the printing works by a thin partition to serve him as editorial room,' a visitor wrote. 'This corner contained a very small writing table, a bookshelf above it, and a chair. When the present writer visited Quelch in this "editorial office" there was no room for another chair.'

The humble surroundings surprised more than one visitor.

'I was profoundly astonished that the Social-Democratic Federation had such a small printing press, [Osip Pyatnitsky later wrote] and that it was publishing a small weekly, the circulation of which was no larger than that of *Iskra*. The Russian S.D.P. in a foreign country, far away from their native land, were publishing a paper which was no worse than that possessed by a legal party in Britain. For me at that time it was incomprehensible, all the more so after the printing-presses, the newspaper circulations, the premises and bookshops, which I had seen in the hands of the German Social – Democrats.'

But despite the cramped conditions Lenin had pleasant memories of the place and when Quelch's son Thomas visited him in Moscow in 1920, one of Lenin's first questions was, 'How is everyone at Clerkenwell Green?'

Seventeen issues of *Iskra* were printed there on a flat-bed machine, the material having been set by a Russian compositor named Blumenfeld, at a small works in the East End and the formes (moulds) then brought to Clerkenwell Green. By late 1903 when a split in the RSDLP brought about Lenin's resignation from the board of the paper, he had thus successfully resolved the main problem of having a Russian publication printed in London, but there were others which occupied a great deal of his patience, ingenuity and time. One was the question of secrecy. Although the English police were considered less of a danger than those in Germany or Russia, Lenin and his colleagues had become so used to covering their tracks that they continued to do so even when it was hardly necessary. There was, for instance, the ceaseless effort to conceal the fact that *Iskra* headquarters had been moved to London, and Akselrod was told: 'If possible, when talking with people try systematically to speak of Munich instead of London and the people in Munich instead of Londoners.' There were also the occasions on which London would be called Prague, as Munich had once been when *Iskra* was being printed in the Bavarian capital.

Secrecy and subterfuge were genuinely necessary in the letters from London to *Iskra* correspondents or to readers in Europe. The regular stream was handled by Krupskaya, who first made a draft. Next, the portion to be coded was underlined and then put into a new open text for the Russian censor's eyes. Finally the important message was written in invisible ink between the lines.

It was understandable that men and women brought up in Russia, beneath the ever-present threat of the secret police, should take precautions that at times appear over-dramatic but even Krupskaya later looked back and marvelled at what she called the naivety of their conspiratorial work.

'All those letters about handkerchiefs (passports), brewing beer, warm fur (illegal literature), all those code-names for towns – beginning with the same letter as the name of the town ("Ossip" for Odessa, "Terenty" for Tver, "Petya" for Poltava, "Pasha" for Pskov, etc.) all this substitution of women's names for men's, and vice versa – all this was transparent in the extreme.'

The police appear to have taken little interest in Lenin's activities although Harry Pollitt, Secretary of the British Communist Party from 1929 to 1946, has maintained that on one occasion a police detective hid himself in a cupboard of the Crown and Woolpack, a public house where Russian *émigrés* often met. But he later reported, as Pollitt has written: 'The meeting was conducted all in Russian, and I know nothing of this language, so am unable to report the subjects they discussed.'

While there was virtually no risk involved for the *Iskra* staff in London, it was very different for those in Russia and the danger often kept Lenin on tenterhooks. Krupskaya has recalled:

'Those weeks and months of waiting for answers to his letters, constantly expecting the whole thing to fall through, that constant state of uncertainty and suspense, were anything but congenial to Vladimir Ilyich's character. His letters to Russia were full of requests to write punctually . . . to act promptly. He did not sleep at night after receiving a letter from Russia saying that "Sonya is silent as the dead" or that "Zarin did not join the committee in time", or that "We have no contact with the Old Woman". I shall never forget those sleepless nights.'

The problems of organizing agents were numerous and constant, as Lenin explained in August 1902, saying that in nine cases out of ten all plans ended in smoke as the frontier was crossed:

'. . . . and the agent muddles along just anyhow. Believe me, I am literally losing all faith in routes, plans, etc., made here, because I know beforehand that nothing will come of it all. We "have to" make frantic efforts *doing (for lack of suitable people)* other people's jobs. In order to appoint agents, to look after them, to *answer* for them, to unite and guide them

112

in practice – it is necessary to be everywhere, to rush about, to see all of them on the job, at work. This requires a team of *practical organizers and leaders,* but we haven't got any; at least, very, very few to speak of . . . That's the whole trouble. Looking at our practical mismanagement is often so infuriating that it robs one of the capacity for work; the only consolation is that it must be a vital cause if it is *growing* – and obviously it is – *despite* all this chaos. That means when the ferment is over we shall have good wine.'

The need for secrecy was stressed after workers at the Kiev end of an *Iskra* distribution line had been discovered by the Russian police. But within a few months three new routes by which copies could be spread throughout Russia were in operation. One went through Stockholm and then down through Finland to Vyborg. A second passed through Archangel and a third went from London to Brindisi and then on to Kherson near Odessa. An even more exotic method of distribution was through Baku where the Third Group, a Georgian section of the revolutionary movement, had set up a clandestine press known as Nina. To this were sent – by sea and horse – 'mats' of the *Iskra* pages from which further copies could be printed for distribution throughout southern Russia.

Much of Lenin's time during his first months in London was occupied in organizing such routes, writing articles for *Iskra,* and persuading other members of the RSDLP to do the same. He also attended working-class meetings in out-of-the-way places. These, his wife later wrote,

'. . . . were usually devoted to the discussion of some such question as a garden-city scheme. Ilyich would listen attentively and afterwards joyfully exclaim: "Socialism is simply oozing from them. The speaker talks rot, and a worker gets up and immediately, taking the bull by the horns, himself lays bare the essence of Capitalist Society." Ilyich always placed his hope on the rank-and-file British workman who, in spite of everything, preserved his class instinct.'

Many of the nooks and crannies of time that could be found for other pursuits were occupied with learning English. To help in understanding the language Lenin and his wife went to the theatre and even to the pantomime, by which he seems to have been fascinated. 'It is the expression of a certain satirical attitude towards generally accepted ideas,' was how he described it to Maxim Gorky, 'an attempt to turn them inside out, to distort them, to show the arbitrariness of the usual. It is a little complicated, but interesting.' He had taken English lessons while in Munich but in London was anxious to improve his idiomatic speech and in May advertised in the *Athenaeum* that 'A Russian LL.D. (and his Wife) would like to exchange Russian lessons for English with an English Gentleman (or Lady).' Three men offered their services: a Mr Raymond who worked for George Bell, the publishers; Mr Williams, a clerk; and Mr Young, a workman. Lenin appears to have used all three.

He continued with his political journalism, sending material to colleagues for comment and in the process building up a disagreement with Plekhanov that grew throughout the next few years.

'I have received my article ["The Agrarian Programme of Russian Social Democracy"] with your remarks [he wrote to Plekhanov in May 1902]. You have a fine idea of tact with regard to your colleagues on the editorial board! You do not hesitate to choose the most contemptuous expressions, not to mention the "voting" on the suggestions, which you did not even take the trouble to formulate, and even about the "voting" about style. I should like to know what you would say if I were to answer your article on the programme in the same way? If your aim is to make mutual work impossible then the way you have chosen will very rapidly help you to succeed. As for our personal, apart from our business, relations, you have finally spoilt them, or more exactly: you have achieved their complete cessation.'

He read the papers for news of local meetings and attended any that were likely to produce evidence of socialist sentiments. Speakers' Corner in Hyde Park was visited frequently. Krupskaya reported:

'One man – an atheist – tried to prove to a group of curious listeners that there was no God. We particularly liked one such speaker – he had an Irish accent which we were better able to understand. Next to him a Salvation Army officer was shouting out hysterical appeals to Almighty God, while a little way off a salesman was holding forth about the drudgery of shop assistants in the big stores.'

By the summer of 1902 Lenin and Krupskaya had become important figures in RSDLP organization. They had a dozen underground agents operating in Russia, paid out of *Iskra* funds and organized by Krupskaya, who acted as secretary to the group. While they were building up their position the Socialist

Revolutionary Party, which was to have a considerable impact on Lenin's future, came into existence in Russia through the merging of a number of Narodnik groups. Appealing more to the peasants than to industrial workers, by 1917 the Socialist Revolutionaries formed the largest party in Russia. In that year the party first split into Left and Right sections; then, in November of the same year, the Left formed a separate party, and shortly afterwards joined the Bolsheviks in a coalition Government which lasted until March 1918.

Little of this could have been foreseen in 1902 as the Social-Democrats gathered strength and Lenin became increasingly involved in planning the next RSDLP Congress. There had been an attempt by Social-Democrats in Russia to organize this earlier in the year but numerous police arrests followed the meeting's opening session and what had been planned as a Congress was downgraded into a conference. After this failure Lenin organized a conference at Pskov from London, and here arrangements were successfully completed for a Congress in Brussels to take place as early as possible in 1903. The tedious administrative work, plus the trials of running *Iskra* and the more pleasant task of writing for it, took up an increasing amount of time, but did not prevent all attempts to 'get out into the countryside, out of the smoke and fog-enshrouded monster', as Krupskaya recorded. It was especially difficult, she added, when they did not want to spend more than three halfpence on the bus fare.

Krupskaya's mother arrived in London before the end of 1902 and she accompanied her daughter and son-in-law on one country jaunt of the kind that Lenin particularly enjoyed. He wrote:

'We took sandwiches with us instead of lunch and spent the

whole of one Sunday *ins Grüne* (quite unintentionally we are taking to foreign ways and arrange our outings on Sundays of all days, though that is the worst time because everywhere is crowded). We had a long walk, the air went to our heads as if we were children and afterwards I had to lie down and rest, as I did after a shooting trip in Siberia. In general, we do not miss a chance to go on outings. We are the only people among the comrades here who are exploring *every bit* of the surrounding country. We discover various "rural" paths, we know all the places nearby and intend to go further afield.'

In June (1902) he set off for Paris where he addressed Russian *émigrés* on the programme and tactics of his supporters and on the programmes of the RSDLP. Then he moved to Loguivy in Brittany where he was joined for a brief holiday by his mother from Russia and his sister Anna Ulyanova-Yelizarova from Germany. 'I liked it here [Loguivy] very much on the whole and have had a good rest, only unfortunately I was a bit premature in imagining myself well again, forgot about dieting and now am again having trouble with catarrh.'

Back in London, he wrote a series of articles about the tasks to be done, then in November left England for Switzerland. He broke his journey to address a meeting in Liege, and lectured in Lausanne, Geneva, Berne and Zurich before returning to England. His mother, he found, had been asking about his living conditions and had been given a not particularly reassuring description by Krupskaya. The account of the Lenin *ménage* which she now passed on to her daughter Anna ran:

'In all they have two small rooms and one of them, that of

El. Vasilevna [Krupskaya's mother], serves both as kitchen and dining-room. Water and coal, the fuel they use, are both downstairs and have to be brought up; the washing-up water has to be taken outside and so on . . . they had first of all thought of looking for a larger place but Nadenka added that she and V[olodya] have become like cats which get used to a particular spot.'

Lenin lived what some of his colleagues felt was a Spartan existence, breakfasting on two or three fried eggs and a small piece of ham, washed down by a mug of thick dark beer.

By 1903 the stresses and strains that were to split the RSDLP into two factions later in the year, and to produce a series of fissions and arguments for almost a decade, were already being felt. Edward Bernstein's supporters lent their weight to the belief that 'revisionism' and 'reformism' could ensure the necessary changes without a revolution, and continued to concentrate on the immediate needs of the proletariat rather than the longer-term aims of winning political freedom by overthrow of the autocracy. Many of the disagreements aroused by these beliefs rested fundamentally on the difference between Lenin's 'all-or-nothing' conception of revolution, outlined in *What Is To Be Done?*, and the various more liberal alternatives being proposed by other members of the RSDLP. Many of the alternatives were epitomized in the writings of Struve. That his schism with Lenin was already becoming unbridgeable was made obvious when, in *Iskra* no. 37, Lenin attacked Struve's position in 'Mr Struve Exposed by his Colleague'. It was important, Lenin wrote here, to 'subordinate *everything without exception* to the interests and demands of the *revolutionary struggle*'.

In the immediate aftermath of this controversy the editorial office of *Iskra* was transferred from London to Geneva, a move against which Lenin had fought and lost. So strongly did it affect him that it brought on an attack of shingles, the extremely painful virus disease which can be aroused by worry. Lenin had been so overwrought by the situation, Krupskaya later wrote, 'that he developed a nervous illness called "holy fire", which consists in inflammation of the nerve terminals of back and chest . . . On the way to Geneva Vladimir Ilyich was very restless; on arriving there he broke down completely, and had to lie in bed for two weeks.'

By the end of May he seems to have recovered completely, probably helped in that he now began to resolve his difficulties with other members of the RSDLP by writing the first and then the second draft of the Party programme, as well as the rules of procedure and the agenda for its Second Congress.

The Congress did more than split the Social-Democrats into two opposing factions. It triggered off a series of disagreements between Lenin and other members of the RSDLP whose reper-cussions were to be felt for years. Moreover, his tactics in the battles that followed the Congress aroused suspicions of the way in which he operated, suspicions that continued and were to affect the way in which Lenin was able to pave the way for revo-lution between 1903 and 1917. 'Ilich was very clever in the way he dealt with people before elections to congresses,' one of his colleagues subsequently wrote. 'He would get his own people in and keep out outsiders, vociferous big mouths, trouble-makers, Makhaevites and block-heads from the *workers' opposition.'* Lenin's success in his use of such tactics increased with the years, but they were already in evidence at the Second – and soon to be famous – Congress of the RSDLP.

119

Apart from being the scene of the split between what were to become Lenin's Bolsheviks and Martov's Mensheviks, the Second Congress was the occasion on which Lenin first met a number of the men who were later to play important roles in his life. One was J. Hanecki-Fürstenberg, who joined Lenin in 1912 after he had moved to Cracow in Poland, who repeatedly travelled on underground assignments for him in both Poland and Russia, and who was to maintain links with him during the First World War from Sweden.

Another future colleague was Heer Genokh Koissevich, an enthusiastic follower who had been pursuing him for some time, and who assumed many names during an active life but was most widely known as Maxim Litvinov. Litvinov had joined the RSDLP in 1898, been imprisoned in Kiev soon afterwards, and following his escape had travelled to Switzerland in the hope of meeting Lenin. Instead he met Georgy Plekhanov who persuaded him to start smuggling copies of *Iskra* into Russia, a task at which he became expert. Hearing of the coming Second Congress, he travelled to Brussels, missed Lenin once again, but finally caught up with him in London, the city to which the Congress had been moved. Here, after an initial meeting allegedly in the Reading Room of the British Museum, he was taken to the Holford Square home and began a friendship that was to last until Lenin's death more than twenty years later. Litvinov carried out many tasks for Lenin and his Party before gaining diplomatic status, including, in 1907, the changing of money taken from the State Bank in Tiflis during the most famous of all the Bolsheviks' 'expropriation' robberies. Caught in Paris, he was deported to England where, with the help of a letter from Maxim Gorky to Charles Hagberg Wright, Librarian of the London Library, he obtained a post with the publishers Williams and Norgate.

The Congress of 1903 opened in Brussels on 30 July in a large flour warehouse, its windows curtained off with red cloth. Here, representatives of five *émigré* organizations and twenty-one groups from Russia assembled. Lenin's supporters appeared to have an unchallengeable majority among the forty-three delegates with their fifty-one mandates, since the *Iskra* organization's twenty-seven delegates could apparently command thirtyfive votes. However, there were five votes for the Bund (Yiddish meaning Union*, two for the Union of Russian Social-Democrats, an *émigré* group which did not support Lenin, one for a St Petersburg group hostile to *Iskra,* and two votes for a small group called Yuzhny Rabochiy (Southern Workers), which was partly independent although it followed the *Iskra* line on many matters. There was, therefore, considerable scope for what could be called either negotiation or horse-trading.

No problems arose during the first sessions. Plekhanov made the opening speech and was elected chairman. Lenin and P. A. Krasnikov were made vice-chairmen. Then, before any crucial issues came up for discussion, some of the delegates were expelled from Belgium. Emile Vandervelde, the Belgian socialist, warned that others might be in danger of arrest and, since it was known that the Russians among them could be repatriated with disastrous consequences, it was decided to suspend proceedings and continue them in London.

This move could have been forced on the Party earlier since one member of the Committee which organized the Congress,

---

* The Bund was the General Union of Lithuanian, Polish and Russian Jewish Workers. Founded in 1897, it joined the RSDLP at its First Congress, left it at the Second Congress in 1903 and rejoined it after the Fourth Congress in 1906.

Dr Yakov Zhitomirsky, was also a member of the tsarist police, the Okhrana. Dr Zhitomirsky had for long been keeping a watch on the RSDLP; it has even been suggested that the lenient treatment accorded Lenin when he was apprehended during his illegal visit to St Petersburg in 1900 was due to Zhitomirsky and that the Okhrana, well briefed on Lenin's plans, was only too glad that he was about to leave Russia.

The move of the Second Congress from Brussels to London meant a good deal of additional routine work for Lenin. Accommodation had to be found hurriedly for the delegates after which regular visits had to be made to ensure that there were no misunderstandings with landladies and that the visitors knew their ways to the different cafés and small halls with conference rooms where the meetings were to be held. One of the first was in an anglers' club where fishing trophies decorated the walls. Others took place in rooms at cafés or public houses, at one of which the landlord was told that the gathering was a meeting of trade unionists.

The Congress reopened in London on 11 August and it was here that the schisms in the Russian revolutionary movement, which were to continue for a decade – until, in fact, the disagreements between the two warring groups were admitted to be irreconcilable and what had been the RSDLP for all practical purposes dissolved into two parties – broke into the open. Basically, the argument was between Lenin's concept of a party led by dedicated professional revolutionaries, an élite which would rule the other members with an iron discipline, and Martov's idea of a less élitist party which would not be so firmly under the control of its leaders but whose members would have more individual influence. Around this central difference were grouped others concerning such matters as the degree of party

122

discipline to be maintained, the extent of central direction on specific details, and the use or non-use of violence to achieve party aims.

The argument broke out at the twenty-second session of the Congress when both Lenin and Martov put forward statutes determining membership of the Party. Lenin proposed that a member was to be one who accepted the RSDLP's programme and supported the Party both financially and by personal participation in one of its organizations. Martov included an amendment that watered down the words after 'financially' so that a member only gave the Party his regular personal co-operation under the direction of the Party organization.

The difference was not blatantly obvious, and both Lenin and Martov tried to minimize it. Thus, Martov almost echoed Lenin when he said: 'Let there be a host of organizations . . . *They cannot enter the party organization,* but the party cannot do without them.' Lenin, also, tried to reassure listeners, saying, 'There's no need to imagine that party organizations must consist only of professional revolutionaries. We need the most varied kinds of organizations . . . from extremely narrow, clandestine ones down to extremely broad, free and open ones. The essential qualification of a party organization is its recognition by the Central Committee.'

Attempts to blur the issue failed to disguise that while Martov was working towards a broad-based party, Lenin's aim was a party of a much narrower scope. Trotsky is reported to have commented of this aim: 'But that's dictatorship you're advocating,' to which Lenin replied: 'There is no other way.' More than one of the delegates certainly saw that this narrower party would be more easily controlled by its leader who, by now, was certain to be Lenin himself. This no doubt affected the voting, which unexpectedly approved Martov's version by twenty-eight votes to twenty-three and thus gave the first round to Lenin's opponents. The confused situation was worsened in that there were fifty-two participants at the meeting of whom only forty-two could vote while nine had two votes each because they represented larger groups than the rest.

However, this vote was to be only the prelude to a series of manoeuvrings and accidents that resulted in a succession of victories and defeats affecting the two groups. Among the most important was the withdrawal of the five Bundist members from the Congress when they were denied the sole representation of Jewish workers in the party. The Union of Russian Social-Democrats followed suit and the balance within the party was thus changed, Lenin's supporters becoming the *bolchinstvo* or majority, and Martov's the *menchinstvo,* or minority. And thus for the next fifteen years the prelude to the autumn Revolution of 1917 was played out against the rivalries of the Bolsheviks and the Mensheviks.

The argument over wording of the Party's membership rules was only one of a number that produced heated discussion at the Second Congress. Others arose from the decision to set up a tripartite executive apparatus consisting of a Central Organ [the *Iskra* board], a Central Committee, and a Party Council. Lenin did his best to secure complete control of this apparatus, and spoke more than 100 times during the Congress. To start with, he looked like being successful. He succeeded first in eliminating Akselrod, Vera Zasulich and Potrezov – all Mensheviks – from the editorial board of *Iskra,* leaving a board consisting of himself and Plekhanov, with Martov as the sole representative of the Mensheviks. When Martov's request that the three former members should be reinstated was turned down Martov announced that he would take no part in producing the next number of the paper. *Iskra* thus became virtually a Bolshevik paper for a while, a situation which was altered in the autumn when Plekhanov changed his position and insisted on the return of the former board members in order to reunite the Party. Lenin was dismayed when from issue no. 52 *Iskra* became, in effect, a Menshevist organ.

> 'Inasmuch [he said in a letter to Plekhanov written in Geneva on 1 November 1903, and handed to him the same day] as I do not share the opinion of G. V. Plekhanov, member of the Party Council and of the editorial board of the Central Organ *[Iskra]*, that it will be in the interest of Party unity at the present time to make a concession to the Martovites and co-opt the board of six, I hereby resign from the Party Council and from the editorial board of the Central Organ. [But he added as a postscript:] At all events, I by no means refuse to support the new central Party institutions by my work, to the best of my ability.'

There was no doubt about the strength of his feelings.

Plekhanov's change of front in the autumn of 1903 can best be explained not by his views of the respective merits of Lenin's and Martov's ideas on party organization, but by a preference for the way in which Martov had conducted his campaign. As Leonard Schapiro, student of Bolshevism, has correctly argued in his detailed account of Communism's rise in Russia:

> 'Lenin could veer, prevaricate, intrigue and sow confusion, seeking support from the devil himself if it were offered, without for a moment imagining that his conduct might in

itself be considered of any importance when judged in relation to the ultimate end. He always attributed the worst motives to his opponents; and there is a ring of sincerity about the surprise which he occasionally revealed that his own conduct should have given rise to genuine dismay among his fellow social democrats.'

All attempts to find a compromise failed. Lenin found himself, after years of preparation, outside the central councils of the Party, and the fact that it was largely his own fault was of little consolation to him. The best he could do was to write *One Step Forward, Two Steps Back*. In this he not only commented on the minutes of the Congress and gave his version of the split that had taken place, but reiterated his belief in the need for a narrowly based party with its core of professional revolutionaries. Martov replied in the Menshevik-dominated *Iskra* with a critical article, 'Forward or Back?', which was in turn countered by a cartoon from Lenin's supporters published in Geneva.

While *One Step Forward, Two Steps Back* provided a further blueprint for what was to become the Bolshevik Party, the title was also a pointer to a future important feature of Lenin's strategy in matters other than politics. His life was certainly full of many acts showing determination to stand his ground in adverse circumstances; yet it also demonstrated, on many occasions, a willingness to compromise, an ability to retreat *pour mieux sauter*, which could disarm his enemies and at times alarm his friends. Lenin's success in a political field that extended beyond the revolutionary movement was more than once due to this dexterity in changing his ground and apparently giving in when in fact the result would achieve his long-term ends. At Brest-Litovsk in 1918 and with his New Economic Policy in 1921 he pulled a measure of military and economic triumph from disaster by this ability to forget earlier assertions and tailor theory to the facts of life. It was an ability shown in minor ways on many occasions during the early years of the twentieth century as he made his way successfully through the labyrinthine coils of revolutionary politics. His own conduct, the veering and prevarication as Schapiro saw it, was once simply explained by Lenin when he had gained power: For me, theory is only a hypothesis, not the Holy Scripture; it is a tool in our daily work.'

The fissions that came to light during the Second Congress, and which for years were to bedevil the efforts of men and women working for revolution in Russia, were not solely due to Lenin's view of how the Party should be run being different from that of others. As much as six months earlier, Potrezov had written: 'relations between Lenin on the one hand and Martov, Vera Zasulich and myself on the other, which were already tense, went completely to pieces. The incident which drew our attention to Lenin's amorality and brought matters to a head was his utterly cynical resistance to the investigation of a charge levelled by the damaged party against one of his outstanding agents.'

This was not the only quality to which some of Lenin's potential supporters objected. There was another. Lenin pursued his arguments with a great force, Potrezov remembered several years after his death. 'But at the same time with a quality of one-sidedness, a kind of single note simplification, a quality of over-simplifying the complexities of life.'

Discontent with the way in which Lenin tried to enforce his own ideas was increased in 1903 after the Congress had approved the setting-up of the five-member Supreme Party Council. Two of the five were appointed by the three-member Central Committee which operated inside Russia, two were appointed by *Iskra* and the fifth was elected directly by the Congress. Lenin's efforts to ensure that his supporters formed a majority on the Central Committee were carried on with a ruthless determination to succeed; his tactics alienated him from many of the delegates and, in effect, widened the breach between himself and Martov, who had made the fatal mistake of withdrawing support from the Central Committee and *Iskra,* thus leaving Lenin in control.

Another reason for continuation of the arguments for so long was that while many Party members were anxious to heal the rift, Lenin's aim was to crush the Mensheviks whom he saw as challenging the machinery that he had built up. *What Is To Be Done?* had laid down the line he believed the Party should follow, and he had succeeded in persuading most of the local groups in Russia to agree. 'Now', as Martov's biographer has underlined, 'all he had achieved was in jeopardy . . . Altogether, Lenin faced a threat both to the measure of control and power which he had gathered into his hands and to his organizational ideas, i.e. to everything he had worked for for years.' In addition, conflict itself tended to satisfy Lenin's love of combat, as he demonstrated to one delegate who complained to him, 'What a depressing atmosphere prevails at our Congress. All this fierce fighting, this agitation one against the other, these sharp polemics, this uncomradely attitude!' Lenin's contradictory response was:

' "What a fine thing our Congress is," I replied to him. "Opportunity for open fighting. Opinions expressed. Tendencies revealed. Groups defined. Hands raised. A decision taken. A stage passed through. Forward! That's what I like! That's life! It is something different from the endless, wearying intellectual discussions, which finish, not because people have solved the problem, but simply because they have got tired of talking!" "The Comrade of the Centre" looked on me as though perplexed and shrugged his shoulders. We had spoken in different languages.'

But there was one way in which he took the split very badly, writing in the aftermath of the Congress:

'You can't imagine even a tenth of the outrages to which the Martovites have sunk here, poisoning the whole atmosphere abroad with their spiteful gossip, encroaching on our contacts, *money*, literary material, etc. War has been declared, and they (Lyuba, Kostya, Yeryoma) are already on their way to fight in Russia. Get ready for the most legal but desperate struggle.'

The Second Congress ended on 23 August, but before leaving London for Geneva Lenin took a large party of the delegates to the London Zoo, the Natural History Museum in Kensington, and Marx's grave in Highgate Cemetery. Lenin had visited the grave more than once and was able to lead his companions to it. This was lucky since the gate keeper did not know where it was, bringing from Lenin the comment: 'Clearly they don't visit it very often.'

Back in Geneva he and Krupskaya began to construct a replica of the machinery they had used during the early days of *Iskra* – machinery driven now by Lenin's annoyance at what he regarded as personal opposition and by a genuine belief that there was only one way in which the Bolsheviks could succeed: by building up a dedicated party of professional revolutionaries. He elaborated his views in the spring of 1904, making three speeches to the Council of the Party. He was now laying the foundations of what was to become Bolshevism.

In Geneva he started work early in the morning and kept on until lunchtime. After lunch he would begin another session that would continue until about four o'clock, then leave his rooms for a walk. 'However, although he went out for his walks in order to rest,' says Valentinov, 'the work on his book [*One Step Forward, Two Steps Back*] was not actually interrupted (he merely talked out loud instead of "whispering"), and he did not stop expending nervous energy. When he got back home, he resumed his writing, sometimes continuing until very late.'

There was not all that much difference between how he wrote and how he spoke, says P. N. Lepeshinsky, (the Social-Democrat who for a while had also been exiled in Siberia). 'In speech as in writing, his thought runs like a full lively stream, and the author does not stop even for a moment to consider the form in which his ideas pour out, never stops to admire the felicity of his own phrase, nor does he ever get embarrassed by some clumsiness of his expression.'

Whatever accommodations could eventually be worked out between Bolsheviks and Mensheviks, Lenin was in no doubt about the fissiparous results of the break. 'The Party is virtually torn apart, the Rules have been turned into scraps of paper and the organization is spat upon,' he wrote to the Central Committee in February 1904. To others he maintained that the Central Committee members were in very serious danger of becoming 'extremely backward eccentrics' and that 'Ever since the Second Congress, the Party is being torn to pieces . . .'

It was a period during which Lenin imposed few restraints on his capacity for invective and a letter to a supporter, I. V. Babushkin, in January 1904 was typical of many more:

'We welcome [your] energetic behaviour and once again ask you to continue in the same fighting spirit, without admitting the slightest wavering. War on the Vyshibalovtsy and to the devil with all the conciliators, people with "indeterminate views" – idiots! Better small fish than a large beetle! Better two or three energetic and completely devoted men than a dozen dawdlers. Write as often as you can and *without delay,* give us some notion of your workers (and describe them) so that in case of failure we should not run aground.'

The Central Committee, like Plekhanov, favoured some form of compromise although it could not agree to Lenin's demand for a further Congress – one at which he appeared confident of strengthening his position *vis-à-vis* the Mensheviks. Discussions continued throughout the spring and summer of 1904. In August, the Party recognized *Iskra* under its new control but invited Lenin to return to it. At the same time it called for informal discussions between Bolsheviks and Mensheviks in lieu of Lenin's proposed new Congress. Lenin replied by resigning from the Central Committee.

Thus the impasse between the two wings of the RSDLP became more difficult to resolve. It was to remain so for some further years although the political situation in Russia was changed in the first months of 1905 by the repercussions of 'Bloody Sunday', the clash between Government and people that triggered off an abortive revolution.

The greater part of the argument between Lenin's Bolsheviks and Martov's Mensheviks continued to be conducted by Lenin from Geneva. It was here that newly arrived comrades reported first to Krupskaya, who briefed those who were leaving and sent them on their way.

In 1904 Krupskaya was joined by Lydia Fotiyeva, a young *émigrée* who much later became one of Lenin's most trusted secretaries in the Kremlin. She has explained in detail how Krupskaya would open and deal with the mail addressed to Lenin from Russia, would keep him up to date with news of how the illegal organizations were faring and would help in the compilation of 'Personal' messages in *Vperyod [Forward]*, the underground weekly published in Geneva between 4 January and 18 May 1905. The messages were worded so that only the addressees could understand them. Thus those in one April 1905 issue included '*Spitsa* Letter containing resolution cannot be developed. *Kolya* Letter by bearer and addresses received. *Vladimir* Letter received, thanks.'

While Krupskaya was thus engaged, Lenin rarely missed an opportunity for haranguing visitors about his disagreement with the Mensheviks. The visitors were numerous and ranged from dedicated men who supported him for the rest of their lives to others such as Valentinov who became strongly critical. Lenin's talk, Valentinov has written, 'consisted of vicious and abusive invective. When he talked about the Mensheviks he could hardly control himself. He would suddenly stop in the middle of the pavement, stick his fingers into the holes of his waistcoat (even when he was wearing an overcoat), lean back, then jump forward, letting fly at his enemies. He cared nothing for the fact that passers-by stared with some amazement at his gesticulations.'

He seems to have moved somewhat abstractedly in traversing towns and when, in October 1903, he spoke in Geneva before the Second Conference of the League of Russian Social-Democrats Abroad, he did so with one eye heavily bandaged. While cycling he had run into the back of a tram and was lucky to have escaped more serious injury.

Potential recruits who turned up in Geneva were not always exactly what they seemed. One comrade who arrived from St Petersburg announced pompously that he had been forming separate collectives, of propagandists, of agitators and of organizers. 'How many are in the organizers' collective?' asked Lenin. 'So far, there's only myself,' he was told. 'How many in the collective of agitators?' was the next question. 'For the time being, I'm the only one,' was the answer. Not only Lenin but also his visitor burst out laughing as the comrade realized how quickly Lenin had seen the reality beneath the words.

A more useful recruit to Lenin's forces during this period was Georgy Vasiliyevich Chicherin, later to play a significant part in Lenin's Government after the 1917 Revolution. Son of an official in the Tsar's ministry of foreign affairs, Chicherin was drawn into the revolutionary movement in 1904, resigned his official job, emigrated to Europe and thereafter occupied a series of progressively more influential posts in the Bolshevik movement. When Trotsky gave up his post as Commissar for Foreign Affairs in March 1918 it was Chicherin who took over from him and subsequently helped to mastermind such important events as the Genoa Conference.

In Geneva there was also Lenin's friend Bonch-Bruyevich who had mustered a sizeable collection of revolutionary books and pamphlets of which Lenin made constant use. Bonch-Bruyevich has written that:

'Vladimir Ilyich read through and examined most carefully all of this old revolutionary literature, paying particular attention to Tkachev and remarking that this writer was closer to our viewpoint than any of the others . . . We collected articles that Tkachev had written and handed them over to Vladimir Ilyich. Not only did V. I. read these works by Tkachev, he also recommended that all of us familiarize ourselves with the valuable writings of this original thinker. More than once he asked newly arrived comrades if they wished to study the illegal literature. "Begin," V. I. would advise, "by reading and familiarizing yourself with Tkachev's 'Nabat' . . ." this is basic and will give you tremendous knowledge.'

Lenin's quarters in Geneva were as modest as those he occupied throughout his life, due not only to shortage of money but to a genuine belief that he should occupy no more accommodation than was required to carry out his work.

'On the ground floor [one visitor recalled], there was a large kitchen containing a stove on which there was constantly being heated a large enamelled kettle, ready for chance visitors . . . Upstairs, the furniture consisted of simple tables covered with journals, manuscripts and press cuttings. On the walls, shelves of books. In each room an iron bed covered with a blanket and two chairs. In the middle of Lenin's table a form of abacus with which he no doubt counted the number of peasant proprietors "with a horse", "with a quarter of a horse", etc.'

Apparendy semi-permanently settled in Geneva, and intent

on setting up an alternative to the now pro-Menshevik *Iskra*, Lenin began to gather round himself a group whom he judged, in most cases correctly, to be both politically reliable and of practical use in the Bolshevik cause. Among them, and one of the first to settle in the city, was twenty-nine-year-old Anatoly Vasiliyevich Lunacharsky, a revolutionary from the age of fifteen, who as Commissioner for Enlightenment was to be an important figure in the Government set up in 1917 after Lenin's seizure of power. He had left Russia for Switzerland at the age of nineteen and had studied philosophy under Richard Avenarius in Zurich. Returning to Russia, he had joined the RSDLP, been exiled until the middle of May 1904, had settled in Kiev and after a few weeks had been persuaded to join Lenin in Europe. Instead of going to Geneva he went for personal reasons to Paris and it was here, late in November 1904, that the two men met for the first time.

'There came a knocking on the door of my room in the Hotel Lion Doré near the Boulevard Saint Germain in Paris [Lunacharsky wrote]. I got out of bed. The stairs were still in darkness. Before me stood a person I didn't know in a flat hat and with a suitcase at his feet. To my quizzical look this person responded, "I am Lenin. What a time for the train to get in." "Yes", I said in some confusion. "My wife is still asleep. Why don't you give me your suitcase. We can leave it here and go and get a coffee somewhere." '

By the middle of December Lunacharsky had not only joined Lenin in Geneva but according to Krupskaya was helping the Party with his lectures. 'We are all in a better mood thanks to the arrival of a new comrade,' she wrote,' – a brilliant orator and talented writer. He has literally electrified the public. The Mensheviks are tearing their hair and raising a row . . . the Old Man (Lenin) has perked up and actually seems younger these past few days.'

The new recruit soon became part of the group's propaganda team and, never backward in extolling his own efforts, later wrote: 'My work consisted not so much of writing copy for *Vperyod* and *Proletary [The Proletarian]*, as of travelling round all the *émigré* colonies in Europe and giving lectures about the essence of the split. Besides political speeches I also spoke on philosophical topics.'

There was one reason why Lenin was glad to be back in Switzerland after the fracas at the London Congress. He wrote to his mother from Geneva on 8 January 1904:

'A few days ago I had a wonderful outing to [the] Salève with Nadya and a friend [F. V. Lengnik]. Down below in Geneva it was all mist and gloom, but up on the mountain (about 4,000 feet above sea level) there was glorious sunshine, snow tobogganing – altogether a good Russian winter's day. And at the foot of the mountain – *la mer du brouillard,* a veritable sea of mist and clouds, concealing everything except the mountains jutting up through it, and only the highest at that. Even little Saléve (nearly 3,000 feet) was wrapped in mist.'

This panegyric was less exceptional than readers of Lenin's political writings may imagine. As Valentinov was to stress,

'It is a huge mistake, and many, almost all, make it, to consider Lenin a heartless man of iron, a producer only of political resolutions, completely indifferent and insensitive to the beauties of nature. He loved the fields, the meadows, the rivers, the mountains, the sea, the ocean. This fact can be grasped least of all from the wooden, remarkably crude lines which he occasionally devoted to art and literature.'

He seems to have been particularly fond of the long chalk ridge of the Salève which rises with its magnificent vantage points above Geneva to 4,290 feet. On one occasion, he told Valentinov, he had climbed it with his wife to see the sunrise.

'We happened to walk up with two workers [he said], but lost sight of them when we got to the top. On the way down we met them again and said to them, "The sunrise was very beautiful, wasn't it?" Their answer was "Unfortunately, we didn't see anything. We worked all day yesterday, and we're very tired, we lay down for a little while, waiting for the sunrise, and just fell asleep." '

Lenin frequently used a round of mountain excursions to help him relax after an intellectual *tour de force* or when he had been particularly worried. After he had resigned from the Central Committee he made two, the first with Krupskaya and Maria Essen. The latter had been helping to distribute *Iskra* in St Petersburg, but was caught, imprisoned, and on her release settled in Geneva where for a while she became the guest of Lenin and Krupskaya. Towards the end of June 1904 she was preparing to return to Russia but before she left set off with Lenin and Krupskaya for what she called 'a farewell treat'. They first travelled to Montreux where they visited the Château of Chillon, and then decided to climb one of the nearby peaks.

'At first [Essen has written] the climb was easy and pleasant, but the higher we went the harder it became. It was decided that Nadezhda Konstantinovna should wait for us at the hotel.

'To get to the top more quickly we left the path and climbed straight up the slope. With each step the climb became more difficult. Vladimir Ilyich strode briskly and confidently, chuckling at my efforts to keep up with him. After a while I was climbing on all fours, clutching at the snow which melted in my hands, but still managing to keep up with Vladimir Ilyich.

'At last we reached the top. A limitless panorama stretched below, an indescribable display of colours. Before us, as on the palms of our hands, lay all the Earth's climatic belts, all types of vegetation; next to us the unbearable brightness of the snow; a little lower down the plants that grow in the North, further still the rich Alpine meadows and then the lush vegetation of the South. I felt in the mood for some high literature and was about to start reciting from Shakespeare or Byron when I looked at Vladimir Ilyich. He was sitting down, deep in thought. Suddenly he burst out: "Hm, a fine mess the Mensheviks are making for us."

'When we started on our walk we agreed not to talk about the Mensheviks, "so as not to spoil the landscape". And as long as Vladimir Ilyich was walking, he was full of fun and the joys of life, having obviously put out of his mind all thought of Mensheviks and Bundists. But he had only to sit down for a minute and his mind would revert to its usual train of thought.'

Both Lenin and Krupskaya had enjoyed the excursion and

shortly afterwards they set off on something more ambitious, a long journey during which, according to Krupskaya, they

'always selected the wildest paths and got away into the heart of the mountains, far away from human beings. We tramped for a month: each day we never knew where we would be on the morrow; by the evening we were always so tired that we sank into bed and fell asleep instantaneously. 'We had very little cash with us, and existed mostly on eggs, cheese and the like, washed down with wine or spring-water. We rarely sat down to a proper dinner. At one little inn, run by a Social-Democrat, a worker advised us: "Don't dine with the tourists, but with the coachmen, chauffeurs and workmen. You will find it twice as cheap and twice as filling." So we took his advice.'

Lenin carried a heavy French dictionary, she a heavy French book for translation. But they didn't open them: '. . . instead of the dictionary, we looked at the mountaintops, covered with perpetual snow, at blue lakes and boisterous waterfalls.' As always, both Lenin and his wife found themselves invigorated by the Alps. 'The mountains helped us,' she once wrote. 'The changing impressions, the mountain air, solitude, healthy tired-ness and healthy sleep were a real cure for Vladimir Ilyich. His strength and vivacity and high spirits returned to him.'

On the way back to Geneva Lenin sent a card to his mother saying 'Greetings from the tramps', and was soon preparing to deal with what was, from his point of view, a deteriorating situa-tion in the Party's Central Committee. The members who had voted earlier in the year for reconciliation with the Mensheviks had now reiterated their position, to be told by Lenin that he could not acknowledge these decisions as lawfully adopted. This was not the only rift in the socialists' lute. Rosa Luxemburg had responded to *One Step Forward, Two Steps Back* with a denunciation which had first appeared in *Iskra* and then been published in the German *Die Neue Zeit*. In her attack she had claimed that Lenin's version of socialism would hamper the movement rather than develop it. Lenin sent his 'Reply' to Karl Kautsky, asking for its publication in *Die Neue Zeit*. This was refused and the article did not appear until 1930, six years after Lenin's death.

His fortunes were now at a low ebb. '[The financial position] is now the only hitch,' he wrote on 2 November, 'everything else we have. Without a big sum we are doomed to the intolerable, depressing vegetable existence we are leading here. We must get that money if it kills us.'

This warning about the need for cash was sent to Aleksandr Aleksandrovich Bogdanov, politician, philosopher and doctor. An RSDLP member since the foundation of the Party, he had been exiled and in Kaluga had met Lunacharsky who later married his sister. In 1904 he moved to Switzerland, met Lenin and joined the Bolsheviks. He quickly established a position for himself and played an important, if often irritant, part in Lenin's life.

In the winter of 1904 no very large sum of money was likely to be involved but Lenin was helped by a speaking tour on which he embarked early in December. In Paris Lunacharsky took him to the studio of the sculptor Naoum Aronson who wanted to model him. 'The structure of Vladimir Ilyich's head is so admirable,' Aronson explained. 'It is enough to regard it properly to appreciate its physical force, the lines of the *coupole colossale du front,* which seems to irradiate light.'

From Paris Lenin returned to Switzerland and spoke in

Zurich and Berne, but not before he had decided that his main priority was to bring out his planned new journal. To Bogdanov, Rozalia Zemlyachka – a Party supporter – and Litvinov he wrote: 'First and foremost comes an organ, and again an organ, and money for an organ.' A few days later he was writing: 'Money is desperately needed. Please do everything you can at once to send at least 1,000–2,000 rubles, otherwise we shall be in the air and everything will be left to chance.' Gorky chipped in with 3,000 roubles and the promise of more when he became convinced that the journal would not be given over entirely to petty polemics.

This was a period during which specialist pro-revolutionary publications proliferated. (Bonch-Bruyevich launched *Rassvet (Dawn)* to attract support among dissident religious groups.) The decision to go ahead with Lenin's new journal, *Vperyod* – the first of six journals of the same name to be published within the next decade – was taken on 12 December 1904. Lenin and his colleagues went to a café to celebrate – on the date of the Escalade, the fete in which the Genevois celebrated the repulse in 1602 of an attempt by the Duke of Savoy to take the town by a surprise assault. The crowd, as usual, filled the streets in a carnival-like gathering; Lenin proposed that he and his colleagues should join them and took up position at the head of a long file of Bolshevik supporters. They continued to celebrate for most of the night, at one point encircling a couple in fancy dress and forcing them to embrace each other. 'We were just like children,' one of them later said. 'And Lenin! How he laughed, with something contagious in his laughter.'

The first number of *Vperyod* appeared in Geneva on 4 January 1905 and seventeen more issues came out before the paper ceased publication in mid-May. Litvinov, known throughout the movement by this time as Papasha, the ever-calm father of the family, was closely connected with the paper's early days, and regularly took it into Russia. 'There will be transport as long as we have Papasha,' Lenin wrote. 'Let him take the most energetic measures for handing over his inheritance in case of failure.'

According to Lunacharsky, *Vperyod* was run on almost co-operative lines. First the subject of an article would be discussed by members of the editorial staff after which Lenin would say: 'Right, and now will you please get down to work and write the article.' Often, Lunacharsky continued, 'on second reading an article would be altered quite a bit. On many occasions the original article written by, say, Orlovsky or Olminsky ended up being largely Lenin's work for he would edit it so heavily, crossing things out, rewriting extensively, putting in large new passages, that afterwards those editing later editions found themselves unable to say whose article it was.' By mid-May, when publication of *Vperyod* stopped, Lenin and his colleagues had set up their own printing establishment in Geneva. Three compositors, one print hand and one reader, all Russian Bolsheviks, worked in premises at 6 quai du Cheval Blanc on the banks of the Arve; but no printing press was available and once material had been set up and corrected it had to be taken to the Imprimerie Ouvrière at 27 rue Caroline where a Genevois named Zeiner printed for the Russians on credit. *Vperyod* was replaced, later in May 1905, by *Proletary*, also printed in Geneva. But before it appeared the situation of Lenin and all those who urged a change in Russia had been transformed by the repercussions of 'Bloody Sunday', the confrontation which took place in St Petersburg and is sometimes considered as the event which triggered the first Russian Revolution.

Approaches to Revolution

5

Return to Russia

'Bloody Sunday', during which up to 1,000 civilians were killed or wounded by tsarist troops in St Petersburg, did not, in fact, provoke the full-scale revolution that Lenin and many others had expected. What it did was to lead to widespread outbreaks of violence in St Petersburg and elsewhere, minor riots and revolts in many parts of Russia, and finally to a military clash in Moscow between the authorities and strong groups of potential revolutionaries. The Government's victory in this Moscow confrontation was by no means the end of the events triggered off by Bloody Sunday, which continued into, and throughout, 1906 and well into 1907. While the repercussions of the St Petersburg massacre are sometimes called the Revolution of 1905, it is perhaps more accurate to speak of them as the Revolutions of 1905 to 1907.

Although these disturbances and troubles were finally put down, they forced the Tsar to introduce minor reforms; to give a qualified promise that a Duma or consultative body would be formed to modify his own autocratic rule; and to grant an amnesty, which induced a number of Social-Democrats, including Lenin, to return to Russia before the end of 1905. The effect of Bloody Sunday on Lenin was, therefore, immense, not only because it changed the climate for revolution inside Russia but because it directly affected the personal and physical course of his own life.

Before outlining these changes it is necessary to describe the events of Bloody Sunday, 9 January 1905. The catastrophe – and it was considered as nothing less by both of the sides involved – came at a moment when any misjudgement of the situation developing inside Russia would have been sufficient to spark off serious trouble. In February 1904 the Japanese had attacked the Russian fleet at Port Arthur and inflicted a series of defeats on Russian troops along the river Yalu and in Manchuria – an indication of the poor state into which the Russian Army had already slipped under tsarist rule – defeats which were to be followed in 1905 by the fall of Mukden and the destruction of Russia's main battle fleet in the Straits of Tsushima.

A strike in the great Putilov works of St Petersburg during the first days of January 1905 quickly spread through other industrial parts of the city and before the end of the month had begun to paralyse the Russian capital. Father Gapon, the turbulent worker-priest who was to stand at the centre of the coming upheaval and whose relationship with the police, whether as stooge or agent, has never been entirely explained, wrote that St Petersburg seethed with excitement. Factories, mills, and workshops gradually stopped working, and thousands of men and women gathered before the premises of the branches of the Workmen's Association.

The authorities, informed that more than ordinary trouble

was expected, put selected troops on the alert, and stationed units at key strategic points and around such buildings as telephone exchanges, railway stations and gasworks. Gapon, founder of the Assembly of Russian Factory and Mill Workers of St Petersburg, an organization supported by the authorities, now decided to play what he hoped would be a trump card: the workers and their families would sign a petition which he would present to the Tsar. Surely that would resolve the problem?

The petition, which Gapon prepared with a number of well-wishers, was a mixture of political and industrial demands and personal appeals typified by the sentence which ran: 'There are more than three hundred thousand of us here, yet we are all of us human beings only in appearance and outwardly, while in reality we are deemed devoid of a single human right, even that of speaking, thinking, and meeting to talk over our needs, and of taking measures to better our condition.'

The crowd began to muster soon after first light on 9 January. One British observer later reported:

'It was a beautiful winter morning, with a sharp frost and a sun brilliantly shining from a pale-blue sky upon the white expanse of the Neva and the snow-covered roofs and streets of the city. Down the Nevsky Prospect walked unceasingly with set, firm faces, working men, young and old, in black winter overcoats and black lambskin caps. There was something uncanny in their intentness. In the great white square before the Winter Palace a bivouac fire was burning, and around it soldiers were boxing to keep themselves warm. The throng from the Nevsky was held back from the Square by a line of dragoons, who from time to time charged down the sidewalks and sent the throng scattering. On the North side of the Neva, near the Finland Station, rifles were stacked and soldiers stood waiting. Near the fortress of St Peter and St Paul, before the oldest of the St Petersburg churches, a score of mounted dragoons were drawn up in line, commanding the square. Past the People's Palace, a procession came marching, workmen in black, intent and solemn, a student or two, and two or three women. They sang a little and then moved silently. They entered the square near the fortress. There was a bugle-call from the opposite side, but they marched on. There was a warning volley, and then three volleys of loaded cartridge. With shouts and cries the procession scattered, and the dead and wounded lay upon the snow. So all the processions were met and scattered, that led by Gapon among the rest.

'Near the Winter Palace the throng grew and pressed on and on. Then the troops fired, bringing down little boys perched on the trees in a neighbouring public garden and killing and wounding many men and women. A little further up the Nevsky Prospect, near the Police Bridge, the troops again fired. Again killed and wounded, again groans and cries, and a terror-stricken scattering crowd spreading indignation throughout the city. A sleigh drove swiftly up the Nevsky followed by half-a-dozen workmen running with bare heads and crossing themselves, some weeping. In the sleigh sat a youth holding in his arms a student, dead, his face one gaping wound. Three or four Cossacks came galloping up on horseback, pulled rein, looked at the sleigh, then rode on with a jeering laugh. The sun set in a roseate sky, the evening fell, crowds wandered about the streets with helpless imprecations, the wounded were brought to the hospitals or cared for in private houses. Cossacks and dragoons guarded the Government buildings, and from time to time charged down the Nevsky, driving loiterers before them like chaff before the wind.'

Another illuminating account was given in the report of Robert S. McCormick, the US Ambassador at St Petersburg.

'The events of Sunday January 9/22nd [he concluded], weakened, if [they] did not shatter, that unswerving loyalty and deep seated reverence which has characterized the subject of "The Czar of All the Russias". I have had evidence of this from the highest to the lowest classes and it finds expression in a letter received this morning from Mr Heenan, our Consul at Odessa, who writes: "Had I answered your enquiries about the situation here before the affair of Sunday last in your city had taken place, the views expressed would have been quite other than those I shall send you in a few days. In all the years (eighteen) I have spent in Russia, I never knew the Russian public to be so united as in their views in connection with the action of the authorities in ordering the soldiers to shoot the workmen, their wives, children and inoffensive spectators last Sunday in St Petersburg. All classes condemn the authorities and more particularly the Emperor. The present ruler has lost absolutely the affection of the Russian people, and what-ever the future may have in store for the dynasty, the present Czar will never again be safe in the midst of his people."

'In any other country this might be true, and I am prepared to accept Mr Heenan's view in so far as I have indicated: that the Emperor will never be able to reestablish himself in his former unique position.'

There was no doubt in the minds of St Petersburg Social-Democrats as to what Bloody Sunday meant.

'Citizens [said a manifesto they issued the following day], yesterday you saw the brutality of the absolutist government! You saw the blood that flowed in the streets! Who directed the guns against the breasts of the workers? The Tsar, the Grand Dukes, the Ministers, the generals and the rabble of the Court. They are murderers. Death to them! To arms comrades, occupy the arsenals, the munition stores and the magazines! Destroy the police stations and gendarmerie offices. We are out to overturn the Tsar's Government and to set up our own. Long live the Revolution! Long live the Constituent Assembly of People's representatives!'

The opinion that Bloody Sunday had undermined the Tsar's control of Russia was also held by Lenin who had heard of the events the following day. 'Vladimir Ilyich and I were on our way to the library and met the Lunacharskys, who were on their way to us . . .', Krupskaya later said. 'Lunacharsky's wife . . . was so excited that she could not speak . . . we went . . . to the Lepeshinskys' emigrant restaurant. We wanted to be together. The people gathered there hardly spoke a word to one another, they were so excited.' Like most of the other Russians living abroad, Lenin believed that the massacre would spark off revolution. Indeed, during the next few days he spent some time in the Geneva library brushing up his knowledge of the military tactics he thought would soon be valuable.

But the Tsar's failure to re-establish himself in his former unique position did not lead to the revolution that Lenin had anticipated; however, during 1905 it led to a series of strikes and local revolts and disturbances which finally brought some amelioration of the brutal methods by which the authorities tried to hold down the country. It also led to the formation in St Petersburg of the first of the soviets, or workers' councils, which were later to become so important in the running of Russia. By no means Bolshevik-dominated, they were, nevertheless, predominantly of left-wing persuasion; they grew in importance during the years that followed Bloody Sunday, and with the Revolutions of 1917 were to attain the status virtually of a Government.

In 1905 troops fired on a procession of working men in Warsaw. Throughout Russia there was not only much sporadic rioting but in country areas many attacks on isolated farms. In June a naval mutiny in Odessa, in which sheds and stores in the port were burned down, was followed by fighting with troops. The battleship *Prince Potemkin* put into port in the charge of a mutinous crew and Lenin, in Geneva, had the hare-brained idea of sending an emissary to her with instructions to take other ships and follow up with the capture of Odessa; but before the emissary could arrive, the ship had sailed off to surrender. The outbreaks of violence died away and the prospects of stability appeared to have increased when peace with the Japanese was signed under American auspices in the American harbour town of Portsmouth, New Hampshire.

The situation was thereby eased, but only temporarily, and in October there began something less spectacular but more significant: a general strike, which quickly began to paralyse the country. One British observer wrote:

'Trains stopped at wayside stations. Passengers bivouacked or pursued their journey in hired carriages. The busy hum and thunderous rattle of the great city stations, their pride in the conquest of distance, yielded suddenly to a chilly, faint-hearted silence. One by one porters, newsboys, book-keepers, ticket-clerks crept away. Cab-drivers deserted their ranks before the stations, disconsolate, to seek chance fares at street corners. At such a moment it was a simple and natural thing that the factory employees should strike once more. Agitation and persuasion were hardly needed. And the strange impulse spread, the impulse to cease from all action, to refrain even from such support of the old system as was involved in the earning of one's bread, till the word of change should come. Shop assistants put on their coats and went wandering aimlessly up and down the streets in search of liberty. The clerks in city offices laid aside their pens and waited. Teachers ceased to teach, and school chil-dren had unexpected holidays. Lawyers ceased to plead, and even unemotional city magistrates were infected by the strange unrest and ceased to judge between landlords and tenants, or to pass sentence on the drunk and disorderly until the word of a new time had been spoken.'

On the third evening of the strike, news came that the Tsar had granted a constitution, and this was followed by amnesty for many accused of political activity.

However, at the end of November G. S. Nosar-Khrustalev, the President of the St Petersburg Soviet, was arrested; and, shortly afterwards, the rest of the Soviet. Then, as opposition to the authorities appeared to be collapsing, the Moscow Soviet declared a general strike, which quickly developed into a confron-tation between workers and troops. For Lenin, who correctly realized that this was the make-or-break moment for reaction to

Bloody Sunday, it was a nerve-racking period – 'infinitely uneasy and dark days' according to Lunacharsky. 'The news from Moscow', he later recollected, 'often reached us late. The situation did not seem quite clear. Lenin pounced on each line of every report about the Moscow uprising, on every word comrades had to say about it on arrival in Petersburg.' After five days of fighting the Moscow rising was defeated and this, following the collapse of opposition in St Petersburg, ended the more significant repercussions of Bloody Sunday. The Government's ferocity in putting down revolt aroused considerable dismay abroad, and in Britain Ramsay MacDonald, later head of the country's first Labour administration and in 1905 secretary of the Labour Representation Committee, sent money to the Russian Strike Relief Committee on condition that it went to the widows and orphans of Bloody Sunday.

Lenin's reaction, which he was prepared to put on record, was given in 'Revolution in Russia' in *Vperyod* no. 3 on 24 January 1905.

'Economic demands are giving way to political demands. The strike is turning into a general strike and it has led to an unheard-of colossal demonstration; the prestige of the tsarist name has been ruined for good. The uprising has begun. Force against force. Street fighting is raging, barricades are being thrown up, rifles are crackling, guns are roaring. Rivers of blood are flowing, the civil war for freedom is blazing up. Moscow and the South, the Caucasus and Poland are ready to join the proletariat of St Petersburg. The slogan of the workers has become: Death or freedom!'

This was not only highly emotive but highly inaccurate.

153

However strong the workers' reaction was in places, and for short periods, there does not appear to have been any realistic prospect of revolutionary success following Bloody Sunday. This is hardly surprising in view of the very few preparations which had been made – also bearing in mind the curious subsequent history of Father Gapon who succeeded in leaving Russia and in July visited Lenin in Geneva. Gapon has left no account of what happened, but it seems likely that he asked for Lenin's good offices in obtaining arms. In Russia he was increasingly regarded with suspicion by the RSDLP; anti-clerical feelings provided a foundation for mistrust but even at this date there was a suspicion that Gapon might have been used by the authorities as some form of *agent provocateur*. Lenin's occasional bad judgement of men was here compounded by his long absence from personal involvement with affairs actually in Russia, although his note in *Vperyod* suggests at least a lingering qualification about the apparendy leftwing father. It read: 'It is to be hoped that Gapon, whose evolution from views shared by a politically unconscious people to revolutionary views proceeds from such profound personal experiences, will achieve the clear revolutionary outlook that is essential for a man of politics.' The qualifications in Lenin's comment proved more than justified. From Switzerland Gapon returned to Russia. There, while openly continuing to profess radical leanings, he visited the Ministry of the Interior and offered to work as a police agent. Peter Rutenberg, who had helped Gapon to travel from St Petersburg to Switzerland, learned of this duplicity and in March 1906 convened a secret tribunal to try the renegade priest. Gapon was condemned to death and then hanged.

Following Bloody Sunday Lenin continued his preparations for the Third Congress of the RSDLP at which he hoped to strengthen his position against the Mensheviks. In *Vperyod* no. 8 he proposed the agenda for the Congress and in the following issue, under 'New Tasks and New Forces', he developed as the goal of the 1905 Revolution the democratic dictatorship of the proletariat and the peasantry.

On 24 April Lenin left Geneva for London to attend the Congress. However, before it opened nine of the Central Committee's eleven members were arrested in Russia, and as a result fewer members than the Committee had agreed to recognize as a quorum were present in London. Even Lenin admitted that the meeting was not representative. Only Bolsheviks were there; the Mensheviks held their own meeting simultaneously in the Swiss city Lenin had just left.

From the start Lenin dominated the Third Congress of which he was elected chairman. Not only did he speak to an enthusiastic audience during many sessions but when the Party statute was debated it was Lenin's formulation of clause one – which had brought the Party's internal quarrels into the open in Brussels two years previously – which was now adopted. He was elected editor of the new Party organ, *Proletary*, and was now unquestioned leader of the Bolsheviks. Typifying his success was the comment of one delegate who reported that throughout one of Lenin's speeches defending his theory of 'revolutionary dictatorship' against the Mensheviks, the whole congress listened to him in deep silence as his iron logic overwhelmed them.

As in 1903, Lenin acted almost as a tourist guide to the delegates, taking them to the National Gallery and to the Old Vic where they sat in shilling seats to see *Hamlet*. He once again arranged a visit to Marx's grave in Highgate Cemetery and also showed the visitors where Marx and Engels had studied in the

British Museum and where he himself had worked while editing *Iskra*.

In mid-May he returned to Geneva by way of Paris and saved his colleagues from trouble by quick action during the journey. As they landed from the cross-Channel steamer at Boulogne the French police asked to check the luggage, saying that they were looking for smuggled tobacco. The baggage contained the drafts of the Third Congress proceedings, and it was later claimed that the French had been alerted by tsarist agents. The situation was saved by Lenin's forceful protest that he and his travelling companions were not businessmen. The search was halted and they were allowed to continue.

Lenin spent three days in Paris, accompanied by P. A. Krasnikov and Lydia Fotiyeva. Two of his evenings were free and on the first he attended the opera but found it boring. On the other night he went with his two colleagues to the Folies Bergères. Fotiyeva remembered one particular item, 'The Legs of Paris':

'The curtain was raised knee-high, showing the legs of people of different walks of life and social standing moving across the stage. There was a workingman, a street-light man, a *grisette*, a priest, a policeman, a small shopkeeper, a Paris dandy, and many others. The legs were so emphatically typical that there was no mistaking their owners, and you could easily picture the person they belonged to. It was very amusing. Vladimir Ilyich laughed as infectiously as he alone knew how, and he really enjoyed himself that evening.'

The relaxation was strictly temporary and once back in Geneva he was writing, again on the basis of the Third Congress decisions. Earlier, in *Two Tactics of Social-Democracy in the Democratic Revolution* he had maintained his attack on the Mensheviks, concentrating on their discussion of a bourgeois revolution and maintaining that since this would never become possible in Russia the proletariat and peasantry had to establish a democratic dictatorship of their own. The pamphlet appeared in Geneva in August, but before this Lenin was back in Paris again where he described the Third Congress to a large meeting.

By now he believed more strongly than ever in armed struggle as the only route to success, and later in the year wrote: 'It horrifies me – I give you my word – it horrifies me to find that there has been talk about bombs for *over six months,* yet not one has been made! . . . Form fighting squads *at once* everywhere.' The fact that Lenin still believed that the road to success lay through battery and barricade is reinforced by his article 'Tasks of Revolutionary Army Contingents' which, while not published until 1926, gave a clear idea of what, in 1905, he saw as the way forward. Units should be formed, he proposed, with 'rifles, revolvers, bombs, knives, knuckledusters, sticks, rags soaked in kerosene for starting fires, ropes or rope ladders, shovels for building barricades'. He also called for the building up of weapon stocks and 'funds for the uprising (confiscation of government funds)'. By contrast he could write to Plekhanov: 'We are in agreement with you on approximately nine tenths of the questions of theory and tactics, and to quarrel over one tenth is not worth while,' an indication that he might in some circumstances be willing to move towards the 'soft' sectors of the Party typified by the Mensheviks who had eschewed violence and preached peaceful means of advance.

Whatever the balance sheet of success and failure at the end of the Third Congress, Lenin was hardly satisfied with the resulting situation, as he made clear when writing on 2 August to Lunacharsky:

'The Geneva Bolsheviks are in a wretched state. We have a major struggle on our hands. The Third Congress, of course, did not resolve it, it merely marked a new stage in it. The Iskrites are busy as bees, as brazen as streettraders, and have the advantage of their long experience of demagogy. Our people on the contrary are in the main conscientiously stupid (or stupidly conscientious). They can't fight, they're clumsy, sluggish, awkward, and timid . . . Good lads all of them – but bloody useless at politics . . . We lack leavening, stimulation, impulsion. They can't work or fight on their own. We lack speakers at our meetings. There's no one to drum up morale, to recognize a matter of principle, to lift them clear of the Geneva swamp into the realm of interests and topics that really matter. And our whole operation is suffering as a result.'

It was thus with a somewhat ambivalent attitude to the future that Lenin returned to Russia on 21 November 1905. It was obvious that the Duma would be the Tsar's puppet. The first Duma, which included eighteen Social-Democrats, formally sat from 27 April until 8 July 1906. Two more were formed in 1907: the first, which included sixty-five Social-Democrats (of which eighteen were Bolsheviks), sat from 20 February 1907 until 2 June 1907; the next, which included eighteen Mensheviks and eighteen Bolsheviks, lasted from 14 November 1907 until 22 June 1912. The fourth Duma lasted from 15 November 1912 until it was dissolved in October 1917. None of these bodies had an effective existence, crippled by the Tsar's wishes until the first Revolution of 1917 and hamstrung after that by the ineffective Provisional Government.

Despite the failure of the post-Bloody Sunday protests to produce more than what could be easily denigrated as only cosmetic changes in Russia's government, the country became at least slightly less authoritarian than it had been in previous centuries. It was a country of contradictory influences, the contrasts being exemplified in Stolypin, the wealthy landowner who became Chairman of the Council of Ministers in 1906 and who combined a hard-line policy against terrorism with an attempt to introduce agricultural reforms.

As a result of Stolypin's influence, ended by his assassination in 1911, Lenin's attempts to build up the Bolshevik section of the RSDLP were less hampered than they had been during the last years of the nineteenth century. Nevertheless he and his supporters were still constantly at risk from censorship, suppression and the threat of imprisonment that hung over all dissidents. The lot of the peasants was improved by the reforms brought in on Stolypin's initiative shortly before his assassination, but it is arguable that whatever Stolypin's intentions genuinely were, his reforms were so inappropriate and difficult to implement that they could never have adequately reformed the existing situation. The Duma's benefits were more theoretical than practical.

Lenin's first reaction to the setting-up of a parliamentary body in the Western sense of the phrase was that the Bolsheviks should boycott it. He believed there was a chance that the Tsar might be overthrown and that while this possibility existed there was no point in co-operating with the Duma. However, as the chance of bringing down the Tsar and the Duma steadily decreased so his attitude changed; if the Duma were to continue, collaborating with it would enable the Bolsheviks to exert a limited influence on events – and in Germany, he noted, the Social-Democratic Party had not boycotted the Reichstag. Lenin's attitude became governed by expediency rather than principle, and from 1905 more than once made him vulnerable to attack by his enemies. So strong did the anti-Duma faction become within the Party that in 1908 it led to the creation of the Otzovisty (the Recallists), a dissident group of which Bogdanov and Lunacharsky were members. It demanded that the Bolshevik deputies should be recalled from the Duma and that the Party should go underground. It failed in its aims and eventually sank without trace.

In the autumn of 1905 two moves were made at opposite ends of the political spectrum in the hope of curbing the continuing breakdown of law and order. Count S. Y. Witte, whom the Tsar had just allowed to form a government – but who resigned the premiership in May 1906 although remaining in the Government as a member of the State Council – brought in a constitution. Almost simultaneously, in St Petersburg the Soviet of about 500 members elected by 250,000 working men and women, was formed. The loosening of the official attitude epitomized by these moves encouraged many dedicated opponents of the regime including Lenin and his wife to return to Russia. Martov and Vera Zasulich also reached St Petersburg before the end of 1905, while Trotsky not only returned but soon afterwards became chairman of the St Petersburg Soviet.

Towards the end of November 1905, Lenin and Krupskaya arrived separately from Switzerland via Germany, Sweden and Finland, travelling on their legal passports. On arrival in Russia they failed to register immediately with the police, in itself an offence. They went first to friends, took a furnished apartment on the Nevsky Prospekt, and then went to live with acquaintances of Lenin's sister Maria, registering with the authorities before they did so. Both then acquired new passports, separated, and started to live underground. The whole tortuous operation was apparently felt necessary in view of the surveillance which, despite the new conditions, the authorities mounted on such suspect characters.

For the next few weeks Lenin, sometimes on his own, sometimes accompanied by Krupskaya, divided his time between St Petersburg and forays into Finland. Within a few days of his arrival he attended a small illegal meeting at the Technological Institute where he discussed the agrarian question with Martov. Aleksandra Kollontay, who had played a part in the disturbances earlier in the year, made a point of attending and here met Lenin for the first time. A few days later Lenin went, as a guest, to the second All-Russian Menshevik Conference being held in the city, and shortly afterwards took part in a session of the St Petersburg Soviet.

Early the next month, on the tenth, he also met Maxim Gorky for the first time. After the authorities had granted at least nominal freedom for new publications in October Gorky had founded *Novaya Zhizn (New Life)*. Lenin, among a number of other Social-Democrats, was co-opted to help. The paper's publication was interrupted after about a month but before that Lenin had been made editor and had contributed no less than thirteen articles.

Late in December 1905, he and Krupskaya travelled to Tampere (Tammerfors) in Finland where the First All-Russian Bolshevik Conference was to be held. Lenin's resolution dealing with the agrarian question was adopted, but when he argued for taking part in elections to the Duma he found unexpectedly strong opposition and the Conference decided to boycott the elections.

The Tammerfors Conference was significant in that it was here that there took place the first meeting between Lenin and Stalin, born five years after Lenin. After escaping from prison, where he had been sent for dissident activities, joining the Bolsheviks in the Caucasus, and showing by miscellaneous writings that he supported Lenin against the Mensheviks, he was elected by the Caucasian Bolsheviks as their delegate to the Tammerfors Conference.

In view of the influence that Stalin was to have on Lenin's life, Stalin's first impressions are significant. He later wrote:

'I had hoped to see the mountain eagle of our party, the great man, great physically as well as politically. I had fancied Lenin as a giant, stately and imposing. How great was my disappointment to see a most ordinarylooking man, below average height, in no way, literally in no way, distinguishable from ordinary mortals . . . Usually a great man comes late to a meeting so that his appearance may be awaited with bated breath. Then, just before the great man enters, the warning goes round: "Hush . . . silence . . . he is coming." The rite did not seem to me superfluous, because it created an impression and inspired respect. How great was my disappointment to see that Lenin had arrived at the conference before the other delegates were there and had settled himself somewhere in a corner and was unassumingly carrying on a conversation, a most ordinary conversation, with the most ordinary delegates. I will not conceal from you that at that time this seemed to me to be rather a violation of certain essential rules.'

The description reveals a good deal not only about Stalin, who had by this time adopted the name of Koba, the romantic Caucasian outlaw and hero of the Georgian writer A. Kazbegi's *The Patricide* (1882), but about the way in which Lenin was to consolidate his influence throughout the next two years, which he spent in Russia.

From this first meeting, Lenin was impressed by Stalin, and he subsequently helped him into the position from which he was eventually to step into Lenin's shoes. With Stalin's later importance in mind, it is diverting to read the query that Lenin sent to V. A. Karpinsky, a prominent Party propagandist, in the autumn of 1915. 'Do me a favour – ,' he wrote, 'get to know . . . the name of "Koba" (Joseph J. . .?? we have forgotten). Very important!!'

Before this lapse of memory, eight years had passed since the first meeting between Lenin and Stalin during which the arguments between Bolsheviks and Mensheviks were not resolved despite more than one attempt to reconcile them; it was a period during which Lenin continued to increase his influence over the RSDLP by lecturing but more importantly by an almost continuous series of articles expounding his view on the way in which the Party should be run and how it should prepare for the revolution, which he saw as inevitable.

The Party's Fourth (Reunification) Congress was held in Stockholm's House of the People between 23 April and 8 May 1906. The Bolsheviks had only forty-six mandates compared with the Mensheviks' sixty-two but Lenin's persuasion and personality made up much of the difference and the Congress confirmed his version of the Party Statute defining membership qualifications.

Lunacharsky has explained how Lenin achieved his aims on

this occasion by using what he describes as literally a method of collective work:

> 'We would [Lunacharsky has written], get together 12 to 14 members. Lenin would suggest drafting a particular resolution. He would start by giving us an outline, proceed to split it into so many sections and suggest a dominant overall idea. Then we would start collectively editing it. Lenin or somebody else would suggest the first formula. It would be discussed first from the standpoint of phrasing, with every word being carefully considered. As soon as a seemingly suitable formula was thrashed out it would be criticized by Lenin for the possibility of any misinterpretation or misunderstanding. We would then work on the language of the formula to make it more precise and as soon as someone hit on the right phrasing Lenin would say: "That's well put. Let's write it down." And we went in this way through the whole formula right to the end. Afterwards our editors would go through it again and polish it up further so that it would be impossible later on to credit anyone with a particular word or phrase.'

At the end of the Reunification Congress Lenin wrote 'An Appeal to the Party by Delegates to the Unity Congress who Belonged to the former Bolshevik Group'. The appeal, which was signed by Bolshevik delegates from twenty-six Party organizations and was later published as a leaflet, maintained that there was no longer a split between the Bolsheviks and Mensheviks. However, this belief was largely the result of wishful thinking and of an optimism that was not to be substantiated. Despite Lenin's efforts, the split remained.

He also did his best to improve the situation after the end of the Congress by secretly setting up a Bolshevik Centre to be run by himself, Bogdanov, and Leonid Borisovich Krasin, an electrical engineer later in charge of the Petrograd lighting grid and later still an influential figure in the encouragement of Anglo-Soviet trade. The Centre was moved after a year to a new headquarters in 'Vasa', the house of G. D. Leitezen at Kuokkala, Finland, where Lenin was soon to be living with the two other organizers of the Centre.

His growing influence was emphasized after he returned from the Stockholm Party meeting when, on 9 May in St Petersburg he spoke publicly in Russia for the first time. His audience was 3,000 strong, gathered at the home of Countess Panina. Krupskaya later wrote:

'Ilyich was very excited. For a minute he stood silent, terribly pale. All the blood had flowed to his heart. One immediately felt how the excitement of the speaker was being communicated to the audience. Suddenly tremendous hand-clapping commenced – the Party members had recognized Ilyich . . . At the end of Ilyich's speech, all those present were swept with extraordinary enthusiasm – at that moment everyone was thinking of the coming fight to the finish.'

The meeting was followed in June by Lenin's attendance in Terijoki, Finland, at the Conference of the St Petersburg Social-Democratic Organizations whose Committee supported the Bolshevik against the Menshevik line.

In July, Lenin, Krupskaya and her mother took a brief holiday at Sablino, on the outskirts of St Petersburg. 'Our people came on the 8th,' said Lenin's mother-in-law writing to his sister Anna. 'Volodya went swimming and then we all sat together in the summer house. They spent the next day with us as well. V[olodya] . . . had intended to spend a week with us but he found the newspapers so interesting on Monday morning that he and N[adya] packed and left.' As usual, even on the most necessary of holiday breaks, Lenin found it difficult not to keep a permanent eye on the changing prospect for the revolution. As Akselrod was to admit at the International Socialist Congress in Copenhagen in 1910 Lenin was 'the only man who for twenty-four hours a day was occupied with revolution, who had no thoughts but thoughts of revolution, and who even in his sleep dreamt of nothing but revolution'.

After the brief holiday at Sablino Lenin returned to Finland, first to Kuokkala, where he attended a meeting of RSDLP leaders. The Duma was dissolved on 8 July, triggering off an uprising in Kronstadt and another in the fortress of Sveaborg outside Helsinki, events which brought forth Lenin's 'The Dissolution of the Duma and the Tasks of the Proletariat'.

Within a few weeks he had moved first to Vyborg and then, early in September, back to a ground-floor flat in 'Vasa', where the Bolshevik Centre was established. Here, he continued to write articles and interview members of the Party, Committee members, and others arriving from the provinces. And here he quickly became a friend of Rosa Luxemburg whom he had previously met only once – in Munich during the early days of *Iskra*. She was a regular visitor, and evening after evening she and Lenin discussed the position in Russia with other visitors who included G. B. Zinoviev, L. B. Kamenev and Bogdanov, three men already rising to prominent positions in the Party. The friendship then struck up with Rosa

Luxemburg flourished until their dispute over policy in 1912.

'From Kaukola [Krupskaya later wrote] Ilyich actually directed the entire work of the Bolsheviks. After a while I also went to live there. I used to go up to Petersburg early in the morning and return late at night. The Leitezens afterwards went away and we occupied the whole of the lower part. My mother came to stay with us, and later Maria Ilyinichna lived with us for a time. The Bogdanovs came to live upstairs, and Dubrovinsky (Innokenty) came there in 1907. At that time the Russian police had decided not to meddle in Finland, and we had considerable freedom there. The door of the house was never bolted, a jug of milk and loaf of bread were left in the dining-room overnight, and bedding spread on the divan, so that in the event of anyone coming on the night train they could enter without waking anybody, have some refreshment, and lie down to sleep. In the morning we often found comrades in the dining-room who had come in the night.

A special messenger came to Ilyich every day with material, newspapers and letters. Ilyich, after looking over what had been sent, would immediately sit down to write an article and send it back by the same man.'

The earlier use of the house by Terrorists had certain disadvantages and when Lenin was sent as a present from Stalin a water-melon wrapped in a serviette, everyone mistook it for a bomb. It was at 'Vasa' in August 1906 that Lenin started publication of *Proletary*, the illegal paper which was the organ of the Bolshevik Centre; fifty issues were printed before it ceased publication in 1909. The first twenty were set up in type in Vyborg and printed in St Petersburg. For reasons of secrecy the place of publication was given as Moscow, but eventually conditions became so difficult that publication was moved, first to Geneva and then to Paris.

Lenin was joined in 'Vasa' by his sister Maria for the New Year celebrations, and by the start of 1907 was ready for the first of what were to be even busier years than those he had just survived. The decade which now began was marked by the hard preparatory work without which the success of the Revolution in 1917 would have been less easily won and possibly with qualifications. The record of the years from 1907 to 1917 is of incessant writing, speaking, organization and travel. In fact, the extent of the travel, looked at as a whole, is one of the more remarkable features of Lenin's life during this period – throughout Finland and Sweden into Switzerland and France, where he settled for some three years, then to Cracow in Galicia, which he left on the outbreak of the First World War for another two and a half years in Switzerland.

Early in 1907 his argument with the Mensheviks brought him into serious trouble with the Party. Before the end of January he had written 'The St Petersburg Elections and the Hypocrisy of the Thirty-One Mensheviks' in which he alleged the 'sale of workers' votes to the Cadets' by the Mensheviks. He also wrote 'The Election Results in St Petersburg' for *Proletary*, and cannot have been surprised when he was arraigned before a Party Tribunal. Still unrepentant, he stated before the Tribunal – consisting of three members he had nominated, three Mensheviks and three members of the Presidium – that his words were 'calculated to evoke in the reader hatred, aversion and contempt for people who commit such deeds. Such wording is calculated not to convince, but to break up the ranks of the opponent, not to correct the mistake of the opponent, but to destroy him, to wipe his organization off the face of the earth.' He had, he went on, 'actually succeeded in causing that section of the proletariat *which trusts and follows the Mensheviks* to waver. That was my aim.' The hearing was adjourned, ostensibly until the Fifth Party Congress, but it was never resumed and this argument between Lenin and his colleagues was therefore never resolved.

He now prepared himself for what were to be busy months, even for him. In April he drafted a speech on the agrarian question that G. A. Aleksinsky was to give in the Duma, chaired the St Petersburg City Conference of the RSDLP in Terijoki, Finland, wrote 'The Strength and Weakness of the Russian Revolution' for the Bolshevik newspaper *Nashe Ekho [Our Echo]*, attended the Second Conference of the St Petersburg Social-Democratic Organizations in Terijoki and was elected to the Presidium of the St Petersburg committee of the RSDLP.

Preparations were now well in hand for the Fifth Party Congress, the largest congress so far to be held by the Russian RSDLP but one beset with difficulties. It had at first been hoped to hold it in Norway, but the Norwegian Government refused permission. Copenhagen was then chosen and Lenin travelled to Denmark to finalize arrangements early in May. Shortly before the Congress should have opened – but after most of the delegates had arrived – he was told that it was prohibited, apparently on the grounds that the Russian Empress-Dowager was a sister of the King of Denmark and the Congress could be construed as a personal insult. To prevent the forced return of the delegates to Russia, it was decided to charter a steamer for travel to the Swedish port of Malmö, but on arrival there the Swedish Government was as unaccommodating as the Norwegian and

Danish had been. In desperation, a telephone call was made to the British Labour politician, John Burns, who said that there would be no prohibition in London as long as the delegates did nothing illegal.

Lenin broke his journey to Britain in Berlin, where he met Rosa Luxemburg and Karl Kautsky, visited the Tiergarten and the theatre with Gorky, and read *en route* the manuscript of Gorky's *The Mother*.

In London the opening of the Congress was preceded by a conference of Bolsheviks held in a socialist club in Whitechapel. There followed a dinner given by the English Friends of the Russian Revolution. Those present were hailed by Ramsay MacDonald and Lenin's reply was translated into English by Plekhanov. All was goodwill, qualified only by some surprise on the part of the Russians that they were expected to attend the dinner in evening dress.

Lenin greeted Gorky with the words: 'So glad you've come. I believe you're fond of a scrap? There's going to be a fine old scuffle here.' Gorky later wrote that before him there 'stood a baldheaded, stocky, sturdy person, . . . holding my hand in one of his, while with the other he wiped a forehead which might have belonged to Socrates, beaming affectionately at me with his strangely bright eyes.'

Gorky appears to have been 'mothered' through the London visit by Lenin who found a room for him at a convenient hotel, then inspected it and commented: 'The sheets are quite damp. They'll have to be dried, even if only in front of this silly little [gas] fire. Alexei Maximovich will start coughing and we can't have that!'

Lenin's feelings at the Congress have been revealed by Gorky who has described in particular the events of 1 May.

'It was amazingly sunny that day – most unusual in London, which is usually shrouded in fog. But there were no workers' demonstrations. This was a surprise to us. After all, we had come from Russia, and in our mind's eye we could picture the strikes, clashes and fighting between demonstrators and not only the police, but also tsarist troops throughout the country. But here, in London, we saw well-dressed young girls everywhere on the streets, with flowers and mugs, collecting for the fight against tuberculosis . . . We were youngish ourselves, and naturally wanted to get outside. But in reply to our arguments that one just had to go out into the streets on this great workers' feastday, Lenin smiled and said: "Of course we must go out for some time but we must not forget that of all the events on the international stage there is none more important than the Russian revolution. And to resolve on this day even one of the serious questions concerning the organization of this revolution would be to make a small, but worthy contribution to celebrating this international workers' holiday." '

(Lenin may have smiled because Gorky appears not to have appreciated the difference between the calendars used in Russia and in Britain. The Fifth Party Congress took place between 13 May and 1 June according to British reckoning, and what Gorky took to be May Day would have been 14 May in Britain.)

The Congress was held in the Brotherhood church, Southgate, where the minister was the socialist Reverend F. R. Swann, later cashier to George Lansbury's socialist *Daily Herald*, and this alone attracted a certain amount of unwanted publicity. The church was, as *Free Russia* reported in its June issue, 'literally besieged by reporters and photographers, who in spite of all requests persist in hovering round the delegates like a swarm of wasps, trying to elicit the names of the delegates and to get a snapshot of their faces. Only on one occasion was a reporter with a camera . . . prevailed upon to give up the plate, having been given to understand that he was simply doing volunteer service for the Russian spies. In other cases, similar efforts proved unavailing.'

The Brotherhood church was more like a meeting hall. Gorky later wrote:

'I can still see the bare walls of the ridiculously shabby wooden church in the suburbs of London, the lancet windows, the small narrow hall much like a classroom of an impoverished school. It was only from the outside that the building resembled a church. The attributes of its use were conspicuously absent inside. The pulpit had even wandered from its customary place in the depths of the hall to the entrance, settling squarely between the two doors.'

Into the building there crammed 336 delegates, including 105 Bolsheviks and ninety-seven Mensheviks, with the rest being delegates from the Bund and social-democratic parties in Poland, Lithuania and Latvia. The Bolsheviks were usually supported by forty-five Polish and twenty-six Lettish delegates; the Mensheviks by fifty-five members of the Bund.

Lenin was elected to the Presidium of the Congress although at times he seemed slightly off form.

'His guttural "r" made him seem a poor speaker [Gorky

later wrote] but within a minute I was as completely engrossed as everyone else. I had never known one could talk of the most intricate political questions so simply. I had not imagined him that way. I felt there was something missing in him . . . He was too plain, there was nothing of "the leader" in him.'

His arm, Gorky wrote,

'was extended with the hand slightly raised, and he seemed to weigh every word with it, and to sift out the remarks of his opponents, substituting them by momentous arguments for the right and duty of the working class to go its own way, and not along with the liberal bourgeoisie or trailing behind it. All this was unusual, and Lenin seemed to say it not of his own will, but by the will of history.

'The unity, completeness, directness and strength of his speech, his whole appearance in the pulpit, was a veritable work of classic art; everything was there, and yet there was nothing superfluous, and if there were any embellishments, they were not noticed as such, but were as natural and inevitable as two eyes in a face or five fingers on a hand.'

The Fifth Congress witnessed the beginning of a genuinely firm friendship between Lenin and Gorky. The latter wrote more than one play to help the Bolsheviks and Lenin himself appeared in more than one of Gorky's fictional works. The two men disagreed after the Bolsheviks came to power in 1917 and Gorky was particularly critical not only of the Red Terror which followed but of the other harsh but allegedly necessary measures brought in by Lenin and his Commissars.

Lenin's work in 1907 did not end when the Congress finished since the following day the Second Congress of the Social-Democratic Party of the Latvian Area opened in which he took an active part. By this time he was also being forced to deal with a new and seemingly intractable problem. It had become increasingly obvious that the Party was in financial difficulties and that £2,000 was needed if all the delegates were to pay their fares back home. Lenin, Gorky, Plekhanov and others first visited the painter Felix Moscheles, in the hope of acquiring the needed contribution to Party funds. They were unlucky, but the Central Committee of the German Social-Democratic Party gave £300, and a more important gesture came from Joseph Fels, an American soap-maker of German-Jewish origin and a friend of George Lansbury. Fels was persuaded to visit the Brotherhood church, listened to the debates for about twenty minutes and lent the Party organizers £1,700 on a loan bond signed by all the delegates after Lenin had guaranteed that the money would be returned. So it was. More than a decade later, when Krasin came to London after the First World War, he returned the £1,700, with interest, to Fels's heirs.

It was ironic that Lenin should have been compelled to plead for money at this time, since the Mensheviks had, during the Congress, condemned the fact that he had tolerated, even if he had not encouraged, the 'expropriations' which brought money into the Party coffers.

The whole question of 'expropriations', most of which could bluntly be called robberies, had been discussed more than once by the RSDLP throughout this period. Lenin believed in a basic revolutionary right to take money from the State but that this was different from taking it from private individuals. It is easy to claim, as has been claimed, that he was for partisans but against bandits, yet in practice there were many borderline cases and those who justified expropriations were frequently driven back on to tortuous arguments. Lenin was on slightly firmer ground when he refused to abide by resolutions against expropriations since they had been taken by a Menshevik majority.

In 1907 the position changed since most of the Bolshevik delegates joined the Menshevik line on expropriations and joint efforts brought a resolution banning such operations. At the same time the Congress appointed a commission, under the presidency of Chicherin, to investigate the expropriations which had so far taken place – a move that led to longcontinuing bad feeling between Chicherin and such enthusiastic expropriators as Stalin and Litvinov.

Lenin, who voted against the ban on expropriations in 1907, had somewhat convoluted feelings about the practice, exemplified when he was once quizzed on the subject by Litvinov. 'You always preach socialist revolution and the expropriation of the expropriators,' the future Russian Ambassador to Britain said to him. 'But tell me, if you met Rothschild carrying a heavy purse, could you rob him yourself and take his purse by threatening him with a revolver?' Lenin laughed and replied:

'I don't think so . . . But if we came to power I should have no hesitation in ordering the nationalization of Rothschild's banks and of his property. But this would have to be done legally, on the strength of a decree passed by the victorious people and their Government. As long as the state has not been abolished, the proletarian state included, the rule of law is necessary or else everything will crumble and the most primitive instincts will be let loose.'

Despite this unqualified if latter-day enthusiasm for abiding by the law, it was to Lenin that the bulk of the proceeds from the most famous expropriation of all were delivered in 1907, only some weeks after the vote in London. The robbery took place in Tiflis under the operational control of the Armenian Ter-Petrosyan, known as Kamo, and the general planning control of Stalin. Three men were killed in the robbery and a number injured, two bags of banknotes were taken in the raid and although the value of their contents has been variously given, most figures exceed 250,000 roubles. However, this expropriation suffered from misfortunes. Most of the money was taken in high-denomination notes which in certain circumstances could be easily traced. Such circumstances were provided in that Lenin had ordered that the money should be passed on by Dr Zhitomirsky, who was still acting as a police agent, with the result that many of those trying to change the notes were arrested. Among them was not only Litvinov but Sophia Ravich, a dedicated Party member arrested in Munich.

Under the expropriations policy, forged notes, gifts and legacies were used to swell Party funds, and to the most notorious of such cases Lenin inconsistently hung on for a number of years. This was the Shmidt case which followed the suicide in prison of Nicholas Shmidt, a wealthy student who left his fortune, estimated to total 200,000 roubles, to the RSDLP. This would, in normal circumstances, have put some of the money into Menshevik hands, an outcome that Lenin was determined to prevent. Luckily for him, Shmidt's executrices were two unmarried sisters on whom it was found possible to exert pressure. The elder was successfully wooed by a Bolshevik but he refused to hand over to the Party more than a portion of the money. The younger sister then took a Bolshevik lover and some of the

Shmidt money became available to Lenin. This, however, was only the start of the tangled story since three Germans, Franz Mehring, Clara Zetkin and Karl Kautsky, were subsequently appointed trustees and succeeded in controlling much of the money, held in a German bank, at least until 1912.

In parallel with the controversy about expropriations there continued the political argument about co-operation or non-cooperation with the Duma. The successor to the first Duma had refused to waive the immunity of its RSDLP members and had thus prevented them going on trial on charges including that of fomenting an uprising in the armed forces. In retaliation, the authorities arrested a number of RSDLP deputies, changed the suffrage regulations under which deputies could be elected to a new Duma, and closed down a number of publications which had been coming out since the relaxations of 1905. All this added further complications that developed after the end of the 1907 Congress.

Lenin dealt with the new situation in 'Against the Boycott', an article in which he explained why he had approved of boycotting the Duma in 1905 to 1906 but was now against doing so. The article was written in a friend's house near Styrs Udde, Finland, to which he had gone with his wife for a holiday after their return from the London Congress. 'I am having a rest such as I have not had for several years,' he wrote to his sister Maria, while his mother was told by Krupskaya: 'We have all put on so much weight it's not decent to show ourselves in public . . . Here there is a pine forest, sea, magnificent weather; in short, everything is excellent.'

Before the end of July Lenin's holiday was over and he was off again on a series of meetings and conferences – to the St Petersburg City Conference of the RSDLP in Terijoki, followed by the Third Conference of the RSDLP in Kotka and then on to Germany for the International Socialist Congress in Stuttgart. Here, one of sixty Russian delegates, he was elected to the Presidium as the Russian representative and subsequently, with Martov and Rosa Luxemburg, proposed an amendment to a resolution on peace and war which was to become significant seven years later:

'If war threatens to break out [it said], it is the duty of the working class and its representatives to make every effort to prevent it. Should war come, notwithstanding these efforts, it is the duty of the workers and their representatives to intervene to bring about a speedy end to the war and to take advantage of the economic and political crisis to hasten the transformation of the capitalist society into a socialist society.'

Not only was the resolution, including the amendment, approved by the Congress but it was confirmed at two subsequent Congresses, a fact which was to help account for Lenin's consternation at socialist reaction to the events of the autumn of 1914.

From Stuttgart he returned to Finland and for a while took up quarters once again in 'Vasa'. From Kuokkala he wrote a letter to Aleksinsky in which he deplored the disadvantages of an *émigré's* life. 'For over there,' he wrote, 'you are frightfully out of touch with Russia, and idleness and the state of mind which goes with it, a nervous, hysterical, hissing and spitting mentality, predominate . . . there is no *live* work or an environment for live work to speak of.' All true, no doubt. But within three months Lenin had emigrated and remained an emigrant for nearly a decade.

However, before the start of this long separation from Russia, which was spent first in Switzerland and France, then in Galicia, then once more in Switzerland, he carried on as before with his intense propaganda for the Party. There were two articles for *Proletary* as well as outlines of the policy to be adopted on the new Duma, given at a conference of the St Petersburg organization of the RSDLP held in Terijoki, and at the Fourth Conference of the RSDLP held in Helsinki. Meanwhile he worked hard at a pamphlet – only published in 1917 – describing the RSDLP agrarian programme. Throughout these weeks Lenin was increasingly wanted by the police and it eventually became clear that it would be better if he once again sought refuge in Switzerland. The realization was reinforced when towards the end of December the Bolshevik Centre decided that *Proletary* should be published abroad. The need to settle the future of *Proletary* was only one reason for the move and before leaving Russia for Stockholm Lenin commented to Krasin of the conditions now developing in Russia: 'This is the beginning of a reaction which is likely to last twenty years, unless there is a war in the meantime. That is why we must needs go abroad and work from there.'

However, to travel by a normal route, such as that from the port of Åbo, would be to invite arrest and so, with papers naming him as Professor Müller, a German geologist, Lenin decided instead to board ship at an offshore island on which arrests would not be made. Shortly before Christmas 1907 therefore, he set off on the first leg of what should have been a comparatively simple journey. However, from the first almost everything that could go wrong went wrong – although the story that he almost perished on the journey rests on a remark reported years later by Krupskaya in her not always reliable memoirs, and has little support from any other source.

Before leaving the Finnish capital Lenin had made contact with an intermediary who lived at Åbo and who was willing to have him guided across the narrow stretch of water which separated the mainland from an island at which the ship from Stockholm would be calling.

On the train journey to Åbo he thought he was being watched by police, left the train about ten kilometres before it reached the town, and walked the rest of the way to the well-wisher's house in the darkness. The water separating the island from the mainland was frozen over and it had been planned that Lenin should be guided across it by two local men. But by the time he arrived the ice was breaking up and he had to wait until it again froze hard. Then, on 26 December, he telephoned his host in some distress, fearing that he would never get away. Eventually two local farmers decided that the ice was safe enough and led him to the point where he could board the ship for Stockholm. Looking back later on the troubles of the journey, Lenin realized how wise he had been to wait. 'Oh, what a silly way to have to die,' he is reported to have commented. However, it seems he referred to the possible results of what he might have done, not of what he had done.

The remark does, however, give weight to the view, sometimes voiced by Lenin's critics, that he was at times more concerned with the safety of his own skin than was fitting for a dyed-in-the-wool revolutionary. Certainly he rarely displayed Trotsky's lust for observing battle at close quarters. Yet Lenin's mind invariably worked in a realistic and practical way and it is difficult not to feel that he would have regarded his own unnecessary death – whether through breaking ice or a stray bullet – as a loss to the revolutionary cause as much as a personal disaster. When he took such care to disguise himself during the dramatic events of 1917 he was safeguarding not only Vladimir Ilyich Ulyanov but also the indispensable leader of the revolution.

In December 1907, no disaster followed the potential risks of the breaking ice, and before the end of the month Lenin was safely in Stockholm.

6

Training for the Task

Lenin had been in Sweden only a few days when he was joined by Krupskaya who had succeeded in travelling by boat from Åbo without being troubled by the police.

Arrangements were quickly completed for publication of *Proletary* in Switzerland, and early in January 1908, Lenin and his wife left Sweden for Geneva, which they reached via Berlin and a visit to Rosa Luxemburg. It was to be the first journey in some years of wandering during which Lenin continued with his speaking and writing throughout Europe: he travelled twice to visit a Bolshevik school Maxim Gorky had opened on the island of Capri; set up his own similar school a few miles from Paris, where he lived temporarily; and after a Bolshevik Conference in Prague in 1912 finally cut the Gordian knot between the two factions of the RSDLP, and settled down outside Cracow for the brief period that remained before the outbreak of the First World War and his return to Switzerland. Throughout these years Lenin carried a burden of organizational work which was admirable training for the arduous period which followed the seizure of power in Russia in the autumn of 1917, a volume of work under which most men would have sunk.

Transport was a major problem, since the bulk of the propaganda material taken into Russia had to be carried illicitly; it was necessary to build up what became known loosely as the 'northern underground', a changing network of routes along which revolutionary literature could be channelled into Russia through Scandinavia. A key figure in this organization, and later an even more important figure after the Bolsheviks' seizure of power in 1917, was Alexander Shlyapnikov. A Bolshevik since 1903, Shlyapnikov was a friend, and later the lover, of Aleksandra Kollontay; it is through her reminiscences that some details can be gleaned of how Shlyapnikov, a skilled lathe operator whose qualifications enabled him to find work in a number of countries, was able to smuggle Lenin's writings into Russia, sometimes concealed in thick-soled boots – apparently one of his favourite methods of carrying them.

In addition to overseeing the dangerous business of illegal transport, Lenin had the task of sorting out the differences, which rose within the movement as continuously as waves on a choppy sea, and of acting as mediator. It is true that the argument between the Bolsheviks and the Mensheviks slowly lost some of its harshness – although the outbreak of war in 1914 did not totally disperse it in the way that the anti-war feeling dispersed many differences in the revolutionary movement. But this major argument was supplemented by many others, most of them involving Lenin himself; in fact, reading the hundreds of letters enshrined in his *Collected Works* it is difficult not to wonder at times how the movement survived the stresses and strains of so many destructive tendencies. The differences were understandable: social-democrats worked not only in Russia but against the varying backgrounds of virtually all European countries. Their contrasted experiences and environments produced theories of revolution which were often different and sometimes conflicting; their views on how such theories could best be implemented varied quite as radically. There was usually a shortage of money, sometimes drastic; the men, and women, who strove to overturn the system were usually high-spirited, often self-opinionated, and many worked under the constant threat of arrest. It is not surprising that Lenin, judged by his correspondence, seems at times during the years leading up to the First World War not only to be preparing the ground for revolution but keeping in order a collection of political and literary prima donnas who, at the hint of a careless phrase or the suggestion that they had not done everything possible for the cause, would flounce out of the business, or provoke indignation or worse. Lenin was strict with them, not only in dismissing them from positions of comparative power which they enjoyed, but also in excoriating them to other comrades. 'Falsifications', 'distortions' and 'downright lies' are accusations carried through the post, and there seem to be few arguments in which those who differed from Lenin are not described by the simple word 'scoundrels'.

The journey to Berlin early in 1908 had unfortunate consequences. The previous day a number of Russians in the city had been arrested and Lenin's contact, Comrade Abramov, thought it safer to take his visitors to a series of cafés rather than to private houses. When they returned to their hotel after the meeting with Rosa Luxemburg they felt ill.

'We both had white foam at the lips and a kind of weakness

had seized us [Krupskaya later wrote]. It afterwards transpired that, in going from one restaurant to another, we had got fish-poisoning somewhere. A doctor had to be summoned in the night. Vladimir Ilyich was registered as a Finnish cook and I as an American citizen. Therefore the chamber-maid fetched an American doctor. First he examined Vladimir Ilyich and said it was a very serious business. Then he looked at me and said: "Well, you'll live!" '

Having been charged what they considered an extortionate fee for the visit, they spent two days in the city and then, still unwell, continued on to Switzerland.

Although his beloved mountains were so near, Lenin was distinctly unhappy in Geneva, commenting that he felt as if he'd come to be buried. To Lunacharsky he wrote on 13 January: 'It is devilishly sad to have to return to this accursed Geneva again, but there's no other way out!' And to his sister Maria he wrote on 14 January: 'We have been hanging about in this damned Geneva for several days now . . . It is an awful hole but there is nothing we can do. We shall get used to it.'

It was in this mood of disillusion with Geneva that Lenin received from Gorky an invitation to visit him in Capri, where, since 1906 with Lunacharsky, Gorky had been supporting the philosophical theory of empiriomonism, a 'God-building' system that diluted the pure spirit of Marxism, and had been produced by Bogdanov. In addition to supporting Bogdanov, Gorky hoped that at his school in Capri 'God-building' ideas could be merged successfully with the political ideas of the RSDLP, which were taught at the school to working-class youngsters from Russia who, it was believed, could be trained for positions as Party leaders. Bogdanov lectured on economics and social thought,

Lunacharsky on trade unionism, and Gorky on the history of Russian literature.

The effort to forge a union between politics and philosophy was only partly successful. The situation was not helped by Gorky's wife being on bad terms with Bogdanov, while disagreements between Bogdanov and Lenin continued despite all efforts to disperse them. Plekhanov, Trotsky and Rosa Luxemburg were only a few of those who refused to come to the Capri school either as lecturers or students. Lenin might have been even more dismissive of Bogdanov's philosophical ideas had he not thought it unwise to disgruntle him politically since Bogdanov was not only an important supporter of expropriating but was a member of the triumvirate, the others being Lenin and Krasin, who helped channel the money from 'exactivities' into revolutionary activities in Russia. But if this was a bull point for Bogdanov in Lenin's estimation, it was counterbalanced by what he regarded as the over-sociological trend of Bogdanov's writings, which he had been known to describe as 'Bogdanovist gibberish'. However, had the invitation from Gorky not come at a moment when Lenin seemed particularly disenchanted with Geneva, he would, nevertheless, have seen at least some attractions about it. 'The idea of dropping in on you on Capri is delightfully tempting, dash it!' he replied. 'You have painted such an attractive picture that I have definitely made up my mind to come out, and I shall try to bring my wife with me.'

Nevertheless, Lenin was anxious to delay the trip, and for more than one reason. A decade previously he had read Bogdanov while in Siberian exile and his dismay had been increased when the two men met in 1904. 'I immediately wrote to him (in the spring or at the beginning of 1904) from Geneva to Paris that his writings firmly persuaded me of the incorrectness of his views and convinced me of the Tightness of Plekhanov's views,' Lenin had written to Gorky. Now he had no reason to think that his philosophical differences with Bogdanov would have decreased.

However inaccurate the phrase 'God-building' might have been to describe Bogdanov's philosophy, that philosophy had an element strong enough to affront the anti-religious views that had been hardening in Lenin's mind since his conversion to atheism while still a teenager. These were outlined in 1905 in the last issue of Gorky's *Novaya Zhizn,* an issue which appeared illegally owing to a police ban.

> 'Those who live by the labour of others [Lenin wrote there in "Socialism and Religion"] are taught by religion to practise charity while on earth, thus offering them a very cheap way of justifying their entire existence as exploiters and selling them at a moderate price tickets to well-being in heaven. Religion is opium for the people. Religion is a sort of spiritual booze, in which the slaves of capital drown their human image, their demand for a life more or less worthy of man.'

These beliefs, which he was to reiterate more than once during the next few years, could be concealed only with difficulty if he became involved in philosophical discussion with Bogdanov. He would also have difficulty in concealing his contempt for what he considered Bogdanov's weakness for sociological theories. And his political antennae warned him that he would be wise to prevent differences from coming to the surface if they could be kept below it. Feeling thus inhibited from speaking out freely for himself, Lenin turned to Lyubov Akselrod who later wrote in 'A New Variation of Revisionism':

> 'Lenin, who quite correctly regarded the combination of empiriomonism with a materialistic explanation of history [as] a new variation of bourgeois "critical" tendencies, most energetically insisted that I should immediately set to work to evaluate this school of thought . . . This episode shows that we Marxists have viewed the combination of empiriomonism with the materialistic explanation of history as an inimical teaching, alien to our views, and we have considered it our duty to come out against it . . .'

Whether owing to the influence of Lyubov Akselrod or of Party interests alone, a satisfactory compromise was subsequently achieved.

> 'In the summer and autumn of 1904 [Lenin later wrote to Gorky] we finally came to an understanding with Bogdanov and concluded as *bolsheviks* a tacit alliance which tacitly excluded philosophy as being a neutral area. This alliance lasted throughout the Revolution [i.e. the Revolution of 1905] and gave us the possibility of carrying out jointly in the Revolution that tactic of revolutionary social democracy [Bolshevism] which according to my deepest conviction was the only correct one.'

In spite of the truce, the dispute simmered on, Lunacharsky and Gorky in Capri being more favourably disposed than Lenin to Bogdanov's ideas. Gorky's invitation to Capri brought matters to a head and in February 1908, Lenin felt forced to tell him direct that Bogdanov's book, *Essays on the Philosophy of Marxism* (St Petersburg, 1908), had greatly exacerbated disagreements concerning philosophical problems. It would, he went on, be unforgivable if philosophical discord hindered social democracy. Just how strongly he felt was shown in his criticisms to Gorky.

'To tell the reader that belief in the external world is mystical (Bazarov), to confuse in the most unseemly manner materialism and Kantianism (Bazarov and Bogdanov), to preach a variation of agnosticism (empiriocriticism) and idealism (empiriomonism), to teach workers "religious atheism" and the "adoration" of the supreme human potentialities (Lunacharsky), to declare Engels' teaching on the dialectic to be mysticism (Berman), to draw water from the stinking wells of all sorts of French positivists, agnostics and metaphysicists (Yushkevich) – the devil knows who they are – no, that is going too far. Of course, we rank and file Marxists are not well read in philosophy, but why should we suffer such indignity, why should we be offered this kind of stuff as Marxist philosophy? I'd rather let myself be quartered than take part in a publication or in any group that preaches this kind of thing.'

On the day that he expressed himself so strongly, Lenin decided to throw his own weight into the fight and, while admitting himself to be only 'a rank and file Marxist' as far as philosophy was concerned, began work on what was to become *Materialism and Empirino-Criticism*. It was written primarily to buttress the theoretical foundation of the Bolsheviks, since it was a refutation of Bogdanov's empiriomonism, which, in the words of Paul Edwards's eight-volume *Encyclopedia of Philosophy*, 'saw synthesis and harmony as more permanent and productive than opposition and conflict'. Bogdanov believed that 'The capitalist monopoly of managerial experience will be broken not by abolishing private ownership of the means of production but by disseminating managerial experience and knowledge among the noncapitalists. Emphasis was thus shifted from violent political and economic "expropriation" à la Lenin to mass education and proletarian culture.' There was also a deeper motive behind the book since Lenin hoped to demonstrate that any discrediting of materialism as a basis of thought such as appeared to be the inevitable result of any success on Bogdanov's part, helped the class enemies of the proletariat. Bogdanov's work was thus seen by him as being reactionary in effect if not in intent.

Lenin found it difficult to ride the two literary horses of philosophy and political polemics at the same time and in March told Gorky: 'I am neglecting the newspaper *[Proletary]* because of my hard bout of philosophy. One day I read one of the empirio-critics and swear like a fishwife, next day I read another and swear still worse.' Soon he was complaining to Gorky that *Proletary* was 'an uncared-for waif' and blamed the attention he was giving to philosophy.

It was in the hope of resolving the situation completely – and as part of his work on *Materialism and Empirino-Criticism* – that he finally agreed to visit Gorky on Capri. He went first in April 1908, and combined the visit with sightseeing trips to Naples, Vesuvius and Pompeii. On Capri itself he made a point of visiting the tourist attraction of the Blue Grotto. 'Of course, the grotto is beautiful, only it is so theatrical as if it were scenery in a theatre,' he later commented. 'On my way here I thought about the Volga all the time. The beauty there is of a different sort; it is simple and dearer to me.'

The main object of his journey to Capri was not achieved. 'I . . . told [Bogdanov and Lunacharsky] . . . that my views on philosophy were unconditionally opposed to theirs,' he wrote. Krupskaya's version of the visit underlines the situation.

'There was a big crowd at Gorki's place [she records], much noise and bustle. Many played chess, others went boating. Ilyich said very little about this trip. He spoke mostly about the beauty of the scene and the quality of the local wine, but he was reticent about the discussion on the big questions that took place there. It was too painful a subject [for] him to talk about.'

Lenin was back in Geneva early in May. He was still worrying away at philosophy and for the rest of the summer managed to combine research for his book in London with his ever-present Party work in Switzerland. From mid-May to mid-June he worked in the British Museum. Lenin made few visits to London without finding a reason for visiting the Reading Room [now the British Library Reading Room] where, according to the actor Miles Malleson, he was long remembered, although not by his famous name but as Mr Ulyanov. Malleson asked an elderly member of the staff whether he remembered Lenin reading there. When this brought no response he suggested that he might have worked under his real name of Ulyanov. 'Of course, I remember Mr Ulianov,' he was told, 'a very charming gentleman, short and with a pointed beard. A very nicely spoken gentleman. I remember him very well. Can you tell me, sir, what became of him?'

Before Lenin's Reading Room visit to complete research for his book on philosophy he had lectured in Geneva, Lausanne,

Paris and Brussels on the 1905 Revolution and on the prospects for the future, after which he continued vigorously with his work for *Proletary*. By the end of September the philosophical writing was coming to an end. His brother Dmitri should now come to Geneva, he told his mother. 'We could go for some splendid walks together,' he added enthusiastically. 'If there are money difficulties, you must take the money Anya has in the bank. I hope I shall now earn a lot.'

Any money from his philosophical writings would be a useful supplement to what came in from his political theses although it was only during the war years that he really began to suffer the financial pinch. The point was later made by Krupskaya, who in describing their life in Europe once wrote: 'We did not know the kind of need in which you don't know how you are going to buy bread. Did the emigrant comrades really live this way? There were some who were out of work for two years, who did not receive any money from Russia, and were literally starving. This never happened to us.'

Materialism and Empirio-Criticism was finished by the end of October 1908, and early the following year Lenin arranged with his sister Anna for the next stage, writing to her:

'As for passing on the proof reading, you are, of course, right to make all arrangements for this, because it must be incredibly difficult to combine such tedious and laborious work with looking after Mother. I can only marvel how the last proofs were so exemplary, when you have to work in such trying circumstances. The most important thing for me is the speedy publication of the book. There has already been too much delay. If only it could appear by the 15th March (old style)! If it doesn't, it will be too bad! With regard to the fine for a breach of contract, I do not really know if it can be exacted. I doubt it. And besides, is it worth spoiling one's relations with the publishers? No, it is not.'

Before the end of 1908 he was able once more to concentrate on Party affairs and the future revolution whose prospect was never far from his mind. And now he and Krupskaya, together with her mother, pulled up what had almost become roots in Geneva and in December moved to Paris together with Lenin's sister Maria who a short while earlier had joined them from Russia to continue her education in Switzerland.

Although the editorial office of *Proletary* had already been transferred to Paris, Lenin would probably not have followed it but for the advice of two Party members, who somehow convinced him that he would be less likely to be spied on in Paris than in Geneva. Even though the size of the French capital, compared with the Swiss city, would presumably make surveillance more difficult, the Russian secret police had their own headquarters in Paris; and it is significant that one of those who recommended Lenin to move was later discovered to be a police spy. Once again, the sophisticated Lenin showed himself to be curiously vulnerable to police infiltration.

Krupskaya also had mixed feelings about the move to Paris. She later wrote with affection of the colony of Russian *émigrés* – she and Lenin, the Zinovievs, the Kamenevs and others making a total of about twenty – which had grown up in Geneva. And of Paris she commented: '[There] we spent the most trying years of our exile.'

After a brief stay in an hotel, they found a four-roomed flat in the rue Beaunier, elegant and expensive according to Lenin. Here, as in all his long succession of homes, Lenin lived in a context very different from that of the traditional left-wing revolutionary. 'I was struck by the order in the flat,' says Ilya Erenburg, about to embark on a distinguished literary career. 'The books stood on shelves, Lenin's desk was tidy; it wasn't like the rooms of my Moscow friends.'

It was from here that in June 1909 Lenin attended a meeting at which were present the editorial board of *Proletary* plus those running the Bolshevik Centre. It was a significant occasion for it was now that Lenin induced the board to approve a resolution stating that Bolshevism must be strictly Marxist. The upshot was a final split with Bogdanov, who left the Centre, itself about to disintegrate. Lenin's triumph over Bogdanov on this point, and it was no less, was counterbalanced when the Centre discussed other matters and showed their disapproval of his own ideas and methods. He survived the arguments although for two or three years he did not regain the influence he had been able to exercise during the first years of the century.

In July 1909 they left the rue Beaunier for a smaller second-floor flat at 4 rue Marie-Rose. Here, where they remained for three years, Krupskaya's mother had the best room, Lenin and his wife had the next and Lenin had a study almost filled with books and a whitewood desk.

As in Switzerland, he spoke frequently in public, sometimes to Jewish meetings, most frequently to Russian emigrants.

'He spoke calmly [says Erenburg], without rhetoric or emotional appeal; he slurred his "r's" a little; sometimes he smiled. His speeches were like a spiral; afraid that people wouldn't understand him he returned to a thought he had already expressed, never repeating it but adding something new. (Some of those who copied his manner of speaking used to forget that a spiral is like a circle and yet unlike. A spiral progresses).'

In Paris he carried on one working practice he had begun years earlier – that of reading aloud whatever speech he was to make once it had been written out. Since he frequently worked at night and he did not wish to wake those within earshot, he virtually whispered during this initial try-out.

Life in Paris had its difficulties. Krupskaya found housekeeping more expensive than it had been in Switzerland, and a visitor who asked her the price of geese or veal had a rough awakening. 'During our stay in Paris we had not eaten either the one or the other,' she later wrote. 'Had [he] interested himself in the price of horse-flesh and lettuce I could have told him.' Krupskaya's aunt had left her 4,000 roubles and this helped with expenses, but at times it seems that the family relied heavily on the food parcels that Lenin's mother sent from Russia. 'Because of [them],' Krupskaya wrote to Lenin's sister Anna, 'Volodya has even learned to help himself from the larder and eats out of turn, i.e., not at the proper times. Whenever he comes in, he starts eating. Now he drinks milk before going to bed (instead of wine) and eats eggs in the mornings.' Lenin himself once revealed that the parcels from Russia included fish, caviar and smoked sturgeon fillets. 'We are greatly enjoying these dainties and thinking of the Volga as we eat them,' he told his mother.

During his first months in the city, as he carried on with his Party work, constantly lecturing and writing, he had anxiously awaited publication of *Materialism and Empirio-Criticism*, telling his sister Anna: 'It is *hellishly* important to me for the book to appear sooner. I have not only literary but also serious political commitments that are linked up with [this].' Publication eventually came in mid-May from the Zveno (Link) company in Moscow, a beautiful production according to Lenin, who complained only about the price of 1 rouble 60 copecks.

The strain on him throughout this period was considerable, judging by the account of Gérard Israel who visited him to discuss Jewish affairs.

'We met in a café in the Gobelins quarter, where the Bolshevik leaders often went [he has written]. This was a period when Lenin was plunged into interminable discussions with his adversaries and even with his followers, on ideological and political questions. But on the day of our meeting, I found him in excellent spirits, gay, his look a bit derisive, with a touch of irony, but with no malice, ready to draw his sword but not to use it. I thought that in his eyes I read a glimmer of indulgence for this youngster of twenty-one (he was then thirty-eight) who was misled by nonsense. He seemed curious, but quite sure of himself. "And so," he began, "are you really a Social Democrat and a Socialist Zionist? Don't you think that the two ideologies are contradictory, and can you ever hope to make me change my opinion?"

' "No, Comrade Lenin. I am not naive enough to hope to modify your ideas or to convince you. Moreover, on this issue, I share the advice of Count Pierre Bezuhov, the character in *War and Peace* who says that each man has his opinion, and who does not believe in the power of words to comince another person. And, I might add, especially to convince someone like you." '

At this period Lenin constantly relied on the power of words. 'I remember once Ilyich came home after a heated debate with the Otzovists,' Krupskaya later wrote. 'I could hardly recognize him, his face was so drawn and he could barely speak. We decided that he must take a week's holiday at Nice to get the sun and be away from the noise and strife. He went and came back much the better for it.' 'The place is wonderful – ' Lenin wrote of the town, 'sunny, warm, dry, and a southern sea.'

He was soon back in Paris, but early in August 1909, left the capital with his wife, her mother, and his sister Maria for a six-week holiday at Bombon, fifty kilometres from Paris. For once he appeared to lay Party affairs aside. 'We went for walks every day,' Krupskaya wrote, 'and almost every day we cycled to the Clamart forests, fifteen kilometres away.' To his mother Lenin wrote: 'We are having a good holiday here . . . Our rooms here are good, and the board is good and not expensive,' while to Zinoviev he said that after three weeks he was 'beginning to come round'. It seems they lived in comparative luxury and were brought coffee every morning by a young girl who forty years later remembered Lenin as 'le monsieur russe, si poli, si gentil, qui apprenait à une petite fille à monter à bicyclette'.

Back in Paris he resumed lecturing and writing, addressed two meetings in Liège, and continued his attempts to bring the entire Party round to his views. He was acclimatizing to Paris but, as he confessed to his brother-inlaw, Mark Yelizarov, he still missed Russia, writing: 'One feels quite cut off here, so that your tales, impressions and observations "From the Volga" (how I miss the Volga!) are real balsam.'

At a meeting in November of the editorial board of *Sotsial Demokrat,* the underground central organ of the Party now being produced in Paris, he introduced a draft resolution on Party matters which was rejected. He countered by resigning from the board, but withdrew his resignation two days later. He was now working all out: 'He always feels better when he is working,'

Krupskaya told his mother in December, 'For over a week now he has been getting up at eight in the morning to go to the library; he returns from there at 2 o'clock. At first he found it difficult to get up so early.'

Throughout this period Lenin continued to exercise his authority by a mixture of aloofness and bonhomie. According to Valentinov he 'kept everyone at arm's length. I never saw him put his hand on anyone's shoulder and no one among his comrades would have dared, however deferentially, to do the same to him.' Yet with ordinary people he could, on the contrary, strike up friendships that were genuine and lasting. Giovanni Spadaro, an old Capri fisherman whom he got to know when visiting Gorky, would say of him 'Only an honest man could laugh like that', and others, intrigued by his ability to catch fish without a rod, a skill which earned him the nickname of 'Drin-Drin', would later ask Gorky 'How is Drin-Drin getting on? The Tsar hasn't caught him yet?'

One quality about Lenin that struck everyone was his resolution, which augured ill for his enemies. Rosa Luxemburg, a woman not lightly impressed with human potential, had pointed him out to Clara Zetkin in Stuttgart saying: 'Take a good look at him. That is Lenin. Look at the selfwilled stubborn head. A real Russian peasant's head with a few faintly Asiatic lines. That man will try to overturn mountains. Perhaps he will be crushed by them. But he will never yield.'

Lenin's struggle towards a position of supreme power was helped by his apparently limitless energy which he could concentrate on a severely limited task. Yet it was also helped by very different qualities, an appreciation of the human condition, and an ability to feel both the tragedies and the farcical circumstances of life which he often concealed and which frequently went

198

unremarked by either friends or enemies. However, one colleague has remarked on how Lenin, watching Bernhardt acting in *The Lady of the Camellias* in Geneva, was seen to be wiping away his tears. As for his sense of humour, Gorky has written:

'He loved fun, and when he laughed it was with his whole body; he was quite overcome with laughter and would laugh sometimes until he cried. He could give to his short characteristic exclamation, "H'm, h'm" an infinite number of modifications, from biting sarcasm to noncommittal doubt. Often in this "h'm h'm" one caught the sound of the keen humour which a sharp-sighted man experiences who sees clearly through the stupidities of life.'

The year 1910 started unfortunately for Lenin when he was returning home on his bicycle from watching an air display at Juvisy-sur-Orge: twenty-two kilometres from Paris, a car collided with him outside the airfield and although he was not hurt his bicycle was wrecked. 'People helped me take the number and acted as witnesses,' he wrote to his sister Maria. 'I have found out who the owner of the car is, (a viscount, the devil take him!) and now I have taken him to court.'

Lenin won his case against the viscount, a bright spot in what was to be, politically, a year of frustrating discussions during which he still hoped to fix a compromise between the various factions holding differing views on what Bolshevism should be. In March he wrote to Plekhanov on the need 'for a close and sincere alignment of all genuinely social-democratic elements in the struggle against liquidationism and otsovism' (two dissident beliefs concerned with the relationship between the RSDLP and the Duma) and added that he was willing to travel down to San

Remo, where Plekhanov was now living, to discuss the situation. The following month he told Kamenev that while a Party core was necessary, it should not be built 'on the cheap *phrases* of Trotsky and Co. but [only] on *genuine* ideological rapprochement between the Plekhanovites and the Bolsheviks'.

It was perhaps in the hope of closing or at least narrowing the schism that had arisen over the philosophical controversy that in the summer of 1910 Lenin decided to visit Gorky on Capri once again. He made the last leg of the journey from Marseille on a boat he described to his mother as 'cheap and pleasant. It was like travelling on the Volga.' After a fortnight of discussion he left for France to join Krupskaya and her mother, already on holiday in two rooms of a coastguard's cottage at Pornic on the Bay of Biscay, west of Nantes. Here Lenin thoroughly enjoyed himself.

'He bathed in the sea a great deal, cycled – he loved the sea and the sea breezes – [Krupskaya reported] and chatted cheerfully on all sorts of subjects with the Kostitsins, enjoyed eating the crabs which the coastguard caught for us. In fact, our landlord and his wife took a great liking to Ilyich. The stout loud-voiced landlady – she was a laundress – would tell us about the conflicts she had with the priests . . . the priests tried to persuade the mother to allow [her son] to be educated in the monastery . . . but the laundress indignantly showed the priests the door . . . and this was why Ilyich praised the crabs so highly.'

After nearly a month on the Biscay coast, Lenin left for Paris and the first of a series of meetings with revolutionary colleagues, including Plekhanov. Shortly afterwards, he arrived in Copenhagen for discussions with Zinoviev, Kamenev, Trotsky and others at the Congress of the Socialist International where it was decided to publish *Rabochaya Gazeta*. The journey enabled him to organize a family reunion he had long been awaiting, and in September, first he, then his sister Maria, and finally his seventy-five-year-old mother, arrived in Stockholm. Here the mother heard her son speak in public for the first time – giving a report on the Congress that had just finished in Copenhagen. 'She listened quite attentively to Vladimir Ilyich and apparently became very excited,' Maria later wrote. 'He spoke well, "so impressively and skilfully" she then said to me, "but why does he exert himself so much, why does he speak so loudly, that is so harmful. He is not looking after himself!" '

She appears to have had doubts about his health, and before leaving the country presented him with a warm plaid for use during the coming winter. Lenin used it regularly and the plaid was on his bed when he died in Russia nearly fifteen years later.

In Stockholm he accompanied his mother down to the quay but was unable to go on the ship with her in safety since the vessel was Russian and on board he would have risked arrest.

'This [day] was the last time he saw his mother,' Krupskaya later wrote. 'He had a premonition of that and it was with sad and wistful eyes that he followed the departing steamer.'

Having returned to Paris shortly afterwards, Lenin's first concern was to deal with the schisms that continued to split the Party. To G. L. Shklovsky he wrote on 14 October: 'Since 1909 I have been *wholly* in favour of a *rapprochement* with the Plekhanovites. And even more so now. We can and should build the Party only with the Plekhanovites.'

November saw the appearance of the first number of *Rabochaya Gazeta* and simultaneously Lenin prepared with Plekhanov to publish *Mysl (Thought)* which was to cover philosophy and economics. As part of his campaign to purge the Party of tendencies with which he disagreed Lenin now increased his polemical writing. In 'Two Worlds', published in 1910 in *Sotsial Demokrat,* he noted that: 'Opportunism is opportunism for the very reason that it sacrifices the *fundamental* interests of the movement to momentary advantages or considerations based on the most short-sighted, superficial calculations.' In the first issue of *Zvezda (The Star),* a legal Bolshevik paper, he described 'Differences in the European Labour Movement'; and he carried on his criticisms in *Mysl* which in its second and third numbers contained 'Those Who Would Liquidate Us', an attack on Potrezov and V. A. Bazarov.

Simultaneously, he kept up pressure against the group which, with Gorky's support, was still operating from Capri. It had by now opened a second school in Bologna – financed not by Gorky but directly by the RSDLP – and towards the end of 1910 its students invited Lenin to address them. In declining, he commented: 'Both the trend and the methods of the group which has organized the school on the island of Capri and in Bologna I consider harmful to the Party and un-Social-Democratic.'

Eventually both schools succumbed to Lenin's opposition. From the start they had faced constant attack from *Proletary* while it was later revealed that of the original thirteen pupils on Capri five had been acting in Lenin's interests. The eight others eventually 'graduated' but shortly after their return to Russia in 1910 were arrested. Subsequently, it was found that one of the five was a police agent – a further illustration of Lenin's particular vulnerability.

The following year, 1911, he was at last able to implement a plan he had formed after his first visit to Capri in 1908. This was nothing less than the opening of his own Bolshevik school which would teach the true faith to carefully selected pupils. Lack of suitable helpers and a suitable site combined to prevent him from carrying out the plan for three years, but by the summer of 1911 both problems had been overcome, the first by the arrival in Paris of the only woman, other than his wife and members of his family, with whom Lenin was to share not only his political ambitions but his affections. She was Inessa Armand, born in Paris in 1879 of a French father and a Scottish mother, both of whom worked as music-hall artistes.

The personal relationship between Lenin and Inessa, an extremely attractive woman with thick chestnut hair, large beautiful eyes and what has been called an irrepressible ardour of spirit, aged thirty when she arrived in Paris, has been the subject of much speculation, fuelled at times by jealousy of Lenin's high regard for her and confused by the political loyalties that affected the warring Bolshevik factions at the time. Feminine feelings in particular were easily aroused either for or against. One of the few Bolsheviks who did not fall quickly under Inessa's spell was Angelica Balabanov who told the American historian Bertram D. Wolfe: 'I did not warm to [her]. She was pedantic, a one hundred per cent Bolshevik in the way she dressed (always in the same severe style), in the way she thought, and spoke. She spoke a number of languages fluently, and in all of them repeated Lenin verbatim.' There is no doubt of Lenin's affection for Inessa. He used in his letters to her the familiar *'ty'* – written by him to only four other women, his mother, his two sisters and his wife. His correspondence with her that has been published – and a great deal has not – suggests a relationship at least of very deep friendship while Lenin confided political plans to Inessa Armand to an extent not exceeded by his confidences to his wife. Aleksandra Kollontay was an intimate of Inessa and has claimed that Krupskaya more than once suggested that Lenin should leave her for his friend. Lenin always turned down the suggestion – as he would have done whatever his personal feelings might have been owing to Krupskaya's value as a political helper. There is no firm evidence that Inessa Armand became Lenin's mistress and none at all that he fathered a child by her, as was once claimed. The legend grew up easily enough, as indicated by Jean Fréville who has made a study of Lenin's life in Paris. 'How', he has written of Lenin's relations with inessa, 'could he not be seduced by this exceptional being who combined beauty with intelligence, femininity with energy, practical sense with revolutionary ardour?'

Speculation was made easier from the start, as following her arrival in Paris in late 1909 or early 1910 Inessa quickly became a close friend of the Lenin family and opportunities for intimacy were constant. Nevertheless, Krupskaya's continued friendship with her can as easily suggest that rumours were mere rumours as that the two formed a *ménage à trois* with Lenin. The only certainty about the situation is that whatever emotional complications developed, the three were balanced enough to cope with them.

Inessa had been taken from France to Russia after her father died, had become tutor in French and English to the sons of Evgeny Armand, a rich businessman living outside Moscow, had married one of his two sons, by whom she had three boys and two girls, and had been introduced to revolutionary politics by his second son for whom she left her husband. She emigrated to Stockholm where she read Chernyshevsky's *What Is To Be Done?* and began to learn of Lenin's activities. Returning to Russia she was twice arrested and escaped to Paris where she made for the

Russian *émigré* colony. She eventually arrived with her children at 2 rue Marie-Rose, next door to Lenin and his wife.

Lenin was attracted to Inessa not only personally but by her love of Beethoven which he shared – without being able to emulate her at the piano – and by the similarity of her interpretations of Marx to his own. It is impossible to quantify her non-political influence on him, but after her arrival in Paris Lenin's interest in the arts seems to have increased and he addressed a significant remark to his sister Maria in a letter of mid-January 1910: 'I have begun to pay more attention to the theatre; I have seen Bourget's new play "La Barricade". Reactionary but interesting.'

Inessa's reception into Lenin's family circle must have been similar to that which she experienced when joining it again in Cracow after Lenin had moved there in 1912.

'My mother became closely attached to Inessa [Krupskaya has written]. Inessa often went to talk with her, sit with her, have a smoke with her. It became cosier and gayer when Inessa came. Our entire life was filled with party concerns and affairs, more like a student commune than like family life, and we were glad to have Inessa . . . something warm radiated from her talk.'

It was almost inevitable that Lenin should co-opt Inessa to help when he was eventually able to set up his opposition to Gorky's school on Capri.

During one of his cycle rides from Paris, he had passed through the little town of Longjumeau which lay in the valley of the Yvette, eighteen kilometres away. Here he spotted an abandoned workshop that he believed would be ideal for his purpose. He rented it, equipped it as a school and arranged accommodation for students and for himself and his wife. Inessa rented a house where the students could eat; the Zinoviev family also moved into the town, and before the end of the summer Longjumeau contained a small Bolshevik community. After opening the school with a lecture on the Communist Manifesto, Lenin was able to attract eighteen students of whom most were Russian workers, including G. K. Ordzhonikidze, who had been imprisoned with Stalin in Baku and who was to rise high in the first Bolshevik administration. Lenin gave thirty lectures on political economy, ten on the agrarian question and five on the theory and practice of socialism. It was a tough schedule. Yet it was a surprising exception to Lenin's general practice in that he allowed the burden of the school's work to be shared with Inessa, who spoke regularly on political economy, while Krupskaya gave lectures on how to set up an illegal newspaper.

As was to be expected in such an environment, Lenin was soon 'making good use of the summer' as Krupskaya described it to his mother.

'He does his work out in the open, rides his bicycle a lot, goes bathing and is altogether pleased with country life. This week we have been cycling our heads off. We made three excursions of 70 to 75 kilometres each, and have explored three forests – it was fine. Volodya is extremely fond of excursions that begin at six or seven in the morning and last until late at night.'

The Longjumeau school was a success, and helped to spread the news that Lenin was operating in France. His reputation was by now so considerable that a delegation of sailors, elected after a meeting of men from Russia's Baltic fleet, travelled to Paris to meet him. Lenin reported to Gorky that the sailors were in a fighting mood.

Loath as he was to leave Longjumeau, he felt that he could not refuse an invitation in September 1911 from Camille Huysmans, the Belgian writer, socialist and statesman, to address a meeting of the International Socialist Bureau to be held in Zurich later in the month. He accepted and, in his customary way, used the journey for a combination of lecturing and holiday. After speaking to the Bureau, while still in Zurich he gave the first of three lectures in Switzerland on Stolypin, the Chairman of the Council of Ministers who had been assassinated in Kiev earlier in the month. Between the lectures he squeezed in a visit to Lucerne and from there wrote to his mother saying: 'Yesterday I went out climbing on the *[sic]* Pilatus – nearly 7,000 feet. The weather is wonderful so far and I am having an excellent holiday.'

He was back in Paris by mid-October. Then in November he was off to Brussels, Antwerp and London, giving in each city further lectures on Stolypin in which he described the death of 'the arch-hangman' as the end of the first stage of the Russian counter-revolution.

Before the end of the year Lenin was preparing for what was to be a crucial Party Conference to be held in Prague early in 1912. Here eighteen Bolsheviks and two pro-Party Mensheviks met between 18 and 30 January. The Prague Conference elected Lenin as its representative in the International Socialist Bureau, as a member of the Central Organ and on to the new Bolshevik Central Committee. His resolutions were adopted and the practical outcome of the Conference was that the split in the RSDLP which had divided it in 1903, was now formalized by, in effect, the formation of an independent Bolshevik Party. According to

Stalin's sanitized *History of the Communist Party of the Soviet Union* (Moscow, 1938)

'The Prague Conference drew up the balance of the entire struggle of the Bolsheviks against opportunism and resolved to exclude the Mensheviks from the Party. After the exclusion of the Mensheviks the Prague Conference formed the Bolshevik Party as a party existing independently. By bringing to an end the ideological and organizational bankruptcy of the Mensheviks and driving them out of the Party the Bolsheviks took over the old banner of the Party, the Social Democratic Workers' Party of Russia. It is for this reason that the Party of the Bolsheviks continued to call itself until 1918 the Social Democratic Workers' Party of Russia with the addition of the word "Bolsheviks" in brackets. [RSDLP(B)]'

The arguments continued but from now onwards the Bolsheviks fought them from the superior, and continually rising, ground. 'We have finally succeeded – in spite of the liquidationist scoundrels – in reviving the Party and its Central Committee,' Lenin wrote to Gorky. 'I hope you will be as glad of this as we are.'

At Prague it was also decided to re-establish the Central Party apparatus and to replace the weekly *Zvezda* with a new publication, *Pravda (Truth)*, which would appear daily. Also at Prague they had inadvertently let into their midst an important tsarist informer, Roman Malinovsky. One of his police tasks was to promote the enmity between the Mensheviks – of which he posed as a member – and the Bolsheviks. When this was thought likely to slacken, as it was in 1912, he worked to keep it alive from within the ranks of the Bolsheviks whom he now joined. Lenin, impressed by Malinovsky's energy, not only helped him on to the new Central Committee, but made him the Bolshevik spokesman on the fourth Duma to which he was also elected. He provided invaluable aid to the authorities until in May 1914 he resigned, ostensibly because of ill-health but, of course unknown to Lenin, on orders from the authorities.

It was at Prague that Lenin again helped Stalin. He had first put forward Stalin's name as a candidate for membership of the Central Committee but Stalin was not then sufficiently well known to be elected. Lenin then exercised his right as a member of the Central Committee to co-opt one man on to the Committee, and chose Stalin.

Back in Paris after the Prague Conference, Lenin got out into the open air to enjoy himself, as he invariably did after a difficult crisis or period of work. 'It is almost Spring here,' he wrote to his mother. 'About a week ago I cleaned up my bicycle and went out to the Bois de Verrières (Manyasha has been there) and I brought back with me some willow catkins. I went again to-day with Nadya – the cherry blossom is already out. The weather is springlike, but unreliable; much rain.' Shortly afterwards he was writing: 'I believe Spring is early here this year. The other day I again went a bicycle ride into the forest. All the fruit trees in the gardens are in white blossom (as though milk had been poured over them), the perfume was wonderful. How delightful Spring is!'

Yet however delightful nature might be, the outcome of the Prague Conference was more disappointing than Lenin could have thought possible when he had written to Gorky in its aftermath. There soon developed, he told his sister Anna, more bickering and abuse among Party members in Paris than there had been for some time. It came to a head in March 1912, when Trotsky succeeded in organizing a Congress of those who had disagreed with Lenin at Prague. In addition to Martov and his Mensheviks there were Plekhanov and his supporters, Bogdanov and Lunacharsky of the *Vperyod* group, and even Lenin's fellow-editors of the *Sotsial Demokrat*. In such a group it was not difficult to gain approval for decisions that went against the Prague Conference. Once again, divisive arguments raged within the RSDLP even though the Bolsheviks under Lenin could now increasingly be considered a self-contained separate group.

It was hardly surprising that passions rose high since almost every development in Russia brought a variety of reactions from Party members. Thus Lenin himself, for a time the enemy of the Duma, now not only supported entry into it but by mid-May had contributed to *Nevskaya Zvezda* (The *Neva Star*) an article on political parties in Russia which supported the idea of parliaments in general:

'In the absence of representative institutions [he wrote] there is *much more* deception, political lying and fraudulent trickery of all kinds . . . The greater the degree of political liberty in a country and the more stable and democratic its representative institutions, the easier it is for the mass of the people to find its bearings in the fight between the parties and to *learn politics*'.

As far as propaganda was concerned, the most important event in the early summer of 1912 was the publication in St Petersburg of the legal *Pravda* of which 60,000 copies were printed. The paper survived under a succession of titles until suppressed by the tsarist police in 1914 on the eve of the First

World War. Although it relied heavily on worker correspondents and in a single year published more than 11,000 items from them, Lenin was its driving force. He gave advice and instructions to its editorial staff and by the time it was closed down in 1914 had contributed 280 articles to its 636 issues. Running it was a nervous business, even for someone like Lenin who lived outside Russia; during its first thirty-eight months its succession of editors were prosecuted thirty-six times and sentenced to forty-seven and a half months of imprisonment.

The problems of influencing *Pravda* from Paris became more intractable and this may have been one of the reasons that induced Lenin to leave France in the summer of 1912. He had been thinking of moving from Paris as early as March. His rent had been raised; he began to feel, as he wrote to his mother, that somewhere outside the capital would be both healthier and quieter. For a while he contemplated moving to one of the more peaceful small towns only a few miles from the centre of the capital. By the summer, however, he had changed his mind and in June 1912, he, his wife and mother-in-law left France for Cracow, only eight versts from the Russian frontier and on the outskirts of the Tatra mountains, a position that made it doubly attractive to Lenin and Krupskaya.

Before moving to Cracow, Lenin left Paris for several days. Although no details are available, Krupskaya's latest biographer has commented: One can't be sure, but it seems pretty fair to surmise that Lenin joined Inessa Armand at Arcachon' on the Biscay coast of France. Arcachon was then a centre for the treatment of tuberculosis and in view of Inessa's later health record it seems likely that her journey was made for medical reasons. The impact on her relationship with Lenin of whatever she learned is unlikely ever to be known but after his return to

Paris he travelled to Cracow with his wife and mother-in-law. Inessa subsequently followed them but stayed only a few days before leaving for an underground mission to Russia, on which she was quickly arrested. Although the details are likely to remain obscure, it is easy to conclude that there was an important change in her relationship with Lenin in the spring or early summer of 1912.

More than one revolutionary, or potential revolutionary, was gravitating east: Trotsky had been living in Vienna since 1910. Ryazanov, a Social-Democrat, settled there four years later while Lenin was soon to be followed to Cracow by Zinoviev and his family. Lenin's journey to Prague had probably suggested to him some of the benefits of living in Eastern Europe, but he spelt out to Gorky the more specific reasons for the move to Cracow a few weeks after his arrival.

'You ask why I am in Austria. The C.C. has organized a Bureau here (between ourselves): the frontier is close by, we make use of it, it's nearer to Petersburg, we get the papers from there on the third day, it's become far easier to write to the papers there, cooperation with them goes belter. There is less squabbling here, which is an advantage. There isn't a good library, which is a disadvantage. It's hard without books.'

He later reiterated one of these points to his sister, Anna, writing: 'Here we feel much better than we did in Paris – our nerves are at rest and there is more literary work and less squabbling.' He settled down easily to the tempo of the ancient Polish city, annexed to Austria in 1846. The way of life in Cracow, he told relatives in Russia, was limited, quiet and sleepy. He liked it

212

better than Paris. And in January 1913 he could write that the Cracow base had been useful.

On arrival he had been met by S. J. Bagocki, secretary of the Committee of Aid to Political Prisoners, who had been asked to help Lenin and Krupskaya settle in. They explained that they were looking for simple and cheap accommodation near woods and the river Vistula. Bagocki and his wife found them an unfurnished house in Zvezhyniets, a working-class suburb.

'Three days later I went to see them [Bagocki has written]. The furniture was already there and everything stood in its place; two narrow iron bedsteads, two plain tables, a bookcase and some chairs; in the kitchen a small table and some stools. Books and newspapers were unpacked and spread on the tables and window sills. Vladimir Ilyich was busy writing and Nadezhda Konstantinovna invited me as the first visitor to tea in the new place.'

This home proved to be too far from the railway station where Lenin posted his mail every day and he soon moved to another, the windows of which opened on to meadows stretching up to the frontier. His working day here was strictly arranged. Bagocki continues:

'He would get up at eight o'clock and no matter what the weather was would go for a short walk. . . About two o'clock there was a break for lunch. (At that time) Nadezhda Konstantinovna was doing the house-keeping. Her culinary talents did not produce outstanding results – she had other more important preoccupations. But Vladimir Ilyich was not difficult to please and used to remark jokingly that too often he had to eat "burning hot" meat, by which he meant stewed meat slightly burnt.

'After lunch he went on with his work. About five o'clock there was a break for a walk or a bicycle ride out of town. In winter, instead of a walk there was skating.'

The organization by the Central Committee of a Socialist Bureau in Cracow which Lenin had reported to Gorky was at least a minor indication of a change of political balance, and it was reinforced when, later in November 1913, the Central Committee held a meeting in Cracow that Lenin chaired. The following year an important meeting of Bolshevik officials was held in Poronin, the village nearer the Tatra mountains in which Lenin occupied a 'country cottage' for two years.

Lenin's move east helped to increase the political importance of Cracow and more than one Bolshevik was drawn to the city or its surroundings. It was here that in 1912 he met for the first time Nikolay Ivanovich Bukharin, a twenty-four-year-old Moscow-born Social-Democrat whom he was later to describe as a 'most valuable and major theorist of the Party'. Bukharin travelled extensively during the next few years in Scandinavia, Switzerland and the USA where he edited a Communist journal for a time before returning to Russia in the autumn of 1917 and subsequently becoming editor of *Pravda*.

Lenin apparently found it almost as easy to keep his finger on the pulse of events while in Cracow as he had while in St Petersburg. It was from this base that he made his unsuccessful efforts to deal with one unfortunate consequence of his earlier support for Malinovsky, the still-undiscovered police informer who had become a member of the Central Committee.

In February 1913 Stalin had broken his journey home from

the Central Committee meeting in Cracow by visiting St Petersburg and had here attended a musical matinée, legally organized by the Bolsheviks. He had taken the precaution of asking whether there would be any risk in attending; unfortunately, the man from whom he sought advice was Malinovsky who was keeping the Russian police informed of all the movements of Bolsheviks returning from the Central Committee meeting. Stalin was arrested and sentenced to four years' exile in Siberia. Lenin, shocked by the news, hoped that he would be able to arrange Stalin's escape without much delay or difficulty. But the man he asked to help in the escape was again Malinovsky. Stalin was moved deeper into Siberia and was able to escape only after the spring Revolution of 1917.

While Lenin kept up his political activities as resolutely as he had in Switzerland and France, his intellectual interests continued and towards the end of 1913 Krupskaya wrote to his mother:

'What we're simply starved of here is belles-lettres. Volodya has learnt Nadson and Nekrasov almost by heart, our single copy of "Anna Karenina" is being read for the hundredth time. We left our belles-lettres (an insignificant part of what we had in Petersburg) in Paris . . . Volodya has for some reason, as if deliberately, become a great belles-lettrist. And an extreme nationalist. You can never tempt him to try Polish artists, but he has, for example, borrowed from some friends a catalogue of the Tretyakov Gallery . . . and buried himself in it repeatedly.'

Before the end of 1913 Lenin, Krupskaya and her mother were sharing a house with the Zinovievs; Inessa Armand arrived and took a room in the same building. Soon she was sent by

Lenin on a series of Party missions in Russia. Imprisoned, she began to show symptoms of tuberculosis, was released and returned to join Lenin and his wife in the house they had by this time taken in the mountain village of Poronin.

Lenin liked the harsher Polish climate. He bought skates and wrote to his mother and Anna that he skated 'with great enthusiasm – it brings back Simbirsk and Siberia'.

In Poland he was again brought into the close contact with mountains that he had enjoyed in Switzerland, and after Bagocki told him that the Babya mountain offered a splendid view of the Tatras, was quick to say that they would climb the peak together. 'About two weeks later,' Bagocki has recounted, 'I saw Vladimir Ilyich coming up to my lodgings . . . on his bicycle, tired and covered with dust, cursing the bad Galician roads.'

Lenin's persistence is shown by Bagocki's account of what turned into a minor adventure.

'Having left the bicycles in a small restaurant, we set off along a sloping path. We soon reached the woods. It was getting darker. Unfortunately we had left our torches on the bicycles. We started looking for the path in all directions, but all in vain. There was nothing else to do but to keep on going up and up. It was dark, we moved slowly, stumbling against bushes and stumps. There was the danger that we might have to spend the night in the woods. Suddenly a light twinkled. We hurried up. Alas! This was the phosphorescent glow of a rotting tree. We went on. Again in the distance something shone. The light became clearer. Soon we could distinguish two windows. We found the door and entered a large room. On a large stove in the middle a big kettle was boiling, around it all sorts of tourists' crockery. At the table and on plank beds about ten people. On the floor open rucksacks. We were in the *schronisko* all right.'

After supper they slept, having asked the warden to wake them early. Bad weather prevented their setting out but Lenin was adamant that on his next free day he would come again. On the second occasion they were luckier.

'In the distance [wrote Bagocki describing the view from the summit], lit up by the bright rays of the sun, a long range of the Tatra peaks as if suspended in the air; below, everything wrapped in fog, like a blanket of thick foam.

'Vladimir Ilyich was glowing.

' "You see, our efforts were not in vain!" '

Lenin hoped that the air near the Tatra mountains would be good for his wife's goitre, which in spite of electric treatment was beginning to affect her eyes, neck and heart. 'It has been discovered that I have thyroid trouble,' she wrote to Lenin's sister Maria. 'The doctor has frightened me and every day I go to the clinic for electrical treatment: that takes three hours and after it I wander about half the day like a lunatic. They feed me bromide and, in general, it is all terribly sickening.' For Lenin, the problem was to decide whether they should go on hoping for the best or whether he should take Krupskaya to Professor Theodor Kocher, a well-known surgeon in Berne who in 1909 had won the Nobel Prize for his work on the physiology, pathology and surgery of the thyroid gland, and who would almost certainly decide to operate.

For the moment they decided to wait, hoping that five summer months near the mountains might resolve the problem. Their choice for a rest home was a large bungalow with a veranda in Poronin, 700 metres above sea level, 'a huge house, big enough for a whole workshop', as Krupskaya described it, surrounded by forest, mountains and a stream.

According to Lenin, Poronin was 'almost a Russian type. Thatched roofs and poverty. The women and children – bare-foot. The men go about wearing the 'gurali' costume – white cloth trousers, and white cloth half cloaks, half jackets.' The village was apparently ideal for both of them. 'The air was wonderful,' wrote Krupskaya, 'and although there were frequent mists and drizzle, the view of the mountains during the clear intervals was extremely beautiful. We would climb up to the plateau which was quite close to our bungalow and watch the snow-capped peaks.' They began leading what Lenin called a rural life: 'We get up early and go to bed almost at the same time as the cocks and hens.'

He was particularly fond of the place and in 1914 took the Poronin bungalow for a second time. '[He] particularly likes scrambling up the mountains,' Krupskaya told her mother-in-law. 'This time we intend to take a servant who will live in, so that there will be no bother with the housekeeping and we shall be able to go on long outings.'

Before they moved, Lenin finally decided that Krupskaya should be taken to Berne for the operation to deal with her goitre. Her bulging eyes, swollen neck and heart palpitations remained unchanged and in view of what Lenin described as the nervous lives they led, a complete rest was not practicable. He sought further information on Kocher from a Berne member of the Party and in June 1913 left Poronin for Switzerland.

On the way they broke their journey in Vienna where Lenin conferred with Party members; and in Switzerland, waiting for

Krupskaya's operation, he spoke in Zurich, Geneva, Lausanne and Berne. The operation was expensive and Lenin had been forced to ask *Pravda* for money, first writing: 'I beg you not to be late,' and later: 'The money is badly needed.' Only on 24 July were they able to leave Switzerland for Poronin, but throughout the period of recuperation in Berne Lenin spent half the day with his wife in hospital, half in the local library.

From his Polish base, he kept up his varied work for the Party. He continued writing and lecturing, and led the Conference of Party functionaries – officially the Joint Conference of the Central Committee of the RSDLP and Party Officials known as the Summer or August Conference. At it twenty-two delegates met in Poronin from 6 to 14 October 1913. Before it was over Inessa arrived from Russia and appeared once again to be in moderately good health.

Back in Cracow by November 1913, Lenin attacked Rosa Luxemburg and Karl Kautsky for claiming that the Russian Party was dead. He renewed his attempts to secure for the Party the Shmidt money still held by the three trustees appointed years earlier, and prepared for a journey to Paris where meetings were to be held in January 1914 to commemorate Bloody Sunday.

By early February 1914 he had returned from Paris to Cracow and settled down to what, over the last few years, developed into his regular routine of writing on Party affairs and lecturing. Conditions in Cracow continued to make the city the best centre for him.

'The weather here is wonderful [he wrote to Maria on 22 April] and I frequently go cycling. No matter how provincial and barbarous this town of ours may be, by and large I am better off here than I was in Paris. The hurly-burly of life in the émigré colony there was incredible: one's nerves got worn down badly and for no reason at all. Paris is an inconvenient place to work in, the Bibliothèque Nationale is badly organized – we often thought of Geneva, where work went better, the library was convenient, and life was less nerve-racking and time-wasting. Of all the places I have been in my wanderings I would select London or Geneva, if those two places were not so far away.'

Early in May, Lenin, his wife and mother-in-law moved to Poronin again and soon afterwards he chaired a meeting of the Central Committee, which hoped to hold a Congress to coincide with the start of the Congress of the Second International in Vienna.

Before either began, Lenin was shaken by news from Russia that Malinovsky had resigned from his seat in the Duma and disappeared. Earlier rumours that he was in the pay of the police were revived but Malinovsky, with considerable bravado, now visited Lenin and convinced the latter of his innocence. Moreover, to forestall the inquiry that the Mensheviks soon demanded, Lenin set up his own tribunal consisting of himself, Zinoviev and Hanecki-Fürstenberg, the Pole who was soon to play a complicated role in Lenin's relations with the Germans. Malinovsky was exonerated by Lenin's tribunal but was nevertheless expelled from the Bolshevik Party.

The inquiry involved Lenin in a good deal of unexpected labour at a time when he had even more literary work than usual waiting to be done. He had agreed to write a major biographical essay on Marx for Russia's *Granat Biographical Encyclopaedia* and started on this early in July but it was to be four months before he was able to finish it. During the first days of July he therefore wrote to Inessa Armand, now in Paris, asking her to speak for him as a delegate to the Unity Conference to be held in Brussels by the International Socialist Bureau on 16 and 17 July in the hope of resolving the disagreements between the Bolsheviks and the Mensheviks. The German delegates were apparently preparing to attack the Bolsheviks and would have to be answered calmly. 'I am no good for that,' he told Inessa. It was essential that whoever spoke for him should understand the essentials of the complicated situation, and it would help if he or she spoke perfect French. 'You are the *only suitable person,*' he wrote to her. 'So please – I beg you most earnestly – consent, if only for one day.'

Inessa consented, as she invariably did for the sake of the Party. She had the task of doing battle with such figures as Kautsky, Vandervelde, Plekhanov, Trotsky and Martov, and to help her Lenin wrote out every word that she was to say and supplemented that with four pages of private notes.

The outcome was a compromise with which Lenin could be satisfied only by agreeing the dictum that 'half a loaf is better than no bread'. The differences between the two factions, the Conference decided, were not serious enough to hamper unity. A general unification congress at which the differences could be resolved should be held and the minority should accept the view arrived at by the majority. This was hardly ideal for Lenin, and was made disagreeable by the fact that Kautsky had chaired the Conference. Moreover, Lenin was already preparing for another Party Congress which would consolidate the position of the Bolsheviks as a separate, autonomous organization. Only the outbreak of the First World War at the beginning of August 1914 prevented the holding of these two inevitably conflicting congresses.

However, Inessa had handled the affair in Brussels with more calm and tact than Lenin could have mustered and she was rewarded with his congratulations. 'You handled the thing better than I could have done,' he wrote to her. 'Language apart, I would probably have *gone up in the air.*'

A few days later the entire European socialist position was put to the test by the onset of war. Lenin had been maintaining for years that the capitalist system must lead to a great conflict.

'It is inevitable [he once told Gorky]. The capitalist world has reached the stage of putrescent fermentation. People are already beginning to poison themselves with the drugs of chauvinism and nationalism. I think we shall yet see a general European war.

'The proletariat? The proletariat will hardly be able to find in itself the strength to avert the carnage. How could it be done? A general strike of workers all over Europe? They are not yet sufficiently organized or classconscious for that. Such a strike would be the signal for a civil war but we as practical politicians cannot count on that.

'The proletariat will of course suffer terribly. Such must be its fate for some time yet. But its enemies will weaken each other, that also is inevitable. No, but think of it. Why should people who are well fed force hungry ones to fight against each other? Could you name a more idiotic and more revolting crime? The workers will pay a dreadfully heavy price for this, but in the end they will gain. It is the will of history.'

Later he revised his opinion, telling both Gorky and his mother that he expected there would be no war. It was therefore with a

222

shock that Lenin heard on 1 August that Germany had declared war on Russia.

Among the RSDLP, as well as among other European socialists, there was not only consternation but doubt and worry as to how their parties would react since in recent years all had so strongly spoken and voted against war. 'You will see that the German social democrats will not dare to vote against the war, they *will abstain* . . .' said Zinoviev, to which Lenin replied: 'No, all the same they are not such rascals. Certainly they will not struggle against the war, but, as a matter of conscience, they will just vote against it, so that the working class does not revolt against them.' In this respect Lenin was over-optimistic, as he was to realize during the first few days of the war. Yet it was to be a war which not only transformed Europe but was to provide him with the great opportunity for which he had been waiting for twenty years.

He later acknowledged that the German declaration was nothing less than this when he wrote in *Pravda* on 'A Strong Revolutionary Government'. 'But for the war,' he said, 'Russia could have gone on living for years and decades without a revolution against the capitalists. The war has made that objectively impossible. The alternatives are either utter ruin or a revolution against the capitalists. That is how the question stands. That is how the very trend of events poses it.'

7

The Catalyst of War

The First World War made revolution possible if not inevitable. In 1914 few could see the end of the road along which events were leading, but had Lenin been able to do so he might have echoed Churchill's reported exclamation on hearing that the USA had entered the Second World War: 'That means we will win.' He went so far as to issue a manifesto predicting that the war would end in revolution, but his forecast was so outspoken that even the *Berner Tagwacht,* a socialist paper, refused to print it.

The conflict also vindicated Lenin's warnings that great changes were bound to follow in the structure of the capitalist system. In addition, it raised, for him and for thousands of other socialists, the need to spell out, in understandable form, where their loyalties now lay and whether they felt able to support their own country in its hour of need. For Lenin, who had thought through the problem time and again, there were no great difficulties in this, but he was well aware of the dilemmas that others would face. Nevertheless, four days later he hardly believed the Social-Democratic *Vorwärts [Forwards]* which Zinoviev brought him and which reported that in Berlin the Party members of the Reichstag had joined the German Government parties in voting for huge war credits. 'Perhaps', he hoped, 'it is a forged edition of [the paper] which the miserable German bourgeois have published in the hope that we shall also betray the International.' But to Bagocki he was less sanguine and commented: 'This is the end of the Second International,' before adding: 'From this day on, I cease to be a Social-Democrat and become a Communist.'

From the outbreak of the war, the left-wing parties in the combatant countries took up one of three positions, two of them similar in their opposition to the war but differing considerably in detail. The 'defencists' supported their own country on the general grounds of 'defence of the fatherland'. Those who opposed the war were the internationalists, who supported the traditional socialist argument that workers of different countries should not kill each other for the benefit of the ruling capitalist classes, and the defeatists who favoured the defeat of their own capitalist government as the lesser evil since victory would strengthen that government. Lenin supported both internationalist and defeatist arguments, both of which, from his point of view, offered a plausible case.

On 7 August the Austrian authorities raided his home in Poronin. As a Russian whose country was now at war with Germany Lenin was naturally a suspect character and was ordered to present himself to the military authorities in the nearby town of Novy Targ the following morning. However, he had a clear conscience and before leaving his home telegraphed the chief of the Cracow city police. 'The local police suspect me of espionage,' he said. 'I lived in Cracow for two years, in

Zwiezsynice and **5**1 Ul Lubomirskiego. I personally gave information about myself to the commissariat of police in Zwiezsynice. I am an emigrant, a Social-Democrat. Please wire Poronin and mayor of Novy Targ to avoid misunderstanding.'

Whether the misunderstanding remained or whether the Austrians were over-cautious, Lenin was kept at Novy Targ when he reported there on the morning of 8 August. He was held for twelve days, but in comparatively genial confinement. Krupskaya was allowed to visit him daily and on her husband's behalf she wrote to Viktor Adler and Hermann Diamand, socialist deputies. Under their pressure Lenin was released, and the way smoothed for his emigration to Switzerland with Krupskaya and her mother. But he still had to ensure that he would be allowed to enter Switzerland and before leaving Poronin he telegraphed Hermann Greulich, a Swiss Social-Democrat, and asked him to use his influence.

On his journey he passed through Vienna where he called on Adler to thank him for his help and was told that the Austrian minister involved had asked Adler: 'Are you certain that Ulyanov is an enemy of the tsarist Government?' 'Oh yes,' Adler had replied, 'a more implacable enemy than Your Excellency.'

From Vienna Lenin, Krupskaya and her mother continued their journey without trouble, their papers being inspected only in Innsbruck and at Feldkirch on the Swiss frontier. On 5 September they arrived in Zurich whence Lenin wrote to Adler saying: 'Passports are required for entry into Switzerland, but I was allowed in without a passport when I mentioned Greulich.' Then, having rejected Geneva as an alternative, they travelled on to Berne, 'A dull little town, but . . . better than Galicia and the best there is!!' as Lenin described it later in the month to Inessa. 'Never mind. We shall adjust ourselves. I am poking around the libraries – I have missed them.'

The day after arriving in Berne, Lenin met a number of Bolsheviks and spoke on the attitude that they should adopt against the war. His ideas, given in 'The Tasks of Revolutionary Social Democracy in the European War' were approved and published in Switzerland. Within a few days a copy of the manuscript was on its way to Stockholm where the faithful Shlyapnikov mobilized part-time helpers including postal clerks, fishermen and a miscellaneous collection of agents, to get the material into Russia. Acknowledging it, Shlyapnikov enclosed a note from Aleksandra Kollontay which brought from Lenin an enthusiastic reply and a request to Shlyapnikov asking whether she might push the manifesto in other languages. However, Lenin was still on a Tolerans pass and had been in Switzerland only a short while. He had to be cautious and his first ideas about the war were circulated over the signature 'A Group of Social Democrats' and were stated to be 'copied from an appeal issued in Denmark'.

This first statement of Lenin's attitude to the war, in which he spoke of a 'bourgeois, imperialist and dynastic war' and called Social-Democratic support for the war a betrayal of socialism, was to have one unfortunate result. His statements, which had quickly reached Russia, were approved at a December meeting on the outskirts of Petrograd (as St Petersburg had been renamed at the outbreak of war) attended by the five Bolshevik members of the Duma as well as by Kamenev who had recently returned from exile and was living legally in Russia. The secret police learned in advance of the meeting, broke in, and arrested all present. They were tried without delay and on 14 February 1915 exiled to Siberia.

Lenin's return to Switzerland marked a renewal of his contacts with Inessa, who was again recuperating from lung trouble, this time at Les Avants, a mountain resort above the eastern end of Lake Geneva. Lenin often wrote in English, asking about her health, what she was reading and when they could meet. Before he left Switzerland in the spring of 1917 during his stay there he had written to her fourteen times – more letters than he had sent to his sisters in Russia.

Inessa came to live in Berne for a while later in 1914 and frequently walked in the surrounding countryside with Lenin and his wife. He had happy memories of her visits and in 1916 when she was living in Paris wrote to her recalling their earlier days in Switzerland.

'Last Sunday [he said on one occasion] we went for a lovely walk up "our" little mountain. The view of the Alps was very beautiful; I was so sorry you were not there with us . . . How are you getting on? Are you content? Don't you feel lonely? Are you very busy? You are causing me great anxiety by not giving any news about yourself! . . . Where are you living? Where do you eat? At the "buffet" of the National Library?'

First in Berne, later in Zurich, Lenin settled down for what were to be two and a half years of tireless work for the cause: work which at the time seemed likely to have little practical result but in fact strengthened the foundation which he was to prepare for the Revolution of 1917.

With a base in neutral Switzerland, friends in Sweden and his sister Anna as a discreet agent in Petrograd, Lenin's communication problems might now be considered minimal. It was not to be so, and as Michael Futrell, an analyst of Lenin's northern underground system, has reported, it never functioned to Lenin's satisfaction although it was not interrupted for long. Shortage of money, disputes between Lenin and other Party members, the scattering of the Stockholm Bolshevik group in the spring of 1916, growing suspicion from the Swedish police, and not least weakness at the Petrograd end all limited efficient working. There were very few experienced Bolsheviks left in the Russian capital and some of them disagreed with Lenin; some refused to emerge from the retirement (from the point of view of revolutionary politics) in which they had lived since 1907 or 1908; and Lenin's most reliable correspondent, his sister Anna ('James') was in prison from July to October 1916. At times he considered moving the centre of his activities from Switzerland to Sweden. This would have had advantages but he turned down the idea because he feared that the Swedes might arrest some of his Russians, to oblige the Tsar as he put it.

He was, as always, alert to the practical considerations of illegal work. Typical were his comments on 18 October 1914 to V. A. Karpinsky in Geneva. The whole question, he pointed out, was how many thousands of letters could be got into two pages. If the material was set in *brevier* (a type size) and the journal's masthead was fitted into a corner instead of taking up so much space, room would be provided for another two articles.

Lenin's views on the war were reiterated when he said at a public meeting:

'Chauvinism seeks to conceal itself in Russia behind such phrases as *"la belle* France", "the unfortunate Belgium", and behind hostility towards the Kaiser and his regime. Therefore it is our immediate duty to fight against this sophistry and for that we need a slogan to embrace the whole problem. Such a slogan should declare in a convincing way that from the point of view of the Russian working class defeat would be the lesser evil because tsarism is a hundred times worse than the Kaiser's realm. "Peace" is not the right slogan at the present moment: it is the slogan of Christian priests and the lower middle classes. The proletarian slogan should be "Civil War"! While not in the position to promise a civil war or bring it about, it is our duty, if necessary for a long time to come, to persevere in this direction.'

Lenin's anti-war propaganda was aided, although the realization seeped in only slowly through the second-hand and third-hand reports reaching him from Petrograd, by what were to be for Russia some disastrous early weeks of the fighting against the Germans, which more than balanced Russian successes against the Austrians in Galicia. Thus the Bolsheviks' road to political power was prepared by a military story, largely governed by the tsarist failings which had marked the previous decade.

The Russians had a more than competent commander-in-chief, the Grand Duke Nicholas, and at least two generals in the high command, Russky and Alekseyev, who have been described as 'among the most scientific soldiers in Europe'. Lower down, the social system, which gave posts to aristocratic young officers with little or no knowledge or training, gravely limited Russian ability to strike effectively against the efficient German military machine. In equipment, the Russians were equally handicapped. On the outbreak of war they could call upon sixty batteries of artillery compared with the Germans' 381. Russia's huge expanses were handicap as well as advantage and while the country had one kilometre of railway mileage to every 100 square kilometres of territory, Germany had 10.6. Reserves of equipment were both poor and insufficient while Russian administration was crippled by corruption and, to a lesser extent, by some pro-German influences. Little wonder that General Polivanov, the former Minister of War, put his faith in Russia's immense distances, her impassable roads and the mercy of St Nicholas, the patron saint of Holy Russia.

On the outbreak of war the Russians decided to open hostilities against Germany by an invasion of East Prussia. The defending forces were believed to be slight while the political background of the area suggested that victory could bring important results: East Prussia was the traditional home of the Prussian aristocracy, it was the site of rich and extensive estates owned by the Kaiser, and it was remembered as an outpost of Germanic culture, colonized in the Middle Ages by the Teutonic Knights. The Russians therefore had great expectations of the First Army of 120,000 men under General Rennenkampf, and the Second Army of 200,000 under General Samsonov which on 17 August began to push eastwards through the almost roadless stretches of East Prussian forests and lakes. At first all went well. Then Generals Hindenburg and Ludendorff, names to conjure with in German military history, were called in to save the situation. The retreat was halted and the Germans turned on Samsonov's Second Army. They were helped in that the Russians had been dispatched into East Prussia ill armed, ill fed and commanded with an inefficiency that allowed wireless orders to be sent in clear, thus giving the Germans full information of Russian movements. Ominously, the Germans had, unknown to the Russians, captured a Russian code that could have been used.

The Second Army was surrounded, two entire Russian corps

trapped in the forests quickly surrendered, and Samsonov committed suicide. The huge number of casualties, in what became known as the battle of Tannenberg – a name the Germans balanced against the defeat of the German knights by Poles, Lithuanians and Russians at Tannenberg in 1410 – was only the first of two blows, since the Germans now turned on Rennenkampf to the north. Here, the Russian commander, apparently unnerved by the disaster in the south, retreated from what Hindenburg had considered an impregnable position. Russian defeat quickly became a rout and before German powers of pursuit gave out, the Russian First Army had lost 120,000 killed, wounded or taken prisoner in the battle of the Masurian Lakes. Before the campaign ended the Russians had effectively lost a total of nearly 250,000 men, or about a quarter of their mobilized troops, as well as 650 guns. The defeat in men, materials and morale was of extraordinary proportions and it gave the Russians, at the start of the war, a taste of what the future was to hold. Tannenberg and the battle of the Masurian Lakes could not be wiped from the record and the defeats made it that much easier for Lenin, in the following years, to denounce the war and claim that its only beneficiaries were the ruling classes. It was one of his strengths that he had thought through the implications of a major war long before Tannenberg had faced Russian socialists with the choice of supporting a tsarist army fighting for aims they disavowed or abandoning their own people in the face of the enemy.

Before the outbreak of war treaties had been signed between Russia and countries such as Britain and France who were now her allies. Although the details were secret, the general lines of the treaties – of which Lenin made much during the next few years – were the subject of common talk, some of which was later shown to be correct. Russia, Lenin maintained with some plausibility, was fighting to conquer Armenia and Constantinople in much the same way that Germany was fighting for 'the "sacred" bourgeois right' to world supremacy in looting and plundering colonies and dependent countries, while England was fighting to 'rob Germany of her colonies and to ruin her principal competitor'. Thus it was easier for him than it might otherwise have been to attack the war and yet evade the charge of disloyalty.

The disasters of Tannenberg and the Masurian Lakes moved him strongly, and not only because he appreciated that any monarch, army or system would find it difficult to survive such disasters, and impossible to surmount their continuation. In addition, one fact became obvious long before he returned to Russia in the spring of 1917 and heard at first hand of the army's sufferings and the trials and tribulations of a civilian population increasingly short of food. Lenin had not heard a shot fired in anger – and was to hear only three when, a few years later, an attempt was made to assassinate him. And though he was at times short of money, and occasionally short of food, he never experienced the poverty and stomachgnawing hunger which was endured during the war by vast numbers of Russians as the equivalent of 'guns before butter' lengthened bread queues and brought hardship to millions of homes. Yet it is clear from letters, speeches and memories, that despite the ruthlessly impersonal policies which he pursued to bring about and consolidate the revolution, he had an instinctive understanding of the torments suffered by ordinary people in wartime, which they were eventually able to bear no longer. With their triumphs Ludendorff and Hindenburg thus tempered the weapon of revolution which Lenin had been forging for two decades.

However, there was another side to the coin. While the German victories in East Prussia encouraged large numbers of Russian troops and civilian workers to doubt the wisdom and efficiency of their rulers, a reverse effect was brought about among those whose patriotism overruled their other feelings. Even Plekhanov was among those who now supported the war and to Angelica Balabanov he said: 'So far as I am concerned if I were not old and sick I would join the army. To bayonet your German comrades would give me great pleasure.' Plekhanov made no secret of his views, outlining them on 11 October 1914 in Lausanne's Maison du Peuple when he spoke 'On the Attitude of the Socialists to the War'. Lenin, who was present, had the chance to say very little, but three days later took the platform in the same hall to speak on 'The Proletariat and the War'. He was glad of the opportunity to contradict Plekhanov, who was to become a popular exponent of patriotic support for the war. At the same time Lenin spelt out the stand he was to maintain until the fighting between Russia and Germany was ended by the treaty of Brest-Litovsk in 1918. Referring to Marx's thesis that the proletariat had no fatherland, he said that the socialist attitude to the war must be based on realities, that the epoch of national wars was over, and that the current struggle was an imperialist war. His conviction was later summed up in a single sentence in *Sotsial Demokrat*: 'It must be the primary task of Social-Democrats in every country to combat that country's chauvinism.'

But while Lenin addressed a meeting on the attitude of the proletariat to the war, reiterated that it was an imperialist war and quoted Marx, socialist voices other than Plekhanov's were contradicting him. They continued to speak out and to criticize his influence until the very eve of the autumn Revolution of 1917.

234

Among those who trimmed their political principles after the outbreak of the war was Kautsky, who particularly aroused Lenin's ire.

'I hate Kautsky and at the moment I despise him more than anyone [he wrote to Shlyapnikov in October]: a beastly, rotten, smug hypocrite. Oh no, – they say – nothing has happened, no principles have been violated; every one was right in protecting the Fatherland; internationalism (kindly note) consists in the workers of all countries shooting at each other in the name of the "Defence of the Fatherland".'

One outcome of the division between those socialists who supported their countries in what was soon a world-wide war and those who maintained their peace-time stance against war was the weakening, virtually to the point of disintegration, of the Second International – officially the Second International Workingmen's Association – in whose resuscitation Lenin was later to play such an important part. The First International Workingmen's Association had been set up by Marx in London in 1864 in an effort to co-ordinate socialist aspirations in different countries. Eight years later disputes between Marx and the Anarchist leader Mikhail Bakunin split the Association; a move to New York failed to heal the rift, as had been hoped, and the Association came to an end in 1876. The Second International, formed in Paris in 1889, tended to concentrate on the various revisionist versions of socialism that proliferated during the last decade of the nineteenth century and the first decade of the twentieth. A test more important than the earlier schisms between socialists and anarchists was provided by the outbreak of the First World War. Lenin's disgust that so many socialists now supported their own country rather than their socialist anti-war principles, merely epitomized the differences which quickly made the Second International ineffective.

The Bolshevik position was recorded at the end of October 1914 by Trotsky who, in a preface to *The War and the International* stressed the need for a 'new International which must arise out of the present world cataclysm, of the International of the last struggles and of the final victory'. Lenin said much the same thing in *Sotsial Demokrat* the following month after the Party's Central Committee had issued a manifesto stating 'the working masses in the face of all obstacles will create a new International'.

Lenin maintained his opposition to socialist participation in the war by any available means and in February 1915 sent Maxim Litvinov to London to present the Bolshevik viewpoint at the international Socialist Congress called by the Party of Independent English Workers. Before the Congress Lenin outlined the Bolshevik view which he summed up for Litvinov under eight headings:

'1. [He] was against any truce or national bloc, 2. believed in invoking the class struggle and revolutionary action, 3. urged the rejection of all military credits, 4. insisted that Socialists retire from the bourgeois cabinets of Belgium and France, 5. appealed for collaboration with the German Socialists who had voted against war credits (Liebknecht and Rosa Luxemburg), 6. wanted organization of soldiers at the front, 7. encouraged women to start a general anti-war agitation, 8. stressed the need for aid to the Russian revolutionaries in their fight against Czarism.'

Lenin was pleased at the way his ideas were presented by

Litvinov, later writing: 'Comrade Maximovich understood and fulfilled his task by speaking clearly about the betrayal of the German Socialists and turning down a resolution where a sentence to this effect was to be omitted.'

The early German successes, and the slow but unavoidable realization that the war would be long and arduous, had one subtle effect on the revolutionary movement, which Lenin outlined to a colleague, Vladimir Aleksandrovich, in September 1915.

> 'I consider it a fact [he wrote], that there are now 2 main *revolutionary* trends in Russia: the revolutionary chauvinists (to overthrow the tsar in order to defeat Germany) and the revolutionary proletarian internationalists (to overthrow the tsar *as a means* of assisting the international revolution of the proletariat). Any rapprochement between these trends beyond occasional "joint actions" is, in my opinion, impossible and harmful. The war has linked together the proletariat of *all* the great powers of Europe, the war has placed *on the order of the day* the task of putting into effect proletarian solidarity. A difficult task, to be sure, but one that is posed by life itself and cannot be shelved.'

However disputable the political result of German successes during the first months of the war – and Lenin was by no means a dispassionate observer – there is no doubt about another effect: they encouraged Baltic nationals from Estonia, Lithuania and Latvia to hope that their countries might eventually be able to break away from the Russian empire. This possibility was to have its effect on Lenin's life since among such men one of the most important was Alexander Kesküla, code-named 'Kiwi', an

Estonian who circulated between Stockholm and Switzerland during the war. Kesküla was not only willing to help the Germans, from whom he expected Estonia could gain independence, but by the same token was anxious to undermine the tsarist forces. This in turn meant support for Bolshevik followers in Switzerland. Kesküla's later claim: 'Lenin was my protégé . . . It was I who launched Lenin,' was a boast. In fact Alfred Erich Senn, who has given a detailed account of Lenin's wartime activities in Switzerland, goes so far as to say 'The evidence does not support [Kesküla's] exalted claims of having "discovered" Lenin. He seems rather to have seized upon a few pieces of information to impress first the Germans and subsequently a variety of historians.' Nevertheless, after seeing Lenin in Switzerland in the autumn of 1914, he informed Count von Romberg, the German minister in Berne, of what he considered to be Lenin's potential usefulness; after a December 1914 visit to Berlin, according to Senn, he accepted 10,000 marks to help develop revolutionary plans in Russia; and Kesküla later helped channel German money into Lenin's finances in a way that prevented its source from being identified.

Moreover, in September 1915 Kesküla succeeded in extracting from Lenin a formal programme which gave the conditions under which the Bolsheviks would be ready to make peace with Germany if they succeeded in gaining control in Russia. According to Fritz Fischer's *Germany's Aims in the First World War,*

'Lenin said that the most important of these points – apart from the domestic political aims of a republic, confiscation of the big estates, the eight-hour day and full autonomy for the nationalities – was No. 5 in which he declared himself ready to offer peace without considering the Entente.

238

Germany would have to renounce annexations and a war indemnity, but Kesküla remarked that this condition would not exclude detaching territories inhabited by the nationalities [non-Russians] and forming them into buffer states between Russia and Germany'

– a point emphasized naturally enough by an Estonian. Whatever the accuracy of this report, which Kesküla passed on to Romberg, it was sufficiently convincing to induce Romberg to write on 30 September 1915: 'In Kesküla's opinion, it is therefore essential that we should spring to the help of the revolutionaries of Lenin's movement in Russia at once.'

Kesküla was helped by his acquaintance with a Scandinavian, Arthur Siefeld, a Bolshevik close to Lenin who acted as an undetected link between the Germans and the Bolsheviks. Kesküla supplied Siefeld with money, which the latter carefully infiltrated into Bolshevik pockets without revealing its source. In return, Siefeld passed on to Kesküla any information he could gather from Lenin and his circle which he believed would be of interest to the Germans. Shlyapnikov suspected, correctly, that Kesküla's sources were German; when, therefore, he himself was offered either money or arms from this source he refused to accept either. 'To those comrades whom I left in charge of the work with the transport of literature,' he has written, ' – the secretary of our bolshevik group in Stockholm, Bogrovsky, and others – I gave strict instructions not to accept any money from anyone at all, except Swedish party organizations.'

As the fighting stretched on into 1915, then 1916, with no indication of an end to it, two further effects became more evident. One was the aid it afforded to the revolutionary movement. In a letter to Aleksandra Kollontay as early as December

1914 Lenin wrote, 'The European war has done a great service to International Socialism in that it has clearly revealed the whole state of rottenness, baseness and swinery of Opportunism, thus giving a magnificent incentive towards cleaning up the workers' movement and ridding it of the filth which has accumulated during the scores of peaceful years.'

To Shlyapnikov, who was playing an important part in the Party's communications network, Lenin spelt out the lesson in more detail the following year:

> 'Military failures are helping to shake the foundations of Czarism and are facilitating the union of revolutionary workers in Russia and other countries. They say: "What will 'you' do if 'you', the revolutionaries, defeat Czarism?" To which I reply (a) our victory will inflame a hundredfold the movement of the Left in Germany; (b) if "we" were to defeat Czarism completely, we should offer peace to all the fighters on democratic conditions and on refusal, we should conduct a *revolutionary* war.'

While the continuation of the war thus helped to make revolution more possible in the eyes of potential revolutionaries, it also made the chances of hampering Russian military opposition more important to the Germans. It therefore became of increasing interest to the German High Command to unleash whatever disruptive forces were available in the East, and help from the Bolsheviks became steadily more attractive.

As far as Lenin was concerned, the situation was complex. He was, it is true, unhindered by any belief that he should be circumscribed by loyalty to Mother Russia. Even had he not regarded nationalism itself as an evil, and had he not seen an identity of interests within the German and Russian working-class movements, his long-term socialist aims would have swamped any nationalist misgivings about sabotaging the Russian war effort. His willingness to see a Russian defeat at the hands of Germany as a lesser evil if it brought about the revolution had an ancestry that went back at least to the Crimean War when some Russian patriots hoped that defeat would help ameliorate the despotism under which they lived. And during the Russo-Japanese war at the beginning of the century there were some Russian politicians who felt that there might be compensations in a Japanese victory.

However, Lenin well knew that when Russian troops were being killed in their thousands by German soldiers, links between the Bolsheviks on the one hand and the Germans on the other, would have to be handled as cautiously as a hair-triggered bomb. The potential dangers were further increased by the belief, not entirely unfounded, that the Russian court, and particularly the Empress, favoured the Germans in the struggle. For this reason, if for no other, pro-Germanism was the last brush with which the Bolsheviks wished to be tarred. Secrecy and guile were called for, but neither were traits in which Lenin was lacking, and with considerable care and skill he succeeded in camouflaging most details of his German contacts between 1914 and 1917. The Germans were equally anxious to preserve secrecy and their policy continued after the war. Only with the capture of German archives after the end of the Second World War in 1945 did fresh light begin to illuminate the help, clandestine and otherwise, that Lenin had received from the Germans after the autumn of 1914 when he settled in Switzerland. Even so, mystery still surrounds many of the details.

It has never been in dispute that from the early days of the First World War the Germans clearly saw the benefits of subversion in Russia. This was evident even before the existence became known of a diplomatic document dated 3 December 1917 which said:

'The disruption of the Entente and the subsequent creation of political combinations agreeable to us constitute the most important war aim of our diplomacy. Russia appeared (to me) [crossed out in the original] to be the weakest link in the enemy's chain. The task therefore was gradually to loosen it and, when possible, to remove it. This was the purpose of the subversive activity we caused to be carried out in Russia behind the front – in the first place (vigorous) [crossed out in the original] promotion of separatist tendencies and support of the Bolshevik). It was not until the Bolsheviki had received from us a steady flow of funds through various channels and under varying labels that they were in a position to be able to build up their main organ *Pravda*, to conduct energetic propaganda [the words "to conduct energetic propaganda" written on the margin and inserted in the text] and appreciably to extend the originally narrow basis of their party . . .'

Lenin's potential value as a disrupter of Russia's fighting forces had become obvious as, during the decade and more preceding the outbreak of war, he had paraded his views throughout Western Europe. It was not only disgruntled nationals of the Baltic states who felt that he might be useful to them. The others included Karl Moor, a Swiss Social-Democrat who had been providing the German and Austrian General Staffs with information during the last years of peace and who made contact with Lenin soon after the latter's arrival in Switzerland. In Berne, Moor helped Lenin, the newcomer who had to register with the police, and at the same time passed on to the Germans any information he could gather. This flow of information continued after Lenin left Berne for Zurich.

Moor's double-dealing was not discovered for many years although by 1917 Lenin seems to have entertained suspicions, since in that year he wrote to the Party's Bureau of the Central Committee Abroad after Moor had given evidence on an internal matter and asked:

'What is Moor like? Has it been completely and absolutely proved that he is honest? Has he never had any direct, or indirect, hobnobbing with German Social Imperialists? If it is true that Moor is in Stockholm, and if you are acquainted with him, then I beg you insistendy to adopt all measures to check this carefully, and by documentary evidence. There must be no room for the shadow of a doubt or rumour etc'

Moor must have passed whatever tests were then made, since the following year he wrote to Lenin asking for the release of an acquaintance who had been arrested by the Cheka, the organization set up in Russia to stamp out counter-revolutionary activity.

In 1915 to 1916, life in Switzerland was circumscribed for the man who within a few years would rule the Tsar's Russia. Lenin and Krupskaya were poor, living on the small sums that could be sent to them from Petrograd, what Lenin could earn from journalism, and the occasional fee that came from public lecturing on what he saw as the inevitable political repercussions of the war.

He and Krupskaya had as homes a succession of rented rooms, chosen to provide easy access to the public libraries in which Lenin worked for at least a part of most days, and to the open countryside. Their friends were mainly fellow refugees, among them the Zinovievs, Inessa Armand, and others who made up the small nucleus of left-wing intellectuals drawn to Switzerland by the country's neutrality and by the comparative freedom from police harassment. The flavour of their life is given by Krupskaya who, after describing their home in a quiet street adjoining the woods surrounding Berne, says:

'Across the road lived Inessa, five minutes' walk – the Zinovievs, ten minutes' walk – the Shklovskys. We would wander for hours along the forest roads, bestrewn with fallen yellow leaves. On most occasions the three of us went together on these walks, Vladimir Ilyich, Inessa and myself. Vladimir Ilyich would develop his plans of the international struggle. Inessa took it all very much to heart. In this unfolding struggle she began to take a most direct part, conducting correspondence . . . Sometimes we would sit for hours on the sunlit wooded mountain side while Ilyich jotted down outlines of his speeches and articles and polished his formulations.'

During the last months of 1914, as Lenin continued with his political activities, finding outlets for his writings wherever possible in the Swiss press and forging links with the Swiss Social-Democrats, his reputation was steadily growing among the left-wing political groups which had begun to coalesce in opposition to the war. It was not surprising therefore that he should lead the Bolshevik delegation to the International Socialist Women's Conference which was held in Berne at the end of March 1915. It was also in character that his resolution was rejected by the Conference as too extreme, and that, as an omen of things to come, a brouhaha should follow.

'Panic seized the delegates [Angelica Balabanov wrote]: agreement was out of the question since the [Bolshevik] minority would not budge from its resolution. The Conference was interrupted. Then Clara Zetkin, shaken and trembling, accompanied the minority delegates to an adjacent room. She returned after an hour. She had after all found a way out; the minority declared themselves prepared to vote for the general resolution if their declaration was included in the minutes. This saved the situation.'

Much the same position developed the following month when the International Socialist Youth Conference was held in Berne. 'Not being at the conference himself [Lenin] led the representatives of his faction from the Volkshaus Café. They came in turns out to him,' according to Balabanov.

Later that April Krupskaya had an outbreak of Basedow's disease, or toxic goitre.

'I . . . must go to mountains between 1100 and 1300 metres [she wrote to Aleksandra Kollontay in Norway]. Do you know if there are such mountains in Sweden or Norway?. . . I'd be glad to get out of Switzerland, it's a sort of sleepy backwater here . . . Ask somebody about mountains, if there's anywhere to live in them – if such mountains exist – and if it's cheap or expensive to live there.'

Lenin and Krupskaya did not move to Norway. Had they done so, the development of the Revolution in 1917 might have taken a slightly different line. From Norway Lenin would have had no need to travel through Germany on his way to Russia. The taunt of the 'sealed train' journey across enemy territory could not have been made against him and it would have been more difficult for his opponents to claim that he was hand in glove with the enemy.

But he remained in Switzerland and a few weeks after the end of the Youth Conference was visited in Berne by the man correcdy described by his biographers as 'the central figure in the conspiratorial connexions between the Imperial [German] Government and the Russian Social Democratic Party, and in particular Lenin's Bolshevik faction of it'.

He was Alexander Helphand whose path had already crossed Lenin's more than once, first in Munich when *Iskra* was published there, then in St Petersburg in the aftermath of the tsarist amnesty of 1905. Helphand had subsequently been banished to Siberia for revolutionary activity, had escaped, found his way to Turkey and had there succeeded in building up a successful business in arms and anything else which was likely to produce sufficient profit. His ambition had remained that of splitting up the Russian Empire, and he had already gained the confidence of many German officials before the outbreak of war.

On 9 March 1915 Helphand had submitted a memorandum to the German Foreign Ministry oudining ideas for destabilizing Russia. One point dealt with 'financial support for the majority group [i.e. the Bolsheviks] of the Russian Social Democrats, which is fighting the tsarist government with all the means at its disposal. Its leaders are in Switzerland'. Helphand's plans were ideologically thin when compared with most of the schemes that Lenin had produced, but for the Germans they had certain practical strengths that have been described by Helphand's biographers.

'It was not the day-dream of a fanatical conspirator [they say]. Helphand had drafted a blue-print for the revolution. It was practical, detailed, with all its parts creating an impressive whole – and it was original. Helphand worked with the combined forces of national and social disintegration; he built on the experiences of 1905, knowing that the World War would provide a more suitable background than the Russo-Japanese War to revolutionary events.'

To the men Helphand had met in Berlin, as well as to Helphand himself, it appeared obvious that the next essential was renewed personal contact with Lenin and it was with this as his objective that he arrived in Berne in May 1916, accompanied by his mistress Ekaterina Groman. Lenin was lunching with his wife, Inessa Armand and a Party member, V. M. Kasparov. Helphand and his companion walked into the restaurant without warning and were afterwards taken, apparently without much enthusiasm, to Lenin's home in Distelweg.

Only Helphand has left any account of the brief meeting that followed.

'I explained to [Lenin] my views on the social-revolutionary consequences of the war [he wrote later], and at the same time drew his attention to the fact that, as long as the war

247

lasted, no revolution would occur in Germany and that at this time, a revolution was possible in Russia only, where it would break out as the result of German victories. He dreamt, however, of the publication of a socialist journal, with which, he believed, he could immediately drive the European proletariat from the trenches into a revolution.'

Lenin was cautious of mentioning to anyone the meeting with Helphand. However he was soon writing in *Sotsial Demokrat* of Helphand's *Die Glocke* in terms that illuminate his views. *Die Glocke was,* Lenin averred, 'an organ of renegades and dirty lackeys' surrounding the 'cesspool of German chauvinism'. It was, moreover, a publication in which 'not a single honest thought, not a single serious argument, not a single straight-forward article' could be found.

But there was more than one reason for Lenin's distaste for Helphand: it must have been obvious to him that Helphand had a great deal of money at his disposal, which no doubt came from Germany but which enabled him to wield a power of disruption among tsarist forces far greater than Lenin could command. If all this was not galling enough for Lenin, Helphand's extravagant way of life, and even his personal appearance, did nothing to create confidence in the ascetic Lenin. Helphand's biographers say of him at this period:

'His massive, gigantic figure was more puffed out than ever. The broad, bull-like face with its high forehead, tiny nose, and carefully trimmed beard, had developed a flabby double chin, behind which his neck completely disappeared. The small lively eyes were deeply embedded in fat. His short legs were barely strong enough to support his body, and when he was standing up or walking, he seemed to use his arms to maintain himself on an even keel.'

That the impression was not due to personal bias is suggested by Arthur Siefeld who describes Helphand as 'An uncommonly fat and paunchy gentleman. Like a tightly stuffed sack with a quivering belly. From the bloated face peeped out very expressive intelligent eyes.' Helphand seemed hardly the man likely to become a devoted ally of Lenin, who delighted in mountain walks and whose main recreation was work. Added to which there was Lenin's devout belief that he, and no one else, was the man chosen by circumstances to lead the coming revolution which would sweep not merely Russia but the whole world.

There was another factor, described by Rosa Luxemburg:

'first to make a fortune during a war in which many thousand German and Russian proletarians are being killed, and then to sit in the safety of Klampenborg in Denmark and run from there a limited company for the exploitation of the (dialectic) connection between these two national proletariats – for this superior revolutionary role we have little understanding.'

With Helphand suitably ejected, Lenin and Krupskaya soon took a break at the little health resort of Sörenberg, midway between Berne and Lucerne, where they were joined for a while by Inessa Armand. Other visitors have somewhat idyllic memories of Inessa playing the piano in the mornings while Lenin worked in a corner of the guest-house garden. But he remained in touch with his colleagues elsewhere in Switzerland, they being instructed to telephone him promptly at 8.30 a.m. if necessary.

In the afternoon he would lead a party up the slopes of the Rothorn, returning in the evening with bouquets of rhododendrons and baskets of mushrooms. At Sorenberg Lenin carried on his work with benefit of both scenery and library facilities, as Krupskaya later explained. 'We were quite comfortable [there],' she wrote, 'all around there were woods, high mountains and there was even snow on the peak of the Rothorn. Mail arrived with Swiss punctuality. We discovered that in such an out-of-the-way village as Sorenberg it was possible to obtain free of charge any book from the Berne or Zurich libraries.'

Lenin made use of the country's facilities not only to continue his political education but to satisfy his cultural interests, which are so often ignored. In Berne, before leaving the city in 1916, he copied into his notebook the titles of a number of books he was apparently preparing to borrow. They included ten volumes on aesthetics, five volumes of Ruskin's *Modern Painters* (1834–60), a book on impressionism, and collections of Goethe, Victor Hugo, Dante, Byron, Schiller, Ibsen, Lessing, Daudet and Shakespeare. The list suggests that for once he had found gaps in his dedication to revolution and was preparing to stuff into them some nonutilitarian study of the arts. If so, it was an unusual occurrence since he rarely discussed literature or any of the arts without underlining the fact that however worthy they might be they should contribute towards the cause to which he had dedicated his life. Thus he had said to Bogdanov on Capri: 'If you would write a novel for the workers on the subject of how the sharks of capitalism robbed the earth and wasted the oil, iron, timber and coal – that would be a useful book, Signor Machist!' He enjoyed Henri Barbusse's *Le Feu* (1916) and the works of Romain Rolland for their antiwar propaganda, and the works of Upton Sinclair for their anti-bourgeois and anti-religious themes. With such exceptions he was distinctly conservative in his tastes, preferring the Russian classics to modern writers, and echoing this in his reactions to art, once saying to Clara Zetkin, 'I have the courage to display myself as a "barbarian". I cannot regard the works of impressionism, futurism, cubism and other "isms" as the highest revelations of the artistic genius. I do not understand them. I get no joy from them.' One reason for his restricted reactions was given by Lunacharsky who had much contact with Lenin after he had been made Commissar for Education in 1917. 'Throughout his life,' he wrote, 'Lenin had very little time to occupy himself at all intently with art, and, since dilettantism was always alien and hateful to him, he did not like to express himself on art. Nevertheless, his taste was very definite. He liked the Russian classics, liked realism in literature, in painting, etc'

Lenin's utilitarian use of 'culture' was expressed most clearly in a statement made to explain the drive for literacy which he inaugurated after the Revolution.

'In general, as you probably know, I do not have much sympathy for the intelligentsia, and our slogan "liquidate illiteracy" is in no way to be interpreted as being aimed at the creation of a new intelligentsia. The purpose of "liquidate illiteracy" is only that every peasant and every worker should be able to read by himself, without help, our decrees, orders and proclamations. The aim is completely practical. No more.'

Lenin remained at Sörenberg until the autumn when he left it, knapsack on back, to attend the International Anti-War Conference called by the Socialist Party of Italy at the Swiss village of Zimmerwald from 5 to 8 September. Earlier in the summer the Italian socialist deputy Odino Morgari had met Emile Vandervelde in Paris and had urged him to organize an anti-war meeting under the aegis of the Second International. When this proved impossible it was decided instead to hold an independent meeting. Eleven countries sent a total of thirty-eight delegates, the largest group coming from Germany. Even running the Conference presented problems. Robert Grimm, the Swiss organizer, felt it necessary to keep the meeting-place secret from spies and ill-wishers. He therefore assembled the delegates in the Berne Volkshaus and had them taken to Zimmerwald in four carriages. The ruse was successful – although when the local inhabitants later discovered what the meeting had been for they protested against 'the abuse of their village'.

Lenin and Zinoviev represented the Bolsheviks, Akselrod and Martov the Mensheviks, Trotsky attended as an independent, and Viktor Chernov, later to become an important figure after the Revolution, represented the Socialist Revolutionaries. British delegates had been nominated by the Independent Labour Party and the British Socialist Party but had been refused passports. Significantly, but with implications unknown to most of the gathering, Karl Moor was there as a Swiss delegate – and subsequently informed the German authorities of everything that had taken place.

Lenin concealed his intense interest in the proceedings under a lighthearted exterior. The Conference was mainly held in the garden of the Zimmerwald Hotel and Lenin spent much of the time playing on the grass with the hotelier's dogs. At one point, while the wording of the Conference manifesto was being decided, he left the table and started laughing and tickling them, first one dog then the other.

Eventually he signed the manifesto, which had been written by Trotsky, but added a rider to it – signed also by Radek and Zinoviev – as did Trotsky:

'The manifesto contains no clear pronouncement about the methods to be used to fight the war. We shall continue, as we have done all along, to advocate in the socialist press and at meetings of the International, a clearcut Marxist position in regard to the tasks with which the proletariat is confronted in an age of imperialism . . . We vote for the manifesto because we regard it as a call to struggle, and in this struggle we are anxious to march side by side with the other sections of the International.'

At Zimmerwald, wrote Angelica Balabanov, who was to be secretary of what became the Zimmerwald movement, Lenin showed another trait: 'I realized how shrewd and incisive was Lenin's mind. But although he was a master polemicist – and frequently an unscrupulous one – he had none of the characteristics of a demagogue. It was in this latter capacity that Zinoviev served him so well. . . At Zimmerwald, and later in Soviet Russia, Lenin's approach to tactical problems, like his approach to life itself, seemed to me very often a primitive one. I have often wondered since if this impression was correct – whether he was inherently primitive in his intellectual and emotional make-up, or had so trained himself to concentrate his attention on one problem, or even one aspect of a problem, as to convey that impression. This concentration and ruthless singleness of purpose were undoubtedly the secret of his success – or if one may use the word – his genius.'

Another 'secret' of which a hint was given at Zimmerwald was Lenin's coopting of others to perform unpleasant tasks. 'I had first observed Zinoviev in action at Zimmerwald,' Balabanov also reported. 'I had noted then that whenever there was an unfair factional manoeuvre to be carried out, a revolutionary reputation to be undermined, Lenin would charge Zinoviev with the task . . .'

At Zimmerwald Lenin was as usual on the left of the line, taking up a revolutionary internationalist stance in opposition to the Kautskyite majority led by the German Social-Democrat Ledebour. His position was firmly stated in a resolution which declared that the task of the Conference was to turn the imperialist war between peoples into a civil war. But the resolution was defeated, the middle-of-the-road resolution drafted by Trotsky unanimously adopted, and Lenin had to be content with the formation of what became known as the Zimmerwald Left.

This faction gave additional support for *Socialism and the War* which he had prepared shortly before the Conference in collaboration with Zinoviev. The pamphlet was introduced into Germany and illegally handed out in Berlin, Leipzig and Bremen. A French translation was also circulated in Paris by Inessa Armand. Despite all Lenin's efforts, only a few could be brought into Russia, and although these were there copied by hand the pamphlet therefore had only a limited distribution in the country.

According to Willi Münzenberg, the veteran German Communist, it was

'the first book that elucidated clearly and sharply, from a truly Marxist point of view, the essence of the world war and made it obvious to all workers that a crisis was imminent in the socialist working-class movement. Lenin's book was a revelation to us; it showed us the inadequacy and errors of the pacifist and social-religious ideology which, as we had theretofore thought, was a fit weapon in the struggle against war.'

Perhaps its most significant feature was the advocacy of a Third International, to be formed on a revolutionary basis, an idea that Lenin eventually brought to fruition in Moscow in 1919.

The booklet provided some consolation for his defeat at Zimmerwald, a defeat from which, as usual, he tried to recuperate in the mountains, first in Sorenberg where he returned for a time. Krupskaya wrote:

'The day after Ilyich's arrival [at Sörenberg] from Zimmerwald we climbed the Rothorn. We climbed with a "glorious appetite", but when we reached the summit, Ilyich suddenly lay down on the ground, in an uncomfortable position almost on the snow, and fell asleep. Clouds gathered, then broke; the view of the Alps from the Rothorn was splendid, and Ilyich slept like the dead. He never stirred and slept over an hour. Apparently Zimmerwald had] frayed his nerves a good deal and had taken much strength out of him. It required several days of roaming over the mountains and the atmosphere of Sörenberg before Ilyich was himself again.'

They made a second ascent of the Rothorn and climbed many other mountains in the area before returning to Berne at the beginning of October. There, he started work to establish the

255

best way of spreading the news of what had been decided at Zimmerwald.

In the city, Lenin and Krupskaya found a new home, 'a nice room here with electricity and bath for 30 francs' he wrote to his mother. He was soon giving lectures on the Zimmerwald meeting. Cash became alarmingly short and before the end of the year Krupskaya was writing to Lenin's sister Maria:

'We shall soon be coming to the end of our former means of subsistence and the question of earning money will become a serious one. It is difficult to find anything here . . . I have to think about a literary income. I don't want that side of our affairs to be Volodya's worry alone. He works a lot as it is. The question of an income troubles him greatly.'

Lenin himself wrote:

'I must say I need an income. Otherwise I shall simply perish. Truly! The fiendishly high cost of living – there is nothing to live on. Money must be squeezed out forcibly (Belenin [Shlyapnikov] should speak about money to Katin and to Gorky himself, if this is not too awkward) from the publisher of *Letopis,* [a left-wing magazine] to whom two of my pamphlets have been sent (let him pay immediately and as much as possible!). The same with Bonch [Vladimir Bonch-Bruyevich] with regard to the translations. If this is not arranged, then I shall not be able to hold out. Of this I am sure. This is very, very serious.'

By the first days of 1916 the need for money had grown even more acute, and when Lenin applied in mid-January for an extension of his Swiss residence permit he asked if he could have it without paying the customary 200 francs. He wrote a preface to Bukharin's *Imperialism and the World Economy* (Moscow, 1927) in December 1915 which was published in *Pravda* in 1927, and sent to Gorky a paper, *New Data on the Laws Governing the Development of Capitalism in Agriculture*, with the hope that its publication would be speeded up. The pamphlet was published in 1917.

It was largely the lack of money that forced him in mid-February to move to Zurich where he at first found a cheap room in Geigergasse. Krupskaya, with her customary resilience, cheerfully made the best of a bad job, later writing: 'Ilyich liked the simplicity of the service, the fact that coffee was served in a cup with a broken handle, that we ate in the kitchen, that the conversation was simple . . . We very soon realized that we had hit upon a peculiar environment, the very "lower depths" of Zurich.' After about a week they moved to new quarters in the house of a shoemaker, Herr Kammerer, in 14 Spiegelgasse, and in spite of its disadvantages remained there until they left Switzerland in March 1917.

Their new home was a small room looking out on to a courtyard, which was stifling in summer and liable to be filled with the stench of a nearby sausage factory. Lenin liked the nearby Zurichersee very much, and the libraries were better than those in Berne, he told his mother, so they would probably stay longer than they had intended. He quickly settled down to a regular routine, visiting the library as soon as it opened, reading there until lunchtime, then returning and working again until it closed. On Thursdays when it was open only in the morning he and Krupskaya would take a snack of nut chocolate, walk up the Zurichberg, which rose above the Zurichersee, find what she called their favourite spot in the thick woods where there was no

257

crowd, and lie reading until it was time to go home.

It was in his new quarters that Lenin completed his main work on political economy, *Imperialism: The Highest Stage of Capitalism: A Popular Outline.* The book was published in Russia the following year but only, as Lenin was to point out in a later edition, after alterations had been imposed by the censors.

With *Imperialism* safely posted off, he set out in April 1916 for the Second International Socialist Conference, the successor to Zimmerwald, held in Kienthal, a summer resort in the Bernese Alps. The Zimmerwald Left sent twelve delegates, including Lenin, Inessa Armand and Zinoviev. Lenin spoke eight times, and although he was unable to win over the majority, he believed that the Left had improved its position compared with the previous year. He wrote to Shlyapnikov,

'After all a manifesto was adopted: that is a step forward . . . On the whole, this is *none the less,* despite the mass of defects, a step towards a break with the social-patriots.

'This time the Left was stronger: a Serb, three Swiss and a Frenchman . . . reinforced our Left. Then there were two Germans [from the *Internationale* Group] who supported us on the main questions.'

In the summer, with the Socialist Conference behind him, Lenin did what he had done after Zimmerwald and took a holiday in the mountains, partly to give himself a rest and partly, as he wrote to Aleksandra Kollontay, because of a recurrence of his wife's goitre. This time they went for six weeks to the canton of St Gallen and stayed at the Chudivise guest-house, quite high up on Mount Flums and serviced only by a donkey using mountain paths.

'The rest resort was quite inexpensive, two and a half francs per day per person [Krupskaya wrote]. It is true, it was a resort where they kept one on a milk diet. In the morning they served coffee with milk, bread and butter and cheese, but they gave us no sugar; for lunch – milk soup, sometimes made of cheese curds and milk . . . During the first [few] days we positively howled against this milk cure, then we began to supplement it by eating raspberries and blackberries which grew in the vicinity in great quantities. Our room was clean, with electric light, but without service; we had to tidy up the room ourselves and clean our own shoes. The latter function was assumed, emulating the Swiss, by Vladimir Ilyich, and every morning he would take my mountain shoes and his and go to the shed set aside for this purpose, exchanging pleasantries with [the] other bootblacks and displaying such zeal that once he knocked down a wicker-basket full of empty beer bottles to the accompaniment of general laughter . . . Among the visitors at the house was a soldier . . . Vladimir Ilyich hovered about him like a cat after lard, tried several times to engage him in a conversation about the predatory character of the war; the fellow . . . was clearly not interested.'

On his return to Zurich Lenin continued with his accepted routine of writing. Money was still a frequent worry. But it was not only a bad period financially. A week before Christmas 1916, he wrote telling Inessa Armand that his manuscript on imperialism had arrived in Petrograd but that Gorky, who was to publish it, was dissatisfied with his attacks on Kautsky.

'Both laughable and disappointing [he commented]. There

it is, my fate. One fighting campaign after another – against political stupidities, philistinism, opportunism and so forth. It has been going on since 1893. And so has the hatred of the philistines on account of it. But still, I would not exchange this fate for "peace" with the philistines.'

By now the war had bred in Lenin an ambivalence about the future, a belief that although progress towards revolution was inevitable it would still be slow. The feeling was epitomized when he spoke on 22 January 1917 m the Zurich Volkshaus to young Swiss workers about the 1905 Revolution:

'the coming years, precisely because of this predatory war, will lead to popular uprisings under the leadership of the proletariat against the power of finance capital, against the big banks, and against the capitalists; and these upheavals cannot end otherwise than with the expropriation of the bourgeoisie, with the victory of socialism.'

Then, in a much-quoted sentence which revealed his feelings about the contemporary situation, he went on: 'We of the older generation may not live to see the decisive battles of this coming revolution.' His pessimism was modified when he continued: 'But I can, I believe, express the confident hope that the youth which is working so splendidly in the socialist movement[s] . . . will be fortunate enough not only to fight but also to win, in the coming proletarian revolution.' And to Inessa he wrote in February that he had good news from Moscow, 'that chauvinism is clearly declining and that probably our day will come'.

Lenin continued with his Party propaganda as strenuously as

always. But as Russia's position grew more desperate, he also strengthened whatever indirect contacts he had with the Germans, some of whom, as we have seen, had been discreetly wooing him since 1914. Indisputable evidence is slight although a signed report published in G. A. Aleksinsky's *Du Tsarisme au Communisme* from the archives of the Provisional Russian Government set up in Petrograd in 1917, is revealing. In view of the built-in anti-Lenin bias of its source it should be considered with care but should not be ignored. The report, signed by a Herr Jean-Henri Bint, claims that in December 1916, he began a watch on Lenin's quarters in the Spiegelgasse.

'On the 28th [he said], [Lenin] carrying a small suitcase, left his home and took the train to Berne, to which we accompanied him. Arriving in Berne at 10 o'clock, he proceeded directly to the Hôtel de France, near the station, reserved a room, left the hotel half an hour later, proceeded to the tramway stop in front of the railway station and went to the other end of the town to the Fosse aux Ours. He returned on foot towards the town, always keeping under the arcades and turning round from time to time, then, suddenly, leaving the arcades and without looking round entered the German Legation. It was half past eleven.

'The watch on the Legation went on until nine at night, without [Lenin] being seen to come out. He did not return to the Hotel de France either in the evening or the following morning.

'The watch at the Legation was begun again on the morning of the 29th, and it was only about four in the afternoon that [Lenin] left and proceeded hurriedly to the Hotel de France where he remained for about a quarter of an hour. Then he took another train, which brought us back to Zurich.'

During the final days of 1916 the Germans might well have increased their efforts to inform themselves of the real situation in Russia, since by this time reports of a coming collapse were already growing, even in Russia itself – a country which, during the previous two years, had had four prime ministers, six ministers of the interior and four ministers of agriculture. Before the beginning of 1916 the Grand Duke Nicholas had been dismissed from his post as Commander-in-Chief owing to the machinations of Rasputin, the monk who exercised such extraordinary influence over both the Tsar and his wife. In the Grand Duke's place the Tsar himself had taken over, an act which some considered sealed the fate of the monarchy since henceforth army defeats could be claimed to be the direct responsibility of the ruler. And Boris V. Stünner became Prime Minister – a man who thought that the war with Germany was the greatest possible misfortune for Russia and had no political justification.

With such a background to events, the reaction of Field-Marshal Sir Henry Wilson, leading an Allied mission to Russia early in 1917 to study the sending of more war material, was hardly surprising. According to his biographer, he 'found the opinion to prevail in Moscow, as it prevailed elsewhere, that the Emperor and Empress were a danger to the country and would very likely be assassinated'. At the British Embassy Wilson heard of the strong feelings being expressed against them, and in his diary wrote: 'They have lost their people, their nobles, and now their Army, and I see no hope for them; there will be terrible trouble one day here.' Before he left Russia for Britain, Wilson added, on 16 February: 'It seems as certain as anything can be that the Emperor and Empress are riding for a fall. Everyone – officers, merchants, ladies – talk openly of the absolute necessity of doing away with them.'

Some Russians were equally pessimistic about the general situation. As early as 5 January, the Okhrana had reported to A. D. Protopopov, the Minister of Internal Affairs:

'The mood in the capital is extremely agitated. The wildest rumors are circulating in society, both as to the plans of the governing authority, for taking various kinds of reactionary measures, and as to the projected aims of groups and layers of the population hostile to the government, implying the possibility and likelihood of revolutionary initiatives and excesses. Everyone expects some sort of extraordinary actions either from one side or the other.'

The prevailing pessimism was echoed by Sir Esmé Howard in Stockholm who told Lord Hardinge at the Foreign Office:

'It is said that the Council of the Empire, the Duma, and the officers and rank and file of the Army are heartily sick of the present regime with its constant shifting of Ministers and consequent disorganization and general incompetence. The blame for all this is attributed not only to the Empress but now also to the Emperor, and the possibility of his removal if he will not appoint men to the Government that have the confidence of the Nation, is openly and widely discussed.'

Not everyone was quite as gloomy and Lord Milner, the British Secretary of State for War, blandly announced, after spending four weeks in Petrograd: 'I have formed the opinion that there is a great deal of exaggeration in the talk about revolution.' This over-optimistic assessment was typical of Milner and in Britain there was considerable criticism that he had been sent at all, criticism exemplified by the question asked in the House of Commons: 'Did Lord Milner go to Russia with the definite mission of propping up by every means in his power the old regime of Tsardom?' Although the answer was that he had been sent for no such purpose, the suspicion remained that in the spring of 1917 the British authorities would have done almost anything to keep the Tsar in power – despite the speed with which they acknowledged his successors.

Milner had been part of a three-nation deputation which arrived in Russia on 29 January 1917 to co-ordinate the next military moves, but even at the beginning of 1917 there was a great deal of secrecy, not to say mistrust, among the Allies fighting the Germans. Even before the Milner delegation left Russia the French had, without the knowledge of their allies, signed a convention with the Russians allowing the Russians a free hand on their Western frontiers while in return the French would set up an independent Rhineland state.

Such secrecy among allies increased the difficulties of even high-ranking statesmen, diplomats and soldiers at the centre of the scene in forming a judgement of the real dangers of revolution. It is, therefore, not as surprising as it at first seems that men like Lenin in his near-isolation from reliable news in Switzerland, should have had so little awareness that the apple-cart was about to be overturned, and that the great event for which they had been planning for years was now so near. In November 1916, he wrote to his sister Maria asking her to send him newspapers since he was receiving none. At the end of December he applied for an extension of his Swiss residence permit until the end of 1917, accompanying the application with a savings book showing a 100-franc credit.

Lenin's unawareness that he would shortly be back in Russia is evident from a note he sent to Inessa Armand on 6 January, 'I have set going my theses on the tasks of the Swiss Lefts, both in German and in French. In this connection I have hit on the plan of founding a small publishing business and issuing sheets, leaflets and *small* pamphlets elaborating these theses . . .'

Lenin not only lacked any premonition of what was about to happen in Russia but had some curiously uninformed ideas of what might soon be happening elsewhere. In mid-January he wrote to Inessa, saying, 'If Switzerland is drawn into the war, the French will occupy Geneva immediately. To be in Geneva then is to be in France, and from there, to be in touch with Russia. I am therefore thinking of turning over the *Party* funds to you (for you to keep *on your person,* sewed up in a special little bag.)' Six days later he reiterated his opinion that while a revolution would come one day it was not imminent.

By January 1917 it might have seemed obvious to any intelligent observer even partially aware of the facts that Russia's wartime losses and her diminishing prospects of victory must be driving the Russian people towards some action. Hindenburg later gave a vivid picture of how these losses were seen by the Germans:

'In the great war ledger the page on which the Russian losses were written has been torn out. No one knows the figures. Five or eight millions? We, too, have no idea. All we know is that sometimes in our battles with the Russians we had to remove the mounds of enemy corpses from before our trenches in order to get a clear field of fire against fresh assaulting waves. Imagination may try to reconstruct the figure of their losses, but an accurate calculation will remain for ever a vain thing.'

Yet not everyone saw this slaughter as the prelude to apocalyptic change and Lenin himself still tended to add a 'probably' to forecasts of revolution. Yet decisive events took place within a matter of weeks.

The sparks that set the timber ablaze fell almost by chance. Reports of appalling casualties continued to arrive from the front during January 1917 and the shortage of bread which had steadily grown greater as the war went on continued to deteriorate. Conditions had been worsening for months, but if there was one reason to explain why the débacle began now it is that civilians and military both reached breaking point at the same time. Robert Bruce Lockhart, the British observer sent to Petrograd to report on events after Lenin had taken over, fairly summed up the situation by saying: 'The revolution took place because the patience of the Russian people broke down under a system of unparalleled inefficiency and corruption. No other nation would have stood the privations which Russia stood, for anything like the same length of time.'

Neither was there much chance of the Tsar himself being moved by his people's troubles judging by one of his remarks to Sir George Buchanan, the British ambassador, who had commented on the qualities of some Government ministers. 'My ministers are chosen by me alone,' Nicholas had replied, 'and it is for my people to deserve my confidence.' It was not only to Buchanan that the Tsar revealed how isolated he was from events. Rodzyanko, the head of the Duma, sent him a telegram late in

February saying: 'The situation is becoming worse; measures must be taken immediately, for tomorrow will be too late. The last hour has come; the fate of our country and the dynasty is being decided.' But the Tsar's response was merely to tell Count Vladimir Frederiks, the Finnish nobleman who was Court Minister in charge of protocol: 'Once again this Rodzyanko has written me a lot of nonsense, which I won't even bother to answer.'

The breaking point came on 23 February, (8 March in Europe and Women's Day in the international Socialist Calendar). Thousands of workers were on strike in Petrograd and many of them joined the queues of women who had been waiting in the bitter cold overnight in the hope of getting food. At places they attacked bakeries with cries of 'Give us bread!' The attacks quickly grew into anti-Government demonstrations and by the following day the strikers were estimated to number 107,000. Large areas of Petrograd were soon in the hands of the mob and although police and troops were called out to restore order, many refused to fire on civilians – indeed, some fraternized with them. Public buildings were set on fire and 'the Russian Bastille', the fortress of St Peter and St Paul, was entered and its prisoners released.

The deteriorating situation was described to the cabinet on the night of 26 to 27 February by the Director of Police:

'At six in the morning the telephone bell woke me sharply; the City Prefect informed me that an NCO of the Volynskii Regiment of the Guard named Kirpichnikov had just killed his superior officer, Training-Captain Lashkevich; the assassin had disappeared and the attitude of the regiment was threatening. The news crushed me; I now saw how far anarchy had infected the barracks . . . Through my window I could see an unusual excitement in the street. Soon there passed hurrying military cars; in the distance shots resounded. The telephone rang again, and again the City Prefect gave me bad news; Brigadier-General Dobrovolskii, commanding a battalion of sappers of the Guard, had been killed by his men. Then events moved fast; the Volynskii Regiment, which had risen after the murder of Captain Lashkevich, had chased its officers out of the barracks. The mutineers joined the Preobrazhenskii and Lithuanian Regiments of the Guard, whose barracks were near their own. They had succeeded in taking the Arsenal on the Liteinyi. Soldiers were dashing about the streets armed with guns and machine-guns. A roaring crowd invaded the quarters of the prison of preliminary confinement (before trial) and opened the cells; soon it was the same in all the prisons of the city. The police stations of the various wards were carried by the mob. Policemen who were not able to change into mufti were torn to pieces. The fire finished off the rest . . .'

Four regiments of the Petrograd garrison – the Pavlovsky, the Litovsky, the Volynsky and the Preobrazhensky – were already deciding the fate of Russia by transforming a revolt into a revolution.

In anything other than winter conditions the authorities would have had at least partial control over the crowd by raising the bridges across the Neva, thus dividing Petrograd into two and making it easier to split up the mobs. The Neva, however, was hard frozen, so that raising the bridges did nothing to deter the thousands of men and women, military and civilian alike, who were now roaming the capital with little thought other than that of defying authority.

The next evening the Tsar prorogued the Duma, an action that angered its members when they heard of it the following morning after walking through a new covering of snow to assemble in the Tauride Palace. They refused to be dismissed. Instead, after a debate that continued all day, they decided to form a 'Temporary Committee [of the members] of the State Duma' in the hope that it would be able to take control of the situation in Petrograd where the revolt of the troops was still spreading. The Committee proposed the formation of a Provisional Government and on 3 March *Izvestia* announced that the Temporary Committee, 'with the help and the support of the army and the inhabitants of the capital, has now attained such a large measure of success over the dark forces of the old regime that it is possible for the Committee to undertake the organization of a more stable executive power'.

The non-party Prince Lvov, landowner from an old aristocratic family, a member of the first Duma with a high reputation for liberal ideas and a low reputation for firmness in implementing them, became Minister-President and Minister of the Interior in the new Government. The other nine members of the cabinet consisted of the non-party M. I. Tereschenko as Minister of Finance; the Centrist V. N. Lvov as Ober-Procurator of the Holy Synod; the rich leader of the Octobrists, A. E. Guchkov, as Minister of War and the Navy; Aleksandr Kerensky, a Socialist Revolutionary of whom much more was to be heard, as Minister of Justice; and five members of the Kadet Party, including, as Foreign Minister the party leader, Paul Milyukov. Together, they made up what could be ailed a cabinet of ten Liberals and one Socialist or, as Lenin was to call them, 'Ten

269

capitalists and one hostage of democracy'. The work of the cabinet, *Izvestia* added, would be guided along the following there would be a complete amnesty for all charged with offences of a political or religious nature; freedom of speech, press and assembly; the abolition of all restrictions based on class, religion or nationality; immediate arrangements for the calling of a Constituent Assembly; and the substitution of a people's militia for the police. These intentions were both well meaning and, in the circumstances, ambitious; but, as noted by Sir John Wheeler-Bennett, 'Of sheer political impotence and well-meaning ineptitude, history has few more striking examples' than the first Provisional Government. In May it became a coalition government of liberals and socialists. In June it was replaced by a second, and more left-wing, coalition, and in September by yet another coalition which lasted until Lenin's Bolsheviks took over the following month.

One of the first actions of the Provisional Government was to acknowledge the existence of the Petrograd Soviet, a revival of the 1905 workers' Soviet which had been set up as soon as it was realized that the events in Petrograd constituted not a strike, not a revolt, but a full-blooded revolution. On 27 February a Temporary Revolutionary Committee of the Soviet of the Workers' Deputies had met in the Tauride Palace and appealed to workers and troops to elect deputies for a meeting that evening. At this Nikolay Chkheidze, a Georgian Menshevik, was elected chairman of the new Soviet; Mikhail Skobelev, another Menshevik, and Kerensky were elected vice-chairmen. The Provisional Government and the Petrograd Soviet both had quarters in the Tauride Palace for some time.

There also came into existence at this time the All-Russian Central Committee of the Soviets (or VTsIK, the Vserossysky

Tsentralyni Ispolnitseinyi Komitet) as well as the Central Executive Committee (TsIK), to be followed by the creation of similar soviets, first in the bigger Russian cities and then in the countryside. These numbered 100 by the late spring, and 600 by the summer. The Petrograd Committee soon began to exercise authority far beyond the city, a development which was reinforced when in March a dozen or so provincial members were added to the Central Executive Committee. This was dominated by Mensheviks and Social Revolutionaries and remained so until October when, after the Revolution, the Second All-Russian Congress of Soviets elected a new Central Executive Committee with a Bolshevik majority.

Thus two main bodies, the Provisional Government and the Soviets' Central Executive Committee, each of questionable official status but each wielding, for practical purposes, considerable political power, had quickly been formed. They governed Russia as best they could until swept away by the Revolution, which in the autumn brought Lenin to power.

Lenin himself later spelled out the ambiguous situation in *Pravda* on 9 April:

> 'Alongside the Provisional Government, the government of the *bourgeoisie, another government* has arisen, so far weak and incipient, but undoubtedly a government that actually exists and is growing – the Soviet of Workers' and Soldiers' Deputies.
>
> 'What is the class composition of this other government? It is a revolutionary dictatorship, i.e., a power directly based on revolutionary seizure, on the direct initiative of the people from below, and *not on a law* enacted by a centralized state power. It is an entirely different kind of power from

the one that generally exists in the parliamentary bourgeoisdemocratic republics of the usual type still prevailing in the advanced countries of Europe and America. This circumstance is often overlooked, often not given enough thought, yet it is the crux of the matter. *This* power is of *the same type* as the Paris Commune of 1871. The fundamental characteristics of this type are: (1) the source of power is not a law previously discussed and enacted by parliament, but the direct initiative of the people from below, in their local areas – the direct "seizure", to use a current expression; (2) the replacement of the police and the army, which are institutions divorced from the people and set against the people, by the direct arming of the whole people; order in the state under such a power is maintained by the armed workers and peasants *themselves:* by the armed people themselves; (3) officialdom, the bureaucracy, are either similarly replaced by the direct rule of the people themselves or at least placed under special control; they not only become elected officials, but are also *subject to recall* at the people's first demand; they are reduced to the position of simple agents; from a privileged group holding "jobs" remunerated on a high bourgeois scale, they become workers of a special "arm of the service", whose remuneration *does not exceed* the ordinary pay of a competent worker.'

In his enthusiasm for the soviets, he may have overstated the position; yet they could, in fact, claim a democratic legitimacy as great as the Provisional Government. That Government had been formed on the initiative of a few members of the discredited Duma; the soviets, by contrast, were comprised of delegates elected by workers in factories and by soldiers in barracks who could replace such delegates by fresh elections as and when they wished. Their power has been emphasized by Isaac Deutscher who, in his life of Stalin, wrote that the soviets

'became a very sensitive reflection of the changing popular mood. This was the source of their unrivalled moral authority. Apart from giving quasiparliamentary representation to the lower classes, they were also the *de facto* executive power, for which the discredited normal administration was no match. The writ of the Soviet ran in factory, railway depot, post office, and regiment alike. From the first hours of its existence the Provisional Government was unable to carry out a single important decision unless it was endorsed by the leaders of the Petersburg [*sic*] Soviet. Thus the Government was the virtual prisoner of the Soviet, though neither the Soviet nor the Government were as yet aware of this. The conflict, now latent, now open, between the two was to underlie the whole course of the revolution.'

The situation, which at times during the summer of 1917 was to prove as much of an embarrassment to Lenin as to the Provisional Government, was a direct legacy of the Duma's political shuffling. On the morning of 12 March it was faced with the Tsar's order to dissolve and also with growing evidence that the Petrograd garrison was supporting what was now clearly a full-blooded revolution. Its members resolved the problem with a compromise: they left the Government chamber in the Tauride Palace and thus could technically claim that the Duma had dissolved itself: but at the same time they asked the Council of Elders to set up a temporary committee with the restricted aim of restoring order in Petrograd.

Within the next few days the Soviet and the Duma Committee both took decisive action. On the night of 14 March the radical lawyer N. D. Sokolov, now an important figure in the Soviet, sat in the Tauride Palace writing down, at the prompting of a surrounding group of soldiers, proposals which were to be tailored together into what became a famous 'Order Number One'. Ridiculed by the monarchist Vasily V. Shulgin with the words, 'This is the end of the Army', the Order in practice transferred control of military units from army officers to the political leaders of the Soviet. While some of the Order's clauses did no more than modify the strict class system operating in the tsarist forces, others struck at the roots of military discipline and made the Russian units even less efficient than they had been. However, it is often forgotten that although the impact of Order Number One was felt throughout the army, it was intended to apply only to the Petrograd garrison.

Its practical effect and the situation from which it sprang, were outlined in a note of 22 March 1917 which Guchkov, the Minister of War, sent to General Alekseyev, the Chief of Staff.

'The Provisional Government possesses no real power and its orders are executed only in so far as this is permitted by the Soviet of Workers' and Soldiers' Deputies, which holds in its hands the most important elements of actual power, such as troops, railroads, postal and telegraph service. It is possible to say directly that the Provisional Government exists only while this is permitted by the Soviet of Workers' and Soldiers' Deputies. Especially in the military department it is possible now only to issue orders which do not basically conflict with the decisions of the above-mentioned Soviet.'

There still remained the problem of what was to happen to the Tsar. The Duma and the Soviet had not taken long to come to a fragile, but at least workable, arrangement which began to resolve the situation in Petrograd; the future of the Tsar was another matter. On 14 March he attempted to travel by rail from Moghilev to Tsarskoe Tselo but the journey was frustrated by revolutionary activity and he arrived at night not in Tsarskoe Tselo but in Pskov. His first plan was to appoint M. V. Rodzyanko, the President of the Duma, as a minister responsible to the Duma, retaining for himself the posts of Minister of War and the Navy. But while this might have been possible a few weeks earlier, it was impossible now. Many high army officers, including General Alekseyev, had already become convinced that nothing less than the Tsar's abdication could halt the rot that was still spreading through army units. Alekseyev sought the views of other army leaders and by the afternoon could inform the Tsar that the overwhelming majority of high officers – and the Grand Duke Nicholas, Viceroy of the Caucasus – favoured his abdication

Once the situation had been made clear to him the Tsar accepted the need to abdicate with considerable dignity. The accounts of this traumatic event, which paved the way for Lenin's seizure or power seven months later, vary in detail but one of the most revealing is that by the correspondent of *The Times*, who describes *how* Guchkov and the Conservative Deputy Shulgin were commissioned to attend the Tsar at Pskov, He reported that Nicholas II

'received them in a small dimly lit room. He locked pale and careworn, but was perfectly calm and self-possessed.

'Addressing Gutchkoff he said. "Tell me the whole truth."

"We come to tell you that all the troops in Petrograd are on our side. It is useless to send more regiments. They will go over as soon as they reach the station."

' "I know it," replied the Tsar. "The order has already been given to the troops to return to the front."

'Then, after a slight pause, [he] asked, "What do you want me to do?"

' "Your Majesty must abdicate in favour of the Heir-Apparent under the Regency of the Grand Duke Michael Alexandrovitch. Such is the will of the new Government, which we are forming under Prince Lvoff," he was told.

' "I cannot part with my boy," replied the Monarch, with emotion. "I shall hand the Throne to my brother."

'Then, speaking in a matter-of-fact tone, he said, "Have you a piece of paper?"

'. . . the manifesto was drafted. Count Fredericks, Minister of the Imperial Household . . . and the Tsar's Aide-de-Camp assisted their master in his final ordeal. Soon the document lay on the writing table. Before signing it he wrote out orders appointing Prince Lvoff Prime Minister and the Grand Duke Nicholas Generalissimo.

'Then, bowing his head for a few moments, he dipped his pen, and without a trace of emotion for the last time appended his signature as Tsar of All the Russias to the writ of abdication.'

The following day the Grand Duke Michael, whom the Tsar had formally named as his successor, also abdicated and from then onwards the Tsar and his family, as well as the future of Russia, lay in the hands of the new Provisional Government which, as Lenin emphasized some weeks later, operated effectively only in conjunction with the newly resurrected Soviet.

This would have been a curious arrangement, even had the Provisional Government and the Soviet not had to watch each other's actions with care. Power was, moreover, exercised through the Soviet's Executive Committee, and this Committee, like the 3,000-strong membership of the Soviet itself, later reinforced by provincial soviets, was constantly changing.

While the overwhelming Allied reaction to the Tsar's abdication was fear of the effect it would have on Allied military plans in the war against the Central Powers, there was in some places a naïve reaction typified by Arthur Ransome, then a correspondent in Russia for the *Daily News*. 'This is far and away the greatest victory over Prussianism gained in this war,' he wrote. 'Germany will now have republican France as one neighbour and free Russia on the other side. Already Russian soldiers must be telling the Germans what they have done and asking when the Germans will do likewise.'

The true situation was only slowly appreciated by the Allied governments. President Wilson viewed the fall of the Tsar and his Government rather simplistically as an encouragement to enter the war and stressed his attitude in a message to Congress: 'For the United States the possibility that a new and liberal government in Russia may now develop is a welcome factor in removing previous American hesitation at associating with a Russian Government which we rightly judged to be tyrannical and corrupt.' And addressing a special joint session of Congress he became almost eulogistic about the Revolution. 'Now [Russia's forbidding autocracy] has been shaken off,' he said, 'and the great, generous Russian people have been added in all their naïve majesty and might to the forces that are fighting for freedom in the world, for justice, and for peace. Here is a fit partner for a League of Honour.'

In Britain, Lloyd George was equally enthusiastic at the prospects, saying in a congratulatory message to Prince Lvov, 'we believe that the Revolution whereby the Russian people have placed their destinies on the sure foundation of freedom, is the greatest service which they have yet made to the cause for which the Allied peoples have been fighting since August 1914'. As for the Independent Labour Party, most of its members welcomed the Revolution in ecstatic terms and Ramsay MacDonald lost no chance of identifying the party, and himself, with it.

It is true that the Tsar still had his supporters in Britain but the country's satisfaction with the Provisional Government – at least as long as it continued the war – was reflected in a resolution the House of Commons passed on 22 March 1917. This recorded

'That this House sends to the Duma its fraternal greetings and tenders to the Russian people its heartfelt congratulations upon the establishment among them of free institutions in full confidence that they will lead not only to the rapid and happy progress of the Russian nation but to the prosecution with renewed steadfastness and vigour of the war against the stronghold of an autocratic militarism which threatens the liberty of Europe.'

Bonar Law, the Chancellor of the Exchequer, told the House of Commons that the British Government was continuing 'to make [financial] advances to our Russian Allies on the same terms as before the change', while he reflected much British opinion when he said that 'no one brought up in the atmosphere of this country, who has read from his childhood, perhaps, the accounts of the horrors of Siberia, has ever had any other feeling than that of relief that a system of that kind has come to an end'.

In both the USA and Britain the difference that the Revolution would make to the war effort was constantly, if mistakenly, emphasized. In the USA papers spoke of the new political and spiritual unity given to the alliance of Germany's enemies. In Britain, a leading article in *The Times* suggested much the same, saying that in Russia 'the Army and the people have joined hands to overthrow the forces of reaction which were stifling the national aspirations and strangling the national efforts'. Only from British labour leaders did there come a note of caution and, according to *The Times* on 17 March, they hoped it would be stressed 'that any remission of effort means disaster to comrades in the trenches and to our common hopes of social regeneration'.

Fear of 'remission of effort' was a constant counterbalance in the minds of Russia's allies against relief that it was a less despotic regime which was now helping in the fight against the Central Powers. This led to much hypocrisy and double-dealing which has come to light only slowly during the last seven decades. Thus while Kerensky's Government was being praised in the House of Commons it was being operated against on Britain's behalf as though it were not very different from a potential enemy.

This has rarely been made more clear than by Somerset Maugham who was an important British agent in Russia between July and November 1917 with, as he has described it, 'unlimited money' at his disposal.

'I was exhilarated by the responsibility of my position. I went as a private agent, who could be disavowed if necessary, with instructions to get in touch with parties hostile to the Government and devise a scheme that would keep Russia in the war and prevent the Bolsheviks, supported by the Central Powers, from seizing power . . . I do not ask [the reader] to believe me when I state that it seems to me at least possible that if I had been sent six months before I might quite well have succeeded.'

Despite fears that the Provisional Government might lessen its support for the Western allies in their fight against the Central Powers, much Allied opinion saw the fall of the Tsar as helping to pave the way for an increased effort against the enemy which had been faced since August 1914. However, it did not look like this to many Germans, and it did not look like this to Lenin, whose main feeling in his Swiss backwater was that his time was at last arriving.

8

The Sealed Train

News of the dramatic events in Russia reached Lenin early on the afternoon of 15 March (according to the Gregorian calendar used in Switzerland). He was preparing for a visit to the library, and as Krupskaya finished washing up the dishes after the midday meal, they heard, on the stairs to their room, the quick steps of Mieczyslav Bronsky, a young Polish revolutionary who lived nearby, and who now burst in with the question: 'Haven't you heard the news? There is a revolution in Russia!'

At first it was difficult to believe that it had happened at last, and the trio hurried out, down the stairs, and into the narrow Spiegelgasse which led to Bellevue Platz on the Zurichersee. Here they could read the newspapers for themselves. The *Zürcher Post* and the *Neue Zürcher Zeitung* confirmed the news although giving only the scantiest of details.

Lenin immediately became obsessed with one thing. He knew that he had to get back to Russia; the first mistake at any time of crisis was to be absent, and to Inessa Armand he wrote straight away: 'We here in Zurich are in a state of agitation today . . . I am *beside* myself that I cannot go to Scandinavia!! I will not forgive myself for not risking the journey in 1915!' From the post office he sent postcards to a number of Bolsheviks in Geneva in the hope that they would be able to join him and make joint plans.

Lenin was not only anxious to return immediately to Petrograd. He was equally anxious to influence at once the reactions to the events which had taken place. He could do this by letters to the papers, which he correctly believed would now be open to him, by letters to friends and, even more importantly, by guiding the thoughts of the Bolsheviks in Sweden and Norway whom he rightly guessed would be returning to Russia many days before he would be able to do so.

Meanwhile, information seeping out to Switzerland tended to be contradictory.

'Today [he wrote in his first notes to the Scandinavian Bolsheviks] there are reports from England that the tsar has not yet abdicated, and that his whereabouts are unknown. This suggests that he is trying to put up resistance, organize a party, perhaps even an armed force, in an attempt to restore the monarchy. If he succeeds in fleeing from Russia or winning over part of the armed forces, the tsar might, to mislead the people, issue a manifesto announcing immediate conclusion of a separate peace with Germany!

'That being the position, the proletariat's task is a pretty complex one.'

But it was not only the Tsar's potential that now worried him.

Once the plans of the Provisional Government became known he was in despair. For as he saw events, not one but two great opportunities were already on the way to being lost. One was the chance of a genuine socialist revolution in Russia rather than the continuation of old policies under new management. The other was the chance of bringing about not a one-nation revolution in Russia alone but a sweeping change that would bring Marxism to the whole of Europe.

Whatever the analysis of the developments soon being reported, one set of facts appeared incontrovertibly clear and were seen by Lenin as giving the key to the future: they were to lie at the centre of his plans during the crucial months ahead. He stated them in simple terms in the small cramped room at 14 Spiegelgasse as he turned from writing to Inessa Armand or from preparing an article for *Pravda:*

'The new government is composed of avowed advocates and supporters of the imperialist war with Germany, i.e. a war in alliance with the English and the French imperialist governments, a war for the plunder and conquest of foreign lands – Armenia, Galicia, Constantinople, etc.

The new government cannot give the peoples of Russia (and the nations tied to us by the war) either peace, bread, or full freedom. The working class must therefore continue its fight for socialism and peace, utilizing for this purpose the new situation and explaining it as widely as possible among the masses.'

The message, the kernel of the belief that was to be so important in bringing the Bolsheviks to power in the autumn, was reiterated in a telegram Lenin sent two days later to the Party members who were now leaving Scandinavia for Russia. It went: 'Our tactics: no trust in and no support of the new government;

Kerensky is especially suspect; arming of the proletariat is the only guarantee; immediate elections to the Petrograd City Council; no *rapprochement* with other parties. Telegraph this to Petrograd.'

While one part of Lenin's mind was thus busy directing the comrades in the way he believed they should go, another part was coping with a jostle of ideas as to how he could get back to Russia in the shortest possible time. The only choice seemed to be between travelling across the enemy territory of the Central Powers or through France and then Britain where he feared that his reputation would lead to arrest. 'At night', wrote Krupskaya, 'all sorts of incredible plans were made. We could travel by aeroplane. But such things could be thought of only in the semi-delirium of the night. One had only to formulate it vocally to realize the utter impracticability of such a plan.' A Swedish passport could, no doubt, be obtained, but Lenin spoke no Swedish and even if he learned a little it would be easy, as his wife pointed out, for him to give himself away. 'You will fall asleep and see Mensheviks in your dreams,' she said, 'and you will start swearing, and shout, scoundrels, scoundrels, and give the whole conspiracy away.'

Sophia Ravich, a Bolshevik who suggested that she might solve her own problem by marrying a Swiss citizen which would thus give her the right to travel through both Germany and Russia, was congratulated by Lenin for 'A brilliant idea' – but it was of no use to him. According to Karpinsky, Lenin advised her to find a convenient old man, and recommended Akselrod for this purpose since he was a Swiss citizen. Akselrod apparently refused to make such a marriage of convenience for the sake of the Party.

Lenin later wrote to Karpinsky asking him to take out papers in Karpinsky's own name for travelling to France and England. 'I will *use them* to travel through England (and *Holland*) to Russia,' he went on. 'I can put on a wig. The photograph will be taken of *me* with the wig on, and *I* shall go to the Consulate in Berne with your papers and wearing the wig.'

These hare-brained schemes were an indication of Lenin's desperation to be in the centre of the stage. 'My nerves naturally are overstrung,' he added in a note to Inessa Armand. 'No wonder! To have to sit here on tenterhooks.' There were also more sober suggestions for his return to Russia. Throughout the second half of March a succession of telegrams and letters went from Lenin in Zurich to Bolsheviks elsewhere, to socialist supporters, and to men who might wield influence in Switzerland, proposing a variety of plans which would legally take him and at least a handful of colleagues back to Petrograd either across or around the territories of the warring powers.

He asked Inessa Armand, whom he believed was about to visit England, to find out whether he would be allowed through that country. He thought it unlikely, but went on to say that there were Russians in Switzerland who could ask the Germans to allow the passage of a railway coach to Copenhagen for various revolutionaries, an idea that had already been put up by Martov at a meeting of Russian political refugees in Geneva. In return for the passage back to Russia, the refugees, Martov proposed, would ask the Provisional Government in Petrograd to set free a corresponding number of Germans and Austrians at present interned in Russia. Everyone at the Geneva meeting, including Lenin, favoured the plan. The refugees, he told Karpinsky, should encourage important Swiss such as lawyers, to ask the German Ambassador in Berne to support it. 'We cannot take part', he went on, 'either directly or indirectly; our participation will *spoil* it all. But the plan, in itself, is a *very* good one and is *very* right.' One reason for caution was that even at this stage Lenin feared the criticism which any dealings with the Germans would attract inside Russia.

The idea was temporarily dropped and Lenin again considered travelling through England:

'Please let me know in greatest possible detail, first whether the British Government will allow passage to Russia to me and a number of members of our party, the RSDLP (Central Committee), on the following conditions. (a) The Swiss socialist Fritz Platten receives permission from the British Government to conduct any number of persons through England irrespective of their political allegiances and their views on war and peace; (b) Platten alone answers both for the composition of the conducted groups and for maintaining proper order, and receives a railway coach for travelling through England, which he, Platten, is to keep locked. No one can enter this coach without the consent of Platten. This coach shall have ex-territorial rights; (c) From a port in England Platten conveys the group by the steamer of any neutral country, with the right to notify *all* countries of the sailing time of this special ship; (d) Railway fares shall be paid by Platten according to the tariff and the number of seats occupied; (e) The British Government undertakes not to place obstacles to the chartering and sailing of a special steamer with Russian political emigrants and not to detain the steamer in England, enabling the passage to be made in the quickest possible way . . .'

Although such methods of returning to Russia now occupied

a good deal of Lenin's thought he also elaborated his ideas about how the future should develop, and during what were to be his last weeks in Switzerland continued work on 'Marxism and the State', a polemic to be completed only five months later as *The State and Revolution*. It was here that he quoted Engels's forecast that the whole machinery of the State would one day lie in 'a museum of antiquities, by the side of the spinning wheel and the bronze axe'; and it was here that he made the declaration to which his actions were to provide an ironic epilogue – that 'so long as the state exists there is no freedom. When there is freedom, there will be no state.'

While Lenin was busily investigating possible, and some impossible, ways of returning to Russia, the Germans were giving increasing attention to the most practical method of infiltrating him back into a Russia where his opposition to the war would be to their advantage. Between two and three years earlier von Romberg in Berne, Helphand in Berlin and Keskula in several different places, were among those who had considered how Leninled agitation could help their respective causes. Now their efforts began to coalesce, and it is not too much to claim that Lenin's return to Petrograd, and all that followed, was the result of combined pressure exercised by individual operators such as Helphand and Keskula, by the German High Command, the diplomats inspired by von Romberg in Berne, by a powerful lobby in the German Foreign Office and, over all, by the Kaiser who from the outbreak of the war had recognized the potential ability of the Bolsheviks to hamper the enemies of the Wehrmacht. As German files have become available over the years, all these characters have been seen to have played significant parts in the drama which made possible a successful Russian Revolution.

Two points which have come to light since the files have been opened highlight both the natural secrecies of such wartime intrigue and the importance which the Central Powers and the Allies both gave to Lenin's potential for good or evil. His aim of hampering Russian involvement in the war, and of ending it if possible, was well known and the British were apparently willing to consider bribery if that would help to discourage him. On 31 May 1917, Lord Milner, Secretary of State for War, passed on to Lloyd George, Prime Minister, certain suggestions he had received for keeping the Russians in the fight. The undisclosed writer added that 'even Lenin could be got by bribery . . . anything could be done in Russia, Turkey or Greece by bribery!' However ludicrous was the idea of using money to turn Lenin from his objective, Milner added to the Prime Minister: 'the enclosed brief note is well worth your *personal* perusal'.

The idea of using Lenin went back at least to the September of 1915 when the German Minister in Berne, Count von Romberg, had sent to the German Chancellor Lenin's conditions on which the revolutionary forces would be prepared to negotiate with Germany if they were successful. Whether these details were expanded during the mysterious visit by Lenin to the Germans in Berne in December 1916 is not certain but even if the Germans believed that his plans were unlikely to be carried out they were in no doubt that they should nevertheless be considered.

'Lenin's programme must not, of course, be made public [von Romberg stressed], first because its publication would reveal our source, but also because its discussion in the press would rob it of all its value. I feel that it should be put out in an aura of great secrecy, so that it creates a belief that an agreement with powerful Russian circles is already in preparation.'

Just what steps were taken to follow up these tentative suggestions during 1915 and 1916 is uncertain even today. It is very likely that pressure came from a number of unconnected quarters and if Helphand's boasts of the part he had played in getting Lenin back into Germany are exaggerated they should not be entirely discounted. Litvinov, who in his post-1918 diplomatic work was to have numerous high contacts in Germany, has written:

'There is no doubt whatever that it was Parvus who suggested to Ludendorff the idea of granting Ilich a permit to pass through Germany . . . The decisive factor which determined Ludendorff to authorize the passage of our comrades was the entry of the United States into the war, which became inevitable after 3rd February 1917, when diplomatic relations were broken off with Washington. Ludendorff was anxious to finish the war before the mass participation of American troops. He wanted to balance the disparity of forces in the West by eliminating the Russian Army from the war . . . objectively we played the part of a bacillus introduced in the East.'

Churchill, as great a contrast to Litvinov as could be found in the longest day's march, used the same comparison with specific reference to Lenin, writing of the Germans that 'it was with a sense of awe that they turned upon Russia the most grisly of all weapons. They transported Lenin in a sealed truck like a plague bacillus from Switzerland into Russia.'

However the idea of using Bolshevik disruption of the Russian army to help German forces was propagated within Germany, it is certain that by the time the Tsar was forced to abdicate early in 1917 the plan to do so – which, however slight the effects, must provide some relief in the East to Germans locked in combat with Anglo-French forces in the West – had been growing for two years. The abdication and the Revolution that brought it about quickly encouraged a transformation of the possibilities as they were viewed by the Germans and by the potential Russian revolutionaries: both were persuaded towards action, although the action had to be qualified for different reasons. As General Ludendorff wrote later: 'Having once sent Lenin to Russia, our Government had a special responsibility. From the war's point of view his journey was justified; Russia had to be beaten.' General Hoffmann put it quite as blandly: 'In the same way that I hurled grenades into enemy trenches and released poison gas against our opponents so do I have the right to use propaganda against our enemies.' The Germans were nevertheless anxious to keep secret the movement of potential Russian revolutionaries from Switzerland to Russia, not only from their own people but from the British. The revolutionaries were equally anxious to keep such movement secret for fear of what the Russian people would make of any negotiations with the Germans. These circumstances combine to give an air of complex intrigue to the 'sealed train' episode which changed history by bringing Lenin and his colleagues from the quiet of Switzerland to the cheering crowds of Petrograd's Finland Station.

In this cloak-and-dagger context, Lenin continued his efforts to find the most convenient way of transporting a picked number of the Russians living in Switzerland as refugees to Russia. The piquant situation that developed had similarities with that following the Soviet-German pact of August 1939, epitomized in the drawing by the English cartoonist David Low showing Stalin and Hitler leading each other up the garden path, each carrying a concealed revolver behind his back. Success came as much by chance as by organization, and the outcome involved not only a number of subsidiary characters but a considerable measure of luck. An important factor was efficient German organization, which smoothed away the inherent problems of shepherding some thirty enemies of various nationalities from neutral territory, across a war-torn Germany, through neutral Sweden and Finland, and across the frontier into Russia.

Lenin's contribution was his desperate desire to return to Russia which at times tended to obscure the clear-headed planning that typified most of his activities. Just as twenty-five years later Churchill declared that if the devil was fighting against Hitler he would be on the side of the devil, so Lenin was happy to receive help from the Germans if that help enabled him to bring about the Bolshevist millennium, first in Russia, then throughout the world. However, he was well aware of the dangers of collaboration with the Germans unless this could be favourably presented and he turned down the first proposal that came to him from Russia's enemies. Apparently sponsored, if not originated, by Helphand, the plan was that Lenin and Zinoviev should be escorted through Germany to Russia by Georg Sklarz, a German businessman who travelled to Switzerland and actually made arrangements to pay the Russians' fares. Before he arrived, though, Lenin decided against the plan.

Before the end of March a different suggestion had been made to the German Foreign Office through a Captain Hülsen of the German General Staff's political section.

'The German Government [he wrote] should approve an application which the Russians living in Switzerland would arrange to have made by the Swiss Government for these Russians (about 300 to 400) to be transported to Sweden in a special train, travelling through Germany because of the shortness of this route. Among these 300 to 400 Russians (of all parties) there would also be those unacceptable to the Entente. As soon as the German Government agrees to the proposal we (the confidential agent) should unobtrusively inform the relevant people in Switzerland so that they could begin to take the necessary steps with the Swiss Government.'

There should be no restrictions on those who left Switzerland, it was added, and it was 'considered advantageous to Germany to bring out the members of Lenin's party, the Bolsheviks, who were about forty in number'.

Almost simultaneously, in Switzerland a Committee for the Return of Russian Political Exiles in Switzerland was formed, which eventually contributed 3,000 Swiss francs to this cause; Robert Grimm, editor of the Social-Democratic *Berner Tagwacht*, was asked to travel to Petrograd on the Committee's behalf. In the last days of March Lenin and Zinoviev sent a telegram to Grimm saying: 'Our Party has decided to accept without reservations the proposal that the Russian émigrés should travel through Germany, and to organize this journey at once. We also expect to have more than ten participants in the journey.' However, Grimm was replaced by Fritz Platten, secretary of the Swiss Social-Democratic Party, whom Lenin had earlier suggested might help in securing permission for travel through Britain. In 1905 Platten had taken part in Riga in the abortive Revolution. He had been confined to a Russian prison, allowed bail after paying the tsarist police and banned from Russia. In the spring of 1917 he had his own reasons for returning since he not only hoped to recover his bail money but also to visit his wife. Although he was not a disinterested party there is no reason to doubt his sincerity in wishing to get Lenin and others back into Russia.

However, Platten's substitution for Grimm presented its own problems, as did many other arrangements for this journey on which the future of Russia was to depend. They have been well described by Professor Z. A. B. Zeman in his *A Diplomatic History of the First World War*. Platten was asked to lunch with Lenin on 3 April, he says; after lunch, at which Radek and Willi Münzenberg were present, they took the train to Berne where Grimm was told that he was being superseded by Platten. The details were then worked out in Lenin's bedroom of what Platten was to say the following day to Count von Romberg, the German Minister.

'The document that Platten put before Romberg [says Zeman] was cautious and naïve, and admirably served its purpose. Platten undertook to accompany his friends "bearing full responsibility and personal liability at all times". He would buy the tickets at "the normal tariffs", and would undertake "all communication with German organizations". The carriage was to enjoy extra-territorial rights; "as far as possible the journey shall be made without stops and in a through train". Romberg remarked how unusual it was for travellers to propose conditions to the government of the country through which they intended to travel, and he forwarded the document to Berlin.'

Two days later Berlin approved the document with only one

minor amendment. But then, with all settled as far as the Germans were concerned, the Mensheviks among the proposed Russian party demanded prior agreement from the Provisional Government in Petrograd that they would release German prisoners-of-war in return for the Russian *émigrés* – part of the bargain that Platten had struck with Count von Romberg. Lenin, unwilling to wait any longer, decided to go ahead without agreement and the rest of the party, as usual, followed his lead.

News that the deal had been concluded astonished many members of the pacifist and left-wing community in Switzerland. The reaction is described by J. Ley who has written that 'pandemonium broke out' in the Plauen café in Zurich. He continued:

'Grumbach, the correspondent for *L'Humanité*, and Otto Pohl of the Viennese *Arbeiterzeitung* were beside themselves with anger. The forceful Grumbach inveighed against the treachery of helping the German imperialists to prolong the war; he assured all of us he would expose the whole thing in the public debate he was to have with Lenin the next evening [a debate which did not take place]. Our neighbours from the next table, Franz Werfel and Stefan Zweig, were expressing their fears and disapproval of Lenin; and even the habitually remote and dignified Romain Rolland, who happened to be sitting in a corner of the café with Busoni [Ferruccio Benvenuto Busoni, the Italian musician] joined in the spontaneous discussions. He thought it very wrong of Lenin to enter into an agreement with Ludendorff [as was then being claimed] and expressed his concern over the repercussions this would have with the international peace movement. (Rolland later declined an invitation from Lenin to come to the station to see him off.)'

James Joyce, who heard the news later in the day, commented: 'It's just like the Trojan Horse to me. I suppose Ludendorff must be pretty desperate.' Other pacifists whom Ley reports as being depressed at the news included the French poet Jouvé, his translator, Felix Beran, and Leonhard Ragaz, Professor of Theology at Zurich University. Many Germans in Zurich took the same line, and the first man whom Ley found approving Lenin's action was the Dutch poet, Herman Gorter, who thought that it would help the cause of the proletarian revolution and said that he would try to join his party.

Another difficulty arose. The French *Petit Parisien* reported that the Provisional Government was planning to arrest the *émigrés* on charges of high treason following their journey across Germany. To safeguard everyone, Lenin, and all the others, signed a document saying: 'I assume full political responsibility for my participation in the journey.'

Although Lenin's main preoccupation had been organizing the journey home, he had managed to write from his table in the cramped room in the Spiegelgasse an extension of his reactions to the Revolution. He also found time to express, at a number of meetings, Bolshevik feelings about what should be done in the new situation which the Revolution had created. Lenin had 'the gift of the gab', refined and uplifted until it became the voice of inspired prophecy, a voice which retained the quality that made men listen and believe. Now was an ideal time for using it.

His standpoint, from which he never deviated, was quickly confirmed in a telegram to Aleksandra Kollontay: 'Our tactics: absolutely distrust, no support of new government. Kerensky particularly suspect; to arm proletariat only guarantee; *no rapprochement with other parties.* The last is *conditio sine qua non.* We do not trust Chkheidze.' He began to develop the theme with the help of Zinoviev, who had joined him from Geneva, and further expanded it in Tetters from Afar', written between 20 and 26 March. They began with 'The First Stage of the First Revolution' which he sent to Hanecki-Fürstenberg in Stockholm, who in turn passed it on to Lenin's sister Maria in Petrograd. The ease with which the Romanovs had been swept away, Lenin averred, was due to a 'conspiracy of the Anglo-French imperialists, who impelled Milyukov, Gushkov and Co. to seize power *for the purpose of continuing the imperialist war,* for the purpose of conducting the war still more ferociously and obstinately, for the purpose of *slaughtering fresh millions* of Russian workers and peasants in order that the Guchkovs might obtain Constantinople, the French capitalists Syria, the British capitalists Mesopotamia, . . .' Milyukov and the other Kadet ministers were described as 'decorations' and Kerensky as 'a balalaika on which they [the other members of the Government] play to deceive the workers and peasants'.

However, it was in the fifth of the 'Letters from Afar', not published until 1924 (the year of Lenin's death), that he summarized, in the immediate aftermath of the Revolution, what he believed should be done next, a conviction that governed the course of his actions from now on.

'The revolutionary proletariat [he began] must (1) find the surest road to the next stage of the revolution, or to the second revolution, which (2) must transfer political power from the government of the landlords and capitalists . . . to a government of the workers and the poorest peasants. (3) This latter government must be organized on the model of the Soviets of Workers' and Peasants' Deputies, namely (4) it must smash, completely eliminate, the old state machine, the army, the police force and bureaucracy (officialdom) that is common to *all* bourgeois states, and substitute for this machine (5) not only a mass organization, but a universal organization of the entire armed people.'

Lenin's attitude to the Provisional Government was restated in numerous pronouncements and letters to friends during the next few days. 'Not a shadow of confidence in or support for the government of Guchkov-Milyukov and Co.,' he told Hanecki-Fürstenberg. To Lunacharsky, he wrote: 'Independence and separateness of our Party, *no rapprochement with other parties,* are indispensable conditions for me. Without this one cannot help the proletariat to move through the *democratic* revolution to the *commune,* and I would not serve any other ends.'

He reiterated his complete mistrust of the Provisional Government, began to clarify relations with the Swiss socialists, and found that more money than expected had arrived from Sweden to finance him and his colleagues on their journey to Russia. Some of it had almost certainly been siphoned off from Germany by those only too anxious to help Lenin on his way.

On 6 April, as he was completing arrangements for his return to Russia, the USA declared war on Germany, an event which transformed the military situation on the Western Front and, by implication, the prospects for the Russian armies fighting the Central Powers elsewhere. It also brought the future of the Provisional Government, and any government which might succeed it, beneath the eyes of yet another power; anything that happened in Russia would now come under the close scrutiny not only of Britain, France and Italy but of the potentially decisive American Government.

On 8 April Lenin's farewell letter to Swiss workers, which he had completed a few days earlier, was discussed and approved at a meeting in Zurich of Russians soon to be heading home. 'We are not pacifists,' he said in a significant paragraph. 'We are opposed to imperialist wars over the division of spoils among the capitalists, but we have always considered it absurd for the revolutionary proletariat to disavow revolutionary wars that *may* prove necessary *in the interests of Socialism'* Lenin had previously agreed to lecture on the Paris Commune of 1870 in La Chaux-de-Fonds and once there he added a postscript to his paper entitled 'Will the Russian Revolution follow the Path of the Paris Commune?' More important was a two-and-a-half-hour lecture on 'The Tasks of the RSDLP in the Russian Revolution' given to Swiss workers in the Zurich Volkshaus.

Once the last details had been settled, Lenin was anxious to be on his way. 'We had just these two hours to liquidate our entire "household" ,' Krupskaya has written, 'settle accounts with the landlady, return the books to the library, pack up, and so on.' As he said goodbye to his tenants, Herr Kammerer hoped 'that in Russia you won't have to work as hard as here'. To this kindly thought Lenin replied with a masterpiece of understatement: 'I think, Herr Kammerer, that in Petrograd I shall have even more work.' The good landlord replied: 'You'll never write more than you've written here,' and hoped that his departing guest would get a room easily in Petrograd. Lenin said he thought that would be possible and added: 'But I don't know that it'll be as peaceful as it is here with you.' Shortly afterwards, before he left Herr Kammerer's house for good, he received an encouraging telegram from Perm in eastern Russia. It was signed by Stalin, Muranov and Kamenev and said that all three were leaving for Petrograd.

On the morning of 9 April Lenin and his wife gathered with

about thirty others soon after 11 a.m. at the Zahringerhof, a small Zurich inn. Among those in the party who had had close relations with Lenin were Martov; Akselrod; Lunacharsky, who had become a devoted helper in Switzerland; Angelica Balabanov who had played such an important role in the Zimmerwald movement; the Zinovievs with their four-year-old son Stefan; Karl Radek, the Austro-Hungarian Jew, 'a little, light-haired, spectacled, revolutionary goblin of incredible intelligence and vivacity', who served Lenin so well in propaganda work after the Revolution; and, almost inevitably, Inessa Armand whom Lenin included in the group on either personal or professional grounds. While they were eating, Count von Romberg in Berne remembered one point which had been overlooked by both Lenin and Platten: as the travellers would be passing through Sweden they would all need Swedish visas. Von Romberg telegraphed the German Foreign Office and permission was received from the Swedes just in time to avoid any delays.

At 2.30 p.m. they moved off to the nearby railway station, an unexceptional-looking group of men, women and children – revolutionaries wearing conventional bowler hats, ties and waistcoats, and distinguished from other travellers only by the large amount of luggage they were carrying. Nineteen of the adults were Bolsheviks, six were members of the Bund and three had been workers on Nashe Stove (*Our Word*). Menshevik-Trotskyite paper published in Parts. Osear Blum, later the author of *The Brains of the Russian Revalution* (Berlin,1923) tried to join the party but was personally thrown off the train by Lenin who appears to have believed rumours that he was a police agent.

Before the train drew our Stegfried Bloch, a Swiss acquaintance, commented to Lenin: "We hope that we shall see you back among us again,' to which Lenin replied that that would nor be a good political sign'.

The departure from Zurich was stormy, with cries from the crowd of 'Traitors!' and 'The Kaiser is paying for the journey.' The first part of the journey was to be made by the normal Swiss service, and it was only at Godmadingen, a small town near the frontier, that the travellers saw for the first time the new green German carriage with its three second-class compartments and five third-class, plus the baggage-wagon provided for the three pieces of hand luggage that each was allowed to take. Here the passengers, who had been given numbered slips by Fritz Platten, filed into the train, the women and children into the second-class compartments with their upholstered seats, the men into the third-class with wooden benches. Three of the carriage's four doors were sealed: the fourth, next to which sat the two German officers accompanying the party, was left open, while a chalk mark on the floor separated the Russian from the German part of the carriage. The doors were closed and Platten wrote 'sealed' on them in German, the word that gave the train its sobriquet in history. When the frontier was reached the Germans passed through beer and sandwiches, an augury of what was to come since while crossing Germany the travellers were given lavish helpings of food, no doubt to suggest that even after two and a half years of war Germany was not as badly off as they might have been led to expect. Not everyone was satisfied and Grigory Sokolnikov, one of the emigrants, had a different story, later claiming that they travelled 'On an empty stomach – on principle we had decided to refuse the watery soup to which the German Red Cross was ready to treat us'.

Once the journey across Germany began, certain mundane problems had to be settled. One concerned smoking and it was eventually agreed that it should be allowed only in the lavatory. It was also decided, in the face of some protests, that there should be no singing of French or anti-German songs. One woman member of the party had a particularly loud laugh that was kept within limits only by constant persuasion. These and other matters were arranged smoothly and as Lenin was later to point out, the Germans carried out their part of the bargain fairly and with a measure of goodwill.

The only disagreeable incident took place in Stuttgart where Platten was called out of the carriage and told by the escorting officer that Mr Janson, a German trade union leader, wanted to talk with him. 'Our meeting was extraordinarily unpleasant,' Platten wrote. 'Janson asked me to give the travelling comrades the compliments of the General Commission of the German Trade Unions . . . The returning émigrés held a short consultation and decided that if Janson tried to violate their exterritoriality they would just throw him out of the carriage.'

The overall behaviour of the German authorities during the journey accorded with their hope that the potential revolutionaries would help weaken resistance to the German forces. As part of the plan the officials who had stage-managed the operation were informed from Berlin on 12 April that: 'His Majesty the Kaiser suggested at breakfast today that the Russian Socialists travelling through Germany should be given White Books and other literature, such as copies of the Easter Message and of the Chancellor's speech, so that they may be able to enlighten others in their own country.' If the message showed anything other than perseverance, it was how little the Kaiser appreciated the character and intensity of the ideas he was now letting through his own country to pursue their destiny in Russia.

But his message had a second suggestion which shows how

highly the German authorities rated Lenin's potential for trouble-making. '2. In the event of the Russians being refused entry into Sweden,' it said, 'the High Command of the Army would be prepared to get them into Russia through the German lines.

'3. The High Command of the Army would also be prepared to get those Russians who are still in Switzerland into Russia through our lines.'

There was no refusal from the Swedes. There were, however, a number of hitches in Germany itself, one of which leaves a further question mark hanging over Lenin's relations with the Germans even today. At Halle two railway timings apparently crossed, but it was the German Crown Prince's train which was held up for nearly two hours to let the Russians' train through. Then the 'sealed train' missed its planned connection in Frankfurt, apparently due to the movement of troops to the Western Front, and the passengers had to spend the night in a room on Frankfurt station. This altered Lenin's formal position, although only in a technical sense: the train had been granted extra-territorial status and as long as Lenin kept aboard it he could claim that he had not set foot in Germany. Outside the train carriage, however, the position was different. Perhaps more importantly, there was a consequent disruption to plans for the following day. The party reached Berlin without further difficulty but then had to wait about twenty hours before continuing the journey to Sassnitz on the Baltic coast. At one of the halts in Germany two members of the German Social-Democratic Party tried to get on the train and greet Lenin. According to Sokolnikov, they were told either to go away or be thrown out. 'This ultimatum', he later wrote, 'was presented by Lenin without any rhetorical courtesy and had the desired effect.'

There is no evidence that Lenin met any Government officials in Germany, but in the circumstances there is little reason to think that any such evidence would have survived. He had already made clear that he would be willing to use any allies to help gain his objective – revolutionary success in Russia – and he stated this again in the coming crucial months. In addition, it is notable that at some time between leaving Switzerland and arriving in Russia a subtle change took place in his plans. To start with, the situation was seen merely as a preparation for the seizing of revolutionary power in the, possibly distant, future; by the time he arrived in Petrograd Lenin saw this as a more immediate objective. The revolutionary timetable had been speeded up, and the possibility that this had happened through some encouragement on the journey across Germany cannot be ruled out, and would have been viewed as acceptable by both sides. This is not to suggest that the cries of 'treason' later raised against Lenin by his enemies were justified; for him, now as in the future, the greatest treason would have been to hinder the great changes with which he planned to transform Russia, Europe, and in due course the world.

On 11 April the Russians continued north in the German carriage, which late in the day rumbled across the metal bridge linking the island of Rügen to the rest of Germany and brought them to Sassnitz. Here they boarded the Swedish ferry, giving false names which were accepted without comment. As Lenin stood on deck during the start of the choppy crossing to the Swedish coast, he was splashed by a wave. 'The first revolutionary wave from the shores of Russia,' commented a colleague.

For Lenin it marked an end to diversions, a concentration even more vigorous than before, on the great tasks waiting to be undertaken. The walks in the sub-alpine woods, the leisurely physical breaks when the mind could go racing on while the mountains rose up as a splendid back-drop, were to be delights of the past, a part of life that he would not regain during the momentous years that lay ahead. Since his youth he had fought for a place at the sharp end of the battle: now he was moving swiftly towards it. Like Lincoln before him at Gettysburg, Lenin had stepped on to the escalator of history from which only bad luck could remove him. And Lenin, like Napoleon's successful marshals, was lucky.

They arrived in Stockholm at 10 a.m., Lenin dressed, as one Swedish socialist remarked, 'like a workman on a Sunday excursion in unsettled weather'. He was greeted by the Mayor, Carl Lindhagen, and Frederik Strom and Tøre Nerman, two Swedes he had met at Zimmerwald. He was then taken to the Hotel Regina for a meal after which Lindhagen gave an address on 'Ex oriente lux'. In Stockholm he was persuaded to buy replacements for the old trousers and heavily studded mountaineering boots which had so far sufficed for the journey. 'I'm not opening a clothesshop in Petrograd,' had been his first reaction to the suggestion that it would create a bad impression if he entered Russia too shabbily dressed. Before leaving, he appealed to the Swedes for funds for the cause. According to one report the Swedish Foreign Minister responded with the words: 'Gladly, as long as [Lenin] leaves today.' He was then ready for some busy hours during which he met Swedish Social-Democrats and set up a bureau of the RSDLP Abroad headed by Radek, who was not to be allowed into Russia with the rest of the party. He also arranged for any cash that could be collected to be passed on to him in Petrograd by whatever means were possible, and tried to ensure that he would have an open line of communication with Stockholm whatever happened in the months ahead.

He would have to move carefully, not only in respect of his relations with the Provisional Government but in his attitude to such figures as Helphand, who two years earlier had sought him out in Switzerland, and who now tried to meet him in Stockholm. Lenin not only refused but arranged for three Bolsheviks in the city – one of them Radek, newly appointed to the Bolshevik Foreign Mission in Sweden – to record his refusal in writing. The complexity of the situation that had developed by this time is shown in that the following day Radek met Helphand while the day after that Helphand travelled to Denmark where he met the German Minister to Denmark, Count Brockdorff-Rantzau. Although details are still unclear it is virtually certain that Helphand now hardened up the arrangements by which money obtained in Germany from his business interests by the sale of surgical instruments, chemicals and medicines, was channelled into Bolshevik funds in Russia. Just how much money was involved is unknown but the sum of 50 million gold marks has been suggested and in September 1917 an official of the German Foreign Office at General Headquarters wrote:

'We have now been engaged in these activities [support of revolutionary forces] for some time, and in complete agreement with the Political Section of the General Staff in Berlin. Our work together has shown tangible results. The Bolshevik movement could never have attained the scale or the influence which it has today without our continual support.'

Lenin is unlikely to have been aware of the mechanics by which German money was channelled into Bolshevik funds by

Helphand – and others – and he will not have been aware of the message received by the political section of the German General Staff soon after his arrival back in Russia – 'Lenin's entry into Russia successful. He is working exactly as we would wish.' Nevertheless, it is difficult to believe that he was unaware of the source which kept the Party afloat in desperate financial times and it would be unwise to believe that he did not appreciate how the Germans were helping not only his revolutionary aims but their own military ambitions.

A potential difficulty failed to develop in Stockholm although Lenin may not at the time have known of the possibility. He had been correct in his belief that Allied efforts would be made to prevent his return to Russia and the British Minister in Stockholm, Sir Esmé Howard (later Lord Howard of Penrith) has written:

> '. . . for a hectic moment the Allied Ministers discussed whether they could not, with the help, naturally, of the Swedish authorities, hold up the arch-revolutionary on the way through. But the plan seemed impossible. It looked as if it might make the situation worse. Indeed, so far had the Revolution gone in Russia by that time that it appeared wiser to let things take their course rather than interfere in matters of which we were then practically ignorant.'

Howard was an experienced diplomat who had a long record of successes before being posted to Stockholm in 1913. From this neutral vantage point between Germany and the Allies he had become the confidant of many European figures and seemed the ideal person to encourage the Swedes to make whatever moves the Western Allies believed would be useful.

But Sir Esmé's diplomatic discretion forbade him to put details publicly on paper and all that is certain is the failure of any efforts to hinder Lenin's progress.

Although the crucial part of the journey, the miles across Germany, had been accomplished without major hitch, there could still be problems. There remained the 600 miles to the Swedish frontier with Finland, the journey south through Finland and then, the crux, Lenin's reception at the Russian frontier where his opposition to the Provisional Government was common knowledge.

He and his party travelled without incident through Sweden, up the western side of the Gulf of Bothnia and then down the east. Shortly before they reached the Swedish frontier – on 15 April (2 April) – they received news that two RSDLP members, Tseretelli and Skobelev, as well as Chernov, a Socialist Revolutionary, had joined the Provisional Government, developments that provided argument for the rest of the journey.

As they were approaching the frontier someone handed Balabanov a stick and a red scarf on which she stitched the message: 'Long live Zimmerwald. Long live the Russian Revolution.' But the message was probably wasted since they reached the frontier town of Tornio at night. The river there was frozen and the Russians crossed it in a long ribbon of horse-drawn sledges, two passengers to each sledge. There was considerable tension as they neared the frontier and only Lenin appeared outwardly calm. 'He was most of all interested', Zinoviev has written, 'in what was happening in far-off Petersburg.' And once on the Russian side of the frontier he cabled to his sisters Maria and Anna: 'Arriving Monday 11 p.m. Inform "Pravda".' It is doubtful that Lenin's faith in his destiny faltered even during the final approach down the line to Russia, but at one point he turned to Kamenev and asked: 'Are we going to be arrested in Petersburg?'

There was no real trouble at the frontier although British guards cooperating with the Swedes who controlled entries into Russia by this route, refused to let Fritz Platten cross the border. He returned to Switzerland, founded the Swiss Communist Party in 1918 and later visited Lenin in Moscow, being present at the inaugural meeting of the Comintern in 1919.

Any fears that Lenin may have had about his reception in Russia vanished as the train steamed into Petrograd's Finland Station. A supporter wrote:

> 'At last the three blindingly bright lights of the locomotive rushed by us and behind it the lighted windows of the carriages began to twinkle – more and more gently and slowly. The train stopped, and at once we perceived, over the crowd of workers, the figure of Comrade Lenin. Lifting Ilyich high above their heads the Sestroretsk workers conducted him into the station hall.'

Hindsight at first suggests that the Provisional Government's failure to prevent Lenin from getting his grip on the crowds from the moment of arrival was a grave mistake of tactics; in fact it was no more than an indication that even now the Government's influence was patchy and irresolute compared with that which Lenin's charisma could exercise almost whenever he wished. There were times when he failed but not many.

At the Finland Station he had Bolshevik organization, and the date, in his favour. The Bolsheviks had been distributing leaflets saying 'Lenin arrives today. Meet him', and it had been easy to do this since it was Easter Monday and all the factories were closed. Large crowds had gathered during the early evening and the arrival platform was packed with people. Banners had been hung across it and triumphal arches set up. A score of welcoming inscriptions and revolutionary slogans could be seen, while at the end of the platform, where the carriage was expected to stop, there was a band and a group of Bolsheviks including Aleksandra Kollontay who carried a bouquet from the Soviet Executive Committee. But the train was very late, the flowers were wilting and she forgot her speech of welcome and had to be pushed forward by Shlyapnikov who said: 'If you're not going to make a speech, do at least kiss Ilich.'

The band had not had time to learn the 'Internationale' so it was the 'Marseillaise' that its members struck up as Lenin stepped down. (Krupskaya commented that all her husband wanted was a cup of tea.) A guard of honour presented arms, adding a further military gloss to a scene that included a squad of sailors and a number of military cars, one of which carried a searchlight. Lenin took it all in his stride, waiting until the roar of welcome had died down, and then answering Ensign Maksimov, the depot commander who in the ensuing silence asked him to say a few words. Standing on a chair, wearing an old grey coat and a peaked worker's cap, he left no doubt as to what his attitude was to be.

He was formally welcomed by Chkheidze, the Menshevik chairman of the Petrograd Soviet, but pointedly ignored him and replied, instead, to the assembled soldiers, sailors and workers.

'Sailors, comrades, as I greet you, I still don't know whether you have faith in all the promises of the Provisional

Government. What I know for certain, though, is that when sweet promises are made, you are being deceived in the same way that the entire Russian people are being deceived . . . Sailors, comrades, we have to fight for a socialist revolution, to fight until the proletariat wins full victory! Long live the worldwide socialist revolution!'

There are different versions of this first – virtually extemporary – exposition of Lenin's views on his return and according to N. N. Sukhanov, a reliable non-Bolshevik reporter, he stressed even at this early stage the international implication of events, maintaining:

'The piratical imperialist war is the beginning of civil war throughout Europe . . . The hour is not far distant when at the call of our comrade, Karl Liebknecht, the peoples will turn their arms against their own capitalist exploiters . . . The world-wide Socialist revolution has already dawned . . . Germany is seething . . . Any day now the whole of European capitalism may crash . . .'

It was what the crowd wanted to hear, and it was only on the top of an armoured car, which forced its way through the throng, that Lenin was able to leave the station. He was driven to the white brick Kzhezinskaya Mansion, once the home of a ballerina who had been one of the Tsar's mistresses. Here he took supper with sixty prominent local Bolsheviks. And here, speaking in one of the huge ground-floor rooms, its massive plateglass windows covered with velvet curtains, he stressed the need for the Soviets to seize power now. Although he had not arrived in the city until 11 p.m., he spoke for two hours, leaving no doubt that if the Provisional Government tried to make permanent the half-hearted version of the Revolution they had introduced, then forceful opposition would result. As far as Lenin was concerned there would be no support for the Provisional Government, no support for any continuation of the war.

That within a few hours of his arrival Lenin made plain the overthrow he intended is clear from two comments on this warning for the future that he issued from the Kzhezinskaya Mansion. 'I shall never forget that thunderlike speech which startled and amazed not only me, a heretic who had accidentally dropped in, but all the true believers,' Sukhanov wrote. 'I am certain that no one had expected anything of the sort.' Trotsky was even more to the point: 'The fundamental impression made by Lenin's speech even among those nearest him was one of fright,' he was later to write. 'All the accepted formulas, which with innumerable repetition had acquired in the course of a month a seemingly unshakeable permanence, were exploded one after another before the eyes of that audience.'

It was not only Lenin's defiant claim that the Revolution which had destroyed the Tsar was a beginning rather than an end that augured stormy days ahead. He had known that supping with the Germans required a long spoon but had nevertheless misjudged the length needed. His mistake became evident the morning after his arrival in Petrograd. Ensign Maksimov, who had welcomed him at the Finland Station, then issued a letter disowning his own speech. It contained a resolution passed by the sailors of the Baltic fleet saying:

'Having learnt that Comrade Lenin came back to us in Russia with the consent of His Majesty the German Emperor and King of Prussia [sic], we express our profound regret at our participation in his triumphal welcome to Petersburg. If we had known by what paths he had returned to us, then instead of the enthusiastic cries of "Hurrah", exclamations of indignation would have resounded: "Away with you, back to the country you passed through to us!" '

The Man Revealed

9

Preparing the Ground

Lenin had arrived in the promised land. Whether his expectations would be fulfilled seemed uncertain in the chaotic Petrograd of April 1917; uncertainty was in fact one of the few elements which suffused almost every aspect of the situation. The Provisional Government was dedicated to continuing the war that had been carried on under the Tsar for nearly three years, albeit on a more efficient basis than had so far been the case; yet the Russians appeared to be increasingly at the mercy of the Germans, and a question mark hung ominously over their military future. There were, moreover, the miseries of the civilian population, becoming ever more short of food and ever more appalled at the battle casualties which were wrecking the lives of so many families. In this situation the Government found it difficult to maintain its authority with the necessary assurance – particularly in the face of growing opposition from the Petrograd Soviet and from the Soviet's allies among the country's other left-wing forces, most of whom believed that the time had now come to end the war, whatever the consequences.

The Soviet, for its part, was faced with the delicate task of campaigning for a peace that would inevitably mean appealing to the Germans – the hated enemy. If the situation helped anyone it was, contrarywise, the military right-wing groups, which called for a fiercer war. In the summer they coalesced round the figure of General L. G. Kornilov, the colourful Commander of the Petrograd Military District who became Commanderin-Chief of the South-Western Front in July, then Supreme Commander, and who, before the summer was out, led an abortive coup whose failure played its part in bringing Lenin to power.

There was also the joker in the pack – the Bolshevik Party. At the time of the Tsar's abdication it had been insignificant in size and not much larger in influence, and was still of relatively little importance when Lenin arrived at the Finland Station. Its influence was further reduced as it became possible to associate its members with collaboration with the Germans – as the train journey from Switzerland could so easily be represented. But the Bolsheviks were not negligible and they grew in importance during the spring and summer of 1917 – although with intermittent setbacks – largely as a result of the way in which Lenin played on the emotions of the population and the skill with which he seized and utilized every circumstance which chance threw his way. He had, of course, one great advantage: since August 1914 he had argued that the war should be ended; he had side-stepped the problems of Russo-German rivalry, had declared that the only acceptable war would be one in which the peoples of both countries combined forces against their capitalist oppressors, and had campaigned for his belief in print and speech with a whole-heartedness that even his strongest opponents had to concede. Only the Bolsheviks, Lenin now maintained, could stop the blood-letting.

The ending of the war thus became the main plank in the platform on which he built up his forces from April 1917. It was strengthened by his stand at Zimmerwald even though his anti-war resolution there had been so whittled down as to be, in his opinion, almost meaningless. 'The Zimmerwald morass', he was soon declaiming, 'must no longer be tolerated. There can be no question of maintaining half-hearted connections with the chauvinist International of Plekhanov, Scheidemann and co. for the sake of the Zimmerwald "Kautskyites". We must immediately break with this International. We should remain with Zimmerwald *only* for purpose of information.'

But in such anti-war declarations he was now to be handicapped by the repercussions of the journey through Germany and, moreover, by the blind spot resulting from his belief that in the battle for revolution all possible means could be used without excuse – a weakness that prevented him from seeing the use his enemies could make of the journey. The reception at the Finland Station had been too encouraging for his own good, since it gave him no indication of the ambivalent feelings which split even the more revolutionary among the populace and which continued to do so throughout the next few months as he struggled to increase the influence of the Bolsheviks and particularly of himself.

The first repercussion of the 'sealed train' journey was the issue, early on the morning following Lenin's arrival, of the statement from Ensign Maksimov. The next warning came later in the month when soldiers in the Fourth Motor Ambulance Unit made an appeal, published in *Malenkaya Gazeta* (the *Little Newspaper*) of 14 April, 'demanding an investigation into the circumstances connected with the passage through Germany of Lenin and others'. His enemies made the most of it, helped by the fact that although Lenin could in no sense be fairly accused of treason, it was undeniable that much of his work aided not only the cause of revolution but also German hopes of eliminating that nightmare of its High Command, a war on two fronts.

But it was not only in Russia that Lenin's concentration on ending the war – for his own reasons rather than the Germans'– produced unexpected reactions. In Britain it was understandable that any chance of diminishing Russia's contribution to the Allied war effort should be considered with dismay by the Government. But the dismay was felt outside it and the attitude of Ramsay MacDonald was very different from what many might have expected. Recording his thoughts on Lenin's return to Russia, MacDonald considered that a separate peace with Germany would be a disaster. It is true that his comment, 'The great service which the Russian Revolution could render to Europe was to have brought about an understanding between the German Democracy and that of the Allied countries' had echoes of Lenin's beliefs, but the first draft of a letter to Kerensky in his papers leaves no doubt of his reaction to Lenin's dominant idea. 'Mere emotional pacifism is of no use,' it said; 'a separate peace between Russia and Germany would only leave Europe more helpless than it now is in the hands of evil doers.' This was no passing fancy and some weeks later Lord Robert Cecil, telling the Prime Minister of MacDonald's plans for meeting Kerensky, reported: 'He said that he regarded a separate peace with absolute horror, as it would mean the destruction of every thing he cared for in Europe, and he would do his utmost to prevent the Russians taking any such step.'

In Petrograd in the summer of 1917, Lenin was handicapped by his recent isolation from most currents of European thought – in fact from virtually all except dedicated Marxist thought. His near-quarantine in Switzerland made it, specifically, more difficult for him to understand some Russian feelings. The demand for change had at last swept over the retaining barriers and carried away the Tsar, but there was still only a patchy demand for a Bolshevik revolution, the minimum with which Lenin would be satisfied. The continuing horrors of the war, the growing shortage of food, corruption in high places and the inefficiency that compounded the corruption, had taken huge numbers to where they were ready for the changes of the February upheavals, but for many the Tsar's abdication and the creation of the Provisional Government was almost sufficient. It was an advance, and thousands did not believe that further advantage would be gained from the entirely different *bouleversement* (total revolution) that Lenin was now advocating. The ending of the war would be generally welcomed but there was no certainty that Lenin's proposals would bring it about while the fresh chaos of a more drastic revolution appeared to be inescapable.

A similar insistence on going further was the main spur of another arrival – Trotsky reached Petrograd exactly four weeks after Lenin. He was now well known throughout Europe, but had tended to keep apart from Lenin's Bolsheviks, operating as an independent with a leaning towards the Mensheviks – possibly for this reason, he was not as well known in Russia as he might have been. He had stayed aloof from many factions and had not picked up, in the hurly-burly of survival, as much experience as Lenin and many of his colleagues. Now, however, he joined the Bolsheviks and, due to his exceptional ability, quickly climbed the Party ladder.

In two ways Trotsky's traits complemented Lenin's so that in their impact on the Revolution the combined influence of the two men was more than the sum of the individual parts. In contrast to Lenin's pragmatism Trotsky invariably showed a loyalty to dogmatic belief whose disadvantages could at times outweigh their benefits. However, during the postrevolutionary months and years this rigidity of outlook provided a sheetanchor of belief as comforting to dedicated revolutionaries as the unexpected appearance of a jug-handle hold before a rock-climber in a difficult place. To this moral resolve Trotsky brought a temperament more fiery than that of Lenin, an ability at least as great as Lenin's to move the crowd by speech or in writing, and a hatred of Russia's rulers which had been nurtured by spells in prison into a feeling as great as that produced in Lenin by the execution of his brother Aleksandr.

It was soon obvious that Trotsky's idea of the way ahead was very like Lenin's, although not identical with it. His reservations remained and it is significant that he supported the Organization of United International Social-Democrats for a while – the Mezrayonka or 'Inter district' group formed within the Bolshevik Party even though its members took issue with some of Lenin's ideas. Despite the group's adherence to the concept of a broadly based party, which Lenin had opposed so constantly and so vehemently in the earlier years of the century, he now not only tolerated its policies but accepted Trotsky into the bosom of the Party in spite of the differences which had previously separated the two men. He would put up with what he considered heresy as long as it contributed to the overall good of the Party and the prospects of a successful revolution.

In the summer of 1917 Trotsky was of particular use to Lenin since he had not been in contact with the Germans. Each successive crisis in the Bolsheviks' popularity ended in their favour until midsummer. Then, when the Provisional Government capitalized in earnest on the 'sealed train' episode and forced Lenin to flee the country, the situation changed and Bolshevik popularity suffered a severe drop. However, this was soon reversed when right-wing influences were felt; then the balance again began to turn in the Bolsheviks' favour, and helped prepare the way for the autumn Revolution that brought Lenin to power.

The success of the autumn Revolution makes it easy to lose sight of the strong feelings in some non-political areas against which Lenin had to fight once he got back into Petrograd. The journey across Germany impeded him when he emphasized the greatest attraction of his programme, the constant plea for peace; a comment from one soldier to another while both were listening to a Lenin anti-war speech seems to have reflected a not uncommon feeling among some troops: 'Ought to stick our bayonets into a fellow like that.' And Lenin's demand for an immediate full-scale revolution, stressed in his April Theses, even staggered many of the Bolsheviks, particularly when he put the demand forward at the All-Russian Conference of Bolsheviks held between 24 and 29 April.

Lenin's struggle for influence was fought out against a background that verged at times on the grotesque. In Petrograd, at the Hotel Europe, Jimmy from the New York Waldorf-Astoria still served cocktails. Karsavina still danced *Swan Lake* before rapturous audiences, and Chaliapin continued to delight his immaculately dressed listeners. Although food was becoming ever more scarce, most of the fashionable restaurants were not only open but flourishing. So were theatres and cabarets, even though demonstrations and counter-demonstrations frequently turned into riots outside them.

This was the city that set the stage for one of the greatest dramas of the twentieth century, one whose political complexities made understanding it difficult even for many Russians and almost impossible for most other Europeans. Luckily, at least three English-speaking writers or journalists of considerable ability were stationed in the Russian capital, and each provided not merely contemperar dispatches but later assessments of what they had seen and reported; from their impressions it is possible to build up a picture of Lenin's reactions to events during these crucial months of his life. The writers were an unusual trio: M. Philips Price of the *Manchester Guardian* who gained a world scoop by obtaining the texts of the secret treaties between the Allies before they were published by the new Russian Government; the American John Reed whose *Ten Days That Shook the World* with its detailed, if in some areas disputed, account of the Revolution, quickly became a classic of revolutionary reporting; and Arthur Ransome, later famous as the British children's writer but working in 1917 as correspondent for the London *Daily News*.

Confusion spread across the country from the spring onwards. In the provinces, however, the scene was so vast, the activities so complex, that some of the most illuminating accounts could come only from diplomats able to draw information from their networks of Russian staff or Russian journalists endeavouring to cover the complicated scene.

'All discipline has vanished in the army [wrote M. Paléologue, the French Ambassador]: officers are everywhere being insulted, ragged and – if they object – massacred. It is calculated that more than 1,200,000 deserters are wandering over Russia, filling the stations, storming the carriages, stopping the trains, and thus paralysing all the military and civil transport services. At junctions in particular they seem positively to swarm. A train arrives: they make its occupants get out, take their places, and compel the station-master to switch the train off in any direction they like. Or it may be a train laden with troops for the front. The men get out at some station, arrange a meeting, confer together for an hour or two, and wind up by demanding to be taken back to their starting-point.'

A similar view was common outside Russia, and from the British Foreign Office Lord Hardinge of Penshurst, the Permanent Under-Secretary, told Sir Esmé Howard in Stockholm:

'Attention is centred principally on Russia where events are following much too closely the course of the French Revolution. It looked at one moment as though the Extremists might get the upper hand, though the latest reports are rather more encouraging. In any case discipline in the Army has been seriously undermined and I am afraid that at the best Russia will have been put back several months.'

He then added two sentences which were to gain greater significance within a few months. 'Under pressure from the Provisional Government we have offered the Imperial Family asylum in this country. Whether the extreme faction in Petrograd will allow them to leave or not remains to be seen.'

The fact that law and order were breaking down was obvious not only to foreign observers but to men such as Nikolay N. Sukhanov, who has given his own graphic account of the situation, which steadily worsened as Lenin struggled towards power:

'Lynch-law, the destruction of houses and shops, jeering at and attacks on officers, provincial authorities, or private persons, unauthorized arrests, seizures and beatings-up

– were recorded every day by tens and hundreds [he wrote]. In the country burnings and destruction of country-houses became more frequent . . . Quite a few excesses were also observed amongst the workers – against factory administration, owners, and foremen . . . There were masses of deserters both in the rear and at the front. The soldiers, without leave, went off home in great floods. They filled all the trains, hectored the administration, kicked out the passengers, and threatened the entire transport system with catastrophe . . . In the cities they blighted the trams and boulevards, and filled all the public places.'

As chaos grew, Lenin had to deal carefully with the situation that developed between the Government, the Soviet, and the as-yet-uncommitted population: he needed to gain support from the maximum number while offending as few as possible. At the same time he tried to fit in a variety of the personal and family tasks which he rarely evaded. The juxtaposition of personal and public duties was illustrated on the day following his arrival in Petrograd. First he visited the graves of his mother, who had died in July 1916, and his sister Olga, demonstrating the family affections he felt strongly all his life. 'Always calm, always in complete control of himself, Vladimir Ilyich never, especially in the presence of other people, disclosed the depth and intimacy of his feelings,' wrote Bonch-Bruyevich. 'But all of us knew how tender and affectionate he felt towards his mother and knowing this we realized that the path leading to the little mound in the Volkov Cemetery was one of the most difficult roads he trod.'

Then he prepared for the Executive Committee of the Petrograd Soviet a report on 'How We Arrived', obviously written to counter the criticism that he had been working hand-in-glove with the German authorities. He delivered the first of two speeches on 'The Tasks of the Revolution' made the same day in the Tauride Palace – now being used not only by the Provisional Government and the Soviet but by many of the groups which sprang up almost spontaneously in the wake of the Revolution – the first to a meeting of the Bolsheviks, the second to a joint meeting of the Bolshevik and Menshevik delegates to the All-Russian Conference of Soviets of Workers', Soldiers' and Peasants' Deputies. Several typed copies of the speech were handed out before and during the joint meeting and served as the original draft of some of the resolutions passed.

'Lenin was a hopeless failure with the *Soviet* yesterday,' Paléologue was told by Milyukov, the Provisional Government's Foreign Minister. 'He argued the pacifist cause so heatedly, and with such effrontery and lack of tact, that he was compelled to stop and leave the room amidst a storm of booing. He will never survive it.' Milyukov was, of course, no unbiased observer, but the fuller account given in his reminiscences seems to have been a fair report.

'Even the Bolsheviks declared that they considered Lenin's civil war slogan a transgression [he wrote]. [Yuri] Steklov [a prominent member of the Petrograd Soviet and later editor of *Izvestia*] explained Lenin's speech as a product of Lenin's unfamiliarity with the Russian scene. Alexandra Kollontai was the only one who, amid stormy protests, defended Lenin and rejected the idea of unifying all Social Democrats, proposing instead the union of only those who were able to carry out an immediate social revolution. The rest of the speakers were for general unity, and one of them even claimed that Lenin's speech had effected the union of Bolsheviks and Mensheviks.'

If this claim was pitching matters far higher than the facts justified, the opposition Lenin aroused during his first days in Petrograd among the potentially faithful was greater than was to be easily remembered after his final revolutionary success. His old opponent Bogdanov, who had returned to Russia in 1913, served as a doctor with the army in the war, and then supported the Bolsheviks – although with many reservations – went so far as to say: 'It's obscene to applaud such rubbish! These are the ravings of a lunatic!' And four days after the arrival at the Finland Station *Pravda,* then edited by Kamenev, printed a summary of the proposals as revealed in Lenin's statements of the preceding few days and commented in an editorial: 'As far as the general scheme of Lenin is concerned it seems to us unacceptable. Lenin takes it for granted that the bourgeois democratic Revolution is at an end and believes that an immediate transformation of our Revolution into the Socialist one is possible: we profoundly disagree with him.'

The abolition of the police, the army and the bureaucracy – which were all called for – as well as the formal confiscation of all landed estates and the nationalization of banks, were all measures which large numbers of the population supported in theory. Yet the men and women listening to such proposals being put forward by Lenin were well aware of the upheavals in civilian life, not to say the chaos, that would almost inevitably follow unless such measures were brought in carefully and slowly. The dangers hung in the balance with the possibility of peace, which was, and continued to remain, the great attraction of Lenin's proposals.

Throughout the next few weeks, and indeed, until the summer, he continued, undismayed, to preach the same objectives in a succession of papers and speeches which slowly but steadily began to have their effect. It may have been partly a case of the constant dripping that wears away a stone, partly the result of what could be seen as the logic of his statements, and his personal persuasiveness. For whatever reasons, Lenin's influence began to win him reluctant adherents, and Paléologue commented in his diary, only three days after reporting the bad impression Lenin had made: 'Lenin's influence seems to have been increasing greatly in the last few days. One point of which there can be no doubt is that he has already gathered round him, or under his orders, all the hotheads of the revolution; he is now established as a strong leader . . .'

His ability to deal with the problems of everyday life that stumped many ordinary people no doubt helped, for in Lenin the practical man was rarely far from the visionary. His chauffeur, Stepan, is quoted by Maxim Gorky as saying:

'Lenin is quite unique. There are no others like him. Once I was driving him along Myasnitskaya Street when the traffic was very heavy. I hardly moved forward. I was afraid of the car getting smashed and was sounding the horn, feeling very worried. He opened the door, reached me by standing on the footboard, meanwhile running the risk of being knocked down, and urged me to go forward. "Don't get worried Gil, go on like everyone else." I am an old chauffeur. I know that nobody else would do that.'

Lenin's political strength was produced to a great extent by the sincerity of his anti-war attitude and by his oratorical ability in making his sincerity felt. It was evident on 10 April [23 April] 1917 when he spoke to soldiers of the Izmailovsky regiment. The Provisional Government, he stated, was continuing the war in the interests of the capitalists, whereas a government of the Soviets of Workers', Soldiers' and Peasants' Deputies would redistribute the land and remove the incentive for war. He went on: 'Do not allow the police to be re-established, do not let the state power or the administration of the state pass into the hands of the bureaucracy, who are non-elective, undisplaceable, and paid on a bourgeois scale; get together, unite, organize yourselves, trusting no one, depending only on your own intelligence and experience – and Russia will be able to move with a firm, measured, unerring tread toward the liberation of both our own country and of all humanity from the yoke of capital as well as from the horrors of war.'

Admitting that Lenin was successfully finding his feet amid the chaos of post-February Petrograd, Paléologue was almost clinically accurate in his view of the man he now saw as reaching up towards power. In fact the description in the Ambassador's diary for 21 April was an accurate reflection of the impression that Lenin made on much of the foreign community during the spring and summer of 1917.

'Lenin, Utopian dreamer and fanatic, prophet and metaphysician, blind to any idea of the impossible or the absurd, a stranger to all feelings of justice or mercy, violent, machiavellian and crazy with vanity, places at the service of his messianic visions a strong unemotional will, pitiless logic and amazing powers of persuasion and command [he wrote]. Judging by the reports I have received of his first speeches, he is insisting on the revolutionary dictatorship of the working and rural masses; he is preaching that the proletariat has no country and proclaiming his longing for the defeat of the Russian armies. When anyone attacks his crude fancies with some argument drawn from the realm of reality, he replies with the gorgeous phrase: "So much the worse for reality!" . . . The man is all the more dangerous because he is said to be pure-minded, temperate and ascetic. Such as I see him in my mind's eye, he is a compound of Savonarola and Marat, Blanqui and Bakunin.'

Although Lenin's growing influence became quickly apparent to those in Petrograd, it was recognized more slowly by his enemies in England, France and the USA who had no personal contact with him. Yet it was an Englishman, C. R. M. F. Cruttwell (whose *A History of the Great War* has become a classic) who was to give one of the most perceptive explanations of Lenin's success during the first vital months following his return to Russia:

> '[His] extraordinary power of unwavering concentration was not merely applied to the idealization of Marxian material-ism, but to thinking out all the appropriate means for achieving the desired practical end. The uniqueness of Lenin among revolutionaries lay in his brilliant combination of the roles of fanatic and staff officer. Bolshevism has often been compared to a new militant religion, and Lenin's closest parallel can probably be found among the great organizing captains of religion such as Mahomet or (a more exact paral-lel) Ignatius Loyola. His accurate knowledge, his orderly method, his pitiless logic, helped to secure him ascendancy over his countrymen, among whom such qualities were rare.'

Lenin's ascendancy was increased by one specific factor

which became important during the summer of 1917. Compared with the divided counsels and allegiances of those who supported the Provisional Government, and with the different beliefs and loyalties of those forming the Government, Lenin could present a concentrated plan for action to the public. This gave him a superiority in meetings, conventions and assemblies of the various soviets which met in Petrograd in the aftermath of the February Revolution. Most of those attending were men and women who had never before exercised power; they were full of goodwill but frequently ignorant of the ways in which political power operated, and they tended to be vulnerable to the simple straightforward propositions that Lenin so expertly presented.

How he operated has been well described by M. Philips Price in his report of the First All-Russian Soviet Congress:

'There now arose from an obscure corner of the room a thick-set little man with a round bald head and small Tartar eyes. He was leading a small group of delegates who had set themselves down on the extreme left and at the back of the hall. Nobody seemed to pay much attention to the corner where they sat, for there was a general impression that here had congregated the extremists, irreconcilables and faddists of all types, who were forming a little "cave of Adullam". But as soon as this short, thick-set little man rose and strode with firm step, and even firmer look upon his countenance, up the gangway, where sat the serried ranks of the "Revolutionary Democracy", a hush came upon the whole assembly. For it was Lenin, the leader of that small, insignificant Bolshevik minority at this First All-Russian Soviet Congress. No uncertain words came from his lips. Straight

330

to the point he went from the first moment of his speech and pursued his opponents with merciless logic. "Where are we?" he began, stretching out his short arms and looking questioningly at his audience. "What is this Council of Workers' and Soldiers' Delegates? Is there anything like it in the world? No, of course not, because nothing so absurd as this exists in any country today except in Russia. Then let us have either one of two things: either a bourgeois Government with its plans of so-called social reforms on paper, such as exists in every other country now, or let us have that Government which *you* (pointing to Tseretelli) seem to long for, but which you apparently have not the courage to bring into existence, a Government of the proletariat which has its historic parallel in 1792 in France." '

Lenin's ability to catch and hold his audience was admired not only by 'outsiders' such as Philips Price but by Russian spellbinders like Trotsky himself. As important as Lenin's seductive platform performance was his correct appreciation that the dominant feeling in the Russia of 1917 was opposition to the war, to which even dislike of the Tsar and hunger for land were subordinate. Since the birth of his political consciousness he had seen war as an instrument of capitalist rule. Until 1914 it had been largely a debating-forum belief, of more use in arguing out the details of the class war than in considering the facts of everyday life. This had been changed in August 1914 and further as the huge casualty lists of 1915 and 1916 became longer, and as an end to the slaughter appeared less and less likely. To huge numbers of Russians the defeat of Germany had slowly but steadily begun to take second place to the end of the fighting. Hatred of Germany continued. So, of course, did the wish for

Russia's survival. But looming over all there was the growing desperation to end the war. It was the core of Lenin's April Theses, the core of his opposition to the Provisional Government, and the core of his claim that the Bolsheviks alone offered the only possibility of restoring peace and giving Russia the chance of rebuilding herself on the ruins of the past three years. What Lenin believed in was what the majority of the population wanted, however much they might disagree on how their aims could be achieved.

To these advantages there was added luck, often enhanced by the ineptitude of his enemies, men who frequently scored goals against their own side when even a little caution or common sense would have prevented trouble. With an adversary as able as Lenin, this was fatal.

All these factors played their part in producing Lenin's major triumph at the All-Russian Conference of Bolsheviks in Petrograd from 24 to 29 April, the first of its kind to be held legally. He was elected to the Presidium, opened the Conference, and before it closed was elected to the Party's Central Committee with more votes than anyone else. Within a few weeks of returning to Russia he became the unchallenged leader of the Party despite the handicap of the 'sealed train' journey and despite the fact that his extreme views were still unpopular, even among many who preached revolution.

In his speech he detailed future objectives:

'We are all agreed that power must be wielded by the Soviets of Workers' and Soldiers' Deputies . . . This would be a state of the Paris Commune type. Such power is a dictatorship, i.e. it rests not on law, not on the formal will of the majority, but on direct, open force. Force is the instrument of power.

332

How, then, will the Soviets apply this power? Will they return to the old way of governing by means of the police? Will they govern by means of the old organs of power? In my opinion they cannot do this. At any rate, they will be faced with the immediate task of creating a state that is not bourgeois. Among Bolsheviks, I have compared this state to the Paris Commune in the sense that the latter destroyed the old administrative organs and replaced them by absolutely new ones that were the direct organs of the workers.'

This Conference was important not just because it emphasized the prestige that Lenin had gained by this time but because it was presided over by Yakov Mikhailovich Sverdlov who became, in effect, the Central Committee's first General Secretary before the post was officially created. Sverdlov, who had reached Petrograd to attend the Conference after escaping from prison and riding 1,300 miles on horseback, became one of Lenin's most trusted supporters, both in the summer and autumn of 1917 which witnessed the prelude to power, and later after the autumn Revolution. While Lenin said that it would take six men to replace Sverdlov, Lunacharsky put it in more detail: 'Whereas Lenin and a few others provided the intellectual guidance for the Revolution, between them and the masses – the Party, the Soviet government apparatus and ultimately all Russia – like a spindle on which it all revolved, like a wire transmitting it all, stood Sverdlov.'

Lenin was also helped by his virtual control of *Pravda* although here money was a constant problem, and in April the paper had to appeal for 75,000 roubles. Nearly 30,000 roubles were raised within four days. Gorky contributed 3,000 but a lot of the money came in 5-copeck pieces which were collected from factories, counted by volunteers, many of them medical students, and then delivered to the banks.

However, there was another side to *Pravda's* popularity. The paper was sabotaged more than once by anti-Bolshevik groups, and when its main press was seized Lenin had to hire another. His sister Maria also recalled one occasion when he was warned that a hostile demonstration was being mounted outside the paper's offices. 'Accompanied by a soldier with a rifle,' she said, 'Vladimir Il'ich left the office in a cab and went to an acquaintance's flat.' Apart from such opposition, *Pravda* now had competition from *Izvestia*, the daily paper of the Petrograd Soviet which had been started immediately after the Soviet's birth in February. With the creation of the Soviet's All-Russian Executive Committee it also became the organ of that body and was thus controlled by Mensheviks and Social Revolutionaries until Lenin took over in the autumn when it became the official organ of the new Bolshevik Government.

During the months following his return, Lenin and his Party enjoyed a popularity that fluctuated in various sectors of the civilian and military population, different parts of Petrograd, and almost from day to day as other factors in the political situation changed like the patterns in a kaleidoscope. Throughout the period Party membership continued to grow. In April 1917 it had been 80,000 but by August had risen to 240,000. If these figures seem small in view of Russia's population it should be noted that even by March 1918, four months after the successful Revolution, membership had only reached 270,000 while a year later, in March 1919, it was no more than 313,766.

Although Lenin quickly began to establish control of the Party, the importance of the Party itself continually changed, and its comparative weakness was brought out clearly at the First All-Russian Congress of Soviets of Workers' and Soldiers'

Deputies which met in Petrograd from 3 to 24 June. Of more than 800 delegates, the Bolsheviks had only 105 compared with the Socialist Revolutionaries' 285 and the Mensheviks' 248. More than one report of the proceedings suggested that even Lenin was given a rather rough ride. Arthur Ransome visited the buildings where the delegates were to meet and sleep shortly after they began arriving.

> 'Hundreds and hundreds of beds with red blankets are arranged in rows and yesterday when I was there I saw crowds of deputies sitting on their beds talking like boys in a gigantic dormitory. Here and there a deputy, weary from his journey, snored under his red blanket. In one dormitory were the Cossacks, all together. Downstairs is a great refectory in the basement under a low ceiling where group after group of dusty soldiers sat drinking tea and emphasizing their political views by thumping the heavy tables.'

Such men had little patience with anything that sounded less than practical, and laughter greeted Lenin's recipe for dealing with the country's economic problems. 'Arrest a score or two of capitalists, keep them in the same condition as those in which lives Nicolas Romanoff, and they will disclose to you all the clues and secrets of their enrichment. The capitalists must be arrested. Without this, all your phrases will be empty words.'

He got a similar reception when he replied to Tseretelli, the Menshevik leader, who claimed that there was no party in Russia prepared to assume full power. 'Yes, there is,' Lenin retorted. 'No party can refuse this, and our Party certainly doesn't. It is ready to take over full power at any moment.' Lenin disliked interrupting speakers or himself being interrupted and only serious considerations could have urged him to break his usual restraint. The applause he received from Party members had to fight hard against the general laughter that greeted his remark.

The first major factor to swing a number of important groups on to Lenin's side in the early summer of 1917 was the ham-handedness with which the Provisional Government dealt with a controversial issue of the war when he had been back in Russia only a few weeks. It gave a major boost to his support in Petrograd and also forced on the Government a cabinet reconstruction which testified to its uncertain hold on power.

The controversy concerned a specific aspect of the war about which differences sharpened throughout 1917, On the one hand there was the Government belief that Russia's war aims should continue to include the annexation of the Austro-Hungarian provinces of the Ukraine, Constantinople and various other areas dealt with in secret treaties signed by the tsarist Government and its allies earlier in the war. On the other hand, there was the view expounded by Lenin and his supporters that peace should be concluded on the principle of no annexations, no indemnities, such penalties being in the Bolshevik view the stigmata of inter-necine war between capitalist states.

Since the birth of the Provisional Government in 1917, the Western Allies had been uncertain of which stance the Government would adopt, and they badly needed reassurance that Russia would not renege on her earlier commitments. The need for such reassurance grew after the Petrograd Soviet issued a blunt statement averring: 'We do not aspire to conquer foreign lands. We want to guarantee liberty to the peoples and, first of all, liberty to the people inhabiting Russia. We shall fight, arms in hand, against everything that stands in the way of this liberty.' By contrast the Provisional Government, like its predecessor, intended to stand by the secret treaties. Lenin chipped in with the statement that the Government's failure to publish the secret treaties signed by the earlier tsarist Government showed that while they claimed to be pursuing a defensive war, they were in fact following the Tsar's aggressive aims. The Bolsheviks, he added, were opposed to this.

An attempt to paper over the differences between the Provisional Government and the Soviet was now made with the issue by Milyukov, the Foreign Minister, of a document maintaining that Russia's aim 'is not domination over other nations, or seizure of their national possessions, or forcible occupation of foreign territories, but the establishment of a stable peace on the basis of the self-determination of peoples'. Whatever encouragement this might have given to the Soviet was counteracted by a final sentence which spoke of continued adherence to 'all obligations assumed towards our Allies'.

The Government document was immediately made public, but not until later, following pressure from the Soviet, was it sent officially to Russia's allies. Then, moreover, it was accompanied by an explanatory official note which spoke of decisive victory – thus cutting away the ground from beneath any attempts to work out a compromise peace – and emphasizing Russia's intention to stand by her commitments to her allies.

Lenin's reaction to this defence of what he called the 'predatory treaties concluded by the tsarist clique and the "Allied" bankers' was predictable.

'The cards are on the table . . . [he wrote]. Short and clear. War to a decisive victory. The alliance with the British and French bankers is sacred . . . The new Note of the Provisional Government will pour oil on the flames. It can only arouse a bellicose spirit in Germany. It will help Wilhelm the Brigand to go on deceiving "his own" workers and soldiers and drag them into a war "to a finish". Fight – because we want to plunder. Die in your tens of thousands every day – because "we" . . . have not yet got our share of the spoils.'

In the controversy Lenin had expressed in vividly extreme form what many non-Bolsheviks were also thinking, and the revelation of the Government's attitude was followed, within a few days, by the battery and barricade, the rioting in the streets and the desultory shooting, which was becoming so common in Petrograd. There are differing versions of what part the Bolsheviks played in these reactions under Lenin's direction, but in spite of his unqualified criticism of the Provisional Government it seems likely that the explanation he gave to the All-Russian Conference of Bolsheviks which opened on 24 April was a fair account:

'We did not know if in this troubled moment the masses would swing in our direction; the question would have been different if they had swung sharply. We proposed a peaceful demonstration but some comrades in the Petersburg Committee injected a different slogan. We annulled it but could not stop it in time, and the masses followed the slogan of the Petersburg Committee. We acknowledge that the slogan "Down with the Provisional Government is adventurist, that we cannot now overthrow the Government . . . We wanted only a peaceful reconnaissance of our enemy's forces and not to give battle. But the Petersburg Committee took a position "a wee bit to the left" . . . To move a "wee bit left" at the moment of action was inept. We regard this as a grave crime . . . We would not remain in the Central

338

Committee for a minute if we consciously permitted such a step. It occurred because of imperfections in our organizational machinery . . . Were there mistakes? Yes, there were. Only those who don't act don't make mistakes. But to organize well – that's a difficult task.'

In spite of the tactical decision to hold their hand until they were better prepared, the Bolsheviks only just escaped being drawn into the opening stages of a confrontation before they were ready. The Provisional Government ordered counter-demonstrations, and troops loyal to them were ordered into the city. 'As the day wore on,' David R. Francis [the US representative in Petrograd] cabled to Washington, 'friends of the new government and opponents of the anarchistic and extremely socialistic expressions of Lenin gained courage to such an extent that whenever a Lenin banner appeared on the streets it was captured and torn into shreds.' Francis, strongly anti-Lenin, seems to have reported the situation with one finger on the scales, but there is no doubt that opinion in the city was widely split and it was only after the Soviet banned street meetings and demonstrations that the danger of a major clash was averted. Then the Bolshevik Central Committee confirmed its position by announcing that it would support 'the transfer of power into the hands of the proletarians and semi-proletarians, only when the Soviets of Workers' and Soldiers' Deputies adopt our policy and are willing to take that power into their own hands'.

The Provisional Government's inept handling of the controversy over what kind of peace they wanted had two results, one important, the other more difficult to quantify. Before mid-May the Government had been restructured. A. I. Guchkov, the Minister for War and the Navy resigned, and was followed by

Milyukov who, as Foreign Minister, took the main blame for what appears to have been a collective piece of political misman-agement. Three days later the second Provisional Government was formed. Prince Lvov remained as Prime Minister but Aleksandr Kerensky was promoted to the key position of War Minister in what was to be a bourgeois-socialist coalition. Two more Socialist Revolutionaries were brought into the cabinet as were two Mensheviks and a Centrist.

The new Provisional Government then announced that elec-tions for the promised Constituent Assembly would be held on 17 September and that the Assembly would meet on 30 September. In August these dates were put forward to 12 November and 29 November; and were later put forward again. Then, before the elections could be held, there came the success-ful Revolution – on 25 October by the Julian calendar (7 November by the Gregorian) – elections were once again post-poned and the Assembly sat for what was to be its single session only on 5 (18) January 1918.

By the time that the Second Provisional Government came into being Lenin had acquired much greater strength. To some extent he was harvesting the results of his activities immediately following his return to Petrograd. In particular the fact that on the question of the secret treaties, he had taken a line which strongly followed public opinion, non-Bolshevik as well as Bolshevik, undoubtedly reinforced his political position. But the disputes about the kind of peace that Russia should seek – an 'annexationist' peace following the lines of the secret treaties signed by the Tsar's Government or a peace such as advocated by the Soviet and its left-wing supporters – had nearly drawn Lenin into actions for which he knew that neither he nor the Bolsheviks were prepared. Although the lessons were clear they were obscured in the military and political fogs that shrouded events in Petrograd throughout the summer of 1917, which helps to explain 'the July days' which were to follow. This was the name given to the series of events which in many ways repeated, on a more dangerous scale, those that had surrounded the arguments over the peace towards which Russia should be aiming. Once again, Lenin was deeply involved, although after more than half a century and the investigations of historians, partial and impartial, no indisputably clear picture has emerged of the role he played.

At one extreme there is the theory that he plotted to seize power and failed owing to a combination of bad management and bad luck. At the other extreme, it can be claimed that he was drawn only reluctantly into the upheavals of the July days, and then tried to defuse the situation they created, for reasons that are also debated but whose consensus is that he correctly felt that conditions were still not ripe for a successful revolt. The difficulty in drawing any satisfactory conclusions regarding Lenin's detailed motives is lucidly described by Alexander Rabinowitch in *Prelude to Revolution,* by far the best unbiased attempt to untangle and analyse the complicated story of events.

As Rabinowitch points out, in the summer of 1917 there were three distinct Bolshevik Party groups in Petrograd. The Bolshevik Military Organization had been formed in March to conduct revolutionary activity in the city's military garrison and at the nearby Kronstadt naval base. The following month the Bolsheviks' Central Committee had been formed of nine men roughly divided into those who supported Lenin's radical line and those who tended to follow the more moderate line of L. B. Kamenev. The Central Committee's brief was to formulate overall party policies and to co-ordinate them throughout Russia; it included some control of the Military Organization whose task was now widened to cover military and naval forces throughout Russia. This ambiguous and not entirely satisfactory arrangement was further complicated by the creation of the Petersburg Committee whose Executive Committee was responsible for co-ordinating and directing virtually all Bolshevik activities in the city. Even without other divisive factors, the existence of these three bodies would have made it difficult to direct opposition activity in a capital nominally ruled by the Provisional Government.

A further complicating feature of the struggles and manoeuvrings which followed the uproar over the Provisional Government's announcements about the peace was that the arguments were not carried on only on diplomatic and political grounds. On 18 June (1 July) the Russians launched a new military offensive in the south which, after initial success, quickly deteriorated into a military disaster. Although this was not the spark that set the tinder ablaze, the fighting was certainly unpopular enough to increase support for demonstrations in Petrograd, which soon developed signs of a revolt if not of a revolution. Yet despite the size of the crowds in the streets, civilian and military, there was no certainty that an attempted overthrow of the Provisional Government would have the support necessary for success; thus there were contradictory counsels from the Bolshevik authorities and from Lenin in particular, as to how much support, if any, should be given to reinforcing the demonstrations.

These demonstrations had begun some while before the start of the long-awaited Russian offensive, but the offensive, launched with thirty-one divisions and 1,300 guns, certainly encouraged them. Lenin's personal view was given in 'An Alliance to Stop the Revolution', published in *Pravda,* in which he wrote: 'An offensive, whatever its outcome may be from the military point of view, means politically strengthening imperialist morale, imperialist sentiments and infatuation with imperialism. It means strengthening the old, unchanged army officers ... and strengthening *the main position of the counter-revolution.*' Here, he was in line with official Bolshevik thought, as is evident from a statement issued on the opening of the offensive by the group of Bolshevik and United Socialist-Democrats to the Congress of Soviets then meeting in Petrograd. This stated that the offensive had been started on the orders of the Anglo-French and the Americans.

Whatever the force of the political argument, events in the field soon showed that the offensive was a mistake. It is true that during the first two days the Russians captured more than 18,000 prisoners and that the Russian Eighth Army under General Lavr Kornilov broke Austrian resistance. But the Russian effort quickly spent itself. The Germans launched a devastating series of counter-attacks to help their Austrian allies, and General Knox, head of the British Military Mission to Russia, soon concluded that the Russian army was 'irretrievably ruined as a fighting organization'. This was no exaggeration since in the twenty days following the start of the offensive the Russians suffered 60,000 casualties.

It was not only the vigour of the German attacks but also the condition of the Russian forces which was by now significant. A majority of the units was in a state of growing disintegration. Persuasion and argument had lost force, and were answered with threats, sometimes with shooting. At times an order to move quickly was debated for hours at meetings, and action was delayed for days. On 29 June while the fighting was continuing, Lenin left Petrograd for the home of Bonch-Bruyevich on the Karelian Isthmus in Finland. The recent disputes about peace had certainly begun to exhaust even the usually indefatigable

Lenin and, as he claimed, overwork and insomnia may well have been his reason for leaving the city. Nevertheless, it would be surprising if he had not anticipated the troubles now coming to the boil. He was uncertain about their outcome and his considerable political experience may well have suggested that it would be advisable to wait from afar to see which way the cat would jump.

It was, moreover, not only the military offensive that was causing the Provisional Government trouble. There were non-Russian areas of the tsarist empire which had seen the February Revolution as a chance of gaining their independence and none had put forward stronger claims than the Ukraine. By the summer more than one nationalist group was demanding autonomy for the Ukrainian Central Rada (Government) in Kiev. While the socialist ministers in the Provisional Government were prepared to accede to most of the Ukrainian proposals, the Kadet members of the cabinet refused to do so. When a Provisional Government delegation to Kiev came to an agreement with the Rada after a three-day meeting all but one of the Kadet members of the Provisional Government resigned; this, in turn, left the Government in an exposed and vulnerable situation which was only improved by a cabinet reconstruction.

The official political division brought about by discussions on the Ukraine's future added fuel to the near-disastrous result of the Russian offensive and to increased unrest among troops in Petrograd, particularly in the 1st Machine-Gun Regiment, some units of which had been advocating rebellion even before the offensive started. The threat was damped down, although with difficulty, by the Petrograd Soviet and a number of Bolshevik leaders, all of whom felt that the time for action had not yet come. However, they succeeded in winning only a temporary respite for the Provisional Government, and by 3 July envoys from the machine-gunners had succeeded in arousing considerable support for action both from the other military units and from civilians in some of the more important factories. This time, help for the Provisional Government came from an unexpected source – the All-Russian Central Executive Committee of the Soviet of Workers' and Soldiers' Deputies and the All-Russian Executive Committee of the Soviet of Peasants' Deputies. On hearing of preparations for a joint military and civilian march on the Government, members of the Committees hastened to telegraph military units in the city and the naval base at Kronstadt, empha-sizing that such a march should not take place.

However, a compromise was reached and the Central Committee, in consultation with the Petrograd Committee and the Military Organization, decided late in the evening of 3 July to participate in the demonstration in order to give it an orga-nized and peaceful character More than 500,000 people were to be on the streets the following day and what happened was almost inevitable. Clashes occurred throughout Petrograd between units from the machine-gunners, right-wing supporters, *agents provocateurs* and undisciplined demonstrators.

In the growing chaos the Bolsheviks' Central Committee did two things. It issued a proclamation saying: 'Comrades! For the present political crisis, our aim has been accomplished. We have therefore decided to end the demonstration. Let each and every one peacefully and in an organized manner bring the strike and the demonstration to a close.' Second, and equally important, it decided to send for Lenin, biding his time in Finland.

The encouragement of a peaceful but armed demonstration had been the main factor behind the chaos. Between 3 and 4 July 200 to 300 people are estimated to have been killed or wounded in clashes between the demonstrators, troops who supported the overthrow of the Provisional Government, troops who remained either loyal to the Government or neutral, and supporters of the Soviet who believed that the time was not yet ready for revolution. An official report of the Executive Committee of the Petrograd Soviet describing the march through the city of the naval units from Kronstadt exemplifies the situation that developed throughout the day. 'On Liteiny Prospect the glass was broken in many shops and the street car cables were torn up. In many houses the Kronstadters carry out searches on the pretext that they have been fired on. If anyone is found he is pulled out on the street and lynched.' The phrase 'fog of war' well describes the overall situation in the city. Much of the crowd was indignant at the lack of any left-wing attempt to take over from the Provisional Government, and Viktor Chernov, the Social Revolutionary Minister of Agriculture was taunted with the cry: 'Take power when you're offered it, you son of a bitch!' pushed into a car and only rescued by Trotsky who persuaded the crowd to let him go.

Despite all the later attempts by Bolsheviks to play down their role in the July days, Lenin's cable to the Central Committee Bureau Abroad leaves no doubt that he was still expecting serious trouble. Both the Provisional Government and the Soviet were defenceless against the thousand-strong mobs which had roamed the streets of Petrograd; but the mobs had no direction and no plan. By dusk their lack of direction was making itself felt; soon even most of the Kronstadt sailors, the most potentially formidable force in the city, were making their way home to base.

However, by this time what were to become known as the Red Guards had begun to be transformed from *ad hoc* groupings of pro-revolutionaries into the military force they later became.

346

Organized through factory and shop committees, they were tolerated by the Provisional Government despite their debatable legal standing, a status that changed as they armed themselves, coalesced, and finally gained military importance. Some units were formed outside Petrograd and Moscow but only in Kiev and Odessa did such provincial units number more than a few hundred. Yet by October, only three months after they had begun to win a separate identity, they totalled some 20,000 men throughout the country – a substantial number if only a fraction of the 200,000 that has sometimes been claimed for them.

In July, however, they failed to affect the outcome of the disturbances whose indeterminate ending appears to have followed Lenin's wishes. When M. A. Savelyev, emissary from the Central Committee, arrived with the latest news at Bonch-Bruyevich's villa near Neivola, he had asked: 'Is this the beginning of decisive operations?' Lenin's reported answer was: 'This would be quite inopportune.'

His attitude apparently hardened during the journey to Petrograd as he heard from Savelyev more details of what had been happening in the city. He was taken from the Finland Station to the Kzhezinskaya Mansion where Bolshevik leaders were already addressing a mass of civilians and troops. Eventually he was persuaded to appear on the balcony before the crowd who greeted him with a great chorus of encouragement. But the crowd was not to hear the message it awaited. Instead, it was told that the demonstrations must be called off since even if the rebels took control of Petrograd they would not be able to maintain control. But Lenin remained equivocal, as M. I. Kalinin pointed out. Asked if the current situation was the beginning of the seizure of power, Lenin replied 'we shall see – right now it is impossible to say!' and implied that in favourable conditions whole regiments could be committed to the struggle, but that in different circumstances it might be necessary to retreat with as few losses as possible.

There is no direct record of Lenin's fluctuating feelings throughout the turbulent July days. But his frame of mind can be gauged from his words to the Central Committee before its members decided to call off the demonstrations. 'Give me an exact count of your strength,' he told the Committee, according to K. Mekhonoshin who was representing the Bolshevik Military Organization and who appears to have given the only account, if an incomplete one, of what Lenin said on this vital occasion. He continued:

'Name the units which will definitely follow us. Which ones are wavering? Who is against us? Where are the storehouses of rifles and other military supplies? What can the enemy rely on in the areas neighboring Petrograd? Where are the food supplies concentrated and are there sufficient quantities? Has the security of the Neva bridges been provided for? Has the rear been prepared for retreat in the event of failure?'

The weight given to these questions is not known. But common sense suggests that it was considerable and that Lenin must have played an important role in finally ending the July days. It seems likely that whatever new material comes to light in the future, whether by accident or produced in order to justify or to criticize Lenin's role, that role will continue to be open to argument. But it was clearly ambivalent, created by the conflict within his own mind in which the overwhelming desire for revolution contrasted, once again, with awareness that a rising which failed to develop satisfactorily into something more important, might set the cause back to an unquantifiable degree. It was perhaps with some relief that he personally supervised the make-up of the *Pravda* page, which on the morning of 5 July announced that the demonstrations were over 'because their goal of presenting the slogans of the leading elements of the working class and the army had been achieved'.

Lenin's decision to hedge his bets during the July days was followed by the launching of a Provisional Government campaign aimed at proving that he was a German 'spy', a word that within the next few days was given a variety of interpretations. The Government had been collecting information for possible use against him for some time. This was not difficult in view of his contacts with such men as Kesküla, which he had allowed to build up over the years. However, there is no evidence that any of the information justified the use of the word 'spy'; and it is, in any case, unlikely that Lenin would ever have been in the position to pass on useful information to the Germans even had he wished to do so. Nevertheless, it is equally clear that revolutionary disruption in Russia's armed forces would benefit the Germans, even though it seems a distortion of words to describe it under the heading of espionage.

The nub of the Provisional Government's accusation, which was made by the unusual mechanism of the Minister of Justice, P. N. Pereverzev, providing information to two journalists, was contained in one paragraph which said:

'From the numerous telegrams in the hands of the legal authorities it is established that a constant and extensive correspondence was carried on between (E. M.) Sumenson, Ul'ianov (Lenin), Kollontai and Kozlovskii residing in Petrograd, on the one hand, and Fürstenberg [Hanecki] and Helfhand (Parvus) on the other. Although this correspondence refers to commercial deals, shipment of all sorts of goods, and money transactions, it offers sufficient reasons to conclude that this correspondence was a coverup for relations of an espionage character.'

If the Government statement was decidedly thin, there was no greater evidence of inefficiency than in its timing. Kerensky, soon to be Prime Minister, revealed later that when the accusation against Lenin was made public Hanecki-Fürstenberg was known to be travelling from Scandinavia to Russia and that plans had been made to have him arrested at the frontier. Naturally enough, he failed to turn up. In Berlin Helphand issued his own statement under the heading: 'My Reply to Kerensky and Co.' He ignored the main charge and then went on:

'I have always supported, and will go on doing so, the Russian revolutionary movement in so far as it is socialist, with every means at my disposal. You lunatics, why do you worry whether I have given any money to Lenin? Lenin and others, whose names you give, have never demanded or received any money from me either as a loan or as a present. But I have given them, and many others, something more effective than money or dynamite. I am one of those men who have given spiritual nourishment to the revolutionary determination of the Russian proletariat, which you are now trying, in vain, to destroy.'

In Petrograd, Helphand's statement was discounted and all except the most devout Bolsheviks took the Provisional Government's statement at its face value. The accusations were backed up by a number of documents which the Government now made available. It was almost forty years before these documents were given any reliable and impartial scrutiny and in view of their importance to Lenin's subsequent story it is necessary to mention them before describing their effect in the summer of 1917.

In the winter of 1917 to 1918 Edgar Sisson, a former editor of *Cosmopolitan* magazine, was sent to Petrograd by the Americans' Committee on Public Information. Within a short time he had acquired copies of some of the Provisional Government's allegedly incriminating documents, which were later published in Washington under the title 'The German-Bolshevik Conspiracy'. Although some doubts were expressed as to their authenticity, they were in general treated as genuine in the USA, one reason being that the Americans did not wish to offend the Provisional Government for fear of reprisals against their countrymen still in Russia. Argument about the Sisson documents continued sporadically but inconclusively, and only in the mid 1950s, after the discovery in Washington of what had been considered the lost originals, did George F. Kennan, the doyen of American diplomats, throw genuinely revealing light on them.

> 'The state of affairs suggested in the main body of the documents [Kennan wrote], is of such extreme historical implausibility that the question might well be asked whether the documents should not be declared generally fraudulent on this ground alone . . . At every hand one finds serious discrepancies between circumstances suggested by the documents and known historical fact.'

Kennan lists a dozen specific examples, and leaves no doubt

that the phrase 'relations of an espionage character' has no justi-fication. This, however, is not to deny that some of the money procured by Helphand's complex and frequently illegal network of import and export companies did not find its way into Bolshevik coffers. How much Lenin knew of this and how much was unknown because of a convenient blind eye still remains obscure. But Kennan has put into perspective the events which within the next few months were to affect Lenin's life, and with it events in Russia and beyond. He has also written what could be the last word on the moral implications of German help – words with which Lenin would no doubt have agreed.

'It should be noted in this connection that there was nothing in the philosophy of either regime which would have inhib-ited the Germans from giving financial aid to the Bolsheviki *prior* to their assumption of power or the Bolsheviki from accepting it. Neither would have considered itself in any way under moral obligation to the other by virtue of such a relationship . . . If the Germans financed the Bolsheviki in the spring and summer of 1917 they did so on the principle – sound in international affairs as elsewhere – that they were supporting them not for what they promised but for what they were; not for what they might undertake to do for others but for what they were likely to do for themselves. In the sweeping demoralization of the Russian armed forces that accompanied the Bolshevik political triumph in Russia, this German speculation was vindicated beyond the most optimistic dreams.'

Although the case against Lenin was undoubtedly thin on legal grounds, it can be argued that the Provisional Government

352

fumbled its chances in July 1917, as it had fumbled chances before and as it would again during its remaining few months of existence.

> 'Had the Provisional Government at this time arraigned Lenin and Trotzky and the other Bolshevik leaders, tried them for treason and executed them [the American diplomat David R. Francis later stated], Russia probably would not have been compelled to go through another revolution, would have been spared the reign of terror, and the loss from famine and murder of millions of her sons and daughters.'

It is no doubt wishful thinking to imagine that the country could have been spared Revolution but it is nevertheless certain that without Lenin it would have taken a different – although not necessarily less bloody – course.

Although it missed its chance the Government did succeed in arousing considerable public opinion against the Bolsheviks and there was comparatively little public outcry when the *Pravda* offices were destroyed.

On the evening of 6 July armed men searched Lenin's home despite the protests of his wife, an event about which he only heard some hours afterwards. He was staying in the flat of Sergei Alliluyev, a veteran Bolshevik workman whose daughter later married Stalin, and it was here that Lenin apparently heard that the Government had issued warrants for the arrest of himself, Zinoviev and Trotsky. 'Gregory [Zinoviev] and I have decided to appear,' he said in a note to Krupskaya. 'Go and tell Kamenev . . . Let us say goodbye; we may not see each other again.' Despite Lenin's instinct to present himself in court, a number of Central Committee officials and other Party members who met that evening in Alliluyev's flat decided he should not do so, a decision confirmed a few days later by an enlarged meeting of the Central Committee.

Instead of waiting in Petrograd, with all its chances of discovery, Lenin decided to make for Finland and go into hiding there, a sanctuary where he could remain for a while. It was argued by the Central Committee that he should not appear in court because there was no guarantee for his safety. This was no doubt true, but it is more than likely that the Committee weighed another factor in the balance. Had Lenin appeared in court he would inevitably have been cross-examined on the material the Government had accumulated and it seems likely that at least some of the mud from it would have stuck. Lenin's and Zinoviev's own explanation was eventually published in the *Proletarskoye Delo (Proletarian Cause)*.

'The counter-revolutionary *bourgeoisie* is trying to make a new Dreyfus case [it said] . . . There is no guarantee of just trial in Russia at the present moment . . . To give oneself up to the authorities would mean to yield oneself to the power of the Miliukovs, Alexinskys, and Pereverzevs, into the hands of infuriated counter-revolutionaries, to whom the charges against us mean simply an incident in the civil war.'

Once he had decided not to give himself up for a trial that might end before an execution squad, Lenin began preparations for what he realized could be a long spell on the run. He delegated Sverdlov to handle his Party affairs while he was in hiding and then firmed up arrangements that would enable him to keep in touch with Petrograd from wherever he spent his 'exile'.

10

On the Eve

When the warrant for Lenin's arrest was issued, the authorities had first gone to the flat of his elder sister Anna, where he had recently been living. They found it empty. Lenin was already one move ahead and continued to remain so, staying in five different apartments in almost as many days, the last of them the home of Alliluyev.

By 10 July he decided that it was time to leave Petrograd. He shaved off his beard, changed into a brown coat and cap and secured the help of N. A. Emelyanov, a loyal Party worker who has left a vivid account of the events that followed. It was Emelyanov who bought railway tickets for Lenin and Zinoviev, then waited by one of the Neva bridges to escort the two men across the river. From the Finland Station they took a train to the village of Rasliv, twenty miles north-west of Petrograd on the Gulf of Finland, then crossed a nearby lake by canoe and set off on foot through the woods until they came to a barn rented by Emelyanov.

They stayed for some weeks in the area, moving from the barn to a small hut when it was feared they might be discovered. Eventually, at a date given inconsistently in different accounts of this variously recorded episode, it was decided that they should move into nearby Finland. After having their photographs taken for new passports – probably in the small holiday town of Sestroretsk – the two men crossed the frontier, Lenin in the name of Konstantin Petrovich Ivanov. This delicate operation was planned by Emelyanov, who at the frontier station of Dibuni picked a quarrel with the soldiers detailed to search trains for suspects. While the argument went on Lenin and Zinoviev slipped unnoticed into an empty compartment and shortly afterwards were safely in Finland.

For the next few weeks they were much on the move, on one occasion spending a night with the Finnish socialist, Karl Wilik, in whose house Lenin read Michelet's account of the Terror during the French Revolution. Early in August Zinoviev returned to Petrograd but Lenin remained in Finland, living for a while in the fifth-floor Helsinki flat of Kustaa Rovio, the head of the city's police force and an ardent Bolshevik. The accommodation was organized on the instructions of the Party's Central Committee by a Bolshevik who commented 'Our people will be surprised and will laugh their heads off when I go back to Petrograd and tell them that I lodged Lenin with the Chief of the Helsingfors City Police. I am sure not one of Kerensky's bloodhound agents will ever think of looking [there].'

Lenin spent two spells in Rovio's flat, staying indoors for most of the daylight hours as a precaution against discovery and receiving from the chief of police the local newspapers and correspondence from Petrograd, which was sent to him by the Central Committee.

Krupskaya had made one surreptitious visit to her husband while he was in the Rasliv area and when he had settled down in Helsinki she made another, using a passport which Emelyanov had helped her to obtain. In Finland she tried to find Lenin's address with the help of a sketch-map he had sent her, but in developing its invisible ink she had burned part of the map and spent some frustrating hours finding her way round Helsinki.

During the next few weeks – in fact, until he returned to Petrograd in the autumn – Lenin was in frequent if not regular contact with Party members in Russia. They managed to get to him some of the notebooks he had left at the start of his hurried flight, while he in turn was able to send them instructions such as the one he sent to Kamenev in July:

'Strictly *entre nous*, if I am done in, please publish my note-book "Marxism and the State". It is held up in Stockholm. A blue binding. All the quotations are taken from Marx and Engels, as well as Kautsky versus Pannekuk. There are a number of notes and remarks. They need to be collated. I think it could be published after, say, a week's work. I think it is important, because Plekhanov and Kautsky are not the only ones to have blundered. One condition: all this must remain absolutely *"entre nous"*.'

These notes on 'Marxism and the State' were eventually to see the light of day later in the year as Lenin's *The State and Revolution* which outlined a programme very different from that of *What Is To Be Done?* and, in contrast to it, gave the more important role in carrying out a successful socialist revolution not to the Party but to the proletarian masses. The preparatory work on it was carried out in December 1916 and early 1917, when Lenin had no idea that Russia was on the brink of the spring Revolution, a point whose significance has been stressed by Rodney Barfield in his 'Lenin's Utopianism: State and Revolution'.

Kamenev succeeded in restoring the precious notebook to Lenin who worked on its entries while living in Helsinki. On 21 July the Petrograd Supreme Court indicted him for treason and the organization of armed uprising, and from that moment every contact with him carried its own risk. Yet throughout August and September, as he travelled with comparative freedom in Finland, there was no attempt to betray his whereabouts. He was, moreover, able to maintain a regular two-way contact with Petrograd. Not only were the Petrograd newspapers brought to him with some regularity by a few dedicated couriers – amusing him when he read of how he had allegedly returned from Russia to his 'paymasters' in Germany – but the articles that he continued to write were almost unfailingly delivered to their designated publishers. 'The Political Situation', 'On Slogans', and 'Lessons of the Revolution' were only some of the polemical essays he hammered out as he relaxed in Finland.

If Lenin's ability to concentrate on the political problems of revolution in the most difficult circumstances was one factor in the success which came to him before the end of 1917, another was the reputation he had built up for himself and for the Bolsheviks during the hard campaigning weeks following his arrival at the Finland Station in the spring. His influence was dramatically revealed when, while he was hiding in Finland, the Sixth Congress of the RSDLP (Bolsheviks), which by now had about 140,000 members, met in Petrograd between 26 July and 3 August. Although Lenin was absent and being sought on a charge of high treason, he was elected to the Central Committee by 133 votes, the highest number recorded at the Congress.

Zinoviev received 132 votes and Trotsky, now imprisoned in Petrograd by the Provisional Government, 131 votes.

Lenin's belief in the growing need for action was reflected in the articles he produced during the latter weeks of his hiding in Finland: 'One of the Fundamental Questions of the Revolution', 'Can the Bolsheviks Retain State Power?' and 'The Tasks of the Revolution' were only three. He added a postscript addressed to the Central Committee to 'The Crisis Has Matured' saying that the victory of an insurrection was now guaranteed but since the Central Committee did not respond to his instructions he was 'compelled to *tender [his] resignation from the Central Committee,* which I hereby do, reserving for myself freedom to campaign among the *rank and file* of the Party and at the Party Congress'.

These outpourings showed that Lenin's stance was now, as it had been when he arrived back in Russia in April, in direct conflict not only with the Provisional Government but with the prevailing mood of the Party leadership. Now, moreover, some members of the Central Committee perceived a danger in the attitude he was adopting: if it became known to Petrograd workers that Lenin was calling for insurrection his call might trigger off another spate of July days. Revolution might be started before all was ready for it and failure at the least, prison at the worst, might be the outcome. Surely, it was argued, Lenin's letters and injunctions should be destroyed? Eventually they were kept; but precautions were taken to ensure that no mass appeals were made to the workers, and all that the Central Committee did was to arrange publication of his earlier and more moderate paper 'The Russian Revolution and the Civil War' in *Rabochy Put (Workers' Path)*.

Shortly after seeing this in print Lenin finally decided that whatever instructions the Central Committee had given, ostensibly to ensure his safety, he must make preparations for returning to Petrograd. It appears to have been more for political than military reasons, since early in October he had written to the Committee saying, with great misjudgement: 'Victory is certain in Moscow: nobody will resist us there. At Petrograd we can afford to wait: it is not necessary to begin with Petrograd.'

During this period he sent Trotsky a number of hastily written notes and letters all urging him to press for immediate action, and reinforced them with similar notes to other members of the Central Committee as opportunity offered. Cautious Committee members felt that Lenin, in hiding, had failed to understand how the situation was developing in Petrograd. Many weeks later, after power had been successfully seized, a desire developed within the Committee to have these notes destroyed; Lenin opposed such a move – ostensibly because he did not wish to build up a legend of his own infallibility.

Fear that the Central Committee would continue to stave off action played an important part in eventually deciding him to return to Petrograd. The details, as well as the actual date of his return, have remained shrouded in mystery for more than seventy years. Harrison Salisbury, with his vast experience of Russia, contributed a significant foreword to *The October Revolution* by the Russian historian and dissident, Roy Medvedev, and discussed the mystery illuminatingly.

'There is, for example [wrote Salisbury in 1979], one enormous, glaring, and obvious hole in the legend of Lenin's spotless leadership of the October coup – the question of when he returned to Petrograd in the weeks just before the plot was hatched (not to mention the even more tricky question of *why* he did not return until two or three weeks before

360

the event). This is a legitimate question of historiography. The records are confused. The witnesses disagree. Lenin had been underground in Finland since the July events. Did he come back in late September, say the 26th or 29th? Or did he return only on October 7 or 8 or 9 or 10? Did he come secretly on his own or did he come at the invitation of his Central Committee colleagues?

'It is obvious that these questions bear heavily on the planning and carrying out of the Bolshevik coup on October 25. Yet 62 years after the event this question had not been resolved. In fact from 1930 until the early 1960s – that is, for some 30 years – it could not even be *mentioned* without the danger that the individual who asked the question would lose his academic standing, his party card, or even his head – obvious testimony to the sensitivity of the problem. Now nearly 20 years have passed since the first scholars and surviving colleagues of Lenin raised the question publicly after Stalin's demise and it is still not resolved despite one stormy meeting of historians and Party theorists after the other.'

For long, all that appeared to be certain was that by the third or fourth week of October 1917 Lenin had arrived back in Petrograd and was staying illegally in the flat of Margarita Vasilyevna Fofanova, a member of the revolutionary movement since 1903 and an old friend of Krupskaya. But in 1974 Volume 34 of Lenin's *Collected Works*, published in Moscow, gave 7 October as the date of his return; and in 1985 the event was further elucidated with the publication in Moscow by Progress Publishers of a long illustrated book on Lenin's life and work. It included what was described as an extract from Minute No. 22

of the meeting of the Central Committee of the RSDLP(B) of 3 (16) October, 1917 (the 'B' for Bolshevik having in fact been added when the name changed to RCP the following year); this was stated to say: 'It was decided to invite Lenin to come to Petrograd to make constant and firm contact possible.' The book also contained a photograph of locomotive no. 293 with a caption which stated that it 'brought Lenin from Finland to Petrograd (Udelnaya Station) in October 1917', and a photograph of the station itself with a caption stating: 'Lenin arrived here from Vyborg on the evening of October 7, 1917.'

As Rovio later remembered, Lenin had asked him to get a wig, some dye for his eyebrows, and a passport, and arrange secret accommodation for him in Petrograd. There had been no time for a wig to be made and Lenin had to do as best he could with a ready-made one. He had then set off for the frontier and crossed it without trouble.

The city in which Lenin now found himself had witnessed a series of traumatic and disruptive events since he had crossed the Neva on his way to Rasliv late in July. A second coalition Government had been formed and Kerensky had been promoted not only to the post of Minister President but to that of Minister for War and the Navy. At the same time three Mensheviks, two Popular Socialists, one Progressive and a complement of Kadets and Socialist Revolutionaries had become cabinet members.

While this second coalition – the third Provisional Government since the abdication of the Tsar – was trying to produce order from the chaotic results of the July days, the Bolsheviks had moved their headquarters to the Smolny Institute on the banks of the Neva. Two hundred yards long, three storeys high and with 100 rooms, the Smolny had been an educational institute for young ladies – the female Eton of

362

Russia as it has been called – and both its size and its situation suited the Bolsheviks who one morning had politely but firmly moved out the occupying young ladies, their governesses and teachers. The new occupants then had the task of sticking fresh notices over those which said 'Vth Class', 'Dormitory', 'Linen Room' and 'Drawing Class'.

While the latest Provisional Government was feeling its way forward and the Bolsheviks were recovering from the débâcle of the July days, the Russian military defeat in the south had been followed by General Brusilov's dismissal and his replacement as Commander-in-Chief by General Kornilov, a colourful and ambitious character of extreme rightwing views, who had warned of the dangers to Riga, the great city that the Germans had so far failed either to take or envelop. At the end of August (3 September) Riga was at last occupied by the Germans, a success quickly followed by Kornilov's demand for personal authority over all the troops in Petrograd, for permission to send a cavalry corps into the city, and for the promulgation of martial law. At the same time he ordered his Third Cavalry Corps and the Wild Division to concentrate near Velikiyu Luki, 200 miles south of Petrograd. Here they were in no position for use against the Germans but could be deployed against Government troops in either Moscow or Petrograd. Kerensky had begun by hoping that he could use Kornilov's prestige for his own ends and had only belatedly realized that Kornilov was determined to further only his own personal aims. Eventually he realized that the General's demands had to be refused and the refusal triggered off events which, in the near future, eased Lenin's path to power.

In an effort to cope with the Government's uncompromising attitude, Kornilov sent to Kerensky a slightly dim-witted supporter, V. N. Lvov, with a request that the Prime Minister should visit Kornilov's army headquarters at Moghilev. However, Lvov was late for the appointment with Kerensky, who by this time had learned of his mission; a trace of farce now entered the drama. Kerensky first asked Kornilov, via the Hughes telegraphic apparatus, a form of primitive teletype, whether he should act according to the information given him by Lvov. On being told yes, he then pretended to be Lvov and asked over the teleprinter whether it was necessary to carry out the decision about which he had been asked to inform Kerensky personally – that is, to go to Moghilev. To this, Kornilov again answered, 'Yes', after which Kerensky ended the conversation. Lvov now arrived and was taken to the Winter Palace where he stated that the Prime Minister should go to army headquarters, but a police inspector concealed within earshot promptly arrested Lvov, since it had become obvious that Kornilov's aim was to hold the Prime Minister captive while his troops took control of Petrograd.

Kerensky called a cabinet meeting for the next morning and afterwards telegraphed Kornilov saying, 'I order you immediately to turn over your office to General Lukomsky, who is to take over temporarily the duties of Commander-in-Chief, until the arrival of the new Commander-in-Chief. You are instructed immediately to come to Petrograd.'

There was no ambiguity about this and Kornilov now ordered some of his crack units to the city to dispute Kerensky's authority. So, in a state of increasing confusion, it was not the Bolsheviks but Kornilov's troops who challenged the Provisional Government. Kerensky immediately sought, and obtained, Government powers to stop Kornilov's move and the General's vanguard was halted, without difficulty, on the railway line from

Luga to Petrograd. The Central Executive Committee of the Soviet of Workers', Soldiers' and Peasants' Deputies meanwhile created a People's Committee for the Struggle Against Counter-Revolution, and a workers' militia. Its members put engines out of action, tore up railway tracks and, where this was difficult, blocked lines by overturning wagons. 'The railwaymen had received orders,' Kornilov later admitted. 'I could not get a train that would take me to the environs of the capital. I would have been given a train at Mogilev but I would have been arrested at Vitebsk.'

Kornilov's challenge was thus a humiliating failure and did much to support Trotsky's later comment that the General was a man with the heart of a lion and the brain of a sheep. His failure was well explained by Milyukov who later wrote: 'The issue was decided not so much by the movement of troops, by the strategic and tactical successes of government or Kornilovite detachments, as it was by the mood of the troops . . . "The shedding of blood" did not occur for the simple reason that no one wanted to shed blood or to sacrifice himself for this cause – neither on the one side nor on the other.'

Neither the British Ambassador, Sir George Buchanan, nor General Knox, the head of the British Military Mission to Russia, gave adequate warning to Kerensky, the head of the Government to which they were accredited, while the official British attitude seems to have been that of *The Times* which in commenting on 8 September on the general situation in Russia said: 'There must be an end of committees and debates, of councils of sham workmen and loafing soldiers, of talk about Utopia while the enemy are thundering at the gate. It is no longer a question of saving the Revolution. The Russians have first to save something much bigger, and that is Russia.' The attitude did not go unnoticed in Petrograd and Gorky's *Novaya Zhizn* carried the headline: 'Part of French and English Bourgeois Press Exultantly Acclaims Mutiny of Kornilov'.

Robert Bruce Lockhart who, as Britain's special envoy in Petrograd, was soon to be in a unique position to know what had, or had not, gone on, has commented that while the British withheld support for Kornilov, 'there is little doubt that French and British officers at the Russian front did nothing to discourage an exploit which they felt might restore discipline in the Russian armies, and Winston Churchill had high hopes that the venture would succeed'. Kerensky himself went further, later claiming in his book *The Catastrophe* that pamphlets distributed in Moscow headed 'Korniloff, the National Hero' had been 'printed at the expense of the British Military Mission and had been brought to Moscow from the British Embassy in Petrograd in the railway carriage of General Knox, British Military attaché'.

When the Kornilov episode was debated in the British cabinet it was felt, Lloyd George was later to write, that

'difficult though it was for the British Government to interfere in the present situation without appearing to take sides with General Korniloff, it was essential, in the interests of the Allies and of democracy generally, to make an effort to improve the situation, although it was realized that any steps in that direction would have to be taken through M. Kerensky, as he was the representative of the existing Government. It was suggested that he should be informed that the British Government viewed with the greatest alarm the probabilities of civil war, and urged him to come to terms with General Korniloff not only in the interest of Russia herself, but in that of the Allies.'

However, as Lloyd George went on with an obvious breath of relief, events delivered the cabinet 'from the dilemma of choosing between Kerensky and Korniloff, for Korniloff was denounced as a traitor and arrested . . .'

Kerensky's view of what had happened was given in a message to the country, on 27 August 1917, which claimed that Kornilov had called for the surrender of the Provisional Government so that he might form a new one. Such demands, he went on, 'revealed the longing of certain circles in Russian society to take advantage of the serious situation the state finds itself in to set up a regime opposed to the gains of the revolution'. As a result, General Kornilov was dismissed and Petrograd put under martial law. Kornilov replied the same day by denying the first part of Kerensky's statement, and then continued: 'I, General Kornilov, declare that under the pressure of the Bolshevik majority in the soviets, the Provisional Government is acting in complete accord with the plans of the German General Staff, and simultaneously with the imminent landing of the enemy forces at Riga, it is destroying the army and is undermining the very foundations of the country.'

The implication that Kerensky had been in cahoots with the Germans was much less plausible than the Provisional Government's previous claim that the Bolsheviks had been helping the enemy. But together with the complete failure of Kornilov's revolt, this attempt to blacken the Provisional Government had the effect of uniting the masses which had been split into two separate factions by the July days. Thousands were now less hesitant about supporting the Bolsheviks whom they saw, if reluctantly, as the best defence against counter-revolutionary forces.

Kornilov's failure strengthened Lenin's hand in more ways

than one: once the General's move towards the capital became known, Kerensky had agreed that more arms should be released to the Red Guards, who alone seemed certain to oppose Kornilov. After the *putsch* had failed the Red Guards refused to return the arms and thus remained stronger than before. The psychological position had also changed and Lenin was quick to exploit the new situation in such pamphlets and letters to the Central Committee as 'The Bolsheviks Must Assume Power', 'Marxism and Uprising', 'Can the Bolsheviks Retain State Power?', and 'The Crisis is Ripe.' The Central Committee, whose members well knew that they would be held responsible for the success or failure of any moves that were made, was distinctly more cautious than Lenin. This became strikingly obvious when the Committee received a 'Letter from Afar' from Lenin, still in Finland. The nub of the letter, read at a meeting of the Committee, stated: 'We should at once begin to plan the practical details of a second revolution.' The proposal astounded the members who ordered that all copies of the letter should be destroyed and it was purely by accident that a single copy was preserved.

It was not only on Lenin that the abortive Kornilov takeover attempt had important repercussions. On 1 September Russia was formally proclaimed a republic and Kerensky set up a five-man Directory consisting of himself, the Minister of Foreign Affairs, M. I. Tereshchenko; the Minister of War, Major-General Verkhovsky; the Minister of the Navy, Admiral Verderevsky; and A. M. Nikitin, the Minister of Posts and Telegraphs in the second coalition Government and Minister of the Interior in the third. The function of the Directory was to deal with urgent matters until a new ministry was formed. This ministry, the third coalition of the Provisional Government, only came into existence on

25 September, and consisted of a sixteen-man cabinet under Kerensky including seven non-Party members, four Mensheviks, four Kadets and one Socialist Revolutionary. It was hoped it would carry on until the election and the meeting of the promised Constituent Assembly.

Agreement was also announced on the formation of a Provisional Council of the Republic, or Pre-Parliament, composed of representatives of the political parties, a number of social organizations and the army. This body, designed to act as a consultative body to the Government, met on 7 October; at the first opportunity Trotsky read a declaration in which he accused Kerensky of wishing to deceive the population, then walked out, followed by the rest of the Bolshevik members.

The upshot of these confused and unsatisfactory political manoeuvrings was that by the middle of October Lenin decided that the time had come for him to take command in Petrograd. Conditions were more favourable than they had been for a move that would finally end the succession of ineffective provisional administrations.

As the Germans saw it, Russia could now 'be expected to collapse as a result of any further, fairly powerful shock'. During October, Lenin, working entirely for his own ends, concentrated all his energies on deciding how best to administer that shock which he saw in only one form – revolution. In particular he renewed his direct demand for immediate action, stressing that the Bolsheviks now commanded a majority in both the Petrograd and the Moscow Soviets. The first of two letters, which were discussed by the Central Committee, stated unequivocally:

'The Bolsheviks, having obtained a majority in the Soviets of Workers' and Soldiers' Deputies of both capitals, can and *must* take state power into their own hands . . . We are concerned now not with the "day", or "moment" of insurrection in the narrow sense of the word. That will be only decided by the common voice of those who are *in contact* with the workers and soldiers, with *the masses.*

'The point is that now, at the Democratic Conference, our Party has virtually *its own congress* and this congress (whether it wishes to or not) *must decide the fate of the revolution.*

'The point is to make the *task* clear to the Party. The present task must be an *armed uprising* in Petrograd and Moscow (with its region), the seizing of power and the overthrow of the government. We must consider *how* to agitate for this without expressly saying as much in the press . . . History will not forgive us if we do not assume power now.'

The somewhat arrogant demand, an example of the tail trying to wag the dog, demonstrates the strength of Lenin's resolution.

In the end, three groups were formed in the Central Committee: the opponents of the seizure of power by the Party; Lenin, who demanded the organization of a rising independent of the Soviets; and a third group who considered it necessary to link the rising closely to the Second Council of Soviets and therefore wished to postpone it. Finally a resolution was passed saying that the rising should take place not later than 15 October.*

---

* It is at this point, where specific preparations begin for The Russian Revolution, that a changed method of giving dates seems appropriate. The Julian calendar was still in use throughout Russia while the Gregorian

Trotsky wrote that he did not remember much discussion about the actual date, which, it appears to have been taken for granted, would be dependent on how events developed.

The details of how the takeover was to be achieved had been given by Lenin in 'Marxism and Uprising'. The Party was to.

'designate the forces; move the loyal regiments to the most important points; surround the Alexander Theatre; occupy Peter and Paul Fortress; arrest the general staff and the government; move against the military cadets, the Wild Division, etc., such detachments as will die rather than allow the enemy to move to the centre of the city; we must mobilize the armed workers, call them to a last desperate battle, occupy at once the telegraph and telephone stations, place *our* staff of the uprising at the central telephone station, connect it by wire with all the factories, the regiments, the points of armed fighting, etc.'

It is a rule of both political and military survival that a leader should not only be present but be seen to be present when great issues are being decided. Lenin knew this as well as most men and he also knew that when he returned to Petrograd he had some leeway to make up. The articles he had written in the comparative security of Finland and which had been sent for

---

calendar, thirteen days in advance, was that used in the West. Therefore, the events which were soon to take place were to be known in Russia – and still are known – as the October Revolution, while they are known in the West as the November Revolution. For this crucial period, events taking place in Russia are dated by the Julian calendar in use there, but the Gregorian dates used in the West follow in brackets.

publication in Petrograd with the help of his well-organized courier system did much to compensate for his personal absence; but the rest had to be made up for now, and quickly, by personal exhortation.

It was with this in mind that he prepared to address a gathering of the Central Committee called for the night of 10 (23) October at Sukhanov's flat. Ironically, in view of its outcome, the meeting had been set up not by Sukhanov, a Menshevik, but by his wife G. K. Sukhanova, who saw that he was absent for the whole evening. The Committee was finally induced to authorize a military uprising, and if it left many questions unanswered – such as a formal decision on the date – it made the decisions without which plans for a revolution might have meandered on indefinitely. According to Aleksandra Kollontay, Lenin 'looked every bit like a Lutheran minister', as, with Trotsky, Stalin, Zinoviev, Kamenev and about a dozen of the Committee's twenty-one members, he sat round the dining table in the Sukhanovs' main room for what was to be a momentous meeting. Before it was over the electricity was cut off; the discussion continued by the dim light of a hanging oil lamp, a discussion which at times was tense and rumbustious.

After a few minor matters had been dealt with Lenin took the floor. It was immediately clear that in Finland he had resolved any doubts about what should be done, and that the articles he had written there were not mere proposals but blueprints for the action which he now proposed should be taken with the minimum delay.

'He states [say the minutes of the meeting] that since the beginning of September a certain indifference towards the question of uprising has been noted. He says that this is inadmissible, if we earnestly raise the slogan of seizure of power by the Soviets. It is, therefore, high time to turn attention to the technical side of the question. Much time has obviously been lost.

'Nevertheless the question is very urgent and the decisive moment is near.

'The international situation is such that we must take the initiative.

'What is being planned, surrendering as far as Narva and even as far as Petrograd, compels us still more to take decisive action.

'The political situation is also effectively working in this direction. On July 16–18, decisive action on our part [during the July days] would have been defeated because we had no majority with us. Since then, our upsurge has been making gigantic strides.

'The absenteeism and the indifference of the masses can be explained by the fact that the masses are tired of words and resolutions.

'The majority is now with us. Politically, the situation has become entirely ripe for the transfer of power.'

This record – the only one that has survived – is only a summary of Lenin's injunctions. But they governed the path that the Revolution was to follow and one point – the link between Lenin's early years and the events of October [November] 1917 – should not be overlooked. It has been made by Lenin's old friend Bonch-Bruyevich:

'It is an irrefutable fact that the Russian revolution proceeded to a significant degree according to the ideas of Tkachev.

The seizure of power was made at a time determined in advance by a revolutionary party organized on the principles of strict centralization and discipline. And this party, having seized power, operates in many respects as Tkachev advised.'

Lenin spoke for an hour to the members of the Central Committee by lamplight. He spoke more with the intention of moving minds than of sticking too accurately to the facts of the situation – there was little evidence, for instance, that (as he implied) the Provisional Government intended pulling back its forces to the outskirts of Petrograd, let alone of giving up the city to the Germans. The idea had originated in a statement by Kornilov who had told the Moscow State Assembly: 'The enemy is already knocking at the gates of Riga, and if the decomposition of the Army prevents us from preserving the Riga Gulf the way to Petrograd will be open.' Riga fell a few days later and it was easy to claim that Kornilov and Kerensky were together plotting to destroy the revolution by letting in the Germans. Lenin himself did not necessarily believe this to be true but he knew that he would gain support for any action presented as a method of keeping German troops from marching through the streets of Petrograd.

Logically, he made the need for revolution sound unchallengeable. Nevertheless, two members of the Committee strongly disagreed. Zinoviev and Kamenev still deplored the idea of an immediate armed uprising, speaking in terms that they set down and elaborated a few days later.

'We are deeply convinced that to call at present for an armed uprising means to stake on one card not only the fate of our party, but also the fate of the Russian and international revolution [was the gist of their message] . . . Under these conditions it would be a serious historical untruth to formulate the question of the transfer of power into the hands of the proletarian party in the terms: either now or never . . . there is only one way in which the proletarian party can interrupt its successes, and that is if under present conditions it takes upon itself to initiate an uprising and thus expose the proletariat to the blows of the entire consolidated counter-revolution, supported by the petty-bourgeois democracy.'

There followed an animated discussion although the only major change in the plans proposed – other than their postponement – came from Trotsky who felt that the uprising must appear to be defensive and that the Red Guards should not intervene unless the Soviet Congress was attacked. When the argument was over and the vote was taken Lenin and nine others voted for action. Zinoviev and Kamenev still dissented. But to all claims that action now would be premature, Lenin had one reply that he gave in 'Can the Bolsheviks Retain State Power?' 'Our party will now be threatened with an immeasurably greater danger if we forget [that the question of the Bolsheviks taking power has become very urgent] than if we were to admit that taking power is "premature". In this respect, there can be *nothing* "premature" now: there is every chance in a million, except one or two perhaps, in favour of this.' Before the meeting ended a Political Bureau – or Politburo – consisting of Lenin, Trotsky, Zinoviev, Kamenev, Stalin, Sokolnikov and Bubnov was set up to direct Party affairs until the rising. The Politburo as thus constituted never met although the later Politburo, formed after the

Revolution, was to play an important role in Party affairs.

Lenin finally picked up a pencil and prepared to write the order for action. But no paper was readily available so he took a child's squared exercise book that someone discovered and in this wrote the instructions that were to change the course of history:

'The Central Committee recognizes that the international situation of the Russian Revolution (the mutiny in the navy in Germany [which had failed in July to August] as the extreme manifestation of the growth in all of Europe of the world-wide Socialist revolution; the threat of a peace between the imperialists with the aim of crushing the revolution in Russia) as well as the military situation; (the undoubted decision of the Russian bourgeoisie and of Kerensky and Co. to surrender Petrograd to the Germans) and the fact that the proletarian parties have gained a majority in the Soviets; all this, coupled with the peasant uprising and with a shift of the people's confidence towards our party (elections in Moscow); finally, the obvious preparation for a second Kornilov affair (the withdrawal of troops from Petrograd; the bringing of Cossacks to Petrograd; the surrounding of Minsk by Cossacks, etc.) – places the armed uprising on the order of the day.

'Recognizing thus that an armed uprising is inevitable and the time perfectly ripe, the Central Committee proposes to all the organizations of the Party to act accordingly and to discuss and decide from this point of view all the practical questions (the Congress of the Soviets of the Northern region, the withdrawal of troops from Petrograd, the actions in Moscow and in Minsk, etc.)'

Once he had written and signed what were in effect the orders for the Russian Revolution, Lenin was anxious to leave so that he would get back to Margarita Fofanova's flat under cover of darkness. But it was then realized that no date had been set for the insurrection. 'What day?' someone asked, and as he was leaving Lenin shouted something back over his shoulder, possibly, '28 October.'

There is uncertainty about what reply he gave to this crucial question but John Reed claims in *Ten Days That Shook the World* that a few days later Lenin explained how its date should tie in with the Second All-Russian Congress of Soviets of Workers', Soldiers' and Peasants' Deputies whose opening had been planned for 20 October (2 November) and was then postponed until 25 October (7 November).

> 'November sixth [24 October] will be too early [he is said to have stated to a number of Bolsheviks]. We must have an all-Russian basis for the rising; and on the sixth all the delegates to the Congress will not have arrived . . . On the other hand November eighth [26 October] will be too late. By that time the Congress will be organized, and it is difficult for a large organized body of people to take swift, decisive action. We must act on the seventh [25 October], the day the Congress meets, so that we may say to it, "Here is the power! What are you going to do with it?" '

Whatever Lenin may have said at a date later than 10 (23) October – and obscurity cloaks this as it cloaks many other events during the preparations for the Revolution – it seems certain that he gave no exact date at the crucial meeting on the tenth [twenty-third].

Stressing this in his history of the Revolution Trotsky, who seems to recollect accurately virtually everything that he did not record, comments:

'But this general resolution [calling for the rising] had to do with an insurrection throughout the whole country, and was destined for hundreds and thousands of leading party workers. To include in it the conspirative date of an insurrection to be carried out in the next few days in Petrograd, would have been unreasonable in the extreme. We must remember that out of caution Lenin did not in those days even put a date on his letters.'

11

The Seizure of Power

The rather casual priming of the starting gun for the Revolution was to be followed by more than one unplanned development during the next few days, as both Kerensky's Provisional Government and the Bolsheviks almost languidly began to flex their muscles for events to come. The importance of chance has been brought out by A.J.P. Taylor in his analysis of what happened. 'The Bolshevik Revolution was not a fully orchestrated piece with the music already composed,' he has written. 'It was compounded, like most other events, of confusions and misunderstandings, of human endeavours and human failures, where the outcome surprised the victors as much as it stunned the defeated.'

One point often overlooked is that it was not merely Zinoviev and Kamenev who were against an insurrection taking place during the second half of October. Trotsky wrote:

'Aside from the fact that those voting for insurrection were much of the time inclined to push it off into an indefinite future, the open enemies of the insurrection, Zinoviev and Kamenev, were not alone even in the Central Committee. Rykov and Nogin who were absent at the session of the 10th stood wholly upon their point of view, and Miliutin was close to them. "In the upper circles of the party, a wavering is to be observed, a sort of dread of the struggle for power" – such is the testimony of Lenin himself. According to Antonov-Saratovsky, Miliutin, arriving in Saratov after the 10th, was "told about the letter of Ilyich demanding that we begin, about the waverings in the Central Committee, the preliminary failure of Lenin's proposals, about his indignation, and finally about how the course was taken towards insurrection." The Bolshevik, Sadovsky, wrote later about "a certain vagueness and lack of confidence which prevailed at that time. Even among our Central Committee of those days, as is well known, there were debates and conflicts about how to begin and whether to begin at all." '

This division within the Party is illustrated by the fact that when the Central Committee met on 20 October Lenin's attempt to have Zinoviev and Kamenev expelled from the Party was overruled. The two men remained persistent in their objections to an insurrection at this time and within a few days had distributed to members of the Party an address in which they stated: 'Before history, before the international proletariat, before the Russian revolution and the Russian working-class, we have no right to stake the whole future at the present moment upon the card of armed insurrection.'

This at least kept the division within the Party secret from the rest of the world. For Zinoviev and Kamenev it was not sufficient and Kamenev quickly took a declaration of their views to Gorky's *Novaya Zhizn* together with a letter which said:

'Not only Zinoviev and I, but also a number of practical comrades, think that to take the initiative in an armed insurrection at the present moment, with the given corre-lation of social forces, independently of and several days before the Congress of Soviets, is an inadmissible step ruinous to the proletariat and the revolution . . . To stake everything . . . on the card of insurrection in the coming days would be an act of despair. And our party is too strong, it has too great a future before it, to take such a step . . .'

This, and the reluctant revolutionaries' statement, chimed in well with the attitude of Gorky and his paper. He had returned to Russia early in 1914, taken a pacifist line on the outbreak of war, but had pursued it with a restraint which protected him from most of the obloquy poured on others of similar views. After the February Revolution of 1917 he had regarded the Bolsheviks as merely one among a number of progressive parties, and it was not unexpected that in October he should warn about the future. Now, he not only printed the Zinoviev-Kamenev statement but also a leading article in which he said:

'Ever more persistent rumours are spreading to the effect that on 2 November a Bolshevik rising will take place; in other words, that the hideous scenes of 16 to 18 July may be repeated. That means that once more there will appear motor lorries overfilled with men with rifles and revolvers in their trembling hands, and these rifles will shoot at shop windows, at people, at random. They will shoot only because the men armed with them will try to kill their fear. All dark instincts of the crowd irritated by disorder, by the falsehood and filth of politics, will flare up and ooze forth poisonous malice, hatred, vengeance. People will be killing one another, in their inability to destroy their own bestial stupidity.

'The unorganized crowd will creep out into the streets, hardly understanding what it wants, while under its cover, adventurers, thieves, [and] professional assassins will set out to "create the history of the Russian revolution".

'In brief, there will be repeated that bloody, senseless slaughter, which we have already witnessed, and which has undermined through our whole land the moral importance of the revolution, and has shaken its cultural meaning.'

Lenin's first reaction to Zinoviev and Kamenev was first that they should be removed not only from the Central Committee but from the Party itself. His feeling was supported by Trotsky, who rarely saw eye to eye with his brother-in-law Kamenev, but many members of the Committee took a milder line, possibly because they secretly sympathized with a view they were unwilling to support openly. Among them was Stalin, who proposed that a reprimand would be sufficient if the two men promised to say no more. Lenin's long-term response to what he was to call Zinoviev and Kamenev's 'strike-breaking' was singularly revealing of the man. He seems never to have forgotten the incident – which was natural enough – and dragged it up whenever it could be used to reinforce any argument he wished to make. But both Zinoviev and Kamenev were to occupy high positions in the Party from which Lenin could have easily barred them. They were useful for carrying out what he saw as essential Party tasks and personal feelings counted for little against this.

The resolution of 10 (23) October had repercussions that were to be significant.

'It promptly put the genuine advocates of insurrection on the firm ground of party right [Trotsky later wrote]. In all the party organizations, in all its nuclei, the most resolute elements began to be advanced to the responsible posts. The party organizations, beginning with Petrograd, pulled themselves together, made an inventory of their forces and material resources, strengthened their communications, and gave a more concentrated character to the campaign for an overturn.'

The open protest of the two dissidents certainly removed any doubts in the Provisional Government that genuine revolution was now being prepared, but Kerensky's cabinet was already well aware of what was afoot. He left no room for ambiguity in the minds of Allied diplomats to whom he spoke. 'All I want them to do is act,' he told Sir George Buchanan, 'then I will crush them.' Possibly reflecting views from the same quarter, the American Ambassador David Francis cabled Lansing: 'Beginning to think Bolsheviki will make no demonstrations; if so, shall regret as believe sentiment turning against them and time opportune moment for giving them wholesome lesson . . .'

While Kerensky, a leader almost uniquely informed of revolutionary moves being prepared against him, was confidently predicting success, his opponents were making their own practical preparations for the insurrection. On 12 (25) October a Military Revolutionary Committee composed of forty-eight Bolsheviks, four Left Socialist Revolutionaries and four anarchists was set up under Trotsky, with a headquarters whose seven departments covered defence, supplies, communications, information, the workers' militia, reporting, and the commandant's office. It immediately began meeting in room 10 on the top floor at Smolny. Later a motor transport allocation department and an air services department were added.

A statement issued by the Military Revolutionary Committee to the people of Petrograd soon removed any doubts that Kerensky may have retained about what was to come. It read:

'In the interests of the defence of the revolution and its conquests against attacks by counter-revolution, commissars have been appointed by us in military units and at strategic points in the capital and its environs. Orders and instructions, which are being distributed to these points are to be carried out only with the sanction of our authorized commissars. Commissars, as representatives of the soviet are inviolable. Opposition to commissars is opposition to the Soviet of Workers' and Soldiers' Deputies. The soviet has taken all measures to protect revolutionary order against attacks by counter-revolutionaries and thugs. All citizens are invited to give every form of support to our commissars. In the event of disturbances arising one should turn to the commissars of the Military Revolutionary Committee in the nearest military unit.'

Estimates of the forces on either side vary considerably, partly owing to differences between numbers of men nominally on the strength and those genuinely likely to take part in operations if required. However, some estimates suggest a total of 300,000 men in armed worker, soldier and sailor units on the Bolshevik side although the Red Guards, organized in battalions of 400 to 600 men each, divided into three companies – a machine-gun section, a liaison section and an ambulance section – numbered only some 20,000. Some of the battalions had an armoured car. About 30,000 men were available to the Provisional Government including about 2,000 cadets and a women's battalion which had been raised after the February Revolution.

A further complication in assessing the number of troops involved on either side is suggested in that while garrison troops in Petrograd numbered 350,000, all but two regiments decided, after listening to harangues from Trotsky, that defending the Revolution offered better prospects than going to the front. One writer adds that the Provisional Government could also call upon 63,000 'guard troops', 25,000 infantry, the 5,000 women volunteers and 7,000 officer-cadets – all forces which were of doubtful reliability.

On both sides there was an observed reluctance to get involved in heavy fighting if it could be avoided. In the case of regular troops it was at least partly due to some units having been fighting since the start of the war in 1914. As was noted on both sides during the Second World War, even when fresh reinforcements were fed into badly mauled units, their fighting quality could be restored only with difficulty. With the Bolsheviks there was also the factor of ideology, the faith in the cause which may in some have become somewhat confused or diluted in the complicated succession of events which had taken place since the abdication of the Tsar. In these circumstances it is not surprising that on both sides moves leading to military confrontation took place slowly.

On 21 October (3 November) members of the Petrograd garrison, summoned to Smolny by the Petrograd Soviet, resolved 'to support the Military Revolutionary Committee in all its undertakings' and added:

'The country is on the verge of ruin. The army demands peace, the peasants land, and the workers bread and work. The Coalition Government is against the people. It became the tool of the enemies of the people. The time for words is past. The All-Russian Congress of Soviets [due to meet on 25 October (7 November)] must take the power into its own hands in order to give to the people peace, land and bread. Only thus can the safety of the revolution and of the people be ensured.'

Once this pledge had been received, the Military Revolutionary Committee sent commissars to the headquarters of Colonel Polkovnikov, Commander-in-Chief of the Petrograd Military District, and demanded from him the right to control the orders issued from the headquarters. The Colonel not only refused but issued a statement which said:'. . . He who is capable, at this time, of calling the masses to a civil war is either insane or a conscious tool of the Emperor William. I order all units under my command, all officers and soldiers, not to allow themselves to become involved in uprisings . .

The response of the Military Revolutionary Committee was to state that

'the [military] staff has broken off relations with the revolutionary garrison as well as with the Petrograd Soviet.

Having broken off relations with the organized garrison of the capital, the staff thereby becomes the tool of the counter-revolutionary forces.

'The Military Revolutionary Committee is thus released from all responsibility for the acts of the staff of the Petrograd Military District.'

Even at this late stage, both sides were apparently anxious to avoid decisive action if possible and during 23 October (5 November) the Provisional Government tried to make some sort of compromise with the Military Revolutionary Committee. The attempt failed, as the Government might have expected, and it can be seen as ending one chapter of the preliminary moves to revolution.

On the night of the 22 to 23 October (4 to 5 November) a cabinet meeting opened the next chapter by ordering Polkovnikov to bring reliable troops in from the suburbs to man strategic points, patrol the Winter Palace, and control the bridges over the Neva. Other troops were to occupy the Petrograd power station, a number of Government institutions and the railway stations. However, it was not these actions which were to bring about the first confrontation of the Revolution.

This came after Government troops, either Junkers or cadets, raided the *Pravda* offices, smashed some of the printing formes (moulds), and sealed off the offices. A girl and one of the workers ran to Smolny, sought out Trotsky, and told him that if new formes could be prepared, and protection given to the workers, the paper could still come out as usual. Trotsky instructed that the seals should be broken and that the 6th Battalion of sappers and the Litovsky Regiment should be ordered to the scene. The seals were broken, new moulds were poured and the paper was soon being printed.

The Government decided to cut off Smolny's telephone links and to prosecute the members of the Military Revolutionary Committee. Trotsky later commented:

> 'These pinpricks were just sufficient to convict the government of preparing a counter-revolutionary *coup d'état*. Although an insurrection can win only on the offensive, it develops better, the more it looks like selfdefence. A piece of official sealing-wax on the door of the Bolshevik editorial rooms – as a military measure that is not much. But what a superb signal for battle! Telephonograms to all districts and units of the garrison announced the event: "The enemy of the people took the offensive during the night. The Military Revolutionary Committee is leading the resistance to the assault of the conspirators." '

Within a few hours the Central Committee had decided that the action which had already been settled in general detail should start at 2 a.m. the following day, 25 October (7 November). As these moves were being made the Military Revolutionary Committee reported the latest events to the troops of the Petrograd garrison and ordered them 'to hold every regiment in readiness and await further orders. Any delay or failure to obey this order will be considered a betrayal of the Revolution.'

Trotsky's Military Revolutionary Committee ordered the requisitioning of vehicles and put its military units on full alert. These units were supported virtually everywhere by workers' units and in many individual cases it is difficult to separate the individual responsibilities of the Red Guards and of the civilian workers with whom they co-operated.

Both sides were now beyond the point of no return and Kerensky opened the next phase by announcing to the Pre-Parliament that Petrograd was in a state of insurrection. During his speech he was handed a copy of the latest order from the Military Revolutionary Committee to the Petrograd garrison, and added that the situation was 'an attempt to incite the rabble against the existing order, to prevent the convening of the Constituent Assembly . . . and to expose the front to the serried ranks of Wilhelm's mailed fist . . .'

Despite the familiar claim that opposition to the Provisional Government would aid the Germans, Kerensky received less support than he must have hoped when he invoked the aid of the Council of the Republic. A resolution moved by Martov, adopted by 123 votes to 102 with 25 abstentions, censured the impending armed outbreak, but supported changes in the Government's plans for peace and for land reform. The agitation in favour of an uprising, it was added, 'is due not merely to the objective conditions of war and general disorganization but also to the delay in carrying out measures which the country most urgently needs'. Kerensky was, with difficulty, dissuaded from resigning but he bowed to the plea that an order for the arrest of the Military Revolutionary Committee should be revoked.

Meanwhile, the Central Committee was confirming at Smolny the final details of its plans, and Trotsky, addressing the Petrograd Soviet, said that the Kerensky Government was now awaiting 'a sweep of the broom of history', in order to clear the way for a real Government of the revolutionary people.

Events continued to escalate throughout 24 October (6 November) and a pattern began to emerge as the Provisional Government did its unsuccessful best to keep control of the key points on which the mastery of Petrograd depended.

A full chronology of what happened where in Petrograd is not easy to give since the Government, the Military Revolutionary Committee, the Soviet, and individual military officers, tended to use different yardsticks for measuring the admittedly uncertain standard of military success or failure. When to this are added the later vagaries of memory and the promptings of personal or political bias it is easy to understand why accounts of the traumatic twenty-four hours starting about dusk on 25 October (7 November) are sometimes so conflicting.

To counter Kerensky's moves, Red Guards occupied the Baltic Station, prevented the raising of the Neva bridges which governed control of movement in much of the city, and occupied the telephone exchange, the telegraph office and the State Bank. As these significant operations were beginning, Lenin, apparently uninformed of latest developments, was writing from his hiding place a 'Letter to Central Committee Members':

'The situation is extremely critical. It is as clear as can be that delaying the uprising now really means death.

'With all my power I wish to persuade the comrades that now everything hangs on a hair, that on the order of the day are questions that are not solved by conferences, by congresses (even by Congresses of Soviets), but only by the people, by the masses, by the struggle of armed masses.

'The bourgeois onslaught of the Kornilovists, the removal of Verkhovsky [A. I. Verkhovsky, Minister of War in the Provisional Government until 19 October (1 November) when he resigned over the Pre-Parliament's rejection of his proposal for demobilizing part of the army] show that we must not wait. We must at any price, this evening, tonight, arrest the Ministers, having disarmed (defeated if they offer resistance) the military cadets, etc. We must not wait! We may lose everything . . .!

'History will not forgive delay by revolutionists who could be victorious today (and will surely be victorious today) while they risk losing much tomorrow, they risk losing all.'

This message now dispatched from Margarita Fofanova's flat to the Central Committee in the Vyborg district, Lenin's act of writing it, and of making sure that it reached its destination without delay, suggests not only his obsession with getting the Revolution under way but also a residual fear that even now his plans might be balked by the sluggishness of the Central Committee.

He had certainly made, in the days immediately before the Revolution, great efforts to ensure that there would be no last-minute hitch. Vladimir A. Antonov-Ovseyenko, a member of the RSDLP since 1903, has described one meeting with him in a house in the working-class district of Vyborg at which Lenin arrived in disguise.

'We found ourselves in the presence of a little, grey-haired old man, wearing pince-nez, wearing them with a proper, almost debonair style. One would have taken him for a musician, a schoolmaster, or a secondhand book dealer. He took off his wig, and we recognized his eyes, sparkling as usual with a glint of humour. "Any news?" he asked. He was full of confidence. He wondered about our chances of calling the fleet up into Petrograd. Somebody objected that this would leave the front at sea undefended, and his reply was brusque: "Come now, the sailors must know that there is more danger to the revolution in

391

Petrograd than on the Baltic." '

The message that Lenin sent on the evening of the 24 October (6 November) was scarcely on its way when even this action appeared insufficient to him. Despite the danger of discovery and arrest, he could not resist the attraction of being at the centre of operations, so he wrote a note to Fofanova saying: 'I am going where you did not want me to go', and then set off for Smolny.

He travelled part of the way on foot, part by tram, unrecognized in wig and battered cap and discussing the situation with the tram's conductress. According to one story she responded to his apparent isolation from what was going on with the remark: 'What sort of a worker are you if you don't know there's going to be a revolution? We're going to kick the bosses out.' It has also been claimed that Lenin was approached by two mounted cadets who wanted to inspect his papers and that he avoided this by feigning drunkenness.

According to Trotsky there was one other incident that night when chance might have altered history:

'The legal authorities did not even think of penetrating Smolny to make arrests; it was too obvious that this would be the signal for a civil war in which the defeat of the government was assured in advance. There was made, however, as a kind of administrative convulsion, an attempt to arrest Lenin in the Vyborg district where, generally speaking, the authorities were afraid even to look in. Late in the evening a certain colonel with a dozen junkers accidentally entered a workers' club instead of the Bolshevik editorial rooms located in the same house. The brave boys

392

had for some reason imagined that Lenin would be waiting for them in the editorial rooms. The club immediately informed the district headquarters of the Red Guard. While the colonel was wandering around from one storey to another, arriving once even among the Mensheviks, a detachment of Red Guards, rushing up, arrested him along with his junkers, and brought him to the headquarters of the Vyborg district, and thence to the Peter and Paul fortress.'

Lenin eventually arrived at Smolny some time before midnight on 24 October (6 November). He sought out Trotsky and the two men sat down together, Lenin still in the disguise in which he had crossed Petrograd. Then two Party members came into the building and passed nearby.

'He [Lenin] had a kerchief tied round him, as if he had toothache [Trotsky later wrote]. He had huge glasses and was wearing a dirty cap and looked quite odd. But Dan, whose eye was experienced and trained, when he had caught sight of us, looked now from one side and now from the other side, nudged Skobelev with his elbow, winked and carried on. Vladimir Ilyich also nudged me and said: "They have recognized us, the scoundrels." '

At 2 a.m. Trotsky pulled out his watch and said: 'It's begun', a remark which is claimed to have brought from Lenin the response: 'From being on the run to supreme power – that's too much.' Then, according to Trotsky, he made the sign of the Cross. Trotsky was correct since at 2 a.m. small parties of military and armed workers had begun to occupy the railway stations, power plants, food and munition stores, the waterworks, the telephone exchange and the post office. Men from the sapper battalion took up guard at these points without trouble.

Lenin was later taken by Bonch-Bruyevich to the latter's home. Although obviously tired, he could hardly be persuaded to go to bed. Bonch-Bruyevich has written:

'I retired to the couch in the next room, determined not to fall asleep until I was sure Vladimir Ilyich was sleeping. For greater safety I locked the outside door, fastening the chains, hooks and bolts, besides loading our revolvers, for somebody might try to break in, to arrest, or kill Vladimir Ilyich. This was the first night of the revolution, and anything might happen! To be on the safe side, too, I at once jotted down on a sheet of paper all the telephone numbers of comrades, the telephones of Smolny, the district workers' committees and trade unions, for fear of forgetting them in a flurry.

'Vladimir Ilyich had already switched off the light in his room, and I listened, wondering if he was sleeping. There was not a sound and I was just dozing off; in another moment I should have been asleep, when the light suddenly flashed on in Vladimir Ilyich's room. I heard him rise almost soundlessly and open the door a trifle to make sure I was sleeping (which I was not). He tip-toed to the desk, sat down, opened the ink-well and set to work on some papers he had spread out.

'He kept writing, crossing out what he had written, reading, making notes, writing again, and then, at last, apparently re-wrote the whole thing in a fair copy. The dawn of late autumn in Petrograd was turning the sky grey when he turned off the light, got into bed and fell asleep.'

In the morning, Bonch-Bruyevich goes on, Lenin came down to breakfast, took some neatly written pages from his pocket and proceeded to read his Decree on Land. It was announced at the Second Soviet Congress that evening, published in the newspapers the following morning, and quickly published as a separate booklet of which 50,000 copies were printed.

The operations of the Military Revolutionary Committee had, meanwhile, gone as planned with only minor and temporary hitches. In addition to occupying key points, its men had begun to monitor supplies to Government offices and checked that the *Aurora* had been brought to an anchorage near the Nikolayevsky Bridge, the only one still under Government control. The telegraph agency and the post office had been occupied. The Military Hotel was taken and at five o'clock the telephone exchange. At first light the State Bank had been surrounded and a few hours later a ring of troops was posted round the Winter Palace. Control of the bridges over the Neva was essential but throughout the early hours of the Revolution the situation on and around some of them remained uncertain. The cadets who arrived to raise the Liteiny Bridge were disarmed by the Military Revolutionary Committee, but for a while it was not clear what had happened next. The Troitsky Bridge, which should have been raised by the women's battalion, remained down. The Nikolayevsky Bridge was first raised by forces under Government control, but Red Guards seized the surrounding area and the bridge was lowered. A detachment of Government troops dispersed the Red Guards and the bridge was raised again, but sailors routed the Government forces around the bridge, which was once again lowered.

These events in the small hours of 25 October (7 November) were later reported to a meeting of the Central Committee in room 38 at Smolny attended by Lenin, Zinoviev, Trotsky and Stalin among others. Lenin was now able to discuss with the members of the Central Committee his ideas on the structure of the government that would succeed Kerensky's – the last opportunity to do so before the Second Congress of Soviets opened proceedings. No minutes of the meeting appear to have survived, but Lenin's notes, apparently made during it, were published in *Leninsky Sbornik* in 1924, and have been reproduced in English in T. H. Rigby's invaluable *Lenin's Government: Sovnarkom 1917–1922*.

Although some of Lenin's ideas later changed, it was certainly not too early to discuss them since it was obvious that the Provisional Government, whose ministers had by this time sought refuge in the Winter Palace, was in desperate straits. Petrograd had, in effect, been occupied by the Military Revolutionary Committee at the cost of a small handful of casualties. The trams had continued to run. The theatres and fashionable restaurants were open almost as usual and in many parts of the city it was difficult to appreciate the enormity of the change that had taken place. The position was exemplified by a report from Colonel Polkovnikov to the Stavka as early as 10.15 on the morning of 25 October.

'The situation in Petrograd is menacing [he wrote with some understatement]. There are no street disorders, but a systematic seizure of government buildings and railways stations is going on. None of my orders is obeyed. The cadets surrender their posts almost without resistance, and the Cossacks, who were repeatedly ordered to come out [behind the Government] refused to do so . . . I must report, conscious of my responsibility to the country, that the Provisional Government is in danger. There is no guaranty that the insurrectionists will not next attempt to arrest the Provisional Government.'

The insurrectionists had already made detailed plans for formally taking over from the Government, whose members were isolated first in the Malachite Chamber overlooking the Neva; then, when danger threatened, in an interior room lit by one lamp shaded by newspaper. Lenin was therefore able to justify his manifesto headed 'To the Citizens of Russia':

'The Provisional Government has been deposed. State power has passed into the hands of the organ of the Petrograd Soviet of Workers' and Soldiers' Deputies, the Revolutionary Military Committee, which heads the Petrograd proletariat and the garrison.

'The cause for which the people have fought – namely, the immediate offer of a democratic peace, the abolition of landed proprietorship, workers' control over production, and the establishment of Soviet power – this cause had been secured.

'Long live the revolution of workers, soldiers and peasants!'

Despite this statement, the ministers in the Winter Palace still presented a problem, if not a serious one. However, the Military Revolutionary Committee was justified in its cautious tactics, which included the infiltration of men into the Winter Palace to discover how the besieged Government forces were faring. One observer of the limp morale inside the Government 'stronghold' was John Reed:

> 'On both sides of the parqueted floor lay rows of dirty mattresses and blankets, upon which occasional soldiers were stretched out; everywhere was a litter of cigarette butts, bits of bread, cloth, and empty bottles with expensive French labels. More and more soldiers, with the red shoulderstraps of the Junker-schools, moved about in a stale atmosphere of tobacco smoke and unwashed humanity . . . The place was all a huge barrack, and evidently had been for weeks, from the look of the floor and walls.'

The situation would no doubt have been resolved earlier had the need to keep casualties to a minimum been less restricting. It had first been intended to storm the building at noon, but the attack had been postponed first until 3 p.m. and then for another three hours. Thus when Trotsky opened an emergency session of the Petrograd Soviet at 2.30 p.m. on 25 October (7 November) the listeners heard not only the news that the Provisional Government no longer existed but also the explosions of Military Revolutionary Committee artillery firing blanks at the Winter Palace in the hope of encouraging surrender.

However, Kerensky himself had already abandoned ship. He had sought the help of the US Embassy, and Secretary Whitehouse came to the rescue with his own car which, flying the American flag on the bonnet, escorted Kerensky to army headquarters where he hoped to raise forces for a return to the city. Following Kerensky's flight A. S. Konovalov, the Moscow millionaire who had served the Progressives in the Duma, became Acting Premier and N. M. Kishkin was appointed

Commissar for the Restoration of Order in Petrograd. Konovalov's first action was to dismiss Colonel Polkovnikov and appoint General Bakratuni in his place. This, of course, failed to alter the military position and it was clear to what remained of the Provisional Government that there was no hope of repelling an attack. However, the Military Revolutionary Committee's cautious approach was compounded by a series of accidental delays and it was only at 6.30 p.m. on 25 October (7 November) that two messengers delivered an ultimatum to the Winter Palace: unless the defenders surrendered within twenty minutes a bombardment would begin from the St Peter and St Paul Fortress, the *Aurora,* and other ships on the Neva.

The ultimatum was disregarded but the threatened attack was held up by the discovery that the guns in the St Peter and St Paul could not easily be used safely with the ammunition available. Eventually a naval gunner able to deal with the difficulty was found but once again there were delays, and at 9 p.m. the ministers in the Winter Palace were able to telephone military headquarters on a line whose existence had not been known to the Military Revolutionary Committee and had still not been cut. They appealed for an uprising in the rear of the fighting army, but it was extraordinarily late in the day for such an appeal, and even as it was being made *the Aurora* opened up once more, but again with blank shot. An hour later there came an unsuccessful sortie from the Winter Palace by the women's battalion and then, after the lapse of another hour, the guns of the St Peter and St Paul Fortress at last began firing with live ammunition. They caused little damage and it was clear that an assault would have to be made even though little serious opposition was expected.

When Red Guards and sailors eventually entered the

building, covered by machine-gun fire, there was virtually no opposition. 'In the name of the Military and Revolutionary Committee of the Petrograd Soviet', said Antonov-Ovseyenko to the ministers in the single small room, 'I declare the Provisional Government deposed. All are arrested.' Attempts to attack the hated members of the Provisional Government were warded off by the guards with cries of 'Don't spoil the Proletarian triumph', and the captives were marched to the St Peter and St Paul Fortress.

While this was happening the Second Congress of Soviets had opened at 10.45 p.m. under the presidency of Kamenev in the great white ballroom of Smolny, lit by the huge chandeliers and with the boom of the Winter Palace bombardment heard clearly by the delegates. Almost immediately, there was criticism of the Bolshevik takeover. The Congress itself was repudiated by Kharash, from the Twelfth Army, supported by a speaker who described the seizure of power as 'a stab in the back of the Army and a crime against the people'. Aleksandr E. Abramovich, the leader of the Bund, called the events a great calamity, and before long the members of the Bund, as well as the Mensheviks and the Right Socialist Revolutionaries, left the Congress. In opposition to them were those represented by a speaker who claimed: 'The men in the trenches are eager for the Soviets to take power.'

The walk-out by some of the Socialist Revolutionary delegates was a foretaste of the trouble brewing. Left- and right-wing Socialist Revolutionaries had both been accommodated within the party since its inception. Now, however, while the right-wing members walked out of the Congress which was regularizing the Bolshevik takeover, left-wing members – who were themselves to break away and become a separate party a few weeks later – stayed on and voted with the Bolsheviks on the main points

400

debated. However, they rejected, for the time being, the Bolsheviks' offer of posts in the Government, although subsequently they accepted a number in the new administration. With the signing of the treaty of Brest-Litovsk early in 1918 a process began of withdrawal from Government, an opposition movement which eventually developed to bring about the assassination of the German representative in Petrograd, Count Mirbach, in the summer of 1918, and an abortive Socialist-Revolutionary revolt.

The Second Congress of Soviets went into recess in the small hours, but was reconvened at 3.00 a.m. and heard Kamenev announce that the Winter Palace had been captured and the remaining members of the Provisional Government arrested. It was not the only encouraging news. A speaker arrived from the Third Cyclist battalion, which Kerensky had hoped to recruit to his side, walked on to the platform and announced that among all the cyclists there was not one who would take action against his brothers. Nor was this all. The garrison at Tsarskoe Tselo, which Kerensky had hoped to bring to the Provisional Government's defence, had voted in favour of the Bolsheviks; even more significant was the response at the headquarters of the Northern Front at Pskov where a Military Revolutionary Committee had been set up.

While digesting the good news the Congress approved the following declaration which had been drafted by Lenin.

'To workers, soldiers and peasants. Basing itself on the will of the vast majority of workers, soldiers and peasants, basing itself on the victorious rising of workers and of the garrison which has been achieved in Petrograd, the Congress takes power into its hands . . . All power in the localities passes to the soviets of workers', soldiers' and peasants' deputies, whose duty it is to establish genuine revolutionary order.'

Before the sitting closed at 5 a.m. on 26 October (8 November) Trotsky had intervened with a speech whose final words became famous:

'The insurrection of the masses is in no need of justification. What is taking place is not a conspiracy but an insurrection. We moulded the revolutionary will of the Petrograd workers and soldiers . . . The masses gathered under our banner, and our insurrection was victorious. But what do they [the other socialists] offer us? . . . To give up our victory, to compromise, and to negotiate – with whom? With whom shall we negotiate? With those miserable cliques which have left the Congress or with those who still remain? But we saw how strong those cliques were! There is no one left in Russia to follow them. And millions of workers and peasants are asked to negotiate with them on equal terms. No, an agreement will not do now. To those who have left us and to those proposing negotiations we must say: You are a mere handful, miserable, bankrupt; your role is finished, and you may go where you belong – to the garbage heap of history!'

The remark brought a rejoinder from Martov, who pushed his way out.

But by the morning of 26 October (8 November) it was clear that whatever the political dissensions, Lenin, the man with no practical military experience and with theoretical knowledge hardly going beyond study of the Paris Commune of almost half a century earlier, had master-minded one of the militarily cheapest revolutions in history. In this he had been immeasurably helped by Trotsky who later fairly summed up the situation when he wrote: 'If neither Lenin nor I had been present in Petersburg, there would have been no October Revolution: the leadership of the Bolshevik Party would have prevented it from occurring – of this I have not the slightest doubt! If Lenin had not been in Petersburg, I doubt whether I could have managed to conquer the resistance of the Bolshevik leaders.'

The success of the Revolution in Petrograd was the more remarkable in that it had been achieved despite the limitations imposed by the wish to keep down casualties to the minimum. This was in line with the philosophical background to the Revolution, in which purely military considerations had, it was felt, to be tempered by the beliefs for which the military operation was being undertaken. Both during it and the immediately following weeks, events often suggest a barely concealed conflict of ideas between those seeking to consolidate the immediate military, economic or industrial results of the Revolution and those who wished such results to be judged within a broader context. Despite the qualifications thus imposed by what might be called the idealistic background of the revolutionaries, it seemed at times to those in Petrograd that victory had been gained almost too easily. As Trotsky himself later put it:

'The final act of the revolution seems, after all this, too brief, too dry, too businesslike – somehow out of correspondence with the historic scope of the events. The reader experiences a kind of disappointment. He is like a mountain climber, who, thinking the main difficulties are still ahead, suddenly discovers that he is already on the summit or almost there. Where is the insurrection? There is no picture of the insurrection. The events do not form themselves into a picture. A series of small operations, calculated and prepared in advance, remain separated one from another both in space and time. A unity of thought and aim unites them, but they do not fuse in the struggle itself. There is no action of great masses. There are no dramatic encounters with the troops. There is nothing of all that which imaginations brought up upon the facts of history associate with the idea of insurrection.'

The incongruity of the achievement was later stressed by James Maxton, an Independent Labour Party member of Parliament. He wrote:

'Here was no great soldier who had won fame by deeds of gallantry or military genius on the tented field. [Lenin] had never buckled on a sword or shouldered a gun – except a sporting gun when he sallied forth to shoot wild-duck. He was no world statesman who had won fame in parliament or council by forensic skill or political subtlety. He was no literary genius whose writings, reaching the hearts of a whole nation, had made his name a household word. He had not even established a reputation as a great lawyer successfully championing in the courts oppressed and suffering individuals. He was a plain man who had appeared out of obscurity to meet a need felt keenly by 150 millions of people, in the armies of Russia, in the factories and streets of Moscow and Petrograd, and in the thousands of villages scattered over the vast plains of Russia.'

Maxton's statement tended to gild the lily. During the opening session of the Second All-Russian Congress of Soviets of Workers' and Soldiers' Deputies, which included 100 left-wing Socialist Revolutionaries, moderate Socialist Revolutionaries and Mensheviks as well as 390 Bolsheviks, it had become evident that there was much disagreement with the Bolshevik seizure of power and that many delegates were prepared to disagree violently. Reaction in the huge areas of provincial Russia had yet to become known, while nearer at hand was the threat still presented by Kerensky, a deposed premier desperately trying to whip up support for an attack on the capital that would bring him back to power. All these were qualifications to Lenin's triumph while there was one political point which was often overlooked in the euphoria at Smolny. As Fritz Fischer was to remark in *Germany's Aims in the First World War*, Lenin's victory 'could not but seem to the German Government to be the crown of their military and political campaign against Russia since the autumn of 1914'. This corollary of the Bolshevik triumph was to become more important in the difficult weeks ahead. During the first days of success what occupied most minds was the series of revolutionary changes which had so long been promised by Lenin, on the platform and in the pages of newspapers and journals.

There were three important matters to be dealt with: the moves to be made to end the war; the decrees which would bring about the promised redistribution of land; and the composition of the Government which was to take over from Kerensky's the task of running the country. All were settled after Lenin had appeared at the Congress on 26 October (8 November) to an outburst of tumultuous cheering.

'A short, stocky figure, with a big head set down on his

shoulders, bald and bulging [was how he appeared in his moment of triumph to John Reed]. Little eyes, a snubbish nose, wide generous mouth, and heavy chin; cleanshaven now but already beginning to bristle with the well-known beard of his past and future. Dressed in shabby clothes, his trousers much too long for him. Unimpressive, to be the idol of a mob, loved and revered as perhaps few leaders in history have been. A strange popular leader – a leader purely by virtue of intellect; colourless, humourless, uncompromising and detached, without picturesque idiosyncrasies – but with the power of explaining profound ideas in simple terms, of analysing a concrete situation. And combined with shrewdness, the greatest intellectual audacity.'

Although Reed's version of the momentous meeting can be disputed on points of detail it is nevertheless among the most reliable and unbiased of the many that exist. Accounts have come from Trotsky, Lenin, and many other participants and it is inevitable that they should differ. Yet what is clear from them all is that Lenin was greeted with an overall rapturous enthusiasm despite criticisms from the Socialist Revolutionaries and from various peasant representatives that the Bolsheviks were stealing their thunder. This was partly true although it should be remembered that Lenin's Party was now achieving what so many others had for so long failed to achieve.

He was given an ovation that lasted several minutes. When it had subsided he said simply, according to Reed: 'We shall now proceed to construct the Socialist order.' Whatever the exact words there was a roar of approval once again, and it was only as this died away that Lenin continued to speak. As usual, it was first things first – 'adoption of practical measures to realize peace . . . We shall offer peace to the peoples of all the belligerent countries upon the basis of the Soviet terms – no annexations, no indemnities, and the right of self-determination of peoples.' But there was to be more to Lenin's peace plans than this.

> 'The Government [he went on] abolishes secret diplomacy, and, for its part, announces its firm intention to conduct all negotiations quite openly in full view of the whole people. It will proceed immediately with the full publication of the secret treaties endorsed or concluded by the government of landowners and capitalists from February to 25 October 1917. The Government proclaims the unconditional and immediate annulment of everything contained in these secret treaties in so far as it is aimed, as is mostly the case, at securing advantages and privileges for the Russian landowners and capitalists and at the retention, or extension, of the annexations made by the Great Russians.'

This threat, for it was no less, probably worried Russia's erstwhile allies almost as much as the words with which Lenin now concluded his plans for peace. 'The question of War and Peace is so clear,' he said, 'that I think that I may, without preamble, read the project of a Proclamation to the Peoples of All the Belligerent Countries.'

The Proclamation, which proposed an immediate three-month armistice, was followed by brief comments from the floor before being unanimously approved. In the ensuing emotional reaction one man was heard declaiming, 'The war is ended! The war is ended!', after which there came a cry from the back of the hall: 'Comrades! Let us remember those who have died for liberty!' Then came the strains of the Russian funeral march.

Lenin now began reading the Decree on Land with its first two crucial points:

'(i) Landed proprietorship is abolished forthwith without any compensation. (2) The landed estates, as also all crown, monastery, and church lands, with all their livestock. implements, buildings and everything pertaining thereto, shall be placed at the disposal of the *volost* [rural district] land committees and the *uyezd* [county] Soviets of Peasants' Deputies pending the convocation of the Constituent Assembly.'

The Decree on Land, under which peasants were released from all earlier debts and more than 150 million hectares of agriculturally valuable land passed into their hands, was approved after only minor protests. There might have been more since satisfying the peasants was a greater problem than it at first appears. It was complicated in that the word 'peasant' could be used to cover at least three groups, which in practice often merged into each other. At the top of the hierarchy there were the *kulaks* who rented land, hired agricultural labour, produced on a relatively large scale for the market and are considered as peasants only by stretching the term. Next there were the *serednyaks* who worked their holdings, smaller than those of the *kulaks*, mainly by family labour, and who while selling their surplus on the markets, did not do so to the same extent as the *kulaks*. Finally there were the *bednyaks*, who did not till enough land to feed their families and who usually had to hire out their labour to the better off. All were eventually covered by the Law on the Socialization

408

of the Land which proposed the development of collective farming as the most profitable with regard to economizing labour and produce, at the expense of individual farms and with the aim of adopting a socialist economy.

After the Decree on Land had been passed the Constitution of Power was discussed, to legitimize the new Government. Some details had already been hammered out between Lenin and Bonch-Bruyevich, who was to become head of the Government's chancellery and who had spent much time with Lenin since the latter's arrival at Smolny. 'It is necessary to set up commissions for the administration of the country, which will be commissariats,' Lenin had stated. Their members should, he added, be called commissars since the word had a fine revolutionary ring. 'The *collegium* of chairmen will be the Council of People's Commissars [Sovet Narodnykh Komissarov or Sovnarkom] to which will belong full power. The Congress of Soviets and the Central Executive Committee are to control its activity, and to them belongs the right of replacing commissars.'

It had earlier been proposed by Lenin that Trotsky should head the Council of People's Commissars but Trotsky had refused. He had also refused, on the ground of his Jewish origin, to become Commissar for Home Affairs, but had taken the Foreign Affairs portfolio on Bonch-Bruyevich's suggestion. The Council's first act was to order elections for the Constituent Assembly on 12 (25) November. The decree, signed by Lenin and soon being printed, said simply that every effort would be made to ensure that they were free.

The Left Socialist Revolutionaries were offered posts in the projected cabinet. For the moment, however, they refused to accept them and the commissars whose names were read out to the Congress by Kamenev were all Bolsheviks, headed by Lenin as

Chairman of the Council. Trotsky held the Foreign Affairs portfolio, and Stalin that for Nationality Affairs. With the exception of three others, V. A. Antonov-Ovseyenko, N. V. Krylenko and P. E. Dybenko, who formed a Committee for Military and Naval Affairs, the other commissars were also responsible for separate departments such as Labour, Agriculture, Justice or Food. The situation changed some weeks later when seven Left Socialist Revolutionaries joined the Government: Kalegayev became Commissar for Agriculture, Prozhyan Commissar for Posts and Telegraphs and Trutovsky Commissar for Local Government. The most important among these later appointments, however, was I. N. Steinberg who became Commissar for Justice.

After the Council of People's Commissars had been voted into office Trotsky announced the composition of the new Government of the Republic, of whose hundred members seventy were Bolsheviks. Places were to be reserved for other factions, he maintained, adding that the Government welcomed all parties and groups which would adopt its programmes.

The momentous Second All-Russian Congress of Soviets of Workers' and Soldiers' Deputies now rose. It was almost seven in the morning and John Reed, who had sat through the proceedings, reported that the drivers and conductors of the trams had to be wakened before the delegates could be taken home. 'In the crowded car,' he wrote, 'there was less happy hilarity than the night before, I thought. Many looked anxious; perhaps they were saying to themselves, "Now we are masters, how can we do our will?" '

Much the same thoughts were, no doubt, running through Lenin's mind as he contemplated the problems ahead.

The Bolsheviks in Control

12

Problems of Success

Although the forces of the Military Revolutionary Committee had gained control of Petrograd at remarkably little cost to either themselves or their opponents, Lenin was experienced enough to know that his problems were only now beginning. There were problems at all levels, of different degrees of seriousness, and in fields that encompassed military, economic, political and diplomatic matters. For the foreseeable future they were inextricably entwined, and the record of his early months in power is largely an account of how he coped with overlapping difficulties whose solutions inevitably reacted on each other.

Following the Congress, the most important matter for him and for his colleagues was the fate of Kerensky's expedition from Petrograd. Kerensky had first driven to Gatchina, then taken a train to Ostrov in the province of Pskov where he tried to gain support at a meeting of the local Soviet of Workers' and Soldiers' Deputies. He had a mixed reception and it was only on 27 October (9 November), after he had won the backing of General

Krasnov, the army commander in Pskov who controlled 700 Cossacks, that he began a march on Petrograd. Tsarskoe Tselo was captured the following day but its 16,000 garrison troops, while not putting up any defence, refused to join Krasnov's forces. Two days later Krasnov reached the strategically important Pulkovo Heights outside Petrograd where, it must have been obvious to both sides, the immediate fate of the Revolution could well be settled.

The outcome of the operation was described by Trotsky two years later on 30 October, 1919 in *Pravda* no. 250:

'[It was] decided by the artillery, which, on the Pulkovo Heights, did considerable damage to Krasnov's cavalry. Casualties of 300–500 killed and wounded were mentioned– undoubtedly an exaggerated figure. The Cossacks fought without any particular zeal. They had been assured that the population of Petrograd would receive them as deliverers, and that a minor artillery bombardment would suffice to bring an end to their campaign. They halted, complained to their commanders, held meetings, and entered into negotiations with the representatives of the Red Guards . . . Eventually the Cossacks withdrew to Gatchina, where Krasnov's headquarters was. Kerensky fled, deceiving Krasnov, who, seemingly, was preparing to deceive him. Kerensky's adjutants, and Voytinsky [V. S. Voytinsky, a former Bolshevik who became Kerensky's commissar for the Northern Front in the First World War], who was with them, were abandoned by him to their fate, and were taken prisoner by us along with Krasnov's whole headquarters.'

Kerensky might have been helped during this crucial episode

by a quickly organized local insurrection on 29 October (11 November) against the new Government mounted from some of Petrograd's military schools in which the Petrograd telephone exchange and a number of other buildings were captured. But these were recaptured by Military Revolutionary Committee units within a few hours, and Trotsky was able to issue a statement saying:

> 'The attempt of Kerensky to move counter-revolutionary troops against the capital of the Revolution has been decisively repulsed. Kerensky is retreating, we are advancing. The soldiers, sailors and workers of Petrograd have shown that they can and will with arms in their hands enforce the will and authority of the democracy. The bourgeoisie tried to isolate the revolutionary army. Kerensky attempted to break it by the force of the Cossacks. Both plans met a pitiful defeat.'

Trotsky's confident statement was no more than the truth as far as Petrograd was concerned, exemplified by what happened on the day after the takeover, when troops arrived at the Winter Palace where the Council of the Republic was meeting and told the delegates to leave. Some agreed to go. Others protested but left after denouncing the military intervention. Members of the Petrograd City Council marched in protest to the city centre; but they gave up when they found their way barred by sailors.

In Moscow, where Lenin had not expected major opposition, a more serious state of affairs developed. As soon as news of success in Petrograd arrived, a revolutionary committee was set up. With equal speed the city's military commander, Colonel Ryabzev, ordered its dissolution, and fighting broke out when his order was ignored. Kerensky's troops held the Kremlin while Military Revolutionary Committee forces held many of the suburbs and most of the working-class areas. For several days fighting was fierce, particularly around the Historical Museum and the Bolshevik headquarters half a mile away. Government forces were driven back into the Kremlin but fighting went on for a week with little sign of either side approaching success. Then the Military Revolutionary Committee brought up heavy artillery and began a bombardment of the Kremlin, but 500 revolutionary troops were killed before failure of either side decisively to gain the upper hand brought an agreement, signed on the afternoon of 2 (15) November. Under it, the defenders were allowed to leave the city on condition that they gave up their arms. Most of them made for other parts of Russia where they hoped to continue the struggle.

During the Moscow fighting a number of Bolshevik prisoners are reported to have been killed by the Provisional Government's forces, and there is little doubt that the encounters in the city were more ferocious and sustained than those that had occurred in Petrograd where, by comparison, battle had tended to assume an almost gentlemanly nature. The clash in Moscow witnessed a prelude to the indiscriminate killings that were to develop on both sides and produced the Red and White Terrors. It also brought an unexpected, if temporary, resignation from the new Government – that of Lunacharsky, appointed Commissar for Education, who left in protest when he was incorrectly told that St Basil's Cathedral and the Uspensky Cathedral had been destroyed in the fighting, apparently by Government artillery. On learning that the buildings were untouched he withdrew his resignation; but the incident revealed how varied were the problems with which Lenin was now having to cope.

One important feature of the Kremlin had been damaged during the fighting – the clock above the Spassky gate in the east wall of the building, which since the mid-nineteenth century had played two tsarist tunes, 'Kol' slayen'and the Preobrazhensky March'. The damage made it necessary for considerable work to be done and Lenin took the opportunity of having the mechanism changed so that two different tunes were played – the Internationale each noon and the funeral song of the Revolution, 'Vy zhertvoiu pali' ('You fell in sacrifice') at midnight.

But although Russia's two main cities were under control of the new Government's forces by mid-November, revolutionary takeovers took place elsewhere in widely differing conditions. The new order was less contested in industrial areas, but it would be misleading to generalize. In the Caucasus, the oil centre of Baku instituted a Soviet authority in November, but in Tiflis, the capital of Georgia, the local Congress of Soviets voted for the convening of a Constituent Assembly.

Lenin quickly began to consolidate his position by ordering the formation of shock units consisting mainly of sailors from the Baltic fleet, and in the first three weeks following the Revolution about 200 such units were sent into the provinces to help the newly established Bolshevik authorities. In some places their mere arrival was all that was needed. At others, where force was required, their discipline was remarked on.

The defeat of the anti-Bolshevik forces in Moscow, following the defeat of Kerensky's troops on the Pulkovo Heights, removed any chance of Lenin's Government being overthrown suddenly by military force. What neither event disposed of was the strong body of opinion throughout the country which had little sympathy for the Bolshevik takeover, even though it exhibited little wish to come out on the streets in defence of the Provisional

Government. Most people wanted peace and were willing to listen to any government that offered the slightest hope of alleviating the food shortage. But while they would not actively oppose Lenin and his supporters they did not look on him and his fellow Bolsheviks as hopeful beacons in the darkness: they might give their support to the new masters of Petrograd but if such support was to be retained their interests would have to be considered whenever possible. There were also those who objected, in varying degree, to the new regime – dissidents who included not only the expected right-wingers and many members of the middle classes, but such possibly surprising figures as Maxim Gorky.

After the success of the Revolution Gorky maintained and increased his attacks on the Bolsheviks. Alexander Kaun, one of Gorky's most trustworthy biographers, has pointed out that *Novaya Zhizn* always referred to the new Government with quotation marks round the word Government, prefaced Lenin's name with 'Citizen' instead of 'Comrade' and published editorials with titles like 'On the Verge of the Precipice', 'The Breath of Death' and 'Demagogy of Impotence'. On 7 (20) November *Novaya Zhizn* provided the following indictment:

'Lenin, Trotsky and their supporters, have already been poisoned by the corruptive virus of power, which is evident from their disgraceful treatment of freedom of speech and person, and of all those rights for which democracy has struggled . . . Along this road Lenin and his henchmen deem it right to commit every – crime, such as the slaughter near Petrograd, the bombardment of Moscow, the abolition of free speech, senseless arrests – exactly the same abominations formerly perpetrated by Plehve and Stolypin. To be sure, Stolypin and Plehve acted against democracy, against all that was alive and decent in Russia, whereas Lenin is followed, for the time being, by a fairly important section of the workmen. But I am convinced that the workmen's good sense, their understanding of their historical tasks, will soon open their eyes to the unattainability of Lenin's promises, to the depths of his madness, to his *Nechayev-Bakunin* brand of anarchy . . . The workmen must understand that, with their skins and blood Lenin is performing an experiment . . . that there are no miracles in ordinary life, that they must expect hunger, complete dislocation of industry, ruin of transport, prolonged bloody anarchy – and in its wake a no less bloody and gloomy reaction. That is where the people are being led by its present leader. We must recognize that Lenin is not an omnipotent magician, but a cold-blooded trickster, who spares neither the honour nor the lives of the proletariat.'

On the 10 (23) November *Novaya Zhizn* went even further in its personal denunciation of Lenin.

'[He] is of course a man of exceptional force . . . He has all the qualities of a leader, including the indispensable amoral quality and an aristocratic merciless attitude to the lives of common people . . . Life in its real complexity is unknown to Lenin. He does not know the masses of the people. He has never lived among them. Only from books he learned how to raise this mass on to its haunches, and how most effectively to rouse its instincts to a fury . . . He is working like a chemist in his laboratory . . . with this difference – that the chemist employs dead matter to gain results valuable for life, whereas Lenin works on living material and is leading the revolution to disaster.'

Gorky's statement sounded like an isolated impassioned outburst. It did, in fact, represent a significant feeling not only in Petrograd but throughout the country; in the immediate aftermath of the Revolution opinion was more evenly balanced than its eventual success has tended to suggest and for a while much rested on how successfully the new Government would use the power it had taken.

As events turned out, Lenin was at first as worried by civilian as by military reaction to the Revolution. While Kerensky had still been advancing, two of the big railway unions had demanded a three-day armistice between the opposing parties and a new, coalition Government, which would include Bolsheviks while excluding Lenin. But Lenin refused to resign, and a railway strike was avoided only after difficult negotiations. What went ahead was a major bank strike and a strike of civil servants, moves that between them steadily began to change conditions in Petrograd from disorder to chaos.

On 3 (16) November, Trotsky had issued a statement from the Smolny Institute saying:

'We are nationalizing all banks, with the object of making one national bank. In these matters we shall act fearlessly and without pity, overcoming the resistance of landowners and capitalists who do not wish to give up their privileges without a fight.

'Our plans are colossal, difficult, grandiose, but the strength of the people, opened up by the revolution, will overcome all difficulties and fulfil its ideals.'

In practice, matters went less smoothly than either Trotsky or Lenin had hoped. According to John Reed who, in spite of being a Bolshevik supporter, has given a comparatively objective account of conditions in the capital:

'The private banks remained stubbornly closed, with a back door open for speculators. When Bolshevik Commissars entered, the clerks left, secreting the books and removing the funds. All the employees of the State Bank [formed after the decree, based on Lenin's draft, had been endorsed by the All-Russian Central Executive Committee on 14 (27) December] struck except the clerks in charge of the vaults and the manufacture of money, who refused all demands from Smolny and privately paid out huge sums to the Committee for Salvation and the City Duma.'

The strike in the civil service had repercussions quite as widespread as that in the banks, although its impact varied from ministry to ministry. At the Commissariat of Foreign Affairs Trotsky was forced to take over with the help of a unit of sailors – those most reliable supporters of the Revolution. At the Ministry of Labour there was no one to light the fires and no one to show Commissar Shlyapnikov where his office was. In the Ministries of Agriculture, Supplies and Finance, similar incidents took place while Aleksandra Kollontay, Commissar of Public Works, was frustrated in all her attempts to deal with the poor and incapacitated. When the keys of the building and the safe were finally obtained, it was found that the former Minister, Countess Panina, had taken charge of all available funds and would not hand them over except on the order of a Constituent Assembly.

Lunacharsky, whose Commissariat of Enlightenment included the former Ministry of Public Education, the State Education Committee, the Academy of Arts and the Palace Ministry which controlled the imperial theatres, found both teachers and education officials on strike. 'It has been observed', he said, 'that an empty-headed clerk will soon come to us, but all the intellectual workers stubbornly insist on their opinion that we have usurped power. It will be much easier to build everything afresh than to take account of old and decayed institutions.'

The Bolsheviks did what they could. 'We are accused of making arrests,' Lenin wrote. 'Indeed, we have made arrests; today we arrested the director of the State Bank. We are accused of resorting to terrorism, but we have not resorted, and I hope will not resort, to the terrorism of the French revolutionaries who guillotined unarmed men.' It was a vain hope, but as far as the banks were concerned chaos was bound to continue and Lenin was soon writing to V. V. Vorovsky in Stockholm: 'Urgently find and send here three highly skilled accountants to work on reform of the banks.'

Getting someone competent to head the newly set-up State Bank was apparently a major problem and M. L. Peskovsky has explained how he was casually sitting in what turned out to be the People's Commissariat of Finances when a Soviet official named Menzhinsky started a conversation with him.

'I told him that I had studied at the London University and that among other subjects I had studied finance [he has written]. Menzhinsky suddenly got up, looked at me severely, and said categorically, "In that case we appoint you director of the State bank." I was frightened, and told him that I had no desire for that position, which was not at all my job.

Menzhinsky said not a word, asked me to wait a little, and left the room. After some time he came back with a paper on which, under the signature of Ilyich, it was stated that I was appointed director of the State Bank. I became still more uncomfortable and began to ask Menzhinsky to revoke the appointment. But he remained unmoved.'

The widespread difficulty of recruiting suitable candidates for top posts was one of Lenin's immediate problems. But while this produced administrative difficulties it was not vitally relevant to the success of the Revolution and it was gradually resolved without doing serious damage to the Bolsheviks' plans. In contrast to this the opportunity was now available to give efficient Party members the chance to use their talents more fully. Aleksandra Kollontay, who now became Commissar for Social Welfare, was one prominent example. Another was Nikolay Bukharin who had been made a member of the Central Committee in August and who, before the end of the year, had become the editor of *Pravda*.

But if the reservoir of specialist-trained talent on which Lenin could draw was a help in some areas it could do little if anything to mitigate the continuing breakdown of law and order throughout the country. This went on, while in Petrograd itself strange contrasts remained.

Although most of the banks were closed the stock exchange was open. The Military Revolutionary Committee had taken control of the police and with their help shops remained open and railways continued to run. With few exceptions trams, restaurants and theatres operated as normal for a while and some anti-Bolshevik papers were still being published and openly sold. The *Volya Naroda (People's Will)* even published a statement issued by Kerensky

423

in Pskov declaring that the disorders caused by the insane attempt of the Bolsheviks placed the country on the verge of a precipice. But food and fuel remained desperately short. On orders from Smolny, electricity was eventually cut off from theatres, food in restaurants began to be restricted and the tram services, on which so much of Petrograd relied, began to be cut. The sailors of the Baltic Fleet came to the rescue with several thousand tons of coal which were used to keep a few of the factories going.

In the international field, Lenin's problems loomed larger. One thing had been clear from the moment that he seized power: that whatever might happen in the mid-term or long-term future, Russia was no longer a fighting force on the Allied side. Any doubt about the position was dispersed by a telegram from General Knox on 13 (26) November which said that Russian troops at the front were now insisting on an armistice. 'It appears quite clear', he added, 'that whatever happens politically in Russia, the bulk of the Russian Army refuses to continue the War.' The implications of this were later encapsulated by Lloyd George when he wrote: A power which had for three years absorbed millions of the best soldiers and thousands of the guns of the Central Powers had finally withdrawn from the fighting line. By the end of November the German strength on the Western Front had risen from 150 to 160 divisions. Other divisions were only awaiting transport.'

Yet the problem presented to the Allies by Lenin's success in Petrograd and Moscow was not only military but diplomatic.

The problem was similar in some ways to that which faced Britain and the USA during the Second World War when it became necessary in 1942 to invade French-held North Africa and to consider the competing claims of General Giraud and General de Gaulle. The diaries of Harold Macmillan, Minister

Resident, Allied HQ North West Africa, give a hint of the difficulties with which the British had had to cope in considering the rival merits of Lenin and the deposed Kerensky. In 1917 the problems facing Russia's allies were not, however, only military and diplomatic; within a few weeks, finance and public opinion was to be challenged by Russian repudiation of foreign debts and the expropriation of factories and businesses.

In the USA the position was illustrated by David R. Francis, the US representative in Petrograd. After a London dinner at Buckingham Palace he had been asked by King George V what he thought should be done about Russia. 'I replied', he later wrote, 'I thought the Allies should overturn the Bolshevik Government. The King rejoined by telling me he thought so too, but President Wilson differed from us.' In the USA there had been some sympathy for the overthrow of what was seen in some quarters as an inefficient successor to the Tsar's Government, and President Wilson soon showed, by the announcement of what was to become his famous Fourteen Points, and by a personal message to the Russians, that he was not entirely in opposition to all Bolshevik ideas. Nevertheless, the Americans, preparing for increased effort on the Western Front, well knew that Russia's official change of heart was a sorry blow.

There was also, in many quarters, the basic personal feeling expressed by the note that Francis wrote to the US Consul-General Summers in Moscow the day after the fall of the Provisional Government. 'It is reported', it went, 'that the Petrograd Council of Workmen and Soldiers has named a cabinet with Lenin as Premier, Trotsky as Minister of Foreign Affairs, and Madame or Mlle Kollontai as Minister of Education. Disgusting! . . .' The feeling was not a passing one and Francis later wrote: 'Of course, we would not, or I would not recognize any Ministry of which Lenin is Premier or Trotzky Minister of Foreign Affairs.'

Not all Allied diplomats were as pessimistic as Hervé, the French Socialist Party deputy who wrote: 'Talk with Lenin? Talk with him after having broken the Declaration of London [1909: covering conditions of wartime blockade] with the Allies, he has abandoned them in the midst of the war?' But the consensus of Allied opinion would probably have agreed with the estimate of Joseph Noulens, the French Ambassador in Petrograd, to the French Foreign Office. 'Whether Trotsky or Chernov is in power tomorrow, whether or not Kerensky forms one of the coalition, the situation will be more or less the same. The requirements of peace and the solution of the agrarian problem will be no different. The Germans will be free to develop all their intrigues against the Allies just as they please.'

One solution to a problem for which none of the Allies had properly prepared themselves was proposed at a British cabinet meeting on 21 December 1917. 'At Petrograd we should at once get into relations with the Bolsheviks through unofficial agents, each country as seems best to it,' was the suggestion. It was a useful proposal since the Americans already had Raymond Robins of the American Red Cross Mission in Petrograd and the French had Captain Jacques Sadoul, a socialist lawyer who was head of the French Military Mission. Both men had a high opinion of Lenin, Sadoul describing him as 'a superb thinking-machine, a willing analytic mechanism of incredible precision and strength, inserted into the great revolutionary movement whose motor it has become, marvellously adapted as an integral part of the whole'.

According to Robert Bruce Lockhart, the young and independent-minded British diplomat who was to become Robins's counterpart in Petrograd, Lenin was amused by Robins's hero-worship, and of all foreigners Robins was the only man whom Lenin was always willing to see 'and who ever succeeded in imposing his own personality on the unemotional Bolshevik leader'. Robins had his own views on Trotsky, 'a four kind son of a bitch, but the greatest Jew since Christ' as he described him before adding: 'If the German General Staff bought Trotsky, they bought a lemon.'

Lockhart was soon to be added to Robins and Sadoul. He had, until recently, been serving as an attaché in Petrograd, where he had been sent by Lloyd George, but Balfour, the British Foreign Minister, had taken over responsibility by the time Lockhart arrived in Petrograd. He therefore found himself in an ambiguous position during the first months of 1918 – months during which his activities were to have a considerable effect on Lenin and some on the course of events in Russia. 'At once intelligent, energetic and smart,' Noulens said of him, 'he was one of those whom the English Government employs, sometimes with success, for confidential missions, and whom it reserves, should the occasion arise, for disavowal.'

Lenin and Lockhart were in many ways as dissimilar in background and belief as any two men could be, but they nevertheless had certain similarities which enabled them to hit it off together during the first months of 1918 when the new Government was consolidating its position. The similar intensity of their working lives is suggested in Kenneth Young's introduction to Lockhart's diaries. 'How did he find time to write this mountain of words?' he asked of Lockhart. 'He was after all endlessly preoccupied with his day-to-day work as journalist, banker or high government official, writing books, travelling hither and thither, regularly learning new languages, broadcasting, lecturing – in short earning a living.' Much the same restless energy imbued Lenin's entire life, and his meetings with Lockhart inevitably remind one of Kipling's lines

'But there is neither East nor West, Border, nor Breed nor Birth When two strong men stand face to face, though they come from the ends of the earth!'

They appear to have liked one another from the start – not only to their mutual advantage but to that of their countries. Lockhart wrote of Lenin:

'There was nothing in his personal appearance to suggest even faintly a resemblance to the super-man. Short of stature, rather plump, with short, thick neck, broad shoulders, round, red face, high intellectual forehead, nose slightly turned up, brownish moustache, and short, stubbly beard, he looked at the first glance more like a provincial grocer than a leader of men. Yet in those steely eyes there was something that arrested my attention, something in that quizzing, half-contemptuous, half-smiling look which spoke of boundless self-confidence and conscious superiority.

'Later I was to acquire a considerable respect for his intellectual capacity, but at that moment [of their first meeting] I was more impressed by his tremendous will-power, his relentless determination, and his lack of emotion . . . Lenin was impersonal and almost inhuman. His vanity was proof against all flattery. The only appeal that one could make to him was to his sense of humour, which, if sardonic, was highly developed . . .

'In his creed of world-revolution Lenin was as

unscrupulous and as uncompromising as a Jesuit, and in his code of political ethics the end to be attained justified the employment of any weapon.'

Lenin was certainly outspoken with his visitor on their first meeting. 'Our ways are not your ways [he said]. We can afford to compromise temporarily with capital. It is even necessary, for, if capital were to unite, we should be crushed at this stage of our development. Fortunately for us, it is in the nature of capital that it cannot unite. So long, therefore, as the German danger exists, I am prepared to risk a co-operation with the Allies, which should be temporarily advantageous to both of us. In the event of German aggression, I am even willing to accept military support. At the same time I am quite convinced that your Government will never see things in this light. It is a reactionary Government. It will cooperate with the Russian reactionaries.'

Lockhart said that the Germans might be able to withdraw from the East and crush the West. Lenin replied:

'Like all your countrymen, you are thinking in concrete military terms. You ignore the psychological factor. This war will be settled in the rear and not in the trenches. But even from your point of view your argument is false. Germany has long ago withdrawn her best troops from the Eastern Front. As a result of this robber peace [by this time being prepared between Germany and Russia at Brest-Litovsk] she will have to maintain larger and not fewer forces on the East. As to her being able to obtain supplies in large quantities from Russia, you may set your fears at rest. Passive resistance – and the expression comes from your own country – is a more potent weapon than an army that cannot fight.'

429

Lockhart's first contacts with Lenin, made early in 1918 as the Russians were already negotiating for peace with the Germans, were hampered by the ambiguity of his instructions from Lloyd George. The imprecision was enough not only to make his task more difficult than it should have been, but also to throw on his shoulders what was in some areas the burden of guiding British policy. Much of his success was due to the good relations he maintained with Lenin and also Trotsky, and which were implied in a significant letter Lockhart later wrote to Robins when, in May, Allied intervention in the developing civil war was an increasing threat.

'Do let me, in support of my view of things here [he said], put before you the following definite instances in which Trotsky has shown his willingness to work with the Allies.

(1) He has invited Allied officers to co-operate in the reorganization of the New Army.

(2) He invited us to send a commission of British naval officers to save the Black Sea Fleet.

(3) On every occasion when we have asked him for papers and assistance for our naval officers and our evacuation officers at Petrograd he has always given us exactly what we wanted.

(4) He has given every facility so far for Allied Co-operation at Murmansk.

(5) He has agreed to send the Czech Corps to Murmansk and Archangel.

(6) Finally, he has today come to a full agreement with us regarding the Allied stores at Archangel whereby we shall be allowed to retain those stores which we require for ourselves.

'You will agree that this does not look like the action of a pro-German agent, and that a policy of Allied intervention with the co-operation and consent of the Bolshevik government is feasible and possible.'

However, Lenin's persistence in seeing revolution not only as a necessity for Russia but as an article for export dissuaded the Allies from forming any such close relationship with the Russian Government. He was, no doubt, experienced enough to know the handicaps that this attitude made inevitable, but to have expected him to modify his views would have been to hope that a jungle maneater could be transformed overnight into a vegetarian. Lenin continued to go his own way, believing in the almost unqualified wickedness of the Allies and astonished that they would not help him accomplish their own destruction.

Equally strong was his belief that a genuine wish for revolution existed at a number of points in Europe, and particularly in Germany. The conviction weakened only slowly and as it began to die away it was compensated for, to some extent, by the propaganda of Stalin, who as Commissar for Nationalities called on the peoples of Asia to revolt and on 3 December 1917 made a specific appeal to the peoples of India to overthrow their rulers.

In Petrograd during the first weeks of the civil servants' strike, it seemed likely that one important consequence would be the frustration of Lenin's plans, announced with the Decree on Peace, to publicize the secret treaties made by the Tsar's Government with various Allied powers during the early days of the war. When Trotsky, as Commissar for Foreign Affairs, ordered officials at the Foreign Office to translate the documents into various languages, 600 officials walked out.

Lenin had good political and tactical reasons for publishing the treaties eventually obtained as soon as possible because the Decrees on Peace and Land, approved as the Bolsheviks came to power, would inevitably take time to implement; until that happened the enemies of the Revolution could claim that Bolshevik ideas were nothing more than promises. Publication of the secret treaties, their details among the most closely guarded material in the chancelleries of Europe, was an entirely different matter. Here, to the satisfaction of the Russian peoples and to the discomfiture of the old order, there could be a demonstration of how the new man Lenin could upset the apple-cart.

The importance of publication was underlined by Trotsky, who as Commissar for Foreign Affairs is reported to have said: 'I accepted this post . . . just because I wanted to have more leisure for party affairs. My job is a small one: to publish the secret documents and to close the shop.'

The embarrassing potential of the secret treaties had been admitted by Kerensky in the summer of 1917 when he entered a committee room and threw a packet on the table with the words: Our secret treaties with the Allies . . . hide them.' Viktor Chernov later commented: 'What unconscious symbolism! The confused heritage of old Tsarist diplomacy, burdened with overdrawn notes, and now bequeathed to the new Russia, was hastily hidden under the table.'

Criticism of secret treaties in general and of the machinery by which they operated, had long been a feature of left-wing thought. They had been condemned at the Copenhagen Congress of the Second International in 1910; an end to secret diplomacy had been a main plank in the platform of the Union of Democratic Control founded in Britain during the First World War, and in the USA the Constitution ruled out the acceptance of any international engagements not publicly ratified by the

Senate. Lenin had been adding his weight to the argument since the start of the century while President Wilson had emphasized the American position by calling for 'open covenants of peace openly arrived at, after which there shall be no private international understandings of any kind but diplomacy shall proceed always frankly and in the public view'.

This view, held by those unexpected bedfellows, Wilson and Lenin, had no support among Russia's civil servants who followed up their initial rebuff to Trotsky by maintaining that the necessary keys could not be found and reluctantly standing by while the doors were forced: it was discovered that Neratov, the former Assistant Foreign Minister, had apparently disappeared with the originals of the treaties. Only after further delay was he tracked down and persuaded to hand over the documents. Publication of their contents began in *Pravda* and *Izvestia* on 23 November.

After a short period during which the authenticity of the documents was questioned, it was established that they were genuine. They concerned the future of Europe and the Near East after the end of the war, and on some points they flagrantly contradicted Allied claims that neither conquests nor annexations were involved in their war aims.

Six main treaties were involved. The first, signed on 20 March 1915, approved Russia's plans for annexation of the Dardanelles and Constantinople in return for a benevolent attitude on Russia's part towards the political aspirations of Britain in other areas. The next was the treaty of London, signed on 26 April 1915, which gave Italy numerous packets of Austro-Hungarian territory, and a share in a future war indemnity in return for her entry into the war on the Allied side. An agreement between Britain, France and Russia, signed in the spring of 1916, outlined the three countries' zones of influence in Asiatic Turkey and gave all three specific areas. On 18 August 1916, Britain signed a treaty with Romania which followed an earlier Russo-Romanian treaty and which brought Romania into the Allied camp in return for parts of Transylvania. In the summer of 1916 a secret Russo-Japanese treaty was signed in addition to another whose details were made public.

Finally, the treaty governing the redrawing of Germany's frontiers was signed by France and Russia on 11 March 1917, only a few days before the abdication of the Tsar. Under this, Russia was to support France in her demands for Alsace-Lorraine and the Saar Valley. The rest of the German territories on the left bank of the Rhine were to form a neutral state. France, in return, recognized Russia's complete liberty in establishing her Western frontiers.

Once the secret treaties had been revealed in Russia they began to be published throughout the world. Soon afterwards they appeared in small pamphlets and once it had been admitted that they were authentic there was nothing that the Allies could do, embarrassed though they were.

In Russia, publication of the treaties, with accompanying exhortations for revolution abroad, implied or explicit, made it even more awkward for foreign governments to acknowledge the existence of Lenin's authority. This already presented problems. 'The difficulties Mr Balfour and I experienced in persuading certain members of the Government to have any dealings with Petrograd which would involve recognition of the Bolsheviks were considerably enhanced by Trotsky's revolutionary appeal to all nations to rise against the rule of the *"Bourgeoisie"*',' Lloyd George subsequently wrote.

Lenin's determination to implement his plans as soon as he

could in fact took precedence over his political wisdom. Many commentators have pointed out that his reiterated call for revolution outside Russia, particularly during the months that immediately followed the seizure of power, made his position more difficult when civil war developed in Russia after the end of 1917 and Allied troops began to support the White counter-revolutionary forces struggling to control widely separated parts of the country.

The difficulties hampering the new Government's attempts to gain support outside Russia during the final months of 1917 were the result not only of the ingrained distrust of revolution among constitutional bodies, but of various political events which followed the seizure of power and which gave warnings, not always recognized even in Russia, of what might follow.

One move which was to have long-term repercussions was the Russian Government's granting of independence to Finland before the end of November. A part of Sweden until 1809, Finland had then become a Russian Grand Duchy and had survived under a variety of Russo-Finnish agreements until the autumn Revolution of 1917. The country then issued a Declaration of Independence which was eventually recognized by Russia.

This result was the outcome partly of the Russian Government following the Bolshevik credo, partly of Lenin's determination to carry out the plans which he had said he would carry out and to do so with the minimum delay. At times he appeared oblivious to the almost inevitable repercussions.

While Russian international actions were increasing opposition, her internal activities had much the same effect. After the initial refusal of the Left Socialist Revolutionaries to take part in the Government there appeared little hope that Russia would now be governed by anything less monolithic than the Bolshevik

Party alone. Such hopes as remained appeared to be extinguished when the Central Committee decided that any talks on the subject would be carried on 'only for the purpose of finally exposing the impracticability of this policy and of finally stopping further negotiations for a coalition Government'.

Shortly afterwards, controls over the press, already decreed by the government, were strengthened by a motion moved by Lenin which said in part: 'We must further proceed to the confiscation of private printing plants and supplies of paper, which should become the property of the Soviets, both in the capital and in the provinces, so that the political parties and groups can make use of the facilities of printing in proportion to the actual strength of the ideas they represent.'

The motion was approved by thirty-four votes to twenty-four, but it was followed by what anyone less determined than Lenin would have considered an important setback – the resignation of five members of the Central Committee, Zinoviev, Kamenev, Nogin, Rykov and Milyutin. They said:

'We cannot bear the responsibility for this fatal policy of the Central Committee, which is carried out against the will of a large part of the proletariat and the soldiers, who are eager for the speediest stoppage of bloodshed between separate parts of the democracy. We resign office as members of the Central Committee, in order to have the right to express our opinion openly to the masses of workers and soldiers and to call them to support our slogan: Long live a Government constituted from Soviet parties. Immediate agreement on this condition.'

Far from being moved by what might have been considered

catastrophic resignations, Lenin issued a defiant manifesto, supporting the rest of the Central Committee's actions and recalling how Zinoviev and Kamenev, 'deserters and strike-breakers' as he described them, had, at the famous meeting in October, voted against the Revolution.

If Lenin's reaction to the resignations was a warning of things to come, something more alarming took place when a decree signed by him and Trotsky, among others, stated: 'Members of the governing body of the Party of the Kadets are to be arrested as enemies of the people and brought to trial before the revolutionary tribunal. Local soviets are duty-bound to keep the party of the Kadets under special surveillance because of its links to the civil war against the revolution. This decree comes into force at once.'

Defending the move in the debate on the decree's ratification, Lenin referred specifically to 'the civil war', a phrase already being used to cover all anti-Government actions and different from the military operations that were to develop in 1918 and 1919.

'It is senseless even to discuss the question of legality [he said]. The Kadets, brandishing the slogans of democracy, actually instigated the real civil war. Very well then: investigate these our charges against them and see if you can disprove that the Kadet Party constitutes the general staff of the civil war which is already drenching the country in blood.'

The decree was carried by 150 to ninety-eight votes.

The steps the Government was ready to take under Lenin's direction – 'almost an invitation to terror issued by the most authoritative institution in the country' according to I. N. Steinberg, the Left Socialist Revolutionary leader who was soon to be Minister of Justice – came at a period when the new Government began implementing its basic policies with a series of decrees transforming joint stock companies into state property, introducing general labour service, giving further power to trade unions and in a variety of less important ways eventually socializing the whole national economy.

This legislative outburst went hand-in-glove with a development that was to be quite as significant – although 'ominous' is perhaps a more fitting word – for the future of Russia. This was the setting-up, under Felix Edmundovich Dzerzhinsky, of the Extraordinary Commission for Combating Counter-Revolution, Speculation and Sabotage – the Cheka.

Dzerzhinsky had proposed such a commission to the Military Revolutionary Committee early in December and the organization was approved by Sovnarkom (the Council of People's Commissars) soon afterwards when its work was described under two headings: '(1) To investigate and liquidate all attempts or actions connected with counter-revolution or sabotage, no matter from whom they may come, throughout Russia. (2) The handing over for trial by Revolutionary Tribunal of all saboteurs and counter-revolutionaries, and the elaboration of measures to fight them.' It was added that 'The Commission carries out only a preliminary investigation in so far as this is necessary for preventive purposes.' Nevertheless, before the end of 1918 one of its members was claiming 'There is no sphere of our life where the Cheka does not have its eagle eye', while at the end of 1919 the same man was quoted by *Pravda* as saying 'life itself dictated that [the Cheka] should be organized'.

According to Steinberg, who as Commissar of Justice was in

constant argument for some weeks with the head of the new organization, Dzerzhinsky

> 'was a revolutionary who . . . brought into the Revolution an unquenchable hatred of his class enemies. He had a slender, haggard figure, a nervous twitching face, a satanic, pointed beard, and blue eyes behind which a dry flame of fanaticism gleamed. Dzerzhinsky was very fond of children who came under his special care in the Soviet Republic. But his chief concern was combating, annihilating, exterminating the counter-revolution. "We don't want justice, we want to settle accounts" was one of his favourite expressions.'

He was born near Vilna, of minor Polish nobility, and founded one of the first revolutionary groups in Poland. Arrested at the age of twenty he had been kept in solitary confinement for a year, an experience which no doubt helped to breed his intense class hatred.

The Cheka was soon putting out its tentacles into more areas and quickly developing into the country's most feared organization. In the circumstances it was not surprising that Steinberg should later write: 'It became my lot to fight against Dzerzhinsky from the very start on this question of priority: law and justice versus security of the revolutionary regime.'

At first the measures to deal with counter-revolution were largely those involving the registration and control of the moneyed classes. Lenin had his own ideas as to what could be done, asking Dzerzhinsky whether it might not be possible to pass a decree against obstructionists and counter-revolutionaries saying:

> 'Persons belonging to the wealthy classes (i.e. those who have

an income of 500 roubles a month and over, owners of real estate, shareholders, or owners of sums of money over 1,000 roubles) as well as employees of banks, joint-stock companies, and government or public institutions, are obliged to submit to the house committees, within the space of three days, three copies of a signed declaration stating their address, income, form of employment or other activities.'

Those who failed to obey would be liable to punishment 'by a fine of 5,000 roubles for each offence, by imprisonment for one year, or by active service at the front, according to the degree of their guilt'. Those 'found guilty of sabotage or evasion of work in banks, government or public offices, jointstock companies, railways, etc. are liable to the same punishment'.

This system of registration, with its possibility of control, was soon extended, and the creation of the Cheka on 7 (20) December, like the suppression of the Kadets, became a clear warning of what was to come. It at first appears remarkable that twelve days later seven Left Socialist Revolutionaries agreed to enter the Government, three of them taking cabinet posts (Kalegayev, Steinberg and Prozhyan). An explanation of the action has been given by Steinberg who claims that the Left Socialist Revolutionaries were clearly aware of the differences between themselves and the materialistically minded, fanatically proletarian and state-obsessed Bolsheviks:

'They hoped, by their participation in the highest governing bodies of the revolution, to give weight and strength to the traditional ideas of the Populists. They would represent the working peasants and intellectuals as well as the urban workers; they would help assure world peace; they would

440

prevent the establishment of one-party rule; and they would stem the tide of the dictatorial tendencies of the Bolsheviks.'

With such different outlooks between the Bolsheviks and the Socialist Revolutionaries there was inevitably a succession of bitter battles between the Cheka and the Commissariat of Justice. A typical disagreement arose over what sometimes appeared to be the Cheka's purely arbitrary arrests: the Socialist Revolutionaries demanded that, as a minimum, arrests should be made only with the knowledge of the Commissars of Justice and of Home Affairs. Lenin, whose adjudication was finally necessary, forced through a resolution under which the Cheka was allowed to make its own decisions on arrests, but simultaneously had to inform the Commissar of Justice of what was being done.

There is no doubt of Steinberg's ameliorating influence as long as he remained in office. Typically, on 14 February 1918, he wired the following instructions to all provincial soviets:

'Now that the Soviet Government has been firmly established we believe that systematic acts of repression against individuals, institutions and newspapers must be stopped. The prevention of counter-revolutionary activity must be confined within the limits of revolutionary justice. Action should be quick and determined, but it must originate in the revolutionary tribunals. The revolution is stern to its active enemies, merciful to the fallen and the conquered. Let none maintain that socialist justice does not reign in the territory of the Soviet republic.'

It would have been easy to predict that with such values the Socialist Revolutionaries would not last long. In fact they remained in the Government only from December 1917 until February 1918, when they left in protest against the treaty of Brest-Litovsk. However, they maintained an alliance of sorts with the Bolsheviks until the summer of 1918. They then revolted – and were immediately suppressed as a party.

The banning of the Kadets, as well as other revolutionary measures taken before the end of 1917 – the nationalization of the banks, a clutch of orders limiting the movement of capital, and a host of decrees restraining the liberty of ordinary Russians – were intended to be valid only until the meeting of a Constituent Assembly, an event towards which the Bolsheviks moved with understandable reluctance once they realized that they were unlikely to obtain a majority in it. According to some stories Lenin had come out against the Constituent Assembly shortly after the seizure of power, wanting to postpone the elections.

These were finally held on 12 to 14 (25 to 27) November. The complexity of the situation is shown in that in Petrograd alone no less than seventeen parties put up candidates, ranging in importance from the Bolsheviks, who later headed the poll in the capital with 424,027 votes, to the Socialist Universalists who polled 158. In the provinces parties were even more numerous and in some towns numbered as many as forty. The Social-Democrats, the Socialist Revolutionaries, Left and Right, the Kadets, and the Bolsheviks, formed the biggest parties, but divergence of opinion in local districts tended to confuse the situation, while the exact beliefs of the two Socialist Revolutionary parties varied from area to area; in general, the Right believed in confiscation of land only with compensation while the Left tended to sympathize with the Bolshevik programme although deploring its ruthlessness.

Figures for the whole country, compiled by a Socialist

442

Revolutionary and accepted as accurate by Lenin, gave the Russian Socialist Revolutionaries 16,500,000 votes; the Bolsheviks 9,023,963; the Ukrainian and other non-Russian Socialist Revolutionaries, 4,400,000; the Kadets 1,856,639; other conservative and middle-class groups and parties, Russian and non-Russian, about 2,750,000; and moderate Social-Democrats, Mensheviks, People's Socialists, etc., about 1,700,000. This resulted in an Assembly of 707 seats in which the Socialist Revolutionaries had a large majority over the Bolsheviks, the figures being variously reckoned at 410 seats against 175 and 412 against 183. Mensheviks and Kadets each secured less than twenty seats, with other groups filling fewer than 100 seats between them. It was obvious that the fate of the Assembly, due to open on 5 (18) January would be decided by a trial of strength and wits between Lenin and the rest. He began by ordering the arrest by Dzerzhinsky's Cheka of the Socialist Revolutionary and Menshevik delegates. The order was countermanded by Steinberg as Commissar for Justice. Lenin retaliated by ordering a number of left-leaning Lettish units into Petrograd, commenting: 'If anything should happen, the *muzhik* might hesitate; here we require proletarian resolution.' At the same time the Extraordinary Commission for the Protection of Petrograd declared the city to be in a state of siege. Meanwhile Moise Uritzky, a member of the Central Committee and head of the Petrograd Cheka, told a session of the Bolshevik Party's Petrograd Committee: 'Shall we convene the Constituent Assembly? Yes. Shall we disperse it? Perhaps; it depends on circumstances.'

An already tense situation was made more so when, on the evening of 1 (14) January shots were fired at Lenin as he was returning from a meeting. He was unhurt, but Fritz Platten, the organizer of the 'sealed train' journey who was travelling with him, was slightly wounded in the hand.

The Constituent Assembly opened in the Tauride Palace on 5 (18) January as finally planned. But the building was surrounded by armed troops, and a demonstration by sympathizers with the Assembly was peremptorily dispersed. A Socialist Revolutionary official named Shvetzov was the senior deputy but as he was about to open the Assembly, Sverdlov appeared on the platform, took command, and formally opened the meeting in the name of the Soviet Executive Committee.

The anti-Bolshevik temper of the Assembly was shown when Chernov, the moderate Socialist Revolutionary, was elected President of the Assembly in opposition to the Left Socialist Revolutionary, Marie Spiridonova. But troops in the galleries continually interrupted proceedings although the Assembly was able to pass three measures – a Land Law; an appeal to the Allied powers concerning the negotiations between Russia and Germany which had already opened; and the proclamation of Russia as a republic. In 1922 it became, with the republics of the Ukraine, Belorussia and Transcaucasia, a member of the Union of Soviet Socialist Republics (USSR).

'Whilst Chernov was speaking [a Scandinavian observer has written], Lenin had returned, or perhaps he had been in the hall the whole time. I saw him lying on a small staircase which led from the presidium up to a higher section of the semicircle of seats above. He lay uncomfortably on the step itself, on his left side with his hand over his eyes. In front of him was the balustrade of the staircase which effectively concealed him from the hall. What was he thinking of at this moment, whilst his triumphant opponent in the Constituent Assembly was making his chairman's speech?'

When Chernov had finished, the Bolsheviks put down a declaration endorsing the decrees passed by the Second Soviet Congress. When it was rejected by 237 votes to 136 the Bolsheviks and the Left Socialist Revolutionaries withdrew from the Assembly. The Commandant of the Tauride Palace, an Anarchist sailor named Zheleznyakov, asked the delegates to leave since the guard was tired, and the session was adjourned. The Bolshevik withdrawal from the Assembly was announced by F. Raskolnikov, a young sailor who was made Deputy Commissar for Naval Affairs shortly afterwards and later in the year was sent on a secret mission to Novorossisk on the Black Sea where he helped to prevent the Russian fleet from falling into German hands.

In the Assembly, Chernov had time to announce that the next session would open at noon the following day. It was not to be, since early in the morning of 19 January (1 February) 1918 the All-Russian Central Executive Committee passed and published in Petrograd a decree dissolving the Assembly on the grounds that it was only 'a cover for the struggle of bourgeois counter-revolution for the overthrow of the power of the Soviets'.

The most significant indication of the Constituent Assembly's mood had been its failure to approve the Declaration of the Rights of the Working and Exploited Peoples. Drafted by Lenin, this abolished private ownership of land, introduced workers' control as the first step towards nationalization, formally made the bank the property of the State, and introduced universal labour conscription. The Assembly's refusal to endorse these omnibus measures was partly countered a few days later when the Third All-Russia Congress of Soviets – formed following a merger of the Third All-Russia Congress of Soviets of Workers' and Soldiers' Deputies and the Third All-Russia Congress of Peasants' Deputies – adopted the Declaration.

The end of Russia's first free Assembly created comparatively little reaction, even in political circles. One of the reasons for the lack of response to what, on the face of it, was a sharp slap in the face for democratic values, was that the people of Petrograd knew that difficult negotiations to end the war were going on with the Germans; many if not most of them knew how helpless the Russian army would be in resisting a renewed German onslaught, and any speculation about a democratically elected assembly was easily overwhelmed by the thought of what life would be like if the Germans occupied Petrograd – as seemed a distinct possibility.

It must also be remembered that the Provisional Government had not been overthrown with the hope of its being succeeded by a democratically elected parliament. There was, therefore, some natural sympathy with Lenin's comment: 'The dispersal of the Constituent Assembly by Soviet authority means a complete and frank liquidation of the ideas of formal democracy in the name of revolutionary dictatorship. It will serve as a good lesson.' Nevertheless, there were those who deplored the use of force to end the Constituent Assembly. A balanced assessment of the reaction is that given by O. H. Radkey in his survey of the elections to the Assembly:

'While the democratic parties heaped opprobrium upon [Lenin] for this act of despotism, their following showed little inclination to defend an institution which the Russian people had ceased to regard as necessary to the fulfillment of its cherished desires. For the Constituent Assembly, even before it had come into existence, had been caught in a back-eddy of the swiftly flowing stream of revolutionary developments and no longer commanded the interest and allegiance of the general population which alone could

446

have secured it against a violent death.'

As might have been expected, most party supporters justified the dispersal of the Assembly. Krupskaya believed that as initially constituted it would have led to a coalition government that would inevitably have been a failure, and illustrated the view in a homely way by borrowing a metaphor from a Russian fable and suggesting that a coalition government would be tantamount to 'harnessing to the Soviet cart the swan, the pike and the crab, setting up a government incapable of working harmoniously and of even moving from the spot.'

The view that the dispersal of the Assembly would help the Bolsheviks was not only held by their supporters; on 23 January Raymond Robins cabled to Colonel William Boyce Thompson, the former head of the American Red Cross Mission in Russia: 'Soviet Government stronger today than ever before. Its authority and power greatly consolidated by dissolution of Constituent Assembly which was led and controlled by Chernov as permanent president. Acceptance of dissolution as final without important protest general throughout Russia.'

Yet despite the lack of protest, all was not well and Lenin knew it. As usual, he had a solution.

'The only chance of securing a painless solution to the crisis which has arisen owing to the divergence between the elections to the Constituent Assembly, on the one hand, and the will of the people . . . on the other [he said] is for the people to exercise as broadly and as rapidly as possible the right to elect the members of the Constituent Assembly anew, and for the Constituent Assembly to accept the law of the Central Executive Committee on these new

447

elections, to proclaim that it unreservedly recognizes Soviet power, the Soviet revolution, and its policy on the questions of peace, the land and workers' control, and to resolutely join the camp of the enemies of the Cadet-Kaledin counter-revolution.'

Lenin's defence for ending the Constituent Assembly was put into a broad context when he spoke to the Third All-Russian Congress of Soviets. He said:

'Not a single problem of the class struggle has been resolved during the course of history except by force. If force proceeds from the exploited working masses and against the exploiters – yes, then we are in favour of force. Therefore, comrades, to all complaints and accusations that we practise terror, dictatorship, civil war, we will reply – Yes, we have openly declared what no other Government has ever been able to declare – yes, we have started the war against the exploiters.'

At the Congress, the Bolsheviks had slightly more than 50 per cent of the delegates; the Left Socialist Revolutionaries had the second largest number and the two groups together thus formed an overwhelming majority. This majority quickly adopted the Declaration of the Rights of the Working and Exploited Peoples which the Constituent Assembly had rejected and which now became the first variant of the Soviet Constitution. And it was to this assembly that Lenin proudly announced on 11 (24) January that Soviet power had been established for two months and fifteen days, five days longer than the Paris Commune had existed in 1871.

Yet however satisfactorily the Congress appeared to implement Lenin's wishes, and however doggedly he might defend the suppression of the Constituent Assembly, the latter event piled up trouble for the future, particularly with the Socialist Revolutionaries. The reason was explained by Boris Sokolov, a Socialist Revolutionary Party leader:

'Of all the political parties the Socialist Revolutionary Party was linked with the idea of the Constituent Assembly by extremely close, I might even say organic, ties. The Constituent Assembly embodied the main demands of the revolutionary people and the basic propositions of democratism were focused around it . . . Those were the considerations that prompted the Socialist Revolutionaries to insist on the idea of an All-Russian Constituent Assembly. It seemed to them, and not only to them, that the crucial thing was to "bring the country to the Constituent Assembly". Theoretically perhaps, and probably in fact, there was a very great truth in this, but practically this peculiar idealism was fraught with the most exasperating consequences and complications.'

One unanswered question raised by the ending of the Constituent Assembly is the extent to which it allowed, if it did not actually encourage, the future growth of the Red Terror. It can be argued that the developing food crisis together with opposition from the Socialist Revolutionaries would have made this inevitable during the first half of 1918, and that the exigencies of the Civil War would have made it inevitable after that. On the contrary, it can be argued that the ameliorating influence of such a body as the Constituent Assembly would have curbed even

Lenin's determination that nothing should stand in the way of implementing the ideals of the Revolution. The most likely answer is that the Assembly would have acted as some sort of a curb on terrorist excesses although the extent of such a curb must be speculative.

The brusque shutting down of the Constituent Assembly formed a milestone on the Bolshevik road that led onwards from the Revolution. By this time, however, only three months after Lenin had successfully seized power, considerable progress had already been made in setting up the machinery through which he was to govern Russia and which would be used by his successors with but minor changes for some years.

Once Kerensky's attack had been defeated on the Pulkovo Heights and it had become clear that success in Petrograd was no flash in the pan, however great future difficulties might be, it had been possible to deal more realistically with the problems of deciding how Russia could best be run in conditions so different from any previously experienced. In *The State and Revolution*, finished the previous August and September while on the run in Finland, Lenin had said:

'[Marx] teaches us to act with supreme boldness in destroying the entire old state machine, and at the same time he teaches us to put the question concretely: the Commune was able in the space of a few weeks to *start* building a *new*, proletarian state machine by introducing such-and-such measures to provide wider democracy and to uproot bureaucracy. Let us learn revolutionary boldness from the Communards; let us see in their practical measures the *outline* of really urgent and immediately possible measures, and then, *following this road*, we shall achieve the complete

450

destruction of bureaucracy.

'The possibility of this destruction is guaranteed by the fact that socialism will shorten the working day, will raise the *people* to a new life, will create such conditions for the *majority* of the population as will enable *everybody*, without exception, to perform "state functions", and this will lead to the *complete withering away* of every form of state in general.'

Here was a glimpse of the idealism that suffused the beliefs of at least some revolutionaries, and which was maintained, if often at a lower intensity, as the practical problems of restructuring Russian life made themselves felt.

During the few months that had passed since Lenin had written these words, even during the short time he had spent in the Smolny Institute since his return to Petrograd, he had begun to appreciate that amendments to the precepts outlined in *The State and Revolution* would be necessary in post-Revolutionary Russia. That raised no insuperable problems. However strongly Lenin might condemn compromise on political ideals, he found little difficulty in bending with the wind when the practical affairs of life were concerned. The best method of running the new Soviet state was one of them, and it has been remarked by more than one observer that the new Government machine, created in the Smolny Institute soon after the Revolution, and continually amended during the following months, was an effective blend of existing tsarist organizations and those now specially created for the revolutionary tasks ahead.

The merging of the more useful elements of the tsarist State machinery with the new that had to be created from scratch, had its ups and downs. But with only a small handful of exceptions it was carried out more successfully than its exponents had any right to expect. Much was due to Lenin's administrative ability, which appears to have surprised some of his colleagues and may even have surprised Lenin himself.

Trotsky was in a better position than anyone to observe how the new Government machinery evolved since his rooms and Lenin's were at opposite ends of a corridor running the length of the Smolny building. Although they were connected by telephone, Lenin jokingly suggested that they should set up a bicycle connection between them. An important link was provided by sailors–probably from the nearly ubiquitous Kronstadt garrison–who constantly brought Trotsky notes from Lenin with the most important words underlined once, twice or even three times. Several times a day Trotsky would traipse along the corridor to consult with Lenin personally, usually on military questions, which first dealt with the repulse of Kerensky's attack and were centred soon afterwards on the negotiations with the Germans at Brest-Litovsk. These consultations were no mere formalities; in fact when the first months of the new Government are considered, it is easy to let Lenin's importance all but blot out the importance of Trotsky. The personal influence of Lenin on all that took place immediately after the Revolution cannot be overestimated: but that of Trotsky can be too easily undervalued. One reason for this is that Trotsky's later accounts, while in no sense underestimating his own role – a tendency of which he could be rarely accused – invariably threw the spotlight on Lenin.

As one example from many, it is Trotsky who has given the most revealing account of how Lenin would preside over the meetings of the Council of People's Commissars, listening to the arguments for five or six hours at a stretch. For a while, the meetings took place every day, but Lenin unfailingly turned up for them, directing the debates from one subject to the next and limiting the speaker's time by referring to a pocket watch which was eventually replaced by a chronometer.

'As a rule, the topics of discussion were put on the agenda without any previous preparation, and . . . always demanding extreme urgency. Very often neither the chairman nor the Commissars were familiar with the essentials of a problem until it became the subject of the debate. But the discussion was always concise: for the preliminary exposition of the theme the speaker had no more than five to ten minutes, and yet the chairman somehow gropingly always found the right line along which to steer the debate. When there was a meeting at which many people were present, among them specialists or people unknown to Lenin, he resorted to his favourite gesture: he would put his right hand over his forehead and eyes and look through between his stretched fingers. Thus, playing peep-bo, he observed the speaker and the participants very intently and attentively and saw exactly what he needed to see. On narrow strips of paper, in small writing (economy measures!) he noted the names of the speakers. He kept one eye on the watch which now and again appeared over the table to remind the orator that the time was up. Meanwhile, he quickly jotted down the essential conclusions resulting from the debate. In addition, in order to save time, he was sending out to some participants short notes in which he asked for particular information.'

Lenin's success at blending the old style of government with the new, demanded by conditions from the end of 1917 onwards, has been stressed by Rigby in *Lenin's Government: Sovnarkom,*

1917–1922, a detailed analysis of how the new State was run in its early days. It was not only through the creation of new machinery, but through the manner in which it was operated that the new Russian Government merged old and new.

> 'Considering Sovnarkom in this comparative context [as a cabinet system of the British type] [Rigby comments], it is striking that in such matters as the conduct of meetings according to prepared agenda, the compilation and advance circulation of relevant documentation, the keeping of minutes, and the creation of a secretariat for maintaining records, preparing meetings, promoting interdepartmental consultation and following up decisions, Sovnarkom had attained a point within its first few months which the British Cabinet was reaching only at about the same time, after some two centuries of experience; in fact in these respects the machinery and procedures elaborated by Sovnarkom by the end of the Civil War [late 1920] were to be matched by the British Cabinet only during and after the Second World War.'

The machinery and procedures were those from which 'War Communism' eventually developed, the economic system that Lenin began to set up soon after the Bolsheviks seized power and which remained in existence until 1921 when, after the end of the civil war, it was superseded by the New Economic Policy (NEP). The core of War Communism was the elimination of free enterprise and finally the planning and control by the state of the whole economy. This had for long been one of Lenin's ideals and to the extent that the exigencies of the civil war made such control necessary, they tended to counterbalance the desperate difficulties which the new Government had to face so soon after it had seized power. The Supreme Economic Council, created in December 1917, had as its duty the organization of national economic life and State finances, and these aims were implemented during the following months by the progressive nationalization of industry and the forcing of labour into the strait-jacket of War Communism.

Even before the end of 1917 the Military Revolutionary Committee had given a hint of things to come by ordering food-requisitioning in Petrograd and by sending out into the provinces flying squads charged with bringing back grain from wherever it could be obtained. By the end of October (early November) the Committee had 185 of its officials in various civil agencies – and was being helped in that some of the new commissariats were operating from the Smolny Institute, the Military Revolutionary Committee's own headquarters. However, Lenin saw to it that the commissariats began working from their own offices as soon as possible, which helped the process of merging new organizations with the old.

Of all the groups which were to operate under the blanket coverage of War Communism one of the most ubiquitous was the Food Commissariat which eventually not only took whatever supplies it could obtain, largely by forced levies, but also handled the task of redistribution. Here, as to a minor extent in other areas, the practices of War Communism lessened the significance of money and replaced it by barter. This usually made a bad system worse, and however strong the need for War Communism its failure can hardly be exaggerated – as was admitted in 1921 when Lenin turned reluctantly to what many Bolshevik diehards regarded as the retrograde, if not politically treasonable, creation of the NEP.

Although the features that made up War Communism were brought in gradually they were all approved by the members of Sovnarkom. Much discussion took place later as to how these ministers – for such they were in all but name – had come to be known as commissars, a word described by Lenin as having a 'good democratic ring'. But not until late in 1919 did A. Joffe write of how 'once in a gathering of those people who had headed the revolution right from the beginning, we were trying to recall, for instance, who first thought up the titles "People's Commissar" and "Council of People's Commissars", and it was only after prolonged arguments and swapping of reminiscences, that we managed to establish that these were proposed by L. D. Trotsky'.

In picking staff Lenin was able to draw on the extensive knowledge about Party members that he had acquired over the years. This was an advantage in that he often knew the best person for any particular task; but that it also had its disadvantages was illustrated by the remarks of Angelica Balabanov, a close observer of Lenin in action after he had appointed Zinoviev, already a prominent man in Petrograd, as secretary of the Third International when it was set up in 1919. Balabanov expressed horror that Lenin had 'put this master of intrigue and calumny, to whom the end justified any means, in charge of the organization that was to cleanse and solidify the revolutionary forces of the world!' In her explanation, Balabanov throws a light which helps to illuminate many of Lenin's actions during those years of supreme power.

'[He] was guided by what he believed to be the supreme interest of the Revolution . . . Zinoviev was an interpreter and executor of the will of others, and his personal shrewdness, ambiguity and dishonesty made it possible for him to discharge these duties more effectively than could a more scrupulous man. Lenin was more concerned that his decisions be made effective than with the manner in which they were carried out. It was his fundamental psychological error that he did not foresee what would happen to the Revolution when these means became the end; that he failed to understand that his own famous *raison d'état* – 'The Proletarian State is justified in any compromise it makes, provided that power is maintained' – would serve as a shield for the failure or corruption of those who spoke in the name of the Proletarian State.'

Another feature of Lenin's determination to push the Party's interests at all costs has also been commented on by Balabanov. At the Ninth Congress of the RCP(B) (see p. 498), held from 29 March to 5 April 1920, measures were introduced to replace trade union autonomy and workers' control in industry by control through political commissars. This was contested by Aleksandra Kollontay who later held a number of posts in the Bolsheviks' diplomatic service. Kollontay, leader of the Workers' Opposition, had produced a pamphlet giving her views. Balabanov has written:

'I have never seen Lenin so angry as when one of these pamphlets was handed to him . . . in spite of the fact that "opposition" within the Party itself was still supposed to be legitimate. Taking the platform, he denounced Kollontai as the Party's worst enemy, a menace to its unity. He went so far in his attack as to make allusions to certain episodes in Kollontai's intimate life that had nothing whatever to do with the issue. It was the kind of polemic which did no credit to Lenin, and it was on this occasion that I realized the lengths to which Lenin would go in the pursuit of his strategic aims, his opposition to a party opponent.'

Lenin's knowledge of the men available enabled him to appoint Bonch-Bruyevich, on whose qualities in various capacities he had relied for seven years, as head of the Sovnarkom chancellen. Some, such as Nikolay Gorbunov, who for some years held the key post of secretary of Sovnarkom, were virtually dragooned into service. According to his own account, in November 1917, he was summoned by Bonch-Bruyevich who took him to the third floor of Smolny where Lenin bluntly told him that he was appointed to the job. 'I received no instructions from him at that time,' Gorbunov has written. 'I had not the slightest idea about my job or in general about secretarial duties. Somewhere I confiscated a typewriter on which, for quite a long time, I had to bang out documents with two fingers; no typist could be found.' He was, moreover, called in to take the minutes of an early Sovnarkom meeting even though he knew no shorthand.

Yet if there was comparatively little trouble about finding competent staff, not all the most suitable candidates were anxious to take on the work, carrying, as it sometimes did, considerable risk if the Bolshevik experiment did not last as long as was hoped.

Another reason for reluctance to serve Lenin too closely was the relentlessly high standard he demanded. Gorbunov, later Sovnarkom's administrative director, has said that in his work Lenin was exacting to the point of being extreme. The way in which he would personally follow up instructions whenever possible made him a hard task master, which he knew and which caused him to say on one occasion: 'Work in my secretariat is real drudgery – no rest, no holidays.' As a counterbalance to this there was the personal interest he took in all who worked for him. He disguised any hint of softness by referring to those in Smolny as State material, a typical note written on 19 February 1919 stating: 'People's Commissar A. D. Tsyurupa is hereby instructed, in view of his resuming work and the need to protect government property, *to take strict precautions*. Not to work more than two hours without a break. Not to work later than 10.30 p.m. Not to receive people. *Implicitly* to carry out the restrictive orders of Lydia Alexandrovna Fotiyeva.' As a diligent personal secretary and personal assistant, Fotiyeva was occasionally ordered to take special care or rest as 'State property'.

Despite his constant care for his staff and what might have been considered ample accommodation, first in Smolny and then in the Kremlin to which the Government moved early in 1918, space usually seems to have been restricted. Aleksandra Kollontay has written,

'Vladimir Ilyich's desk was shoved up against the wall and the lamp was hanging over it. We people's commissars sat around Vladimir Ilyich and partly behind his back. Nearer the window there was the desk of Sovnarkom secretary N. P. Gorbunov, who took the minutes. Whenever Lenin gave someone the floor or issued instructions to Gorbunov, he had to turn around but no one at that time thought of moving the desk, we were busy with larger matter.'

Later another room was used for Sovnarkom meetings but towards the end of 1918, after the formation of the Council of Labour and the Council of Defence, these two organizations still

459

met in a small third-floor room that hardly matched the importance of the matters discussed in it.

'The room was dim, despite the sunny day, its light struggling through the heavy draperies [says one visitor whom Lenin received in it]. A number of armchairs stood along the walls. The furniture was ill-assorted, apparently gathered from various places. A worn, faded carpet covered the floor. The whole scene reminded me of the reception room of a provincial lawyer.'

In Smolny, as later in the Kremlin, Lenin could be surprisingly accommodating and informal, as was discovered by Captain Hill, a British officer who had come to Russia in the days of the Provisional Government to help restore the country's railway system, and who after the Revolution of 1917 had remained in the country to carry out a variety of operations engagingly described in his memoirs *Go Spy the Land*.

'Lenin ambled in, Karahan in his wake [Hill has written]. The outward appearance of the Dictator was that of a strong and simple man of less than middle height with a Slavonic cast of countenance, piercing eyes and a powerful forehead. He shook hands with us. His manner was not friendly, nor could it be said to be hostile; it was completely detached. He listened to what Joffe and Karahan had to say about us, and when they had finished, nodded his head two or three times and said, "Of course, they must be given full facilities for the work they are doing." Now that the Commissars had got him there, they plied him with questions concerning other matters which they had in hand, and I noticed at once how ready he was with well-reasoned advice, which he gave with disarming simplicity. In a few minutes he had polished off their questions and then bowing to us strolled away with his hands behind his back.'

Although commissars were soon operating from their own ministries, the Sovnarkom discussions that they attended continued to be held in comparatively primitive surroundings at Smolny. Meetings started between 5 and 8 p.m. and continued until the early hours. Lenin quickly showed himself a stickler for punctuality and before the end of 1917 had instituted a system of fines: five roubles for being half an hour late, and ten roubles for an hour. A series of reprimands was finally worked out for all decisionmaking bodies. Lateness of ten minutes or more brought a reprimand written into the minutes; a second offence meant the loss of a day's pay, and a third earned a reprimand that was published in the daily press.

Lenin was equally strict when it came to the conduct of Sovnarkom meetings, according to one colleague 'cutting short the slightest violation of proper order with harshly shouted remarks. In this respect, Vladimir Ilyich admitted no exceptions. I remember, for instance, that there once suddenly turned up at a meeting of the Sovnarkom L. B. Krasin, directly on his return from London, whence the press of the whole world had been reporting his first meeting with Lloyd George. Some of the People's Commissars rushed up to him with greetings and questions, but Vladimir Ilyich sharply rebuked both them and Krasin from the chair for the violation of order. When however the meeting closed, after midnight or thereabouts, Vladimir Ilyich ran up to Krasin with a joyful expression, started talking with him in the kindest tone, and led him off to his room. But that was already after the meeting,

461

towards one a.m., on the close of *official* work.'

From the early days of Sovnarkom Lenin realized that he would be in danger of being swamped by paperwork. This was evident even before the day when sixty separate items came up for discussion. There is, apparently, no record of what was involved but Lydia Fotiyeva, who years earlier in Geneva had helped Krupskaya maintain clandestine contacts with Russia and who became one of Lenin's secretaries after 1917, has recalled that on one occasion five items were accompanied by 120 pages of documentation.

The problem of too much paperwork was partially dealt with by the creation of a 'Little Sovnarkom' which met once a week to deal with any less important matters that could be passed on to it. However, it was only a qualified help since Lenin still insisted on keeping closely in touch with even the comparatively minor matters it handled. As with the running of Sovnarkom itself, his influence was all-pervading and could be decisive. 'It is simply amazing,' wrote one colleague, 'that such minor matters, and it was specifically such matters and them alone that formed the chosen speciality of the Little Council, should have attracted so much attention and the most painstaking consideration by Lenin, who, one might have thought, had enough work and worries without that.'

It was remarkable, and perhaps unprecedented, Rigby has stated,

'that Lenin, a man approaching fifty who had spent his whole youth and adult life as professional revolutionary, could apply himself so single-mindedly and persistently to such humdrum matters [as those dealt with by the Little Sovnarkom], especially when one recalls the critical and

462

chaotic circumstances in which he did so. This relates, moreover, not only to his contribution to the creation and running of the Sovnarkom machine, but to his exercise of the "prime-ministerial" role. In such matters as the management of agendas, the clarification of issues and judicious injection of his influence on them before they came up for formal consideration, the guidance, stimulation and focusing of discussion, the crystallization of clear decisions embodied in his summings-up, the use of standing and *ad hoc* committees, and the exercise of his executive authority in taking, facilitating or ensuring administrative decisions, Lenin quickly displayed a mastery that would have done credit to a politician who had served a long apprenticeship in a mature system of cabinet government.'

Mastery was necessary in view of the relationship between Sovnarkom, the State organization, and the Bolshevik Party's Central Committee, or with the Politburo of the Party which was set up in 1919. As the Bolsheviks transformed tsarist Russia into a Communist state pressure of work inevitably meant that Sovnarkom had to delegate some of the work its members would otherwise have carried out personally. It was therefore at the weekly meetings of the Politburo that final decisions were taken on questions of internal and foreign policy, and it was the Politburo that had the final responsibility for the organizations through which such decisions were implemented. Yet the situation was complex and its significance lay in that from this time onwards Russia was governed, in practice, not by an organ of the State but by a Party body. But Lenin, as Rigby has pointed out in his analysis of an unusual situation, 'certainly identified the "dictatorship of the proletariat" with rule by the Communist

Party, but this did not mean government by the party's executive machinery. Lenin's "Cabinet" was not the Politburo, but Sovnarkom.'

While Little Sovnarkom dealt with comparatively minor matters, Sovnarkom itself was busy restructuring the fundamental basis of Russian life and society. Castes and ranks, grades and titles, were abolished by decree, as was the right of inheritance. Women were given equal rights with men in a decree 'on civil marriage, children and the keeping of records on marital status'. Church and State were formally separated, as were Church and schools. Not only was the State bank nationalized, but so also were all privately incorporated commercial banks which now became branches of the State Bank. Many large businesses and syndicates were also nationalized. All this was part of a huge administrative shake-up at which Lenin hinted when he spoke on 26 April 1918 to the Party Central Committee:

'We, the Bolshevik Party, have *convinced* Russia [he said]. We have *won* Russia from the rich for the poor, from the exploiters for the working people. Now we must *administer* Russia. And the whole peculiarity of the present situation, the whole difficulty, lies in understanding *the specific features of the transition* from the principal task of convincing the people and of suppressing the exploiters by armed force to the principal task of *administration.*'

It was not only to major matters of commerce and social life that Lenin directed attention. The language of Russia itself was brought up to date by the formal dropping of certain characters, accretions to the language which were no longer necessary. The Julian calendar was brought into line with the Gregorian at the beginning of February 1918 when 1 February officially became 14 February.

In addition to these moves aimed at bringing Russia into the twentieth century there were eventually to be seen the results of the encouragement to education that Lenin gave from the time he took power. He had begun by appointing Lunacharsky, his colleague in Geneva days who had, for a while, supported Gorky's god-building efforts in Capri, as head of the Narodnyi Komissariat Prosveschcheniya (po Prosveschcheniyu) usually shortened to Narkompros, ('The People's Commissariat of Enlightenment'), in practice, the Ministry of Education. Lunacharsky had returned to Russia in May 1917, travelling in a second 'sealed train', which had followed Lenin's of a few weeks earlier. In Petrograd, after the initial success of the Revolution, Lenin began to recreate the Russian educational system in the face of considerable difficulties which were both practical, since chaos reigned in the schools as much as elsewhere, and ideological, since feeling against the Revolution was as strong among educationalists as in other non-working-class centres.

To these perhaps inevitable problems there were others, which crop up spikily through even the most uncritical accounts of how Lenin deployed his enthusiasm for education during the first years of the new Government. One was the great dissimilarity between Lenin and Lunacharsky. 'He approached all these questions [half-hearted commitments, compromises and obscuring of the bright maximalist bases of fully revolutionary Marxism] as a practical man with an enormously clear grasp of tactics, a real political genius,' Lunacharsky has written. 'I approached them as a philosopher and, I will say more definitely, as a poet of the revolution.' Secondly, there was Lunacharsky's weakness for giving acquaintances posts in the educational organization. '[He] could never believe that Narkompros could be the worse for gaining a man of goodwill, or the wife of a comrade, or the destitute grand-daughter of a distinguished writer, [and] had the habit of recruiting staff on a personal basis and directing them with letters of introduction to the head of a Narkompros department,' his biographer has written. The Commissariat staff included, it is added, the wives of Lenin, Trotsky, Zinoviev, Kamenev, Dzerzhinsky and Bonch-Bruyevich, as well as Lenin's sister Anna.

This recruitment of what were mostly faithful party workers was to have its sometimes unexpected impact on the cultural flow of life under the Soviet Government. Thus, Krupskaya's appointment enabled her to inaugurate a purge of unacceptable books that Maxim Gorky later described as 'intellectual vampirism', and induced him to state: 'The first impression I experienced was so strong that I started writing to Moscow to announce my repudiation of Russian citizenship.' Krupskaya's campaign, which began in 1920 and continued until after Lenin's death in 1924, has been detailed by Bertram D. Wolfe in 'Krupskaya Purges the People's Libraries'. It brought protests even from such officials as the chairman of the Central Library Commission but it was to continue until taken over and amplified by Stalin after Lenin's death.

'This strange tree of unknowledge was planted by Krupskaya under Lenin, with his direction and advice. After his death, it was nurtured and tended by her in what she took to be Lenin's spirit. Stalin and his lieutenants have not let it die, but have tended it with zeal. It flourishes to this day, in the very centre of the Garden of Eden. The

fruit is not forbidden, but, being mutable, it is alike hazardous to eat thereof, and hazardous to fail to eat . . .'

In addition to supporting education in 1918 the Government
encouraged a number of commercial and technological improvements which were to lay the foundation for Russia's progress in
following years. It approved massive plans for the exploitation of
Lake Saskunchak, north-east of Astrakhan, which was eventually producing up to 25 per cent of Russia's salt supplies, and the
first major schemes for electrification – which encouraged Lenin
to say that Communism was Soviet power plus the electrification
of the whole country. Plans for massive geological surveys and
for new railways were also approved.

Some of the frankest and most illuminating accounts of how
Lenin managed to run the newly founded Soviet State through
Sovnarkom have been given not by dedicated Party members
but by men such as Simon Liberman, who before his return to
Russia after the Revolution had spent some years as a timber
merchant in the USA and who became one of the triumvirate
controlling Russia's important timber production.

> 'When I knew him [he has written], Lenin always wore the
> same dark-colored suit, with pipelike trousers that seemed a
> trifle too short for his legs, with a similarly abbreviated,
> single-breasted coat, a soft white collar, and an old tie. The
> necktie, in my opinion, was for years the same: black, with
> little white flowers, one particular spot showing wear. When,
> sitting at his desk, he received visitors, one could notice that
> the heels of his shoes were somewhat higher than the ordi-
> nary size. In one hand he always held a pencil, while the
> fingers of his other hand were inserted in the pages of a

book lying open before him, as if he were comparing one page with another and yet another. When he worked or talked, he also wrote notes or messages, scribbling on each page of his notebook from top to bottom and tearing them off one by one . . .

'During the deliberations his sly smile might tell you that he was preparing a new move, but never just what it was going to be. Even those who were used to his methods did not know until the very last minute in precisely what ways he would engineer a clash between opponents, exactly how he would direct the general argument and play the game, and what final decisions would be reached. He alone knew his mind and plans.'

One of the great paradoxes of Lenin, as illustrated in the commercial matters he discussed with Liberman, was the contrast between his gentleness in preliminary negotiations and his firmness in final action; another was the equal contrast between his constant theorizing and dogmatism and his down-to-earth practicality.

When Liberman protested at one meeting against State demands on the timber industry, Lenin replied,

'Of course, we make mistakes. There cannot be a revolution without errors. But we are learning from our errors and are glad when we can correct them. Now about these decrees [to which Liberman had been objecting], don't forget that we are in the midst of a revolution. Our government may not last long, but these decrees will be part of history. Future revolutionaries will learn from them – perhaps from these very decrees of Larin's which now seem so absurd to you. We ourselves keep the decrees

468

of the Paris Commune before our eyes as a model.'

When the interview was finished Lenin added: 'Our mistakes should be corrected not by experts but by us ourselves. The correction should come from above only. Therefore, whenever you have ideas on this subject, telephone directly to me, and I will make the necessary changes myself.'

The differences between Lenin and Trotsky, Liberman has remarked, came out clearly when they were seen in action at council meetings.

'Lenin was spoken of as "Ilyich", a somewhat familiar appellation, certainly, yet one with much fondness in it, too – and this fondness, as well as great and genuine respect, could be sensed at any meeting of either of the two councils. Every Bolshevist had a personal attachment for Lenin, and thus an intimate tie was felt between the party and its founder and organizer. It was partly because of this that Lenin's authority in the affairs of the party proved to be so extraordinary.'

While Liberman could be outspoken in his praise of the way in which Lenin handled business affairs, he was no sycophant. This often emerges from his reminiscences, as when he recalls a discussion about the best way of getting in more wood. It was proposed that foresters should be made responsible, but Liberman pointed out that foresters were intellectuals not used to manual labour. Dzerzhinsky said that it was time to liquidate this inequality. 'Moreover,' he went on, 'should the peasants fail to deliver their quota of wood, the foresters responsible for them are to be shot. When a dozen or two of them are shot, the rest will tackle the job in earnest.' Lenin closed the discussion writes

Liberman, but 'suggested that the point about shooting the foresters, although adopted, be omitted from the official minutes of the session.'

At the end of the meeting, Liberman continues, he was approached by Lenin's chauffeur who said that he had been instructed to drive him home since Lenin thought that he looked unwell. 'I thought bitterly,' Liberman writes: 'here is a cruel contrast, indeed – while he was deciding to shoot scores of innocent people, Lenin had also remarked to himself that I was suffering from a bad cold and must be fetched home in his car.' After describing the incident, Liberman quotes Plekhanov, who had said: 'Lenin is baked of the same dough as Robespierre', a remark to which Lenin replied when he heard of it: 'Yes, a Jacobin joined with the working class is the only true revolutionary.'

Lenin's creation of Sovnarkom – and it was mainly his creation however much he was helped by the Soviet commissars he had appointed – was as great a tribute to his political powers of organization as was the success of the Revolution in Petrograd. This can best be appreciated when it is realized that between the Revolution and the weeks when Sovnarkom was working successfully Lenin had also pushed through the operation he had been advocating since August 1914 and which had become a main plank in his revolutionary programme – peace with Germany.

13

Brest-Litovsk

Lenin had argued his way into power armed with a weapon formidable in any demagogue's armoury, the promise held out to a weary nation of ending an unpopular war, and he had immediately begun to wield this weapon by the promulgation of the Decree on Peace. Implementing the promise by action was a more difficult matter since Germany, the main enemy among the Central Powers, occupied an impressive position in the autumn of 1917. Blockaded and short of food, she was beginning to suffer from the heavy casualties sustained since the late summer of 1914. Nevertheless Germany, with her allies, was preparing for a major offensive that would demand everything additional that the Americans, in the war for only a few months, could send across the Atlantic. Any peace bought from Germany by Russia would obviously have to be bought on German terms but even Lenin the realist began to appreciate only slowly how humiliating those terms would be. It was a tribute to his political ability that he was finally able to thrust those terms down the throat of a protesting Russian nation.

The peace of Brest-Litovsk, which ended the war between Russia and Germany, involved princes dining with peasants, gave birth to Trotsky's remarkable 'No peace, no war' proposal that brought an anguished 'Unheard of cry from the German General Hoffmann, and in both conception and execution broke almost every diplomatic rule in existence. In addition, it was among the incentives that drove President Wilson to produce his 'Fourteen Points', eventually to become a milestone in diplomatic history. None of this, it should be emphasized, would have happened without Lenin's resolute determination to end the war with Germany, however desperately his more shortsighted colleagues, worried about the price to be paid, might try to deter him.

The first moves took place on 9 (22) November when Trotsky formally told Allied ambassadors, then the diplomatic representatives of neutral countries, of the change of Government in Russia and in a note called their attention to the Decree of Peace. The Allies were informed that the note should be considered as 'a formal proposal for an immediate armistice on all fronts and the immediate opening of peace negotiations'.

News that the Russians would be seeking a separate peace had, naturally enough, alarmed the Western Allies, then bracing themselves for what they correctly feared would be an all-out German attack on the Western Front. 'The action just taken by the extremists in Petrograd . . .', Lord Robert Cecil, Britain's Under-Secretary of State for Foreign Affairs, commented on 23 November (6 December) 1917 'would of course be a direct breach of the agreement of September 5, 1914 [the agreement between the Allies that none of them should seek a separate peace], and . . . if approved and adopted by the Russian nation would put them practically outside the pale of the ordinary councils of Europe. There is no intention of recognizing such a Government.'

The Americans agreed to ignore Trotsky's note because the 'pretended Government was established by force and not recognized by the Russian people'.

If Lenin was unable to persuade the Allies that they should start negotiating with the Germans – a task in which Lord Lansdowne was to fail a few days later in his famous letter to the *Daily Telegraph* – he could at least prod Russian peace moves into action. Even this, however, was less easy than he expected. On 8 (21) November General Dukhonin, the Russian Commander-in-Chief at Army Headquarters at Moghilev, was instructed by telephone 'to address to the military authorities of the hostile armies a proposal to immediately cease military operations with a view to opening peace negotiations'. Dukhonin prevaricated but finally said that he would obey the orders only of a Government supported by the Army and the country. Within a few hours he was being told on the telephone from Petrograd:

'We dismiss you from your post for refusing to carry out the orders of the government and for pursuing a course that will bring incredible misery to the toilers of all countries, especially for the armies. We order you, on pain of being handed over to the military courts, to continue your duties until relieved by a new commander-in-chief or by someone authorized to take over your affairs. Ensign Krylenko is appointed Commander-in-Chief.'

The last sentence was the unkindest cut of all. Nikolay Vasilyevich Krylenko had been elected to the Army Committee of the Eleventh Army after the Revolution. He had then been made a member of the Sovnarkom's Collegium for Military and Naval Affairs together with Antonov-Ovseyenko and P. E. Dybenko. Nevertheless, the fact remained that a full general was being replaced by a man who only a few weeks previously had been an ensign, the lowest-ranking of army officers.

Lenin was quick to tell the troops what had happened, broadcasting a message to them which said: 'The matter of peace is in your hands. You will not suffer counter-revolutionary generals to destroy the great cause of peace. You will surround them with a guard in order to prevent lynching unworthy of the revolutionary army and to prevent these generals from avoiding the court that awaits them.'

In Dukhonin's case, Lenin's instructions were not obeyed. By the time Krylenko arrived in Moghilev, accompanied by a guard of fifty sailors from the *Aurora,* as well as soldiers and Red Guards, the former Commander-in-Chief had started a propaganda war, printing leaflets which were distributed among the troops and appealing for popular support. He failed to get it. After Krylenko's arrival the Moghilev garrison mutinied, arrested their former Commander-in-Chief and, despite the half-hearted protests of his successor, murdered him.

If the replacement had been abrupt and the aftermath brutal, there was a case for change which, not unexpectedly, was put forward by Krylenko himself. Explaining the reason for Lenin's move, he wrote:

'It was aimed not so much at obtaining immediate practical results from such talks as at establishing the total and unquestionable predominance of the new governing authority on the front lines. The minute the regiments and divisions were offered this right [responsibility for peace talks] and were given the order to take reprisals against anyone who dared to interfere with the peace talks, the cause of the revolution in the army was won and the counter-revolutionary cause hopelessly lost . . . And there was no reason to fear that chaos would be produced at the front. The war was paralysed by this measure. There was nothing to fear from the Germans – they could be expected to take a good wait-and-see attitude, and they did. At the same time the danger of counter-revolution at the front was done away with.'

Although 'counter-revolution at the front' had been circumvented, Lenin's revelation that he had determined on serious moves to end the war between Russia and Germany brought strong reaction from what might be termed counter-revolutionary sentiments among the Allies. These were exemplified by the American representative who 'categorically and energetically protests against any separate armistice which may be made by Russia'. One general reason for the Allied response was given by David R. Francis when he reported to the US State Department: 'I have a strong suspicion', he said, 'that Lenin and Trotsky are working in the interests of Germany, but whether that suspicion is correct or not, their success will unquestionably result in Germany's gain.' A similar attitude was shown by Monsieur Pichon, the French Foreign Minister, after negotiations had got under way. 'Germany is trying to involve us in her Maximalist [Bolshevik] negotiations,' he told the Chamber in Paris. 'After suffering as we have, we cannot accept peace based on the *status quo* . . . Russia may treat for a separate peace or not. In either case the war will continue for us.'

For the Allies, and for Britain in particular, Lenin's move had created an awkward dilemma, which is best appreciated by contrasting two statements. One came from Sir George Buchanan whose dispatch of 27 November was read by Balfour to the Supreme War Council, meeting in Paris, on 30 November.

It was no good trying to keep Russia fighting against her will, Buchanan maintained. 'For us to hold to our pound of flesh and to insist on Russia fulfilling her obligations, under the 1914 Agreement, is to play Germany's game. Every day that we keep Russia in the war against her will does but embitter her people against us.' On the other hand, Britain's Foreign Minister, Arthur Balfour, stressed in a minute to the cabinet: 'No policy would be more fatal than to give the Russians a motive for welcoming into their midst German officials and German soldiers as friends and deliverers.' The following day it was agreed that each country should ask its ambassador in Petrograd to state that 'the Allies were willing to reconsider their war aims in conjunction with Russia as soon as she had a stable government with whom they could act'.

In contrast to Buchanan's tacit understanding of Lenin's move there was the reaction from the other end of the political spectrum, from Ramsay MacDonald, the British socialist leader and pacifist whose anti-war stance had been evident since 1914. 'Of Russia I can hardly bring myself to write,' he said when giving his first comment on a separate peace in the *Leicester Pioneer* of 21 December 1917: 'I have dreaded this all along – driven to make a separate peace – alienated from us, made a present of to Germany. Oh! The stupidity that has gone to create this tragedy! And it could easily have been averted.'

As was so often to be the case in dealing with the Revolution, the British dithered, decided to be indecisive, and encouraged the Americans to be the same. Hence the initiative was left to the Russians, and on 13 (26) November Trotsky made formal application to the German High Command for an armistice. Two days later Krylenko issued orders for firing to cease immediately on all fronts, and for fraternization to begin.

The first German reaction to the Russian approach came from General Ludendorff who asked General Hoffmann: 'Is it possible to negotiate with these people?' 'Yes, it is possible to negotiate with them,' he was told. 'Your Excellency needs troops and this is the quickest way to get them.'

Once negotiations had been agreed on, the site for them was quickly settled. It was to be Brest-Litovsk, a town in Belorussia on the right bank of the river Bug, which had long been disputed by Russia and Poland and which before the war had been a rail and water communications centre. It had been burned and evacuated by the Russians in 1916 and was hardly in the best condition to accommodate the 400 men who gathered in December 1917 for what was to be a major peace conference with far-reaching implications. To make bad matters worse, the low-lying area was under snow, and few less prepossessing spots can have existed for the meeting. The shattered citadel of the old fortress, improvised railway cars and tented camps, formed much of the accommodation.

Preliminary talks began on 2 (15) December, when the Germans put forward simple proposals for armistice terms which involved an end to the fighting with each side continuing to hold their current positions. The Russians responded by proposing a six-month armistice, the evacuation of German forces from the Moon Islands in the Gulf of Riga, and the banning of fresh orders for the movement of German troops from the Eastern Front. These points were settled quickly, the

Germans countering the first with the offer of a twenty-eight-day armistice and dismissing the second with the statement that 'such terms could be addressed only to a conquered country'. As for the third, the Germans had already given orders to those units they intended moving to the Western Front.

A problem next arose when the Germans raised the question of the Russians' powers to speak on behalf of their allies. They had none, which brought the Russian negotiators back to Petrograd since they felt it necessary to clear their formal reply with Lenin. They returned to BrestLitovsk on 12 (25) December.

A few days later a dinner took place for a hundred of the delegates given by the German Commander-in-Chief in the East, Field Marshal HRH Prince Leopold of Bavaria. The British historian of the Conference, Sir John Wheeler-Bennett, has written:

'The picture was rich in contrasts. At the head of the table sat the bearded, stalwart figure of the Prince of Bavaria, having on his right Joffe, a Jew recently released from a Siberian prison. Next to him was Count Czernin, a *grand seigneur* and diplomat of the old school, a Knight of the Golden Fleece, trained in the traditions of Kaunitz and Metternich, to whom Joffe, with his soft eyes and kindly tone, confided: "I hope we may be able to raise the revolution in your country too." '

The two delegations whose members formally sat down to open negotiations on 22 December 1917 (4 January 1918) were headed by Adolf A. Joffe for the Russians and Baron von Kühlmann for the Germans. General Max Hoffmann represented the German High Command; Count Ottokar Czernin the Austro-Hungarians, while Bulgaria and Turkey were also represented.

That Czernin was to act as an ameliorating influence during the proceedings is suggested by his later description of attitudes in Vienna.

'In the Ministry here [he wrote], three groups are represented: one declines to take Lenin seriously, regarding him as an ephemeral personage, the second does not take this view at all, but is nevertheless unwilling to treat with a revolutionary of this sort, and the third consists, as far as I am aware, of myself alone, and I *will* treat with him, despite the possibly ephemeral character of his position and the certainty of revolution. The briefer Lenin's period of power the more need to act speedily, for no subsequent Russian government will recommence the war – and I cannot take a Russian Metternich as my partner when there is none to be had.'

At Brest-Litovsk both the Central Powers and the Russians had their supporting teams of military or naval experts while the Russian delegation included two contrasting groups of civilians; on the one hand there were L. B. Kamenev; M. N. Pokrovsky, the Bolshevik historian; L. B. Karakhan, the future Assistant Foreign Commissar; Karl Radek and, representing the Left Socialist Revolutionaries, Madame A. A. Bitzenko, a revolutionary heroine who had served a long prison sentence for killing a tsarist official. But the Russians also included, to emphasize the revolutionary nature of the Government with which the Germans were dealing, a Russian soldier, Nikolay Byelakov; a young sailor, Fyodor Olich; a young worker called Obukhov;

479

and finally Roman Stachkov, a peasant who had been brought along at the last moment without any previous thought. There were thus some prickly characters among those present, and they met in circumstances which were, in any case, conducive to prickliness. On one occasion Count Czernin referred to Radek as a Russian; Radek, hearing of the remark, replied: 'My nationality, Count, is not Russian. It is the same as yours – Austrian. It's not nationality that puts us on the other side of the table from you.'

Joffe opened the proceedings on 22 December by outlining the Russian proposals for negotiation, proposals that had not only been drawn up along the lines of Bolshevik theory but which strongly echoed the ideas about war in general, and more especially the current one, which Lenin had long been expounding. Whatever can be said about the controversial peace of BrestLitovsk, the blueprint from which it developed was a clear pointer to the way in which Lenin henceforth looked at international relations. The Russian proposals began:

'1. No forcible annexations of territories seized in time of war are permitted. Troops in occupation of these territories are withdrawn from them in the shortest period of time. 2. The political independence of those peoples who were deprived of it during the present war is fully restored. 3. National groups which did not enjoy political independence before the war are guaranteed the possibility of deciding the question of their attachment to one or another state or of their state independence by means of a referendum. The referendum must be organized in such a manner that complete freedom of voting will be assured to the whole population of the given territory, not excluding emigrants and fugitives. 4. In regard to territories which are inhabited by several nationalities the right of the minority is guarded by special laws, which guarantee it national cultural independence and, if possible, administrative autonomy. 5. No one of the belligerent countries is obligated to pay to other countries so-called "war expenditures"; contributions which have already been levied are to be returned. As for the compensation of private persons who have suffered from the war, this is to be made out of a special fund, created by means of proportionate contributions from all the belligerent countries. 6. Colonial problems are to be decided in accordance with the principles set forth in Points 1, 2, 3 and 4.'

Despite misgivings voiced by Hoffmann, the reception of the Russian proposals was better than might have been expected and Joffe received a conciliatory reply on 25 December to his suggestion that negotiations should be suspended for ten days so that the other belligerent powers might then join them.

These comparatively agreeable discussions were given a different tone when Hoffmann told Joffe after lunch that if parts of the former Russian Empire at present occupied by German forces – for instance Poland and Courland (a Baltic province of the old Russian Empire, later divided into Latvia and Lithuania) – decided to secede from Russia and unite with Germany, such moves would not be considered as forcible annexations.

The Russians were unable to move the Germans from this decision which was formally propounded on 28 December. There was consternation in the Russian camp and it was not only the Russians who looked on the proposal as a form of double-dealing.

'On 28th December 1917, we made our irreparable mistake [Prince Max of Baden later wrote in his *Memoirs*]. We gave the impression to the whole world and to the German masses that in contrast to the Russian attitude our agreement to the national right of self-determination was insincere and that annexationist designs lurked behind it. We rejected the Russian demand for a free and untrammelled popular vote in the occupied territories on the ground that the Kurlanders, Lithuanians and Poles had already decided their own fate. We ought never to have claimed the arbitrarily instituted or enlarged land-councils as authoritative representative assemblies.

'The Russian request for a referendum should either have been accepted without reserve or replaced by the demand for a National Constituent Assembly elected by universal suffrage.'

Joffe was astounded by the turn in the proceedings, felt it necessary to confer with Lenin on the next steps to be taken, and on 29 December 1917 (11 January 1918) returned to Petrograd. Lenin was just coming back from a holiday in Finland with his wife and his sister Maria.

'That spotless Finnish cleanliness with its white curtains everywhere reminded Ilyich of the days of his secret residence in Helsingfors in 1907 and again in 1917 on the eve of the October Revolution, when he had been writing his book *The State and Revolution* there. As a holiday, it wasn't much of a success. Ilyich sometimes even dropped his voice when speaking, the way we used to do when we were in hiding, and although we went for walks every day, there was no real zest in them. Ilyich's mind was occupied and he spent most of his time writing.'

Much of the thought was, no doubt, about the progress, or lack of it, at Brest-Litovsk. Lenin was anxious to move negotiations from Brest to Stockholm where he believed that the atmosphere might be more favourable to the Russians. But if he had any hopes of success, which hardly seems likely, they came to nothing. In another hope he was more successful since he was anxious to replace Joffe with someone of heavier weight, a man who might more effectively be able to spin out negotiations until, as he still unrealistically thought possible, revolution took hold in Germany. 'To delay negotiations,' he told Trotsky, 'there must be someone to do the delaying.' Trotsky agreed. 'You'll do it, Lev Davidovitch?' Lenin asked him. Trotsky again agreed. And when the Russian delegation returned to Brest-Litovsk on 9 (22) January it was headed by Trotsky, a master of the arts now needed.

His first problem was raised by the presence of a delegation representing the independent Ukrainian Republic, which had been set up only a few days earlier. This was the latest in a series of moves that went back to April 1917 when a National Ukrainian Congress had established an autonomous Ukrainian Republic. A Ukrainian Constituent Assembly came in November 1917, and the new Bolshevik Government set up a Ukrainian Soviet Government in Kharkov. The Ukrainian reply was to create a 'free and sovereign republic', and it was this that now requested a separate peace agreement with the Central Powers.

Trotsky, entangled in the moves and counter-moves which would influence the coming peace between Russia and Germany, was unable to prevent the concession to the Ukrainians, granted in a treaty of 9 February, which was to have complex repercussions. While it was being concluded Russia was successfully invading the country and on 1 March 1918 occupied Kiev. But the Germans quickly restored the Government that the Russians had displaced, soon found it not to their liking and before the end of April had installed as their authority Pavlo Skoropadsky, a former Russian general of Ukrainian descent whose Government remained in power until German control ceased with the armistice of November 1918 and the end of the war between the Central Powers and the Allies.

The negotiations at Brest-Litovsk following the Russian delegation's return under Trotsky were different from those which had gone before owing to the character of Trotsky who brought a harsher atmosphere to the Conference. He insisted that the Russians eat apart from the Germans rather than in a communal mess and he refused to be presented to the Prince of Bavaria. Lenin, as usual, took a more realistic view. When Trotsky asked him whether he should wear evening dress for one reception, he was told: 'Go in a petticoat if you can only get us peace.'

Trotsky's feelings towards the Germans were more like Lenin's than Joffe's. However, while the Germans were giving whatever attention they thought necessary to Russian attitudes, another factor was brought into play by a statement from President Wilson to both Houses of Congress incorporating the Fourteen Points.

The American desire to keep Russia in the war against the Germans was, as with the British, limited by reluctance to give diplomatic recognition to Lenin's Government, and as early as 4 December 1917, Lansing had urged Wilson to issue a statement explaining that even though it did not wish to offend the

Russian people, the USA could not recognize the new Russian Government.

Wilson was by now also brooding over a cable he had received from Boris A. Bakhmetiev, Russian Ambassador to the USA, who was still in post despite the coming to power of the Bolsheviks.

'Although Lenin's Government, which seized control by force, cannot be regarded as representing the will of the Russian nation [it went], the appeal which it addressed to the Allies in proposing an armistice cannot remain unanswered; for any evasion on the part of the Allies in the matter of peace will simply strengthen the Bolsheviks and help them to create an atmosphere in Russia hostile to the Allies. Any formal protest against Lenin's policy or any threats will have the same effect; they will simply aggravate the situation and aid the Maximalists to go to extremes . . .'

Lenin's peace campaign was already having an effect far further afield than he had probably expected. Bakhmetiev was not the only one jogging Wilson's elbow and before the end of December, the President began, according to his aide Colonel House, to consider an address to Congress 'because the American Mission [in Paris had] failed to secure from the Inter-allied Conference the manifesto on war aims that might serve to hold Russia in the war'. On 3 January 1918 Wilson received both a telegram from the US Ambassador in Petrograd urging a restatement of war aims with this end in view, and the same advice from Edgar Sisson, his special representative in Russia, proposing 'thousand words or less, short almost placard paragraphs'. Two days later the British Foreign Secretary told House:

'Should the President himself make a statement of his own views which in view of the appeal made to the peoples of the world by the Bolsheviks might appear a desirable course, the Prime Minister is confident that such a statement would also be in general accordance with the lines of the President's previous speeches, which in England as well as in other countries have been so warmly received by public opinion.'

This encouragement was certainly noted by the President, and among their aims the Fourteen Points had the dual purpose of curbing Russian propaganda based on the Allied refusal to take part in peace negotiations and stimulation of the Allied defence of democratic and liberal principles. The Russian representatives at Brest, 'sincere and in earnest', had, Wilson said, 'insisted . . . very justly, very wisely, and in the true spirit of modern democracy' on full publicity, but representatives of the Quadruple Alliance, of France, Britain, the USA and Italy, seemed to represent not their parliaments or peoples but 'that military and imperialistic minority which has so far dominated their whole policy'. It was America's heartfelt desire, Wilson went on, that the Russians would find some way 'whereby we may be privileged to assist the people of Russia to attain their utmost hope of liberty and ordered peace'.

If there was any doubt about Wilson's attitude, it was dispelled by the sixth of the Fourteen Points which called for:

'The evacuation of all Russian territory and such a settlement of all questions affecting Russia as will secure the best and freest cooperation of the other nations of the world in obtaining for her an unhampered and unembarrassed opportunity for the independent determination of her own political development and national policy and assure her of a sincere welcome into the society of free nations under institutions of her own choosing; and, more than a welcome, assistance also of every kind that she may need and may herself desire. The treatment accorded Russia by her sister nations in the months to come will be the acid test of their good will, of their comprehension of her needs as distinguished from their own interests, and of their intelligent and unselfish sympathy.'

The President's well-intentioned move had little immediate effect. Point 6 was given great publicity in Russia and details were circulated by the Russians to the German troops; but no impact on the Brest-Litovsk negotiations was discernible. As Wheeler-Bennett put it, the chasm dividing the two sides 'was unbridgeable, yet for four mortal weeks did Kühlmann and Trotsky circle round each other like duellists upon a cloak, debating the ethics, forms, and principles of self-determination and its application to the border states'.

While these negotiations were continuing Trotsky had concocted his own method of breaking the impasse. It was first outlined in a letter to Lenin whose authenticity was doubted for almost twenty years until, in September 1937, Trotsky confirmed it to Wheeler-Bennett during the course of the latter's research on the Treaty. Trotsky had begun:

'It is impossible to sign their peace, Vladimir Ilyich. They have already agreed with fictitious governments of Poland, Lithuania, Courland, and others concerning territorial concessions and military and Customs treaties. In view of "self-determination", these provinces, according to German interpretation, are already independent States, and as independent States they already have concluded territorial and other agreements with Germany and Austria-Hungary. We cannot sign their peace.'

He then came to his own proposals.

'We announce the termination of the war and demobilization without signing any peace. We declare we cannot participate in the brigands' peace of the Central Powers, nor can we sign a brigands' peace. Poland's, Lithuania's and Courland's fate we place upon the responsibility of the German working people. The Germans will be unable to attack us after we declare the war ended. At any rate, it would be very difficult for Germany to attack us, because of her internal condition.'

The last claim was perhaps ingenuous. So, too, was the hope of help from 'the German working people' although Lenin for long held on to the belief that the German revolution would come, remarking on one occasion to Raymond Robins: 'When you see a Council of Workmen's and Soldiers' Deputies at Berlin, you will know that the proletarian world revolution is born.' But Trotsky's plan itself was plausible enough for Lenin to telegraph him saying they would talk it over when they next met.

By 5 (18) January the negotiations in Brest-Litovsk had reached a particularly difficult point and it was now that Lenin and Stalin signed a joint message to Trotsky asking him to request a recess and then return to Petrograd.

Trotsky did so and, back in the city, on 8 (21) January addressed a meeting of sixty-three Bolshevik leaders to whom he outlined his proposals. After a long debate during which Lenin read a paper, 'Twenty-One Theses for Peace', Trotsky's 'No Peace, No War' proposal received sixteen votes, Lenin's argument for dragging out the negotiations and then signing the treaty, received fifteen, and proposals for ending negotiations and starting 'revolutionary war' against the Germans, received thirty-two.

The following day, 9 (22) January, the argument was continued in the Party's Central Committee. The proposal for a revolutionary war was lost by two votes to eleven. Lenin's proposal for dragging out the negotiations was supported by twelve votes to one. However, Trotsky's 'No Peace, No War' was accepted by nine votes to seven. What this meant in practice was that Trotsky could continue his delaying tactics at Brest-Litovsk until what he considered was the best moment, and then spring his proposal on the unsuspecting Germans.

There was to be an extended delay before this happened, at least partly due to a series of strikes in Germany which gave the Bolsheviks a false hope that the revolution there was about to begin. The delay meant that it was not until mid-February that Trotsky rose for his dramatic announcement. He began by denouncing imperialism and some of his hearers believed that this would be followed by capitulation to the existing German terms. What they heard was something very different.

> 'We are removing our armies and our people from the war [he said]. Our peasant soldiers must return to their land to cultivate in peace the fields which the Revolution has taken from the landlord and given to the peasants. Our workmen soldiers must return to the workshops and produce, not for destruction but for creation. They must, together with the

peasants, create a Socialist State. We are going out of the war. We inform all peoples and their Governments of this fact. We are giving the order for a general demobilization of all our armies opposed at the present to the troops of Germany, Austria-Hungary, Turkey and Bulgaria. We are waiting in the strong belief that other peoples will soon follow our example . . .'

The astonished silence of those present was finally broken by Hoffmann's *'Unerhört'* ('Unheard of'). Kühlmann tried to call a plenary session of the conference, but Trotsky stated that there was nothing to discuss and left the room for Petrograd with the bulk of the Russian delegation.

In the Russian capital there was great rejoicing; at last the hated war was over; Lenin had made good his promise.

But the euphoria lasted less than a week. At noon on 16 February – the date in both Russia and Germany since on 1 February the Russians had brought their calendar forward to 14 February, so that henceforth Russian dates were the same as those of the Gregorian calendar used throughout Europe – Lenin and Trotsky at Smolny received a telegram from General Samoylo who had been left at Brest. 'General Hoffmann', it said, 'today gave official notice that the armistice concluded with the Russian Republic comes to an end on 18 February at 12 o'clock, and that war will be renewed on that day. He therefore invites me to leave Brest-Litovsk.'

Lenin's reaction was to be expected. 'So, they have deceived us after all and gained five days,' he said. 'This wild beast lets nothing escape it. There is nothing left for us now but to sign the old terms at once if the Germans will still agree to them.' Trotsky maintained that they should wait until the German offensive had

490

begun but Lenin strongly disagreed. 'There is not another moment to lose,' he said. 'Your test has been tried and it failed. Hoffmann can and will fight. It's not a question of Dvinsk [one of the first Russian-held towns which was expected to fall to a German advance] but of the Revolution. Delay is impossible. We must sign at once. This beast springs quickly.'

Lenin now had a double problem on his hands. First, he had to secure from the Germans peace terms that were not too desperately onerous but which he correctly believed would be worse than those previously offered. Secondly, he had to gain approval of the new terms from colleagues who had already balked at approving those already proposed by the Germans. He also had the equally ticklish problem of dealing with public opinion. During February the larger soviets throughout Russia had been sent summaries of the two alternative ends to the talks – one leading to peace, the other to war – and asked which their members favoured. The results, published day by day in *Izvestia*, showed that almost half the urban votes were in favour of continued war.

The enemy began his new advance on time and moved forward against negligible opposition. As Lenin had correctly forecast, the Germans refused Russian acceptance of the terms offered at Brest-Litovsk; '. . . this time,' Hoffmann stated in his diary, 'the Comrades must simply swallow what we put before them.' One of the first reactions to the renewed German advance came from Trotsky who offered to resign from his post as Commissar of Foreign Affairs. While discussion about such a move was continuing, news came that the Germans had landed in Finland, news that gready disturbed Lenin. At first he favoured breaking the 'No Peace, No War' stance and sending help to Finland. Then he decided against it, saying to Trotsky,

'No, we dare not change our policy. Our entering would not save revolutionary Finland, but would certainly ruin us. We shall support the Finnish workmen as best we can, without, however, departing from the basis of peace. I do not know if this will save us. But in any case it is the only way in which deliverance is possible.'

The Party's Central Committee met twice on 18 February to decide what should be done. At the first meeting those factions for and against signing a peace treaty with inevitably harsher German terms were each allowed two speakers, both of whom were given only five minutes to make their case. Lenin and Zinoviev spoke in favour of peace; Trotsky and Bukharin spoke against. Lenin and Zinoviev were defeated by seven votes to six.

But that evening the Central Committee met again. The German advance was still continuing at full speed and when the vote was taken once again, Trotsky changed sides and the proposal for peace was carried by seven votes to six. The fluctuating votes were symptomatic of the near-chaos reigning in Petrograd, but Lenin, insisting on acceptance of peace terms, had succeeded in pulling the Russian chestnuts out of the fire.

In spite of the comrades' reluctant acceptance of the German terms there was nearly a last-minute hitch because of an interval between the Russian acceptance of new terms and acknowledgement by the Germans, an interval which the Russians at first thought was due to a German rejection. The delay brought from Trotsky a proposal that aid against the Germans should now be sought from the British and French. It was approved, six votes to five, by the Central Committee after Lenin, unable to be present, had sent in a slip of paper saying: 'Please add my vote *in favour* of the receipt of support and arms from the Anglo-French imperialist brigands. Lenin.' Luckily for all concerned, German acceptance arrived in time to prevent Trotsky's proposal being taken further.

A Russian delegation immediately set out for Brest-Litovsk. When it passed through Pskov, 257 miles from Petrograd, it discovered that Pskov was already occupied by German troops. The enemy were continuing their advance, presumably until acceptance of new peace terms had actually been signed.

Lenin was under no illusion about the situation and was to face difficulty in persuading the necessary bodies to approve what was clearly an abject surrender. Late on 23 February he drove with other members of the Central Committee to the Tauride Palace where he addressed the Petrograd Soviet – amid cries of 'Traitor' and 'German spy'. Nevertheless he made his point that there was no viable alternative to accepting German terms. Next he had to convince the members of the Central Executive Committee of the Soviet, possibly an even more difficult task. After seven members had supported him compared with four left-wing Communists who were against and another four who abstained, he rose in the Tauride Palace's Central Hall during what were by now the small hours of 24 February.

'I was present in the gallery [Philips Price has written], and shall never forget the atmosphere of depression and tension – such a contrast to the triumphant scenes which that same hall had witnessed not a fortnight before, on the opening of the Great Convention! Those few people who were present at this gathering as spectators, like myself, were suffering the same mental torture as the delegates. At one moment I found myself secretly hoping that Lenin's cautious, if opportunist, policy would prevail. At another moment I was almost about to cry out to the delegates in the hall to refuse to sign and declare a Holy War on Western Imperialism.'

Most people seemed to speak against signing. Among Lenin's more important opponents were Radek, Aleksandra Kollontay and Bukharin, a man whose conventional revolutionary apprenticeship of prison followed by emigration had led him to the far Left of the party. The first Revolution of 1917 had found him in the USA, and two further spells in prison – one in Japan and one in Siberia – had intervened before he arrived in Moscow in May 1917. His rise – until he became, as Lenin called him, 'the favourite of the whole party' – was due to intellectual ability, which brought him a following despite his determined opposition to much of what Lenin stood for. With his supporters he was now founding *Kommunist,* the vehicle for those who were now most virulently against the treaty.

'Then up rose Lenin [Philips Price has written], calm and cool as ever. Never did such responsibility rest on the head of one man. Yet it would be a mistake to assume that his personality was the most important factor in this crisis. Lenin's strength at this time, as at every subsequent time, lay in his ability to interpret the psychology, both conscious and unconscious, of the Russian workmen and peasant masses. He seemed to know what the members of the thousands of provincial and district Soviets were saying at this moment without summoning a new All-Russia Soviet Congress. 'Let us not become slaves to phrases,' he began; 'let us consider what are the practical conditions confronting the Revolution. Our impulse tells us to rebel, to refuse to sign this robber peace. Our reason will in our calmer moments tell us the plain naked truth – that Russia can offer no physical resistance, because she is materially exhausted by a three-year's war. It is true there may be people who will be willing to fight and die in a great cause. But they are romanticists, who would sacrifice themselves without prospects of real advantage. Wars are won today, not by enthusiasm alone, but by technical skill, railways, abundance of supplies. Has the Russian Revolution any of these in the face of an enemy equipped with all the technique of bourgeois "civilization"? The Russian Revolution must sign peace to obtain a breathing-space and to recuperate for the struggle. The central point of the world struggle now is the rivalry between English and German finance-capital. Let the Revolution utilize this struggle for its own ends.'

It was a convincing defence of the unpopular line he was taking and he clinched it with the words: 'To carry on a revolutionary war, an army is necessary, and we do not have one. It is a question of signing the terms now, or of signing the death sentence of the Soviet Government three weeks later.' The argument was convincing enough to give Lenin his victory by 116 votes to eighty-five with twenty-six abstentions.

It was 6 a.m. before Lenin left the Tauride Palace on 24 February, the day which saw his 'An Unfortunate Peace' published in no. 34 of *Pravda,* in which he reiterated the points he had made a few hours earlier, and ended:

'The plunderer has besieged us, oppressed and humiliated us – we are capable of enduring all these burdens. We are

495

not alone in the world. We have friends, supporters, very loyal helpers. They are late – owing to a number of conditions independent of their will – but they will come. Let us work to organize, organize and yet again organize! The future, in spite of all trials, is ours.'

In spite of such optimistic statements, the Germans continued to advance and in Petrograd it was now feared that the capital itself might be attacked. Axes and shovels were collected for trench-digging, factory sirens sounded the alarm, and in one night volunteers, including doctors and nurses, sailors from Kronstadt and munition workers, totalling in all some 60,000 it was claimed, volunteered for service in the city. Meanwhile, the bread ration was reduced to two ounces a day.

One fortuitous result of the German advance was that the Allied missions in Petrograd decided to move; there appeared to be little chance of preventing the Germans from sweeping into the capital if they wished to do so, and with the USA, Britain and France at war with Germany and preparing for desperate engagements on the Western Front, the case for leaving Petrograd was unanswerable, however much more difficult it might make Allied relations with the Russians. The American Francis had taken the lead in prospecting for an alternative site and had picked Vologda, 350 miles to the east. The provincial town had good railway links with the rest of Russia, a telegraph line to Archangel, the port to the north that had earlier been turned into an Allied base for supplying the Russians, and a wireless link with Murmansk, an equally important base in the north which was the Russian end of a British-Russian submarine cable. Francis and his staff arrived in Vologda on the last day of February 1918, and were joined the following month by most of the French diplomats and Francis Lindley, the British chargé d'affaires in Petrograd. Buchanan's duties had been taken over by Lockhart for most practical purposes but he was unwilling to move to Vologda. Working from that town, he later wrote, would be as if 'three foreign Ambassadors were trying to advise their governments on an English cabinet crisis from a village in the Hebrides'. He moved, instead, to Moscow where he carried on efficiently until, in the late summer, he came under suspicion of anti-Bolshevik activities and was arrested for some weeks before being released to England in exchange for Litvinov.

The German advance also forced Trotsky – and in effect Lenin – to reveal how the Bolsheviks then stood *vis-á-vis* the Allies, with whom the question of intervention in Russian affairs was becoming more and more tangled and contentious. In Murmansk the local Soviet, fearful that the Germans might launch an attack on what was becoming a valuable base, telegraphed Petrograd for instructions. 'Resistance is possible and obligatory,' Trotsky replied. 'Abandon nothing to the enemy. Evacuate everything that has any value; if this is impossible, destroy it. You must accept any and all assistance from the Allied missions and use every means to withstand the advances of the plunderers.'

The treaty of Brest-Litovsk had been settled. The German threat to Murmansk, as well as to Petrograd, evaporated, although before the arguments over ratifying the humiliating peace terms were finally settled Lenin had to use his ultimate threat – that of personal resignation. 'Only an unrestrained policy of phrases can drive Russia in the present moment into war,' he said at one point, 'and I personally would not remain for a second in the Government, or in the Central Committee of our party, should the policy of phrases gain the upper hand.'

Dislike of the coming treaty was not confined to the Socialist Revolutionaries and on one occasion Radek is reported by Raymond Robins's biographer to have said openly to Lenin: 'If there were five hundred courageous men in Petrograd, we would put you in prison.' Lenin, apparently unflustered, replied: 'Some people, indeed, may go to prison; but if you will calculate the probabilities you will see that it is much more likely that I will send you than you me.'

It was not only the other leading members of the Party that Lenin had to convince. The treaty had to be ratified as well as signed, and before this process was completed approval of the draconian terms was necessary from the Seventh Congress of the Russian Communist Party (Bolsheviks) (RCP (B)), as the RSDLP (B) was renamed during the Congress, and the Extraordinary Fourth All-Russian Congress of Soviets. Lenin finally got his peace – but only after a hard fight and through the cogency with which he stated the existing position. He told the Seventh Congress,

> 'In view of the fact that we have no army, that our troops at the front are in a most demoralized condition, and that we must make use of every possible breathing-spell to retard imperialist attacks on the Soviet Socialist Republic, the Congress resolves to accept the most onerous and humiliating peace treaty which the Soviet Government signed with Germany.'

Lenin's resolution for accepting the treaty was passed by the Seventh Congress – by thirty votes to twelve with four abstentions, according to *Pravda* on 9 March; and by twenty-eight votes to nine with one abstention according to the editors of Lenin's *Collected Works.*

An approving vote still had to be won from the Fourth All-Russian Congress of Soviets which met in Moscow on 14 March, but while Lenin was as anxious as ever to conclude the peace treaty he was still hopeful that offers of help from the Allies might strengthen his bargaining position. His hopes had been reinforced by a message from President Wilson. It had been cabled to Francis in Vologda, then wired to Raymond Robins in Moscow where Robins handed it to Sverdlov, Chairman of the All-Russian Central Executive Committee.

'May I not take advantage of the meeting of the Congress of the Soviet [Wilson characteristically began his message] to express the sincere sympathy which the people of the United States feel for the Russian people at this moment when the German power has been thrust in to interrupt and turn back the whole struggle for freedom and substitute the wishes of Germany for the purposes of the people of Russia. Although the Government of the United States is unhappily not now in a position to render the direct and effective aid it would wish to render, I beg to assure the people of Russia through the Congress that it will avail itself of every opportunity that may offer to secure for Russia once more complete sovereignty and independence in her own affairs and full restoration to her great role in the life of Europe and the modern world. The whole heart of the people of the United States is with the people of Russia in the attempt to free themselves for ever from autocratic government and become the masters of their own life.'

On behalf of the Government, Lenin thanked the President for his message and then took the opportunity of working in some publicity for the cause.

> 'The Russian Soviet Republic, having become a neutral country [he said], takes advantage of the message received from President Wilson to express to all peoples that are perishing and suffering from the horrors of the imperialist war its profound sympathy and firm conviction that the happy time is not far away when the working people of all bourgeois countries will throw off the yoke of capital and establish the socialist system of society, the only system able to ensure a durable and just peace and also culture and well-being for all working people.'

If Lenin's hopes that America might now actively intervene on Russia's side had been raised by President Wilson's message, he was also aware that Robert Bruce Lockhart was recommending a similar course to the British Government. He was therefore anxiously awaiting news when the debate on the treaty opened on 14 March in the Extraordinary Fourth All-Russian Congress of Soviets.

Most speakers were against signing the treaty, including Steinberg, who made a forceful protest. Lenin, sitting on the platform, waved to Robins to join him, and then asked the American: 'What have you heard from your Government?' After the answer 'Nothing', he [Robins] asked what Lockhart had heard. Again the answer from Lenin was 'Nothing'. 'I shall now speak for the peace,' Lenin replied. 'It will be ratified.'

He spoke for an hour and a half, and with a frankness that must have amazed, and possibly alarmed, his listeners. He emphasized, above all else, the need of the Revolution for a respite. The account of Robins's biographer says:

'His policy remained what it was in Petrograd. He would surrender Petrograd – the imperial, the revolutionary city. He would surrender Moscow – the immemorial, the holy, city. He would retreat to the Volga. He would surrender anything, and retreat anywhere, if only, on some slip of land, somewhere, he might preserve the revolution and create the revolutionary discipline which did indeed, twelve months later, enable him to fight a war on sixteen fronts and endure all the disabilities inflicted by the Allied economic naval blockade and still precariously revolutionarily live.'

Lenin swayed his audience not only by the logic of the military position as he outlined it, but by other characteristics emphasized by Arthur Ransome.

'Time and again, after listening to speeches which might have been made in any language in any country by men of any nationality, I have been suddenly, as it were, brought back to Russia when this little urgent figure stepped to the tribune, stuck his thumbs in the armholes of his waistcoat, and mingled jest and argument in language that tasted of Russian tobacco and the life of the Russian peasantry. It was natural to him to talk of the principles of his international revolution in the language of the Volga peasants, and in his mouth political theory seemed in no way out of tune with the peasant proverbs that were characteristic of his speeches. At the Assembly which ratified the peace, for example, he suppressed Steinberg, who was asking questions, by remarking, to the general delight, "One fool can ask more questions than ten wise men can answer." '

It was an impressive performance – as indeed it had to be. Lenin won his vote. Nevertheless the opposition from the Left Socialist Revolutionaries was more than a formality and before the end of the meeting they announced that they would leave the Soviet Government.

'We regard the ratification of the peace treaty as a denial of the international programme of the Socialist revolution which has begun in Russia [their spokesman declared]. We regard it as a capitulation to world imperialism. The L.S.R. [Left Socialist Revolutionary] Party declares that it does not feel itself bound by the terms of the peace treaty. The party herewith withdraws its representatives from the Council of People's Commissars.'

But Lenin continued to defend the stand he had taken, saying: 'When now . . . it has become clear that if we had fought we should have helped imperialism, we should have finally wrecked the transport system and lost Petrograd – we see that to play with words and wave a cardboard sword is useless.'

The treaty was signed on 3 March. Until the last moment Lenin was suspicious that the Germans might provoke some hitch and thus let the war go on, and as late as 2 March issued instructions to all soviets telling them to delay the demobilization of Red Army men and intensify preparations for blowing up railways, bridges and roads. They were to mobilize and arm detachments, continue accelerated evacuation and withdraw armaments into the interior of the country.

The war in fact ended although Russia paid a heavy price for the peace. It was, indeed, a 'Tilsit Peace' as Lenin called it more than once, referring to the peace forced on Prussia by Napoleon in 1807; and in 1918 there was no indication that it would be annulled before the end of the year – not by revolution in Germany as Lenin continued to hope but by Germany's military collapse.

In the spring Lenin made little attempt to sugar the pill, writing in *Izvestia*, 'We must not deceive ourselves. We must size up in full, to the very bottom, the abyss of defeat, partition, enslavement, and humiliation into which we have been thrown.' Under the treaty Russia renounced all rights over Riga and some Livonian territory behind it, the whole of Courland, Lithuania and part of Belorussia. She agreed to evacuate the Ukraine, Estonia, Livonia and Finland; ceded Kars, Ardahan and Batum in the Caucasus to Turkey; and recognized the German-protected Government of the Ukraine. In brief, she lost 1,267,000 square miles and a population of 62 million.

Economically, the terms of the treaty were devastating. Russia lost 27 per cent of the crop-sown area, 20 per cent of her railways, three-quarters of her iron and steel capacity and a third of her factories. To all of which was added the loss of the Ukraine, Russia's 'bread-basket'. Thus the total effect of the treaty was to increase rather than lessen Lenin's problems after three and a half years of war.

Nor was this all. In the late summer the Bolshevik Government, increasingly troubled by civil war, increasingly anxious to dissuade the former enemy from aggressive action, signed a supplementary agreement with the Germans, indemnifying them with 6 billion marks in gold, goods and bonds. Soon afterwards the then enormous sum of 120 million gold roubles was actually shipped to Berlin.

One aspect of the treaty still not entirely clear is the part, if any, played by Germany in coaxing the Russians to accept its terms. According to a number of documents reproduced in Professor Z. A. B. Zeman's *Germany and the Revolution in Russia, 1915–1918* the Germans authorized Count Mirbach, their representative in Petrograd from the early summer of 1918, to spend considerable sums to persuade the Russian Congress to ratify the treaty. The details are either non-existent or extremely shadowy; but the same is largely true of the German aid that helped Lenin to power; and it would, after all, have been surprising if the country that had gained such a startling political victory as the treaty represented did not make certain that that victory was firmly stapled into position.

As was to be expected, the opposition in Russia made the most of the treaty terms. Under the heading 'A Disgraceful Finale', Gorky's *Novaya Zhizn* said:

'We are facing a band of adventurers who, for the sake of their personal interests, for the sake of prolonging, if only for a few weeks, the agony of their perishing autocracy, are ready for anything. They are ready for the most shameful betrayal of the interests of the country and the revolution, the interests of socialism, the interests of the unfortunate Russian proletariat, in whose name they are committing their infamies on the vacant throne of the Romanovs, preparing for their truster a horrible Golgotha.'

The next day the paper published a signed article by Sukhanov in which he said: '. . . the surrender of the Council of Commissars is a disgraceful suicide of the Russian revolution and a betrayal of the cause of the international proletariat.' The paper was asked to publish a statement of disagreement with Sukhanov and when it failed to do so was suspended for eight days. But it is an indication of the comparatively weak censorship then in operation that after the eight days it was allowed to resume publication. *Pravda* was equally outspoken with its leading article of 24 February headed, 'An Unfortunate Peace'.

A possibly unconsidered consequence of the treaty was that the Lettish units which had come to Russia at the time of the Revolution, could not return to Latvia, now occupied by Germany. Lenin solved the problem of what to do with them by giving them the task of guarding the Kremlin and the Government offices, work they carried out with as fierce a determination as the sailors from whom they took over.

With the signing of the treaty, relations between Russia and Germany were put on as normal a peacetime basis as was possible. Joffe, who had at first led the Russian delegation to Brest-Litovsk, became the Russian Ambassador in Berlin and Count Mirbach, an established German diplomat, became his counterpart in Moscow where, despite his conciliatory attitude, he inevitably became the focus for Russian opposition to the treaty.

Implementation of the treaty rested, of course, on German success in the continuing war against Britain and France. While this seemed at least likely, Lenin may have had his doubts judging by a comment in Bonch-Bruyevich's memoirs:

'We were already in Moscow when the German Government sent us the peace treaty printed in Russian and German in excellent type, on excellent paper, excellently bound . . .

505

[Vladimir Ilyich] took the volume in his hands, looked at it and said with a laugh: "The binding is good, the print is beautiful, but before six months are up there will not be a trace left of this pretty piece of paper." '

The remark cannot have been made much before April 1918; by mid-November the treaty had been ended following the defeat of the Central Powers.

Before this, however, there were a number of repercussions as the Germans 'tidied up' their gains and did their best to consolidate their success by threatening the Black Sea Fleet; at the end of April Lenin ordered that it should be scuttled.

Quite as important was the support the treaty of Brest-Litovsk gave to the disparate forces gathering along the frontiers of Russia in the hope that even if the Bolsheviks survived internal opposition they could not survive serious attack from outside. President Wilson might cable words of solace to the Russians who had fought the Germans since 1914, but there were French, British and others for whom the Bolshevik signatures on the treaty of Brest-Litovsk were testimony that they could not be trusted. To this extent, Germany's victory, even if later annulled by the events of the autumn of 1918, encouraged both the Russians anxious to overthrow the Revolution by civil war, and those countries and politicians who were beginning to believe that foreign intervention should be used to help bring down the Bolshevik Government.

The peace of Brest-Litovsk thus gave a push towards civil war and in doing so encouraged further the terrorist activities of the Cheka. That they had already been boosted by the renewed German advance at the end of February is shown by a statement in *Pravda* on 23 February. This began:

'The Vecheka hitherto has always been tolerant in its struggle against the enemies of the people. But now, when the hydra of counter-revolution, encouraged by the treacherous attack of the Germans, grows bolder every day, and the world bourgeoisie is trying to crush the vanguard of international revolution, i.e. the Russian proletariat, the Vecheka sees no means of combating counter-revolutionaries, spies, speculators, thugs,roughs, saboteurs, and other parasites, except by mercilessly destroying them on the spot.'

The concentrated efforts to suppress all opposition in Russia no doubt increased Allied dismay at the treaty of Brest-Litovsk, revealed in a statement which protested against it. 'Peace treaties such as these we do not, and cannot, acknowledge,' it said rather sententiously on 18 March. 'Our own ends are very different; we are fighting, and mean to continue fighting, in order to finish once for all with this policy of plunder, and to establish in its place the peaceful reign of organized justice . . .'

Lenin felt deeply the humiliations of Brest-Litovsk. He was realist enough to admit to himself that the Germans were still capable of adding to them and this produced more than one notable reaction during the next few months. The murder of Count Mirbach by Socialist Revolutionaries in Moscow in July was to stir him to placatory moves since he feared, unjustifiably, that the Germans might invade Russia in revenge.

Less expected was his intervention on behalf of the German-born Tsarina and, by implication, her husband, a bizarre incident in an already bizarre tale. In August 1917 – following the abdication but months before the Bolshevik seizure of power – the Tsar, the Tsarina and their children had been taken to Tobolsk in Siberia and accommodated in the Governor's house. Even at this early date there were various schemes, some less wild than others, for getting them out of Russia. One was proposed by the Russian attaché in Stockholm who passed it on to Sir Esmé Howard. Howard told Lord Hardinge at the Foreign Office in London, in a 'Private and Very Confidential' note on 29 May 1917 that,

'He suggested that if their lives seemed to be in danger it might be possible to get them off in a British Submarine when they could be met by Swedish destroyers and brought to Sweden in safety. He said he was sure that the King of Sweden would do everything in his power to secure their safety. Mr Nekludow begged General Hanbury Williams [who had brought the message to Howard] to submit this plan to The King, when he returned to London. General Hanbury Williams promised to do so but wished me also to inform the Foreign Ofice. He was quite of my opinion that the plan was quite impracticable besides which it appears to me to be most impolitic and inopportune from many points of view. The Russian Imperial Family, if they come to Sweden, would almost certainly become the centre of German intrigue. Only in case of Russia's falling into the hands of the extreme Anarchist party [Howard presumably means the Bolsheviks] who are willing to treat with Germany anyhow, does it seem to me that such an arrangement would no longer be open to any objections, and it would then probably be too late to do anything, even if it is not too late already.'

Nothing came of this or the various other escape plans tentatively put forward, and after the Bolshevik Revolution the prisoners' conditions became harsher. Ration cards were issued to them; they were allowed no more than soldiers' food and in April 1918 were moved to Ekaterinburg in the foothills of the central Urals.

Two months later there were proposals that the Tsar, and possibly members of his family, should be brought to trial. 'I proposed', Trotsky has written, 'that we hold an open court trial which would reveal a picture of the whole reign, with its peasant policy, labour policy, national minority and cultural policies.' The proceedings, he added, should be broadcast. Steinberg, the Commissar of Justice, says that this idea was subsequently suggested by a representative of the Peasant Congress at a Session of Sovnarkom. He opposed the idea:

'Finally [he has written], all eyes turned on Lenin who presided over the session. And, strangely enough, for once he agreed with me. Calmly he said that he also doubted the timeliness of such a trial; that the masses were too preoc- cupied with other concerns and that it would be well to postpone the matter. In the meantime, the Commissariat of Justice should be charged with the preparation of the perti- nent documents for future use. Lenin, of course, had his own political calculations in the stand he took. That night, however, the issue was waived, and that is where the matter rested. The Commissariat of Justice never troubled to "prepare the documents".'

There was to be neither preparation of documents nor trial. Instead, the Tsar, his wife, their children and a number of their closest retainers, were taken from their imprisonment and brutally murdered. Lenin's involvement in the massacre has remained a subject of dispute but Steinberg's claim that he did not favour even a trial has been reinforced by Anthony Summers and Tom Mangold in their book *The File on the Tsar*. They admitted that 'the truth about [the fate of] the Romanovs remains a casualty of history', but they added a new element to the generally accepted story of how all members of the family – with the possible exception of the Grand Duchess Anastasia – were murdered together in July 1918. This was the revelation, made with the help of documents in Harvard's Houghton Library, that Lenin himself had hoped to prevent the family from coming to harm. One document was from the Criminal Investigation Department of the Russian Government and referred to a conversation between Lenin in Moscow and General Jan Berzin, Commander-in-Chief of the Red Army in the Urals at Ekaterinburg. This conversation had apparently been overheard by three telegraph officials in Ekaterinburg named Sibirev, Borodin and Lenkovsky; according to their evidence Lenin ordered Berzin to take under his protection the whole Imperial Family and to shield them from any violence whatsoever. If this were not done, it was stated, Berzin was told that he would 'answer for it with his own life'.

There was no suggestion here that Lenin was moved by humanitarian motives. But since the Tsar's abdication the Kaiser had shown much interest in the fate of the Imperial Family, and following rumours that the Tsar had been executed or was about to be, Count Mirbach had asked the Russian Government to ensure that the Imperial Family should not be badly treated. As Summers and Mangold point out, Mirbach's inquiry (to Lenin) about the Imperial Family 'was just a gentle prod from Berlin, and must have seemed the least of his problems. The man who in March had signed away a third of Russia's population to appease the Germans, would surely not have found it hard to accede to a mild request about one redundant imperial family.'

However strong or weak Lenin's wish to appease the Germans by saving the Romanovs, most of them, and probably all, were murdered in July 1918. Lenin took calmly the doctored news which was given to him on the evening of the 18th during a meeting of the Council of People's Commissars. Sverdlov came into the Council meeting while the draft Public Health Law was being discussed, had a few words with Lenin and then announced:

'I have to say . . . that we have had a communication that at Ekaterinburg, by a decision of the Regional Soviet, Nicholas has been shot. Nicholas wanted to escape. The Czechoslovaks were approaching. The Presidium of the ARCEC [All-Russian Central Executive Committee] has resolved to approve.'
'Silence [from] everyone.
' "Let us now go on to read the draft clause by clause," suggested Ilyich. The reading clause by clause began.'

However sincerely Lenin might have wished for political purposes to avoid the family's death, it is likely that he would have accepted the news philosophically during a session of Sovnarkom. However, Trotsky has a totally different version of how the murder decision was taken: 'Talking to Sverdlov I asked in passing: "Oh, yes, and where is the Tsar?" "It's all over," he answered, "he has been shot." "And where is the family?" "And the family along with him." "All of them?" I asked, apparently with a touch of surprise. "All of them!" replied Sverdlov. "What about it?" He was waiting to see my reaction. I made no reply. "And who made the decision?" I asked. "We decided it here. Ilyich believed that

511

we shouldn't leave the Whites a live banner to rally round, especially under the present difficult circumstances." '

The story of Lenin's reluctance to exasperate the Germans is not incompatible with a later fear that the Romanovs might become a rallying point. Certainly, at the time when the members of the Imperial Family were murdered, Lenin and his rule were being put increasingly at risk by dangers different from those provided by Germany. In fact, the months following the treaty of Brest-Litovsk, and the peace which Lenin had not wished to be disrupted by the murder of the Tsar and his family, provided a greater challenge to the Revolution than any opposition that Kerensky had mounted in the final months of 1917.

This was not at all what had been expected. With the signing of the treaty, Lenin looked forward to what was later to be described as a peaceful breathing spell, during which, it was hoped, Russia would be able to recover, if only slowly, from the disastrous losses of the war. While the recovery was going on, moreover, the socialist revolution would spread to other countries, and success in these would reinforce what had been achieved in Russia. But neither hope was to be realized. Chagrin at the success of the Revolution led to anti-Communist opposition abroad which consolidated into the offensives of the civil war. At the same time the rest of Europe stubbornly refused to follow the road mapped out in Bolshevik plans. Neither Britain nor France showed more than the faintest flicker of interest in socialist tendencies while Germany, which had seemed to provide Lenin's best hope of emulation outside Russia, mustered only a temporary glimmer of revolt and then settled down to the liberal policies of the Weimar Republic, which typified those he had always seen as the most dangerous barrier to revolution.

512

Peace with the Germans, achieved under such difficult conditions, certainly showed that Lenin was not only sincere but also determined as far as the major claim which had brought him to power was concerned. The price to be paid, however, went far beyond the humiliating physical and financial terms of the treaty, whose repercussions were to be felt for the rest of Lenin's life. The terms fuelled the oppositional fury of the Socialist Revolutionaries and spurred them and their supporters to acts which led to the extension of the Terror by Dzerzhinsky's Cheka, whose tentacles by the end of 1918 were covering the entire face of Russia.

The spread of the Terror operated according to the physicist's rule that the use of any force produces a counter-force, and played its part in encouraging Lenin's opponents inside Russia, and also the country's former allies who had been shocked both by the rise of Communism and by the end of the Russian army as a fighting force. From now onwards they were able to augment their White forces beneath a banner which proclaimed that the Red enemy was using arrest and murder as everyday weapons in its battle for control of the country. This made even more bitter and even less easily resolvable the civil war which had begun after the Bolsheviks seized power and then spread with a remorseless horror even greater than that which characterizes most civil wars.

The fury with which it developed after the treaty of Brest-Litovsk ended Lenin's hopes that the transformation of Russia's economic life could be carried out methodically if slowly; both the economic demands made by the war and the intensification of class hatreds which the war brought about combined to speed up changes within Russia and to bring about the conditions of what was known as War Communism. The communist seizure of power had been followed by the nationalization of the land

513

and the banks, by the nationalization of shipping and the declaration of foreign trade as a State monopoly. After this Lenin had hoped for a breathing space. Instead, the sugar industry was nationalized on 2 May and the oil industry on 17 June, while later in the month a decree called for the nationalization of the largest firms in the mining, metallurgical, metal-working, textile, electro-technical, pottery, tanning and cement industries. The process continued, and before the end of 1920 all factories employing more than ten workers were nationalized.

This development of War Communism cannot, of course, be laid exclusively against the development of the civil war since it followed, in many ways, the paths the Bolsheviks would have taken in any case. Yet the speed and intensity with which such measures were brought in were very much the result of the fighting in which Russia's former allies were to play their part. Thus they cannot be totally absolved from responsibility for the desperate situation in which Russia finally found herself at the end of 1920 when the civil war ended as General Wrangel's forces finally took to the boats and evacuated the Crimea.

This situation was to face Lenin, some three years after the seizure of power, with the need for two embarrassing dilutions of the principles on which he had built the Party over the years. At home he eventually found it essential to restore private enterprise in the guise of the New Economic Policy, while abroad it was necessary to deal with the hated foreign capitalists – even with the Germans – sign agreements with them and even grant them concessions within Russia itself.

However, all this lay in the future as in the summer of 1918 he dealt as best he could with the immediate repercussions of the humiliating peace that the Germans had forced the Bolsheviks to accept.

14

The End of Democracy–Terror

D espite the humiliations that the treaty of Brest-Litovsk brought to Lenin's administration, it reinforced the fact that a new government now controlled the country once ruled by the Tsar – even though in more than one area the first engagements of what was to develop into the barbarous civil war were already being fought.

Yet there were other ways in which the meetings round the conference table at Brest-Litovsk, between some of Europe's most powerful diplomats and men who for a decade or more had helped fill Russia's prisons, created a boundary between one era and the next. Lenin had now shown himself to be a man who could fulfil, in spite of all difficulties, one of the main promises he had made from his political platform. As Louis Fischer has said of the treaty in his study *The Soviets in World Affairs:* 'The Russians compromised with the enemy without compromising themselves. Brest-Litovsk was a great practical defeat but a greater moral victory. Viewed in the light of one, the conference is the darkest page in Soviet history –; viewed from the other it is the brightest spot in all the years of the republic's foreign relations.' Lenin had bought a peace that few in either Russia or the Allied countries had expected to be on sale.

In Russia, signature of the treaty brought a reaction against Lenin and his policies so great as to be different not in degree but in kind from what had gone before. Opposition to a surrender to the Germans had been strong from the first day that it seemed possible, particularly among the Left Socialist Revolutionaries. Yet as the peace treaty became gradually feasible and was then finally signed, opposition to it turned into opposition to Lenin himself. The feeling grew as it was realized that the food shortage, already developing into a famine that would stalk all Russia, was inevitably to be exacerbated by the loss of Russia's food-producing areas, which formed an integral part of the treaty. The result of this disastrous concatenation of events was that Lenin's life after the treaty of Brest-Litovsk was dominated by a sequence of chapters which all contained the same unpleasant ingredients but in which the importance of the ingredients changed from one chapter to the next.

Three days after the end of the Seventh Party Congress the chief organs of the Government moved from Petrograd to Moscow, which now became the capital of the country and the city to which Lenin and Krupskaya moved in mid-April to make a new home. The first suggestion that Petrograd should be permanently abandoned for Moscow had come when it seemed likely that the peace negotiations might break down and that the Germans would be able to make a successful military thrust into the city. That danger never developed, but the proposal for a move to Moscow was renewed in March 1918 – apparently for administrative as well as military reasons. There was considerable resistance from civil servants which rested not only on a dislike for change but on the prestige which, it was claimed, now clung to the Bolshevik headquarters in Smolny.

Lenin ridiculed the opposition, pointing out that if Sovnarkom moved from Smolny into the Moscow Kremlin the prestige would move with it. He dismissed the alleged importance of Smolny but won his argument as much by military logic as anything else. He said:

'If the Germans in one big swoop over-run Petersburg – and all of us – then the revolution perishes. If the government is in Moscow, then the fall of Petersburg will be a grievous blow, but only a blow. How is it that you don't see this, that you don't understand? Moreover, in the present conditions, if we remain in Petersburg we are only increasing the military danger; it is as if we were inviting the Germans to take Petersburg. If the Government is in Moscow, the temptation to seize Petersburg is much smaller; what advantage is there in occupying a hungry revolutionary city if this occupation is not decisive for the fate of the revolution and of peace? Why do you prattle about the symbolic importance of the Smolny! The Smolny is what it is because we are in it. When we are in the Kremlin, all your symbolism will move to the Kremlin.'

And on 11 March Lenin and most of the commissars moved there.

A special train was provided for Lenin, a second one for other members of the Central Committee and the forty-three typists, telephonists and messengers that went with them. But there were incongruities about the move, typified by the sight of Lenin himself, spotted by Arthur Ransome, sitting in the hall of Moscow's National Hotel on his luggage, surrounded by piles of 'unimaginable rags and tatters of baggage and bedding rolled in blankets, and every kind of tatterdemalion basket and battered trunk'. Lenin, Ransome continues, was 'calm as usual, fearless as usual, without any guard whatsoever in the old stronghold of Russian capitalism which is his sworn enemy'.

After a few days in the National he and Krupskaya moved into temporary rooms in the Kremlin and before the end of April were occupying what became permanent quarters. Once he was settled in he began discussing projects for replanning the city and Ivan Zholtovsky, the architect, has recalled in his memoirs how Lenin 'dwelt a great deal on the question of green spaces in the city. He thought tree-planting should be seriously considered when Moscow was being replanned, and advised us architects to study experiences in the European capitals – London with the massive green space of Hyde Park, Paris with the Champs Elysées, etc.'

Lenin's quarters in the Kremlin consisted of three main rooms, plus a maid's room, kitchen and bathroom, on the third floor of a large building later known as the Zdaniye Pravitel'stva (Building of the USSR Government), originally housing the Imperial judicial quarters.

His office was another third-floor room, and he was somewhat pernickety about his working conditions. The temperature had to be 63.5 degrees Fahrenheit and he would complain if it were a single degree higher or lower. He disliked the sound of telephone bells and eventually had them replaced with lights which lit up when a call came through. He insisted that he should be able to see out of the windows, and one of his secretaries remarked: 'It was as though he felt cramped and stifled in a room cut off from the outside world by lowered blinds.' He had separate folders marked 'Urgent', 'Not Urgent', 'Important', 'Less Important', 'Seen' and 'Not Seen' on his desk, the top left drawer of which contained papers to which he had pinned instructions. This was the only drawer which he ever left unlocked, although he would leave papers on which he was working in the centre of his desk, held in place by a heavy pair of scissors which meant 'Don't touch'.

A small green-shaded electric lamp stood on his desk before which was drawn up a plain wooden chair with wicker seat and back. The rest of the furniture consisted of a chair for visitors, bookshelves and two revolving bookcases, which he had designed himself and which he called his whirligigs and which, with the shelves, held about 2,000 volumes.

On the walls there hung a portrait of Marx and a bas-relief of S. N. Kalturin, a Russian revolutionary who had been executed in 1882. On his desk there always rested an assortment of souvenirs that had been sent to him – at one period a writing set of Caucasian workmanship, an inkwell, an ashtray and a cast-iron monkey examining a human skull. And on the desk there was usually a mother-of-pearl paper-knife. He would never have cut flowers in the room but was fond of a large tubbed palm which he looked after himself. The only unexpected item was an old clock which could lose up to fifteen minutes a day whatever repairs were made to it – for a long time Lenin stood out against a replacement, saying that it would be just as bad.

Lenin's move to the Kremlin meant that those who looked after the huge collection of buildings were now at the mercy of his personal superintendence of how they were run and maintained. What this could mean is shown by a note he sent to the Kremlin's Commandant, after learning that a lift would be out of order for three days, which ran,

> 'This is the height of disgrace. There are people suffering from heart disease for whom mounting stairs is both harmful and dangerous. I have pointed out a thousand times that the lift must be kept in order, and that one person should be made responsible for it.
>
> 'I strongly reprimand you, and charge you to establish the identity of those guilty of not giving due warning; let me have a list of the people responsible for the lift once again; and the penalties imposed on them.'

It was not only Lenin and the commissars who moved into the Kremlin in March 1918. There was Sverdlov, who from room 39 on the first floor not only carried out his duties as Chairman of the All-Russian Central Executive Committee but acted in numerous ways as Lenin's right hand. At the same time Dzerzhinsky and his Cheka staff also moved to Moscow – to the former headquarters of an insurance company at 22 Lubyanka Street, a name soon to become notorious as one of the most feared prisons in the world. Its first regular unit was a detachment of the Latvian Sharpshooters.

Early in 1922 the Cheka reported officially that between 1918 and the end of 1921 it had carried out 12,733 executions, including 3,082 for taking part in rebellions, 2,024 for membership of counter-revolutionary organizations, 643 for gangsterism, 455 for incitement to revolution, 206 for corruption, 102 for desertion and the same number for espionage. The figures, remarkable as they sound as an official admission, must be viewed against many other estimates of what the Red Terror meant.

Lenin settled down to an existence in the Kremlin as homely as his wife could make it. His lifestyle remained simple, partly because of a stern belief that it should not be ostentatious, partly because he genuinely liked it that way. The low-ceilinged suite of rooms had been occupied by a lady-in-waiting before the Revolution and was quite adequate for Lenin's tastes. Life and food in the new home were unpretentious and Angelica Balabanov later remarked that she was touched when on a visit Krupskaya opened a treasured bottle of preserves in her honour. Her description of tea fits those of other visitors – most of whom called to discuss the best way of running Russia or the Party and the problems which constantly beset both. The usual menu was black bread, butter and cheese, tea, and possibly a jar of something special for the guest.

The impression that Lenin gave was very different from that of a man who ruled a great empire.

'[He] normally worked a seventeen to eighteen hour day at his desk in the Kremlin, was sustained by his robust constitution, his lifelong habit of physical exercises and of hard work, his humour *and joie de vivre* [says one visitor]. Many . . . commented on his shrewd and humorous scrutiny, with one eye screwed up in concentration, and on his invigorating laugh; and he was always ready to join children in their fun.'

As far as possible he maintained a strict personal routine, returning from his office to his personal quarters at 4 p.m. sharp for a meal and a brief rest but making certain that he was back at his desk by six o'clock. Judging by the comment of his secretary, Lydia Fotiyeva, his sense of humour, present even in the grimmest circumstances, enabled him to maintain the unrelenting pace:

> 'Speaking of the way he worked I think it can be said that he worked jovially. He had an amazing sense of humour. One could hear him breaking into a laugh now and again when he was talking to someone in his office, and he often laughed at C.P.C. meetings too. He had an extraordinarily infectious laughter, without any malice in it ever. It was the laughter of a man of ebullient energy and vigour.'

In these surroundings, where relaxation was rarely more than a walk that enabled him to enjoy the view over Moscow, Lenin faced, from the early summer of 1918 onwards, a succession of steadily mounting troubles – what his opponents no doubt considered as chickens coming home to roost.

Throughout these particularly difficult months – as at other times – he was helped by an in-built understanding of propaganda, from the use of radio broadcasts, then in their infancy, to the development of agit-trains and agit-ships, which stirred up agitation for the cause by taking books, newspapers and trained speakers to the most vulnerable fronts in the growing civil war. The Lenin Train was used extensively, while Krupskaya made at least one tour in the *Red Star* agit-ship. That Lenin appreciated her efforts is shown in a revealing letter he wrote to her in the summer of 1919 when she was aboard the Government vessel *Krasnaya Zvezda* saying:

> 'I learned from Molotov that you did have a heart attack. That means that you are *over-working* yourself. You must

stick strictly to the rules and obey the doctor's orders absolutely.

'Otherwise you will not be able to work when winter comes. Don't forget that.'

Early in 1920 Lenin was still expanding propaganda methods, writing on 25 January: 'Step up economic and practical aspects of the work of the trains and steamers by including agronomists and technicians in their political departments, by selecting technical literature, films on appropriate subjects, etc.' The work, he went on, should be 'extended beyond the range of the tracks and riverbanks by making wider use of auxiliary forms of transport (motor-cycles, motor-cars, bicycles) carried in the trains and steamers, as well as by the use of local conveyances'.

Throughout this period he was intensely aware of the need to publicize Bolshevik aims.

'Dear Comrade [he wrote to Angelica Balabanov, now carrying out propaganda for the party],
The work you are doing is of the utmost importance and I implore you to go on with it. We look to you for our most effective support. Do not consider the cost. Spend millions, tens of millions, if necessary. There is plenty of money at our disposal. I understand from your letters that some of the couriers do not deliver our papers on time. Please send me their names. These saboteurs shall be shot.'

Although regarding personal publicity as offensive, Lenin would do almost anything for the cause. He perhaps remembered the story of Napoleon, helping to shift a heavy gun before an important battle but making certain that his figure was well lit by lanterns, and he took the necessary action on an early *subbotnik* – day of voluntary action dedicated to the regime – which was celebrated on May Day 1919. At 9 a.m. he walked into the courtyard of the Kremlin and asked the military commander if he could help the troops moving heavy debris there, He refused the purely nominal duties offered and insisted on working hard with the men for the entire day.

Lenin's own assessment of the situation in the aftermath of Brest-Litovsk was given in May 1918, with an honesty qualified only by political caution, to Count Mirbach. Mirbach transmitted his account of the interview to Berlin:

'In general Lenin trusts his lucky star with the utmost conviction and repeatedly expresses the most boundless optimism in an almost overpowering way. However, he does admit that, even though his system is still standing firm, the number of his opponents has increased and that the situation "demands intenser vigilance than it did a month ago".

'He bases his faith principally on the fact that the governing party is the only one which has any organized force at its disposal, whereas all the others only agree in their opposition to the present system whilst, beyond this, they diverge in all directions and have no power behind them to equal that of the Bolsheviks. [Kaiser's marginal remark: "The Japanese, the Chinese, the English!? He will have the whole Kossack army against him!"]

'In some respects this is certainly true, but the tone in which Lenin speaks of the impotence of his enemies shows that he nevertheless somewhat underestimates them.

'Beyond this, however, Lenin quite freely admits that his opponents are no longer to be found exclusively among the parties on his right, but that they are now also being recruited in his own camp, where a kind of left wing has formed. The main complaint of this opposition inside his own house is that the treaty of Brest-Litovsk, which he is still determined to defend with the utmost tenacity, was a mistake. More and more Russian territory was being occupied; the peace with Finland and the Ukraine had still not been ratified; the famine had not merely not been vanquished, but was actually on the increase. In short, a state of peace worthy of the name was still apparently in the far distance . . .'

The report ends: 'However, he was quite apparently concerned to describe the awkwardness of his position as graphically as possible,' words against which there was a comment by the Kaiser. 'He is finished,' it read. But it was the Kaiser who was forced into abdication little more than six months later by the defeat of the Central Powers in France and the armistice which followed.

Although it was the Kaiser who was 'finished' before the end of 1918, during that year Lenin had quite enough troubles to test the organization he had built up. For if the obvious problems which had faced the Bolsheviks were considerable until the threat from Kerensky had been finally disposed of in November 1917, those which throughout 1918 crowded in upon the Soviet commissars were not only as formidable but seemed to offer less chance of easy solution. Economic and political, civil and military, they were so intimately interlinked that it was virtually impossible to deal with one without affecting others, and even to define them accurately illustrates the complexity of the situation with which Lenin was faced once he began to deal with the results of ending the war with the Central Powers.

The food shortage was so great that at times it loomed as a threat in Lenin's mind almost as great as that from the counter-revolutionary forces which continued to gather their strength throughout the early part of 1918. 'The more the famine surges up on us the clearer it becomes that against this desperate need desperate measures of struggle are necessary,' he said on one occasion. 'To get bread – that is the basis of socialism today.' In addition, those anxious to drag down the new Government by military means seemed likely to be – and were – augmented before the end of the year by interventionist troops from those who had been Russia's allies. If this was not enough to make survival of the new Government uncertain as 1918 advanced, there was also the internal political threat, posed most danger-ously by the Left Socialist Revolutionaries, who before the summer was over were to goad the authorities into unleashing a concentrated 'Red Terror' which brought horrified reaction outside Russia and led the way towards worse horrors to come.

The importance of the Left Socialist Revolutionaries in driving the Bolsheviks towards the Red Terror, whose enormities underlined so many of the criticisms that their enemies had been making, should not be underestimated. However, there were other factors which suggest that Bolshevism's original sin was merely one among many contributing to the awful episodes that blotted the Russian record from the start of 1918 onwards.

One point in particular should be remembered. In view of the relatively small number of dedicated Bolshevik supporters and of the similarly small numbers of Cheka members, it is unrealistic to assume that the Red Terror was only the result of operations directed from above, and that it lacked the compliance, if not the encouragement, of large segments of the population. Indeed, this point is supplemented by the fact that when the Terror began in earnest in the late summer of 1918 the strongest demands for executions came in many cases not from the official Cheka but from the freely elected Soviets. This does not absolve either Lenin himself, or his Government, from the dark campaign that blackened Russia's name in 1918 and 1919 but suggests that it was as much the product of national circumstance as of ideological motivation, even though the second factor was naturally stressed by all those who hated both the theoretical basis of Communism and its practical applications.

Certainly the circumstances with which Sovnarkom had to deal in the aftermath of Brest-Litovsk demanded all the administrative ingenuity and personal resolution that Lenin could call upon; it is necessary to deal with them separately, but fitting that the first to be described should be the food shortage, which during the first year or two of the Bolshevik Government transformed discontent into revolt in many parts of Russia. To a great extent the Bolsheviks were reaping what the Tsar had sown, since before 1917 the conscription of agricultural workers into the army had played havoc with Russia's food supply. However, the return of these men in the winter of 1917 to 1918 was balanced by the chaos that followed the Revolution; the net result was that the shortage of food continued to increase. The break-up and redistribution of the big estates worsened matters still further and Lenin was justified when, towards the end of July 1918, he declared: 'The time before the new harvest is the most difficult and critical period for the Russian socialist revolution. Now, I think, we must say that the highest point of this critical situation has been reached.' And to A. G. Shlyapnikov he wrote in May 1918: ' *Obviously* we shall perish and ruin the *whole* revolution if we do not conquer famine in the next few months.'

The seriousness of the situation was emphasized when, also in May, he spoke to a deputation from Petrograd's great Putilov Works. The Government, he told them, had to organize a 'great crusade against the grain profiteers'. This implied, he said,

'the absolute prohibition of all private corn trade, the obligatory surrender of all surplus grain to the State at a fixed price, the absolute prohibition of the hiding and secreting of surplus grain by anybody; and the strictest registration of all surplus grain for the just distribution of bread between all citizens, controlled by the Proletarian State.'

In practice these measures, even though aimed at distributing fairly the food that was available, comprised State control of all crops, confiscation in kind, and the complicated machinery of repression and collection, which aroused steadily rising discontent throughout the country and was only abandoned when the NEP was introduced early in 1921.

Lenin never made any attempt to conceal the seriousness of the food shortage. Thus in May he sent a circular telegram to provincial Soviets and food committees: 'Petrograd is in an unprecedentedly catastrophic condition. There is no bread. The population is given the remaining potato flour and crusts. The Red capital is on the verge of perishing from famine.' But he then added: 'Counter-revolution is raising its head, directing the dissatisfaction of the hungry masses against the Soviet Government.' There was doubtless justification for the remark but it was typical of the way in which Lenin insistently, at times rather simplistically, attributed all troubles to anti-Bolshevik forces. The shortage of grain had to be due to the *kulaks* rather than to a mixture of evils that included the ravages of war and the poorness of some seasons' harvests.

The belief that this was so, governed, to a large extent, the operations of the Food Commissariat, set up in May to balance the needs of the 'consuming' areas against those of the 'producing' areas – a rough and ready division between the cities and the country – and which established a food dictatorship throughout all Russia.

'The peasant bourgeoisie, having accumulated in their cash boxes enormous sums of money, which they extorted from the state during the war, remain stubbornly indifferent to the groans of the starving workers and poor peasants [it stated]; they will not bring their grain to the collection points, thinking to force the government to raise prices again, so that then they can sell their grain at fabulous prices to grain speculators and "bag traders". The greedy stubbornness of the village kulaks and rich peasants must be brought to an end . . . Only one way out remains – to answer the violence of the grain owners against the starving poor with violence against the grain hoarders. Not one pood of grain should remain in the hands of the peasants beyond the amount required for the sowing of their fields and the feeding of their families until the next harvest.'

On 1 June *Pravda* printed a proclamation of Sovnarkom, 'All Out for the Struggle Against Famine', signed by Lenin and others, which left no doubt about the position in which the country now found itself:

'The food situation in the republic grows worse every day. Less and less grain is reaching the grain-consuming areas.

Famine has already arrived: its fearful breath can be felt in the cities, the factory centers, and in the grain-consuming provinces.

'The hungry and tormented workers and poor peasants who have bravely endured all the burdensome consequences of the criminal imperialist war, are asking the government agonizing questions . . . Almost all the surplus grain is in the hands of the village kulaks. Having grown rich during the war and accumulated huge sums of money, they don't have to sell their grain and they are hoarding it, waiting for the prices to rise, or selling it at speculative prices . . . The grain must be taken from the kulaks by force . . . As fast as you can, form armed detachments of firm and steadfast workers and peasants who will not give in to any enticements, and place them at the disposal of the central authorities . . . The detachments you form, together with the disciplined units of the Red Army, led by experienced and tested revolutionaries and specialists in food procurement, will march out to win the grain from the village bourgeoisie.

'Merciless war against the kulaks!'

Shortly afterwards the first Committees of the Village Poor were set up. Their purpose was not only to distribute grain, but to co-operate with local authorities in taking surplus grain from the richer members of the community and ensuring that it was equitably distributed.

Thus the latest stage of revolutionary redistribution was a counterpart to what had happened during the Revolution of 1917. That had been accompanied by the elimination of the large estates; now it was *kulak* property, the large peasant farms, which were being broken up. Accurate figures are difficult to obtain since in some cases part of a *kulak* property would be taken and redistributed but the remainder left in the hands of the original owner who was thus converted into a *serednyak*.

Even if such measures were required, their scope for creating trouble was obvious, and the Commissariat for Internal Affairs records twenty-six peasant uprisings in July, forty-seven in August and thirty-five in September. They were not pleasant. 'The greatest ferocity was displayed on both sides,' according to W. H. Chamberlin who studied the reports, 'people were cut to pieces, beaten to death, burned alive in these unknown battles over the country's last crusts of bread.'

Far from being exceptional, such incidents were symptomatic of the brutality and inefficiency with which the Committees of the Village Poor sometimes carried out their work and which produced comparable actions among those whose food they were taking. The danger, even in the initial grain collection, was recognized by the authorities, and the first of the instructions issued on 20 August 1918 by A. Tsyurupa, Commissar for Food, said that every food-requisitioning detachment was to consist of not less than seventy-five men and two or three machine guns.

If the spontaneous actions of men and women whose families were starving often passed beyond the horrendous, the official moves to deal with the situation were only slightly less dramatic. 'Speculators who are caught red-handed', read one injunction to the official food detachments, 'and can be convicted on clear evidence will be executed on the spot by the detachments. When they draw up a report on an act of requisitioning, an arrest or an execution, the Revolutionary Sections will call upon at least six witnesses who must be picked from the poor population of the neighbourhood.'

The phrase about the poor population was an indication of Lenin's underlying belief that the class war was an important factor in the situation, if not the major one.

'Emphasize more strongly [he demanded] the basic idea of the necessity, for salvation from famine, of conducting and carrying through a ruthless and terrorist struggle and war against peasant or other bourgeois elements who retain surplus grain for themselves.

'Lay down precisely that owners of grain who possess surplus grain and do not *send* it to the depots and places of grain collection will be declared *enemies of the people* and will be subject to imprisonment for a term of not less than ten years, confiscation of all their property, and expulsion for ever from the community.'

Although it was in Petrograd, Moscow and other great cities of central Russia that the food shortage was most sharply felt, its impact on wider areas can be judged from a message from Stalin to Lenin, sent on 7 June 1918:

'Arrived in Tsaritsyn [renamed Stalingrad in 1928 and Volgograd in 1961] on the 6th. Despite the muddle in all spheres of economic life, order can be established. In Tsaritsyn, Astrakhan, and Saratov the grain monopoly and fixed prices had been suspended by the local Soviets; there is a bacchanalia of profiteering. I have managed to intro-duce rationing and fixed prices in Tsaritsyn. The same must be done in Astrakhan and Saratov, or else all the grain will leak out through these profiteering channels.'

Stalin followed up his urgent message shortly afterwards by saying that the situation he had described could be explained in that the former frontline soldier who in October 1917 had fought for Soviet power had now turned against it. He heartily detested the grain monopoly, the fixed prices, the requisitions, and the measures against the bag trading, it was added.

As Lenin was forced to admit, much as he disliked doing so, the peasants were the same as most other people in wanting things both ways, wishing to retain the freedom of choice of a free economy but unhappy with the shortages that it involved and equally unhappy about the restrictions that alone would ensure a fairer distribution of what was available. There was no quick solution to the intractable problem but in November the Committees of the Village Poor were abolished and their duties merged with those of the local soviets. The Food Detachments remained. They had numbered only 3,000 on 15 June 1918, but by the end of August had swollen to 17,000, and by early 1919 to 30,000. This meant an increased State control which, it was hoped, would even out the worst of the inequalities now bringing starvation to many parts of the country. But the success of the moves to deal with the food shortage is debatable. Indeed, it could hardly have been otherwise, since there was obviously no quick way of increasing the amount of grain available. Hoarding there no doubt was, but it was only one factor in creating the threat of starvation, which varied in intensity from area to area and from month to month in so many areas. Although there was genuine famine in certain districts in the spring of 1918, the position improved a little from the autumn of 1918 until the spring of 1920. From then onwards the crisis deepened again and by the spring of 1921 had become disastrous.

However the blame was divided between natural disasters

and the cupidity of man, the famine was aggravated by the steadily deteriorating system of rail distribution, and on 1 February 1920 Lenin informed Trotsky that the rail situation was quite catastrophic; grain supplies no longer got through and emergency measures were now required. For two months, he went on, the individual bread ration should be reduced for those not engaged on transport work and increased for those who were. Even if thousands more perish, the country will be saved, he added. Military law should be introduced on either side of railway lines so that the necessary labour could be conscripted, while senior party workers should be conscripted as necessary.

At times Lenin revealed an uncustomary trace of panic when reporting on the food situation, as when he wrote to Antonov-Ovseyenko and Ordzhonikidze at Kharkov: 'For God's sake, take the *most* energetic and *revolutionary* measures to send *grain, grain,* and *more grain!!!* Otherwise Petrograd may perish. Special trains and detachments. Grain collection and delivery. Have the trains convoyed. Report daily. For God's sake!'

Even before the food crisis had reached its climax, Lenin was advocating the most drastic measures. Thus, as early as January 1918 he was writing: 'The workers and soldiers of Petrograd must realize that no one will help them except themselves . . . Unless the masses are roused to spontaneous action, we won't get anywhere . . . Until we apply terror to speculators-shooting on the spot – we won't get anywhere.' On 22 August 1918 he supplemented the injunction with specific suggestions. 'For the time being,' he wrote to one official, 'I advise appointing your own chiefs and shooting conspirators and waverers without asking anybody and without allowing any idiotic red tape.' In the same month he proposed a decree for dealing with the food problem which he suggested should run '. . . 25–30 *hostages* from among the *rich* in each grain-producing *volost,* answering with their *lives* for the collection and delivery of *all* surpluses'.

Coping with the food shortage would have been difficult enough without the activities of the Left Socialist Revolutionaries, who from the beginning of March 1918 had concentrated their aims on wrecking the treaty of Brest-Litovsk and had no compunction about the measures they used. One method was the assassination of suitable Bolsheviks, and on 20 June a Socialist Revolutionary shot and killed Volodarsky, a member of the Presidium of the Petrograd Soviet. Local workers were anxious to take revenge but the Petrograd Central Committee restrained them, much to Lenin's annoyance. 'This is in-ad-miss-ible,' he wrote to Zinoviev on 26 June. 'The terrorists will take us for milksops. The time is ultra-martial. It is necessary to encourage the energy and mass-character of the terror against counter-revolutionaries, and especially so in Petrograd, whose example is *decisive.*'

The trouble with the Left Socialist Revolutionaries came to a head early in July after a warning had been given at the meeting of its Central Committee on 24 June. The minutes of the meeting ran:

'Having examined the present political situation of the Republic [the Central Committee] resolves that in the interests of the Russian as well as of the international Revolution, an immediate end must be put to the so-called "breathing space" created by the Treaty of Brest-Litovsk.

'The Central Committee believes it to be both practical and possible to organize a series of terrorist acts against the leading representatives of German imperialism. In view of the fact that this, contrary to the wishes of the party, may involve a collision with the Bolsheviks, the Central Committee makes the following declaration:

' "We regard our policy as an attack on the present policy of the Soviet Government, not as an attack on the Bolsheviks themselves. As it is possible that the Bolsheviks may take aggressive counteraction against our party, we are determined, if necessary, to defend the position we have taken up with force of arms. In order to prevent the party from being exploited by counter-revolutionary elements it is resolved that our new policy be stated clearly and openly, so that an international social revolutionary policy may subsequently be inaugurated in Soviet Russia." '

This was the most direct challenge from the Left that Lenin or his policies had faced and there was much speculation as to how he would answer it when the Fifth All-Russian Congress of Soviets opened in Moscow's Bolshoi Theatre on 5 July. The Bolsheviks, mainly soldiers in khaki, sat on the right, facing the stage; to the left were the Left Socialist Revolutionaries, mainly peasants in loose shirts and numbering about 350 of the 900-odd delegates. On the stage – where Pavlova and Karsavina had danced, and Chaliapin had sung – there sat some 150 members of the Central Executive Committee. Below, in the front row, sat the members of the Presidium with Sverdlov, its President, in the centre.

From the start it was clear that the Government and particularly Lenin would have to face bitter criticism.

In the Ukraine, Aleksandrov, a representative of the Soviet there, exclaimed 'the bourgeoisie and Skoropadsky are supported by the German imperialists. I declare to you, in the name of the peasants and workers, that the whole of the Ukraine is in revolt

536

against the Austrian and German yoke.' Then, turning to the Bolshevik benches, he went on: 'You signed the Treaty of Brest-Litovsk at the expense of the freedom of the Ukraine. I call upon you now to help us in our battle. We are convinced that you will do so without waiting for Mirbach's consent.'

Maria Spiridonova, the veteran revolutionary, kept up the attack, turning towards Lenin to say:

'I accuse you of betraying the peasants, of making use of them for your own ends . . . Our other differences are only temporary . . . When the peasants, the Bolshevik peasants, the Left Social Revolutionary peasants and the non-party peasants, are alike humiliated, oppressed and crushed – crushed as peasants – in my hand you will still find the same pistol, the same bomb, which once forced me to defend . . .'

Here her words were drowned in cheers which only died away as Trotsky rose to defend the Government's record. He was greeted with cries of, 'Kerensky!'

Lockhart has given a graphic account of how Trotsky and Lenin were treated by the audience.

'Trotsky pushes himself forward and tries to speak. He is howled down, and his face blenches with impotent rage. In vain Sverdloff rings his bell and threatens to clear the theatre. Nothing seems more certain than that he will have to carry out his threat. Then Lenin walks slowly to the front of the stage. On the way he pats Sverdloff on the shoulder and tells him to put his bell away. Holding the lapels of his coat, he faces the audience – smiling, supremely self-confident. He is met with jeers and cat-calls. He laughs

537

good-humouredly. Then he holds up his hand, and with a last rumble the tumult dies. With cold logic he replies point by point to the criticisms of the Left Social-Revolutionaries. He refers with gentle sarcasm to their illogical and frequently equivocal attitude. His remarks produce another storm of interruption. Again Sverdloff becomes excited and grasps his bell. Again Lenin raises his hand. His self-confidence is almost irritating. Then, swaying slightly forward as he accentuates his points, but with strangely little gesticulation, he proceeds as calmly as though he were addressing a Sunday-School meeting . . . Gradually the sheer personality of the man and the overwhelming superiority of his dialectics conquer his audience, who listen spell-bound until the speech ends in a wild outburst of cheering, which, although many of the Left Social-Revolutionaries must know of the preparations for the morrow, is not confined to the Bolsheviks.'

The omens of serious trouble to come were, apparently, ignored and there were no special guards on the German embassy when, on the afternoon of the following day, 6 July, two Russians asked to see Count Mirbach. They said that they had come on behalf of Dzerzhinsky, head of the Cheka, produced Cheka passes and were shown into the Ambassador's ground-floor room. Before the passes could be inspected one of the visitors had drawn a revolver and shot Mirbach, finishing off the murder by hurling a hand grenade. Both assailants then escaped by jumping out of the window.

Lenin feared that the Germans might march into Russia in retaliation and was anxious to influence the character of the German report to Berlin. He was driven to the embassy with

Sverdlov, and there was argument about what word should be used to express their feelings. Lenin preferred *Mitleid* (sympathy) but on Sverdlov's advice used instead *Beileid* (condolence).

The threat of German intervention came to nothing but Lenin was faced with the demand for a battalion of uniformed German troops to be allowed into Moscow as embassy guards, a demand he turned down on the grounds that it would be the start of an occupation by alien forces. The Germans did not press the issue.

The murder of Count Mirbach had been planned and carried out by the Left Socialist Revolutionaries in the hope that the Germans would take retaliatory action which would lead to a renewal of hostilities between Russia and Germany. But this was only part of an ambitious plot, the next part of which was now set in motion.

In the evening, Left Socialist Revolutionaries arrested a number of Bolsheviks on the Moscow streets. A group of about forty seized the main Moscow post office and sent two messages to all soviets. One reported the killing of Count Mirbach; the other banned the sending of communications by Lenin, Trotsky and Sverdlov, and referred to the Left Socialist Revolutionaries as 'the Party now in power'. This was not so. There had been plans to kidnap Lenin and Trotsky, but these had gone astray while the Bolshoi Theatre, where Left Socialist Revolutionaries were now meeting, was surrounded by Government troops.

There are contradictory accounts of how great the threat to Lenin's Government really was. Vatzetis, a former tsarist officer, now Commander of the Bolsheviks' Lettish troops in the city, and later a Commander-in-Chief of the Red Army, has written: 'Towards midnight I was summoned by Lenin to the Kremlin. The first question he asked me was: "Comrade, can we hold out till morning?" I asked for permission to make a tour of inspection of the city. I returned about two hours later, and told Lenin: "We shall be in control of Moscow by about midday." '

It seems unlikely that the situation was as bad as Lenin obviously feared, although soon after midnight on 6 July he sent the following message to the Moscow Soviet with orders that it be passed on to all Regional Village and District Soviet Departments of the Moscow Province:

'Scattered bands of Left Social[ist] Revolutionaries, who have risen against Soviet power, are at large in the neighbourhood. Leaders of these adventurers are running away. Adopt all measures to catch and detain those who have dared to rise against Soviet power. Hold up all motor cars. Keep all the level crossings shut on the highroads. Concentrate near to these level crossings armed squadrons of local workers and peasants. Information to hand that one armoured car belonging to rebels has escaped out of the town. Adopt all measures to capture it.'

The situation was brought under control and at 1 a.m. Lenin was able to telegraph to Stalin:

'We are liquidating [the rising] mercilessly this very night and we shall tell the people the whole truth: we are a hair's breadth from war. We have hundreds of Left S.R's as hostages. Everywhere it is essential to crush mercilessly these pitiful and hysterical adventurers who have become tools in the hands of the counter-revolutionaries. All who are against war will be for us.'

During the confused skirmishing Dzerzhinsky was held for a

short while by Left Socialist Revolutionary supporters. After his release, and shortly before the shooting of thirteen of the 400 Left Socialist Revolutionaries who were captured, he gave a revealing Press conference:

> 'We exist on a basis of organized terror, which is an absolutely essential element in revolution, [he said]. We counter the enemies of the Soviet Government with terror and extirpate the criminals on the spot . . . The Cheka is not a court of justice. It is a defender of the Revolution, just like the Red Army. And just as the Red Army in the civil war cannot stop to see whether it is wronging individuals, and is obliged to pursue a single aim, i.e. the victory of the Revolution over the bourgeoisie – in the same way the Cheka is obliged to defend the Revolution and crush the enemy, even if its sword sometimes chances to strike the heads of innocent people.'

The Left Socialist Revolutionaries were now systematically exterminated as a force, although some members successfully went underground, including the man who murdered General Eishorn, the Commander of the German forces in the Ukraine. As for Blyumkin, the more important of the two men who together killed Count Mirbach, he not only evaded capture but later rose to an important level in the Bolshevik hierarchy. This, together with other facts that ultimately came to light, have suggested to suspicious minds that Mirbach's murder may not have been as simple as it appeared at the time and that the Bolsheviks may, despite Lenin's immediate and apparently genuine alarm, have connived at what happened. George Katkov, an astute student of Russian affairs, has pointed out in

'The Assassination of Count Mirbach' that by the summer of 1918 the German legation in Moscow was urging the German Government to switch its support from the Bolsheviks to the moderate monarchists now lurking in the background of the developing civil war. There is no doubt that the Left Socialist Revolutionaries were calling for Mirbach's blood, and it is undisputed that they plotted his murder. Nevertheless, Katkov points out that Krasin, discussing the situation later, stated – to G. A. Solomon who reported the conversation in *Sredi Krasnykh Vozhdey*, (Paris 1930) – 'Although I know Lenin well yet I have never been able to suspect in him such profound and cruel cynicism. Talking to me of the projected solving of the situation he used to tell me with a crooked smile note, with a crooked smile, "We are going to make an internal loan among the Left S.R. comrades and thus we shall preserve our innocence and get all the benefit." ' This could mean letting Blyumkin and Spiridonova organize the murder so that the Left Socialist Revolutionaries would take the blame while the Bolsheviks reaped the benefit.

Though the revolt in Moscow by Left Socialist Revolutionaries failed, it was symptomatic of a general atmosphere of unease that had spread not only through the capital but also through the provinces. The war at least had been brought to an end but the great food shortage continued; the unrest that was soon to fuel the civil war continued to grow and it would have done so even without the anti-revolutionary agitation on which the Government naturally blamed most of the trouble. And on the day that Mirbach was killed, the town of Yaroslavl on the Upper Volga was seized by rebels under the command of B. N. Savinkov, a prominent Left Socialist Revolutionary, and retaken by Bolshevik forces only after two weeks.

Lenin was well aware of the tensions just below the surface

and throughout August he was constantly writing of the looming dangers and lecturing to workers in the hope of lessening them. From G. F. Fyodorov, chairman of the Nizhni Novgorod Soviet, he demanded action against what he believed to be a coming White Guard insurrection, asking for 'Mass searches, Execution for concealing arms. Mass deportation of Mensheviks and unreliables.' He still believed in the certainty of world revolution but was less sure than he had been of when it would come. At the start of August he spoke to five meetings of workers and Red Guards in a single day on 'The Soviet Republic is in Danger'. By the end of that month, and since the beginning of June, he had spoken at more than forty meetings of Sovnarkom on aspects of social life in Russia.

Lenin must have known even before the murder of Mirbach that he was exposed to a danger from which total protection was impossible. The event many must have feared took place on 30 August; the day began ominously enough with the murder of Moise Uritzky, head of the Petrograd Cheka, by a young army officer who shot him down as he was going to his office. Later in the day, Lenin made three speeches in Moscow, the last to workers in the Michelson factory. As he was walking from the building to his car he was approached by two women who complained about the taking of food from train passengers by Food Detachments. As Lenin was telling them that abuses would be remedied, one of the women, Fanny Kaplan, drew a revolver and shot him at point-blank range. One bullet entered his neck close to the main artery, another penetrated the lung above the heart.

Lenin tried to refuse help as he got into the car, driven by his chauffeur, Stepan Gil, which drew up beside him and moved off towards the Kremlin. 'About midway . . .' Gil subsequendy wrote, Lenin 'sank back against the seat but did not moan or make any other sound. His face was growing whiter. The comrade beside him kept him upright. Approaching the Troitsky Gate I did not stop, merely shouting to the sentries: "Lenin!" '

At that date the Kremlin had no hospital, first-aid station or even a chemist, but Vera Mikhailovna Velichkina, Bonch-Bruyevich's wife, who was medically qualified, came quickly and gave Lenin an injection of morphia before the arrival of the hastily summoned doctors. One of the next to arrive was Krupskaya. 'You've come, you must be tired. Go and lie down,' she was told by her husband. 'The words were irrelevant, but his eyes said something quite different: "This is the end". I went out of the room so as not to upset him.'

Trotsky hurried to Moscow and, speaking to the All-Union Central Executive Committee on 2 September, described Lenin's struggle to survive as a new front in the civil war. Four days later, as it appeared that the chances of recovery were better than first thought, Zinoviev made a long eulogistic statement about their wounded leader of which 200,000 copies were printed.

Zinoviev's address was the first in a flood of tributes unleashed by the attack on Lenin. The day after the shooting Emelian Iaroslavsky, who a decade later was to head the Institute of Party History, began a quickly completed biography: *The Great Leader of the Workers' Revolution;* the Peasant Department of the Central Executive Committee issued 100,000 copies of a pamphlet, 'The Leader of the Rural Poor, V. I. Ulianov-Lenin'. And many poems in praise of his work were published during the next few weeks.

Although it was soon evident that Lenin would recover, the rumour spread that he had died and that his body had been removed from the Kremlin at night. To counter the story Bonch-Bruyevich arranged for him to be photographed while walking in the Kremlin courtyard. It was planned to be done in secret but Lenin spotted the photographers, and objected when 'Vladimir Ilich's Kremlin Stroll' was publicly shown. This was in line with the attempts he made to stop the eulogies that continued throughout the autumn. While Lenin knew the value of publicity, and would use it as necessary for the sake of the cause, he strongly disapproved of anything that smacked of what later became known as the personality cult. His reaction to such attitudes was brought out strongly in the summer of 1920 after one of Gorky's journals had published an extravagant series on Lenin.

'The Politburo of the C.C. [ran a draft resolution which Lenin himself wrote and sent to the organization] considers the publication in no. 12 of "Kommunisticheskii internat-sional" of Gorky's *articles* extremely inappropriate, especially the editorial, since there is not only *nothing* communist about these articles, but a great deal that is *anti* – communist in them. In the future *such* articles must on no account be published in "Kommunisticheskii internatsional." '

The resolution was accepted by the Politburo on 31 July 1920.

Lenin's efforts to damp down personal publicity were only partly successful and Nina Tumarkin has pointed out in her history of the Lenin cult in Soviet Russia, *Lenin Lives!*, that the shooting had set the cult on its course although no one at the time would have predicted its future development. It did, she has added, bring forth a new rhetorical convention for expressing solidarity with Bolshevik policies: extravagant praise of Lenin which was to take many forms.

'Some of the imagery was religious, some was folkloric, and some came from the language of war. All of it was emotional and intense. Its range reflected both the social and cultural heterogeneity of its users and the richness of revolutionary rhetoric in this early, formative period of Soviet culture. More than a decade would pass before the establishment of a standard political rhetoric. The cult of Lenin played a big role in its formation by providing an official object of Communist enthusiasm whose exalted status ultimately gave the highest authorities in the party the full power to determine the language fit to describe him.'

Popular reaction was described at the time by Leonid Krasin who wrote to his wife on 7 September, saying:

'As it happens, the attempt to kill Lenin has made him much more popular than he was. One hears a great many people who are far from having any sympathy with the Bolsheviks, saying that it would have been an absolute disaster if Lenin had succumbed to his wounds, as it was thought at first he would. *And they are quite right,* for in the midst of all this chaos and confusion he is the backbone of the new body politic, the main support on which everything rests.'

Fanny Kaplan's assassination attempt had long-term repercussions – quite apart from its effects on Lenin himself, which have never been entirely disentangled from the deterioration in his health which brought about his death almost four and a half years later. She was taken to the Lubyanka Prison and there stated: 'I shot Lenin today of my own accord. I will not say from whom I obtained the revolver. I have long had the intention of killing Lenin. In my eyes he has betrayed the Revolution. I was for the Constituent Assembly and I still am.'

For Lenin, it had been a narrow escape, but it was not 'almost over' as Krupskaya had feared. He gave up chairing Sovnarkom meetings for a week or two and Rykov and Sverdlov alternated in his place. Because of the injury to his lung, smoking was forbidden at the table when he resumed the chairmanship, and a 'No Smoking' notice was hung in his office. There had been some fear that after his recovery Lenin might find that one arm was shorter than the other. He commented that there was really no need for a man to have both arms exactly the same length, but for a while carried out exercises that involved moving a weight on a pulley.

Fanny Kaplan was sentenced to death within hours of the attack and was shot on 3 September, a brief notice of her execution appearing in *Izvestia* on 4 September. Despite this there were rumours not only that Lenin had pleaded for her life but that she had not, in fact, been executed. The stories continued for years and it was only in 1958 that they were effectively refuted in the memoirs of the officer who apparently shot her:

'All kinds of fables and nonsense tales are in circulation; that Kaplan allegedly remained alive, that Lenin allegedly cancelled the verdict at the last moment [wrote Pavel D. Malkov, former commandant of the Kremlin, who says that he shot her]. There are even "eye-witnesses" who "met" Kaplan either in the Butirki prison, or in Solovkii or in Vorkuta, and I don't know where else. These fairy tales were born of a petty bourgeois urge to represent Lenin as a kindly fellow who graciously forgave enemies their evil deeds. No . . . No-body annulled Kaplan's death sentence.'

Lenin's recovery was more rapid than his doctors had any right to expect. Within little more than a week he was able to report to Trotsky that he was progressing excellently and on 16 September he was allowed to resume work; roughly a week later he moved to a private house at Gorki, and after about three weeks' recuperation there – some of it spent reading Dickens and George Eliot – returned to the Kremlin. The last bulletin on his condition was issued on 18 September. On it, Lenin wrote: 'In view of this bulletin and my fitness I make a personal and very earnest request not to bother the doctors with telephone calls and questions,' and then asked that the report with his comment should be published.

The Gorki house, thirty miles from Moscow, where from now onwards Lenin spent an increasing amount of his time, was a comfortably furnished home standing in its own park, and surrounded by countryside that he described as being like Switzerland in miniature. It had once been the home of Savva Morozov, head of a big textile firm, one of the richest magnates in Russia, and the man whose legacies had been disputed by the Communists before the war. Morozov had shot himself in the house and it had later been occupied by various senior officials. Until 1918 there had been no special guard on it. All was different now, and on Lenin's arrival after the shooting he was welcomed with a large bouquet of flowers and a speech of welcome from the newly appointed guards housed on the ground floor. 'Both the guards and Ilyich felt exquisitely embarrassed,' Krupskaya wrote. 'The surroundings, too, were new and strange to us. We had been accustomed to living in humble dwellings . . . We chose the smallest room to live in . . .'

Lenin's personal reaction to the attempt on his life was to be revealed by Angelica Balabanov. He 'did not care to enlarge upon the episode', she wrote. 'I had the impression that he had been particularly affected by the execution [of Fanny Kaplan] because of its relation to himself; that the decision would have been easier had the victim of her bullet been one of the other Soviet Commissars.' He appears to have been philosophic according to Gorky, one of the few to visit him. 'I called on him, when he was still unable to use his arm freely, and could hardly move his perforated neck,' Gorky said. 'In answer to my words of indignation, he spoke unwillingly, as of something of which he was tired and bored: "It's [only] a scuffle. What are you going to do about it? Everybody acts in the only way he knows how." '

Another visitor to the injured Lenin was Trotsky who reported on the situation along the various fronts on which the civil war was being fought out. 'He listened eagerly to my stories about the front', Trotsky wrote, 'and kept sighing with satisfaction, almost blissfully.'

Lenin kept up his spirits after the attack. So did Krupskaya although she too, according to Angelica Balabanov, was apparently upset by the execution of Fanny Kaplan. 'I could see', Balabanov later wrote, 'that [Krupskaya] was deeply affected by the thought of revolutionaries condemned to death by a revolutionary power.'

Lenin had no such feelings, and, after Balabanov had discussed with him the execution of a group of Mensheviks accused of counter-revolutionary propaganda, said: 'Don't you understand that if we do not shoot these few leaders we may be placed in a position where we would need to shoot ten thousand workers?' Lenin's tone, Balabanov comments, 'was neither cruel nor indifferent; it was an expression of tragic necessity which impressed me deeply at the time'.

While the Left Socialist Revolutionaries had been planning

their attempt to seize power and Fanny Kaplan preparing to kill Lenin, another anti-Soviet plot was being hatched by Allied agents. The Englishman Sidney Reilly and a French agent, M. de Vertemont, were involved; so, it seems, was Lockhart, although his involvement has often been exaggerated and he may have done little more than pass on money from French sources for purposes of which he knew little. The key event of the plot was apparently the kidnapping of Lenin and Trotsky and their transport to Murmansk, by now in the hands of Allied interventionist forces, but the contradictory evidence – from those who are now dead – has left a series of unresolved questions rather than hard facts. All that is certain is that neither Lenin nor Trotsky were kidnapped and Allied activities were concentrated on military intervention in the civil war.

The two attacks on 30 August – on Lenin and on Moise Uritzky – were followed by a dramatic increase in the activities of the Cheka, which even during the preceding months had steadily been transforming isolated executions into a widespread and organized campaign soon rightly known as the Red Terror.

The ground had thus been well prepared, and as early as 4 August *Pravda* had enjoined its readers:

'Workers and poor, take up arms, learn to shoot, prepare yourselves for a rising by the kulaks or the White Guards, take action against all who agitate against the Soviet Power, ten bullets for every man who raises a hand against it . . . The rule of Capital will never be extinguished until the last capitalist, nobleman, Christian, and officer draws his last breath.'

The intensification of terror had begun immediately after the murder of Count Mirbach, but its extension was made inevitable by the attack on Lenin. The deepening anti-Bolshevik activity was laid at the feet not only of the counter-revolutionary Russian forces gathering their strength at many points in Russia, but of the Allied countries already developing armed intervention against the Bolsheviks; on 4 September 1918 an assortment of British and French diplomats was arrested, among them Robert Bruce Lockhart, who now suffered from the ambiguous position in which the British Government had placed him. Only after some weeks in prison was he allowed to return to England, his release being secured in exchange for a permit enabling Litvinov to leave Britain for Russia, where he was quickly appointed Assistant Commissar for Foreign Affairs.

These international exchanges, important as they appeared at the time, were less significant than the unleashing of the organized Red Terror on a scale that few, even in Russia, had believed would be possible. Lenin was back in full command by early October and it is necessary to consider what part he played in what many have since described justifiably as a policy of mass murder. There can be no doubt about his knowledge and encouragement of the killings which took place by the thousand from the summer of 1918 onwards. However, it would be simplistic to view such murders without regard to the general Russian background, Lenin's personal involvement with revolutionary activities from his early years, his attitude to killing as a political weapon, and the very different groups into which the long catalogue of murders can be divided. Terror had a long ancestry in Russia, and from the mid-nineteenth century onwards both the tsarist authorities and many revolutionary groups used it in efforts to attain their ends, even though neither side found it particularly effective as a weapon.

Lenin grew up in an atmosphere of terrorism alien to the West during the first half of the twentieth century. Casual murder was certainly endemic during his early years, yet it affected only a small percentage of the population and it was not until the trial and execution of his brother in 1887 that the full implications of murder as a policy began to exercise him. But although some of the evidence is contradictory, it is beyond doubt that by the first years of the twentieth century, Lenin had come to regard murder as a usable weapon in the revolutionary's armoury.

His mind was made up by the early 1900s and he declared in 1901: 'We have never rejected terror on principle, nor can we ever do so, for that is one of those military actions which can be very useful and even indispensable in certain moments of battle.' Two points should be made: the first is that Lenin regarded terror from a purely utilitarian standpoint – would it help the cause in any particular set of circumstances? If so, it should be used without qualification or scruple. If not, then some other method should be adopted. Thus in Lenin's long record of approval for terrorism there are no slipped-out revelations from those acting on his orders which suggest that they obtained vicarious pleasure from their awful work. Secondly, Lenin was buttressed throughout his life by a moral justification which he outlined in *Krasnyi Mech (The Red Sword)*, a weekly periodical of the Political Department of the Special Corps of Ukrainian Cheka Troops.

'For us there do not, and cannot, exist the old systems of morality and "humanity" invented by the bourgeoisie for the purpose of oppressing and exploiting the "lower classes" [he wrote]. Our morality is new, our humanity is absolute, for it rests on the bright ideal of destroying all oppression and coercion.

'To us, all is permitted, for we are the first in the world to raise the sword not in the name of enslaving and oppressing anyone, but in the name of freeing all from bondage . . . Blood? Let there be blood, if it alone can turn the grey-white-and-black banner of the old piratical world to a scarlet hue, for only the complete and final death of that world will save us from the return of the old jackals.'

Creation of the Cheka had been a warning of such things to come. Now, from the summer of 1918, they came. Terror quickly developed into the norm and, when the tenth anniversary of the Cheka's foundation was being celebrated, it could be claimed 'Without the Vecheka and the O.G.P.U., the realization and consolidation of the Dictatorship of the Proletariat would not have been possible.' Long before this, the organization created to counter anti-revolutionary activity had so expanded that during the civil war Lenin could pass to Trotsky's deputy Sklyansky at a meeting of the Revolutionary War Council (in August 1920) a handwritten note which read: 'A beautiful plan. Finish it off *together with* Dzerzhinsky. Under the guise of 'Greens' [bands of brigands and army deserters] (and we will pin it on them later) we shall go forward for 10–20 verst and hang the kulaks, priests and landowners. Bounty: 100,000 roubles for each man hanged.'

Although terror as a Government weapon was introduced in a series of stages extending its use over ever-wider areas by small single steps, Lenin did not doubt the extent to which it was altering the fabric which served as a background to society. This has been made clear by Steinberg, Commissar of Justice until he left the post, who had tried to exercise at least some restraint on what was being done. After failing to dissuade Lenin from carrying out one particular measure, apparently during the spring of 1918, he exclaimed in exasperation: 'Then why do we bother with a Commissariat of Justice? Let's call it frankly the *Commissariat for Social Extermination,* and be done with it,' At this, Steinberg has written, 'Lenin's face suddenly brightened and he replied: 'Well put . . . that's exactly what it should be . . . but we can't say that." '

Thus by September 1918, as Lenin was fighting for his life after Fanny Kaplan's attempt to kill him, there was already in Bolshevik Russia a substantial background of government by terror, much of it approved by Lenin and the rest of it tolerated in principle. Those murders which had followed the first ten months of Bolshevik rule were linked with the battery and barricade, the lawlessness and random killings, which had increasingly become a part of Russian life since the first weeks of 1917. At a session of the Central Executive Committee on 14 December 1917 Trotsky had warned that 'in not more than a month's time terror will assume very violent forms, after the example of the great French Revolution'. During 1918, as the Cheka improved its organization, terror became even less random, its implementation carried out on more of a plan.

Lenin and Trotsky had very different attitudes to such matters. Trotsky, wrote Liberman,

'took very lightly decisions to execute this man or that. To Lenin there was, in such terrible decisions, something abstract and necessary – a necessary evil, essential to all revolutions. Trotsky regarded the same death sentences differently. To him each sentence was a revolutionary act, to be viewed even at the time of its signing and execution as part of a historical process.'

The early killings, though, were hardly comparable to the overwhelming flood of organized terror unleashed after the attempt on Lenin's life. Warning was given in a proclamation issued five days later by Grigory I. Petrovsky, the Commissar for Internal Affairs.

'The murder of Volodarsky [it said], the murder of Uritzky, the attempted murder and wounding of the President of the People's Commissars, V. I. Lenin, the mass shooting of tens of thousands of our comrades in Finland, Ukrainia and finally in the Don and in Czechoslovakia, the continually exposed plots in the rear of our armies, the open participation of Right Socialist Revolutionaries and other counter-revolutionary scoundrels in these plots and at the same time the extraordinarily negligible numbers of serious repressions and mass shootings of White Guards and bourgeoisie by the Soviets show that, notwithstanding continual talk about mass terror against socialist revolutionaries, White Guards and bourgeoisie, this terror really does not exist.

'There must be a decisive end of this situation. There must be an end of laxity and weakness. All Right Socialist Revolutionaries known to local soviets must be immediately arrested. A considerable number of hostages must be taken from among the bourgeoisie and the officers. Mass shooting must be applied upon the least attempts at resistance or the least movement in the midst of the White Guards. Local

Provincial Executive Committees must show special initiative in this respect.

'Administrative departments through the militia and the Extraordinary Commissions must take all measures to detect and arrest all who hide under foreign names and surnames, with unconditional shooting of all who are involved in White Guard activity.

'All the above mentioned measures must be carried out immediately.

'The Commissariat for Internal Affairs must be immediately informed of any indecisive activities of local soviets in this direction.

'Last of all, the rear of our armies must be finally cleared of all White Guardism, and all scoundrelly conspirators against the power of the working class and the poorest peasants. Not the least wavering, not the least indecision in the application of mass terror.'

On 5 September 1918, the Council of People's Commissars issued their own decree 'Concerning the Red Terror' which authorized the Cheka to take to concentration camps and there execute all those 'involved in White Guard organizations, conspiracies and risings'. Later it was authorized to shoot anyone guilty of 'grave dereliction of duty'.

These moves legitimized in detail what had hitherto been legitimized only in more general terms, and were a decisive encouragement to the Red Terror without need of qualification. The extent of the Terror cannot be in dispute since at the time the Bolshevik-controlled press made no attempt to hide what the words meant; only later, as apologists for the excesses of the Revolution took the field, was the enormity of the Red reaction played down. Prominent among those who have since set the record straight is James Bunyan whose *Intervention, Civil War, and Communism in Russia, April-December 1918,* written under the auspices of the Walter Hines Page School of International Relations (named after the American ambassador to Britain during the First World War), uses the published Russian reports to provide a graphic account of events in the late summer and autumn of 1918.

On 3 September, *Izvestia* published an announcement made two days earlier in Nizhni-Novgorod, saying: 'The conditions of the life-and-death struggle which is now taking place require that we discard all sentiment and carry on the dictatorship of the proletariat with a firm hand. In view of this fact the Gubernia Cheka of Nizhny-Novgorod has shot forty-one persons of the enemy camp.' A list of those shot was added, together with the warning 'To every murder of a communist or attempt at such murder we shall reply by shooting bourgeois hostages.'

On the same day Petrovsky telegraphed to all local soviets:

'There must be an immediate end to laxity and sentimentality. All Right Social Revolutionaries, known to the local Soviets, are to be arrested at once. Considerable numbers of hostages are to be taken from among the bourgeoisie and the officer caste. The slightest attempt at resistance, or the slightest move in circles of the White Guardists, must at once be stifled by summary mass shooting. Provincial Executive Committees must exhibit special initiative in the matter . . . No hesitations, no doubts in the application of mass terror.'

In Petrograd, it was officially announced that the local Cheka had shot more than 500 hostages while a few days later a further announcement said that twenty-nine counter-revolutionaries had been executed, including two former ministers and an archbishop. The executions, it was added, 'came about as a result of the Red Terror proclaimed after the attempt on . . . the life of Lenin and the murder of Uritsky'.

The story was much the same in the provinces, the range of those executed being shown by the report of one day's work of the Cheka's Western Region, quoted by Bunyan. Some thirty men were ordered to be shot for offences varying from complicity in anti-Soviet plots to being 'notorious for cruelty to peasants'.

By this time there had been more than one attempt to curtail the power of the Cheka. However, a resolution carried by the Conference of Commissars of Justice in July 1918 had no effect. The following month a resolution opposing the independence of the Cheka was adopted by the Congress of Representatives of Gubernia Soviets but the Cheka, which operated directly under Sovnarkom, successfully maintained its independence.

Following the efflorescence of the Cheka's activities there were protests both in Russia and abroad which came not only from Patriarch Tikhon, the Patriarch of Moscow and of all Russia, as might have been expected, but also from the Ukraine where a resolution was passed by the All-Ukrainian Trade-Union Council saying:

'The news of the ever increasing brutal and frenzied terror in Russia is arousing profound anxiety in the ranks of the organized proletariat of the Ukraine. This anxiety is the more deeply felt because the cruel and inhuman deeds are being perpetrated in the name of the Russian proletariat, to which the Ukrainian proletariat is bound by the most intimate and solid ties.'

In language as blunt as that habitually used by Lenin, the resolution deplored the murder of thousands in reprisal for the murder of one man and underlined the damage that the Terror was doing to democracy and the working class. Meanwhile, from the USA the Secretary of State sent all American Diplomatic Missions a circular listing reports of the Red Terror and asking for action, 'to impress upon the perpetrators of these crimes the aversion with which civilization regards their present wanton acts'.

It is true that it was not Lenin in person who had started the Terror, but as he said in a letter he sent from Zurich to Franz Koritschoner, the Austrian left-wing Social-Democrat in Vienna:

' "Killing is no murder" our old "Iskra" [no. 20] said about terrorist acts [he wrote]. We *do not at all oppose* political killing . . . but as revolutionary tactics, individual attempts are both impractical and harmful. It is only a mass movement that can be considered to be a real political struggle. Individual terrorist acts can be, and must be, helpful, only when they are directly linked with the mass movement.'

Holding such views, Lenin naturally saw the Red Terror as part of the larger struggle in which he and his Party were engaged, and when Maxim Gorky taxed him about the cruelty of revolutionary tactics, he made no attempt to dissemble.

'What do you want? [he would reply]. Is it possible to act

humanely in a struggle of such unprecedented ferocity? Where is there any place for soft-heartedness or generosity? We are being blockaded by Europe, we are deprived of the help of the European proletariat, counter-revolution is creeping like a bear on us from every side. What do you want? Are we not right? Ought we not to struggle and resist? We are not a set of fools. We know that what we want can only be achieved by ourselves. Do you think that I would be sitting here if I were convinced of the contrary?

'What is your criterion for judging which blows are necessary and which are superfluous in a fight?'

And in a speech celebrating the first anniversary of the Revolution he said,

'What astonishes me is that so few [accusing intelligentsia] are able to estimate the work of the Cheka broadly . . . The Cheka must act firmly, quickly and loyally. When I place its achievements beside its mistakes the latter sink into insignificance . . . For us the important consideration is that the Cheka has made the dictatorship of the proletariat a living reality. Regarded from this point of view its work is priceless. There is only one way to free the masses and that is to crush the exploiters. This is the task of the Cheka, and for this it deserves the gratitude of the proletariat . . .'

Lenin's apologia for the Cheka, coming as it did in November 1918, referred primarily to the Terror and the executions that had spread throughout Russia as a result of the political challenge presented to the Government by the Left Socialist Revolutionaries. But the Cheka was also used for other tasks,

560

some of them unexpected. Thus, in January 1919, Lenin sent the following orders to the Cheka in Kursk.

'Immediately arrest Kogan, a member of the Kursk Central Purchasing Board, for refusing to help 120 starving workers from Moscow and sending them away empty-handed. This to be published in the newspapers and by leaflet, so that all employees of the central purchasing boards and food organizations should know that formal and bureaucratic attitudes to work and incapacity to help starving workers will earn severe reprisals, up to and including shooting.'

Moreover by November 1918, the Terror, inaugurated and extended mainly to deal with purely political opponents, was spreading over a still expanding area through the development of the civil war. It was a war which occupied a great part of Lenin's mind until the end of 1920.

15

Civil War and Intervention

O ne of the few things on which all commentators on the
Russian civil war agree is that it took place; they also agree
that it was barbarously fought on both sides, brought even more
suffering to an already ravaged country than is customary with
most civil wars, and was kept going by a tangle of motives, political, diplomatic and military, that after more than two-thirds of a
century it is still impossible to disentangle satisfactorily. But when
exactly the civil war can be said to have started, when it ended,
what was the comparative importance of its campaigns – which
were spread across vast areas – and what were the personal
factors which governed its course, are some of the matters which
remain the subject of impassioned debate.

It can be claimed that General Kornilov's abortive rebellion
against the Provisional Government in the late summer of 1917,
made while Lenin was still waiting in the wings in Finland, was
the prologue to civil war. Lenin is reported to have said that civil
war was inevitable by 25 October 1917, a reference to his

conviction that once the Bolsheviks had seized power, efforts to overthrow them would follow. And it can be claimed with equal plausibility that Kerensky's attempt to return to Petrograd a few days after the Bolsheviks' seizure of power, and the defeat of his forces under General Krasnov on the Pulkovo Heights outside Petrograd, was the first real engagement of the civil war.

The clash on the outskirts of Pulkovo and the Bolsheviks' victory, which destroyed Kerensky's chance of returning to power, was a comparatively straightforward encounter between the revolutionary forces that had seized power under Lenin and those of the Provisional Government. This simple situation changed more than once during the following months and years. On the Bolshevik side, it is true, the Red forces remained united by the common concern of maintaining the Revolution. It was not only Lenin who was constantly borne up by a determination that neither the days of the Tsar nor those of the Provisional Government should ever return; with few and minor exceptions those who supported him continued to do so with a single-minded dedication that few military commanders enjoy for long.

With the Bolsheviks' opponents, 'the Whites', the situation was very different. During 1918 and 1919 such plainly anti-revolutionary troops as those led by Kornilov were to be augmented by a varied collection of forces. They included groups which formed behind professional soldiers who had served the Tsar and who found themselves under-employed, or not employed at all, in the chaos of post-revolutionary Europe. There were also the nationalist armies who saw the Revolution as an opportunity for breaking away from what they regarded as their subsidiary positions in the Russian Empire, and the 'coalition socialists' who fought largely for the convening of a Constituent Assembly. From early 1918 onwards, there were also the interventionist forces provided for a complex of reasons by Britain, France, Japan and the United States as well as by the Czechs whose Czech Legion had grown from a brigade of Czechoslovaks living in Russia after the start of the First World War. If this was not a complicated enough amalgam of anti-revolutionary forces, there were also those Russians supporting the Left Socialist Revolutionaries whose opposition developed from political into military. It would have been unrealistic to expect overall political direction to unite the activities of this complex anti-Bolshevik opposition and such direction was singularly lacking throughout the civil war.

The disparity in military efficiency, which sprang from the difference in central political direction between 'the Reds' and 'the Whites', was compounded by geographical contrasts. At various times the Whites controlled forces in Siberia, on Russia's eastern extremity, and also on the country's western frontiers; they had troops or supporters operating in Northern Russia, on the shores of the Arctic Ocean, as well as in the Caucasus and even further south. Thus the forces whose activities might have been co-ordinated against the new Russian Government were rarely separated by less than hundreds and often by thousands of miles. By contrast, Lenin, operating from Moscow, could be likened to a spider at the centre of its wreb while his opponents remained separate forces on the periphery of operations. Communications between Moscow and its far-flung battle fronts did not compare with those that both sides had enjoyed during the First World War. Nevertheless, railways and roads radiated from Moscow and gave Lenin and his forces an advantage over the White forces, which had to operate along exterior lines.

The state and control of land forces in Russia – on one side the Red Guards which were steadily transformed into the Red

Army, and on the other the conglomeration of 'White' armies – were not the only important elements in the civil war, and while the activities of naval forces did not loom large in the story they should not be ignored. Early in the First World War the bulk of the Baltic fleet – 170 ships in all – was brought to the safety of the fortified base of Kronstadt, largely by the heroic efforts of Rear-Admiral A. M. Stchasny, who was shot for his pains after being charged with making himself popular 'with a view to using this popularity later against the power of the Soviets'. The Black Sea fleet faced a more complex situation and was moved from Sevastopol to Novorossisk after the treaty of Brest-Litovsk to save it from the Germans and the Ukrainians. But the situation at Novorossisk was complicated even by the standards of the civil war. 'There was a Soviet Republic ashore, which anxiously asked the fleet if it would mind putting down the Red army which was in a state of mutiny,' writes David Woodward, whose beguiling account of *The Russians at Sea* gives a clear account of the situation:

> 'there were refugees from all along the Black Sea literally living on board ships in the harbour; there was the White volunteer army, though not much of it, inland and there was the fleet, which was a counter of enormous value in the hands of anyone who could get it – White, Red, Allied or German. In this way its situation resembled that of the French fleets in the Mediterranean in 1940–2.'

Lenin in Moscow was naturally anxious to keep the Red Fleet out of German hands, but there was no certainty that its crews would continue indefinitely to obey Russian orders. He therefore devised a two-pronged plan. To Vice-Admiral N. P. Sablin, the

Black Sea naval commander, he sent secret orders telling him that he might shortly receive an uncoded message ordering him to hand the fleet over to the Germans. If such a message came, he was to sink the fleet immediately. However, when the message did come, many of the men refused to scuttle their ships. But the situation was saved by the second part of Lenin's scheme which involved the sending to Novorossisk of Fedor Fedorovich Raskolnikov, the 'Krasny [Red] Admiral' who reached Novorossisk in mid-June, carried out his task of destroying what was left of the fleet, and then fought his way back to Tsaritsyn on the Volga with a detachment of Marines.

In the long account sheet of the civil war the Whites might be thought to have enjoyed a built-in advantage when it came to commanders, and certainly they could count on the services of many tsarist officers, men who had devoted their lives to the art and craft of war. There were, by contrast, few among the Bolsheviks who had much military experience beyond that of guerrilla activities, which was useful, even though something more was required in the campaigns that developed in the civil war. However, what the Bolsheviks could call on was what can with little exaggeration be called the genius of two men. One was Lenin: holding the reins of both civil and military power, he was found singularly able at co-ordinating long-term and far-flung operations in a way that was beyond the scope of most White commanders. The second was Trotsky whose dash and personal courage inspired the Red Army wherever he appeared. On 13 March 1918 he was made chairman of the Supreme War Council, which had been set up in Petrograd the previous month with the task of creating the Red Army. He, almost alone, was responsible for building up that Army from the mishmash of units into which the Russian forces had begun to deteriorate even before the spring of 1917 and into which they had sunk even more speedily following the autumn Revolution. When Trotsky took over, the Red Army numbered 100,000 and was of decidedly variable quality; within three years it had been built up into a formidable fighting force of 5,000,000 – an achievement as decisive for the Revolution in the military field as was Lenin's in the political.

For if Trotsky helped to save the Revolution during the civil war by his military flair, Lenin did the same through his knack of ensuring that the maximum effort was made on whichever of the battle fronts would yield the best political results. All these factors, political, geographical and military, were present in varying degrees during successive stages of the operations. It would be difficult to determine the relative importance of these different factors, so closely were they interlinked, even if the reorganization of Russia's military forces, an essential consequence of the Revolution, had not taken place as the civil war developed. During the first months of 1918 two moves were afoot – largely as a result of Trotsky's efforts: the Workers'-Peasants' Red Army began to take shape through the efforts of the All-Russian Collegium for the Formation of the Red Army and at the same time the Committee for the Revolutionary Defence of Petrograd came into existence, a body from which the Supreme Military Soviet was finally organized.

As the Red Guards were gradually fused into the Red Army, Lenin became personally involved in an argument that rumbled on for years and was not properly resolved until after the civil war had ended. It concerned the use in the Bolshevik forces of ex-tsarist officers and specialists. In some cases their loyalty to their new masters could be relied on; in others it was obtained and guaranteed only by taking as hostages members of the officers' families. Lenin, who had insisted that former tsarist officers were necessary, also set up civilian managers on the battle fronts as they developed – Stalin, Ordzhonikidze and Trotsky among others. Despite the military opposition this aroused, it was generally successful and was probably unavoidable in a civil war in which military and civil problems were so inextricably mixed.

The first phase of the war saw the formation on the other side of what became known as the Volunteer Army in the Don area of southern Russia. Its leaders were Generals Kornilov, Denikin and Alekseyev, all of whom had escaped from the prison in which they had been held following the Revolution, and who took the field under General Kaledin, the leader (or *hetman)* of the local Cossacks. After some initial successes the Volunteer Army found itself in retreat before the troops sent from Moscow under the command of Antonov-Ovseyenko, who had helped in the capture of the Winter Palace in 1917 and who from December 1918 until June 1919 was the Red Commander-in-Chief in the Ukraine. Before the end of February 1918, the Volunteer Army in the Don area had collapsed. What was left of it set out on a long trek to the Kuban, which ended in the death of General Kornilov, killed by a stray shell during an unsuccessful attack on the town of Ekaterinodar. The importance of this event can be judged from the telegram which Raymond Robins sent to Ambassador Francis, on 20 April 1918: 'Death Kornilov verified, this final blow organized internal force against Soviet Government.'

The Volunteer Army, which on the face of it might have had a good chance of rallying anti-Bolshevik feeling, but never successfully did so, was certainly dogged by bad luck. But it, and other anti-Bolshevik groups, wreaked their own havoc on the country, as pointed out by Professor Mavor in The *Russian Revolution:*

'Officers and men alike seemed in general to regard everyone who was not in their force as a Bolshevik and therefore as someone who might be killed or robbed with impunity. When the Army was in retreat, the country was laid waste. Hence, from the point of view of the people, the conduct of the Volunteer Army was no better than that of the Red Army; there was little to choose between them; both were equally ruining the country.'

An early Bolshevik success against the Volunteer Army was the taking of Kiev on 26 January (8 February). At this stage the Red Army's prospects looked excellent, but the whole situation was changed by the conclusion of the treaty of Brest-Litovsk. The Germans retook Kiev on 16 March, and began an occupation of the Ukraine that continued until the defeat of the Central Powers in the autumn.

The effects of the treaty of Brest-Litovsk on the civil war were not limited to the fighting in the Ukraine. At the other extremity of the country, where, in the far north, Finland had become independent under a pro-Bolshevik regime, the Bolshevik forces were summarily crushed by Finnish White troops under General Mannerheim, aided by German units under von der Goltz.

Quite as important as these repercussions were the treaty's effects on the countries that had been allied with Russia until her withdrawal from the First World War. By the time that the Russian signatures at Brest-Litovsk finally justified Lenin's oft-repeated claim that he would end Russia's war with the Central

Powers, his Government had already affronted the Allied powers in a number of ways. The Russians had confiscated foreign property, repudiated foreign debts, and were still threatening to start revolutions in Europe by propaganda and subversion. Now they were, in Allied eyes, leaving unprotected from German attack the huge supplies of arms and equipment that the Allies had sent, during the previous few years, to Russia at an immense cost in money and labour. The effect of the treaty of Brest-Litovsk was steadily to increase pressure from the West for 'intervention' in Russia – in its starkest and simplest form, military intervention in whatever mix of men, money and supplies seemed best in support of the anti-Bolshevik forces trying to bring down the Government in Moscow.

Yet early in the complex operations of the civil war, Russia's former allies were reluctant to admit openly and officially that they were arming the enemies of the Bolshevik Government with the aim of bringing it down. Every possible alternative reason was emphasized. One of the first men to describe the situation honestly was Winston Churchill, that consistent opponent of Lenin and all he stood for.

'The fitful and fluid operations of the Russian armies found a counterpart in the policy, or want of policy, of the Allies [he later wrote]. Were they at war with Soviet Russia? Certainly not; but they shot Soviet Russians at sight. They stood as invaders on Russian soil. They armed the enemies of the Soviet Government. They blockaded its ports, and sunk its battleships. They earnestly desired and schemed its downfall. But war – shocking! Interference – shame! It was, they repeated, a matter of indifference to them how Russians settled their own internal affairs.'

570

As early as 21 November 1917, Balfour had proposed that Britain should aid General Kaledin. The idea was supported by the USA, even though there would be difficulties since Kaledin did not represent a *de facto* Government.

> 'The only practicable course [Lansing telegraphed on 13 December 1917 to Page, the US ambassador in Britain] seems to be for the British and French Governments to finance the Kaledine enterprise in so far as it is necessary, and for this Government to loan them the money to do so. In that way we would comply with the statute [since Kaledine was not a *de facto* government, the US could not legally lend them money] and at the same time strengthen a movement which seems to present the best possibility of retaining a Russian army in the field.'

Colonel House, President Wilson's adviser, was distinctly cautious, pointing out that the Allies had no definite scheme for the support of anti-Bolshevik programmes in Russia, nor the forces to back up any decisions which were taken. However, he added, if pro-Allied groups in Russia received neither encouragement nor money they would go to pieces. In the light of this attitude the British cabinet decided the following day to give Kaledin all the financial assistance he needed. Neither the British Ambassador nor General Knox welcomed the decision. 'To ask us to intrigue with Cossacks while we are here in the power of the Rebel Government', Knox stated, 'is merely to get our throats cut to no purpose.'

However great the common sense of Knox's comment, at the end of 1917 the Allies were much disturbed about the possibilities as the implications of the Revolution sank in, and as Britain and France began to wonder what Lenin's new Government would do next. In a note to Lloyd George on 23 December 1917, Lord Milner said

> 'It . . . becomes of particular importance to us, even if we cannot ultimately prevent, *to delay as long as possible,* the establishment of an authority favourable to trade with the Central Powers, *in parts of Southern Russia.*Civil War, or even the mere continuance of chaos and disorder, would be an advantage to us from this point of view.'

Any chance of this in the Ukraine was temporarily removed by the defeat of the Volunteer Army and Kaledin's subsequent suicide. However, the signing of the treaty of Brest-Litovsk in March 1918 revived Allied fears of German capabilities and thereby encouraged Allied military intervention on two fronts and in two different ways which became almost inextricably linked. The German forces were soon consolidating their hold in Finland, and Allied forces were landed at Murmansk and then Archangel on the plausible excuse of providing protection for the arms dumps there. While this was being done the formidable and steadily-growing Czech Legion gathered strength in eastern Russia. Instead of being evacuated, as initially proposed, from Vladivostock to reinforce the Western Front in France, or drafted to support the Allied troops preparing for a German attack on the north Russian arms dumps – an attack that never came – the Czech force evolved from a pro-Allied unit whose task it was to beat off the Germans into an anti-Bolshevik force which played a significant part in the civil war.

Neither Murmansk nor Archangel were centres from which

anti-Bolshevik forces could be easily launched into the heart of Russia. But Murmansk had been built as a Russian supply port in 1916 before becoming the northern end of the British-Russian submarine cable, and if Allied fears that the Germans might try to develop it into a submarine base were somewhat extravagant they could not be entirely ruled out. In February and March 1918, British and French naval forces including the British cruiser HMS *Glory* arrived off Murmansk. Naval landings were followed by military and in August a contingent of eight DH4 bombers, plus thirty-seven pilots and ground crew of the former Imperial Russian Air Force, came from Britain. One reason was that the Allies had discovered nearby a number of planes shipped to tsarist Russia but not used. Bolshevik suspicions of what the Allies were up to could not be easily countered and Lenin's fears were increased when after the Allied landings – which Trotsky had not regarded with undue alarm – the local Soviet declared itself independent of Moscow and set up a Murmansk Provincial Council.

With such a background it was inevitable that there should be diverse opinions, both at the time and later, as to Allied intentions in northern Russia. According to an article in *The Times* of 13 December 1918 from Rear-Admiral Kemp, commander of the Allied forces in the area, the operations, including the later arrival of a French and an American cruiser, were regularized by a definite arrangement between the senior representatives of the Allied powers and the Murmansk Provincial Council under which the Allied Governments

'agreed to assist in the defence of Russian territory against German-Finnish invasion with all the forces they could spare for the purpose, to assist to feed the population of the

Murman Province – then threatened with famine – and gave assurances that they had no annexationist aims or intention to interfere in the domestic affairs of Russia. This agreement was communicated to the Central Government at Moscow, and a reply was received from M. Trotsky, then Minister for Foreign Affairs and the head of the Soviet Government, ordering the Provincial Council to co-operate in all ways with the Allied forces for the defence of Russian territory on the lines laid down.'

Admiral Kemp no doubt wrote in good faith. But Churchill gave a more informed and more sophisticated version of the situation in *The World Crisis: The Aftermath* when he said that on 30 November 1918, the British representatives at Archangel and Vladivostock were told of the British policy towards Russia in the following terms:

'To remain in occupation at Murmansk and Archangel for the time being; to continue the Siberian Expedition; to try to persuade the Czechs to remain in Western Siberia; to occupy (with five British brigades) the Baku-Batum railway; to give General Denikin at Novorossisk all possible help in the way of military material; [and] to supply the Baltic States with military material.'

As Churchill commented: 'This was a far-reaching programme. It not only comprised existing commitments, but added to them large new enterprises in the Caucasus and in South Russia.'

Churchill's post-civil-war version of events justified many of Lenin's earlier suspicions, including those regarding north Russia which he voiced in volume 27 of *Sochineniya (Works)*:

'The British and French [he wrote] have raised claims concerning Murmansk because they have invested tens of millions on the construction of the port in order to secure their military supply line in the imperialist war against Germany. They have such a wonderful respect for neutrality that they make free use of everything that is not nailed down. And the fact that they have an armored vessel and we have nothing with which to drive it away serves as sufficient grounds for seizures. Now there is an external wrapping, a juridical expression, called into being by the international situation of the Soviet Republic, which postulates that no armed force of a warring power may enter neutral territory without being disarmed. The English landed their armed forces at Murmansk, and we had no possibility of preventing this by armed force. In consequence we find ourselves faced with demands bearing a character close to that of an ultimatum: if you cannot protect your neutrality, then we will fight on your territory.'

The Allies were unable to mount any serious offensive from either Murmansk or Archangel. During the autumn of 1919 they withdrew from both areas (from Archangel by 27 September, and from Murmansk by 12 October), thus bringing to an end a project which is generally agreed to have been useless in its effects and disastrous in its implications.

The Allied landings in northern Russia left a legacy of suspicion and ill will which, if not justified, was certainly natural. Only among the local inhabitants did the Allies perhaps reap some propaganda rewards. 'I cannot believe that the people at Murmansk or Archangel are pro-anything except their own stomachs,' wrote one correspondent to Sir Esmé Howard in Stockholm, 'and if this is the case, and we can fill those said stomachs sufficiently, the game ought to be in our hands.'

Lenin's sour comments in *Sochineniya* on the Allied activities in northern Russia were partly due to the fact that from the summer they had become linked with the activities of the Czech Legion, a more serious threat to Bolshevik authority. The development of the Legion had begun after the spring Revolution of 1917 when Professor Masaryk, President of the Czecho-Slovak National Council, had asked Russia's Provisional Government if it might form a Czecho-Slovak Army from the prisoners-of-war captured by the Russians since August 1914. The Provisional Government agreed and first a Czech Brigade, then an Army Corps, and finally a 50,000-strong Czech Legion was formed. The Allies had made the freeing of Czechs and Slovaks from Austrian rule one of their war aims and the newly formed Legion fought enthusiastically beside the Red Army in more than one campaign, including Kerensky's ill-fated offensive of July 1917.

After the autumn Revolution of 1917, an agreement was signed between the Czechs and the Bolshevik Government under which the Russians agreed to transport 50,000 Czech troops to Vladivostock and the Allies agreed to take them from Vladivostock to France, where they would strengthen the hard-pressed Allied forces on the Western Front. The Czechs had to surrender the bulk of their arms before they began the long journey across Siberia, but they were allowed to keep ten rifles and one machine-gun for every 100 troops.

Mistrust grew during the spring of 1918 until on 14 May a spark set the situation alight. A train carrying German prisoners of war passed a train-load of Czechs in the town of Cheliabinsk.

An unidentified object was thrown from a carriage carrying Germans, and a Czech was injured. Fighting broke out and the local Soviet was forced to intervene. Even so, the outcome might not have been disastrous had not the impetuous Trotsky sent a cable to the soviets on the line along which the Czechs were travelling, saying

'All Soviets are ordered, on pain of criminal charges, to immediately disarm the Czechoslovaks. Every Czechoslovak who is found armed on the railroad is to be shot on the spot. Every troop train in which even one armed Czechoslovak is found is to be entirely emptied of Czechoslovaks, who are to be detained in a prisoner-of-war camp. Local military commissars are under obligation to carry out this order immediately, and any delay is equivalent to base treason and will bring severe punishment down upon the guilty. At the same time reliable forces are to be sent into the rear of the Czechoslovak units with the assignment of teaching a good lesson to those who will not comply. Honest Czechoslovaks who surrender their weapons and submit to Soviet authority are to be treated as brothers and given all public assistance.'

According to Robert Bruce Lockhart, Trotsky's action was condemned by no less a Bolshevik than Karakhan, the Soviet Deputy Commissar for Foreign Affairs who told Lockhart 'in attacking the Czechs Trotsky had made a political mistake, though he had been fully justified by the bad faith of the French in this connection'.

Despite growing ill will, the first Czechs reached Vladivostock without further serious trouble. But in their progress they took possession of stations and towns along the strategic trans-Siberian line, being joined as they did so by many compatriots from prisoner-of-war camps so that by the end of June their forces numbered some 120,000. By midsummer, the Moscow Government was thus faced with the fact that an increasingly anti-Bolshevik force controlled much of the country's transcontinental railway, that it was being given support, covert or otherwise by the Western powers who had been Russia's allies, and that the White forces were thus being considerably helped.

The situation was made even worse for Lenin when on 29 June a mixed force disarmed the Bolsheviks in Vladivostock and suppressed the local government. This force consisted not only of Czechs and White Russians but also of a few British plus a Japanese unit, which had arrived in Siberia in April only after much dispute between Russia's British and American allies, and whose presence added further confusion to the situation.

At the beginning of 1918, the Czechs had not yet revealed the effort of which they were capable and it was felt that a Japanese force would provide a useful counter-balance in the east to any attack the Germans might make. The British representative in Tokyo, Colville Barclay, was therefore instructed 'to urge that Japan shall be asked by the Allies to occupy the Siberian Railway as their mandatory'. Balfour wrote to Colonel House on 30 January 1918:

'I hope the scheme will receive very serious consideration in spite of the many serious difficulties it presents . . . We do not wish to quarrel with the Bolsheviks. On the contrary, we look at them with a certain degree of favour so long as they refuse to make a separate peace. But their claim to be the

Government of all the Russians, either *de facto* or *de jure,* is not founded on fact'

House, as many other Americans, was reluctant to see the Japanese getting a foot in the Siberian door and it was only after much dispute – House cabling Balfour in March that he felt the proposal to have the Japanese in Siberia 'may be the greatest misfortune that has yet befallen the Allies' – that the Japanese occupied Vladivostock with other Allied troops early in April 1918.

Thus strong anti-Bolshevik forces were in control of long stretches of the vital railway from Vladivostock to Penza, only 300 miles from Moscow, and of the far eastern terminus of the line.

There were repercussions both military and political from the Czech Legion's initial advance across Siberia. Striking back westwards towards the Volga, they occupied Kazan, Simbirsk and Samara in all of which Bolsheviks and their supporters were massacred. After the capture of Samara at dawn on 8 June, a committee of four former Socialist Revolutionary members of the brief Constituent Assembly assumed power, proclaimed the dissolution of the soviet, and set up their own Assembly.

These Czech-induced successes lasted only a few months; Kazan was recaptured by the Red Army on 10 September, and Simbirsk two days later.

The recapture of Simbirsk, Lenin's birthplace, took place while he was still recovering from Fanny Kaplan's attack; in a message to the troops involved he said: 'The seizure of Simbirsk, my home town, is the most health-giving and best bandage for my wounds. I felt an unprecedented surge of courage and strength.' Trotsky was quoted as saying: 'That day was a noteworthy date in the history of the Red Army. At once we felt firm ground under our feet. The time of our first helpless efforts was over; thenceforth we were able to fight and win.'

Three separate anti-Bolshevik 'Governments' were set up on or near the line running west from Vladivostock. The first was the Assembly in Samara which for its brief life between June and September could be classed as democratic. Later in June a comparable White Government was formed at Omsk and early in July a third in Vladivostock. These moves were further developed in September when all three 'Governments' met at Ufa and formed a five-man Directorate on which there sat one Socialist Revolutionary, one Kadet, one Populist and two Non-Partisans. This 'All-Russian Government' as it termed itself, lasted only until 18 November when it was overthrown in a coup by Admiral Aleksandr V. Kolchak, a tsarist officer now leading an anti-Bolshevik force. The Czechs in the area objected and only monarchist supporters acquiesced.

Events in Siberia tended to emphasize the fissions which split the anti-Bolshevik opposition. Nevertheless, they were testimony to the fact that opposition was strong and continuing, and the story throughout other parts of Russia was much the same. Even if there was no unity among those who opposed the Moscow Government, opponents were numerous and likely to remain so; at the end of May 1918, it had been thought wise to put Moscow under martial law. Incidents of varying gravity continued throughout the summer weeks, ranging from what could fairly be called counterrevolutionary, if local, campaigns, to smaller revolts whose existence rested on the presence of a competent leader able to exploit unusually aggravating circumstances. On 17 June, a Military Committee was set up by a rebel group in

Tambov, a town retaken after two days' fighting. Yaroslavl on the upper Volga, seized by rebel forces early in July, was only retaken after two weeks' fighting. But before the end of the month there came reports of something more serious. On hearing them, Lenin told Zinoviev:

'News has just been received that Alexeyev in the Kuban area, with about sixty thousand men, is advancing against us, carrying out the plan for a combined attack by the Czechoslovaks, the British and the Alexeyev Cossacks. In view of this, and in view of the statement of the Petrograd workers, Kayurov, Chugurin and others, who have arrived here, that Petrograd could provide ten times as many if it were not for the opposition of the Petrograd section of the C.C. – in view of this I categorically and imperatively insist on the cessation of all opposition and on the dispatch from Petrograd of ten times as many workers. That is the demand of the C.C. of the Party.

'I categorically warn you that the Republic is in a dangerous situation and that the Petrograders, by holding up dispatch of workers from Petrograd to the Czech front, will make themselves responsible for the possible downfall of our whole cause.'

In the south a revitalized Volunteer Army under General Denikin captured the Black Sea port of Novorossisk on 26 August and the British Dunster force, charged with the task of safeguarding British interests in an oil-rich area, occupied Baku in the far south. New Bolshevik effort was needed and on 2 September the Party's Central Executive Committee in Moscow declared the Soviet Republic in a state of siege; this was followed in November by the creation of a Council of Workers' and Peasants' Defence. Lenin was the new Council's President and members included Trotsky, Nevsky, Bryukhanov, Krasin and Stalin. No doubt as to the new Council's authority was left by the decree which set it up and which stated that the Council was 'to have full power in matters pertaining to the mobilization of the forces and resources of the country in the interests of defense. The decisions of the Council of Defense shall be absolutely binding upon every department and institution, both central and local, and upon every citizen.'

It is impossible to tell what the result of these innovations alone might have been since the Russian situation was soon transformed by the failure of the great German offensive on the Western Front and the ending of the First World War. The most obvious repercussion on Lenin and his Government was the withdrawal of German troops from the territories they had occupied after the treaty of Brest-Litovsk, and the annulment of that treaty within a few days of the Armistice between the Central Powers and the Allies. But the German withdrawal created a vacuum which the Russians were unable to fill immediately, thus producing conditions, particularly in Poland, from which much trouble later flowed.

The Whites planned to take advantage of the situation, so far as their heterogeneous make-up allowed, by advancing on Moscow and Petrograd from the south, east and north-west. From the south, the Whites under Denikin were to thrust north into the Ukraine, the left wing capturing Kharkov and Kiev while the right, led by General Wrangel, advanced up the Volga and joined forces coming down from Estonia. Meanwhile, Kolchak was to strike west across the Volga and head for Moscow. Little came of these ambitious schemes.

Lenin hoped that the German military defeat would, as he had often prophesied, lead to a successful revolution in Germany and at first it seemed that this might happen. Even before the fighting had stopped Karl Liebknecht had been released from prison in Berlin and the German High Seas fleet, ordered to sea for what was seen as a suicide engagement with the British fleet, mutinied. Although the mutiny petered out, it was followed by Liebknecht's proclamation of a German Soviet Republic. However, the German Chancellor, Prince Max of Baden, now handed over his post to Fritz Ebert, a Social-Democratic member of the cabinet; Philipp Scheidemann, the German cabinet's other Social-Democratic member, proclaimed a Democratic Republic. General Wilhelm Groener, the Germans' wartime chief of field railways, telephoned Ebert from the German High Command, making an offer of military assistance that was accepted, and it became clear that a struggle for power could not be avoided.

Lenin was still recuperating from Fanny Kaplan's attack and did not attend a meeting of the soviets held on 3 October during the early days of the German confrontation. However, his optimistic view of the developing situation was revealed in a note from him read out at the meeting.

'[The German] crisis [it said], means either that the revolution has begun or at any rate that the people have clearly realized it is inevitable and imminent . . . The admission of Scheidemann and Co. to the Cabinet would only hasten the revolutionary outburst and make it more widespread, more conscious, more firm and determined after the thorough exposure of the pitiful impotence of these lackeys of the bourgeoisie . . . It will inevitably end in the transfer of political power to the German proletariat.'

Lenin's prognostication was to be quite wrong. General Groener's intervention was followed by some weeks of confused fighting in Berlin during which Ebert was first captured then released, and Liebknecht and Rosa Luxemburg were captured and then murdered by right-wing officers. The fighting ended only in mid-January 1919, when the Social-Democratic leader Gustav Noske gained control of the capital. Three weeks later, on 6 February, a National Assembly met in the town of Weimar. Here Ebert was elected President and Scheidemann Chancellor of a coalition government supported by the Social-Democratic Party, the Catholic Centre Party and the Democratic Party.

The Government of Weimar, which lasted a decade and a half, and gave its name to both an administration and a culture, put an end to Lenin's hope that in the near future Germany would be supporting Russia with a Bolshevik or near-Bolshevik government. The situation, moreover, now reinforced his fears that the ending of the war between the Allies and the Central Powers would allow the Allies to give increased attention to Bolshevik Russia.

Much rested on the decisions to be taken in Paris where Allied statesmen were meeting to decide what peace terms could be imposed on Germany and the other Central Powers which had supported her in the long, bitter and costly war. As Lenin well knew, there was an overall dislike in the West of both Communist theory and practice. The dislike was, however, qualified – and more strongly than Lenin seems to have believed – by the beliefs, at least quasi-humanitarian, held most strongly among the peacemakers by President Wilson of the USA. Russian still fought Russian as the statesmen gathered in Paris. Lenin's

Government still struggled, at times with what seemed to be increasing desperation, to beat off those who, if not hoping for the restoration of the Tsar's regime, hoped at least for the defeat of Lenin and his system of government, and for the creation of a new White administration. The problem that these circumstances presented to the statesmen gathered in Paris was succinctly put by Wilson who said: 'The associated powers are now engaged in the solemn and responsible work of establishing the peace of Europe, and of the world, and they are keenly alive to the fact that Europe and the world cannot be at peace if Russia is not.'

Herbert Hoover described Russia as 'probably among the worst problems before the Peace Conference . . . the Banquo's ghost sitting at every Council table', and it has been estimated that during the first two weeks of the conference the Allied diplomats spent more time discussing Russia than any other subject. However flattered Lenin might have been had he appreciated the time that was being devoted in Paris to his country, his feelings would have been modified as he realized that the men considering the fate of Russia, among them Herbert Hoover, the well-known American public figure and future president, Colonel House and Winston Churchill, while all being giants of a sort were of less importance than Wilson, Lloyd George or Clemenceau, the leaders who concentrated their time and attention on the intransigent problem of Germany.

Wilson, and to a more limited extent Lloyd George, were able to control their instinctive anti-Bolshevik beliefs but despite this the conservative feelings among the diplomats in Paris constantly made Lenin's task in Moscow more difficult. Lloyd George and Churchill discussed their fears of Communism on the night of the Armistice with Germany while a memorandum from Robert

Lansing stated: 'Bolshevism is the most hideous and monstrous thing that the human mind has ever conceived. It . . . finds its adherents among the criminal, the depraved, and the mentally unfit . . .'

It was against such sentiments that Wilson's vision of what peace in Russia meant to the peace of the world had to struggle. It became the mainspring behind three separate but overlapping ideas for ending the Russian civil war. They all failed, mainly owing to Allied inefficiency and muddle, although the failure was inestimably helped by the virulent anti-Bolshevism present in all Western countries involved but particularly strong in France and Italy. Yet Lenin's reaction to these three efforts to end the fighting between Reds and Whites, the success of which would have had such an impact on the future of Russia, also throws revealing light on him and on those whose advice he took during the crucial first half of 1919.

On both Bolshevik and Western sides, strong incentives for peace in the Russian civil war were operating as the Allied ministers met in Paris for the Peace Conference. Even the French, the most ardent of the interventionists, were reluctant to step up intervention to the extent needed to produce results; yet no Allied power was happy at the thought of the other obvious alternative – an all-out Bolshevik victory which would bring with it the threat of Communist ideas spreading across Western Europe. If these considerations moved the Western powers towards compromise between the forces tearing themselves apart in Russia, Lenin had his own motives which, while different, bent him in the same direction. He continued to fear that with the Central Powers beaten, Britain, France and the USA would combine to fall on Bolshevism, although his belief was increasingly qualified by the conviction that the former allies would quickly fall out among themselves. Nevertheless, he knew that however the cards fell, Russia's victory over the Whites would only be won after long and bloodletting campaigns which would dangerously weaken the ability of the Revolution to survive. And, as always, survival of the Revolution was given priority. Therefore he turned a more receptive ear than might have been expected to the various ideas for an end to the civil war, which the Allies proposed from the end of 1918 onwards.

Litvinov in Stockholm and Chicherin, Commissar for Foreign Affairs in Moscow, both made it clear that Lenin was open to diplomatic approaches. From December onwards Lloyd George had shown that he felt Russia's voice should be heard at the Paris peace discussions, even though his feelings were more qualified than those of Wilson. The ideas nourished in such a climate hardened after 30 December 1918, when the Canadian Prime Minister, Sir Robert Borden, proposed to the Imperial War Cabinet in London that military intervention in Russia should not be stepped up but that governments with troops in Russia should call an end to the fighting and send representatives to Paris for a conference with Allied and Russian officials.

Borden's proposal went through a number of sea changes. Clemenceau would not hear of Bolshevik representatives coming to Paris but Lloyd George supported the idea in principle and so did Wilson who, in Paris, called on 22 January for his typewriter and himself tapped out a declaration. The proposed meeting place was the cluster of the Prinkipo Islands in the Sea of Marmara a few miles from Constantinople, well equipped for conference purposes with a number of holiday hotels. The terms of the invitation were quite definite.

'They [the associated Powers] invite every organized group that is now exercising or attempting to exercise, political authority or military control anywhere in Siberia, or within the boundaries of European Russia as they stood before the war just concluded (except in Finland) to send representatives, not exceeding three representatives for each group, to the Princes Islands, Sea of Marmora, where they will be met by representatives of the associated Powers, provided, in the meantime, there is a truce of arms amongst the parties invited . . . These representatives are invited to confer with the representatives of the Associated Powers in the freest and frankest way, with a view to ascertaining the wishes of all sections of the Russian people, and bringing about, if possible, some understanding and agreement by which Russia may work out her own purposes and happy co-operative relations be established between her people and the other peoples of the world.'

The Prinkipo proposal was never implemented. The White groups, strongly supported by the French, refused to attend such a meeting with the Bolsheviks. However, the Bolshevik response was not as unqualified as is sometimes made out. Lenin's reply agreed to recognize Russia's foreign debts; to grant mining and similar interests to the Allies; to discuss a territorial settlement; and not to interfere in the internal affairs of the Allies. Reasonable as these points were, the Soviet reply made no mention of a cease-fire and it was widely believed that even if the Whites had come to Prinkipo the Bolsheviks would have refused to order an armistice.

Lenin certainly had his suspicions as to Allied intentions which were voiced in a note to Trotsky on 24 January 1919: 'I am afraid [Wilson] wants to establish his claim to Siberia and part of the South, having otherwise scarcely a hope of retaining anything.' But there was another point which would have affected the outcome of any meeting at Prinkipo and that was the offence aroused in the minds of both Wilson and Lloyd George by the economic concessions proposed in the Russian reply. This emphasis on commerce gave Western statesmen the impression that the Bolsheviks regarded those allegedly calling for peace as mere money-grubbers. But assuming – as one should – that Lenin had carefully vetted the terms of the reply, the fact that he allowed the belief to be apparent indicates that he was still graduating from politician to statesman.

If the failure of the Prinkipo proposal was largely due to White intransigence, the failure of its successor, the ill-fated Bullitt Mission, was mainly the result of Western mismanagement and suspicion, reinforced by extreme French anti-Bolshevism. Certainly there is every indication that by the time of the Mission Lenin had been won round to giving high priority to ending the civil war.

The credit for conceiving the Bullitt Mission was for long divided between Wilson, Lloyd George and Colonel House, but almost half a century after the event the true credit was revealed by John M. Thompson who quoted in *Russia, Bolshevism, and the Versailles Peace* an entry for 9 January 1919 from the diary of Gordon Auchincloss, Colonel House's aide. In it, Auchincloss recorded that he had called on Lord Northcliffe, and went on: 'We talked for some time about the present situation, particularly in Russia and Germany. He [Northcliffe] suggested that a commission should be sent to Russia after securing the approval of the present government. The commission would simply find out what the facts of the situation were.' Four days later Auchincloss visited Wilson and noted in his diary, as quoted by Thompson:

'I told the President that the Colonel [House] suggested that the President propose that a Commission be sent to Russia to ascertain the facts of the situation there before they had been refused representation at the peace conference and that the President should appoint as American members of this Commission Radicals. The President said that this procedure was also in his mind.'

The following month William C. Bullitt, a young American diplomat who had sailed with Wilson to France for the peace conference, received a letter, dated 18 February 1919, from Robert Lansing, the US Secretary of State, which said:

'Sir,
American Commission to Negotiate Peace
You are hereby directed to proceed to Russia for the purpose of studying conditions, political and economic, therein, for the benefit of the American Commissioners plenipotentiary to negotiate peace . . .'

In Bullitt's opinion this purely information-seeking mission was changed in scope before he left Paris since he was visited in the French capital by Philip Kerr (later Lord Lothian), at that time Lloyd George's private secretary, who left with him a list of seven points regarding an armistice on which it was hoped that Bolshevik agreement could be secured. Kerr later stated that these points were purely unofficial but Bullitt, who took it for granted that Kerr must have discussed the matter in detail with

Lloyd George, read more into them than that.

'I was instructed [he later told the US Senate Committee on Foreign Relations (12 September 1919)] to go in and bring back as quickly as possible a definite statement of exactly the terms the Soviet Government was ready to accept. The idea in the minds of the British and the American delegation were [sic] that if the Allies made another proposal it should be a proposal which we would know in advance would be accepted, so that there would be no chance of another Prinkipo proposal miscarrying.'

Kerr's recollection of his message, given in a letter some months later to Sir Ronald Graham, Assistant Under-Secretary of State at the Foreign Office, was somewhat different:

'I told [Bullitt] [he wrote to Graham] that, in my opinion, the essential condition of any settlement was the immediate cessation of hostilities on all fronts, the acceptance of all existing Governments as the *de facto* Governments of the territories they controlled, and an agreement that the Allied forces should be withdrawn from Russia as soon as the Bolshevik forces were demobilized or disarmed, subject to the necessary safeguards against political retaliation and proscription. Throughout I made it clear to Mr Bullitt that any opinions which I expressed were purely my own.'

The last point was to be the most important in the confusion which subsequently developed, for although Colonel House appears to have covered Bullitt with some cloak of authority, and although the British gave him what help they could in reaching

591

Russia, the proposals that Bullitt subsequently discussed with Lenin are likely to have been purely unofficial even though Lenin no doubt gained a different impression.

However, at least one thing had been settled by the time Bullitt left France for Russia: the Allies would have nothing to do with a plan put forward by Winston Churchill for arming the anti-Bolshevik forces in Russia with Volunteers, technical experts, arms, munitions, tanks, aeroplanes, etc.' According to *Papers Relating to the Foreign Relations of the United States: 1919, Russia,* 'Churchill's project [put forward 14 February 1919] is dead and there is little danger that it will be revived again by the [Peace] Conference.'

Thus Bullitt left for Russia in a climate which showed no enthusiasm for increased military intervention; the problems he had to face from the Allies were as much those of muddle as of ill will.

With him went Captain W. W. Pettit from Paris, of US Intelligence; a secretary, R. E. Lynch; and the left-wing journalist Lincoln Steffens. Lynch was left in Finland, but the three other members of the party were met in Petrograd on 8 March by Chicherin and Litvinov, who both seemed agreeable to the aims of the mission although they were unclear about how a cease-fire could be enforced on the various fighting fronts.

On 10 March Bullitt moved on to Moscow where he had further talks with Chicherin and Litvinov, followed by a long interview with Lenin. The Bolshevik military position was just as precarious as it had been at the time of the Prinkipo plan, and Bullitt seems to have been justified in believing that the proposals he put to Lenin – modelled on those he had received from Kerr – would be accepted without difficulty. This was not only his opinion: Arthur Ransome, who interviewed Lenin on

9 March, appears to have gained the same impression, and Chicherin reported to Rakovsky in the Ukraine: 'The decision [regarding Bullitt] is very important. If we do not reach an understanding the policy of blockade will be pressed with vigour. They will send tanks, etc., to Denikin, Kolchak, Petlura, Paderevski etc.' And Lenin himself underlined his attitude when he spoke in Petrograd on 13 March and affirmed the policy of a 'second Brest', saying, 'that policy, which led us to accept the Brest peace, the most atrocious, outrageous, humiliating peace, turned out to be entirely correct. I think that it is not without value to recall this policy just now, when the situation in reference to our relations with the Allies is similar, when they in raging fury want to use Russia's debts to crush her in poverty and ruin, to pillage her so that they may drain her of the growing might of her toiling masses.'

Stripped of the rhetoric in which Lenin felt it necessary to wrap his feelings, this meant that the gist of Kerr's draft notes had been accepted – although Lenin maintained, apparently to save Russian 'face', that the these 'Russian proposal'* on 14 March. They called for two–week armistice, the end of the economic

---

* The full text of the Projected Peace Proposal by the Allied and Associated Governments (see notes and references, pp. 778–82) was read to the United States Senate Committee on Foreign Relations (12 September 1919) by Bullitt who prefaced it by saying: 'The Soviet Government undertook to accept this proposal provided it was made by the allied and associated Governments not later than 10 April 1919.' and propagand, just as yours will come here and propagand. We can agree not to send them to you, and we can agree that if they do go they shall be subject to your laws but we – nobody can make a propagandist stop propaganding." '

blockade of Russia, the withdrawal of Allied troops from Russia, what it was hoped would be the ending of long–standing differences. They had been approved by the Bolshevik should stop all aid to anti–Bolshevik governments, believing that if this happened those governments would quickly collapse. Bullitt sincerely felt that he had succeeded in getting all that he had come for, and there is much to be said for his son's comment half a century later that had these proposals been 'accepted by President Wilson and Lloyd George, they might have given us a different world than that in which we live today'.

Before Bullitt left Moscow his colleague Steffens had an interview with Lenin at which the trained journalist got more straight answers from the Russian leader than did most foreigners who met him. He wrote later,

'I asked whether, in addition to the agreement with Bullitt, I could not take back some assurances; that, for example, if the borders were opened, Russian propagandists would be restrained from flocking over into Europe.

' "No," he said sharply, but he leaned back against the desk and smiled. "A propagandist, you know, is a propagandist. He must propagand. When our propagandists for revolution won, when they saw the revolution happen, they did not stop propaganding. They went right on propaganding. We had to give them propaganda work to do among the peasants and workers. If our borders are opened, our propagandists will go to Europe and propagand, just as yours will come here and propagand. We can agree not to send them to you, and we can agree that if they do go they shall be subject to your laws but we – nobody can make a propagandist stop propaganding." '

When Steffens asked 'What assurance can you give that the red terror will not go on killing . . .', Lenin came to his feet in anger and asked: 'Who wants to ask us about our killings?' Steffens answered with the one word 'Paris', and Lenin asked: 'Do you mean to tell me that those men who have just generaled the slaughter of seventeen millions of men in a purposeless war are concerned over the few thousands who have been killed in a revolution with a conscious aim – to get out of the necessity of war and – armed peace?' Then he continued: 'But never mind, don't deny the terror. Don't minimize any of the evils of a revolution. They occur. They must be counted upon. If we have to have a revolution, we have to pay the price of revolution.' He went on:

'It is no use. There will be a terror. It hurts the revolution both inside and out, and we must find out how to avoid or control or direct it. But we have to know more about psychology than we do now to steer through that madness. And it served a purpose that has to be served. There must be in a revolution, as in a war, unified action, and in a revolution more than in a war the contented people will scuttle your ship if you don't deal with them. There are white terrors too, you know. Look at Finland and Hungary. We have to devise some way to get rid of the bourgeoisie, the upper classes. They won't let you make economic changes during a revolution any more than they will before one; so they must be driven out. I don't see, myself, why we can't scare them away without killing them. Of course they are a menace outside as well as in, but the émigrés are not so bad. The only solution I see is to have the threat of a red terror spread the fear and let them escape. But however it is done,

595

it has to be done. The absolute, instinctive opposition of the old conservatives and even of the fixed liberals has to be silenced if you are to carry through a revolution to its objective.'

Lenin appears to have spoken as frankly to Bullitt as he did to Steffens, and Bullitt, possibly naive and certainly inexperienced, seems to have had little doubt that the terms he had obtained would be accepted in the West. He telegraphed the results of his mission to Colonel House in Paris, received the Colonel's congratulations, and returned to Europe confident that he would receive a comparable reception from Lloyd George and Wilson. In fact, the response was more complicated than he can have expected. At first, all appeared to be going well. Having seen Bullitt, House wrote in his diary on 25 March, '. . . at last I can see a way out of that vexatious problem [Russia], that is, if we can get action by the Prime Ministers and the President . . . While Bullitt was talking, I was maturing plans which I shall begin to put in execution tomorrow.' The same evening he arranged for Bullitt to meet the President the following day. That meeting was postponed indefinitely for reasons that are still not clear, but they may have been connected with a *contretemps* of which Bullitt became aware when he had a breakfast meeting with Lloyd George, Philip Kerr, Maurice Hankey and Jan Christian Smuts. Here he watched Lloyd George hand Smuts a copy of the peace proposals he had brought back from Russia. As Lloyd George did so he commented: 'This is of the utmost importance and interest, and you ought to read it right away.' But although this sounded encouraging, he then said he did not know what he would do about public opinion and, flourishing a copy of the *Daily Mail,* added: 'As long as the British press is doing this kind of thing how can you expect me to be sensible about Russia?'

The paper that raised Lloyd George's ire carried, over a strong anti-Bolshevik leading article by Wickham Steed, the headline: 'The Intrigue that May be Revived'. Gordon Auchincloss had leaked information to Steed about the Prinkipo plan which had failed; now he warned readers against any recognition of the Bolsheviks, made it more difficult for the Prime Minister to implement the proposals with which Bullitt had returned from Russia, and by implication encouraged Wilson also to remain aloof from them. Wickham Steed's article – part of a continuing campaign – was, of course, not the only factor: White objection to any contact with the Bolsheviks was strong and at times appeared to be all-pervasive. No further action was taken on the proposals to which Bullitt had obtained agreement; and, as perhaps with Prinkipo, Lenin may again have felt that he had been led up the garden path.

There were post-mortems in the USA and in Britain on the failure of the Bullitt Mission. But the manner in which it had been organized and had developed made it easy for both President Wilson and Lloyd George to duck responsibility and claim – quite accurately – that no official proposals had been made. Thus when the *Nation* published (in the USA) a story on the mission and apparently quoted Kerr's memorandum to Bullitt, Wilson felt able to write:

'This is an amazing article. I know of no such "Allied terms" as are here quoted, and do not for a moment believe that it is true that "The Nation" itself is in a position through information received direct from Paris, to state . . . that Messrs. Bullitt and Steffens did take a memorandum into

Russia and that memorandum was in the handwriting of Philip Kerr, Private Secretary to Mr Lloyd George.'

In Britain, Lloyd George, questioned in Parliament, referred to Bullitt merely as one among many hundreds of men whom he had seen with information from Russia. And when asked whether it was with his sanction that on 21 February Kerr had sent a letter to Bullitt enclosing a note of the conditions on which it would be possible for the Allied governments to resume normal relations with Soviet Russia, stating that they had no official significance and merely represented personal suggestions of the Prime Minister, it was Bonar Law, the Leader of the House, who replied with the words: 'The Answer to this question is in the negative.'

The combination of mistrust and bungling by the Allies was compounded by the timing of Bullitt's return. The moment was, as described by Churchill in *The World Crisis: The Aftermath*, 'unpropitious.' Kolchak's armies, he went on,

> 'had just gained notable successes in Siberia, and Bela Kun had raised his Communist rebellion in Hungary. French and British indignation against truckling to the Bolsheviks was at its height. The Soviet proposals to Mr Bullitt, which were of course in themselves fraudulent, were treated with general disdain; and Bullitt himself was not without some difficulty disowned by those who had sent him.'

Late in March, when it was obvious that the Bullitt proposal was dying, but not actually dead, President Wilson raised with Colonel House the possibility of sending relief to Russia in the form of food; this could be linked with the ending both of the civil war and of Bolshevik propaganda abroad, although the ways in which such activities were to be combined were never properly formulated. But it was felt that some plan could be worked out which would not require formal recognition of the Bolshevik Government and one which might, therefore, be carried through without the definite hostility of the White forces.

Fridtjof Nansen, the Norwegian explorer who had taken part in a number of international humanitarian enterprises, and Herbert Hoover were eventually persuaded to work out the 'Hoover-Nansen Plan' under which much food would have been sent. Yet even this plan, framed so as not to offend anti-Bolshevik susceptibilities, aroused the suspicions of the French, who claimed that it could lead to British, American and perhaps even German control of Russian markets. It is notable that strong French anti-Bolshevism continued long after it had begun to wane among the other Western allies. One reason, well articulated in Professor Zeman's *A Diplomatic History of the First World War*, was the Bolsheviks' repudiation of their financial obligations which, he points out, was a 'grudge [which] dominated French policy toward Russia' for years.

However, this was not the main objection which finally put paid to the plan. It was found necessary to submit the first draft ideas to the lawyers – theoretically to correct the legal language. Something else happened and, according to Bullitt, who had become involved in the plan, the end product was a proposition 'which left out all possibility of the matter coming to a peace conference, and was largely an offer to feed Russia provided Russia put all her rail-roads in the hands of the allied and associated Governments'. By this time Bullitt was no impartial observer, but the details of the plan, as broadcast by radio, were such as to bring a hostile response not only from some of the White authorities but also from Moscow. Chicherin maintained on Lenin's behalf that Russia's current sufferings were the result of the Allied blockade and that, in effect, no relief programme would be necessary if this were lifted. The chances of the Bolsheviks now implementing an armistice or cease-fire seemed remote. There still remained, moreover, the possibility that anti-Bolshevik forces coming from Siberia might be able to link up with the interventionist forces in the Archangel area, thus lessening the need for the West to help the Whites.

However, the advantage to Lenin's forces of their control from centrally situated Moscow quickly became apparent; Bolshevik troops were diverted east and the possibility of a link-up between anti-Communist forces in the north and those in Siberia was averted, ending the temporarily revived hope among the Western Allies that Lenin's Government could be toppled by Russian White forces without further interventionist help. It was not the only development that, following the failure of the peace efforts of the winter of 1918 to 1919, suggested that in the absence of increased interventionist action, which the Western allies were unwilling to give, the Communist threat might not only continue but start to grow. The revival of Lenin's internationalist ideas from early 1919 encouraged anti-Bolshevik forces both in and outside Russia in the belief that they had to go on fighting, a notion that sustained hostilities for almost another two years.

16

Lenin's State Survives

Since the autumn Revolution of 1917 most countries in the West had been as perturbed by Communist threats to spread revolution beyond the frontiers of Russia as by revolutionary success in Russia itself. There had at first been few hard indications that the international danger was real. But in March 1919, as the implications of the failure of the Bullitt Mission and its planned successors began to sink in, a new factor was added by the setting-up in Moscow, after Lenin's assiduous lobbying, of the Third International, or Comintern. There had been other post-First World War attempts to revive the Second International, which had disappeared in the flames of the war, the most recent being a proposal by the British Labour Party that a convention with this aim should be held at Lausanne in January 1919. The Central Committee of the RCP(B) had issued a recommendation that revolutionary parties should not take part 'in conferences of enemies of the working class wearing the mask of socialism', and Lenin advised Chicherin that their own preparations should start for founding the Third International. This became more urgent with the failure in Berne of yet another attempt to revive the former International.

Lenin was more successful, and on 2 March 1919, fifty-two delegates from thirty countries met in a room in the old courts of justice in the Kremlin. At the centre of the presidium, on a raised dais at the end of the room, sat Lenin, flanked by Trotsky, Zinoviev, Chicherin, Bukharin and Litvinov. He began by asking everyone to rise in tribute to 'the finest representatives of the Third International, Karl Liebknecht and Rosa Luxemburg'. Trotsky, remarked Arthur Ransome – one of the few 'outsiders' at the proceedings – wore a leather coat, military breeches and gaiters, and a fur hat with the sign of the Red Army in front, 'a strange figure for those who had known him as one of the greatest anti-militarists in Europe'.

Lenin listened to the speakers, replied in German, and during the day prepared the way for the adoption by the International of the conditions on which national groups would be admitted to it. The admission of moderate socialist parties was ruled out and it was clear, even at the first meeting, that the new International would be cast in an extreme revolutionary mould created by Lenin. This would impede any form of reconciliation with the West but increased Lenin's popularity among the Party faithful, which was evident in the evening when a celebratory meeting was held in Moscow's Grand Theatre. Ransome later wrote:

'If I had ever thought that Lenin was losing his personal popularity I got my answer now. It was a long time before he could speak at all, everybody standing and drowning his attempt to speak with roar after roar of applause. It was an extraordinary, overwhelming scene, tier after tier crammed with workmen, the parterre filled, the whole platform and the wings. A knot of workwomen were close to me, and they almost fought to see him, and shouted as if each one were determined that he should hear her in particular. He spoke as usual, in the simplest way, emphasizing the fact that the revolutionary struggle everywhere was forced to use the Soviet forms. "We declare our solidarity with the aims of the Sovietists" he read from an Italian newspaper, and added "and that was when they did not know what our aims were, and before we had an established programme ourselves." '

Later that night Lenin took a significant part in drawing up the Comintern's first manifesto. Karl Steinhardt has written:

'I had to work together with Eberlein [the German delegate] on the final text [of it]. Eberlein and I not only had to translate it into German, but also had to edit it. Lenin came in the evening and worked on the Manifesto together with us from 10.00 p.m. to 6.00 a.m. He was tirelesss and finished working only when we had read every paragraph, every sentence, and polished up not only the content, but also the style of the Manifesto. Time and again we argued about different wordings, and Lenin won every time. Then he would smile his winning smile and merrily wink his left eye at us. Seeing that Eberlein and I were already pretty tired he would stop working every now and then and would crack jokes.'

Moreover, when the job was done Lenin gave them advice on how best to recover. 'Follow my own tried and tested method,' he said. 'Don't go to bed, but take a good, hot bath and then a cold shower, have a good breakfast and take a walk before the session.'

603

The revival of the International, now to be known as the Comintern and under tight Bolshevik control, confirmed to the Allied ministers in Paris that they would continue to be faced with the problems, political and military, of how to deal with the new Russian Government. Yet Lenin, thwarted of whatever hopes he had of turning from the burdens of war to the tasks of reconstruction, faced a similarly discomfiting 1919 during which the civil war continued to grow in complexity. In the east by mid-March Kolchak's offensive had occupied Ufa. In May the Red Army opened its counter-offensive and retook Ufa the following month. In the autumn Kolchak set up his own form of government at Irkutsk but before the end of 1919 this was overthrown by the Socialist Revolutionaries and Kolchak was shot.

While the Red Army was consolidating its position in Siberia, its fortunes elsewhere were going from bad to worse. In the south, where the situation was confused by the presence not only of Red and White forces but of Ukrainian nationalists, Denikin led an offensive which by the end of the summer had driven a 15,000-man Red Army from the northern Caucasus, gained control of the Ukraine and held Kharkov, Odessa and Kiev. After improving his position still further he captured the town of Orel, only some 200 miles from Moscow, on 13 October. Since the renewal of his offensive he had won back 400,000 square miles from the Red Army, begun to establish contact with the anti-Bolshevik forces in Siberia, and greatly strengthened his position in southern Russia. To the north an almost equally important threat to Petrograd was being developed by General Nikolay Nikolayevich Yudenich, who had failed in a thrust towards the city earlier in the year. Yudenich, a former officer in the Tsar's army, had a distinguished record in the war during which, in February 1916, he had captured the town of Erzurum from the Turks. By the late summer he had gathered behind him the White Russian forces in Finland and commanded around 25,000 men, pardy armed and trained by British and French officers. It was also planned that a British monitor on his left wing would shell the Russian fort of Krasnaya Gorka as he moved on Petrograd. Both threats were eventually countered and January 1920 saw a series of Red Army successes. On 3 January their troops occupied Tsaritsyn; three days later they entered Krasnoyarsk while the rest of Kolchak's forces laid down their arms. On the same day Red Army forces captured Taganrog and four days afterwards other Red Army troops captured Rostov-on-Don. Almost equally important was the action of the Supreme Allied War Council in Paris, which before the end of January decided to end the blockade which had been so gravely extending the famine in Russia.

By February 1920 the one remaining military threat to Lenin's Government was from White forces in the south of Russia led by General Wrangel, whose political adviser, P. B. Struve, had debated revolutionary theory and tactics with Lenin during the early years of the century.

But it was only during the last days of October 1920 that the Bolsheviks were able to launch their decisive attack against Wrangel who by this time had been driven back into the Crimea. In November the Red Army stormed the narrow Perekop Isthmus, the only connection between the Crimea and the mainland, and within a few days overwhelmed the White forces. Wrangel evacuated 130,000 men, women and children as best he could on a fleet of 126 vessels which even included lightships, and for most practical purposes the civil war was over.

Owing to the nature both of the commands involved and of the fighting, estimates of the casualties in the civil war vary considerably. The only thing which is certain is that the numbers of dead ran into tens of thousands and the numbers of injured into at least hundreds of thousands, and possibly into millions. Figures for material destruction are more reliable and the official numbers seem likely to be roughly correct: 3,672 railway bridges destroyed, 3,597 ordinary bridges, 1,750 kilometres of railway line, 381 railway depots and workshops and nearly 180,000 kilometres of telegraph and telephone lines. At times during the war, the Whites held sixty of the main railway lines, and were effectively cutting off from the rest of Russia Ukrainian grain, Turkestan cotton and the pig iron of the Donetz Basin.

The three years of widespread operations had stretched Lenin's forces and his personal powers to their limits. Moreover, with activity spread over so many different areas, with success in one campaign so frequently balanced by failure in another, it was always difficult to draw up a realistic overall balance sheet of how the Government was faring.

Of the various factors that eventually led to victory over the Whites, the personal influence of Lenin and Trotsky was among the most important. Trotsky, arriving at the front in his armoured train, was the epitome of the commander always anxious to be active at the sharp point of the battle. His train, with its two engines, was an extraordinary piece of equipment, carrying electrical generator, printing press, radio and telegraph station and garages for cars; in it he made thirty-six visits to the various civil war fronts, and in 1919 outside Petrograd the train crew and accompanying guards took an active part in the fighting against General Yudenich.

Quite as important as Trotsky, and with an influence extending over broader territories, was Lenin himself. Despite his lack of military training, his varied experiences since the start of the century seem to have equipped him for a key role in the civil war even more fittingly than they had equipped him to mastermind the autumn Revolution. In that role he virtually controlled from Moscow operations being carried out from the shores of the Black Sea to the northern territories surrounding Archangel and Murmansk. Throughout 1918 he continued to keep up a daily series of notes and injunctions to the local commanders and councils carrying on the civil war. They were often in strong terms, chiding and threatening those who were thought to have failed, even slightly, in their duty. Lenin was constantly 'surprised', 'alarmed' or 'shocked' at what had or had not been done, and it was not unusual for the actions of even close Party colleagues to be described as 'monstrous' or 'criminal'.

With the exception of the increased acerbity which such comments reveal, and the added pressure demanded by the fighting, Lenin's life continued much as it had before the situation had developed into civil war. Krupskaya continued to support him, both as the ever-present, ever-loving wife and the experienced, professional Party member on whose advice he could draw if he wished. She served as an educational administrator, a propagandist for the Party and, perhaps quite as importantly, as a psychological prop if this were required in the darker and more depressing moments of the struggle. All this enabled Lenin to maintain his undiminishing influence on a military-political-economic situation as complex as any that faced leaders during the Second World War.

That we have so revealing a picture of him during this period is due partly to his being rarely out of touch, by letter, telegram, or recorded telephone conversation, with Trotsky and, only slightly less frequently, with commanders in the field; and also to the fact that in 1936 the International Institute of Social History acquired from Trotsky a collection of about 800 documents, the Lenin-Trotsky correspondence, added to them from various sources, and subsequently published them in *The Trotsky Papers, 1917–1922*.

These two thick volumes throw an illuminating light on the way in which Lenin dominated the strategy of the civil war from his office in the Kremlin. They also reveal, in a multitude of small points, the sort of man he had become by the time he approached his fifties: a man with an unexpectedly informed concern with detail and an unqualified ruthlessness with which he was prepared to pursue his aims in the sacred cause of the Revolution. The latter trait was remarked on after his death by Struve: 'The terrible thing in Lenin', he wrote, 'was that combination in one person of actual self-castigation, which is the essence of all real asceticism, with the castigation of other people as expressed in abstract social hatred and cold political cruelty.'

Certainly Lenin rarely minced his words, and never when dealing with vital military matters. Typical of his warnings was the note in May 1919 to the Council of People's Commissars of the Ukraine:

'Disaster is absolutely inevitable for the Revolution as a whole without a swift victory in the Donbass, to achieve which it is essential that procedural routine be abandoned in the Ukraine; that the work in hand be performed in a true revolutionary spirit and everything and everyone brought into play; that a personal watch be kept on each military unit, on each step of the work in progress; that everything but the Donbass be put to one side and to every rifle three soldiers assigned.'

And at other critical moments commanders and commissars

were reminded that the future depended on their own personal efforts.

Although Lenin was frequently cautious about commenting on military judgements – 'Let the military themselves decide about your military proposals for forming detachments manned by instructors. I do not propose to pass judgement upon the matter,' he once wrote to Trotsky – he used his position at the centre of affairs to advise as he thought necessary. Thus the town of Voronezh and Trotsky received the following message from him during the first days of 1919: 'I am very disturbed as to whether you have not got absorbed in the Ukraine to the detriment of the over-all strategic task on which Vacetis insists and which consists in launching a rapid, determined and general offensive against Krasnov . . . Should you not direct your entire effort towards speeding up the putting through [of] the general offensive against Krasnov?'

From the central viewpoint which allowed him to survey the whole panorama of the civil war in a single glance, Lenin was in a unique position for judging the rights and wrongs of the various personal disputes that sprang up among the strong-minded men responsible for Russia's military survival. Among the most important, and one which, only a few years later, was to have its impact on the post-war development of the country, was the antagonism between Trotsky and Stalin.

Argument began soon after Stalin had been appointed Sovnarkom Special Commissar for Food Supplies in southern Russia and sent by Lenin early in June 1918 to Tsaritsyn. It was essentially a civil appointment, and was not expected to last long. Stalin arrived in the city on 6 June, accompanied by two armoured cars and 400 Red Guards and the following day reported to Lenin on 'the bacchanalia of profiteering' which he noted there. He began an energetic plan of clearing up, soon saw that the problem was even wider than he had thought, and quickly asked for, and was given, military powers to deal with the situation on the Southern Front. From the start he failed to see eye to eye with Trotsky and on 10 June cabled Lenin: 'If Trotsky will, thoughtlessly, hand out credentials right and left to Trifonov (in the Don region), to Antonov (Kuban region), to Koppe (Stavropol), to members of the French mission (who deserve to be arrested), and so forth, you may be sure that within a month everything in the North Caucasus will crash and this region will be lost to us definitely.' Stalin wanted full military authority to dismiss commanders if necessary, and added to Lenin: 'This is what the common interest tells me to do, and, of course, the absence of a piece of paper from Trotsky will not stop me.'

For his part, Trotsky cabled Lenin in Moscow: 'I categorically insist on Stalin's recall.' Lenin was quick to see that the Southern Front was too small to hold both men, but he solved the problem ingeniously by sending Sverdlov, the President of the Russian Republic, to bring Stalin back to Moscow personally in a special military train, and by ensuring that on his arrival in the capital he received appropriate military honours.

Tsaritsyn was surrounded, relieved, surrounded again, and finally relieved only in mid-October 1918. It was then that Stalin, returning to the city, balked the White forces' ambitious plan to capture the city and enable Kolchak's left wing, coming from Siberia, to link up with Denikin's right wing coming from the south. If these complex events inflamed relations between Trotsky and Stalin, they were further worsened when Stalin, promoted to the Supreme War Council, opposed Trotsky's project for attacking Denikin through the Don Cossack region and proposed, instead, a flank attack through the south-eastern

Ukraine which was successfully carried out.

One by-product of the military struggle for Tsaritsyn arose in that both attackers and defenders here made more use of aircraft than elsewhere during the civil war. The attackers were supported by nearly forty aircraft when the city finally fell to the Red Army and Lenin subsequently asked that aircraft designers should design a plane specially for ground-attack sorties.

Lenin's ability to take a comprehensive view of the whole area over which the civil war was fought is illustrated by a telegram to the Military Revolutionary Council of the Eastern Front.

'On your insistence, Kamenev has been reappointed. If we do not capture the Urals before the winter, I consider that the revolution will inevitably perish. Exert all efforts. Any friction between Kamenev and the staff should be reported to me in good time, in code. Pay particular attention to the reinforcements, mobilize all the population near the front. Take care of political work. Send me ciphered telegrams every week about results. Read this telegram to all prominent Communists and workers from Petersburg. Report receipt. Pay particular attention to the mobilization of the Orenberg Cossacks. You are responsible to ensure that there is no decomposition and that morale should not collapse.'

If Lenin could paint in the effects of military operations with the broadest brush, his letters also show an informed concern with the minutiae of military operations and their consequences. When the Volga had been reopened to shipping after the recapture of Samara in the autumn of 1918, it was Lenin who sent lengthy instructions to Trotsky and others on how traffic up and down the river should now be organized – as well as for the setting-up of courts for 'trial and the carrying out of sentences' of those who had disobeyed. And after clothing and boots had been sent to one area but apparently not used, the local commander was told: 'I recommend, on pain of the strictest personal responsibility, that you take decisive steps to distribute immediately the stocks you have received among the units in need of them.'

Many such matters of only local significance when judged against the broad canvas of the civil war, appear to have been scrutinized by Lenin. Thus the unfortunate commander of one particular troop train received a demand saying: 'Submit an exact report to me immediately by telegraph of the circumstances in which the men of your troop train improperly interfered in the performance of their duties by the railway inspectorate and the members of the armed guard when conducting a check of train no. 26, which all but finished in bloodshed. You will answer in all strictness for a false report.'

From demands that cipher clerks should 'be more accurate in their ciphering so that everything is made intelligible' to complaints 'about the catastrophic state of the army and about drunkenness', Lenin seems to have probed virtually every aspect of the forces supporting the Government, and to have had no inhibitions in dealing with them as necessary. Thus one commander's detailed list of instructions was prefaced by the warning: 'It is extremely odd that you send only boastful telegrams about future victories. Look into the following immediately.'

His comments were of an outspokenness typified by a complaint that the reply to one inquiry was 'an outright disgrace' which 'betrays complete negligence or *complete fumbling*', and by a demand to the Military Revolutionary Council of the Eastern Front to pay attention to an uprising at Samara which ended, 'your silence on this subject is suspicious'. At times Lenin intervened in an effort to keep the peace among commanders and in one case, following a demand by Stalin for the recall of a particular officer, asked for details so that he could 'keep the conflict from spreading and steer it along the right lines'.

If there is one feature of Lenin's civil war instructions as constant as the ubiquity of his concerns, it is the regularity with which the threat of summary execution is stressed. Thus, two commanders are ordered at one point to 'issue instructions for and put into effect the wholesale disarming of the population; apply shooting on the spot, without mercy, to every case of concealment of a single rifle'. Another is told that 'It would be a disgrace to fail to punish absence from duty and evasion of mobilization by shooting . . .' At one point a commander was instructed that 'The taking of hostages from the bourgeoisie and from officers' families must be stepped up in view of the increased frequency of instances of treason. Arrange matters with Dzerzhinsky.' Elsewhere the use of additional Cheka forces is suggested. Ruthlessness was not limited to individuals and during operations against Kazan, he warned Trotsky that: 'There must be no question of taking pity on the town and putting matters off any longer, as merciless annihilation is what is vital once it is established that Kazan is enclosed in an iron ring.'

This was the other side of a coin that also revealed Lenin leaning over backwards in his efforts to help old friends – one of the few signs of human feeling to be seen in the multitude of instructions that poured from his office. Maxim Gorky rarely appealed to Lenin without effect, despite his blistering comments following the seizure of power. In April 1919, after the arrest of Ivan Volny, Gorky's writer-colleague, Gorky applied to Lenin, who wrote to the relevant authority asking if Volny could not be freed under close observation. Shortly afterwards he was able to tell Gorky that this had been done. On a later occasion, after another friend had sought help from Gorky, Lenin himself wrote on the back of the appeal a request that similar matters should be sent to him for action. He was always solicitous about Gorky's own health, writing to him:

'I am so tired that I cannot do a thing to save my life. But you, you spit blood, yet you don't go. Upon my word, that is both unfair and extravagant. In Europe, in a good sanatorium, you will be treated properly, and you will be able to accomplish thrice as much work. Upon my word. Whereas with us here you get neither treatment nor any work done, nothing but fuss and vanity, futile vanity. Go away from here, get well. Don't be stubborn I beg of you!'

The ruthlessness and the military intuition exercised by both Lenin and Trotsky effectively helped to decide the outcome of the civil war by the end of 1920. But although the last contingent of General Wrangel's troops had left the Crimea before December, it was another two years before Japanese troops finally evacuated Siberia. To some extent the civil war petered out as it had petered in.

Before this, however, between the spring of 1920 and the spring of 1921 the Red Army was involved in a major war with Poland and a disastrous revolt of Bolshevik forces on the island of Kotlin. Neither set of operations can be claimed as forming part of the civil war, but in timing they provided an epilogue to it and helped delay the economic reconstruction of Russia, which had been one of Lenin's main aims since the Revolution.

As far as Poland was concerned, Lenin regarded the fate of the country in purely political terms: how, he must have asked

– naturally enough – would the future of Poland affect the future of the Revolution? In this, his overall judgement was warped and it was Trotsky, with clearer military insight, who saw before the clash with Poland the differences between what the Red Army should attempt and what it should not.

While Lenin was dealing with the Poles he reluctantly agreed to the publication of his papers – and many of his letters – from the end of the previous century when he had embarked on the revolutionary course that was to bring him to the Kremlin. On 5 April 1920, he was re-elected to the Central Committee at the Ninth Congress of the Party, and shortly afterwards it was proposed that a complete edition of his works should be published. 'Ilyich began to protest,' Kamenev wrote later. 'Why? Entirely unnecessary. Everything possible was written 30 years ago. It is not worth while.' He was finally persuaded after Kamenev pointed out that youth must learn and that it was better that they learned from Lenin's writings rather than from those of Martov and others.

The war between Bolshevik Russia and Poland was, even more directly than other European wars of this period, the result of political ambitions, military rivalries and geographical facts. In his peace message of 22 January 1917 President Wilson had called for a 'united, independent and autonomous Poland', while the thirteenth of his famous Fourteen Points the following year had recommended an 'independent Polish State' with 'free and secure access to the sea'. Later in 1918 Great Britain, France and Italy had also called for an independent and united Poland.

The stumbling block hampering the establishment of an independent Poland was that following the German defeat in the autumn of 1918 Russia and Germany had diametrically opposed ideas of what should happen next. The right-wing forces still powerful in Germany were anxious to see the destruction of

Poland so that Germany would appear to the world as the only barrier obstructing the westward extension of Communism. Lenin, on the other hand, had the ambition of nurturing the embryonic revolutionary forces in Germany and believed that the Red Army's task was to destroy the wall separating Soviet Russia from revolutionary Germany, that wall being Poland.

As the German forces moved out and back westwards during the last weeks of 1918 and early 1919, Red Army troops took over in their place. The Poles immediately objected and on 9 February 1919 a major Polish movement towards the East was started. Russian preoccupation with the civil war limited Red Army reaction and when Lenin, Trotsky and Chicherin made contact with the Polish Government on 28 January 1920, it was to offer them peace proposals based on the lines that the Russian and Polish forces then held. But the Poles suspected that the Russians, while proposing peace, were preparing a counter-offensive. In fact Lenin did wish to dispose of the Poles, as he feared it was they who would keep the war going. 'All the signs are that Poland will present to us conditions which are absolutely impossible to fulfil and even brazenly so,' he wrote to Trotsky on 27 February.

On 1 March 1920 he spoke to the First All-Russian Congress of Working Cossacks and commented on the danger. After rejecting a war on account of frontiers, he added that the Russia of the Soviet Revolution would be defended 'to our last drop of blood'. Shortly afterwards, on 11 March, he warned Trotsky:

'Five thousand French officers have arrived in Poland: Foch is expected and there is little chance of avoiding war. Our systemically peace-loving attitude is proving to the Polish masses that they have no call to fear us, but menaces will be employed by the imperialists in order to spoil the mood of the masses which is well-disposed towards us. But adequate military preparations are absolutely essential. We must be prepared for the very worst.'

The very worst began on 24 April when the Poles launched an attack with ten infantry and four cavalry divisions on the Russians south of the Pripet River. Kiev was occupied on 7 May and the Poles seemed to be sweeping all before them.

In mid-May the situation was transformed – partly by Lenin's decision to carry the war into Poland since he mistakenly believed that Polish workers in Warsaw would rise in support of the Bolsheviks when the Red Army approached the city; partly by the appointment of General Tukhachevsky, the former tsarist officer who eventually became one of the Red Army's most successful and flamboyant commanders.

The decision to march on Warsaw coincided with the Second Congress of the Comintern which, as E. H. Carr has remarked, 'imparted to the military campaign a distinctively revolutionary fervour which made it unlike any other war in Soviet history'.

From the start Lenin took a direct personal interest in the campaign, following it with, if anything, even more interest than he had followed the other campaigns tearing Russia apart. Victor Serge, a historian of the Revolution, has described him sitting intently in a small room off a grand gold-panelled room that had been specially fitted up for him in the Kremlin:

'A throne had been bundled away here . . . a map of the Polish front was displayed on the wall. The rattle of type-writers filled the air. Lenin, jacketed, briefcase under arm, delegates and typists all round him, was giving his views on the march of Tukhachevsky's army on Warsaw. He was in excellent spirits, and confident of victory. Karl Radek, thin, monkey-like, sardonic and droll, hitched up his over-size trousers (which were always slipping down over his hips), and added: "We shall be ripping up the Versailles Treaty with our bayonets!" '

When it seemed that at any moment Warsaw would fall to the Reds, 'Lenin was the most enthusiastic cheer-leader, positioning himself daily in front of his map to give the foreign delegates his comments on Tukhachevsky's advance.'

It has been claimed that the most surprising of all the features of the Polish campaign was the enthusiasm of the soldiers of the Red Army.

Minsk, Wilno and Grodno fell to the Russians in quick succession in July. The advance under Tukhachevsky continued and it must have seemed to Lenin and his colleagues in Moscow that the fall of Warsaw was only a matter of time. However, the strength of Polish nationalism now began to be felt. The further the Russians penetrated into Polish territory, the less effective became their propaganda with the population. Whatever attractions Bolshevism had offered were increasingly counterbalanced by the fears of Russia taking over Polish territory. This nationalist sentiment was reinforced by the vigour of the Polish leader Pilsudski, who also played on the anti-Bolshevik feelings of the Supreme War Council, then meeting in Belgium, and obtained its approval for the move to Warsaw of a Franco-British mission including General Weygand, one of France's most influential soldiers.

While the battle was continuing, Lloyd George offered to act as mediator and proposed an armistice along a line subsequently named after the British Foreign Minister, Lord Curzon. The Poles rejected the proposal, their reason becoming clear later in the summer when they advanced to occupy twice the territory that the Curzon Line would have given them.

Lenin and his colleagues learned the outcome of Weygand's mission on the evening of 17 August. The Poles had not only halted what had already become the Russian threat to Warsaw but had launched a major offensive. Lenin's reaction was typical. 'Now that the Poles have gone over to the attack along the *whole* line we must not snivel . . . for that is ridiculous,' he wrote. 'We must devise a *counter-move;* military measures (flanking movement, holding up *all* negotiations, etc.).' The following day he reinforced his convictions, writing to Ivar Tennisovich Smilga, member of the Revolutionary Council of the Republic and Deputy Chairman of the Supreme Economic Council: 'The advance of the Poles makes it very important for us to increase our pressure, if only for a few days. Do all that is possible; issue an order to the troops, if you think it useful, saying that by multiplying their efforts tenfold now they will secure for Russia advantageous terms for a peace for many years ahead.'

But by this time Polish military prowess was being allied with French military genius and the result was met only by a Russian failure of organization. Within a few days the disengagement that Tukhachevsky had been forced to order was turned into a rout. The Poles took 66,000 prisoners and 231 guns, making almost inevitable Tukhachevsky's failure to halt the Russian retreat further south the following month. By the beginning of October the Poles had reconquered most of the territory they had occupied in 1919 and then been forced to give up.

Lenin now realized that he was not, as yet, able to bring Bolshevism to Poland. The Poles consolidated their position as an independent nation and an armistice worked out at Riga on 12 October was followed by a peace treaty between the two countries signed on 18 March 1921.

The war with Poland brought the Bolsheviks one benefit despite the defeat administered by the Poles. Poland had been a traditional enemy of Russia, and the Polish invasion encouraged into the Red Army a number of tsarist officers who had previously resisted the Bolshevik claim that by serving in it they would be serving the best interests of Russia. But as with Brest-Litovsk, the peace treaty with the Poles engendered anguished discussion as to whether Russia had been justified in signing it. Lenin put his point of view when he spoke to Clara Zetkin.

'I myself believe [he said] that our position did not force us to make peace at any price. We could have held out over the winter. But I thought it wiser, from a political standpoint, to come to terms with the enemy; and the temporary sacrifice of a hard peace appeared to me preferable to a continuation of the war. The pacifist catchwords of the Poles and their friends – all imperialists – are, of course, tricks, nothing but tricks. They are looking to Wrangel. But we shall use the peace with Poland to throw all our forces against Wrangel and to defeat him so completely that he will for ever leave us in peace. In the present situation Soviet Russia can only win if it shows by its attitude that it carries on war only to defend itself, to protect the revolution; that it is the only great country of peace in the world; that it has no intention whatever to seize land, suppress nations, or enter upon an imperialist adventure. But, above all, ought we, unless absolutely and literally compelled, to have exposed the Russian people to the terror and suffering of another winter of war? Our heroic Red soldiers at the fronts, our workers and peasants, who have suffered and endured so much: Another winter of war, after the years of the imperialist war and of the civil war, when millions would starve, would freeze, and die, desperately silent. Food and clothes are already scarce. The workers are complaining, the peasants murmuring that we are only taking away from them and giving them nothing . . . No; the thought of the agonies of another winter of war was unbearable. We had to make peace.'

As Lenin spoke, Zetkin has written, 'his face shrunk before my eyes. Furrows, great and small, innumerable, engraved themselves deeply on it. And every furrow was drawn by a grave trouble or a gnawing pain. An expression of unspoken and unspeakable suffering was on his face.'

It was not only the outcome of Russo-Polish relations which affected Lenin during this period. As happened only rarely, personal affairs now intruded on his public life, and to an extent that could not be concealed. Early in 1920 Inessa Armand, who had continued to work in a variety of Bolshevik posts, travelled to the Caucasus with her son. When she fell ill, Lenin was quick to write to the administrator of the Caucasian health resorts, asking for the best possible treatment for her. A further letter asked for a personal inspection of her accommodation. Despite all Lenin's hopes, she died of cholera, on 24 September. Her body was brought back to Moscow for burial and Lenin asked Angelica Balabanov to speak at her funeral. Balabanov later said (to Bertram D. Wolfe):

'He was utterly broken by her death . . . I did not want to speak because I did not feel close to her nor really know her well. Yet I did not want to refuse. Fortunately, at the last moment, Kollontai arrived, and delivered a moving address.

621

I cast sidelong glances at Lenin. He was plunged in despair, his cap down over his eyes; small as he was, he seemed to shrink and grow smaller. He looked pitiful and broken in spirit. I never saw him look like that before. It was something more than the loss of a "good Bolshevik" or a good friend. He had lost some one very dear and very close to him and made no effort to conceal it.'

By the end of 1920 General Wrangel's forces, driven into the Crimea, had at last been forced to leave even that toe-hold on Russian territory. To Lenin and the commissars in the Kremlin it must have seemed that they could now devote all their energies to dealing with the disastrous economic situation into which the country was still slipping with increasing speed. Before this was possible, however, it became necessary to deal with a full-scale revolt which was no part of the civil war but which forms an epilogue to it and which played its part in making more plausible and respectable the ideological retreats of the NEP which were to help change the face of Russian industry and agriculture over the next few years.

The revolt was in Kronstadt, a rising of Bolshevik against Bolshevik, whose effective but brutal suppression caused Lenin much heart-searching. Publicly, however, he made few comments on it, only saying to an American journalist, 'Believe me, only two kinds of government are possible in Russia: tsarist or soviet. Some fools and traitors at Kronstadt have been talking about a Constituent Assembly. But surely nobody with any common sense can even imagine a Constituent Assembly under the abnormal conditions in Russia today.'

It must have been particularly galling to Lenin that it was the sailors from Kronstadt, men from units that had provided some of the revolutionary shock troops in the July days, and again in the autumn of 1917, who now turned against the Government they had helped create. Lying on the six-mile by three-mile island of Kotlin in the Gulf of Finland only a few miles from Petrograd, Kronstadt had been founded as a fortress and port by Peter the Great in 1703. Its defensive strength had been increased by a number of artillery batteries built on rocky islands in the Gulf and was further reinforced by the forts of Sestroretsk and Lisy Nos on the northern coast of the Baltic and by two others, Oranienbaum and Krasnaya Gorka, on the southern coast. During the first weeks of 1921 Kronstadt's community, in touch with the rest of the world only by sea except for the few winter months when ice linked the island with the Baltic coast, comprised a naval garrison and its auxiliaries totalling about 50,000 men and women, half soldiers and sailors, half civilians.

Contact was maintained with Petrograd, and the Kronstadt garrison was well informed about the deteriorating food situation on the mainland. Towards the end of February 1921 this led to a wave of strikes in Petrograd, the imposition of martial law, and the setting-up of special units to counter what were described as counter-revolutionary movements. On 26 February, a delegation of civilians and sailors crossed the ice from Kronstadt to the mainland to investigate what was really happening in Petrograd. They returned disillusioned and reported the following day to a meeting on the battleship *Petropavlovsk*. The shock of finding the food shortage so desperate in Petrograd added to political discontent, which had sprung from earlier attempts by Trotsky and Zinoviev to exercise control over the Russian navy, and to the increasingly strict censorship over speech and the press operated by the local soviet.

All this provided fuel for an anti-Government outburst which began with a meeting of some 15,000 sailors and workers in the island's Anchor Square on 1 March. Mikhail Ivanovich Kalinin, head of the city of Petrograd until he had replaced Sverdlov as Chairman of the Soviet Central Executive Committee on the latter's death in 1919, flew to Kotlin and addressed the potentially rebellious assembly, as did N. Kuzmin, Commissar of the Baltic Fleet. Neither of the Government spokesmen was acceptable to the Kronstadters, who the following day formed a fourteen-man revolutionary committee headed by Stepan Maksimovich, a senior clerk on the battleship *Petropavlovsk*, which now became the headquarters for what developed into a full-scale mutiny.

Kuzmin was arrested by the Kronstadters who issued a set of demands for political reform which struck at the requisitioning and similar steps taken by the Government during the previous two years. The Government replied by sending over Kronstadt aircraft which dropped leaflets saying that hostages had been taken on the mainland. Yet even there the Government had only mixed support and Emma Goldman, the veteran American anarchist, later reported a Petrograd meeting at which one worker stood up and said:

'Barely three years ago, Lenin, Trotsky and Zinoviev and all of you were denounced as traitors and German spies. We, the workers and sailors, had to come to your rescue and saved you from the Kerensky Government. It is we who placed you in power. Have you forgotten that? Now you threaten us with the sword. Remember you are playing with fire. You are repeating the blunders and crimes of the Kerensky Government. Beware that a similar fate does not overtake you!'

Even then it might still have been possible to avert the tragedy for the Kronstadters and for the Bolshevik cause which was to follow. However, on 2 March the Petrograd Committee of Defence was ordered to stamp out the festering Kronstadt revolt and two days later the Petrograd Soviet flatly defined it as counter-revolutionary and called for immediate surrender.

Confrontation was now inevitable and a delegation from Kronstadt crossed the ice to Oranienbaum and persuaded members of the First Naval Air Squadron stationed there to join them. Success was short-lived: Government troops quickly intervened after the bulk of the Kronstadters had left and then executed many of the dissidents who had remained at Oranienbaum.

By now it had become essential to Lenin, and to Trotsky as well as other Soviet commissars, that the Kronstadt challenge to their authority should be decisively beaten. It was not an easy task, and would have been more difficult still if the island of Kotlin had not been surrounded by winter ice still thick enough to bear troops. Preparations went on throughout the first days of March and on 8 March Red Army troops, clad in white overalls, made their first assault from bases on the mainland. Their advance had to be made across the open ice, bare of any protection, and at most places they were driven back with heavy losses. Some 25,000 Red Army troops were later claimed to have been used in the assault but they took only one Kronstadt fort and that was recaptured the following day. It was evident that more preparation was necessary. It had, furthermore, to be made against time, since the start of the spring thaw was imminent and once the ice began to melt Kronstadt would become almost impregnable.

The assault came at last on 17 March, made by around 50,000 men and preceded by an artillery bombardment that did not succeed in totally silencing the Kronstadt defences. This time, however, the Red Army finally fought its way on to the island

and began what was to be a desperate street-by-street advance through the naval base. Resistance lasted until the afternoon of 18 March. The Government admitted casualties of 700 dead and 2,500 wounded while the Kronstadters lost 600 killed, 1,000 wounded and 2,500 taken prisoner. Other estimates put total casualties as high as 10,000. They would certainly have been higher had not many defenders escaped over the ice to the mainland and found refuge in Finland. Those from Kronstadt who survived there helped to spread the news of what had happened, adding graphically to the details published in the daily paper which appeared on the island between 3 and 16 March.

Yet if it was the Kronstadt uprising which became notorious throughout Russia, and indeed throughout the world, there were other lesser-known outbreaks of discontent which were overshadowed into obscurity only by the circumstances and drama of the assault mounted against the famous base. The fuel on Kronstadt had been set alight, but similar fuel had accumulated elsewhere in Russia and in more than one place had already blazed up on account of locally intolerable conditions.

Nor was this all. Lenin was incontrovertibly the great instigator of the NEP but something very similar had been proposed by Trotsky roughly a year earlier when it had been turned down by the Party's Central Committee and had even won criticism from Lenin himself. Trotsky's account *in My Life,* written in the late 1920s after Lenin's death, makes the most of his own contribution to affairs, as does much else in his story, but it should not be ignored.

'My practical work [he wrote] had satisfied me that the methods of war communism forced on us by the conditions of civil war were completely exhausted, and that to revive our economic life the element of personal interest must be

626

introduced at all costs; in other words, we had to restore the home market in some degree. I submitted to the Central Committee the project of replacing the food levy by a grain-tax and of restoring the exchange of commodities.'

In essence this was similar to the heart of the NEP, which Lenin announced at the Tenth Party Congress even while the Kronstadt assault was being prepared. The mutiny certainly did not bring about the new policy although it did emphasize, if emphasis were required (which in general it was not), the need for radical reorganization of Russia's economic policies if the country were not to slip even further into agricultural and industrial crisis.

But if the need for what became the NEP was highlighted by the dramatic assault on the naval base, it had been increasingly difficult to camouflage from the start of 1920 onwards. Successive peasant protests and revolts in areas as far apart as the Ukraine, western Siberia and the northern Caucasus, and insurrections – for some were nothing less – broke out, which at times threatened to cut off entirely central Russia's supplies of grain.

These discontents, of which the Kronstadt mutiny was an extreme example, coincided with an escalating conflict between the Government and a number of bodies which had been simmering for some while.

The most important of these was the Workers' Opposition, a group based in the trade unions and organized to resist the centralizing trend in Soviet politics. The Democratic Centralists and the Ignatov Group based on Moscow took the same line but it was the Workers' Opposition, supported by Shlyapnikov, the first Commissar of Labour, and two leaders of the metal workers, Y. K. Lutovinov and S. Medvedev, which quickly became foremost among the dissidents. It was much aided by Aleksandra Kollontay, who could operate with some authority and wrote and spoke enthusiastically on its behalf. It was she who had bluntly put the nub of the argument in *The Workers' Opposition* published early in 1921 – to whom should the Party entrust the construction of the Communist economy? To the Sovnarkom, with all its bureaucratic departments, or to the industrial trade unions?

One of the main objects of the Workers' Opposition was to diminish the influence of the non-proletarians, and at the Tenth Congress of the RCP(B) in 1921 it proposed that every Party member should live and work for three months every year as an ordinary proletarian or peasant, engaged in physical labour, a proposal regarded by Lenin as nothing less than a deviation.

He dealt with the embryonic revolt first in the decree 'On Party Unity', which in practice ruled out any hint of factionalism, and followed it up with a resolution 'On the Syndicalism and Deviation in our Party'. The Tenth Congress passed both decrees and thus effectively clipped the wings of the Workers' Opposition; however, a special commission to investigate its activities was set up at the Eleventh Party Congress. 'A number of facts', this commission concluded, 'establish beyond doubt that an *illegal factional organization* was preserved, and at its head stood the inspirers and leaders, comrades Shliapnikov, Medvedev and Kollontai.' That those thus found 'guilty' were merely reprimanded rather than being expelled from the Party as might have been expected is an indication of the opposition's strength.

At the same time, the opposition was effectively put in its place. That this could happen to an organization which had considerable support in some quarters illustrated the hold – perhaps 'amazing hold' could be justified – that Lenin exerted over the Party and its machinery. Yet although he had demonstrated that he could deal with a political threat as successfully as he had dealt with the military threat from Kronstadt, his economic problems remained.

17

The Fight for Recovery

The Kronstadt mutiny was an indicator not only of political unrest but equally of disquiet at the economic morass into which Russia had been sinking, as a result of the physical pressures produced by more than six years of war and civil war. The mutiny was followed by the introduction and implementation of the New Economic Policy (NEP), that great qualification of Bolshevik principles, which for a while revitalized the economy by diluting communal good with private profit. It is sometimes inferred that the substitution of taxation in kind for forced requisitioning, the heart of the NEP, and all the ancillary changes that accompanied it, were the direct result of the politically jolting if militarily unsuccessful rising of the Kronstadt garrison and its supporters.

The truth is that by the first weeks of 1921 a series of events, set in train many months earlier, was already moving Lenin towards an economic compromise as significant as the military and political compromise of the treaty of Brest-Litovsk.

The need for steps to revitalize the economy, however much such steps might offend the principles on which the Revolution had been based, can be shown by a comparison between Russian industry in 1913 and in 1921. By 1921 large-scale industry was producing only 21 per cent of its 1913 output while the figures for some separate sectors were equally disastrous. Pig-iron production had dropped from 4.2 million tons to 0.1 million, steel from 4.3 million to 0.2 million tons and coal output from 29 million to nine million tons. The agricultural productivity index was 60 per cent of its 1913 value, the index of railway tonnage carried had dropped from 132.4 to 39.4, while the value index for exports had dropped from 1520 to 20. Further, and equally alarming, figures are given in the *League of Nations Report on Economic Conditions in Russia* (Geneva, 1922).

The drop in agricultural output was partly due to peasant disenchantment with the ways in which crops were controlled or confiscated by the authorities, but the position was made worse by a succession of bad harvests, particularly that of 1920 to 1921, an 'act of God' for which the Bolsheviks could not be blamed and which made it easier for well-wishers to appeal for help to countries like the USA. Maxim Gorky wrote to American newspapers and received a reply from Herbert Hoover, Director of Relief for Europe. Gorky responded by sending a formal request for help signed by Kamenev, and in the following months the USA sent 800,000 tons of food and medicines while American families sent thousands of individual food parcels. Of Petrograd's 160,000 children aged between three and fifteen it was later estimated that 150,000 had been fed regularly from American sources.

While much of Russia's disastrous industrial decline was due to the First World War and the civil war, the drop in exports was largely the result of the Allied blockade and the reluctance of much of the world to trade with a Communist government. Overall, there loomed the problem of how best to induce the peasants to produce more food.

If Russia was to be set back on her feet, conditions had to change in many spheres. Crucial among the required changes were the legalization of trading for private profit and the substitution of taxes for confiscation in kind, two features of the NEP which gained most attention both in Russia and outside. But at the same time trade with the detested capitalist countries of the Western world had to be encouraged and this inevitably meant opening up Russia to non-Communist influences. Lenin and many of his colleagues also realized that an amelioration of the Terror, and perhaps even a cosmetic reconstruction of the Cheka, would both encourage Russians to co-operate in implementing the NEP and persuade foreigners that it was worthwhile collaborating industrially with a system and community that they continued to detest and distrust.

Thus the idea of compromise, which lay at the heart of the NEP, was to affect more than the purely economic methods by which Russia tried to draw level with the capitalist world both agriculturally and industrially. What it did not mean was any major and immediate lessening of the burdens which the Russian people had carried for so long. As early as April 1920 Lenin had warned the Third All-Russian Congress of Textile Workers that the unparalleled privations of the last two years were not yet over for the proletariat. It had to achieve unparalleled miracles on the labour front, comparable to those achieved by the Red Army.

But some improvement in conditions could come from the better relations with Europe which became a supplementary aim of the NEP programme. In the autumn of 1919 there had been significant statements from both sides of what Ethel

Snowden, who visited Russia with a Labour Party delegation, was to call in 1920 'the iron curtain' between Russia and the West. On 8 November, Lloyd George had said [in his Guildhall speech at the Lord Mayor's Banquet], 'You cannot have peace until you have peace in Russia.' Even more significantly, Chicherin had stated later in the same month:

'Relations with Russia are quite possible in spite of the profound differences between Britain's and Russia's regime . . . The British customer and purveyor are as necessary to us as we are to them. Not only do we desire peace and the possibility of internal development, but we also feel strongly the need of economic help from the more fully developed countries such as Great Britain . . . I therefore gladly welcome the declaration of the British Premier as the first step towards such a sane and real policy corresponding to the interests of both countries.'

The nub of the NEP, which was soon to be supplemented by such improved Anglo-Soviet relations, had in fact been prophesied two years earlier by Ramsay MacDonald who in *Parliament and Revolution* had written that if Lenin's Government was not destroyed by Allied pressure it might

'modify its position . . . It will abandon its absolute programme; it will recognize that, in order to keep up revolutionary ardour to carry it through its first work, it simplified its problems in its imagination, and brought its Socialist New Earth nearer than it actually was; it will adopt views and methods which it now rejects (it has done some of this already), and it will commence the work of evolutionary

632

revolution and democratic education. The gain of the revolution will then be that it enabled Socialists to acquire the political power necessary for the economic transformation of Society. The Government will return and pick up the threads of social organization where the revolution broke them, and will proceed to carry out a policy of socialization on precisely the same plan as we should do here if a Socialist Party were in power at Westminster.'

The NEP that Lenin introduced at the Tenth Congress of the RCP(B) in March 1921 did not quite do this but it did 'pick up the threads of social organization' to such an extent that it aroused, by its allowance of private enterprise, considerable opposition from the hard-liners in the Party. Its best explanatory defence was perhaps that to be given in one of the notes to Lenin's *Collected Works:* 'The principal task of NEP was to ensure a strong alliance between the working class and the peasantry, as the highest principle of the dictatorship of the proletariat, the basis of the Soviet power.'

The need for such a change had been clear to Lenin even before the start of 1921. Liberman, one of the country's timber experts, capitalist-trained but used to good effect from 1918 onwards, reported to him (apparently in 1920) that hostility was building up in the country, particularly on account of the armed expeditions roaming the countryside in search of food. He was told by Lenin

'I agree with you entirely. We are indeed in need of changes. We must broaden the base of our government. We should introduce economic relaxations and concessions. But don't forget, all you comrades, that the civil war is not quite ended yet. It still makes demands upon us. At Balashov [a railway junction about 175 kilometres from Tambov on the line linking Moscow with Kamyshin on the Volga] a Communist division lost 60 per cent of its men. We cannot begin a retreat in our policy when hundreds and thousands of men continue to fall, continue to give their lives, while holding our banner in their hands. We cannot change our banner in the midst of this battle. The least change will kill our soldiers' enthusiasm. First we must vanquish the forces of counterrevolution, and only then will we begin to think of changes. Right now all of us must strive toward a sensible use of everything and anything that may help us in our fight against the Whites.'

Lenin added, however, that some of the timber expert's suggestions would be adopted and a few days later, Liberman claims, 'it became known that the Commissariat of Food Supply had issued instructions to its officials to allow a certain easing-up in the demands made upon the peasants for their grain and other produce.'

Not everyone in Russia approved of the relaxations, and when Liberman later reported the conversation he had had with Lenin to Martov, the Menshevik leader, he was faced with a protest. 'How dared he answer you like that!' Martov is said to have replied. 'This means that he sends Russian workers to die in battle for the slogans which he doesn't mean to keep!'

On 8 February, at a meeting of the Politburo which discussed the spring sowing campaign, Lenin wrote the rough draft of 'Theses concerning the Peasants'. This was, according to a note in his *Collected Works*, 'the first document defining the new economic foundation of the workers' and peasants' alliance, charting the transition from War Communism to the New Economic Policy'. It included the following four points.

'1. Satisfy the wish of the non-Party peasants for the substitution of a tax in kind for the surplus appropriation system (the confiscation of surplus grain stocks). 2. Reduce the size of this tax as compared with last year's appropriation rate. 3. Approve the principle of making the tax commensurate with the farmer's effort, reducing the rate for those making the greater effort. 4. Give the farmer more leeway in using his after-tax surpluses in local trade, provided his tax is promptly paid up in full.'

This was to become the basis for the draft resolution adopted by the Tenth RCP(B) Congress on 15 March 1921 on the substitution of a tax in kind for the surplus appropriation system.

On 11 February *Pravda* had printed what it is difficult to believe was not a 'planted' letter from a peasant saying that the State would benefit from such a change. 'In this way', the writer said, 'the Government will obtain a good deal more [so far it has got only uprisings] and the peasants will be content and will produce more.'

Three days later, Lenin received a peasant delegation from the Tambov area where there had already been more than one peasant revolt. According to Boris Levytsky 'The peasants asked him to stop the requisitioning of food, and Lenin actually tried to comply with their request. The peasants' rising soon convinced him that a new land policy was a crucial necessity for the Bolsheviks.' Whether or not the visitors had as much influence as Levytsky believes, within a few days Lenin had written 'The Integrated Economic Plan' which was published in *Pravda* on 22 February. What was needed, he said, was less intellectual and bureaucratic complacency and a deeper scrutiny of practical experience and of the available achievements of science.

Lenin's plans for a major economic shake-up were now well under way and before the end of February the replacement of compulsory grain deliveries by a tax in kind, demobilization of the army and oil concessions, were discussed at meetings of the Central Committee. At roughly the same time Lenin spoke to a peasant, I. A. Chekunov, who told him that the peasants had lost confidence in soviet power. 'I asked him', he said, 'whether we could right things with a tax. He thinks we could. This is the kind of people we must *do our utmost* to hold on to, in order to restore the confidence of the peasant *mass*. This is the *main* political task.' And he was soon putting the final touches to 'The Tax in Kind', a pamphlet partly inspired by the State-controlled German war economy.

The upshot of all these thoughts and discussions was that by the time the Tenth Congress of the RCP(B) opened on 8 March, Lenin had prepared the ground for changes which he knew were necessary and which he knew equally well could raise the hackles of dedicated Communist theorists however much they might be welcomed by a majority of Russians. Nearly 1,000 delegates representing 732,000 members attended this vital Congress at which the transition from War Communism to the NEP would be outlined. To them, Lenin both defended the introduction of the existing system in 1917 and stressed the need for change.

'The truth is that the system which we have now was dictated not by economic but by purely military consider-ations [he emphasized]. In the conditions of unheard of ruin in which we found ourselves we had, after being engaged in a great and devastating foreign war, to wage a whole series of civil wars. It is necessary to admit that we made many mistakes and many exaggerations in carrying out our policy. But in the actual war conditions this policy was essentially correct. We simply had no alternative save to make the maximum use of State monopoly even to the point of seizing the entire surplus (of produce) without giving any compensation. We could not do anything else. But that does not mean that this was a symmetrical economic system. It was a system adopted under the dictation not of economic but of war conditions. The only economic consideration at present is to increase the amount of products in the country. We find ourselves in conditions of such impoverishment, ruin, weariness, and exhaustion of the chief productive forces – peasants and workers – that to this prime consideration, the increase at any price of the amount of products, we have to sacrifice everything . . .'

Lenin was adept at putting such justifications for the NEP's compromises in simple words not only to the Congress but also to colleagues. In his opening address to the Congress he said: 'Comrades, the question of replacing requisitions with a tax [in kind] is first of all and above all a political question, for the essence of this question is the relationship of the working class to the peasantry.' And to Angelica Balabanov he said of the NEP: 'You know very well that this was necessary. Russia would not have resisted otherwise.'

One of the relatively few enthusiastic supporters of the changes which Lenin saw as essential was Leonid Krasin who during the arguments which took place before the NEP changes became law stated to the Central Committee:

'All the evils and hardships we are suffering now are due to the fact that the Communist Party consists of ten per cent of convinced idealists, ready to die for the cause, but incapable of living for it, and ninety per cent of unscrupulous time-servers who have simply joined the Party so as to get jobs. It is useless and hopeless to try and persuade the ten per cent fanatics of the necessity for this NEP, so I will appeal to the other ninety per cent, and I give them a fair warning that if they do not want the Russian masses to do to them what they did to the Tsar's people, they must throw overboard impracticable day-dreams and they must be prepared to face economic laws. The gospel according to Karl Marx is not the be-all and end-all of wisdom.'

As for fears that the NEP marked the beginning of the end for the great changes brought in by the Revolution, Lenin unequivocally dismissed them in (among other documents) a letter of November 1922, to the members of the Russian colony in North America, estimated to number roughly 3 million in the early 1920s. 'The New Economic Policy', he stressed to them, 'has changed nothing radically in the social system of Soviet Russia, nor can it change anything so long as the power is in the hands of the workers – and that Soviet power has come to stay, no one now, I think, can have any doubt.' Lenin was ready to admit that under the NEP there would be some growth of capitalism. But he was quick to maintain that in the manner in which it would be allowed to grow it would be harmless:

'Of course, freedom of trade means the growth of capitalism. If there are small enterprises, if there is freedom of exchange – capitalism will appear. But is this capitalism dangerous to us, if we keep in our hands the factories, the transportation system and foreign trade? I believe that this capitalism is not dangerous to us . . . Is state capitalism dangerous to us? No, because we will decide in what measure we shall grant concessions.'

It was not only economic necessity that had called for the new system. Lenin admitted:

'Don't let us make any mistake. The peasants are dissatisfied with their present relationship to the State, and so it cannot continue. That is certain. The mind of the peasants is now made up. It is the mind of the overwhelming number of the toiling masses. We have to take notice of this, and we are sufficiently realists to say straight out, "Let us revise our policy towards the peasants" . . . Why do we propose to abolish requisitioning? Because we must give back to the small-holder a stimulus, an incentive, and a push. The small-holder will then be able to be industrious in his own interests; for he will be sure that only a portion of his surplus will be taken from him and not the entire amount. The main thing is to give him an incentive, a stimulus, and a push . . . It is necessary to say to the smallholder, "You are the master. Go on producing stuff and the State will take only a minimum tax from you." '

The most important result of the change was the end of the State monopoly of grain; much would flow from this and many of those in the Government's Food Department were sceptical of what would happen. No doubt some were influenced by the fact that their powers would be lessened, but there were genuine doubts about the overall benefits of the proposed new system, and they were forcibly presented by M. I. Frumkin, one of the senior officials in the Food Department, who maintained that

'In abandoning the monopoly of grain we are abandoning the possibility of controlling its distribution. This will be ruinous to the workers. We cannot tell whether we shall be able to improve our financial position. But one thing is clear already, that the workers and the Soviet employees will have nothing to offer the peasants in exchange for grain. They have already lost their last shirt. And if we are going to pay them with paper money I don't see what they have got to barter with. They will have to give up not only their last paper money but their last skin, too . . . If we must abandon many things we can still refrain from adopting State Capitalism, a mysterious Capitalism without bourgeoisie.'

This was a mild way of putting what many Bolsheviks felt more forcibly. They had many sympathizers, some of them unexpected. It was Churchill who wrote of Lenin's introduction of the NEP: 'He repudiated what he had slaughtered so many for not believing. They were right it seemed after all. They were unlucky that he did not find it out before.'

The objections of Frumkin and those who supported him were overruled. The Congress approved the basis of Lenin's NEP and shortly afterwards the new tax was formalized by a decree of the All-Russian Soviet Executive Committee which said:

'From now on, by decision of the All-Russian Soviet Executive Committee and the Council of People's Commissars, requisitioning is abolished and a tax in kind on agricultural products is introduced instead . . . After the tax has been paid what remains with the peasant is left at his full disposal . . . Every peasant must now know and remember that the more land he plants the greater will be the surplus of grain which remains in his complete possession.'

The change was further formalized and expanded the following year when in May 1922 a decree recognized in effect the right of the peasant to treat his holding as his own, to lease his land as he wished, and if necessary hire labour to work it.

Lenin was well aware of the likely reactions both to the NEP and to the other innovations that accompanied it; as might have been expected, he had answers ready. And when told of the joke that Russia under the NEP was a man on crutches, he replied: 'Russia was battered for seven years, and thank God we *can* get about on crutches.'

His firm grasp of the need for the changes was made clear in his article published in *Pravda* on 31 October 1921:

'Self-interest will develop production and we must first develop production at all costs . . . Not directly relying on enthusiasm, but aided by the enthusiasm born of the great revolution, and on the basis of self-interest, personal benefit and business principles, you must set to work in this small-peasant country to build solid little bridges leading to socialism by way of state capitalism . . . the idea that we can build communism by the hands of pure communists, without the assistance of bourgeois experts, is childish . . . Socialism cannot be built unless advantage is taken of the heritage of capitalist culture . . . The bourgeois experts must be so encompassed by organized, creative and harmonious work that they will be compelled to fall in line with the proletariat, no matter how much they resist and fight at every step.'

But the introduction of the NEP – with whatever dilution of Bolshevik principles – was not the only innovation of the Tenth Congress. It was here that, as it was afterwards popularly described, Lenin 'put the lid on opposition'. Until now the Party had, as he maintained, allowed itself the luxury of engaging in serious disputes; these had tended to increase as living conditions worsened and, it could be claimed, had burst out in sporadic peasant rebellions and what was, for the Party, the disastrous Kronstadt mutiny. All that, Lenin demanded, almost in the same breath in which he announced the NEP, must be relegated to the past. 'We cannot', he said, 'have arguments about deviations and . . . we must put a stop to that.' Unity, discipline and restraint were what was needed and they were soon to become the hallmarks of the faithful. To give muscle to the policy, he proposed the motion 'On Party Unity', unanimously adopted, which ordered the immediate dissolution of all factions and groups. To show that these were no idle words the Congress authorized the Central Committee to expel those who engaged in such activity from the Party, if really necessary.

While the implementation of the NEP brought differences to the surface which were deeply felt by the theoretical hard-liners in the Party and others closely concerned with the running of the country, there were other comparable issues on which Lenin had been forced to adjudicate since the autumn of 1917. One was the status of Proletcult, a cultural and educational organization set up in September 1917 independently of the State and whose chief ideologist was Bogdanov. The ambivalent official view about its status can be inferred from a note in Lenin's

Collected Works: 'In addition to bourgeois intellectuals, who held leading positions in many of its organizations, the membership [of Proletcult] included young workers who sincerely wished to promote cultural progress in the Soviet State.'

The basic differences between Bogdanov, who wanted the organization to be independent, and Lenin, who wanted it to be a State element of popular education, were partly resolved when Lenin drafted a decree which was approved by the Central Committee. This laid it down that

> 'The work of Proletcult in the field of scientific and political education merges with that of the People's Commissariat for Education and the Gubernia Education Departments, while in the artistic field (music, the theatre, fine arts, and literature), it remains autonomous, and the leading role of the commissariat's organs, carefully screened by the R.C.P., is to be retained only for combating patently bourgeois deviations.'

Thus, although Proletcult was abolished in 1923, it managed to drag out its life owing to one of Lenin's characteristic compromises.

Adherence to the new ideas laid down by the Party was necessary if the NEP were to succeed. The country in general and the peasants in particular had to co-operate, and Lenin used every subtle argument within his power to persuade workers of the NEP's justification, both moral and practical. On one occasion he said:

> 'The capitalist is operating by your side. He is operating like a robber, he makes a profit, but he is skilful. But you – you

are trying to do it in a new way: you do not make any profit; your communist principles, your ideals are excellent, they are written out so beautifully that you deserve to be living saints in heaven – but can you do business?'

But in addition to the internal changes and adjustments essential to the success of the NEP there was also the international side of Lenin's plan for economic recovery. He was certain that what Russia required was a lengthy period during which her technical and organizational machinery could be made more nearly equal in efficiency with that of Europe. This, he realized, would demand a process that Russia would not be able to carry through on her own. She would require the co-operation of at least some capitalist countries, which further incensed those for whom the ideas of the NEP were a form of treason to the Communist cause.

It was fortuitous, therefore, although symbolic, that on the day following Lenin's announcement of the NEP plans to the Tenth Congress, an Anglo-Soviet trade agreement was signed in London, for which at least some of the credit should go to the tactful work of Litvinov. The signing of the agreement was only an early step leading towards an understanding between two strikingly different commercial outlooks but it was a very necessary one and, Lenin was convinced, only the first of many to follow. Early in 1922 he told a Congress of Metal Workers:

'Do not forget that in recent years the most urgent, daily, practical and obvious interests of all the capitalist powers have demanded the development, consolidation and expansion of trade with Russia. And since such interests exist, we can argue, quarrel, break off negotiations on some

644

issues . . . but in the end, basic economic necessity will force its way. We are quite sure on that score. We cannot be sure of the time . . . but we can confidently predict here that progress will be made.'

It was not only an increase in straight trade arrangements that was called for. George Kennan has written of the situation after the introduction of the NEP:

'[It] cried out, in particular, for investment capital, and this could not easily be created or provided by a continuation of the wartime methods. The only visible alternative was a policy of concessions to private initiative, in agriculture and industry, designed to free resources then being concealed or withheld from the economy, and to enlist the initiative of the peasant and of the private investor in the process of economic reconstruction. Reluctandy, but manfully and with resolution, Lenin recognized the necessity of such a course, and sponsored it.'

This was underlined in a telegram which Lenin sent to the Georgian Ordzhonikidze on 5 April 1921 asking whether the German owners of the Chiatura manganese mines had been turned into lessees or concessionaires: 'It is extremely important that there should be the quickest possible decisions on these and similar questions, it is of enormous significance both for Georgia and for Russia, for concessions are absolutely essential, especially with Italy and Germany, as also is goods exchange on a large scale with these countries in return for oil and later with others too.' He admitted that such agreements involved a certain retreat from what appeared to be an advance towards the goal of socialism.

This, he said, was a regrettable necessity – a single step backward, in order to make possible two steps forward at a later stage.

Almost forty years earlier, when the split between the Bolsheviks and the Mensheviks had been tearing the Social-Democrats apart, Lenin had bowed to the policy of taking one step back in order to prepare for two forward. The success of the manoeuvre had not been lost upon him.

His attitude to foreign concessions, which he had to defend against the attacks of his more ideologically rigid comrades, was exemplified in a letter to Washington B. Vanderlip, an American who had been seeking oil concessions in Kamchatka.

'I thank you for your kind letter of the 14th & am very glad to hear of President Harding's favourable views as to our trade with America. You know what value we attach to our future American business relations. We fully recognize the part played in this respect by your syndicate & also the great importance of your personal efforts. Your new proposals are highly interesting & I have asked the Supreme Council of National Economy to report to me at short intervals about the progress of the negotiations. You can be sure that we will treat every reasonable suggestion with the greatest attention & care. It is on production & trade that our efforts are principally concentrated & your help is to us of the greatest value.'

It was an omen of things to come that Lenin ended his letter with the comment: 'The Congress of the Communist Party has taken so much of my time & forces that I am very tired & ill. Will you kindly excuse me if I am unable to have an interview with you just now. I will beg Comrade Chicherin to speak with you shortly. Wishing you much success . . .'

Lenin adopted a comparable attitude when he considered similar commercial relations. He had told a Moscow Party conference in November 1920 that

> 'So long as we remain, from the economic and military standpoint, weaker than the capitalist world, so long we must stick to the rule: we must be clever enough to utilize the contradictions and oppositions among the imperialists . . . Politically we must utilize the conflicts among our adversaries which are explained by the most profound economic causes . . .'

He was well aware of the built-in dangers of contamination as he emphasized when he spoke at the Eighth All-Russian Congress of Soviets in December 1920 of the negotiations already going on with Britain.

> 'I must say [he reported] that this trade agreement with Great Britain is connected with one of the most important questions in our economic policy, that of concessions . . . We do not in the least close our eyes to the dangers this policy presents to the Socialist Soviet Republic, a country that, moreover, is weak and backward. While our Soviet Republic remains the isolated borderland of the capitalist world, it would be absolutely ridiculous, fantastic and Utopian to hope that we can achieve complete economic independence and that all dangers will vanish. Of course, as long as the radical contrasts remain, the dangers will also remain, and there is no escaping them. What we have to do is to get firmly on our feet in order to survive these dangers; we must

be able to distinguish between big dangers and little dangers, and incur the lesser dangers rather than the greater.'

The change of stance in 1921 was noted in the West and one result of the NEP was that countries which had so far registered only shock at Bolshevik economic policies now began to feel that it would be possible to make trade contacts with Russia without being ideologically endangered. The feeling was reinforced as it became evident that Russia would survive as a trading nation and as the new Russian Government's practice of trying to export its ideologies together with its physical products seemed to be wavering. In fact, as Lenin emphasized in connection with the NEP, changes were of emphasis rather than of objectives and were tactical rather than strategic. If Lenin saw this as a development without any serious danger of diluting the purity of Communist beliefs or practice, a comparable attitude was sometimes taken in Europe. The grounds for optimism had been laid when the Allied Supreme Council ended the blockade of Soviet Russia in 1920. The move would, according to a British Foreign Office document, provide 'a limited opportunity of testing the theory frequently advanced of late that the lifting of the blockade would do more to oust or modify Bolshevism than armed intervention ever accomplished'. Lloyd George struck much the same note when he stated in the House of Commons on 10 February 1920: 'We have failed to restore Russia to sanity by force. I believe we can save her by trade. Commerce has a sobering influence in its operations. The simple sums in addition and subtraction which it inculcates soon dispose of wild theories.'

The remark was perhaps almost as ingenuous as the comments of George Lansbury, the British socialist leader, who telegraphed from Moscow to Lloyd George that the Bolshevik leaders were 'first-rate, clear headed honest humane men' who were 'doing what Christians call the Lord's work', and who added for good measure that Lenin's devotion to the cause of humanity made his whole life like 'that of one of the saints of old'.

If Lloyd George could not go quite so far, he was soon saying that opponents of the projected Anglo-Russian trade agreement would find that Lenin was

'a man after his own heart if he has only a little patience, if he does a little business with him, a little trading, a little interchange of commodities. The moment they begin to realize they cannot run their country except upon the same principles which have brought prosperity to other countries, they will begin to realize that the only way to bring prosperity to Russia is to put an end to their wild schemes.'

Lloyd George was a key figure in the process by which Russia was eventually brought into a working relationship with the Western world. This was partly due to his respect for Lenin's ability, partly to his political appreciation that the ideological modifications to be embodied in the NEP would have to come sooner or later, beliefs implied in a comment recorded in Lord Riddell's diary of the Versailles peace conference. 'L.G. said that Lenin is the biggest man in politics,' Riddell wrote on 30 May 1920. 'He had conceived and carried out a great economic experiment. It looked as if it were a failure. If so, Lenin was a big enough man to confess the truth and face it. He would modify his plans and govern Russia by other methods.' Thus both in Russia and in the capitalist countries events were being driven – although by very different motivations – towards an opening of trade relations which was to be regarded with equal suspicion by the diehard Communists in Russia who disliked the direction in which Lenin was moving, and the diehard conservatives in Europe who disliked equally the tendencies exemplified by Lloyd George.

While the Anglo-Russian Trade Agreement was the first open acknowledgement by Lenin's Russia that the advantages of trade with the capitalists outweighed the ideological stigma of dealing with them, it had been preceded by important negotiations with their earlier enemies, the Germans. Both sides were anxious to keep from public scrutiny negotiations which were, in some ways, a counterpart to political changes. The secrecy was natural enough, since the aim of the negotiations was the building in Russia of arms and aircraft. Under the treaty of Versailles, signed by the Allies and Germany after the end of the First World War, Germany was forbidden to build an air force and her manufacture of arms was strictly limited. The Russians, for their part, had built few planes during the civil war; the number of workers in their aircraft factories had dropped from 10,000 to less than 3,500, and the level of their skills had decreased correspondingly. What would therefore be more mutually beneficial than an arrangement by which the Germans would build aircraft and arms in conditions not covered by the treaty of Versailles and that the Russians would learn from their skills and experience? It was with such a scheme in mind that two men had met for tentative talks as early as the spring of 1920. One was Trotsky, the other the German General von Seekt, who, after the defeat of 1918, had given himself the task of rebuilding Germany's military effectiveness.

Russia's Aviation Research Institute was created in September 1920 and a few months later Lenin personally ordered the setting up of a commission charged with working out in detail an aircraft construction programme for the next ten years. The convergence of German and Russian incentives meant that before the end of 1922 350 German aircraft engineers were working in Russia, many of them at a modern aircraft factory created by Professor Hugo Junkers at Fili near Moscow, and a number of German officer cadets were training in Russia, some of them wearing Russian uniforms. Only a few months later, plans for military collaboration were drawn up by the Soviet Politburo and the Reichswehr.

While this first commercial agreement between the Russians and capitalists was made and implemented in conditions which demanded no excusatory explanations from either side, the open trade that followed – mainly between Russia and Britain – was a very different matter. Public explanations were necessary on both sides.

The turning point had come on 16 January 1920 when the Allied Supreme Council in Paris declared the blockade of Russia at an end. 'The Allies now understand', Lord Riddell commented in his diary, 'the impossibility of fighting the Bolsheviks in Russia. No nation is prepared to supply troops or money.' Although Riddell was correct, the lifting of the blockade failed to sweep away all suspicions, either Russian or Allied. French and British support for the Poles was already known to be under discussion and Lenin told Lincoln Eyre of New York's The *World* who interviewed him in mid-February: 'It is hard to see sincerity behind so vague a proposal [the ending of the blockade], coupled as it seems to be with preparations to attack us afresh through Poland . . . closer examination convinces us that this Paris decision is simply a move in the Allied chess game, the motives of which are still obscure.' On the Allied side, opinion on the wisdom of developing trade with the Russians was still divided. Curzon and Churchill were foremost among those who believed that no good would come of dealing with Bolsheviks since they were obviously intent on continuing their propaganda attacks on the capitalist system. Lloyd George believed, on the contrary, that trade would help build bridges between the two opposing systems. In the commercial world, Sir Robert Horne, one of the estimated 260 businessmen elected to the House of Commons in the 1918 election, pointed out that before the First World War Russia had supplied Britain with one-eighth of her grain, one-seventh of her butter, half of her eggs and timber and four-fifths of her flax, while Russian purchases of machinery from Britain were exceeded only by those of India. But if this was a good reason for restoring Anglo-Russian trade, there was the question raised by the Association of British Creditors of Russia representing 350,000 British investors whose claims totalled £300 million.

The prospects for Anglo-Russian trade therefore had some similarity with the traditional bottle of whisky, considered half full or half empty according to the eye of the beholder. This being so, it is not surprising that during the first months of 1920 a number of separate British firms had signed individual contracts with Russia. It was, however, not until May 1920 that a Russian delegation headed by Litvinov and Krasin, Commissar for Foreign Trade and later Russian Ambassador in London, began negotiations for an Anglo-Russian Trade Agreement.

Despite the obvious benefits to both sides of any reasonable agreement, discussions went on for many months and it was only on 16 March 1921 that a trade agreement was signed in London by Horne and Krasin. The difficulties had been political rather than commercial: British prisoners were still being held by the Russians in Baku; the Communist International's Third Congress called for more extensive anti-Western propaganda; while Britain's apparent determination to give the Poles whatever support was practicable in their war with the Russians made Krasin's delegation doubtful of what it should do.

After signature of the agreement trade improved but the willingness of the Russians to deal with a capitalist country reinforced the view in many quarters that the NEP was a sign of Communism's failure. Thus, comments in British newspapers and business journals tended to be ambivalent, not only during 1921 but throughout the following year and into 1923. On 19 November 1921 *The Times* reported its belief that Lenin had been persuaded of the failure of Bolshevism and that it was 'only a matter of hitting on a suitable formula to re-introduce the capitalist system into Russia'. The *New Statesman*, even then well to the Left of the line, commented that 'The Communistic experiment has failed' and that Lenin was now 'driving the Russian State furiously back on the road to capitalism'. All in Russia acknowledged this save a handful of desperate doctrinaires. The *Spectator* felt that Lenin had 'admitted the economic collapse of his system', while *The Economist* and many of Britain's business papers took the same view. They were epitomized by the *Financial News* which on 7 November 1923 recommended that businessmen move away from the diffidence that had characterized their previous actions if they were to avoid being 'ousted from a potential market of growing worth'. Certainly, it was added, it would not be 'in national interests – financial, commercial and economic – that we should see it fall into other hands'.

For this reason, as much as for any other, trade had lumbered on, surviving even difficulties which reached crisis point when on 8 May 1923, Curzon handed the Russians a note threatening that the Agreement would be ended unless they stopped their hostile propaganda. Negotiations were opened and there was no tearing up of the Agreement, and one reason given by Radek had more than a touch of truth. Curzon, he maintained, had been unable to bring about a trade rupture 'because the industrialists, forming part of the membership of the English Conservative party, considered to what it might lead ... Curzon was defeated in his own party, because industrial circles did not want to leap with him into the unknown. From their point of view they were completely right.'

By this time, Lenin's hopes of strengthening Europe's commercial bridges with Russia had suffered a setback through the failure of the Genoa Conference of which he had had high hopes. The failure was doubly disappointing since both Russia and the West had proposed such a conference. As early as 28 October 1921, the People's Commissariat for Foreign Affairs had sent a note to Britain, France, Italy, Japan and the USA suggesting an informal conference to discuss the possibility of 'opening an opportunity for private initiative and capital to co-operate with the power of the workers and peasants in the exploitation of Russia's natural resources'. Little more than two months later, at a meeting of the Allied Supreme Council held in Cannes on 6 January 1922, the same plan was proposed in a resolution which said: 'A united effort by the stronger Powers is necessary to remedy the paralysis of the European system.'

One of the aims of the conference was to be an examination of the conditions by which foreign enterprise and capital might be attracted to support the restoration of Russia; yet Western aims were not entirely humanitarian, and it was hoped that the outcome might be not only the supply of aid to Russia but also the payment of reparations from Germany. On the Russian side, Lenin had his usual suspicions of anything coming from the West but certainly welcomed the prospect of the conference. 'First he wanted to meet Lloyd George, for whom he had a certain weakness . . .' according to Litvinov who was deputy head of the Russian delegation to Genoa. 'He wanted also to present his thesis on the possibility of Soviet Russia's peaceful co-existence with non-Soviet countries and intended to work out the political and economic basis for such a coexistence.' 'We are going to it as merchants,' Lenin himself said on 6 March 1922, 'because trade with the capitalist countries . . . is absolutely necessary for us.' But he then added that any ideas for imposing plans on Russia as a conquered country were 'simple nonsense'. Chicherin, who finally led the Russian delegation in place of Lenin (owing to a combination of Lenin's poor health and Sovnarkom fears for his safety outside Russia), spelt this out in a note telegraphed to the Governments of Britain, France and Italy, in which he said:

'If it is true that this group of governments intends, as the press has stated, to present proposals that are incompatible with the sovereign rights of the Russian Government and with the independence of the Russian State, it must be stated that disregard for the principles of equality and free exchange of views between all Governments participating at the conference will inevitably result in its failure.'

Chicherin stage-managed the Russian presentation at the Genoa Conference with professional skill – appearing in tails for the opening ceremony, speaking for twenty minutes in excellent French and then receiving spontaneous applause as he translated his speech into English – but it was Lenin who had drawn up detailed directives for the Russians, one of which read:

'All members of the delegation should be posted in a general way on all political and financial questions that are likely to be brought up at the conference. Moreover every member of the delegation should make a special and thorough study of one of the most important diplomatic and one of the most important financial questions.'

All, it was added, should be familiar with Keynes's *The Economic Consequences of the Peace* as well as with other named books.

If Western objectives at Genoa were more complex than was suggested by their openly stated aim of restoring trade with Russia, Lenin's aims were more complicated than those outlined by Chicherin, who told the Conference: 'the Russian delegation has come here . . . in order to engage in practical relations with Governments and commercial and industrial circles of all countries on the basis of reciprocity, equality of rights and full recognition.' Lenin, on the other hand, wrote in one directive of: 'our main object of dividing the different countries and setting them by the ears'. Elsewhere he stated:

'Everything possible and even impossible should be done to strengthen the pacifist wing of the bourgeoisie and increase, if only slightly, its chances of success at the elections. This first and foremost. Secondly, to disunite the bourgeois countries that will be united against us at Genoa – such is our dual political task at Genoa, and not at all the development of communist views.'

It is unlikely that Lenin's presence would have produced agreement between all at Genoa since France was inexorably opposed to the reconciliation with Russia which Lloyd George sought, while Russia was unable to settle with the other countries' representatives the complex question of Soviet debts and liabilities. Yet if the Genoa Conference was a failure from the viewpoint of most participants, a concurrent meeting ended in one outcome satisfactory to the Russians. This was the signature at Rapallo, a small town some twenty miles away, of a treaty between Russia and Germany which restored full diplomatic relations between the two countries, applied 'most-favoured-nation' treatment to trade relations between them, and reciprocally wiped out war reparations.

Genoa and Rapallo were symptomatic of Lenin's growing belief that the Bolsheviks should improve their relations with the West, and during the early 1920s he concentrated considerable effort on the task. He did so firstly through official diplomatic contacts, but also in less formal meetings and attempts to explain to visitors what he was trying to accomplish in Russia. His attempts were sometimes distinctly unsuccessful, even when those involved might have been expected to sympathize. Thus the visit of a British socialist delegation early in 1920 – a delegation including Ethel Snowden, Clifford Allen (later Lord Allen of Hurtwood) and Tom Shaw, who became Minister of Labour in the first Labour Government – transformed Bertrand Russell, who accompanied the delegates, from an ardent supporter of the Revolution into a dedicated anti-Communist.

Russell's reactions were not unsurprising in an aristocrat and intellectual appalled to hear, from a mathematician, of a university soviet which gave each cleaner an equal voice with the professor in determining the mathematical curriculum. Russell met Trotsky between the acts of *Prince Igor,* and Lenin, who granted him an hour's interview. In his journal Russell wrote of Trotsky:

'Very Napoleonic impression. Bright eyes, military bearing, lightning intelligence, magnetic personality. Exceedingly good-looking, which surprised me. Would be irresistible to women, & an agreeable lover while his passion lasted. I felt a vein of gay good-humour so long as he was not crossed in any way. Ruthless, not cruel. Admirable wavy hair. Vanity even greater than love of power; the vanity of an artist or actor. He came back with us into our box. When the audience saw him, they gave a great ovation – quite spontaneous, we all thought. He stood in Napoleonic attitude while they cheered; then spoke a few words, short & sharp, full of transitional energy, & called for three cheers for the brave fellows at the front. 1914 over again; but without the hope engendered by communism, I think it would be impossible to revive this mood in a war-weary nation. Conversation banal.'

Russell's account of his long interview with Lenin is not merely more revealing than his reaction to Trotsky but does much to explain the outlook of the Russian leader as the civil war continued and as the need for the NEP grew.

'His room is very bare – a big desk, some maps on the walls, 2 book-cases, one easy chair, for visitors. Throughout the time I was there, a sculptor was working on a bust of him. Conversation in English, very fairly good. He is friendly & apparently simple – entirely without a trace of *hauteur*, a great contrast to Trotsky. Nothing in his manner or bearing suggests the man who has power. He looks at his visitor very close, & screws up one eye. He laughs a great deal; at first, his laugh seems merely friendly & jolly, but gradually one finds it grim. He is dictatorial, calm, incapable of fear, devoid of self-seeking, an embodied theory. The materialist conception of history is his life-blood. He resembles a professor in his desire to have the theory understood & in his fury with those who misunderstand or disagree; also in his love of expounding. I put three questions to him. (1) I asked whether & how far he recognized the peculiarity of English conditions. The answer was unsatisfactory to me. He admits that there is little chance of revolution now, & that the working man is not yet disgusted with Parliamentary government. He hopes this result may be brought about by a Labour Ministry, particularly if Henderson is premier. But when I suggested that whatever is possible in England may occur without bloodshed, he waved aside the suggestion as fantastic. I got little impression of knowledge or psychological imagination. (2) I asked him whether he thought it possible to establish communism firmly & fully in a country containing such a large majority of peasants. He admitted it was difficult. He laughed over the exchange the peasant is compelled to make, of food for paper – the worthlessness of Russian paper struck him as comic. But he said things would right themselves when there are goods to offer to the peasant. For this he looks partly to electrification in industry, which he says is a technical necessity in Russia & will take 10 years; but chiefly he looks to the raising of the blockade. He said that as late as July 1917 the Bolsheviks were not only persecuted, but even assaulted by the Moscow mob. He said that very few understand the theory of the gov't., but that many support it out of instinct. I got the impression that he despises the populace & is an intellectual aristocrat.

'He described the division between rich & poor peasants, & the government propaganda among the latter against the former – leading often (as he suggested with a great laugh) to the rich peasant being hanged on the nearest tree, or meeting some such

659

fate. He seemed to think that the dictatorship over the peasant would have to continue a long time, because of the peasant's desire for free trade. He spoke with glee of the advantages the government had gained from the harshness of Kolchak & Denikin. He said he knew from statistics that the peasants have had more to eat these last two years than they had before, "& yet", he said, "they are against us" – but in this he was only speaking of the rich peasants, I imagine. I asked him what to reply to critics who say that in the country he has merely created peasant proprietorship, not communism; he said that was not quite the truth, but he did not say what the truth is. (3) I asked him whether resumption of trade with capitalist countries would not create centres of capitalist influence, & make the preservation of communism more difficult. He admitted that it would create difficulties, but said they would be less than those of the war. He said that 2 years ago neither he nor his colleagues thought they could survive against the hostility of the world. He attributes their survival to the jealousies & divergent interests of the different capitalist nations; also to the power of Bolshevik propaganda. He said the Germans had laughed when the Bolsheviks proposed to combat guns with leaflets, but that the event had proved the leaflets quite as powerful. I don't think he recognizes that the Labour & Socialist parties have had any part in the matter. He likes Northcliffe's attacks on him, & wants to send N. a medal for Bolshevik propaganda. Accusations of spoliation, he says, may shock the bourgeois, but have an opposite effect on the proletarian – I think if I had met him without knowing who he was I should not have guessed that he was a great man, but should have thought him an opinionated professor. His strength comes, I imagine, from his honesty, courage, & unwavering faith – religious faith in Marxian orthodoxy, which takes the place of the Xtian martyrs' hopes of Paradise, except that it is less egotistical. He has as little love of liberty as the men who suffered under Diocletian & retaliated (on heretical Xtians) when they acquired power. Says "Herald" completely misunderstands dictatorship of proletariat. Laughs at Cole for believing in Soviets without dictatorship.'

It was not only to Russell that Lenin appeared to speak with more freedom than one would expect of him: with Arthur Ransome he freely discussed his problems in running the country and also his views on men in the political and literary fields. George Bernard Shaw was A good man fallen among Fabians', and when someone described Shaw as a clown, Lenin interjected with: 'He may be a clown for the bourgeoisie in a bourgeois state, but they would not think him a clown in a revolution.' When Ransome said he was sure that Sidney Webb was not working in the interests of the capitalists, Lenin remarked: 'Then he has more industry than brains. He certainly has great knowledge'. And he freely expressed his admiration for Raymond Robins whom he saw as being open to new ideas. When his enthusiasm was aroused he could describe the future seductively to visitors. To H. G. Wells – who admitted that on his visit his 'passive objection to Marx [had] changed to a very active hostility' – he gave such a vivid account of an electrified Russia that, Wells later wrote, 'he almost persuaded me to share his vision'.

This enthusiasm for technological innovation, and particularly for electricity, was typical of the emphasis on science and technology, and the scientific approach to problems, that Lenin had encouraged since he came to power and whose rewards began to be noticed in the first months of NEP. As early as January 1918 he had inaugurated discussions with the Academy of Sciences on the best ways of using science to improve Russia's industrial prospects and by April a draft plan had been drawn up stressing that industry should be rationally distributed in relation to the proximity of raw materials and of labour. In April he wrote his 'Draft Plan of Scientific and Technical Work' – not published until 4 March 1924 in *Pravda* – saying that the Supreme Economic Council should immediately tell the Academy of Sciences to set up expert commissions to compile plans for the reorganization of industry and the economic progress of the country. Here, as in all Lenin's plans for industrial progress, great emphasis was placed on the electrification of industry and the application of electricity to farming. Peat and low-grade coal should be used to help produce electricity for industrial purposes while wind power and water power could be utilized to help create electricity for agricultural uses.

Eight new power stations were built in 1918, another twenty-eight the following year. These were among the first items in the ten-to-fifteen-year plan finalized in 1920 by the State Commission for the Electrification of Russia (GOELRO), an organization that Lenin studied and supported with almost as much enthusiasm as he had followed the development of the Party twenty years earlier. It was not only the practical and material benefits of electrification that attracted Lenin, as he made clear when he spoke on 22 December 1920 at the Eighth All-Russian Congress of Soviets. Capitalism in Russia had not yet been torn up by the roots, he said. 'It depends', he went on, 'on small-scale production, and there is only one way of undermining it, namely, to place the economy of the country, including agriculture on a new technical basis, that of modern large-scale production. Only electricity provides that basis'.

It was in his enthusiastic support for electrification that Lenin was to have his greatest impact on advancing Russian technology. This was in contrast with his reactions to Gosplan (Gosudarstvennaya Planovaya Comissiya, State Planning Committee), which was set up on the eve of the NEP's introduction. He naturally showed interest in its activities, but it was less concentrated and less personal than he showed in Russia's electrification. 'We must see to it', he said, 'that every factory and every electric power station becomes a centre of enlightenment; if Russia is covered with a dense network of electric power stations and powerful technical installations, our communist economic development will become a model for a future socialist Europe and Asia.' His ideas were exemplified when he quoted the saying 'The age of steam is the age of the bourgeoisie, the age of electricity is the age of socialism.'

Lenin frequently urged on ways in which the work could be kept up to schedule. In May 1921 he wrote:

'The electrification plan which is calculated on ten years (first phase of the work), requires 370 million working days. Per year per man in the army this amounts to $(37:1.6) = 24$ working days, i.e. two days a month. Of course the disposition of the army, transport to places of work, etc. etc. will create a mass of difficulties, but all the same the army can and must (with the aid of the Universal Military Training Organization) lend enormous assistance to the cause of electrification. We must bind the army to this great cause – ideologically, organizationally and economically – and must work systematically on it . . .'

And of the first plan produced by the State Commission for Electrification, he said, 'this small volume . . . In my opinion it is the second programme of our Party.'

There could be no question, he told the Party's Moscow Gubernia Conference on 21 November 1920,

'of rehabilitating the national economy or of communism unless Russia is put on a different and a higher technical basis than that which has existed up to now. Communism is Soviet power plus the electrification of the whole country, since industry cannot be developed without electrification. This is a long-term task which will take at least ten years to accomplish, provided a great number of technical experts are drawn into the work. A number of printed documents in which this project has been worked out in detail by technical experts will be presented to the Congress. We cannot achieve the main objects of this plan – create 30 large regions of electric power stations which would enable us to modernize our industry – in less than ten years.'

The documents made up the report of the State Commission for the Electrification of Russia, which was presented to the Eighth Congress of Soviets. They envisaged not merely the building of power stations and the distribution of electricity but its overall application to both industry and agriculture. As Lenin went on to explain in his speech: 'This is an enormous task, to accomplish which will require a far longer period than was needed to defend our right to existence against invasion.'

His vision of what electricity could do for Russia was again revealed in his interview with Lincoln Eyre of February 1920.

'We mean to electrify our entire industrial system through power stations in the Urals and elsewhere. Our engineers tell us it will take ten years. When the electrification is accomplished it will be the first important stage on the road to the Communistic administration of public economic life. All our industries will receive their motive power from a common source, capable of supplying them all adequately. This will eliminate wasteful competition in the quest of fuel, and place manufacturing enterprise on a sound economic footing, without which we cannot hope to achieve a full measure of interchange of essential products in accordance with Communist principles.'

He went on to say that in three years he hoped there would be 50 million lamps in Russia – more than two-thirds of America's 70 million, 'Electrification', he added, 'is to my mind the most momentous of the great tasks that confront us.' He was almost obsessed with ensuring that the benefits of this great task should not be squandered and in the Kremlin expended some of his most pungent criticisms on those who left electric lights burning unnecessarily.

It was no passing fancy. Lenin's enthusiasm for electrification – if 'fanaticism' is too strong a description – continued for the rest of his life and was well illustrated when he wrote a Preface to I. I. Stepanov's *The Electrification of the R.S.F.S.R. and the Transitional Phase of World Economy* (Moscow, 1922). After pointing out that by 1922 there were more than 800 electric power stations in Russia, he went on:

'We must see to it that every village schoolteacher reads and assimilates this manual (to help him in this a circle or group of engineers and teachers of physics should be organized in every *uyezd)*, and not only reads, understands and assimilates it himself but is able to relate what is in it in a plain and intelligible way to his pupils, and to young peasants in general.'

Lenin tried to staple into the educational system as full an understanding as possible of the electrical revolution being carried out in the country. In March 1921, he wrote an addendum to the Central Committee's draft decision of the obligatory minimum for science teaching in the higher schools. 'The following', it said, 'should be added on the basis of the resolution of the Eighth All-Russia Congress of Soviets: *electrification plan,* its economic foundations, the economic geography of Russia, significance of and conditions for the plan's implementation.'

With his enthusiasm there went an appreciation of practical problems revealed in a letter he wrote to Gleb Krzhizhanovsky, head of the electrification projects, in 1921.

'Gleb Maximilianovich!

This idea has just come to me: there must be propaganda for electricity. How? Not only in words, but in deeds.

What does this mean? Most important of all – to popularize it. To do this, we must at once work out *a plan* for putting electricity into every single house in the R.S.F.S.R.

And this must be for a long time ahead, because for some time to come we shall not have sufficient wiring etc. for 20 million (or is it 40 million?) bulbs. All the same, a plan is necessary *at once,* even though it covers a number of years.

That comes first. Secondly, we must immediately work out an *abridged* plan; and then thirdly, and this is the most important of all, we must succeed in stimulating both the *competitive instinct* and *initiative of the masses,* so that they will set to work at once.

Could not the following plan (for instance) be drawn up at once?

1. All volosti (rural districts – 10/15,000) to be supplied with electric light within one year.

2. All hamlets (half-a-million to a million, and probably not more than three quarters of a million), within two years.

3. First of all – the reading-room huts and the Sovdep (two electric bulbs).

4. Electric light standards to be made *immediately*, and in such and such a way.

5. Insulators to be manufactured *immediately*, and *by us* (ceramic factories – I suppose local and small ones?) to be made in such and such a way.

6. *Copper* for wiring? *Collect it yourselves* in each volost (rural district) and local district (a little hint at church bells, etc.)

7. Electrical training to be organized in such and such a way. Cannot something *like this* be thought out, worked out in detail and *decreed?*'

As with his political instructions during the early years of the century, and his orders during the civil war, Lenin made certain that his wishes were carried out. The Electricity Department of the Supreme Economic Council was told in September 1921,

'You are expected to carry out with complete precision and maximum adherence to the schedule laid down for completion of construction, the supply of electrotechnical equipment to the Kashira construction project. I categorically demand that in this matter there should not be the slightest delays, which could lead to the non-completion of the project in terms of the prescribed schedule.'

Lenin was also an enthusiastic supporter of the Nizhni-Novgorod Radio Laboratory, the first of its kind in Russia, and on 21 October 1918 wrote to N. P. Gorbunov: 'I earnestly request you to *speed up* as much as possible the Science and Technology Department's findings in regard to the Radio Laboratory. *It is extremely urgent.* Drop me a line when its findings are ready.' He was not only intrigued by science itself but by its potentialities for propaganda. Here, he early saw the possibilities of radio and the gramophone, and in 1919 had eight of his speeches put on records. Significantly enough, when seven of them were re-recorded and put on public sale during the Khrushchev era, more than forty years later, the one omitted was that outlining Lenin's feelings against anti-Semitism.

He showed considerable business instincts, as from the end of the civil war onwards he began to lead the country towards a future very different from its agrarian past. Thus the inventions section of the Scientific and Technical Department of the Supreme Economic Council was asked to provide details of how it was faring and of how many claims to inventions it had examined since it was set up and how many had been recognized as useful. Gorbunov, secretary of Sovnarkom, who was instructed to keep a special eye on particular matters, was told: 'This business must be organized on the correct lines: you must always have a file or a list of decisions which have *not been carried out* or require constant supervision (over execution).' There are similar injunctions scattered through the flood of Lenin's correspondence.

He made an attempt, now, to soften the methods of terror used by the Cheka. He had suggested this early in 1920 when at a meeting of Chekist officers from a number of departments, he had said:

'Although the period of armed conflict on a major histori- cal scale is nearing its close, we must in all circumstances remain in a state of readiness. The organs for the suppres- sion of counter-revolution, i.e. the Cheka, are faced with a somewhat difficult task. On one side we must allow for the transition from war to peace, on the other we must always remain on our guard, for we do not know how quickly a real peace is attainable . . . Retaining our readiness to fight, and without weakening the apparatus for the suppression of exploiters, we must find a new means of transition from war to peace, we must change our tactics as well as the form of our reprisals.'

The need became even greater as the practice of confiscations ended. Lenin knew the value of outside appearances, and it was significant that the leather jackets, which for some had been the mark of the Cheka, were discarded for bright blue uniforms when the organization was replaced on 6 February 1922 by the State Political Administration whose initials, GPU, had as yet no terrorist connotation. In what appears to have been Lenin's wish to dissociate the Government from earlier organized terror, curbs were put on various histories of the Cheka then being, or about to be, published, and a strong case has even been made out for believing that many of the Cheka's records were destroyed on Lenin's personal orders. Certainly such an act, astonishing as it at first appears, chimes in with other official moves to create a more liberal impression of what future Government actions were likely to be.

Some relaxation in Bolshevik dogma, which accompanied the introduction of the NEP, helped to bring non-Communist support, but that this was not widespread is suggested by a comment in *The Times* of 25 August 1921, after the famine on the Volga had produced calls for help from the rest of the world. Relief, *The Times* sourly remarked, would mean 'maintaining the Bolshevists in power at the moment when their misdeeds have wrought themselves out in their inevitable consequences and are threatening the collapse of the whole hateful and criminal system'.

The new and less rigorous interpretation of the beliefs on which Lenin had founded the Party now began to stretch well beyond politics and is exemplified by a letter which he wrote in April 1921 to V. M. Molotov, earlier the secretary of *Pravda* and now Secretary of the Party's Central Committee. Something had been written, apparently under Bolshevik auspices, to *'expose the falsehood of religion*, or something to that effect. That is not right,' Lenin warned. 'It is tactless', he went on, before adding that it was absolutely necessary 'to avoid any affront to religion'.

Some changes following in the wake of the NEP, such as the renaming of the Third Red Army as the First Revolutionary Army of Labour, and the decree that set up the Ukrainian Soviet Army of Labour, were primarily symbolic. More important was the creation of State Trusts, of which there were 430 by the winter of 1922. These Trusts – of which the first was the Linen Trust, set up in July 1921, quickly followed by the Northern Timber Trust – were syndicates of factories run on commercial lines and allowed to sell some of their products to obtain working capital. They were mainly formed from the larger factories while many of the smaller ones were leased back to their former owners, the effect of the changes being to remove the bulk of the nationalized industries from direct state control and to put them, instead, on the basis of normal commercial management.

Another side-effect of the NEP was an increase in the importance of paper money. Previously, barter had become the almost universal method of trade; now 'old-fashioned' money began to come into its own again. The new atmosphere is well illustrated by a quotation from Michael S. Farbman's *Bolshevism in Retreat* and an extract he produces from the Party's *Five Years of Bolshevik Rule*:

> 'With all the Communist phraseology and discipline, with all the waving of the Red Flag, Russia is thoroughly in the throes of bourgeois impulses and passions. From the little *papirosnik* boy who sells you loose cigarettes in the streets to the director of a syndicate, from the parasitic sackman speculator to the engineer projecting electrification – all are throbbing with a new sense of life.'

Of even more significance is the verdict of Teodorovich, a member of the Agrarian Commissariat, who wrote in *Five Years of Bolshevik Rule*:

'The economy of 182 million holdings is now being seriously tested by the market. The division of land has stopped. Fixity of tenure is declared and guaranteed. The peasants, freed from all illusion about equalization, are now starting to work on their respective holdings. Tested in the market some will be successful, others will prove failures. A successful peasant must not on that account be called a *Kulak*. The gain he makes in the market he uses for improvements and repairs. The improved holding can now begin to accumulate capital, which is used partly for the purpose of making further improvements and partly as a contribution to the cooperative movement in agriculture . . .'

Lenin made a further justification for the great changes being introduced on 20 November 1922 when he made his last official speech, an address to the Moscow Soviet:

'We have begun to relearn, and shall relearn in such a way that we shall achieve definite and obvious success. And it is for the sake of this relearning, I think, that we must again firmly promise one another that under the name of the New Economic Policy we have turned back, but turned back in such a way as to surrender nothing of the new, and yet to give the capitalists such advantages as will compel any state, however hostile to us, to establish contacts and to deal with us.'

Some of the diehards in the Party may have fumed on hearing this, but Lenin was merely restating that his plans for reviving the country's fortunes were working. The Revolution would survive. This proved a major compensation for him in the difficult times, personal and political, that lay immediately ahead.

18

Death, Succession and the Legacy

It was as well that circumstance forced Lenin to inaugurate the NEP when it did since from the start of the 1920s the rigours of his life began to catch up with him, and slowly but relentlessly to put increasingly important limitations on the active part he could play in directing Russia's fortunes. He struggled fiercely against this, and the record of his last years is one of regular argument between his doctors, always trying to impose restrictions on his work, and the stubbornness of a man always reluctant to give up.

The intensity of the struggle is revealed by the written records of his secretariat, the detailed notes that were kept of almost everything that he said and did, and the later recollections of his secretaries and assistants whose memories, when checked against contemporary diaries, appear singularly free of remembrance with advantages. The picture which emerges is that of an exceptionally strong-willed man desperately anxious to keep control as firmly as possible in his own hands; a man becoming daily more suspicious that some of those around him were plotting to take over after his death.

The clear picture of Lenin's determination to remain in charge of events in Russia is in strong contrast to the miasma of doubt concerning what exactly was wrong with him during the last years of his life – a doubt not entirely removed by the post-mortem that was carried out in 1924. Even today the mechanisms by which the brain does its job are not completely understood and in the early 1920s there was considerable discussion about the insomnia, lack of concentration, headaches and general feeling of lassitude which, from the end of 1920, progressively began to affect Lenin's ability to carry on with his work. It is true that only in the years of his Siberian exile, when he was struggling to create a base for his revolutionary ardour, and again a decade later when he was deep in philosophical argument with Bogdanov, did he find it necessary to stretch himself towards his intellectual limits. Yet since the beginning of the century he had worked under the constant pressure of carrying out underground work in which mistakes or slackness could bring grim penalties. Such possibilities were never far from his mind as is shown by remarks reported by Krupskaya from her normally non-communicative husband. He could never relax and more than one of his colleagues remarked that even on the most beguiling of mountain excursions part of his mind would be concerned with the problems of revolution. Now, in the early 1920s, the strain of the past was becoming partly responsible for the slowing-up, the breakdowns and strokes which began to affect his control over the Communist experiment he had started to plan three years earlier.

He appears to have survived the trials of 1920 without serious damage – the disappointments of the war with Poland, the

674

personal loss of Inessa Armand, and the work needed before the NEP could be got under way – although towards the end of December he asked N. P. Gorbunov to investigate electric ploughs in his place since he felt unwell owing to insomnia. Even so, he showed little more than what could be considered the effects of overwork. Trotsky describes him at this period in a way with which most of his colleagues would probably have agreed.

'Lenin himself was considered a man of robust health, and this health seemed to be one of the indestructible pillars of the revolution. He was always active, alert, even-tempered and gay. Only occasionally did I notice alarming symptoms. During the First Congress of the Communist International [in 1919] he surprised me with his tired look, the uneven-ness of his voice, and his sick man's smile. More than once I told him that he was spending himself on matters of secondary importance. He agreed, but said that he couldn't do otherwise. Sometimes he complained of headaches, always casually and with a little embarrassment. But two or three weeks of rest sufficed to restore him. It seemed as if Lenin would never wear out.'

However, the range of subjects about which he found time to take a personal interest was still vast. Early in 1921 he asked Ryazanov whether there was a collection of all the letters that Marx and Engels had written to newspapers in any Moscow library. If so, could he borrow a copy? A few days later he made a special plea for a member of the Commissariat of Foreign Affairs to be posted abroad since the member's wife feared that their children would not survive conditions in Moscow. He studied a new atlas of Russia that was in proof and suggested how it might be improved, asked for special materials to be obtained for headstones on the graves of Plekhanov and Vera Zasulich, and for steps to ensure that all new Russian books were available in prisons within a month of publication.

Meanwhile, the routine work of running the State was accompanied by the usual warnings. One complainant was called 'a silly whimpering old woman'; Leonid Krasin, the Commissar for Trade and Industry, was told at the start of a letter, 'You deserve a beating'; and a member of the Food Administration was threatened with penalties unless he produced necessary figures on time.

The intensity of Lenin's 'routine' work, which constantly produced such personal comments, can be inferred from Fotiyeva's records. On 2 February 1921, which she describes as a typical day, Lenin presided over the Supreme Economic Council from 11 a.m. until 2 p.m., and attended the Central Committee's Political Bureau from 2 p.m. until 4 p.m. From 6 p.m. until 7 p.m. he presided at a meeting of the Central Committee's commission on the reorganization of the People's Commissariat of Education, and during it received an urgent request for a meeting sent in by Boris Sokolov, a member of the Siberian Revolutionary Committee. When someone else wanted to see him, the secretary was sent out with the message, 'I *hope* to be free by 9 or 10 tonight.' During the afternoon he was handed a telephone message from the Secretary of the Petrograd Gubernia Committee stating that there had been stoppages in the city owing to the non-receipt of food, and sent out the reply: 'Yesterday, Council of Defence decided to buy 18½ million poods of coal abroad. The food situation will improve because we have today decided to allocate two more trains for grain deliveries from the Caucasus.' During the day he also held meetings with G. M. Krzhizhanovsky, chairman of the State Planning Committee, the Deputy People's Commissar of Finance M. K. Vladimirov, Sokolov from Siberia and a Party member from Czechoslovakia. He also wrote, read, made notes on, or signed, forty documents, excluding those discussed at the meetings; wrote a number of letters; approved and signed the minutes of various committees; and endorsed a provisional ruling on the payment of bonuses in kind.

Only as 1921 progressed was it possible to sense a new factor determining Lenin's life and affairs. Dominating everything there was still, of course, the navigation of the ship of State through the dangerous waters of an ill-disposed world. But this work was now seen to be affected, if not hampered, by what was obviously his deteriorating health. While it only slowly caused grave concern, the question of a successor steadily became a more relevant subject of the speculation that steadily began to polarize around the relative positions of Stalin and Trotsky. Lenin's health, and the question of who would succeed him became inextricably entangled during that year with the progress of the NEP and three other controversial subjects, which produced arguments that darkened his closing days: the State monopoly of foreign trade, the growth of Russian bureaucracy and, most important of all, the future of Georgia. On all of these Lenin held views in strong contrast to those of Stalin, which led to growing differences between them.

The differences had roots deep within the intellectual and psychological backgrounds of the two men. Both were hard, both could be ruthless, but Lenin's actions and reactions could be qualified by an ability to compromise and a crafty realization that compromise sometimes led to the most satisfactory method of ending a debate. He had, in addition, the ability to turn on the charm which Stalin singularly lacked, as well as the perception to see when this could help in the battle. Since their earliest contacts, their differences had risen to the surface on occasion, becoming evident at times during the civil war but it was only after that war, as the various nationalities within the Russian Empire began to reach out for autonomy, and as Lenin's failing health led to a quick enlargement of Stalin's ambitions, that they began seriously to affect the ways in which the country could be managed.

Thus an internal Party battle gradually began to affect Lenin's struggle to survive ill-health. On 8 July 1921 he asked the authorities to grant him a month's holiday, in accordance with his doctor's orders, and began the holiday at his house in Gorki later in the month. Early in August he wrote to Maxim Gorky saying: 'I am so tired that I am unable to do a thing,' and later in the month told Lunacharsky that he could not see him since he was 'ill'. Early in December he was again granted a period of sick leave, and on 7 December 1921 before going again to Gorki, wrote in a memo to the Political Bureau: 'I am going away today. Despite the reduction of my share of work and the increase of my time for rest in recent days, insomnia has increased devilishly. I am afraid that I cannot present any reports either at the party Convention or at the Congress of Soviets.'

However, although his health was deteriorating, throughout 1921, Lenin maintained a formidable output of work. In April he completed 'The Tax in Kind', which contained the theoretical backbone of the NEP, attended the Tenth All-Russian Conference of the RCP(B), opening and closing the Conference; and in midsummer made several speeches at the Third Congress of the Comintern.

The remaining years were very different. An early hint of things to come was given in February 1922 when the Politburo decided to extend his leave to the opening of the Eleventh Party Congress on 27 March. That this was necessary was shown by a letter from Lenin to D. I. Kursky on 28 February in which he said: 'I shall try to see you personally,' presumably at the Congress, 'but I cannot promise it because I am not feeling well.' However, he summoned up all his strength and not only opened the Congress on 27 March but closed it, on 2 April.

During the Congress Lenin, Kamenev, Rykov, Stalin, Tomsky, Trotsky and Zinoviev were elected to an enlarged Politburo. More importantly as it turned out, Stalin was appointed General Secretary of the Party; he was already Commissar for the Nationalities as well as Commissar for the Workers' and Peasants' Inspectorate, and the new appointment combined with the others to give him a position of extraordinary power. Lenin certainly acquiesced in the appointment, even if it was not made at his suggestion, so that at the start of 1922 there was little indication of the rift which divided the two men by the end of the year.

While overwork was at least a large factor in Lenin's condition, the doctors suspected that another might be the bullet that had remained in his body after Fanny Kaplan's assassination attempt in August 1918. It was decided to remove it and this was done on 23 April 1922 in Moscow's Soldatenkovo Hospital. The doctor's suspicions were justified since a small abscess had formed where the bullet rested. 'Regarding the nervous system – ', the doctors wrote in the hospital records, 'there is a general nervousness, occasional insomnia, headaches. The specialists have found a neurasthenia, the result of overwork.' But Lenin recovered quickly from the operation.

On 26 May 1922, he suffered his first stroke, later diagnosed as being due to arteriosclerosis of the brain. The result was temporary paralysis of his left side and a temporary speech impediment, and from this moment onwards the details of his health became as much State secrets as today's estimates of the yields from nuclear weapons. But there is no reason to doubt the accuracy of the later statement by N. A. Semashko, the Commissar of Health:

'Vladimir Ilyich's final illness began with insignificant symptoms. He felt dizzy as he got out of bed and he had to grab hold of a cupboard which was nearby. The doctors, who were called immediately, at first attached no significance to these symptoms . . . But Vladimir Ilyich was sad and pensive; he felt the impending disaster and answered all attempts to reassure him: "No, that is the first alarm signal." '

According to Dr Getier, 'The tendency to fatigue would increase, there would not be the former clarity in work, but a virtuoso would remain a virtuoso.' Maybe. But Lenin was both paralysed and speechless for a short time, and although he was telling the Sovnarkom by mid-July 1922 that he had recovered, and was asking for books to be sent to him, his visitors suggest that although he was recovering it was a slow business.

From the time of his first stroke – the warning bell as he felt it to be – Lenin eased up slightly from his strenuous routine, although only reluctantly, and only in response to the appeals of Krupskaya and the solicitations of his doctors and secretaries. He began to spend more time at Gorki, fishing, hunting or gathering mushrooms, travelling there in the winter months in a Rolls-Royce Silver Ghost which he had had equipped with caterpillar tracks for easy travel over snow.

He was fond of playing with the local children on the estate but would rarely divorce himself from work for long and, in spite of the doctors' persistent orders that he should take things easy, still found it unnerving to be out of touch with what was going on in the Kremlin.

Some of the evidence on Lenin's health during these final years comes from those whose testimony is suspect because of their involvement in events and can only be accepted, like the evidence in certain criminal cases, when it is supported from other, independent, sources. It is difficult, therefore, to take at its face value Trotsky's claim that at one point Lenin

'summoned Stalin and addressed to him an insistent request to bring him some poison. Afraid lest he lose the power of speech again and become a toy in the hands of the doctors, Lenin wanted to remain the master of his fate. It was no accident that at one time he had expressed his approval of Lafargue, who preferred by his own act to *"join the majority" [in English]* rather to live an invalid . . . Anyhow, Stalin did not comply with the request, but reported it to the Politburo. Everybody protested; the doctors still maintained there were grounds for hope; Stalin kept his own counsel . . .'

If this tale appears intrinsically unlikely, more credence can be given to his claim that Stalin tried to isolate Lenin during the second period of his illness, before his second stroke: 'He was calculating that Lenin would never recover, and was trying with all his might to prevent [him] from communicating his views in writing.'

Throughout his illness, as always, Lenin had the solicitous care of Krupskaya. Liberman, who normally had little interest for matters outside the political sphere, has noted: 'I used to see [Krupskaya] passing through the room with a seemingly unconcerned look, but actually thinking of neither God nor man, neither Russia nor the revolution, but only of her Vladimir Ilyich.'

To Stalin, who visited him in mid-July 1922 and noticed continuing traces of tiredness and strain, Lenin said: 'I may not read a newspaper. I may not speak about politics. I go round every piece of paper lying on my desk, fearing it could be a newspaper and that it could lead to a breach of discipline.' But by early August he was considerably improved and Stalin, who visited him on the fifth, reported: 'This time I found Comrade Lenin surrounded by a mountain of books and newspapers (he was permitted to read as much as he liked and to talk about politics). There was no trace of over-tiredness and overstrain . . . It is our old Lenin who looks craftily, one eye half closed, at his interlocuter.'

The following month he was well enough to send a message to the Fifth All-Russian Congress of Trade Unions, 'the first time since my long illness that I am able to address a Congress, even though in writing', as he said. And early in October he returned to Moscow from Gorki. His doctors agreed that his working day could last from 11 a.m. to 2 p.m. and from 6 p.m. to 8 p.m., but in return he had to rest one day every week in addition to Sunday. Despite these restrictions he would often go to his office well before 11 a.m. and if a secretary entered the room would explain: 'I am not working, I'm just reading'.

He continued to get through an enormous amount of work for a sick man and one compilation claims that between 2 October 1922 when he returned to Moscow, and mid-December when he suffered a second stroke, he wrote 224 official letters and notes, saw 171 people and chaired thirty-two meetings and discussions at the Sovnarkom, the Councils for Labour and Defence, and the Politburo and its various commissions.

During this period he was aided by a partial revival of the Little Sovnarkom. For some while he had habitually passed matters on to the Politburo when he disagreed with the Sovnarkom's decision. Now the tendency changed and once again the Little Sovnarkom rather than the Politburo was called into aid.

Lenin's work did not consist of trivialities; it never did. And during the autumn of 1922, when he was drawing on his remaining resources with no thought for his own future, he made an important address to the Fourth Session of the All-Russian Central Executive Committee; granted an interview to Michael Farbman for *The Observer* and the *Manchester Guardian* which he knew would be important in influencing world opinion, and on 13 November addressed the Fourth Comintern Congress, in German, on 'Five Years of the Russian Revolution and the Prospects of the World Revolution'.

The Congress had opened on 5 November in Petrograd and moved five days later to Moscow, where Lenin spoke to the 408 delegates.

'Those who were seeing him for the first time said: "This is still the same Lenin!" [wrote Alfred Rosmer]. But to the others no such illusion was possible; instead of the alert Lenin they had known, the man before them now was badly affected by paralysis, his features remained frozen, and his general appearance was that of an automaton; his habitually simple, rapid confident speech was replaced by a hesitant, jerky delivery. Sometimes words eluded him. The comrade who had been given the task of assisting him did so poorly; Radek pushed him away and took his place himself.'

To many, though, it must have seemed that Lenin had fully recovered, and Oscar Cesare, the *New York Times* cartoonist who spent an hour with him (in October 1922), later reported that he saw no trace of illness. But much depended on the observer, and that equally trained men could provide evidence that depended on the eye of the beholder is shown by comparing the reports of Walter Duranty and Louis Fischer. Duranty, who was sitting at Lenin's feet as Lenin spoke in Moscow's Grand Opera House at a special session of the Moscow Soviet to open the electoral campaign for the coming All-Russian Soviet Congress, wrote:

'For the first time – so closely and well had the secret been guarded, so many and bewildering the rumors – I was sure of the truth; there is no disguising the accents of a paralytic from anyone who knows. I said as much that evening to the Soviet censor, but he would not let me write it. The most I could say was, "The speaker's voice was full and strong but it seemed rather thicker and less clear than last year, although not enough so for anyone to miss his words." The lay reader might not grasp my meaning, but I hoped that it would be clear to anyone with medical training.'

A different picture remained with Louis Fischer who watched Lenin at a meeting of the Central Executive Committee in October 1922.

'While Nicholas Krylenko, Federal Attorney General, was delivering an address from the podium, Lenin walked into the hall unescorted and sat down unnoticed on one of the yellow folding chairs near me. I had a few minutes to observe him. His head was round, almost bald, and luminous, with a high domed forehead, high cheek bones, a reddish moustache, little red beard, and slanting, Mongolian, twinkling eyes. His lips played with a smile. Soon the delegates noticed him and whispered, and then the whisper "Lenin" became a loud cry drowned in applause, and Lenin, almost running, moved up to the platform. Immediately, Krylenko interrupted his long report, and the chairman, Mikhail Kalinin, President of the Soviet Republic, said simply, "Comrade Lenin has the floor." The applause lasted exactly forty-five seconds; Lenin raised his hand, the clapping stopped and the delegates resumed their seats. He held a watch in his palm and said that the physicians had given him permission to speak for fifteen minutes. He spoke fifteen minutes, all the while squinting near-sightedly at his watch. His tone was conversational, rapid and informal. He gesticulated freely but there was no striving for effect. The audience laughed or grew emotional or settled into seriousness just as he apparently wished it. I understood only a few words.'

He still seemed to keep an eye on almost everything: after the Commissariat of Foreign Affairs had published in 1922 *Documents on the History of Franco-Russian Relations for 1910–14 (Materialy po istory frankorusskikh otnosheni za 1910–1914 gody),* Stalin received a letter from him which ran: 'This massive tome of 733 pages has been published with that disgraceful, truly Soviet slovenliness which ought to be punished by imprisonment. The price is not indicated. The responsible person or persons are not named.

There is no index! The simple *list* of names has been compiled *carelessly*. And so on.' His 'feel' for propaganda was as acute as ever and on 19 May 1922 he wrote to Stalin recommending that 100,000 roubles should be allocated for the construction of radio transmitters. 'I think that from the standpoint of propaganda and agitation, especially for those masses of the population who are illiterate, and also for broadcasting lectures, it is absolutely necessary for us to carry out this plan.'

He retained his oblique sense of humour and commented in a memo to the Political Bureau: 'I declare war to the death on dominant nation chauvinism. I shall eat it with all my healthy teeth as soon as I get rid of this accursed bad tooth. It must be *absolutely* insisted that the Union Central Executive Committee should be *presided over* in turn by a Russian, Ukrainian, Georgian, etc., *absolutely!*'

He continued to work almost daily and after a brief break at Gorki early in December returned to Moscow on the twelfth. He spent much of the morning in his office, returned to it at 5.30 p.m. after a visit to his flat, and worked there until 8.15 p.m. At some period during the day he conferred with Dzerzhinsky.

On 13 December 1922, he suffered two attacks, caused by what was later diagnosed as thrombosis of the brain. His life from now on became a patchwork record of fluctuating illness and recovery, the first months of which can be followed in some detail with the help of the Journal of Lenin's Duty Secretaries made between 21 November 1922 and 6 March 1923. 'Doctors came at 11,' says Lydia Fotiyeva's first entry in the diary for 13 December. 'Ordered complete rest. He was to leave town.' It is clear that he could be a difficult patient and his sister Maria later wrote of this occasion that the doctors 'had great difficulty in persuading Vladimir Ilyich to drop work altogether and go out into the country. Meanwhile he was to lie down for as long as possible and not go for walks. In the end Vladimir Ilyich agreed to leave town and said "I'll start winding up my affairs this very day." ' At midday on the thirteenth he sent for Fotiyeva and dictated a number of letters to her, including one to Trotsky explaining how his views on the foreign trade monopoly should be put forward. Then Stalin arrived for what turned out to be a two-hour discussion. It seems clear that whatever the doctors advised or ordered, Lenin was still determined to maintain his control of State affairs as long as possible. He kept in touch with his secretaries by phone, ordered that certain minutes and other material should be delivered to him and on the fifteenth gave Fotiyeva another letter to Trotsky, told her to type it and send it off, but to keep a copy in the secret files.

Then, on the night of 15 to 16 December he took a sharp turn for the worse and paralysis of his right arm and leg set in, although he soon began to recover the use of both limbs.

Two doctors came at 11 a.m. on the sixteenth but Lenin said, according to the Journal of the Duty Secretaries, that he had

'no wish to go to Gorki, saying that the journey by aero-sleigh was tiring and you could not go down by car. Pakaln [head of his bodyguard] tells that every day at 9.30 a dog (Aidu) is brought to him with whom he plays and is very fond of. A telegram has arrived from Foerster [the German neuropathologist] confirming that before addressing the congress he should have no less than 7 days complete rest.'

His illness now virtually forced him to give up writing and dictate instead to one of his secretaries, a change he greatly disliked. Fotiyeva has written:

'He used to say that he was accustomed to seeing what he had written in front of him, and was therefore finding dictation difficult. Another thing that irked him was the sight of the stenographer sitting there with pencil poised, waiting for him to go on, while he took a few minutes' pause to think of what he wanted to say next. He had to adjust himself to it, however, and thought it would help if the stenographer had a book to read in the pauses, but that was not much good either. In the end the stenographer was placed in the adjoining room and given ear-phones, so [that] Vladimir Ilyich could dictate to her over the phone. However, he resorted to this method but rarely and then with reluctance.'

It was unwillingly that he carried out many of the doctors' orders, and the position was not made much better when on 18 December the Central Committee decided that Stalin should be given the task of ensuring that the orders were obeyed. The decision came at an inopportune time since one of the three important subjects on which Lenin and Stalin were in disagreement was just coming to a head. This was the foreign trade monopoly and its resolution came when it was to have the maximum impact on Lenin's health and his relations with Stalin.

Control over the import and export of goods had been proposed soon after the autumn Revolution of 1917 by the Petrograd Revolutionary Committee, which supervised the work of the Customs. Customs had been regularized by a decree of the Council of People's Commissars on 29 December 1917 (11 January 1918) which brought foreign trade under the People's Commissariat for Trade and Industry, and in April 1918 was further tightened up by a decree, proposed by Lenin, which gave the State a monopoly of all foreign trade.

It was subsequently promised that the monopoly would be abolished, although on whose initiative is not quite clear as many Party leaders sought its end. Lenin thought differently and on 3 March 1922 pointed out what he saw as the inevitable dangers of such a move. Stalin, however, believed in its inevitability and the argument between the two factions was heated. Lenin seemed to have won when in May 1922 the Politburo agreed that the monopoly should remain in force. But on 6 October 1922 during Lenin's absence through illness the Politburo reversed the earlier decision by voting to limit drastically the State's foreign trade monopoly. It was an outcome that Lenin, ill though he was, had no intention of letting stand, and later in October he proposed that no change should be made for at least two months. Although he was absent from the meeting, he explained his views at some length in a letter to Stalin for members of the Party's Central Committee.

'We have begun to build up a system; the foreign trade monopoly and the co-operatives are both only in the process of being built up. Some results will be forthcoming in a year or two. The profit from foreign trade runs into hundreds per cent and we are *beginning* to receive millions and tens of millions. We have *begun* to build up mixed companies; we have begun to learn to receive *half* of their (monstrous) profits. We can already see signs of very substantial state profits. We are giving this up in the hope of duties which cannot yield any comparable profit; we are giving everything up and chasing a spectre!'

In the face of this the Central Committee decided by fourteen votes to one to postpone the changes.

Victory had been gained with the help of Trotsky's support, and on 21 December Lenin dictated a note to Krupskaya, thanking his colleague for having helped to gain the triumph in the Central Committee 'without a single shot'.

The repercussions of the note were greater than any of those involved can have imagined: Stalin telephoned Krupskaya, assailed her with what she later called 'unworthy abuse and threats', and even suggested that she might be prosecuted by the Party's Central Control Commission for taking down Lenin's note allegedly in defiance of doctor's orders.

Stalin had misjudged the situation. Neither Lenin nor Krupskaya was prepared to accept such treatment and Stalin's rash act appears to have been one of the factors in unleashing Lenin's 'Testament' – a revealing and controversial document.

On 23 December Krupskaya wrote to Kamenev:

'Lev Borisovich!

Stalin subjected me to a storm of the coarsest abuse yesterday about a brief note that Lenin dictated to me, with the permission of the doctors. I didn't join the Party yesterday. In the whole of these last thirty years I have never heard a single coarse word from a comrade. The interests of the Party and of Ilich are no less dear to me than to Stalin. At the moment I need all the self-control I can muster. I know better than all the doctors what can and what cannot be said to Ilich, for I know what disturbs him and what doesn't, and in any case I know this better than Stalin.'

She then asked to be protected from gross interference in her private life and continued:

'I have no doubt as to the unanimous decision of the

Control Commission with which Stalin takes it upon himself to threaten me, but I have neither the time nor the energy to lose in such a stupid farce. I am too human and my nerves are at breaking-point.'

It is impossible to know the precise further impact on events of Stalin's brusque telephone call, but on the evening of 23 December Lenin called his secretary M. A. Volodicheva to his flat. Her entry in the Duty Secretaries' Journal says:

'In the course of 4 minutes he dictated. Felt bad. Doctors called. Before starting to dictate, he said: "I want to dictate to you a letter to the Congress. Take it down." Dictated quickly, but his sick condition was obvious. Towards the end he asked what the date was. Why was I so pale, why wasn't I at the congress, was sorry that he was taking up the time that I could have spent there.'

The statement that Lenin began to dictate, which he continued on following days, and to which he added a postscript on 4 January, became known as the 'Testament'. In view of its contents it is not surprising that its history in the last sixty-odd years should have become just as wrapped in controversy as Lenin's own life.

'Comrade Stalin, having become Secretary-General [the "Testament" began], has unlimited authority concentrated in his hands, and I am not sure whether he will always be capable of using that authority with sufficient caution. Comrade Trotsky, on the other hand, as his struggle against the C.C. on the question of the People's Commissariat for Communications has already proved, is distinguished not only by outstanding ability. He is

691

personally perhaps the most capable man in the present C.C, but he has displayed excessive self-assurance and shown excessive preoccupation with the purely administrative side of the work.

'These two qualities of the two outstanding leaders of the present C.C.can inadvertently lead to a split, and if our Party does not take steps to avert this, the split may come unexpectedly.

'I shall not give any further appraisals of the personal qualities of other members of the C.C. I shall just recall that the October episode with Zinoviev and Kamenev was, of course, no accident, but neither can the blame for it be laid upon them personally, any more than non-Bolshevism can upon Trotsky.

'Speaking of the young C.C. members, I wish to say a few words about Bukharin and Pyatakov. They are, in my opinion, the most outstanding figures (among the youngest ones), and the following must be borne in mind about them: Bukharin is not only a most valuable and major theorist of the Party; he is also rightly considered the favourite of the whole Party, but his theoretical views can be classified as fully Marxist only with great reserve, for there is something scholastic about him (he has never made a study of dialectics, and, I think, never fully understood it).

. . . As for Pyatakov, he is unquestionably a man of outstanding will and outstanding ability, but shows too much zeal for administrating and the administrative side of the work to be relied upon in a serious political matter.

'Both of these remarks, of course, are made only for the present, on the assumption that both these outstanding and devoted Party workers fail to find an occasion to enhance their knowledge and amend their onesidedness.

December 25, 1922   Lenin.'

While Lenin dated the 'Testament' 25 December, he in fact continued dictating it not only on the twenty-fifth, but also on successive days. On the twenty-fourth, according to Volodicheva, he warned her that what he had dictated on the twenty-third and the twenty-fourth 'was *strictly* confidential. He emphasized this again and again. Demanded that *everything* he was dictating should be kept in a special place under special responsibility and to be considered *categorically* secret. He then added another order.'

The importance Lenin gave to the 'Testament' can be gathered from Volodicheva's later statement – footnoted in Lenin's *Collected Works* as though this was the additional 'order' to which she referred in her entry for the twenty-fifth.

'All the articles and documents which Lenin dictated between December 1922 (the 20th) and the beginning of March 1923 [it says] were typed at his request in five copies, one of which he asked to leave for him, three copies to be given to Nadezhda Konstantinovna, and one to his secretariat (strictly secret). The copy to be sent to 'Pravda' retyped fair with all his final corrections and changes was looked through by Lenin, after which it was passed on to Maria Ilyinichna. The three copies that Nadezhda Konstantinovna had received were also corrected. The rough copies were burnt by me. He asked that the sealed envelopes in which the copies of the documents were kept should be marked to the effect that they could only be opened by V. I. Lenin, and after his death by Nadezhda Konstantinovna. I did not write the words "and after his death" on the envelopes. Lenin's copies were kept in a file and corded for more convenient use.'

If the 'Testament' was explosive material, the postscript Lenin added on 4 January was even more so.

'Stalin is too rude and this defect, although quite tolerable in our midst and in dealings among us Communists, becomes intolerable in a Secretary-General. That is why I suggest that the comrades think about a way of removing Stalin from that post and appointing another man in his stead who in all other respects differs from Comrade Stalin in having only one advantage, namely, that of being more tolerant, more loyal, more polite and more considerate to the comrades, less capricious, etc. This circumstance may appear to be a negligible detail. But I think that from the standpoint of safeguards against a split and from the standpoint of what I wrote above about the relationship between Stalin and Trotsky it is not a detail, or it is a detail which can assume decisive importance.

January 4, 1923   Lenin.'

Dictation of the 'Testament' and its postscript appears to have allowed Lenin's mind to get back to its customary enthusiasm for purely political problems and during January 1923 he dictated his paper 'On Cooperation'; wrote 'Our Revolution (Apropos of N. Sukhanov's Notes)'; and completed a paper 'How We Should Reorganize the Workers' and Peasants' Inspectorate'.

Early in February he was visited by Volodicheva, who on 2 February 1923 wrote: 'I had not seen [Lenin] since January 23. Outwardly, a considerable change for the better; fresh, cheerful-looking. Dictates, as always, excellently.' Three days later M. I. Glyasser, another secretary, reported: 'I was seeing [Lenin] for the first time since his illness. I thought he looked well and cheerful, only slightly paler than before. Speaks slowly, gesticulating with his left hand and stirring the fingers of his right. No compress on his head.'

But his condition fluctuated quickly. On 7 February the entry in the Duty Secretaries'Journal spoke of a tremendous improvement and recorded that Lenin was beginning to think that he would regain the use of his arm. Five days later, however, he was worse, with bad headaches. The doctors had apparently upset him so much that his lips quivered. 'Foerster', it was added, 'the day before had said that he was emphatically prohibited newspapers, visitors and political information.'

Lenin's comparative cheerfulness early in February, interspersed though it was by darker periods, may well have been caused by the fact that with the 'Testament' he had put the record straight for the future while in immediate matters he had won his point on foreign trade. His victory here was confirmed during the Twelfth RCP(B) Congress, held from 17 to 23 April 1923, when it was stated: 'The Congress categorically affirms that the monopoly of foreign trade is immutable and that no-one is permitted to bypass it or to waver in implementing it. The new Central Committee is instructed to take systematic measures to strengthen and promote the monopoly of foreign trade.' The sick man had won.

There were, however, the two other matters of major importance over which he was to disagree strongly with Stalin and which continued to sour relations between them.

Rabkrin, the Workers' and Peasants' Inspectorate, had been set up by Lenin in 1919 to eliminate inefficiency and corruption in the State organization, and to expose abuses of power and the unnecessary use of red tape. He put Stalin in charge of the new organization. As Isaac Deutscher has said in his life of Stalin,

> 'The Rabkrin would have had to be a commissariat of angels in order to rise, let alone raise others, above the dark valley of Russian bureaucracy. With his characteristic belief in the inherent virtues of the working classes, Lenin appealed to the workers against his own bureaucracy. The mill of officialdom, however, turned the workers themselves into bureaucrats. The Commissariat of the Inspectorate, as Lenin was to discover later on, became an additional source of muddle, corruption and bureaucratic intrigue. In the end it became an unofficial but meddlesome police in charge of the civil service.'

For some time Lenin had either turned a blind eye to Rabkrin's deficiencies or considered that it could do no better in the circumstances. However, Stalin had remained in control of it, and it is difficult not to believe that it was Lenin's growing disillusion with 'the Caucasian' which finally brought his opposition to Rabkrin into the light. His first public criticism was 'How We Should Reorganize the Workers' and Peasants' Inspectorate' published in *Pravda* no. 16 on 25 January 1923. It was followed by the even more outspoken 'Better Less, but Better' which he dictated late in February or early March: 'Let us say frankly that the People's Commissariat of the Workers' and Peasants' Inspectorate does not at present enjoy the slightest authority,' he said. 'Everybody knows that no other institutions are worse organized than those of our Workers' and Peasants' Inspectorate and that under present conditions nothing can be expected from this People's Commissariat.'

While arguments over the State monopoly of trade and the efficiency of Rabkrin both exercised Lenin in the later days of his illness, it was the future of Georgia that loomed ever larger in his mind and which was to bring him into even more direct conflict with Stalin.

The policies controlling the administration of Georgia had been complex for years, and following the abdication of the Tsar in the spring of 1917 they became almost Byzantine in their complexity. The country was first controlled by a Petrograd Committee known as the Ozakom on which the Mensheviks were strongly represented. With the October Revolution the Committee took Georgia from Russia and founded a Trans-Caucasian Commissariat. This lasted only until 26 May 1918 when the Georgians set up a Georgian Social-Democratic Republic and placed themselves under the protection of the Germans. The situation was dramatically changed towards the end of 1918 with the defeat of the Central Powers, the occupation of Georgia by a British force and the appearance of General Denikin's White Russians. The Georgians found it impossible to work with the Whites while the British moved out, paving the way for a Russo-Georgian treaty and then the arrival of a Russian Mission under S. M. Kirov. There followed a period during which relations between Russia and Georgia – as between Russia and the Ukraine, Belorussia, Azerbaijan and Armenia – were regulated by bilateral treaties.

Meanwhile, three separate policies were gathering support in Georgia. One was for a union of the three Trans-Caucasian areas of Georgia, Azerbaijan and Armenia into a federation. Another was for the 'autonomization' or full self-government of Georgia, while the third proposed making Georgia an integral part of the Soviet Union. All three policies gained adherents and while Stalin favoured 'autonomization' which in practice would have meant Georgia joining the Russian federation as an autonomous unit, Lenin favoured the creation of a sovereign and independent unit which would have joined the Russian federative state.

To those unfamiliar with conditions in the region or with the history of how these conditions had evolved over the years, the differences between the three possible lines of future development can appear academic and of little practical importance. To those deeply rooted in the area, the differences of approach were of great importance and disagreements inevitable. Following the end of the Civil War, attempts were made to give what had been the huge tsarist empire a form reconciling local autonomy with policies that could be implemented on the national scale required for recovery. This had begun with the formation of a Trans-Caucasian Socialist Federal Republic from the three Trans-Caucasian republics of Armenia, Georgia and Azerbaijan. Next, the USSR was formed in December 1922 when the Ukrainian Soviet Socialist Republic and the Belorussian Soviet Socialist Republic joined the new grouping. In May 1925 the Uzbek and Turkmen Autonomous Soviet Socialist Republics became constituent members of the USSR and in 1929 the Tadzhik Autonomous Soviet Socialist Republic did the same, preparing the way for the creation of today's USSR.

While this common-sense development continued in general with a minimum of ructions over the years, the situation inside Georgia at the inception of these changes was both different and more difficult. On 12 February 1921 a rising took place inside the country. The Bolsheviks attributed it largely, as might have been expected, to Menshevik influence. During the first weeks of 1921 the Red Army, acting under the orders of Stalin, as Russian Commissar for Nationalities, and supported by the Georgian leader, Ordzhonikidze, invaded the country. According to a note in Lenin's *Collected Works,*

> 'At the request of the Georgian working people, Soviet Russia's Government ordered units of the 11th Army to support the insurgents. Relying on the support of these units, the workers and peasants of Georgia fought a heroic struggle and routed the Menshevik forces, liberating Tiflis, the capital of Georgia, on 25 February and proclaiming Georgia a Soviet Socialist Republic,'

which was then incorporated into the Trans-Caucasian Socialist Federal Republic.

Lenin had been prevented by illness from taking his usual direct part in the discussions which led to these moves, something he was apparently to regret later since he subsequently wrote: 'I am, it seems, strongly to blame *vis-á-vis* the workers of Russia for having failed to intervene sufficiently energetically and sufficiently incisively in the notorious question of the "Autonomization".'

He could not, however, avoid being directly concerned in the more serious discussions which developed in the second half of 1922. They covered relations between all the republics which were to form units of the USSR but the position of Georgia was one of the most contentious subjects involved, and on 22 October the Central Committee of the Georgian Party resigned *en bloc.* The following month Ordzhonikidze became involved in an argument with Kabanidze, a supporter of the Georgian 'Nationalists', and the latter was struck at least one physical blow. It was clear that urgent action was needed and on 24 November the Central Committee in Moscow set up a commission under Dzerzhinsky to visit Georgia and report on the situation. Lenin refused to vote on the composition of the commission – probably owing to lack of information and mixed feelings. But it was to Lenin that Dzerzhinsky went immediately on his return to Moscow on 12 December and reported his findings. He also appears to have given Lenin the latter's first news of the 'incident', as it was termed, between Ordzhonikidze and Kabanidze. Dzerzhinsky left no record of the meeting while Lenin's view of his role in the affair can be deduced only from what was subsequently reported by Lydia Fotiyeva whom he delegated to secure for him the necessary papers on 'the Georgian question'. 'He [Lenin] had been dissatisfied with the work of F. E. Dzerzhinsky's commission', she wrote, 'and considered that it had not displayed the necessary impartiality in its investigations of the "Georgian incident".' All that Lenin specifically told Fotiyeva appears to have been: 'Just before I fell ill, Dzerzhinsky told me about the work of the commission and about the "incident", and it affected me painfully.' During this meeting, Dzerzhinsky seems to have been less than forthcoming and in January 1923, Fotiyeva, acting on Lenin's instructions, asked Dzerzhinsky for 'the data on the "Georgian question".' She was told that Stalin had the information but Stalin maintained that he could not pass it on without the sanction of the Political Bureau, an answer that brought from Lenin the comment that 'he would fight for the data to be given him'.

It was on the morning following the meeting with Dzerzhinsky that Lenin suffered from the two attacks of thrombosis of the brain and it is difficult not to believe that the intensification of his illness was accelerated by his dismay at the way in which the situation in Georgia was developing. His attitude during that long-running drama was governed by two beliefs that tended to conflict and which he did his best to describe in notes written in the last days of December 1922. It is clear from these that he wanted national minorities to be proud of their status but at the same time proud of being part of Soviet Russia. Above all he wanted, as he put it, to ensure protection of 'nationalized Russians from the assault of the True-blue Great-Russian chauvinist – a scoundrel and ruffian in essence – personified by the typical Russian bureaucrat'.

In the deteriorating Georgian situation Stalin decided to protest to Lenin personally. He was stopped by Krupskaya, was unnecessarily rude to her, and thus added more bitterness to the relationship between himself and Lenin. Then, on 5 March 1923, Lenin sent for Volodicheva, and dictated two letters to her, one to Stalin and one to Trotsky. In the argument with Stalin, and in his stand on the Georgian question, he had reached his Rubicon.

The letter to Stalin was, on Lenin's instructions, not sent immediately but read over the telephone to Stalin's office the next day. Marked 'Top Secret and Personal' but bearing the words 'Copy to Comrades Kamenev and Zinoviev', it began: 'You have been so rude as to summon my wife to the telephone and use bad language', the implication being that only now had Lenin learned of Stalin's telephone argument with his wife the previous December.

'Although she had told you that she was prepared to forget this, the fact nevertheless became known through her to Zinoviev and Kamenev. I have no intention of forgetting so easily what has been done against me, and it goes without saying that what has been done against my wife I consider having been done against me as well. I ask you, therefore, to

701

think it over whether you are prepared to withdraw what you have said and to make your apologies, or whether you prefer that relations between us should be broken off.'

The second letter, whose contents Lenin insisted should be telephoned to Trotsky without delay, began with the words, 'Esteemed Comrade Trotsky', and went on,

'I urgently request you to take upon yourself the defense of the Georgian affair at the Central Committee of the party. The thing is at present under "prosecution" at the hands of Stalin and Dzherzhinsky, and I cannot rely upon their impartiality. Indeed, quite the opposite. If you would agree to take upon yourself its defence, then I could be at rest. If you for some reason do not agree, then return the whole thing to me. I will consider this a sign of your disagreement.

'With the best comradely greetings, Lenin.'

The following day Lenin reiterated his stand, writing to the Georgian Bolsheviks: 'To Comrades Mdivani, Makharadze and others (copies to Comrades Trotsky and Kamenev) Dear Comrades, In this affair I am entirely on your side. I am horrified at Ordzhonikidze's arrogance and Stalin's criminal alliance with him. I am preparing memoranda and a speech in your defence. With high regards, Lenin.'

It is not possible to claim that every deterioration in Lenin's condition during the last year or so of his life was directly the result of arguments with Stalin. Nevertheless there is a suspicious link once events are correlated, and it was now, a few days after his protest to Stalin, that on 9 or 10 March he suffered another stroke. It confined him to bed and the doctors again reported paralysis of the right arm and leg, as well as loss of speech and what was described as a cloudy consciousness. In May he was moved to Gorki. There was some improvement in his condition and on 19 June Krupskaya wrote to Clara Zetkin: 'The most important thing now is not a diagnosis but careful, attentive nursing. Everything depends on the general state of his strength. In this regard a visible improvement has been noticeable during the past month and there are days when I begin to hope that recovery is not impossible.'

G. E. Lozgachev-Yelizarov, the adopted son of Lenin's sister Anna, visited him at Gorki and found him 'sitting in his wheel-chair in a white summer shirt with an open collar . . . A rather old cap covered his head and the right arm lay somewhat unnaturally on his lap. [He] hardly noticed me even though I stood quite plainly in the middle of the clearing.'

Krupskaya strove to teach her husband to speak once more, and by the early autumn of 1923, with the help of a stick and orthopaedic shoes, he was just able to walk again. He was sometimes pushed in a wheelchair round the grounds of the Gorki house; he began to read papers which were sent in, and he learned to write with his left hand so that his inability to speak and the paralysis of his right hand did not completely prevent his communicating with Krupskaya or with visitors.

In October 1923 he was driven to Moscow and visited his flat and his office before being taken back through an agricultural exhibition so that he could see the latest equipment. Once in Gorki again, Krupskaya often read to him and late in December 1923 Lenin asked her to read a passage from one of Trotsky's books, probably his early *History of the Revolution,* dealing with Marx and Lenin. He listened intently, then read the passage for himself.

Back in Gorki, Lenin continued to show interest in his

surroundings and bought a Christmas tree for the children on the estate. The few details of his last days come from only three sources – Krupskaya, Walter Duranty, the *New York Times* correspondent who over a long period had built up a reliable network of informants, and Nikolay Bukharin, Lenin's confidant from 1917 and a member of the Central Committee for twenty years. Bukharin later told an interviewing historian, Boris I. Nikolayevsky:

'Lenin would summon me to come and see him. The doctors had forbidden him to speak lest he become upset. But when I arrived, he would immediately take me by the hand and lead me into the garden. He would begin to speak. "They don't want me to think about this. They say that this upsets me. But why don't they understand that I have lived my whole life this way? If I cannot speak about this, I become more upset than when I do speak. I calm down when I am able to talk about these matters with people like you." '

The talk, Bukharin explained to Nikolayevsky, was mostly about 'leaderology', about who was fit to succeed him as leader of the Party. 'This', Bukharin went on, 'is what worried and upset Lenin the most.'

'In this connection [Nikolayevsky later wrote], he told me that the last articles of Lenin's "Better Less but Better", about co-operatives and so forth, were only part of what Lenin had planned to do. He had wanted to put out another series of approximately the same number of articles which would give a complete picture of the future policy to be pursued. This was his principal goal.'

On 19 January 1924, Krupskaya read her husband *Love of Life* (1906), a story by Jack London which describes how a gold prospector struggles to survive after spraining his ankle in the Canadian wilderness and finally does so by strangling a wolf that tries to attack him, and then drinking the wolf's blood. According to Krupskaya, Lenin liked the story enormously. While she was reading it, Mikhail Kalinin, chairman of the Central Executive Committee of the Congress of Soviets, was opening the Soviets' Eleventh Congress in Moscow and telling its members that Lenin was fighting his illness and that 'rays of hope are already visible – the end of his long grave battle with this disease'. There came a call from the delegates: 'Long live the leader of the world proletariat, comrade Lenin!', followed by cries of 'Hurrah'.

The next day followed quietly. Krupskaya again read from Jack London but this time with different results. 'The next story we came to was of a quite different type,' she wrote. 'It was replete with bourgeois morality . . . Ilich began to laugh and waved it aside.'

On the morning of the next day, the twenty-first, it was thought that an outing would do him good, so a sleigh was brought round and he was propped up in it with pillows. Then Bukharin and a number of workers from the estate took him on a hunting party. 'Lenin was evidently in good spirits when they lifted him into the sleigh to go hunting. He sat watching with the keenest attention and when a young retriever brought back a bird to Bukharin, who was standing near the sleigh, Lenin raised his good hand and said *"Vot sobaka"* ("Good dog").'

He came back still in good spirits. But he was obviously tired, the doctor in attendance advised that he should go to bed and after eating a hearty meal he retired to lie down. In the late afternoon he had another stroke. His temperature rose and he lost consciousness before dying in the early evening.

The dangerous state of Lenin's health had been kept not only from the public but from many of those Party members who might have expected to be better informed, and news of his death therefore came as a greater shock than would otherwise have been the case. The late hour of his death on the twenty-first, combined with the fact that the twent y-second was the nineteenth anniversary of Bloody Sunday, always marked by demonstrations, meant that the event missed the first editions of that day's papers. The members of the Eleventh Congress of Soviets meeting in the Bolshoi Theatre thus had no warning when Kalinin asked them to rise before announcing: 'I bring you terrible news about our dear comrade, Vladimir Ilyich.' This was an indication of what was coming and a wailing cry was heard from high up in one of the galleries, followed by an outburst of sobs as he continued: 'Yesterday, he suffered a further stroke of paralysis and – died.'

The scene that followed was described by Walter Duranty, who during the next few days was to provide graphic accounts of how Moscow and its citizens responded to the event:

'The emotional Slav temperament reacted immediately. From all over the huge opera house came sobs and wailing, not loud or shrill, but pitifully mournful, spreading and increasing. Kalinin could not speak. He tried vainly to motion for silence with his hands and for one appalling moment a dreadful outbreak of mass hysteria seemed certain. A tenth of a second later it could not have been averted, but Yenukidze, Secretary of the Russian Federal Union, thrust forward his powerful frame and with hand and voice demanded calm. Then Kalinin, stammering read

706

out the official bulletin. It gave few details, merely reporting: 'On January 21st, the condition of Vladimir Ilyich suddenly underwent a sharp aggravation. At 5.50 Vladimir Ilyich died from paralysis of the respiratory centres." '

Members of the Presidium and others, Kalinin went on, would travel to Gorki the following morning by special train. Lenin's body would be brought to Moscow, and would then lie in state until the following Saturday. A funeral march was played and the meeting ended.

News of Lenin's death spread quickly through Moscow by word of mouth and by special editions of *Pravda, Izvestia* and *Rabochaya Moskva*. A Funeral Commission was set up in the Moscow Trade Union Hall whose Hall of Columns was selected as the place where the body would lie in state until the funeral. Elsewhere throughout the country, factory sirens blared out to call the population to hear the news, the task performed for earlier generations by church bells.

Before the body was moved to Moscow a four-and-a-half-hour autopsy was undertaken at Gorki by a medical team led by Dr. A. I. Abrikosov. It was found that owing to a severe sclerosis of the arteries leading to the brain, the brain's blood supply had been seriously impaired. Fatty deposits in the arteries had calcified and had prevented the normal flow of blood, and the necessary amount of oxygen, from reaching the brain. The destroyed blood vessels were in that part of the brain controlling respiration and for that reason Lenin's breathing stopped. Thus, put simply, the cause of death was brain haemorrhage.

On the twenty-third, the body was brought from Gorki to Moscow, Duranty remembering years afterwards the figure of Kalinin helping to carry the coffin from the Moscow station to the Nobles' Club where it was to lie in state.

'When two steps down from the platform, its weight was suddenly thrown on him in front. During those moments of strain he symbolized the struggle of Russia's 140,000,000 peasants against the blind enmity of nature and human oppression. For two nights he had not slept and, as the level ground relieved part of the burden, he staggered from sheer exhaustion. But on he went like an old peasant plowing the stubborn earth, with sweat pouring down his cheeks in an icy-flecked gale, until he reached a gun caisson with six white horses waiting in the station-yard to carry the coffin to the Nobles' Club.'

The coffin was in fact carried through the Moscow streets by Kalinin, Bukharin, Tomsky, Kamenev, Stalin, Rudzutak, Zinoviev and Rykov. Behind it walked Krupskaya, Lenin's sisters, and other relatives, followed by a guard of honour and Party members. Overhead flew aircraft dropping mourning leaflets.

The cortège halted every half-mile of its five-mile route through the snow-covered streets for the coffin-bearers to be changed as spectators looked on from windows, balconies and roofs, or from the packed streets.

'In the central hall of the former Nobles' Club [Duranty reported] Lenin lay on a high couch with four columns that gave the effect of a sort of old-fashioned four-poster bed without curtains. Over his feet was a grey rug with some-thing stenciled on it, over his body a dark red blanket; and his head rested bare on a white pillow. The face was a yellow-white, like wax, without the slightest wrinkle and utterly calm. The eyes were closed, yet the expression was of one looking forward, seeking something beyond his vision.'

It had originally been arranged that during the lying-in-state eight guards should stand by the bier and should be changed every ten minutes. But so many wanted to share the honour, that sixteen men instead of eight took up position simultaneously, then twenty-four instead of sixteen. Even this was not sufficient and it was arranged that the guard should be changed every five minutes, then every three. The wish to file by the coffin was as considerable as that of the military to mount guard, and the original single file of mourners soon had to be doubled. Outside the hall the cold remained intense even for Moscow, and inside stretchers were stacked for those who fainted. Children had to be dissuaded from joining the queue of mourners.

The ceremonies in Moscow were carried out in the absence of one Party leader whose failure to appear caused comment never entirely countered by later statements. This was Trotsky, who on 18 January had left Sukhumi on the Black Sea where he was to take a recuperative rest. By the twenty-first he had arrived at Tiflis and it was on the station there that he was brought the news of Lenin's death. He cabled Moscow immediately and asked whether he should return for the funeral. According to his version of events he received a reply saying: 'The funeral will be on Saturday: you can't get back in time, and so we advise you to continue your treatment.'

'Accordingly [he goes on] I had no choice. As a matter of fact, the funeral did not take place until Sunday, and I could easily have reached Moscow by then. Incredible as it may appear, I was even deceived about the date of the funeral.

The conspirators surmised correctly that I would never think of verifying it, and later on they could always find an explanation.'

Trotsky's suspicions were unjustified, since Saturday was the day originally chosen for the funeral, and the postponement until Sunday had a valid explanation. Nevertheless, his belief that he had been kept from Moscow at a time when the succession would be under debate is an indication of the atmosphere then surrounding those governing the country.

While Muscovites speculated on Trotsky's absence, the repercussions of Lenin's death began. The Sparrow Hills outside Moscow were renamed the Lenin Hills and in Petrograd it was agreed, without major objection, that the name of the city should be changed to Leningrad. It was proposed that the northernmost Russian territory, hitherto named after Nicholas II, should be renamed Vladimir Ilyich Lenin Land. *Pravda* suggested that a black stripe or a black square should be added to the country's flag as a sign of perpetual mourning, and there even crept into print the proposal that Sunday should in future be known as Leninday.

What Duranty termed an amazing week of national emotion reached its climax at four o'clock on 27 January when six members of the Central Committee carried the red-draped coffin to the mausoleum in Red Square. He wrote:

'Massed bands played the *Internationale* to slow time and from the vast multitude in the Square rose in the icy air a fog of congealed breath, like the smoke of sacrifice. So cold was it – 35 degrees below zero Fahrenheit – that beards, hats, collars, and eyebrows were white like the snow-clad trees in the little park close to the Kremlin wall. Few dared to take off their hats as Lenin's body passed to its last rest-ing-place. The majority stood at salute with raised hands.

'In the streets leading to the square tens of thousands more, lined up under mourning banners, were waiting admission. At the corners soldiers built log fires, round which each squad, relieved hourly owing to the intense cold, stamped and beat their arms against their bodies.

'The most striking feature of the last moment was its utter absence of ceremony. Lenin's disciples took the Master's body and laid it in its appointed place. No word was said.'

There was to follow the embalming of Lenin's body and its removal to a new mausoleum in Red Square, which became the central Russian place of pilgrimage for the Communist faithful, Lenin statues and Lenin mementoes and souvenirs; and the building-up in folklore and legend of a fairytale Lenin.

The final resting place of Lenin's body quickly became the focal point for 'the Lenin cult'. As Nina Tumarkin has commented *in Lenin Lives! the* cult

'was less an actual substitute for religion than a party effort to fuse religious and political ritual to mobilize the popula-tion. It is likely that people were – and still are – drawn to the Lenin Mausoleum not for spiritual reasons but out of a combined sense of political duty and fascination, or even morbid curiosity. If nothing else, the body cult is a show. A visit to the Lenin Mausoleum is memorable, with its solemn guards hushing the visitors and hurrying them along, its gleaming walls of polished grey and black marble slashed with a red zigzag, and the figure of Lenin bathed in a pinkish light. Before the shrine was erected, Agitprop had generated nothing even remotely so riveting.'

Considerable mystery has always surrounded the decision to embalm the body and make the mausoleum a centre of pilgrimage. The possibility, with others, had been discussed by members of the Politburo in the autumn of 1923. Stalin had reported that certain unnamed comrades in the provinces had expressed themselves as being against cremation. Embalming was always a possibility but it is unlikely to have been given such earnest consideration, or finally adopted, had there not been so much publicity in 1923 about the discovery of Tutankhamun's mummified body at Luxor by Lord Carnarvon. The interest aroused among the public by the lying-in-state also helped. Trotsky, Kamenev and Bukharin had all seemed to be against embalming, while a letter from Krupskaya, who lived on until 1939, published in *Pravda* on 30 January 1924, could also be considered in the same sense. It read,

'Comrades, workers and peasants!
I have a great request to make of you: do not allow your grief for Ilyich to express itself in the external veneration of his person. Do not build memorials to him, palaces named after him, (do not hold) magnificent celebrations in his memory, etc. All of this meant so little to him in his lifetime: he found it all so trying. Remember how much poverty and disorder we still have in our country. If you want to honour the name of Vladimir Ilyich – build day care centres, kindergartens, homes, schools . . . etc., and most importantly – try in all things to fulfil his legacy . . .'

Krupskaya failed to make her point and on 25 March 1924, it

was officially announced that it had been 'decided to take measures, available in current science, to preserve the body for as long as possible'. Three days later the Funeral Commission was renamed the Commission for the Immortalization of the Memory of V. I. Ulyanov (Lenin) and soon afterwards work was begun on planning a new mausoleum which was finally opened on 1 August 1924 – only to be replaced by a more elaborate edifice in 1930.

Although the decision to put Lenin's body on display indefinitely in Moscow aroused controversy, other developments of the Lenin cult also brought protests, even though most of them served some propaganda purpose for the Party. The number of girls being christened 'Ninel' – Lenin spelt backwards – was an indication of how strongly many people felt. There was the Lenin Enrolment inaugurated by the Central Committee – a three-month campaign that flew in the face of Lenin's belief that quality should come before quantity. Schools, factories and institutions started Lenin Funds, which were to be dedicated to boosting Party membership and were very successful. Wherever Lenin had lived or worked was given special attention and Russia eventually had more than 500 such places in its charge. Outside the country there were twenty Lenin museums and museum rooms and innumerable memorial plaques.

Numerous biographies of Lenin began to appear soon after his death, and so did a huge quantity of articles describing various aspects of his life.

More than one of the obituary notices underwent a change with time. Gorky had originally written: 'In the end, that wins out which is honest and righteous, in what is created by man that wins out without which there is no man.' In later editions of Gorky's works this was changed to: 'Vladimir Lenin died: the heritage of his reason and will live on, are alive and work successfully as no

713

one, nowhere in the world, ever worked.' It is claimed that Gorky made the change himself in 1930 but as one of his biographers has pointed out: 'The new text seems to be modelled on a rather perfunctory sentence Gorky once had written to somebody about Tolstoy's death, and the scary image of Lenin's reason and will working on, and on, and on, was a standard Party cliché.'

Despite the flood of biographies, largely hagiographical, Lenin was singularly absent from imaginative literature during the decades that followed – largely, no doubt, because of the dangers of stepping beyond what was for years the officially approved version of his activities. An important exception was *Lenin in Zurich* by Alexander Solzhenitsyn, who had intended to make Lenin an important figure in a multi-volume epic he began after the Second World War. Instead, there appeared the account of Lenin's years in Switzerland.

'My aim [Solzhenitsyn has been quoted as saying] is [there] to give as little play to the imagination as possible and to re-create as closely as possible what he was really like. The writer's imagination only helps to forge the separate elements into one whole and, by penetrating into the character, to try to explain how these elements interact.'

According to Michael Scammell, one of Solzhenitsyn's biographers, his 'aim was to demystify Lenin, to cut him down from his mythic dimensions to human size and to create a counter-myth to the official Soviet legend of the avuncular idealist with the heart of gold and the cares of mankind on his shoulders'.

The method used, according to Solzhenitsyn, was

'a form of creative research. My aim is to reconstruct history

714

in its fullness, in its authenticity, in its complexity, but for this I have to use the artist's vision, because a historian uses only documentary material, much of which has been lost. The historian uses evidence from witnesses, most of whom are no longer alive . . . whereas the artist can see farther and deeper, thanks to the force of perception in the artist's vision. I am not writing a novel. I am using all the artistic means available to me to penetrate as deeply as possible into historical events.'

How successful he was is a matter of opinion. He recalled how Lenin and Trotsky had, in his words, 'created the first and great-est totalitarianism the world has seen and how they devised their methods of mass terror'. The extent to which this attitude quali-fied his use of actual events can be judged in that, according to Solzhenitsyn, Lenin was on the verge of giving up his revolution-ary hopes entirely and retiring to America when in 1917 the opportunity arose for him to return home.

But literature about Lenin was only the most expected form of tribute made immediately after his death. His portrait appeared in articles as a sales promotion device, a practice which was stopped when it was reported that numbers of empty cigarette packets carrying his picture were being trampled underfoot. Inkwells made in the shape of the mausoleum were on sale during the summer of 1924, as were at least two Lenin toys, one consist-ing of building blocks from which five portraits of Lenin could be made up, the other making a model of the mausoleum.

So great had the 'Lenin curio trade' quickly become that on 24 April 1924, the Central Executive Committee passed a decree prohibiting the manufacture or exhibition of posters, paintings, drawings or busts of Lenin unless permission had been given for them by one of a number of subcommittees named by the Immortalization Commission.

His life and achievements were already being transposed into legend. It was a slow process, but less than three decades had passed before a writer could describe how

'In Tadjik and Kazakh legend Lenin was as high as the hills, as the clouds; in Dungan folk-lore he was brighter than the sun and knew no night. The Oyruts say that he had a sunbeam in his right hand, a moonbeam in his left; the ground trembled under him. For the Uzbeks Lenin was a giant who could shake the earth and move great rocks in his search for the fortune hidden in the hills; he could solve the most puzzling riddles. In Kirgiz story he had a magic ring, with the help of which he overthrew the power of the evil one and liberated the poor from wrong and injustice. He is reputed to have arrived in Armenia on a white horse, to lead the people. In another legend Lenin was a Titan struggling against Asmodeus, the friend of the rich and privileged, the worst enemy of the poor. Asmodeus strove to kill Lenin but the light from the hero's eyes put him to flight. Lenin then seated himself upon an eagle and flew to Dagestan, where he stirred up war against the rich, and finally flew back to the cold regions to write books of truth for the people. For the northern Ostyaks Lenin was a great seal hunter who slew the rich fur-traders and gave the booty to the poor; similarly, the Nentsy think of Lenin as the most expert of all sailors, who overcame his enemies in combat, seized their dogs and reindeer, and divided them among the poor. Sholokhov's Cossacks visualized Lenin as a Don Cossack.'

716

The apotheosis of Lenin in folklore and legend, as well as the growth of the Lenin cult in more sophisticated circles, took place while his views on his potential successors, and his bitter disagreements with Stalin, remained unknown to the mass of the population and known only in partial and guarded detail to most members of the Party who were trying to deal with Russia's problems as they expanded in the vacuum created by Lenin's death. Until he died only Krupskaya and his secretaries knew of the existence of the most vital document, the 'Testament'. Only when the details of the Thirteenth RCP(B) Congress were being settled, the Congress at which Lenin had hoped that his views would be revealed, was it made known.

But by this time Stalin, Zinoviev and Kamenev were, semi-officially at least, in control of the Party machine, and since Stalin was the most powerful of the three it was decided that the 'Testament' should not be read at the Congress. However, Krupskaya was a determined woman and on her insistence it was read by Kamenev to the leaders of the provincial delegations although none of them was allowed to take notes. 'So far as I can restore the picture from memory,' Trotsky wrote later, 'I should say that those who already knew the contents of the document were incomparably the most anxious.' As the 'Testament' was read out to the local delegations he also said, 'The leaders of the delegations in their reading would swallow some words, emphasize others, and offer commentaries to the effect that the letter had been written by a man seriously ill and under the influence of trickery and intrigue. The machine was already in complete control.'

It was clear that the struggle for leadership was between Trotsky and Stalin and when the 'Testament' was being read to the Central Committee Radek, then still a member of the Committee, turned to Trotsky, who was sitting next to him, with

717

the words: 'Now they won't dare go against you.' Trotsky replied significantly: 'On the contrary, they will have to go [to] the limit, and moreover as quickly as possible.'

Finally, in May 1924, the 'Testament' was read out in plenary session, after which a vote was to be taken on whether or not it should be made public. 'Terrible embarrassment paralysed all those present,' according to B. Bazhanov. 'Stalin sitting on the steps of the rostrum looked small and miserable. I studied him closely; in spite of his self-control and show of calm, it was clearly evident that his fate was at stake.' Then Zinoviev spoke:

'Comrades [he said], every word of Ilyich is law to us . . . We have sworn to fulfil anything the dying Ilyich ordered us to do. You know perfectly well that we shall keep that vow. But we are happy to say that in one point Lenin's fears have proved baseless. I have in mind the point about our General-Secretary. You have all witnessed our harmonious co-operation in the last few months; and, like myself, you will be happy to say that Lenin's fears have proved baseless.'

Kamenev then proposed that Stalin should be left in office; and the 'Testament' should not be published at the Congress, a proposal that was approved despite Krupskaya's protest. Instead, it was agreed that it should be communicated confidentially to selected delegates. In Russia this remained the position for more than another four decades although the text was published in the *New York Times* in 1926. Then, on 25 February 1956, three years after Stalin's death, Khrushchev read at the Twentieth Party Congress, the 'Testament', its postscript, and Lenin's letter to Stalin objecting to Stalin's treatment of Krupskaya.

The process of de-Stalinization, begun in 1956, reached its

climax during the Twenty-Second Congress of the Communist Party of the Soviet Union, held in Moscow in October 1961, when it was decided to move Stalin's corpse. It was stated:

'To continue to keep the coffin with the mortal remains of Y. V. Stalin in the Lenin Mausoleum is intolerable. His grievous contraventions of Lenin's testament, his abuse of power, his mass reprisals against honourable Soviet people, and other misdeeds in the days of the personality cult make it impossible for the coffin with his mortal remains to [stay] any longer in the Lenin Mausoleum.'

Long before this, the fears expressed in the 'Testament' were seen to have been justified. After Lenin's death Stalin had quickly begun to extend his power. Trotsky was demoted, then expelled and murdered in Mexico, almost certainly on Stalin's direct personal orders. A series of show trials resulted in the execution of most of those veteran Bolsheviks who had built up the Party. And a series of military purges so reduced the effectiveness of the Red Army that it was barely able to meet Hitler's attack which came in 1941.

While the struggle for power was being fought out a determined effort was made within the Party to fix in a shape that best conformed to Party theory the image of Lenin, his family background and his beliefs throughout an active life.

The process continued, and within a few years of Lenin's death Stalin had begun to impress his own stamp on the life of Russia and the methods by which the country was run. The agricultural requirements of the NEP began to be replaced by plans to transform Russia into a modern industrialized state, and with this went a nationalism that soon became chauvinistic in character

– a process carried out with a ruthlessness and disregard for human rights that even surpassed those qualities shown by the Cheka at the height of its power. Soon afterwards there began the show trials which brought before the firing squads of a Stalin-dominated Government many of the men who had made the Communist Revolution.

In the light of these events it was for long difficult if not dangerous to draw up an unbiased balance sheet of what Lenin had done for the country, a task made more difficult when about fifteen years after his death Russia struck a bargain with Nazi Germany which eventually led to her invasion by the Germans for the second time in a generation and to the expansion of a European conflict into a world war. Yet it can hardly be disputed that without Lenin's genius and drive the Provisional Government of 1917 would have stumbled on in some shape or form until Germany, before turning for a final assault on the West, had enforced a peace on Russia quite as humiliating as that of Brest-Litovsk. Without Lenin, Russia might have been spared the worst disasters of the civil war but it is unlikely that she would have recovered from the ravages of the First World War without the ruthless reorganization which he forced on the country and which inevitably caused such suffering.

On a different plane it can be argued, and often is, that Lenin, by his devious and Machiavellian operations within the Party, lowered political and diplomatic negotiations to a level that became the norm rather than the exception, and that by his early attitudes to terror he paved the way first for the enormities of the Cheka and then for the even greater enormities perpetrated by Stalin.

The first charge appears ingenuous. If the jockeyings for power in Western parties and governments are investigated with the attention to detail that has been given to the building of Lenin's empire, then the differences tend to be revealed as differences of method and degree rather than as differences between black and white. Few men have gained power, or retained it, by using, in Lenin's words, 'the methods of a finishing school for young ladies'.

Charges crediting Lenin with the use, and extension, of political terror, the antithesis of such methods, cannot be avoided. He himself made no attempt to prevaricate except on the rare occasions when it was expedient to do so, and usually he would readily admit that terror had been used as a matter of policy. Horrifying as this will be to most people, it is often excused on the grounds of ends justifying means. Lenin stands out from other defenders of terror partly because of the great facilities for organized terror that he had at his disposal and partly because of their unlimited extension under his successor, Joseph Stalin. If it is one of the debit entries in his record, it is one of unparalleled importance.

In summing up a man's life it is customary to provide a profit and loss account. This is sometimes meaningless in the case of the genius, to whom normal standards can be applied only with difficulty; and Lenin was certainly a genius in the concentration and ability that he devoted to the one single ambition of his life, the restructuring of Russian society at least, and if possible that of the world, into a form which, he believed, would enable human beings to exploit their potentialities more fully than was possible under capitalism. His success in Russia is beyond doubt, as is his failure to achieve more than partial success elsewhere. The questions raised by the human balance sheet are whether the price paid for the Russian achievement was too high and, secondly, whether the same result could have been obtained at lower cost. The answer to the first question lies very largely in the mind of whoever asks it; the answer to the second can be obtained more easily since it seems unlikely that the Russia of Tsar Nicholas could have been steered into that of the Bolsheviks without the changes forced through by Lenin.

Yet his qualities, which made such changes possible, are different in two ways from those normally attributed to the dedicated revolutionary. It is true that once the blatant hagiography is cut away the picture that the Party has painted for more than half a century conforms nearly to the facts. Lenin was, indeed, dedicated to the cause as few men are dedicated. His personal austerity was of a quality found in few people, and his life had an almost puritan strictness, which survives the most diligent inspection. In these respects Lenin under the microscope is remarkably like the public figure that has been painted since the early days of the Revolution.

Yet there are two aspects of his character which tend to be overlooked but which stand out when his life is carefully and impartially examined. The first is that the dogmatism expected of the dedicated and successful revolutionary was qualified in Lenin's case by a surprising talent for bending with the wind when necessary; a talent, furthermore, which enabled him not only to abandon long-held positions but to justify, as part of the naturally ordained order of events, those changes described by enemies as retreats. Lenin's ability to *reculer pour mieux muter* – shown more than once on minor points of policy or strategy during the bitter in-fighting that marked the formation and consolidation of the Bolshevik Party during the first years of the century – was demonstrated most clearly in his changes of stance concerning co-operation with the Duma, in his support for the treaty of Brest-Litovsk and in the NEP. This flexibility, a colourless but fair word to describe the quality that contributed so much to Lenin's success, was matched by another, which is rarely seen in a revolutionary – that of administrative ability. The record from the late autumn of 1917 until late 1922, when illness began to warp the story, is a remarkable account judged by any relevant standards. Lenin's early legal training no doubt helped; so did the ruthlessness that formed an iron rod running through him from top to toe and which was exercised as often in the administrative or business field as in the political. Without the results of such leadership Russia would have been unable to pull herself through the problems which so nearly brought irreparable disaster after so many years of war. As it was, survival was a close-run victory.

Without Lenin at the helm it would have been impossible to bring in, with eventual success, the changes of 1917 to 1918, followed by those introduced after 1921. Without them Russia would almost certainly have sunk down, from one level to the next, into a miasma of Oblomovism, which would have justified all the criticisms that the West would have made.

The explanation of how Lenin gave Russia a different destiny is predominantly a question of character, a factor perceptively remarked upon in a different case by Kenneth Harris in his life of Clement Attlee. 'Mr Attlee's appearance has been compared to that of Lenin,' he has written. 'Wild as the comparison may seem, it is nevertheless true that he has something of that quality of private decision, that ability to follow his own analysis of events to its logical conclusion, unperturbed by the feelings of those around him, unperturbed, also, by his own feelings, fears, or vanities, that Lenin possessed.'

It is against the long-term results of these private decisions, emerging only decades after Lenin's death, that there must be weighed the Terror which he helped to inaugurate and the evolution of a system of life unacceptable to those outside the mental and physical strait-jacket of Communist beliefs.

Notes and References

Full details of the sources quoted, manuscript and printed, are given with bibliographical information in the Bibliography, pp. 533–45.

1 The Boy from the Volga

4. 'collegiate councillor Ilya Nikolayevich Ulyanov' Y. A. Krasin (ed.) *V. I. Lenin: His Life and Work* (afterwards referred to as *Lenin's Life and Work*), p. 23.

5. 'No sooner had I come to know' quoted I. Y. Baranov, in *The Ulyanov Family* (afterwards referred to as Baranov), p. 114.

5. 'Accurate and complete information' Rolf H. W. Theen, *Lenin,* (afterwards referred to as Theen), p. 27.

5. 'to Vladimir Ilyich Lenin, nobleman by birth' quoted Nikolai Valentinov, *The Early Years of Lenin,* (afterwards referred to as Valentinov, *Early Years)* p. 5.

8. 'His entire life' M. I. Ulyanova, Preface to *Letters to Relatives* (1930 edition), V. I. Lenin, *Collected Work,* (afterwards referred to as *CW)* vol. 37, p. 24

9. '. . . various kinds of houses' quoted Valentinov, *Early Years,* p. 9.

10. 'The outward appearance of my home town' *ibid.*

10. 'lay on his bed all the time' quoted Leopold H. Haimson, *The Russian Marxists & the Origins of Bolshevism* (afterwards referred to as Haimson) p. 102.

11. 'These other children are good' quoted Valentinov, *Early Years,* p. 17.

11. 'Russian blood is flowing in vain' quoted Valentinov, *Early Years,* p. 197.

12. 'very painfully felt the change' quoted Isaac Deutscher, *Lenin's Childhood* (afterwards referred to as Deutscher, *Childhood)* p. 14.

12. 'Kubyshkin', 'French only' and 'German only' *ibid.,* p. 26.

13. 'At first Vladimir imitated his brother' quoted A. I. Tomul in Baranov, p. 55.

14. 'Rather short, but fairly powerfully built' quoted George Katkov and Harold Shukman, *Lenin's Path to Power: Bolshevism and the Destiny of Russia* (afterwards referred to as Katkov and Shukman) p. 16.

15. 'a walking encyclopaedia' *ibid.*

16. 'A very gifted and reliable student' quoted Valentinov, *Early Years,* p. 35.

16. 'He is very attentive in class' *ibid.*

17. 'I am sending father the brochure' quoted Tomul in Baranov, p. 53.

20. 'Why did you not try to escape' quoted Deutscher, *Childhood,* p. 58.

20. 'I did not want to escape' *ibid.*

20. 'After studying social and economic sciences' quoted Baranov, p. 125.

21. 'These accursed social questions' quoted *Lenin through the Eyes of Lunacharsky* (afterwards referred to as Lunacharsky), p. 21.

21. '. . . the evening was so still' quoted Deutscher, *Childhood*, p. 65.

22. 'He was at the age to feel' Winston S. Churchill, *The World Crisis: The Aftermath* (afterwards referred to as Churchill), p. 73.

22. '[He] questioned me . . . especially' I. N. Chebotarev, quoted Valentinov, *Early Years*, p. 117.

23. 'Chernyshevsky's novel . . . fascinated' quoted Valentinov, *Early Years*, pp. 135–6.

23. 'Before I came to know' quoted Baranov, p. 128.

26. 'No, we shall not take that road' quoted Theen, p. 49.

26. 'Terror is the sole form of defense' quoted William Henry Chamberlin, *The Russian Revolution, 1917–1921* (afterwards referred to as Chamberlin), vol. I, P. 34.

26. 'Basically we have never rejected terrorism' quoted Hellmut Andics, *Rule of Terror* (afterwards referred to as Andics), p. 14

27. 'Many of [the Social-Democrats] had begun' *What Is To Be Done?*, *CW*, vol. 5, P. 517.

27. 'A neat job' quoted Theen, p. 67.

27. 'We consider it not only our right' quoted Chamberlin, vol. I, p. 41.

28. 'Quite talented, invariably diligent' quoted Leon Trotsky, *Young Lenin* (afterwards referred to as Trotsky, *Young Lenin*), p. 94.

2 Novice Conspirator

31. 'You must not shout so' quoted Valentinov, *Early Years*, p. 44.

31. 'We began to dream about our move' quoted Nikolay Valentinov, *Encounters with Lenin* (afterwards referred to as Valentinov, *Encounters*), p. 109.

32. 'I did not imagine that I would remember' *ibid.*

32. 'In contrast to the overwhelming majority' Valentinov, *Early Years*, p. 140.

33. 'He attracted attention' quoted Christopher Hill, *Lenin and the Russian Revolution* (afterwards referred to as Hill), p. 33.

34. 'Why are you rebelling' quoted Theen, p. 56.

34. 'A wall, yes,' quoted Theen, p. 57.

34. 'surrounded himself with books' quoted Gerda and Hermann Weber, *Lenin: Life and Works* (afterwards referred to as Weber), p. 3.

35. 'Not to be accepted' quoted Trotsky, *Young Lenin*, p. 122.

35. 'It is a sheer torment to look at my son' quoted Adam B. Ulam, *The Bolsheviks,* p. 97.

36. 'One must rule the advocate' quoted Eugene Huskey, *Russian Lawyers and the Soviet State*, p. 38.

36. 'Everything that [Chernyshevsky] published' Lenin to V. V. Varovsky, (1904), quoted Valentinov, *Early Years*, p. 195.

37. 'I do not know another person' quoted Valentinov, *Early Years,* p. 141.

37. 'got hold of the first volume' quoted Trotsky, *Young Lenin*, p. 126.

38. 'was compelled to avoid using the words' N. Krupskaya, *How Lenin Studied Marx,* p. 2.

38. 'The highroad of History is not the sidewalk' quoted Tibor Szamuely, *The Russian Tradition* (afterwards referred to as Szamuely), p. 167.

39. 'The attempt to seize power' *What Is To Be Done?, CW,* vol. 5, p. 510.

40. 'I think that I, too,' 'A Few Words about N. Y. Fedoseyev', *CW,* vol. 33, p. 452.

40. 'I have balanced myself at last' quoted Trotsky, *Young Lenin*, p. 137.

41. 'On the assumption that I might soon be permitted' quoted Valentinov, *Encounters,* p. 66.

41. 'What is more' *ibid.*

41. '*How* I miss the Volga!' *CW,* vol. 37, p. 465.

41. 'What is spring on the Volga' *CW,* vol. 37, p. 475.

42. 'I too used to live on a country estate' Lenin to Olminsky, (1904), quoted Valentinov, *Encounters,* p. 107.

42. 'that the idea' quoted Szamuely, p. 318.

43. 'I think, darling Mamochka' quoted Weber, p. 4.

43. 'cursed the blessed Virgin' quoted Hill, p. 34.

44. 'a good room, or so it seems' *CW,* vol. 37, p. 65.

44. 'taken over by a certain Ulyanov' quoted Weber, p. 6.

46. 'Earlier than any of us' A. Tyrkova-Vil'iams, quoted Robert H. McNeal, *Bride of the Revolution: Krupskaya and Lenin* (afterwards referred to as McNeal), p. 19.

46. 'The knell of capitalist private property sounds' Karl Marx, *Das Kapital,* vol. I, quoted McNeal, p. 29.

46. 'heart beat so that it could be heard' quoted McNeal, p. 29.

46. 'I had already been working' Nadezhda K. Krupskaya, *Memories of Lenin,* (afterwards referred to as Krupskaya), vol. I, pp. 6, 7, 8 and 9.

48. 'Physically, there was much in her favor' McNeal, p. 51.

49. 'in a torrent of statistics' G. M. Krzhizhanovsky quoted Weber, p. 6.

49. 'I met [Lenin] for the first time' quoted Weber, p. 7.

50. 'By minimizing or altogether ignoring' Richard Pipes, Preface, *Social Democracy and the St Petersburg Labor Movement, 1885–1897,* p. viii.

50. 'The impression which Lenin at once made on me' Peter Struve, 'My Contacts and Conflicts with Lenin' (afterwards referred to as Struve), pp. 591 and 592.

729

53. 'If money is needed' quoted McNeal, p. 38.

54. 'I ask the guard on the train' *CW*, vol. 37, p. 72.

54. 'The scenery here is splendid' *CW*, vol. 37, p. 73.

54. 'Do you ski?' quoted Maurice Pianzola, *Lénine en Suisse* (afterwards referred to as Pianzola), p. 9.

55. 'He's one of us all right' Maxim Gorky, *Days with Lenin*, (afterwards referred to as Gorky), p. 17.

55. 'I have rarely met two people' Gorky, p. 29.

55. 'overawed in the presence' quoted Weber, p. 8.

55. 'not without warm sympathy' *ibid*.

55. 'He all the time' quoted Valentinov, *Early Years*, pp. 244 and 245.

56. 'I felt then that I had to do' quoted Chamberlin, vol. I, p. 124.

56. 'And they understand it?' quoted Jean Fréville, *Lénine a Paris* (afterwards referred to as Fréville), p. 35.

56. 'It makes a very pleasant impression' *CW*, vol. 37, p. 74.

57. 'studying the Berlin mores' *CW*, vol. 37, p. 78.

58. 'Few men knew Lenin's attitudes' Jonathan Frankel, 'Martov and Lenin', p. 203.

59. 'He knew all the through courtyards' Krupskaya, vol. I, p. 11.

59. 'It is essential to use liquid paste' Elizabeth Hill and Doris Mudie (eds.), *The Letters of Lenin* (afterwards referred to as Hill and Mudie), p. 14.

3 A Youth in Exile

62. 'I particularly recommended translations' *CW*, vol. 37, p. 327.

63. 'They loosened my joints' Hill and Mudie, p. 53.

63. 'I sleep about nine hours a day' and 'Someone, for instance'

CW, vol. 3 7, p. 85.

64. 'At six o'clock they brought' Krupskaya, vol. I, pp. 19 and 20.

64. 'One was struck by his incredible power' G. M. Kzhizhanovsky *(Velikii Lenin,* (Moscow, 1956), pp. 18–20, 4–5, 34–5), in Támara Deutscher (ed.), *Not By Politics Alone* (afterwards referred to as Támara Deutscher), p. 50.

65. 'If I had been in prison longer' quoted Theen, p. 90.

65. 'They would not even go to sleep' V. O. Tsederbaum, quoted Israel Getzler, *Martov: A Political Biography of a Russian Social Democrat* (afterwards referred to as Getzler), p. 32.

66. 'The country covered by the West Siberian Railway' *CW,* vol. 37, p. 92.

67. 'I remember that one day' O. P. Lepeshinskaya *(Vstrechi s Ilyichem,* (Moscow, 1957), pp. 8–9 in G. V. Bulatsky, *Oruzhem Slova,* (Moscow, 1968), p. 94), in Tamara Deutscher, p. 52.

68. 'Shu-shu-shu is not a bad village' Hill and Mudie, p. 36.

68. 'We can go shooting together' *CW,* vol. 37, p. 102.

69. 'Yesterday I travelled about 12 versts' *CW,* vol. 37, p. 108.

69. 'The amount of game he used to bring back' P. N. Lepeshinsky *(Na Povorote,* (Moscow, 1955), pp. 108–9), in Tamara Deutscher, p. 56.

70. 'Well he was so beautiful' quoted Krupskaya, vol. I, p. 33.

70. 'in addition to being an ardent cyclist' R. H. Bruce Lockhart, *My Scottish Youth,* p. 160.

70. 'as mildly amused to stalk' Churchill, p. 74.

71. 'At that time he was still living alone' G. M. Kzhizhanovsky *(Velikii Lenin,* (Moscow, 1956), pp. 18–20, 4–5, 34–5), in Tamara Deutscher, p. 50.

72. 'Able to work productively' O. P. Lepeshinskaya *(Vstrechi s Ilyichem* (Moscow, 1957) p. 8–9 in G. V. Bulatsky *Oruzhem Slova* (Moscow, 1968) p. 94), in Tamara Deutscher, p. 52.

72. 'I received a pile of letters' Hill and Mudie, p. 57.

73. 'Buy them, if the prices are reasonable' *ibid.*, p. 70.

73. 'smooth black tulle for a mosquito net' *ibid.*, p. 78.

73. 'I am already looking for quarters' *ibid.*, p. 50.

74. 'I found Nadezhda Konstantinovna looking not at all well' *ibid.*, p. 61.

74. 'Having two mothers-in-law' quoted Louis Fischer, *The Life of Lenin*, (afterwards referred to as Fischer, *Life)*, p. 403.

75. 'The peasants are particularly clean' and 'For example' Krupskaya, vol. I, pp. 25 and 30.

75. 'It was a strange marriage' Ian Grey, *The First Fifty Years: Soviet Russia, 1917–67* (afterwards referred to as Grey), p. 29.

76. 'We were newlyweds, you know' quoted McNeal, p. 68.

76. 'Send me one of our sets of chess' Hill and Mudie, p. 59.

76. 'he would become more serious' S. J. Bagotsky ('V. I. Lenin v Krakove i Poronine' in *Vospominaniya*, vol. I, pp. 437–56), in Tamara Deutscher, p. 64.

77. 'When he lost [he] grew angry' Gorky, p. 26.

77. 'At first Volodya announced' *CW*, vol. 37, p. 563.

78. 'The last time' *CW*, vol. 37, p. 559.

78. 'to skate, play chess, sing' and 'It looks as though' *CW*, vol. 37, p. 212.

78. 'Spring is in the air' *CW*, vol. 37, p. 245.

79. 'At the beginning of my exile' Lenin to Maria, 11 November 1898, Hill and Mudie, p. 67.

79. 'You can be proud of your offsprings' quoted Tomul, in Baranov, p. 66.

80. 'Its contents astound us more and more' Hill and Mudie, p. 95.

81. 'the gifted German journalist' *CW*, vol. 4, p. 65.

81. 'the special features of English history' and 'the high

development of democracy' *CW,* vol. 4, p. 102.

82. 'Marxism was the first to transform socialism' *CW,* vol. 4, p. 210.

84. 'We have packed the books' *CW,* vol. 37, p. 286.

84. 'It was a great pity to have to part' Krupskaya, vol. I, p. 43.

4 *Great Expectations*

85. 'The minister regards the workers as powder' quoted George Vernadsky, *Lenin: Red Dictator* (afterwards referred to as Vernadsky), p. 38.

88. 'Had we not felt such love (for Plekhanov)' Lenin, 'How *Iskra* was Nearly Extinguished', quoted Haimson, p. 140.

89. 'In the turmoil here I live rather fairly well' quoted McNeal, p. 85.

91. 'George [Plekhanov] is a greyhound' quoted Leon Trotsky, *Lenin* (afterwards referred to as Trotsky, *Lenin),* p. 38.

92. 'it is unpleasant without snow' Hill and Mudie, p. 127.

92. 'We [Lenin and Potrezov] are both quite well' *CW,* vol. 36, p. 37.

93. 'Plekhanov was esteemed' quoted Nina Tumarkin, *Lenin Lives! The Lenin Cult in Soviet Russia* (afterwards referred to as Tumarkin), p. 44.

93. 'Each packet went to a different address' Max Purschwitz, letter dated 28 August 1952 quoted F. Donath, *Auf Lenins Spuren in Deutschland,* p. 16.

93. 'there is no need to speak' and '*Iskra* laid the foundation' quoted Tumarkin, p. 77.

95. 'Do not merely organize yourselves into mutual aid socie-ties' Lenin 'The Urgent Tasks of Our Movement', quoted Andics, p. 9.

96. 'It was a remarkable meeting' 'Note of December 29, 1900', *CW*, vol. 4, p. 380.

96. 'The harshness of his [Lenin's] polemics' J. P. Nettl, *Rosa Luxemburg* (afterwards referred to as Nettl), p. 244.

97. 'You must tone down something' quoted Valentinov, *Early Years*, p. 247.

99. 'Over here everything now depends on transport' *CW*, vol. 36, p. 66.

99. 'What is essential' Lenin to L. I. Goldman, December 1901, *CW*, vol. 36, p. 105.

99. 'The fact that quite young workers' *CW*, vol. 36, p. 49.

100. 'This is not a program for a practical fighting party' quoted Vernadsky, p. 43.

100. 'If the majority expresses itself in favour' *CW*, vol. 34, p. 57.

100. 'This is the first time' *CW*, vol. 37, p. 319.

101. 'Ah, it must be Herr Meyer's wife' quoted McNeal, p. 87.

101. 'Couldn't you write and tell' quoted *ibid.*

101. 'At that time one might have perceived' Leon Trotsky, *On Lenin*, (afterwards referred to as Trotsky, *On Lenin*), p. 41.

102. 'I am glad for his sake' *CW*, vol. 37, p. 604.

102. 'to have to look at the mountains' *ibid.*

102. 'struggling' and 'advancing in a crab-like fashion' *CW*, vol. 36, p. 103.

102. 'The whole burden of our newspaper' quoted Weber, p. 25.

103. 'The organization of the revolutionaries *What Is To Be Done?*, *CW*, vol. 5, pp. 452 and 467.

103. 'We are marching in a compact group' *ibid.*, vol. 5, p. 355.

104. 'We firmly believe that the fourth period' *ibid.*, p. 519.

104. 'bear in mind that communication by wire' Lenin to L. Y. Galperin, July/August 1901, *CW*, vol. 43, p. 63.

104. 'It is terribly annoying to get a letter' Lenin to Kartavtsev,

4 August 1902, *CW,* vol. 43, p. 87.

105. 'a passport and small files be sewn' Lenin to the Tver Committee of the RSDLP, 26 November 1904, *CW,* vol. 43, p. 138.

107. 'at once . . . began to look round' N. K. Krupskaya, *Reminiscences of Lenin,* (afterwards referred to as Krupskaya, *Rems.*), p. 69.

107. 'We found that all those "ox-tails". ' Krupskaya, *Rems.,* p. 75.

108. 'Nadya and I have often been out locally' *CW,* vol. 37, p. 348.

108. 'A cab that I engaged' Trotsky, *Lenin,* p. 28.

109. 'That's *their* famous Westminster [Abbey]' quoted Trotsky *On Lenin,* p. 30.

109. 'Almighty God' and 'The English proletariat has in itself quoted *ibid.,* p. 45. 74. 'A corner was boarded off 'Harry Quelch' (Obituary), 11 September 1913, *CW,* vol. 19, p. 371.

110. 'I was profoundly astonished' quoted Andrew Rothstein, *A House on Clerkenwell Green,* p. 69.

110. 'How is everyone at Clerkenwell Green?' quoted L. Muravyova and I. Sivolap-Kaftanova, *Lenin in London* (afterwards referred to as Muravyova and Sivolap-Kaftanova), p. 42.

111. 'If possible, when talking with people' *CW,* vol. 43, p. 82.

111. 'All those letters about handkerchiefs (passports)' Krupskaya, vol. I, p. 77.

112. 'The meeting was conducted' Harry Pollitt in *They Knew Lenin,* p. 232.

112. 'Those weeks and months of waiting' Krupskaya, *Rems.,* p. 85.

112. '. . . and the agent muddles along' Lenin to V. A. Noskov, 4 August 1902, *CW,* vol. 34, p. III.

113. '. . . were usually devoted to the discussion' Krupskaya, vol. I, p. 72.

114. 'It is the expression of a certain satirical attitude' quoted Gorky, p. 20.

114. A Russian LL.D. (and his Wife)' *The Athenaeum*, no. 3889, 10 May 1902, p. 577.

114. 'I have received my article' Hill and Mudie, p. 155.

115. 'One man – an atheist' Krupskaya, *Rems.*, p. 70.

116. 'get out into the countryside': quoted Muravyova and Sivolap-Kaftanova, p. 100.

116. 'We took sandwiches with us' Lenin to his mother, 29 March 1903, *CW,* vol. 37, P.358.

117. 'I liked it here [Loguivy]' Lenin to G. D. Leiteisen, 24 July 1902, *CW,* vol. 34, p. 106.

117. 'In all they have two small rooms' quoted Weber, p. 30.

118. 'subordinate *everything without exception*' *CW,* vol. 6, p. 360.

119. 'that he developed a nervous illness' Krupskaya, vol. I, p. 90.

119. 'Ilich was very clever in the way' Maxim Litvinov, *Notes for a Journal* (afterwards referred to as Litvinov), p. 83.

123. 'Let there be a host of organizations' quoted Harold Shukman, *Lenin and the Russian Revolution* (afterwards referred to as Shukman), p. 56.

123. 'There's no need' *ibid.*

123. 'But that's dictatorship' and 'There is no other way' quoted Victor Serge and Natalia Sedova Trotsky, *The Life and Death of Leon Trotsky,* p. 14.

125. 'Inasmuch as I do not share' *CW,* vol. 7, p. 91.

125. 'Lenin could veer, prevaricate' Leonard Schapiro, *The Communist Party of the Soviet Union* (afterwards referred to as Schapiro), p. 25.

127. 'For me, theory is only a hypothesis' quoted Simon Liberman, *Building Lenin's Russia* (afterwards referred to as

Liberman), p. 87.

127. 'relations between Lenin on the one hand' quoted Getzler, p. 67.

127. 'But at the same time' quoted Leonard Schapiro and Peter Reddaway, (eds.), *Lenin: The Man, the Theorist, the Leader* (afterwards referred to as Schapiro and Reddaway), p. 8.

128. 'Now all he had achieved was in jeopardy' Getzler, pp. 73 and 74.

128. 'What a depressing atmosphere prevails' Lenin, 'One Step Forward, Two Steps Back', quoted Krupskaya, vol. I, p. 102.

129. 'You can't imagine even a tenth of the outrages' Lenin to G. M. Krzhizhanovsky and V. A. Noskov, 5 October 1903, *CW,* vol 36, p. 128.

129. 'Clearly they don't visit' quoted Andrew Rothstein, *Lenin in Britain* (afterwards referred to as Rothstein, *Lenin),* p. 18.

130. 'However, although he went out' Valentinov, *Encounters,* p. 146.

130. 'In speech as in writing' P. N. Lepeshinsky, ('Around Lenin' in G. V. Bulatsky, *Oruzhem Slova* (Moscow, 1968), p. 94), in Tamara Deutscher p. 53.

130. 'The Party is virtually torn apart' *CW,* vol. 34, p. 232.

130. 'extremely backward eccentrics' Lenin to L. B. Krasin, 26 May 1904, *CW,* vol. 34, p. 241

130. 'Ever since the Second Congress' Lenin to M. K. Vladimirov, 15 August 1904, *CW,* vol. 34, p. 245.

131. 'We welcome [your] energetic behaviour' Hill and Mudie, p. 197.

132. 'Spitsa Letter . . . *Kolya* Letter . . . *Vladimir* Letter' quoted L. Fotieva, *Pages from Lenin's Life* (afterwards referred to as Fotieva), p. 10.

132. 'consisted of vicious and abusive invective' Valentinov, *Encounters*, p. 146.

133. 'How many are in the organizers' collective?' quoted Pianzola, p. 41.

134. 'Vladimir Ilyich read through and examined' quoted Szamuely, p. 318.

134. 'On the ground floor' C. Zelikson-Dobrovskaya, quoted Pianzola, p. 38.

135. 'There came a knocking on the door' quoted A. L. Tait, *Lunacharsky: Poet of the Revolution (1875–1907)* (afterwards referred to as Tait), p. 76.

135. 'We are all in a better mood' quoted Tait, p. 77.

136. 'My work consisted not so much': A. V. Lunacharsky in Georges Haupt and Jean-Jacques Marie, *Makers of the Russian Revolution: Biographies of Bolshevik Leaders* (afterwards referred to as Haupt and Marie), p. 307.

136. 'A few days ago' *CW*, vol. 37, p. 359.

136. 'It is a huge mistake' quoted Schapiro and Reddaway, p. 37.

137. 'We happened to walk up' quoted Valentinov, *Encounters*, p. 47.

137. 'a farewell treat' and 'At first, the climb was easy' M. Essen ('Vstrechi's Leninym', in *Vospominaniya*, vol. I, pp. 247, 251–4), in Tamara Deutscher, p. 60.

139. 'always selected the wildest paths' Krupskaya, vol. I, p. 115.

139. '. . . instead of the dictionary' *ibid*.

139. 'The mountains helped us' quoted note 234, *CW*, vol. 37, p. 659.

139. 'Greetings from the tramps' *CW*, vol. 37, p. 363.

140. '[The financial position] is now the only hitch' *CW*, vol. 43, p. 132.

140. 'The structure of Vladimir Ilyich's head' quoted Fréville, p. 54.

141. 'First and foremost comes an organ' *CW*, vol. 34, p. 272.

141. 'Money is desperately needed' Lenin to Rozalia Zemlyachka, 13 December 1904, *CW*, vol. 43, p. 146.

141. 'We were just like children' quoted Pianzola, p. 45.

142. 'There will be transport' Lenin to Rozalia Zemlyachka, 26 December 1904, quoted Arthur Upham Pope, *Maxim Litvinoff* (afterwards referred to as Pope), P. 53.

142. 'Right, and now will you please get down to work' quoted Lunacharsky, p. 85.

5 Return to Russia

147. 'There are more than three hundred thousand' The St Petersburg Workmen's Petition to the Tsar, 22 January 1905, quoted Father George Gapon, *The Story of My Life*, p. 258.

147. 'It was a beautiful winter morning' Harold Whitmore Williams, *Russia of the Russians* (afterwards referred to as Williams), p. 64.

149. 'The events of Sunday January *9/22nd* weakened' quoted William C. Askew, 'An American View of Bloody Sunday', p. 43.

150. 'Citizens, yesterday you saw the brutality' quoted James Maxton, *Lenin* (afterwards referred to as Maxton), p. 82.

150. 'Vladimir Ilyich and I were on our way to the library' Krupskaya, vol. I, p. 122.

151. 'Trains stopped at wayside stations' Williams, p. 67.

153. 'infinitely uneasy and dark days' and 'The news from Moscow' Lunacharsky, p. 92.

153. 'Economic demands are giving way' CW, vol. 8, p. 71.

154. 'It is to be hoped that Gapon' A Militant Agreement for

the Uprising', *CW,* vol. 8, p. 165.

156. 'The curtain was raised knee-high' Fotieva, p. 30.

157. 'It horrifies me' to the Combat Committee of the St Petersburg Committee, 16 October 1905, *CW,* vol. 9, p. 344.

157. 'rifles, revolvers, bombs' 'Tasks of Revolutionary Army Contingents', *CW,* vol. 9, p. 420.

157. 'funds for the uprising' *CW,* vol. 9, p. 422.

157. 'We are in agreement with you' *CW,* vol. 34, p. 364.

158. 'The Geneva Bolsheviks' quoted Tait, p. 78.

162. 'I had hoped to see the mountain eagle' quoted I. Deutscher, *Stalin: A Political Biography* (afterwards referred to as Deutscher, *Stalin),* p. 78.

163. 'Do me a favour — ' *CW,* vol. 43, p. 498.

164. 'We would get together 12 to 14 members' Lunacharsky, p. 89.

165. 'Ilyich was very excited' Krupskaya, vol. I, pp. 166–7.

165. 'Our people came on the 8th' quoted Weber, p. 50.

166. 'the only man who for twenty-four hours a day' quoted Michael Futrell, *Northern Underground* (afterwards referred to as Futrell, *Underground),* p. 65.

167. 'From Kaukola Ilyich actually directed' Krupskaya, vol. I, p. 171.

168. 'sale of workers' votes to the Cadets' *CW,* vol. 12, p. 34.

168. 'calculated to evoke in the reader' and 'actually succeeded in causing that section'. 'Speech for the Defence (or for the Prosecution of the Menshevik Section of the Central Committee) delivered at the Party Tribunal', *CW,* vol. 12, pp. 424 and 426.

170. 'So glad you've come' quoted Gorky, p. 5.

170. 'stood a baldheaded, stocky, sturdy person' Gorky, p. 6.

170. 'The sheets are quite damp' quoted Muravyova and

Sivolap-Kaftanova, p. 177.

171. 'It was amazingly sunny that day' quoted Muravyova and Sivolap-Kaftanova, p. 161.

172. 'literally besieged by reporters'. 'The Pothouse Press and the Russian Social Democrats', *Free Russia*, June 1907, p. 8.

172. 'I can still see the bare walls' Gorky in *About Lenin*, p. 27.

172. 'His guttural "r" made him seem a poor speaker' *ibid.*, pp. 29 and 28.

173. 'was extended with the hand slightly raised' Gorky, p. 15.

175. 'You always preach socialist revolution' Litvinov, p. 177.

175. 'I don't think so' *ibid.*

177. 'I am having a rest' *CW*, vol. 37, p. 368.

177. 'We have all put on' *CW*, vol. 37, p. 366.

178. 'If war threatens to break out' quoted Angelica Balabanoff, *My Life as a Rebel* (afterwards referred to as Balabanoff), p. 97.

178. 'For over there' *CW*, vol. 43, p. 176.

179. 'This is the beginning' quoted Lubov Krassin, *Leonid Krassin: His Life and Work* (afterwards referred to as Krassin), p. 37.

179. Åbo to Stockholm journey Ludwig Lindstrom, 'På Flykt med Vladimir Uljanov, mera bekant som Lenin', *Allsvensk Samling*, Gothenburg, December 1946, pp. 14–16 and 44–8.

180. 'Oh, what a silly way' quoted Krupskaya, vol. I, p. 181.

6 Training for the Task

184. 'We both had white foam at the lips' Krupskaya, vol. I, p. 182.

185. 'It is devilishly sad' *CW*, vol. 43, p. 179.

185. 'We have been hanging about' *CW*, vol. 37, p. 372.

186. 'Bogdanovist gibberish' quoted Stephen F. Cohen, *Bukharin and the Bolshevik Revolution. A Political Biography 1888–1938*, . 96.

186. 'The idea of dropping in on you' Lenin to Gorky and Maria Andreyeva, 15 January 1908, *CW,* vol. 34, p. 373.

186. 'I immediately wrote to him': quoted Schapiro and Reddaway, p. 73.

187. 'Those who live by the labour of others' *CW,* vol. 10, p. 83.

188. 'Lenin, who quite correctly regarded the combination' quoted Schapiro and Reddaway, p. 74.

188. 'In the summer and autumn of 1904' *ibid.,* p. 75.

189. 'To tell the reader that belief' *ibid.,* p. 77.

189. 'a rank and file Marxist' *ibid.,* p. 75.

189. 'saw synthesis and harmony' and 'The capitalist monopoly' George L. Kline, 'Alexander Aleksandrovich Bogdanov', *The Encyclopedia of Philosophy,* vol. I, P. 33.

190. 'I am neglecting the newspaper' *CW,* vol. 34, p. 387.

190. 'an uncared-for wail' *CW,* vol. 34, p. 391.

190. 'Of course, the grotto is beautiful' quoted Valentinov, *Early Years,* p. 45.

191. 'I . . . told [Bogdanov and Lunacharsky] . . . that my views' quoted Weber, p. 60.

191. 'There was a big crowd at Gorki's place' Krupskaya, vol. II, p. 23.

191. 'Of course, I remember Mr Ulianov' quoted John Strachey, 'The Great Awakening: or: From Imperialism to Freedom', *Encounter,* Pamphlet no. 5, (1961), p. 7.

192. 'We could go for some splendid walks together' *CW,* vol. 37, p. 390.

192. 'We did not know the kind of need' quoted McNeal, p. 88.

192. 'As for passing on the proof reading' Hill and Mudie, p. 277.

193. '[There] we spent the most trying years' Krupskaya, vol. II, p. 31.

194. 'I was struck by the order' Ilya Erenburg, *People and Life,* p. 69.

194. 'He spoke calmly without rhetoric' *ibid.*

195. 'During our stay in Paris' Krupskaya, vol. II, p. 84.

195. 'Because of [them] Volodya has even learned' *CW*, vol. 37, p. 612.

195. 'We are greatly enjoying these dainties' *CW*, vol. 37, p. 473.

195. 'It is *hellishly* important to me' *CW*, vol. 37, p. 426.

196. 'We met in a café in the Gobelins quarter' Gérard Israel, *The Jews in Russia*, p. 121.

196. 'I remember once Ilyich came home' Krupskaya, vol. II, p. 35.

197. 'The place is wonderful' Lenin to Anna, 2 March 1909, *CW*, vol. 37, p. 412.

197. 'We went for walks every day' Krupskaya, vol. II, p. 41.

197. 'We are having a good holiday here' *CW*, vol. 37, p. 436.

197. 'beginning to come round' *CW*, vol. 34, p. 399.

197. 'le monsieur russe, si poli' Madame Taboulet, quoted Fréville, p. 89.

197. 'One feels quite cut off here' Hill and Mudie, p. 289.

197. 'He always feels better when he is working' *CW*, vol. 37, p. 608.

198. 'kept everyone at arm's length' Valentinov, *Encounters*, p. 82.

198. 'Only an honest man could laugh' and 'How is Drin-Drin getting on?' quoted Gorky, p. 28.

198. 'Take a good look at him' quoted Clara Zetkin, *Reminiscences of Lenin* (afterwards referred to as Zetkin), p. 7.

199. 'He loved fun' quoted Gorky, p. 38.

199. 'People helped me take the number' *CW*, vol. 37, p. 447.

199. 'for a close and sincere alignment' *CW*, vol. 34, p. 416.

200. 'on the cheap *phrases* of Trotsky and Co.' *CW*, vol. 43, p. 243.

200. 'cheap and pleasant' *CW*, vol. 37, p. 462.

200. 'He bathed in the sea a great deal' Krupskaya, vol. II, p. 54.

201. 'She listened quite attentively to Vladimir Ilyich' quoted Weber, p. 72.

201. 'This [day] was the last time he saw his mother' Krupskaya, vol. II, p. 55.

201. 'Since 1909 I have been *wholly* in favour' *CW,* vol. 34, p. 430.

202. 'Opportunism is opportunism for the very reason' 'Two Worlds', *CW,* vol. 16, p. 309.

202. 'Both the trend and the methods of the group' *CW,* vol. 16, p. 328.

203. 'I did not warm to [her]' quoted Bertram D. Wolfe, 'Lenin and Inessa Armand' (afterwards referred to as Wolfe), p. 101.

204. 'How could he not be seduced' Fréville, p. 108.

205. 'I have begun to pay more attention' *CW,* vol. 37, p. 448.

205. 'My mother became closely attached to Inessa' quoted Wolfe, p. 103.

206. 'making good use of the summer' *CW,* vol. 37, p. 610.

207. 'Yesterday I went out climbing' *CW,* vol. 37, p. 472.

207. 'the arch-hangman' 'Stolypin and the Revolution', *CW,* vol. 17, p. 247.

208. 'The Prague Conference drew up the balance' quoted Andics, p. 34.

208. 'We have finally succeeded' *CW,* vol. 35, p. 23.

209. 'It is almost Spring here' Hill and Mudie, p. 298.

209. 'I believe Spring is early' *ibid.,* p. 299.

210. 'In the absence of representative institutions' 'Political Parties in Russia', *CW,* vol. 18, p. 45.

211. 'One can't be sure' McNeal, p. 143.

212. 'You ask why I am in Austria' *CW,* vol. 35, p. 55.

212. 'Here we feel much better' *CW,* vol. 37, p. 482.

213. 'Three days later I went to see them' S. J. Bagotsky ('V. I.

Lenin v Krakove i Poronine' in *Vospominaniya*, vol. I, pp. 437–56), in Tamara Deutscher, p. 63.

213. 'He would get up at eight o'clock' *ibid.*, p. 64.

214. 'most valuable and major theorist' 'Testament,' *CW*, vol. 36, p. 595.

215. 'What we're simply starved of here' quoted Schapiro and Reddaway, p. 42.

216. 'with great enthusiasm' *CW*, vol. 37, p. 489.

216. 'About two weeks later' S. J. Bagotsky ('V. I. Lenin v Krakove i Poronine' in *Vospominaniya*, vol. I, pp. 437–56), in Tamara Deutscher, p. 65.

216. 'Having left the bicycles' *ibid.*, p. 65.

216. 'In the distance' *ibid.*, p. 66.

217. 'It has been discovered' and 'a huge house' *CW*, vol. 37, p. 617.

218. 'almost a Russian type' Lenin to Maria, 29 or 30 April (12 or 13 May) 1913, Hill and Mudie, p. 317.

218. 'The air was wonderful' Krupskaya, vol. II, p. 117.

218. 'We get up early and go to bed' Lenin to Maria, 29 or 30 April (12 or 13 May) 1913, Hill and Mudie, p. 317.

218. '[He] particularly likes scrambling' *CW*, vol. 37, p. 516.

219. 'I beg you not to be late' and 'The money is badly needed' quoted McNeal, p. 149.

219. 'The weather here is wonderful' *CW*, vol. 37, p. 519.

221. 'I am no good for that' *CW*, vol. 43, p. 406.

221. 'You are the *only suitable person*' *CW*, vol. 43, p. 409.

222. 'You handled the thing better' *CW*, vol. 43, p. 423.

222. 'It is inevitable' quoted Gorky, p. 22.

223. 'You will see that the German' and 'No, all the same' Zinoviev and Lenin, quoted G. Zinoviev, *N. Lénine* (afterwards referred to as Zinoviev), p. 30.

223. 'But for the war' 'A Strong Revolutionary Government', *CW,* vol. 24, p. 360.

7 The Catalyst of War

225. 'Perhaps it is a forged edition' quoted Zinoviev, p. 30.

225. 'This is the end' quoted Weber, p. 103.

225. 'From this day on' quoted Alfred Erich Senn, *The Russian Revolution in Switzerland 1914–1917* (afterwards referred to as Senn), p. 21.

225. 'The local police suspect me' *CW,* vol. 43, p. 430.

226. 'Are you certain that Ulyanov' and 'Oh yes' quoted Krupskaya, vol. II, p. 140.

226. 'Passports are required' *CW,* vol. 36, p. 291.

226. 'A dull little town' CW, vol. 43, p. 432.

227. 'copied from an appeal' quoted Senn, p. 22.

227. 'bourgeois, imperialist and dynastic war' 'The Tasks of Revolutionary Social Democracy in the European War', *CW,* vol. 21, p. 15.

228. 'Last Sunday we went for a lovely walk' *CW,* vol. 43, p. 506.

229. 'Chauvinism seeks to conceal itself quoted Katkov and Shukman, p. 43.

230. 'among the most scientific soldiers in Europe' C. R. M. F. Cruttwell, A *History of the Great War 1914–1918* (afterwards referred to as Cruttwell), p. 39.

233. 'the "sacred" bourgeois right' and 'rob Germany of her colonies' 'A Separate Peace', in *CW,* vol. 23, p. 126.

234. 'So far as I am concerned' quoted Samuel H. Baron, *Plekhanov, the Father of Russian Marxism,* p. 324.

234. 'It must be the primary task'. 'The War and Russian Social-Democracy' *CW,* vol. 21, p. 32.

235. 'I hate Kautsky' Hill and Mudie, p. 342.

236. 'new International which must arise' Leon Trotsky, Preface to *Der Krieg und die Internationale,* p. ix.

236. 'The working masses in the face of all obstacles will create' quoted E. H. Carr, *The Bolshevik Revolution, 1917–1923,* (afterwards referred to as Carr), vol. III, p.567.

236. 'I. [He] was against any truce' Lenin to *Nashe Slovo,* 9 February 1915, quoted Pope, p. 104.

237. 'Comrade Maximovich understood' Lenin, quoted *ibid.,* p. 108.

237. 'I consider it a fact' *CW,* vol. 43, p. 494.

238. 'Lenin was my protégé . . .' quoted Futrell, *Underground,* p. 151.

238. 'The evidence does not support' Senn, p. 62.

238. 'Lenin said that the most important' Fritz Fischer, *Germany's Aims in the First World War* (afterwards referred to as Fritz Fischer), p. 151.

239. 'In Kesküla's opinion, it is therefore essential' the German Minister in Berne, Count von Romberg, to the Chancellor, Report No. 794,30 September 1915, in Z. A. B. Zeman, *Germany and the Revolution in Russia, 1915—1918* (afterwards referred to as Zeman, *Documents),* p. 7.

239. 'To those comrades whom I left in charge' quoted Michael Futrell, 'Alexander Keskuela', p. 26.

240. 'The European war has done a great service' Hill and Mudie, p. 355.

240. 'Military failures are helping' Hill and Mudie, p. 373.

242. 'The disruption of the Entente' quoted George Katkov, 'German Foreign Office Documents on Financial Support to the Bolsheviks in 1917', p. 189.

243. 'What is Moor like?' Hill and Mudie, p. 430.

244. 'Across the road lived Inessa' Krupskaya, vol. II, p. 150.

245. 'Panic seized the delegates' Angelica Balabanoff, *Erinnerungen und Erlebnisse*, p. 101.

245. 'Not being at the conference himself' *ibid.*, p. 102.

245. 'I must go to mountains' quoted Futrell, *Underground*, p. 152.

246. 'the central figure in the conspiratorial connexions' Z. A. B. Zeman and W. B. Scharlau, *The Merchant of Revolution* (afterwards referred to as Zeman and Scharlau), p. 3.

246. 'financial support for the majority group' Appendix I in Zeman, *Documents*, p. 150.

247. 'It was not the day-dream' Zeman and Scharlau, p. 149.

247. 'I explained to [Lenin] my views' Helphand, quoted Zeman and Scharlau, p. 158.

248. 'an organ of renegades', 'cesspool of German chauvinism' and 'not a single honest thought' Lenin, quoted *ibid.*, p. 178.

248. 'His massive gigantic figure' Zeman and Scharlau, p. 157.

249. 'An uncommonly fat and paunchy gentleman' quoted Futrell, *Underground*, P.173.

249. 'first to make a fortune during a war' quoted Nettl, vol. II, p. 634.

250. 'We were quite comfortable [there]' Krupskaya, vol. II, p. 166.

250. 'If you would write a novel' quoted Gorky, p. 20.

251. 'I have the courage to display myself' quoted Fischer, *Life*, p. 489.

251. 'Throughout his life Lenin had very little time' quoted *ibid.*, p. 491.

251. 'In general, as you probably know' quoted Schapiro and Reddaway, p. 60.

252. 'the abuse of their village' Gerd Hardach, *The First World War, 1914–1918*, (afterwards referred to as Hardach),

p. 213, fn. 57.

253. 'The manifesto contains no clear pronouncement' quoted Robert Payne, *The Life and Death of Trotsky,* p. 141.

253. 'I realized how shrewd' Balabanoff, p. 85.

254. 'I had first observed Zinoviev' *ibid.,* p. 244.

254. 'the first book that elucidated clearly' Willi Münzenberg in *They Knew Lenin,* p. 79.

255. 'The day after Ilyich's arrival' Krupskaya, vol. II, p. 171.

256. 'a nice room here with electricity' *CW,* vol. 37, p. 526.

256. 'We shall soon be coming to the end' *CW,* vol. 37, p. 624.

256. 'I must say I need an income' Lenin to Shlyapnikov, September/October 1916, quoted George Katkov, *Russia 1917: The February Revolution,* p. 83.

257. 'Ilyich liked the simplicity of the service' Krupskaya, vol. II, p. 176.

258. 'After all, a manifesto was adopted' *CW,* vol. 36, p. 390.

259. 'The rest resort was quite inexpensive' Krupskaya, vol. II, pp. 186–187.

259. 'Both laughable and disappointing' *CW,* vol. 35, p. 259.

260. 'the coming years' and 'We of the older generation'. 'Lecture on the 1905 Revolution', *CW,* vol. 23, p. 253.

260. 'that chauvinism is clearly declining' *CW,* vol. 35, p. 288.

261. 'On the 28th' quoted G. A. Alexinsky, *Du Tsarisme au Communisme,* p. 29.

262. 'found the opinion to prevail in Moscow' Major-General Sir C. E. Callwell, *Field-Marshal Sir Henry Wilson Bart., G. C. B., D.S.O.: His Life and Diaries,* vol. I, p. 319.

262. 'They have lost their people' diary entry for 15 February 1917, quoted *ibid.*

262. 'It seems as certain as anything' diary entry for 16 February 1917, quoted *ibid.* 179. 'The mood in the capital is

extremely agitated' quoted Roy Medvedev, *The October Revolution* (afterwards referred to as Medvedev), p. 23.

263. 'It is said that the Council of the Empire' Lord Howard of Penrith Papers, File DHW/4, Cumbria Record Office, Carlisle (afterwards referred to as Howard Papers).

264. 'I have formed the opinion' quoted David Lloyd George, *War Memoirs,* (afterwards referred to as Lloyd George) vol. III, p. 1588.

264. 'Did Lord Milner go to Russia' A. A. Lynch, 25 May 1917, *Hansard,* Commons, vol. XCIII, col. 2651.

265. 'I have set going my theses' *CW,* vol. 43, p. 590.

265. 'If Switzerland is drawn into the war' *CW,* vol. 43, p. 603.

265. 'In the great war ledger' Marshal von Hindenburg, *Out of My Life,* p. 273.

266. 'The revolution took place' R. H. Bruce Lockhart, *Memoirs of a British Agent* (afterwards referred to as Lockhart, *Memoirs),* p. 171.

266. 'My ministers are chosen by me alone' quoted Cruttwell, p. 419.

267. 'The situation is becoming worse' quoted Medvedev, p. 26.

267. 'Once again this Rodzianko has written' *ibid.,* p. 26.

267. 'At six in the morning' quoted Roger Pethybridge (ed.) *Witnesses to the Russian Revolution,* p. 100.

269. 'with the help and support of the army' quoted Martin McCauley (ed.) *The Russian Revolution and the Soviet State, 1917–1921, Documents* (afterwards referred to as McCauley), p. 18.

270. 'Ten capitalists and one hostage' quoted John W. Wheeler-Bennett, *Brest-Litovsk: The Forgotten Peace, March 1918* (afterwards referred to as Wheeler-Bennett), p. 24.

270. 'Of sheer political impotence' *ibid.*, p. 23.

270. 'Alongside the Provisional Government' 'The Dual Power', *CW,* vol. 24, p. 38.

273. 'became a very sensitive reflection' Deutscher, *Stalin,* p. 130.

274. 'The Provisional Government possesses no real power' Chamberlin, vol. I, p. 101.

275. 'received them in a small dimly-lit room'. 'The Tsar's Final Ordeal. Signing the Act of Abdication', *The Times,* 20 March 1917, p. 8.

277. 'This is far and away' quoted Hugh Brogan, *The Life of Arthur Ransome,* (afterwards referred to as Brogan), p. 122.

277. 'For the United States the possibility' quoted Wheeler-Bennett, p. 31.

277. 'Now [Russia's forbidding autocracy] has been' Arthur S. Link (ed.), *The Papers of Woodrow Wilson* (afterwards referred to as Wilson Papers), vol. 41, p. 524.

278. 'we believe that the Revolution' quoted Lloyd George, vol. III, p. 1636.

278. 'That this House sends to the Duma' *Hansard,* Commons, vol. 91, col. 2093.

278. 'to make [financial] advances to our Russian Allies' *Hansard,* Commons, vol. 94, col. 1426.

278. 'no one brought up in the atmosphere' *Hansard,* Commons, vol. 94, col. 721.

279. 'the Army and the people have joined hands'. 'British Labour and the Russian Revolution', *The Times,* 19 March 1917, p. 9.

279. 'that any remission of effort'. 'Labour Party's Message', *The Times,* 17 March 1917, p. 7.

279. 'unlimited money' and 'I was exhilarated' Somerset

Maugham, *The Summing-Up*, p. 204.

8 The Sealed Train

281. 'Haven't you heard?' quoted Krupskaya, vol. II, p. 199.

281. The *Zürcher Post* and the *Neue Zürcher Zeitung* confirmed the news 12(15) March 1917 for news of revolution; 4 (17) March 1917 for reports of new government. *CW*, vol. 23, p. 405, n. 122.

282. 'We here in Zurich' *CW*, vol. 35, p. 294.

282. 'Today there are reports from England' 'Draft Theses', *CW*, vol. 23, p. 287.

283. 'The new government is composed' 'Draft Theses', *CW*, vol. 23, p. 288.

283. 'Our tactics: no trust' 'Telegram to the Bolsheviks leaving for Russia', *CW*, vol. 23, p. 292.

284. 'At night all sorts of incredible plans were made' and 'You will fall asleep' Krupskaya, vol. II, p. 200.

284. 'A brilliant idea' *CW*, vol. 43, p. 622.

285. 'I will *use them* to travel' *CW*, vol. 35, p. 300.

285. 'My nerves, naturally, are overstrung' *CW*, vol. 43, p. 617.

285. 'We cannot take part' *CW*, vol. 36, p. 420.

286. 'Please let me know in greatest possible detail' Lenin probably to Jakub Hanecki-Fürstenberg, prior to 30 March 1917, *CW*, vol. 43, p. 622.

287. 'a museum of antiquities' quoted *The State and Revolution*, *CW*, vol. 25, p. 394.

287. 'so long as the state exists' *ibid.*, p. 468.

288. 'even Lenin could be got by bribery' quoted A. M. Gollin, *Proconsul in Politics: a Study of Lord Milner in Opposition and in Power* (afterwards referred to as Gollin), p. 532.

288. 'the enclosed brief note' quoted *ibid*.

288. 'Lenin's programme must not, of course, be made public' Zeman, *Documents*, p. 7.

289. 'There is no doubt whatever' Litvinov, pp. 87–8.

289. 'it was with a sense of awe' Churchill, p. 73.

290. 'Having once sent Lenin' General Erich Ludendorff, *Meine Kriegserinnerungen*, p. 407.

290. 'In the same way' General Max Hoffmann, *Der Krieg der versäumten Gelegenheiten*, p. 174.

292. 'The German Government should approve an application' Zeman, *Documents*, p. 28.

292. 'considered advantageous to Germany' *ibid*.

292. 'Our Party has decided' *CW*, vol. 36, p. 427.

293. 'The document that Platten put before Romberg' Z. A. B. Zeman, *A Diplomatic History of the First World War* (afterwards referred to as Zeman, *History*), p. 231.

294. 'pandemonium broke out' J. Ley, 'A Memorable Day in April', p. 496.

295. 'It's just like the Trojan Horse to me' James Joyce, quoted *ibid*.

295. 'I assume full political responsibility' statement signed by *émigrés* on way to Swiss frontier, 9 April 1917, *CW*, vol. 23, p. 417, note 158.

295. 'Our tactics: absolutely distrust' quoted Schapiro, p. 164.

296. 'conspiracy of the Anglo-French imperialists' 'Letters from Afar. First Letter. The First Stage of the First Revolution', *CW*, vol. 23, p. 302.

296. 'decorations' and 'a balalaika on which they play' *ibid*., p. 303.

296. 'The revolutionary proletariat must' 'Letters from Afar. Fifth Letter. The Tasks Involved in the Building of the

Revolutionary Proletarian State', *CW*, vol. 23, p. 340.

297. 'Not a shadow of confidence' *CW*, vol. 35, p. 312.

297. 'Independence and separateness of our Party' *ibid.*, p. 302.

298. 'We are not pacifists' 'Farewell Letter to the Swiss Workers', *CW*, vol. 23, p. 370.

298. 'We had just these two hours to liquidate our entire "household". ' Krupskaya, vol. I, p. 208.

298. 'that in Russia' quoted Pianzola, p. 161.

298. 'I think, Herr Kammerer', 'You'll never write' and 'But I don't know' *ibid.*

299. 'a little, light-haired, spectacled, revolutionary goblin' Arthur Ransome, quoted Brogan, p. 166.

299. 'We hope that we shall see you' quoted Pianzola, p. 162.

300. 'would not be a good political sign' *quoted ibid.*

300. 'Traitors!' and 'The Kaiser is paying' quoted Michael Pearson, *The Sealed Train* (afterwards referred to as Pearson), p. 78.

300. 'on an empty stomach' G. Y. Sokolnikov, in Haupt and Marie, p. 247.

301. 'Our meeting was extraordinarily unpleasant' Fritz Platten in *They Knew Lenin*, pp. 91 and 92.

301. 'His Majesty the Kaiser suggested' memorandum by Ow-Wachendorff, 12 April 1917, in Zeman, *Documents*, p. 45.

302. '2. In the event of the Russians' *ibid.*

302. 'This ultimatum was presented by Lenin' Sokolnikov in Haupt and Marie, p. 247.

303. 'The first revolutionary wave' quoted Pearson, p. 108.

304. 'like a workman on a Sunday excursion' Frederick Strom, quoted Futrell, *Underground*, p. 155.

304. 'Gladly, as long as [Lenin] leaves today' quoted *ibid.*, p. 156.

305. 'We have now been engaged in these activities' the State Secretary [R. von Kühlmann] to the Foreign Ministry Liaison Officer at General Headquarters, 29 September 1917, in Zeman, *Documents,* p. 70.

306. 'Lenin's entry into Russia' the Foreign Ministry Liaison Officer at the Imperial Court (Grünau) to the Foreign Ministry, 21 April 1917, in Zeman, *Documents,* p. 51.

306. '. . . for a hectic moment' Lord Howard of Penrith, *Theatre of Life,* vol. II, p. 264.

307. 'Long live Zimmerwald' Balabanoff, p. 167.

307. 'He was most of all interested' quoted Pearson, p. 117.

307. 'Arriving Monday 11 p.m.' *CW,* vol. 37, p. 539.

308. 'Are we going to be arrested' quoted Pearson, p. 125.

308. 'At last the three blindingly bright lights' F. F. Raskolnikov, *Kronstadt and Petrograd in 1917,* p. 70.

308. 'Lenin arrives today' quoted Pearson, p. 127.

309. 'If you're not going to make a speech' quoted Cathy Porter, *Alexandra Kollontai* (afterwards referred to as Porter), p. 245.

309. 'Sailors, comrades, as I greet you' quoted Pearson, p. 129.

310. 'The piratical imperialist war is the beginning' quoted N. N. Sukhanov, *The Russian Revolution 1917: A Personal Record* (afterwards referred to as Sukhanov), P. 273.

311. 'I shall never forget' Sukhanov, p. 280.

311. 'The fundamental impression made' quoted Pearson, p. 133.

311. 'Having learnt that Comrade Lenin came back to us' quoted Sukhanov, p. 298.

9 Preparing the Ground

317. 'The Zimmerwald morass must no longer' quoted Hardach, p. 224.

317. 'demanding an investigation' *CW,* vol. 24, p. 135.

318. 'The great service' Ramsay MacDonald, 'From a Labour Bench', *Forward,* vol. II, no. 24, 28 April 1917.

318. 'Mere emotional pacifism is of no use' PRO 30/69 1161, f. 99, Public Record Office, Kew (afterwards referred to as PRO).

318. 'He said that he regarded a separate peace' CAB. 24/14 GT.875 f.335, PRO.

321. 'Ought to stick our bayonets into a fellow' quoted Grey, p. 98.

322. 'All discipline has vanished in the army' diary entry for 30 April 1917, Maurice Paléologue, *An Ambassador's Memoirs* (afterwards referred to as Paléologue), vol. III, p. 322.

323. 'Attention is centred principally on Russia' and 'Under pressure from the Provisional Government' Howard Papers, DHW/4.

323. 'Lynch-law, the destruction of houses and shops' Sukhanov, pp. 368–9.

324. 'Always calm, always in complete control' quoted Tomul, in Baranov, p. 70.

325. 'Lenin was a hopeless failure' quoted Paléologue, vol. III, p. 302.

325. 'Even the Bolsheviks declared' Paul N. Miliukov, *The Russian Revolution* (afterwards referred to as Miliukov), vol. I, p. 67.

326. 'It's obscene to applaud' quoted Porter, p. 247.

326. 'As far as the general scheme of Lenin' quoted Michael Farbman, *Bolshevism in Retreat* (afterwards referred to as Farbman), p. 71.

327. 'Lenin's influence seems to have been increasing greatly' diary entry for 21 April 1917, Paléologue, vol. III, p. 304.

327. 'Lenin is quite unique' quoted Gorky, p. 19.

328. 'Do not allow the police' *CW*, vol. 24, p. 108.

328. 'Lenin, Utopian dreamer and fanatic' diary entry for 21 April 1917, Paléologue, vol. III, p. 304.

329. '[His] extraordinary power of unwavering concentration' Cruttwell, p. 425.

330. 'There now arose from an obscure corner' M. Philips Price, *My Reminiscences of the Russian Revolution* (afterwards referred to as Price), p. 44.

332. 'We are all agreed that power must be wielded' *CW*, vol. 24, p. 239.

333. 'Whereas Lenin and a few others' A. Lunacharsky, *Revolutionary Silhouettes*, p. 106.

334. 'Accompanied by a soldier with a rifle' quoted Roger Pethybridge, *The Spread of the Russian Revolution. Essays on 1917* (afterwards referred to as Pethybridge, *Spread*), p. 118.

335. 'Hundreds and hundreds of beds' quoted Brogan, p. 134.

335. 'Arrest a score or two of capitalists' quoted Arthur Ransome, 'Russia's Steady Recovery', *Daily News & Leader*, no. 22241, 22 June 1917.

335. 'Yes there is' quoted *CW*, vol. 25, p. 20.

336. 'We do not aspire to conquer' quoted R. P. Browder and A. F. Kerensky (eds.), *The Russian Provisional Government 1917* (afterwards referred to as Browder and Kerensky), vol. II, p. 1080.

337. 'is not domination over other nations' and 'all obligations assumed towards our Allies' quoted Browder and Kerensky, vol. II, p. 1046.

337. 'predatory treaties concluded by the tsarist clique' 'The War and the Provisional Government', *CW*, vol. 24, p. 113.

337. 'The cards are on the table . . .'. 'The Provisional

Government's Note', *CW,* vol. 24, pp. 189–90.

338. 'We did not know if in this troubled moment' quoted Alexander Rabinowitch, *Prelude to Revolution* (afterwards referred to as Rabinowitch), p. 45.

339. 'As the day wore on' Cable, 25 April (8 May) 1917, United States Department of State, *Papen Relating to the Foreign Relations of the United States. The Lansing Papers, 1914–1920* (afterwards referred to as *Lansing Papers),* vol. II, p. 333.

339. 'the transfer of power into the hands' quoted James Bunyan and H. H. Fisher, *The Bolshevik Revolution 1917–1918,* (afterwards referred to as Bunyan and Fisher), p. 8.

342. 'An offensive, whatever its outcome' *CW,* vol. 25, p. 53.

343. 'irretrievably ruined as a fighting organization' Major-General Sir Alfred Knox, *With the Russian Army, 1914–1917,* vol. II, p. 648.

345. 'Comrades! for the present political crisis' *The Collected Works of V. I. Lenin* (afterwards referred to as *CW* (Roman numerals), vol. XXI, book II, p. 300.

346. 'On Liteiny Prospect the glass was broken' quoted Chamberlin, vol. I, p. 174.

347. 'Is this the beginning of decisive operations?' quoted Rabinowitch, p. 180.

347. 'This would be quite inopportune' quoted *ibid.,* p. 181.

347. 'we shall see' *ibid.,* p. 184.

348. 'Give me an exact account' *ibid.,* p. 204.

349. 'because their goal of presenting the slogans' *ibid.*

349. 'From the numerous telegrams in the hands' quoted Browder and Kerensky, vol. III, p. 1375.

350. 'I have always supported' quoted Zeman and Scharlau, p. 229.

351. 'The state of affairs suggested' George F. Kennan, 'The

Sisson Documents', pp. 134 and 137.

352. 'It should be noted' *ibid.,* p. 154.

352. 'Had the Provisional Government at this time arraigned Lenin' David R. Francis, *Russia from the American Embassy* (afterwards referred to as Francis), p. 141.

353. 'Gregory [Zinoviev] and I have decided' quoted Krupskaya, vol. II, p. 232.

354. 'The counter-revolutionary *bourgeoisie*' quoted Vernadsky, p. 166.

10 On the Eve

356. 'Our people will be surprised' A. V. Shotman, quoted Kustaa Rovio in *They Knew Lenin,* p. 100.

357. 'Strictly *entre nous*' Hill and Mudie, p. 427.

359. 'compelled to *tender [his] resignation*' *CW,* vol. 26, p. 82.

360. 'Victory is certain in Moscow' quoted Victor Serge, *Year One of the Russian Revolution* (afterwards referred to as Serge), p. 380, note 21.

360. 'There is, for example' Harrison Salisbury, Foreword to Medvedev, p. ix.

362. 'It was decided', 'brought Lenin from Finland' and 'Lenin arrived here' captions nos. 73, 74 and 75, *Lenin's Life and Work,* p. 258.

364. 'I order you immediately' quoted Chamberlin, vol. I, p. 212.

364. Note regarding 'Kornilov affair'. This version has been disputed by Professor Richard Pipes in the *Times Literary Supplement* of 12–18 August 1988, p. 876.

365. 'The railwaymen had received orders' quoted Pethybridge, *Spread,* p. 38.

365. 'The issue was decided' Miliukov, vol. II, p. 209.

365. 'There must be an end'. 'Riga and the Carso', *The Times*, 8 September 1917, p. 7.

366. 'Part of French' quoted Brogan, p. 144.

366. 'there is little doubt' Sir Robert Bruce Lockhart, 'The Unanimous Revolution', P. 333.

366. 'Korniloff, the National Hero' and 'printed at the expense' Alexander F. Kerensky, *The Catastrophe*, p. 315.

366. 'difficult though it was' quoted Lloyd George, vol. V, p. 2564.

367. 'from the dilemma' *ibid.*

367. 'revealed the longing' McCauley, p. 38.

367. 'I, General Kornilov' *ibid.*, p. 39.

368. 'We should at once begin' quoted A. J. P. Taylor, Introduction to John Reed, *Ten Days That Shook the World* (afterwards referred to as Reed), p. xiii.

369. 'be expected to collapse' The State Secretary to the Foreign Ministry Liaison Officer at General Headquarters, Kühlmann, telegram no. 1610, 29 September 1917, in Zeman, *Documents*, p. 70.

369. 'The Bolsheviks, having obtained'. 'The Bolsheviks Must Assume Power', *CW*, vol. 26, p. 19.

371. 'designate the forces' 'Marxism and Uprising', *CW*, vol. XXI, book I, p. 229.

372. 'looked every bit like a Lutheran minister' quoted Alexander Rabinowitch, *The Bolsheviks Come to Power*, p. 202.

372. 'He states that since' *CW*, vol. XXI, book II, p. 327.

373. 'It is an irrefutable fact' quoted Szamuely, p. 318.

374. 'The enemy is already knocking' quoted Farbman, p. 104, fn. 1.

374. 'We are deeply convinced' *CW,* vol. XXI, book II, p. 328.

375. 'Under these conditions' *ibid.,* p. 332.

375. 'Our party will now be threatened' *CW,* vol. 26, p. 95.

376. 'The Central Committee recognizes' *CW,* vol. XXI, book II, p. 107.

377. 'November sixth [24 October] will be too early' Reed, p. 73.

378. 'But this general resolution' Leon Trotsky, *The History of the Russian Revolution* (afterwards referred to as Trotsky, *History),* vol. III, p. 156.

11 The Seizure of Power

379. 'The Bolshevik Revolution' A. J. P. Taylor, Introduction to Reed, p. x.

379. 'Aside from the fact' Trotsky, *History,* vol. III, p. 150.

380. 'Before history' quoted *ibid.,* p. 154.

381. 'Not only Zinoviev and I quoted *ibid.,* p. 161.

381. 'Ever more persistent rumours' Gorky, 'One Must Not Be Silent', quoted Alexander Kaun, *Maxim Gorki and his Russia* (afterwards referred to as Kaun), p. 460.

383. 'It promptly put' Trotsky, *History,* vol. III, p. 153.

383. 'All I want them to do' quoted Pearson, p. 261.

383. 'Beginning to think' Cable 30 October 1917, United States Department of State, *Papers Relating to the Foreign Relations of the United States: 1918, Russia* (afterwards referred to as *US Foreign Relations, 1918, Russia),* vol. I, p. 216.

384. 'In the interests' McCauley, p. 121.

386. 'to support the Military Revolutionary Committee' and 'The country is on the verge' quoted Bunyan and Fisher, p. 79.

386. '. . . He who is capable' *ibid.*, p. 76.

386. 'the [military] staff has broken off *ibid.*, p. 79.

388. 'These pinpricks were just sufficient to convict' Trotsky, *History,* vol. III, p. 205.

388. 'to hold every regiment' quoted Bunyan and Fisher, p. 86.

389. 'an attempt to incite' *ibid.*, p. 89.

389. 'is due not merely' *ibid.*, p. 91.

390. 'The situation is extremely critical' *CW,* vol. XXI, book II, p. 144.

391. 'We found ourselves' quoted Serge, p. 67.

392. 'I am going' *CW,* vol. 43, p. 638.

392. 'What sort of a worker' quoted Hill, p. 121.

392. 'The legal authorities' Trotsky, *History,* vol. III, p. 218.

393. 'He [Lenin] had a kerchief Trotsky, 'Reminiscences of the October Revolution', 7 November 1920, quoted McCauley, p. 129.

393. 'It's begun' quoted Taylor, Introduction to Reed, p. xvi.

393. 'From being on the run' *ibid.*

394. 'I retired to the couch' V. Bonch-Bruyevich in *About Lenin,* pp. 53 and 54.

396. 'The situation in Petrograd' quoted Bunyan and Fisher, p. 99.

397. 'The Provisional Government has been deposed'. 'To the Citizens of Russia', 25 October 1917, *CW,* vol. 26, p. 236.

398. 'On both sides of the parqueted floor' Reed, pp 92–3.

400. 'In the name of' quoted Farbman, p. 112.

400. 'Don't spoil the Proletarian triumph' quoted *ibid.*

400. 'a stab in the back' Kuchin, quoted Reed, p. 101.

400. 'The men in the trenches': quoted Chamberlin, vol. I, p. 321.

401. 'To workers, soldiers and peasants' quoted T. H. Rigby,

Lenin's Government: Sovnarkom 1917–22 (afterwards referred to as Rigby), p. 2.

402. 'The insurrection of the masses' quoted Bunyan and Fisher, p. 113.

403. 'If neither Lenin nor I Leon Trotsky, *Trotsky's Diary in Exile, 1935* (afterwards referred to as Trotsky, *Diary)*, p. 54.

403. 'The final act of the revolution' Trotsky, *History*, vol. III, p. 229.

404. 'Here was no great soldier' Maxton, p. 11.

405. 'could not but seem' Fritz Fischer, p. 475.

405. 'A short, stocky figure' Reed, p. 128.

406. 'We shall now proceed' and 'adoption of practical measures' Reed, p. 129.

407. 'The Government abolishes secret diplomacy' Decree on Peace, 26 October (8 November) 1917, in Yuri Akhapkin (ed.), *First Decrees of Soviet Power* (afterwards referred to as Akhapkin), p. 21.

407. 'The question of War and Peace' Lenin, quoted Reed, p. 129.

408. 'Landed proprietorship is abolished' Decree on Land, 27 October (9 November) 1917, in Akhapkin, p. 23.

409. 'It is necessary' and The *collegium* of chairmen' quoted Rigby, p. 4.

410. 'In the crowded car' Reed, p. 144.

12 Problems of Success

414. '[It] was decided' Leon Trotsky, *The Military Writings and Speeches of Leon Trotsky: How the Revolution Armed*, vol. II, p. 594.

415. 'The attempt of Kerensky' quoted Reed, p. 198.

418. 'Lenin, Trotsky and their supporters' quoted Richard Hare, *Maxim Gorky*, p. 94.

419. '[He] is, of course, a man' *ibid.*, p. 95.

420. 'We are nationalizing' quoted Lloyd George, vol. V, p. 2600.

421. 'The private banks' Reed, p. 233.

422. 'It has been observed' quoted Sheila Fitzpatrick, *The Commissariat of Enlightenment: Soviet Organization of Education and the Arts under Lunacharsky, October, 1917–1921* (afterwards referred to as Fitzpatrick), p. 12.

422. 'We are accused' Lenin, speech at joint meeting of Petrograd Soviet of Workers' and Soldiers' Deputies and Delegates from the Fronts, 4 (17) November 1917, *CW,* vol. 26, p. 294.

422. 'Urgently find and send here' *CW,* vol. 44, p. 50.

422. 'I told him' quoted Farbman, p. 126.

424. 'It appears quite clear' quoted Lloyd George, vol. V, p. 2566.

424. 'A power which had' Lloyd George, vol. V, p. 2570.

425. 'I replied' Francis, p. 307.

425. 'It is reported' quoted Francis, p. 186.

425. 'Of course, we would not' *ibid.* p. 188.

425. 'Talk with Lenin?': Gustav Hervé, 'Causer avec Lénine? A quoi bon?', *La Victoire*, no. 1734, 3 January 1918.

426. 'Whether Trotsky or Chernov' Joseph Noulens, *Mon Ambassade en Russe Soviétique, 1917–1919* (afterwards referred to as Noulens), vol. I, p. 128.

426. 'At Petrograd' Lloyd George, vol. V, p. 2582.

426. 'a superb thinking-machine' quoted Serge, p. 254.

427. 'and who ever succeeded' Lockhart, *Memoirs*, p. 222.

427. 'a four-kind son of a bitch' quoted Lockhart, *Memoirs*, p. 225.

427. 'At once intelligent' Noulens, vol. II, p. 115.

427. 'How did he find time' Kenneth Young, Introduction to *The Diaries of Sir Robert Bruce Lockhart,* vol. I, p. 8.

428. 'There was nothing in his personal appearance' Lockhart, *Memoirs,* pp. 237–8.

429. 'Our ways' Lenin, quoted *ibid.,* p. 239.

429. 'Like all your countrymen' *ibid.,* p. 240.

430. 'Do let me' quoted William Hard, *Raymond Robins' Own Story* (afterwards referred to as Hard), p. 202.

432. 'I accepted this post' quoted Farbman, p. 125.

432. 'Our secret treaties' quoted Robert D. Warth, *The Allies and the Russian Revolution: From the Fall of the Monarchy to the Peace of Brest-Litovsk* (afterwards referred to as Warth), p. 45.

432. 'What unconscious symbolism' Viktor Chernov, *The Great Russian Revolution,* P. 193

433. 'Open covenants of peace openly arrived at' President Woodrow Wilson, Point I, the Fourteen Points Address, 8 January 1918, Wilson Papers, vol. 45, p. 536.

434. 'The difficulties Mr Balfour' Lloyd George, vol. V, p. 2567.

436. 'Only for the purpose of quoted Chamberlin, vol. I, p. 352.

436. 'We must further proceed' quoted Reed, p. 238.

436. 'We cannot bear the responsibility' quoted Chamberlin, vol. I, p. 352.

437. 'deserters and strike-breakers' Lenin, proclamation, quoted Reed, p. 242.

437. 'Members of the governing body' quoted I. N. Steinberg, *In the Workshop of the Revolution* (afterwards referred to as Steinberg, *Workshop),* p. 58.

437. 'It is senseless' Lenin, quoted *ibid.,* p. 61.

437. 'almost an invitation to terror' Steinberg, *Workshop,* p. 65.

438. '(1) To investigate and liquidate' quoted E. J. Scott, 'The Cheka', p. 6.

438. 'There is no sphere of our life' Chekist Moroz, quoted *ibid.*, p. 5.

438. 'life itself dictated' *ibid.*, p. 3.

439. 'was a revolutionary' I. Steinberg, *Spiridonova: Revolutionary Terrorist* (afterwards referred to as Steinberg, *Spiridonova*), p. 196.

439. 'It became my lot to fight' Steinberg, *Workshop*, p. 64.

439. 'Persons belonging to the wealthy classes' quoted C. E. Vulliamy (ed.), *The Red Archives*, p. 297.

440. 'They hoped, by their participation' Steinberg, *Workshop*, p. 64.

441. 'Now that the Soviet Government' quoted *ibid.*, p. 235.

443. 'If anything should happen' quoted G. H. Leggett, 'Lenin, Terror, and the Political Police' (afterwards referred to as Leggett), p. 162.

443. 'Shall we convene?' quoted Chamberlin, vol. I, p. 368.

444. 'Whilst Chernov was speaking' Carl Lindhagen, quoted McCauley, p. 282.

445. 'a cover for the struggle' quoted Chamberlin, vol. I, p. 370.

445. 'The dispersal of the Constituent Assembly' quoted Leggett, p. 163.

446. 'While the democratic parties' O. H. Radkey, *The Election to the Russian Constituent Assembly of 1917*, p. 2.

447. 'harnessing to the Soviet cart' quoted Rigby, p. 26.

447. 'Soviet Government stronger' quoted W. P. Coates and Zelda K. Coates, *Armed Intervention in Russia 1918–1922* (afterwards referred to as Coates and Coates), p. 49–50.

447. 'The only chance' 'Theses on the Constituent Assembly', *CW,* vol. 26, p. 383.

448. 'Not a single problem' quoted Andics, p. 45.

449. 'Of all the political parties' quoted Medvedev, p. 103.

450. '[Marx] teaches us to act' *The State and Revolution, CW,* vol. 25, p. 488.

453. 'As a rule, the topics of discussion' Trotsky, *On Lenin,* p. 122.

454. 'Considering Sovnarkom' Rigby, p. 223.

456. 'Once in a gathering' quoted *ibid.,* p. 7.

456. 'put this master' and '[He] was guided' Balabanoff, p. 245.

457. 'I have never seen Lenin so angry' *ibid.,* p. 277.

458. 'I received no instructions' quoted Fischer, *Life,* p. 519.

459. 'Work in my secretariat' Lenin to Y. S. Ganetsky, 25 April 1921, quoted *Lenin, Comrade and Man,* p. 78.

459. 'People's Commissar A. D. Tsyurupa' quoted *ibid.,* p. 27.

459. 'Vladimir Ilyich's desk' quoted Rigby, p. 31.

460. 'The room was dim' Liberman, p. 7.

460. 'Lenin ambled in' Capt. George A. Hill, *Go Spy the Land,* p. 100.

461. 'cutting short the slightest violation' Ya Gindin quoted Rigby, p. 71.

462. 'It is simply amazing' D. P. Bogolepov, quoted *ibid.,* p. 37.

462. 'that Lenin, a man approaching fifty' Rigby, p. 224.

463. 'Lenin certainly identified' *ibid.,* p. x.

464. 'on civil marriage' quoted Medvedev, p. 94.

464. 'We, the Bolshevik Party'. 'Thesis on the Tasks of the Soviet Government in the present situation', *CW,* vol. 27, p. 242.

465. 'He approached all these questions' quoted Fitzpatrick, p. 3.

466. '[He] could never believe' Fitzpatrick, p. 19.

466. 'intellectual vampirism' and 'The first impression' A. Peskŏv [Gorky] to Vladislav Xodasevič, 8 November 1923, in Hugh McLean (ed.), 'The Letters of Maksim Gorikij to V. F.

Xodasevič, 1922–1925', p. 307.

466. 'This strange tree of unknowledge' Bertram D. Wolfe, 'Krupskaya purges the People's Libraries', p. 155.

467. 'When I knew him' Liberman, p. 9.

468. 'Of course, we make mistakes' and 'Our mistakes should be corrected' Lenin, quoted *ibid.*, pp. 7–8.

469. 'Lenin was spoken of Liberman, p. 79.

469. 'Moreover, should the peasants fail' quoted Liberman, p. 14.

470. 'suggested that the point' and 'I thought bitterly' Liberman, pp. 14 and 15.

470. 'Lenin is baked' quoted Liberman, p. 16.

470. 'Yes, a Jacobin' quoted *ibid.*

13 Brest-Litovsk

472. 'a formal proposal' C. K. Cumming and Walter W. Pettit (eds.), *Russian-American Relations, March 1917-March, 1920* (afterwards referred to as Cumming and Pettit), p. 44.

472. 'The action just taken by the extremists' quoted Judah L. Magnes, *Russian and Germany at Brest-Litovsk*, p. 14.

473. 'pretended Government' *US Foreign Relations, 1918, Russia*, vol. I, p. 245.

473. 'to address to the military authorities' Lenin, Trotsky and Krylenko to General Dukhonin, 21 November 1917, quoted Wheeler-Bennett, p. 71.

473. 'We dismiss you' Lenin, Stalin, Krylenko, telephone call to Dukhonin, 22 November 1917, Bunyan and Fisher, p. 235.

474. 'The matter of peace' quoted Wheeler-Bennett, p. 72.

474. 'It was aimed' quoted Medvedev, p. 52.

475. 'categorically and energetically' statement by Lieutenant-Colonel M. Kerth to General Dukhonin, 27 November 1917, Cumming and Pettit, p. 53.

475. 'I have a strong suspicion' quoted Francis, p. 185.

475. 'Germany is trying' quoted Louis Fischer, *The Soviets in World Affairs, (afterwards referred to as Fischer, Soviets),* vol. I, p. 36.

476. 'For us to hold' quoted the Rt Hon. Sir George Buchanan, *My Mission to Russia and Other Diplomatic Memories,* vol. II, p. 225.

476. 'No policy would be more fatal' quoted Wheeler-Bennett, p. 76.

476. 'the Allies were willing' Colonel House to President Wilson, 2 December 1917, Charles Seymour, *The Intimate Papers of Colonel House* (afterwards referred to as House), vol. III, p. 290.

477. 'Is it possible' quoted Major-General Max Hoffmann, *War Diaries and Other Papers* (afterwards referred to as Hoffmann), vol. II, p. 190.

478. 'such terms could be addressed' Hoffmann, quoted Wheeler-Bennett, p. 89.

478. 'The picture was rich in contrasts' Wheeler-Bennett, p. 113.

479. 'In the Ministry here' Count Ottaker Czernin, *In the World War,* p. 216.

480. 'My nationality, Count' quoted Hard, p. 124.

480. 'No forcible annexations'; A. A. Joffe, quoted Chamberlin, vol. I, p. 390.

482. 'On 28th December 1917' *The Memoirs of Prince Max of Baden,* vol. I, p. 208.

482. 'That spotless Finnish cleanliness' Krupskaya, *Rems.,* p. 425.

483. 'To delay negotiations' quoted Wheeler-Bennett, p. 139.

484. 'Go in a petticoat' quoted Christopher Hollis, *Lenin* (afterwards referred to as Hollis), p. 237.

485. 'Although Lenin's Government' Cable, 30 November 1917, House, vol. III, p. 339.

485. 'because the American mission [in Paris]' House, vol. III, p. 324.

485. 'thousand words or less' quoted Edgar Sisson, *One Hundred Red Days*, p. 205.

486. 'Should the President himself Balfour to House, 5 January 1918, House, vol. III, p. 349.

486. 'sincere and in earnest' President Wilson, address to both Houses of Congress, 8 January 1918, Wilson Papers, vol. 45, pp. 534 and 536.

486. 'The evacuation of all Russian territory' President Wilson's Sixth Point, *ibid.*,P. 537.

487. 'was unbridgeable' Wheeler-Bennett, p. 157.

487. 'It is impossible' quoted *ibid.*, p. 185.

488. 'We announce the termination' *ibid.*

488. 'When you see a Council' quoted Hard, p. 2.

489. 'We are removing our armies' quoted Wheeler-Bennett, p. 226.

490. 'General Hoffmann today gave official notice' *ibid.*, p. 238.

490. 'So they have deceived us' quoted *ibid.*, p. 239.

491. 'There is not another moment' *ibid.*

491. 'this time the Comrades' diary entry for 25 February 1918, Hoffmann, vol. I, p. 208.

492. 'No, we dare not change our policy' quoted Trotsky, *Lenin*, p. 139.

492. 'Please add my vote' quoted Fischer, *Soviets*, vol. I, p. 62.

493. 'I was present' Price, p. 246.

494. 'the favourite of the whole party'. 'Letter to the Congress', 24 December 1922, *CW, vol* 36, p. 595.

494. 'Then up rose Lenin' Price, p. 247.

495. 'To carry on a revolutionary war' quoted Anthony Summers and Tom Mangold, *The File on the Tsar* (afterwards referred to as Summers and Mangold), p. 294.

495. 'The plunderer has besieged us' 'An Unfortunate Peace', *CW,* vol. 27, p. 52.

497. 'three foreign Ambassadors' Lockhart, *Memoirs,* p. 248.

497. 'Resistance is possible' quoted Zeman, *History,* p. 300.

497. 'Only an unrestrained policy' quoted Wheeler-Bennett, p. 257, fn. 2.

498. 'If there were five hundred courageous men' quoted Hard, p. 94.

498. 'Some people indeed' *ibid.*

498. 'In view of the fact' Bunyan and Fisher, p. 527.

499. 'May I not take advantage' Wilson Papers, vol. 46, p. 598.

500. 'The Russian Soviet Republic' *CW,* vol. 27, p. 171.

500. 'What have you heard' and 'I shall now speak' quoted Hard, p. 151.

501. 'His policy remained' Hard, p. 152.

501. 'Time and again' Arthur Ransome, quoted Brogan, p. 188.

502. 'We regard the ratification' quoted Steinberg, *Spiridonova,* p. 201.

502. 'When now . . . it has become clear' *CW,* vol. 27, p. 197.

503. 'We must not deceive ourselves' quoted Wheeler-Bennett, p. 303.

504. 'We are facing a band of adventurers' quoted Kaun, p. 478.

504. '. . . the surrender of the Council of Commissars' *ibid.*

505. 'An Unfortunate Peace' *CW,* vol. 27, p. 51.

505. 'We were already in Moscow' quoted Fotieva, p. 105.

507. 'The Vecheka hitherto has always' quoted Boris Levytsky, *The Uses of Terror* (afterwards referred to as Levytsky), p. 22.

507. 'Peace treaties such as these' quoted Lloyd George, vol. V, p. 2596.

508. 'He suggested that if their lives' Howard Papers, DHW.5/6.

509. 'I proposed that we hold' Trotsky, *Diary*, p. 80.

509. 'Finally all eyes turned on Lenin' Steinberg, *Workshop*, p. 143.

510. 'the truth about [the fate of] the Romanovs' Summers and Mangold, p. 354.

510. 'answer for it with his own life' Report no. 1497 of Criminal Investigation Division, 3 February 1919, Kilgour bMS Russ. 35, vol. 1 and vol. 3, Houghton Library, Harvard University, Cambridge, Massachusetts.

510. 'was just a gentle prod' Summers and Mangold, p. 294.

511. 'I have to say . . . that' quoted P. M. Bykov, *The Last Days of Tsardom*, p. 82.

511. 'Talking to Sverdlov' Trotsky, *Diary*, p. 80.

14 The End of Democracy – Terror

515. 'The Russians compromised' Fischer, *Soviets*, vol. 1, p. 78.

517. 'If the Germans in one big swoop' quoted Trotsky, *On Lenin*, p. 120.

518. 'unimaginable rags and tatters' quoted Brogan, p. 187.

518. 'dwelt a great deal on the question' quoted Rothstein, *Lenin*, p. 16.

519. 'It was as though he felt cramped' Fotiyeva, quoted Fischer, *Life*, p. 465.

520. 'This is the height of disgrace' quoted Fotieva, p. 44.

521. '[He] normally worked' quoted M. C. Morgan, *Lenin*, p. 178.

522. 'Speaking of the way he worked' Fotieva, p. 93.

522. 'I learned from Molotov' *CW,* vol. 37, p. 546.

523. 'Step up economic' Lenin, Instructions, *CW,* vol. 42, pp. 160 and 161.

523. 'Dear Comrade, The work you are doing' quoted Balabanoff, p. 195.

524. 'In general, Lenin trusts his lucky star' Count von Mirbach to the German Chancellor, Report No. 61, 16 May 1918, in Zeman, *Documents,* p. 126.

525. 'However, he was quite apparently concerned' and 'He is finished' *ibid.,* p. 127.

526. 'The more the famine surges up' quoted Chamberlin, vol. II, p. 43.

527. 'The time before the new harvest' *ibid.,* p. 42.

527. '*Obviously* we shall perish' *CW,* vol. 44, p. 95.

528. 'great crusade' quoted D. S. Mirsky, *Lenin,* p. 147.

528. 'Petrograd is in an unprecedentedly catastrophic condition' quoted Hollis, P. 243.

529. 'The peasant bourgeoisie' Sovnarkom decree 'On granting the Commissariat of Food Supply Extraordinary Powers', 13 May 1918, quoted Medvedev, p. 153.

529. 'The food situation' quoted Medvedev, p. 156.

531. 'The greatest ferocity' Chamberlin, vol. II, p. 45.

531. 'Speculators who are caught' quoted Andics, p. 47.

532. 'Emphasize more strongly' 'Main Propositions of the Decree on Food Dictatorship', 8 May 1918, *CW,* vol. 27, p. 356.

532. 'Arrived in Tsaritsyn' quoted Medvedev, p. 151.

534. 'For God's sake' *CW,* vol. 44, p. 57.

534. 'The workers and soldiers of Petrograd' quoted Leggett, p. 164.

534. 'For the time being' Lenin to A. K. Paikes, 22 August 1918, *CW*, vol. 44, P. 139.

534. '. . . 25–30 *hostages*' Lenin to A. D. Tsyurupa, 10 August 1918, *CW*, vol. 44, p. 127.

535. 'This is in-ad-miss-ible' quoted Leggett, p. 167.

535. 'Having examined the present political situation' quoted Steinberg, *Spiridonova*, p. 208.

536. 'the bourgeoisie and Skoropadsky' quoted Steinberg, *Spiridonova*, p. 209.

537. 'I accuse you' quoted Lockhart, *Memoirs*, p. 298.

537. 'Trotsky pushes himself forward' Lockhart, *ibid.*, pp. 298–9.

539. 'Towards midnight' quoted Steinberg, *Spiridonova*, p. 214.

540. 'Scattered bands of Left Social[ist] Revolutionaries' Hill and Mudie, p. 446.

540. 'We are liquidating' *CW*, vol. 27, p. 533.

541. 'We exist on a basis' quoted Levytsky, p. 28.

542. 'Although I know Lenin well' quoted George Katkov, 'The Assassination of Count Mirbach', p. 92.

543. 'Mass searches, Execution' *CW*, vol. 35, p. 349.

543. 'About midway' Stepan Gil in *About Lenin*, p. 165.

544. 'You've come' quoted Krupskaya, *Rems.*, p. 481.

544. 'The words were irrelevant' *ibid.*

545. 'The Politburo of the C. C quoted Tumarkin, p. 106.

546. 'Some of the imagery was religious' Tumarkin, p. 91.

546. 'As it happens, the attempt to kill Lenin' Krassin, p. 97.

546. 'I shot Lenin today' quoted Levytsky, p. 29.

547. 'All kinds of fables' quoted Fischer, *Life*, p. 282.

548. 'In view of this bulletin' quoted Fotieva, p. 128.

548. 'Both the guards and Ilyich felt' Krupskaya, *Rems.*, p. 484.

548. 'did not care to enlarge' Balabanoff, p. 209.

549. 'I called on him' quoted Kaun, p. 505.

549. 'He listened eagerly' Trotsky, *Diary*, p. 83.

549. 'I could see' Balabanoff, p. 209.

549. 'Don't you understand' quoted *ibid.*

549. 'was neither cruel' *ibid.*

550. 'Workers and poor' quoted Levytsky, p. 30.

552. 'We have never rejected' quoted Leggett, p. 159.

552. 'For us there do not' *ibid.*, p. 174.

553. 'Without the Vecheka' Unshlikht, quoted *ibid.*, p. 185.

553. 'A beautiful plan' Jan M. Meijer, (ed.), *The Trotsky Papers, 1917–1922* (afterwards referred to as *Trotsky Papers*), vol. II, p. 279.

554. 'Then why do we bother' and 'Lenin's face suddenly brightened' Steinberg, *Workshop*, p. 145.

554. 'in not more than a month's time' quoted James Bunyan, *Intervention, Civil War, and Communism in Russia April-December 1918* (afterwards referred to as Bunyan), p. 227.

554. 'took very lightly' Liberman, p. 77.

555. 'The murder of Volodarsky' quoted Hollis, p. 251.

556. 'involved in White Guard organizations' quoted Levytsky, p. 30.

557. 'The conditions of the life-and-death struggle' and 'To every murder' quoted Bunyan, pp. 240 and 241.

557. 'There must be an immediate end' quoted Steinberg, *Workshop*, p. 148.

558. 'came about as a result' Bunyan, p. 241.

558. 'notorious for cruelty to peasants' quoted *ibid.*, p. 246.

558. 'The news of the ever-increasing' *ibid.*, p. 253.

559. 'to impress upon the perpetrators' *U.S. Foreign Relations, 1918, Russia*, vol. I, p. 688.

559. ' "Killing is no murder" ' Hill and Mudie, p. 401.

559. 'What do you want?' quoted Gorky, p. 44.

560. 'What astonishes me' quoted Bunyan, p. 257.

561. 'Immediately arrest Kogan' *CW,* vol. 36, p. 499.

15 Civil War and Intervention

565. 'with a view to using' quoted David Woodward, *The Russians at Sea,* p. 188.

565. 'There was a Soviet Republic ashore' *ibid.,* p. 190.

568. 'Death Kornilov verified' quoted Coates and Coates, p. 79.

569. 'Officers and men alike' James Mavor, *The Russian Revolution,* p. 348.

570. 'The fitful and fluid operations' Churchill, p. 235.

571. 'The only practicable course' *Lansing Papers,* vol. II, p. 346.

571. 'To ask us to intrigue' quoted Richard H. Ullman, *Intervention and the War,* P. 47.

572. 'It. . . becomes of particular importance' quoted Gollin, p. 557.

574. 'To remain in occupation' quoted Churchill, p. 165. 392. 'This was a far-reaching programme' Churchill, p. 166.

575. 'The British and French have raised' quoted G. F. Kennan, *Soviet-American Relations, 1917–1920,* vol. II, p. 259.

575. 'I cannot believe' Howard Papers, DHW.5/5.

577. 'All Soviets are ordered' Cable, 25 May 1918, quoted Medvedev, p. 172.

577. 'in attacking the Czechs' quoted Peter Sedgwick, Editorial Postscript to Serge, p. 415.

578. 'to urge that Japan' and 'I hope the scheme will receive' quoted House, vol. III, p. 402.

579. 'may be the greatest misfortune' House to Balfour, 4 March

1918, quoted House, vol. III, p. 406.

579. 'The seizure of Simbirsk' quoted Valentinov, *Early Years*, p. 11.

580. 'That day was a newsworthy date' quoted Erich Wollenberg, *The Red Army*, p. 92.

581. 'News has just been received' *CW*, vol. 27, p. 552.

582. 'to have full power' quoted Bunyan, p. 276.

583. '[The German] crisis means' *CW*, vol. 28, p. 101.

585. 'The associated powers are now engaged' Wilson in United States Department of State, *Papers Relating to the Foreign Relations of the United States: The Paris Peace Conference, 1919* (afterwards referred to as *Paris Peace Conference*), vol. III, p. 691.

585. 'probably among the worst problems' quoted John M. Thompson, *Russia, Bolshevism, and the Versailles Peace* (afterwards referred to as Thompson), p. 2.

586. 'Bolshevism is the most hideous' quoted Thompson, p. 15.

588. 'They [the associated Powers] invite every organized group' *Paris Peace Conference*, vol. III, p. 677.

589. 'I am afraid [Wilson]' *Trotsky Papers*, vol. I, p. 259.

589. 'We talked for some time' quoted Thompson, p. 150.

590. 'I told the President' *ibid.*

590. 'Sir, *American Commission to Negotiate Peace*, You are hereby directed' quoted William C. Bullitt, *The Bullitt Mission to Russia* (afterwards referred to as *Bullitt Mission*), p. 4.

591. 'I was instructed' *ibid.*, p. 38.

591. 'I told him [Bullitt]' quoted E. L. Woodward and R. Butler (eds.), *Documents on British Foreign Policy., 1919–1939*, vol. III, p. 426.

592. 'volunteers, technical experts, arms' Churchill, at Supreme

War Council meeting, 14 February 1919, *Foreign Relations of the United States, 1919, Russia*, p. 58.

592. 'Churchill's project' *ibid.*, p. 73.

593. 'The decision [regarding Bullitt] is very important' quoted Fischer, *Soviets*, vol. I, p. 171.

593. 'second Brest' and 'that policy which led us to accept' quoted Thompson, p. 164.

593. *Text of the Projected Peace Proposal by the Allied and Associated Governments, Bullitt Mission*, p. 39–43.

The allied and associated Governments to propose that hostilities shall cease on all fronts in the territory of the former Russian Empire and Finland on[1] and that no new hostilities shall begin after this date, pending a conference to be held at[2] on[3].

The duration of the armistice to be for two weeks, unless extended by mutual consent, and all parties to the armistice to undertake not to employ the period of the armistice to transfer troops and war material to the territory of the former Russian Empire.

The conference to discuss peace on the basis of the following principles, which shall not be subject to revision by the conference.

1. All existing de facto governments which have been set up on the territory of the former Russian Empire and Finland to remain in full control of the territories which they occupy at the moment when the armistice becomes effective, except in so far as the conference may agree upon the transfer of territories; until the peoples inhabiting the territories controlled by these de facto governments shall themselves determine to change their Governments. The Russian Soviet Government, the other soviet governments

and all other governments which have been set up on the territory of the former Russian Empire, the allied and associated Governments, and the other Governments which are operating against the soviet governments, including Finland, Poland, Galicia, Roumania, Armenia, Azerbaidjan, and Afghanistan, to agree not to attempt to upset by force the existing de facto governments which have been set up on the territory of the former Russian Empire and the other Governments signatory to this agreement.[4]

2. The economic blockade to be raised and trade relations between Soviet Russia and the allied and associated countries to be reestablished under conditions which will ensure that supplies from the allied and associated countries are made available on equal terms to all classes of the Russian people.

3. The soviet governments of Russia to have the right of unhindered transit on all railways and the use of all ports which belonged to the former Russian Empire and to Finland and are necessary for the disembarkation and transportation of passengers and goods between their territories and the sea; detailed arrangements for the carrying out of this provision to be agreed upon at the conference.

4. The citizens of the soviet republics of Russia to have the right of free entry into the allied and associated countries as well as into all countries which have been formed on the territory of the former Russian Empire and Finland; also the right of sojourn and of circulation and full security, provided they do not interfere in the domestic politics of those countries.[5]

Nationals of the allied and associated countries and of the other countries above named to have the right of free entry

779

into the soviet republics of Russia; also the right of sojourn and of circulation and full security, provided they do not interfere in the domestic politics of the soviet republics.

The allied and associated Governments and other governments which have been set up on the territory of the former Russian Empire and Finland to have the right to send official representatives enjoying full liberty and immunity into the various Russian Soviet Republics. The soviet governments of Russia to have the right to send official representatives enjoying full liberty and immunity into all the allied and associated countries and into the nonsoviet countries which have been formed on the territory of the former Russian Empire and Finland.

5. The soviet governments, the other Governments which have been set up on the territory of the former Russian Empire and Finland, to give a general amnesty to all political opponents, offenders, and prisoners. The allied and associated governments to give a general amnesty to all Russian political opponents, offenders, and prisoners, and to their own nationals who have been or may be prosecuted for giving help to Soviet Russia. All Russians who have fought in, or otherwise aided the armies opposed to the soviet governments, and those opposed to the other Governments which have been set up on the territory of the former Russian Empire and Finland to be included in this amnesty.

All prisoners of war of non-Russian powers detained in Russia, likewise all nationals of those powers now in Russia to be given full facilities for repatriation. The Russian prisoners of war in whatever foreign country they may be, likewise all Russian nationals, including the Russian soldiers and officers abroad and those serving in all foreign armies to be given full facilities for repatriation.

6. Immediately after the signing of this agreement all troops of the allied and associated Governments and other non-Russian Governments to be withdrawn from Russia and military assistance to cease to be given to antisoviet Governments which have been set up on the territory of the former Russian Empire.

The soviet governments and the antisoviet governments which have been set up on the territory of the former Russian Empire and Finland to begin to reduce their armies simultaneously, and at the same rate, to a peace footing immediately after the signing of this agreement. The conference to determine the most effective and just method of inspecting and controlling this simultaneous demobilization and also the withdrawal of the troops and the cessation of military assistance to the antisoviet governments.

7. The allied and associated Governments, taking cognizance of the statement of the Soviet Government of Russia, in its note of February 4, in regard to its foreign debts, propose as an integral part of this agreement that the soviet governments and the other governments which have been set up on the territory of the former Russian Empire and Finland shall recognize their responsibility for the financial obligations of the former Russian Empire, to foreign States parties to this agreement and to the nationals of such States. Detailed arrangements for the payment of these debts to be agreed upon at the conference, regard being had to the present financial position of Russia. The Russian gold seized by the Czechoslovaks in Kazan or taken from Germany by the Allies to be regarded as partial payment of the portion of the debt due from the soviet republics of Russia.

The Soviet Government of Russia undertakes to accept the foregoing proposal provided it is made not later than April 10 1919.

Notes

[1] The date of the armistice to be set at least a week after the date when the allied and associated Governments make this proposal.

[2] The Soviet Government greatly prefers that the conference should be held in a neutral country and also that either a radio or a direct telegraph wire to Moscow should be put at its disposal.

[3] The conference to begin not later than a week after the armistice takes effect and the Soviet Government greatly prefers that the period between the date of the armistice and the first meeting of the conference should be only three days, if possible.

[4] The allied and associated Governments to undertake to see to it that the de facto governments of Germany do not attempt to upset by force the de facto governments of Russia. The de facto governments which have been set up on the territory of the former Russian Empire to undertake not to attempt to upset by force the de facto governments of Germany.

[5] It is considered essential by the Soviet Government that the allied and associated Governments should see to it that Poland and all neutral countries extend the same rights as the allied and associated countries.

593. 'The Soviet Government undertook to accept this proposal' *ibid.*, p. 39.

594. 'accepted by President Wilson and Lloyd George' Orville H. Bullitt (ed.), *For the President: Personal and Secret, Correspondence Between Franklin D. Roosevelt and William C. Bullitt*, P. 6.

594. 'I asked whether, in addition to the agreement with Bullitt'

Lincoln Steffens, *The Autobiography of Lincoln Steffens*, vol. II, pp. 796–7.

596. '. . . at last I can see a way out' quoted Thompson, p. 235.

596. 'this is of the utmost importance' quoted *Bullitt Mission*, p. 66.

596. 'As long as the British press' *ibid.*

597. 'The Intrigue that May be Revived' Wickham Steed leading article, *Daily Mail* (Paris), 28 March 1919.

597. 'This is an amazing article' President Wilson to Joseph P. Tumulty, 17 July 1919, quoted Thompson, p. 155.

598. 'The Answer to this question is in the negative' *Hansard*, Commons, vol. 120, col. 451.

598. 'unpropitious' and 'had just gained' Churchill, p. 176.

599. 'grudge [which] dominated French policy' Zeman, *History*, p. 289.

599. 'which left out all possibility of the matter' Bullitt to US Senate Commitee on Foreign Relations, *Bullitt Mission*, p. 80.

16 Lenin's State Survives

601. 'in conferences of enemies' note 120, *CW*, vol. 42, p. 518.

602. 'the finest representatives of the Third International' *CW*, vol. 28, p. 455.

602. 'a strange figure' Arthur Ransome, *Six Weeks in Russia in 1919* (afterwards referred to as Ransome), p. 143.

602. 'If I had ever thought' *ibid.*, p. 146.

603. 'I had to work together with Eberlein' Karl Steinhardt in *They Knew Lenin*, p. 66.

603. 'Follow my own' quoted *ibid.*

608. 'The terrible thing in Lenin' Struve, p. 593.

608. 'Disaster is absolutely inevitable' *Trotsky Papers,* vol. I, p. 481.

609. 'Let the military themselves' *ibid.,* p. 91.

609. 'I am very disturbed' *ibid.,* p. 237.

609. 'the bacchanalia of profiteering' quoted Deutscher, *Stalin,* p. 196.

610. 'If Trotsky will, thoughtlessly,' quoted Fischer, *Life,* p. 286.

610. 'I categorically insist' *Trotsky Papers,* vol. I, p. 135.

611. 'On your insistence' quoted Thos. G. Butson, *The Tsar's Lieutenant: The Soviet Marshal* (afterwards referred to as Butson), p. 47.

612. 'trial and the carrying out of sentences' *Trotsky Papers,* vol. I, p. 145.

612. 'I recommend, on pain' *ibid.,* p. 647.

612. 'Submit an exact report' Lenin to commander of the troop train no. 54, 27 July 1918, *ibid.,* p. 61.

612. 'be more accurate' Lenin to Antonov and others, 22 April 1919, *ibid.,* p. 373.

612. 'about the catastrophic state of the army' *ibid.,* p. 229.

612. 'It is extremely odd' *ibid.,* p. 377.

612. 'an outright disgrace' Lenin to Sklyansky, August 1919, *ibid.,* p. 663.

612. 'your silence on this subject' Lenin to the Military Revolutionary Council of the Eastern Front, 20 June 1919, *ibid.,* p. 569.

613. 'keep the conflict from spreading' Lenin to Sklyansky, 4 June 1919, *ibid.,* p. 523.

613. 'issue instructions for' *ibid., p.* 471.

613. 'It would be a disgrace' *ibid.,* p. 545.

613. 'The taking of hostages' Lenin to Sklyansky, 8 June 1919, *ibid.,* p. 545.

613. 'There must be no question' *ibid.,* p. 91.

614. 'I am so tired' quoted Dan Levin, *Stormy Petrel: The Life and Work of Maxim Gorky* (afterwards referred to as Levin), p. 213.

615. 'Ilyich began to protest' Kamenev, *Lenins literarisches Erbe*, p. 19.

615. 'united, independent and autonomous' Wilson, an Address to the Senate, 22 January 1917, Wilson Papers, vol. 40, p. 537.

615. 'independent Polish State' Wilson, the Fourteen Points Address, an Address to a joint Session of Congress, 8 January 1918, *ibid.*, vol. 45, p. 538.

616. 'All the signs are' *Trotsky Papers*, vol. II, p. 75.

616. 'to our last drop of blood!' *CW,* vol. 30, p. 395.

616. 'Five thousand French officers' *Trotsky Papers*, vol. II, p. 119.

617. 'imparted to the military campaign' Carr, vol. III, p. 210.

617. 'A throne had been bundled away here' Victor Serge, *Memoirs of a Revolutionary, 1901–1941*, p. 108.

618. 'Lenin was the most' Butson, p. 97.

619. 'Now that the Poles have gone over' Lenin to Sklyansky, *Trotsky Papers*, vol. II, p. 257.

619. 'The advance of the Poles' Lenin to I. T. Smilga, 18 August 1920, quoted *ibid.*, p. 259.

620. 'I myself believe' quoted Zetkin, p. 21.

621. 'his face shrunk before my eyes' *ibid., p. 22.*

621. 'He was utterly broken' quoted Wolfe, p. 112.

622. 'Believe me, only two kinds of government' quoted Shukman, p. 200.

624. 'Barely three years ago' quoted Emma Goldman, *Living My Life,* vol. II, p. 880.

626. 'My practical work had satisfied' Trotsky, *My Life*, p. 395.

628. 'A number of facts' quoted Robert Vincent Daniels, *The Conscience of the Revolution*, p. 163.

632. 'You cannot have peace' quoted 'Peace in Russia', *The Times*, 10 November 1919, p. 15.

632. 'Relations with Russia' Chicherin on Moscow Radio, 20 November 1919, quoted Alfred L. P. Dennis, *The Foreign Policies of Soviet Russia*, p. 380.

632. 'modify its position' J. Ramsay MacDonald, *Parliament and Revolution*, p. 17.

633. 'The principal task of N.E.P.' Preface, *CW*, vol. 45, p. 40.

633. 'I agree with you' quoted Liberman, p. 93.

634. 'it became known' Liberman, p. 93.

634. 'How dared he answer you' quoted *ibid.*, p. 94.

634. 'the first document' note 34, *CW*, vol. 32, p. 538.

635. 'I. Satisfy the wish' *CW*, vol. 32, p. 133.

635. 'In this way the Government' quoted Chamberlin, vol. II, p. 446.

635. 'The peasants asked him' Levytsky, p. 44.

636. 'I asked him' Lenin to N. Osinsky, 1 March 1921, *CW*, vol. 45, p. 91.

636. 'The truth is that the system' quoted Farbman, p. 282.

637. 'Comrades, the question of replacing requisitions' quoted Fischer, *Life*, p. 477.

637. 'You know very well' quoted Angelica Balabanoff, *Impressions of Lenin*, p. 63.

637. 'All the evils and hardships' Krassin, p. 155.

638. 'The New Economic Policy' *CW*, vol. 42, p. 426.

638. 'Of course, freedom of trade' quoted Chamberlin, vol. II, p. 447.

639. 'Don't let us make any mistake' quoted Farbman, p. 279.

640. 'In abandoning the monopoly of grain' quoted *ibid.*, p. 281.

640. 'He repudiated' Churchill, p. 75.

640. 'From now on' Appeal to the Peasants, 23 March 1921, quoted Chamberlin, vol. II, p. 448.

641. 'Russia was battered for seven years' quoted Hill, p. 206.

641. 'Self-interest will develop' quoted *ibid.*, p. 201.

642. 'We cannot have arguments' Report on the Political Work of the Central Committee of the RCP (B), 8 March 1921, *CW,* vol. 32, p. 178.

643. 'In addition to bourgeois intellectuals' note 246, *CW,* vol. 42, p. 547.

643. 'The work of Proletcult' Decree of Central Committee, 10 November 1920, *CW,* vol. 42, p. 226.

643. 'The capitalist is operating by your side' quoted Hill, p. 197.

644. 'Do not forget' quoted Xenia Joukoff Eudin and Harold H. Fisher, *Soviet Russia and the West,* p. 100.

645. '[It] cried out' George F. Kennan, *Russia and the West under Lenin and Stalin,* p. 181.

645. 'It is extremely important' McCauley, p. 241.

646. 'I thank you' and 'The Congress of the Communist Party' quoted Fischer, *Life,* p. 476.

647. 'So long as we remain' quoted Carr, vol. III, p. 276.

647. 'I must say' Report on the Work of the Council of People's Commissars, 22 December 1920, *CW,* vol. 31, p. 493.

648. 'a limited opportunity of testing the theory' Birse Memorandum, p. 2, 21 January 1920, FO 371/4032/ 172292, PRO.

648. 'We have failed to restore Russia' *Hansard,* Commons, vol. 125, col. 43.

649. 'first-rate, clear headed' Lloyd George Papers, F/95/2/9, House of Lords Record Office, London.

649. 'doing what Christians call' George Lansbury, *What I Saw in Russia,* p. xv.

649. 'that of one of the saints of old' *ibid.*, p. 27.

649. 'a man after his own heart' *Hansard,* Commons, vol. 139, col. 2511.

649. 'L.G. said that Lenin' *Lord Riddell's Intimate Diary of the Peace Conference and After, 1918–1923,* p. 198.

651. 'The Allies now understand' *ibid.*, p. 161.

651. 'It is hard to see' *The World,* vol. lx, no. 21369, 22 February 1920, p. 2.

653. 'only a matter of hitting' quoted Stephen White, *Britain and the Bolshevik Revolution* (afterwards referred to as White), p. 55.

653. 'The Communistic experiment has failed' 'The Russian offer', *New Statesman,* vol. XVIII, no. 447, 5 November 1921, p. 126.

653. 'admitted the economic collapse' 'The Collapse of Russian Communism', *Spectator,* no. 4873, 19 November 1921, p. 659.

653. 'ousted from a potential market' 'Trade with Russia', *Financial News,* 7 November 1923, p. 5.

654. 'because the industrialists' Radek, quoted White, p. 171.

654. 'opening an opportunity' quoted Evgeny Chossudovsky, 'Genoa Revisited: Russia and Coexistence' (afterwards referred to as Chossudovsky), p. 561.

654. 'A united effort' Cmd. 1621 (1922) no. 441, p. 2.

655. 'First he wanted to meet Lloyd George' Litvinov, p. 43.

655. 'We are going to it' and 'simple nonsense' quoted Carr, vol. III, p. 360.

655. 'If it is true' Cmd. 1637 (1922) no. 459, p. 3.

656. 'All members of the delegation' *CW,* vol. 42, p. 390.

656. 'the Russian delegation has come here' quoted Chossudovsky, p. 556.

788

656. 'our main object' *CW*, vol. 42, p. 392.

656. 'Everything possible' draft decision for the Central Committee on the Tasks of the Soviet Delegation at Genoa, 24 February 1922, *CW*, vol. 42, p. 403.

658. 'Very Napoleonic impression' quoted Ronald W. Clark, *The Life of Bertrand Russell*, p. 377.

658. 'His room is very bare' *ibid.*, p. 378.

661. 'A good man' quoted Ransome, p. 78.

661. 'He may be a clown' and 'Then he has more industry' *ibid.*

661. 'passive objection to Marx' and 'he almost persuaded me' H. G. Wells, *Russia in the Shadows*, pp. 69 and 136.

662. 'It depends on small-scale production' *CW*, vol. 31, p. 516.

663. 'We must see to it that every factory' *ibid.*, p. 518.

663. 'The age of steam' *CW*, vol. 30, p. 334.

663. 'The electrification plan' Lenin to Sklyansky, 30 May 1921, *Trotsky Papers*, vol. II, p. 461.

663. 'this small volume' *CW*, vol. 31, p. 514.

664. 'of rehabilitating the national economy' *CW*, vol. 31, p. 419.

664. 'This is an enormous task' *ibid.*, p. 420.

664. 'We mean to electrify' and 'Electrification is to my mind' *The World*, vol. lx, no. 21369, New York, 22 February 1920, p. 2.

665. 'We must see to it that every village schoolteacher' *CW*, vol. 33, p. 246.

666. 'The following should be added' *CW*, vol. 42, p. 281.

666. 'Gleb Maximilianovich! This idea' Hill and Mudie, p. 469.

667. 'You are expected to carry out' quoted Rigby, p. 269.

668. 'I earnestly request you' *CW*, vol. 44, p. 156.

668. 'This business must be organized' *CW*, vol. 45, p. 74.

669. 'Although the period of armed conflict' quoted Levytsky, p. 46.

670. '*expose the falsehood of religion*' *CW,* vol. 45, p. 119.

671. 'With all the Communist phraseology' Farbman, p. 295.

671. 'The economy of 18½ million' quoted Farbman, p. 292.

672. 'We have begun' *CW,* vol. 33, p. 441.

18 Death, Succession and the Legacy

675. 'Lenin himself was considered' Trotsky, *My Life*, p. 401.

676. 'a silly whimpering old woman' Lenin to Tsyurupa, 15 April 1921, *CW,* vol. 45, p. 123.

676. 'You deserve a beating' *CW,* vol. 45, p. 141.

676. 'I *hope* to be free' and 'Yesterday, Council of Defence decided' Fotieva, pp. 82 and 80.

678. 'I am so tired' *CW,* vol. 45, p. 249.

678. 'ill' quoted Weber, p. 185.

678. 'I am going away today' quoted Vernadsky, p. 297.

679. 'I shall try to see you personally' quoted Weber, p. 188.

679. 'Regarding the nervous system' quoted Tumarkin, p. 112.

680. 'Vladimir Ilyich's final illness' quoted Weber, p. 190.

680. 'The tendency to fatigue would increase' quoted Vernadsky, p. 302.

681. 'summoned Stalin and addressed to him' Trotsky, *Diary*, p. 44.

681. 'He was calculating that Lenin' *ibid.,* p. 43.

682. 'I used to see [Krupskaya]' Liberman, p. 12.

682. 'I may not read a newspaper' quoted Weber, p. 190.

682. 'This time I found Comrade Lenin' quoted Weber, p. 191.

682. 'the first time since my long illness' *CW,* vol. 33, p. 370.

682. 'I am not working' quoted Weber, p. 191.

683. 'Those who were seeing him' Alfred Rosmer, *Moscou sous Lénine*, p. 231.

684. 'For the first time' Walter Duranty, I *Write As I Please* (afterwards referred to as Duranty), p. 178.

684. 'While Nicholas Krylenko' Louis Fischer, *Men and Politics,* p. 56.

685. 'This massive tome': *CW,* vol. 33, p. 344.

686. 'I think that from the standpoint' *CW,* vol. 33, p. 360.

686. 'I declare war to the death' *CW,* vol. 33, p. 372.

686. 'Doctors came at 11' *CW,* vol. 42, p. 478.

686. 'had great difficulty' quoted note 492, *CW,* vol. **42**, p. 608.

687. 'no wish to go to Gorki' *CW,* vol. 42, p. 481.

688. 'He used to say that he was accustomed' Fotieva, p. 170.

689. 'We have begun to build up a system' *CW,* vol. 33, p. 376.

690. 'without a single shot' *CW,* vol. 45, p. 606.

690. 'unworthy abuse and threats' Krupskaya to Kamenev, 23 December 1922, quoted Moshe Lewin, *Lenin's Last Struggle* (afterwards referred to as Lewin), P. 153.

690. 'Lev Borisovich! Stalin subjected me' *ibid.,* p. 152.

690. 'I have no doubt as to the unanimous decision' *ibid.,* p. 153.

691. 'In the course of 4 minutes' *CW,* vol. 42, p. 481.

691. 'Comrade Stalin, having become Secretary-General' *CW,* vol. 36, p. 594–5.

693. 'was *strictly* confidential' *CW,* vol. 42, p. 482.

693. 'All the articles and documents' note 597, *CW,* vol. 42, p. 619.

694. 'Stalin is too rude' *CW,* vol. 36, p. 596.

694. 'I had not seen [Lenin]' *CW,* vol. 42, p. 486.

694. 'I was seeing [Lenin] for the first time' *CW,* vol. 42, p. 489.

695. 'Foerster the day before had said' diary entry by L. A. Fotiyeva, *CW,* vol. 42, p. 492.

695. 'The Congress categorically affirms that the monopoly' note 154, *CW,* vol. 33, P. 536.

696. 'The Rabkrin would have had to be' Deutscher, *Stalin*, p. 231.

696. 'Let us say frankly' *CW,* vol. 33, p. 490.

699. 'At the request of the Georgian working people' note 58, *CW*, vol. 45, p. 623.

699. 'I am, it seems, strongly to blame'. 'On the Question of the Nationalities or Autonomization', 30 December 1922, *Trotsky Papers*, vol. II, p. 801.

700. 'He [Lenin] had been dissatisfied' Fotieva, p. 175.

700. 'Just before I fell ill' quoted Fotieva, p. 180.

700. 'the data on the "Georgian question"' quoted Fotieva, p. 181.

700. 'he would fight for the data' Fotieva, p. 181.

701. 'nationalized Russians from the assault'. 'On the Question of the Nationalities or Autonomization', 30 December 1922, *Trotsky Papers*, vol. II, p. 803.

701. 'You have been so rude' *CW,* vol. 45, p. 607.

702. 'Esteemed Comrade Trotsky, I urgently request you' *The Suppressed Testament of Lenin* (afterwards referred to as *Suppressed)*, p. 36.

702. 'To Comrades Mdivsni, Makharadze and others' quoted Levytsky, p. 58.

703. 'The most important thing' quoted Weber, p. 197.

703. 'sitting in his wheelchair' quoted *ibid.*

704. 'Lenin would summon me' quoted Boris I. Nikolaevsky, *Power and the Soviet Elite*, p. 12.

704. 'In this connection' Nikolaevsky, *ibid.*

705. 'rays of hope are already visible' Mikhail Kalinin at the Eleventh Congress of Soviets, 22 January 1924, quoted Tumarkin, p. 133.

705. 'The next story we came to' quoted Weber, p. 198.

705. 'Lenin was evidently in good spirits' quoted Duranty, p. 218.

706. 'I bring you terrible news' *ibid.*, p. 205.

706. 'The emotional Slav temperament' Duranty, p. 220.

708. 'When two steps down from the platform' *ibid.*

708. 'In the central hall' *ibid.*, p. 221.

709. 'The funeral will be on Saturday' Trotsky, *My Life*, p. 433.

710. 'Massed bands played the *Internationale*' Duranty, p. 224.

711. 'was less an actual substitute for religion' Tumarkin, p. 197.

712. 'Comrades, workers and peasants!' quoted *ibid, p.* 177.

713. 'decided to take measures' *ibid., p.* 185.

713. 'In the end, that wins out' quoted Levin, p. 258.

713. 'Vladimir Lenin died' *ibid.*

714. 'The new text seems to be' *ibid.*

714. 'My aim is [there] to give as little play' quoted Michael Scammell, *Solzhenitsyn: A Biography* (afterwards referred to as Scammell), p. 943.

714. 'aim was to demystify' Scammell, p. 944.

714. 'a form of creative research' A. Solzhenitsyn, 'The Book Programme', BBC TV, 27 April 1976, quoted *ibid.*, p. 942.

715. 'created the first and greatest totalitarianism' *ibid., p.* 945.

716. 'In Tadjik and Kazakh legend' quoted Hill, p. 214.

717. 'So far as I can restore the picture' Trotsky, 'On Lenin's Testament', *Suppressed, p. 12.*

717. 'The leaders of the delegations', 'Now they won't dare' and 'On the contrary' *ibid., p.* 17.

718. 'Terrible embarrassment paralysed all those' quoted Deutscher, *Stalin, p.* 272.

718. 'Comrades, every word of Ilyich' quoted *ibid.*

719. 'To continue to keep the coffin' quoted Levytsky, p. 272.

723. 'Mr Attlee's appearance' Kenneth Harris, *Attlee, p.* 427.

Bibliography

Any biographer of Lenin is in danger of being overwhelmed by the extraordinary amount of raw material available. Lenin's own published writings, which fill more than forty thick volumes, in various translations, are available with detailed exegesis and notes, and are supplememed by the complementary volumes in Russian of *Leninsky Sbornik* containing further letters as well as miscellaneous telegrams, notebooks and messages. The writings of Trotsky who at times played such a vital role in Lenin's activities, have also been published at great length, as have the reminiscences of Lenin's wife, Krupskaya. A-bublication in the 1980s listed no less than 3,000 English-language items ooving specialist aspects of Lenin's activities, and the more obscure Russian journals have been persistently trawled by those – predominantly American-who have ridden their hobby-horses through the controversies of the times. As Roy Medvedev, one of the more respected of contemporary Russian historians, has said in his Preface to *The October Revolution,* no author writing on the problems of 1917 and 1918 need focus on the gathering of previously unknown facts. Almost every surviving participant in the Revolution and the civil war has left memoirs, and extensive collections of documents continue to be published.

British, American and French parliamentary and diplomatic archives as well as the personal reminiscences of the main non-Russian actors in the international drama of the Revolution, have all added their poundage to the material available, as has the release of more German archives following the end of the Second World War. Even so, unexploited papers, such as those of Sir Esmé Howard (later Lord Howard of Penrith), British representative in Stockholm throughout the First World War, and the man who might have changed history by preventing Lenin's return to Russia in 1917, still exist in various archives.

Much of the material written following Lenin's death is unadorned hagiography, and its evaluation has not been made easier by the rise of Stalin during the 1920s and the attempted rewriting of Russian history to which the record has been subjected. As Medvedev has pointed out, in the Soviet Union 'shameless and crude falsification of history and the suppression of many extremely important historical facts exist side by side with an agonizing search for the truth . . .'

In the published records Lenin's charismatic personality, one of the most important keys to his success, almost inevitably tended to be swamped by his political victories; it is this imbalance which I have, with the help of the material listed below, tried to correct in the pages of this biography.

RWC

9 March 1987

About Lenin. See Hanna, the late George (ed.)

Akhapkin, Yuri (ed.). *First Decrees of Soviet Power*, London, Lawrence & Wishart, 1970

Alexinsky, Grégoire. *Du Tsarisme au Communisme. La Révolution Russe ses Causes et ses Effets*, Paris, Librairie Armand Colin, 1923

Andics, Hellmut. *Rule of Terror,* translated by Alexander Lieven, London, Constable, 1969

Askew, William C. 'An American Review of Bloody Sunday', *The Russian Review,* vol. 11, no. 1 (January 1952), pp. 35–43

Balabanoff, Angelica. *Erinnerungen und Erlebnisse,* Berlin W30, E. Laubsche Verlagsbuchhandlung, 1927

—*Impressions of Lenin,* translated by Isotta Cesari, Ann Arbor, University of Michigan Press, 1964

—*My Life as a Rebel,* London, Hamish Hamilton, 1938

Baranov, I. (ed.). *The Ulyanov Family,* translated from the Russian, Moscowy Progress Publishers, 1968

Barfield, Rodney. 'Lenin's. Utopianism: State and Revolution' 'Slavic Review vol 30 no. 1 (March 1971), pp. 45–6

Baron, Samuel H. *Plekhanov, the Father of Russian Marxism,* stanford, California, Stanford University Press; London, Routledge & Kegan Paul 1963

Bradley, J. F. N. *Civil War in Russia 1917-*London. B. T. Batsford, 1975

Brogan, Hugh. *The Life of Arthur Ransome,* London, Jonathan Cape, 1984

Brooks, Jeffrey. *When Russia Learned to Read: Literacy and Popular Literature,* 1861–1917, Princeton, New Jersey, Princeton University Press, 1985

Browder, Robert Paul and Kerensky, Alexander F. (eds.). *The Russian Provisional Government* 1917. *Documents,* 3 vols., Stanford, California, Stanford University Press, 1961

Buchanan, The Right Hon. Sir George, GCB, GCMG,GCVO. *My Mission to Russia and Other Diplomatic Memories,* 2 vols., London, New York, Toronto and Melbourne, Cassell, 1923

Bullitt, Orville H. (ed.). *For the President: Personal and Secret. Correspondence Between Franklin D. Roosevelt and William C. Bullitt,* London, André Deutsch, 1973

Bullitt, William C. *The Bullitt Mission to Russia. Testimony before the Committee on Foreign Relations United States Senate of William C. Bullitt,* New York, B. W. Huebsch, 1919

Bunyan, James. *Intervention, Civil War, and Communism in Russia, April-December 1918. Documents and Materials,* (the Walter Hines Page School of International Relations, the Johns Hopkins University), Baltimore, The Johns Hopkins Press; London, Humphrey Milford, Oxford University Press, 1936

Bunyan, James and Fisher, H. H. *The Bolshevik Revolution, 1917–1918. Documents and Materials,* Stanford, California, Stanford University Press, 1965

Butson, Thos. G. *The Tsar's Lieutenant: The Soviet Marshal,* New York, Praeger, 1984

Bykov, P. M. *The Last Days of Tsardom,* translated, with an Historical Preface, by Andrew Rothstein, London, Martin Lawrence, 1934

Calder, Robert Lorin. *W. Somerset Maugham & The Quest for Freedom,* London, William Heinemann, 1972

Callwell, Major-General Sir C. E. *Field-Marshal Sir Henry Wilson, Bart., GCB, DSO, His Life and Diaries,* with a Preface by Marshal Foch, 2 vols., London, Toronto, Melbourne, and Sydney, Cassell, 1927

Carmichael, Joel. 'German Money & Bolshevik Honour', *Encounter,* vol. 42 (1974), pp. 81–90.

Carr, Edward Hallett. *The Bolshevik Revolution, 1917–1923,* 3 vols., London, Macmillan, 1953

—*The Russian Revolution from Lenin to Stalin, 1917–1929,* London, Macmillan, 1979

Carswell, John. *The Exile. A Life of Ivy Litvinov,* London, Faber and Faber, 1983

Chamberlin, William Henry. *The Russian Revolution, 1917–1921,* 2 vols., London, Macmillan, 1935

Chernov, Viktor. *The Great Russian Revolution,* translated and abridged by Philip E. Mosely, Newhaven, Yale University Press, 1936

–Lenin: A Contemporary Portrait', *Foreign Affairs,* vol. 48, no. 3 (April 1970), pp. 471–7

Chossudovsky, Evgeny. 'Genoa Revisited: Russia and Coexistence', *Foreign Affairs,* vol. 50, no. 3 (April 1972), pp. 554–77

Churchill, The Rt. Hon. Winston S., CH, MP. *The World Crisis: The Aftermath,* London, Thornton Butterworth, 1929

Clark, Ronald W. *The Life of Bertrand Russell,* London, Jonathan Cape and Weidenfeld & Nicolson, 1975

Coates, W. P. and Coates, Zelda K. *Armed Intervention in Russia, 1918–1922,* London, Victor Gollancz, 1935

Cohen, Stephen F. *Bukharin and the Bolshevik Revolution. A Political Biography, 1888–1938,* London, Wildwood House, 1974

Conquest, Robert. *The Great Terror: Stalin's Purge of the Thirties,* London, Macmillan, 1968

Cowden, Morton H. *Russian Bolshevism and British Labor, 1917–1921,* Boulder, East European Monographs; New York, Columbia University Press, 1984

Crankshaw, Edward. *The Shadow of the Winter Palace: The Drift to Revolution, 1825–1917,* London, Macmillan, 1976

Cruttwell, C. R. M. F. *A History of the Great War, 1914–1918,* Oxford, Clarendon Press, 1934

Cumming, C. K. and Pettit, Walter W. (eds.). *Russian-American Relations, March, 1917-March, 1920. Documents and Papers,* New York, Harcourt, Brace and Howe, 1920

Czemin, Count Ottaker. *In the World War,* London, New York, Toronto and Melbourne, Cassell, 1919

Daniels, Robert Vincent. *The Conscience of the Revolution. Communist*

Opposition in Soviet Russia, Cambridge, Massachusetts, Harvard University Press; London, Oxford University Press, 1960

Dennis, Alfred L. P. *The Foreign Policies of Soviet Russia,* London, J. M. Dent, 1924

Deutscher, Isaac. *Lenin's Childhood,* London, New York, Toronto, Oxford University Press, 1970

—*Stalin. A Political Biography,* London, New York, Toronto, Geoffrey Cumberlege, Oxford University Press, 1949

Deutscher, Tamara (ed.). *Not By Politics Alone . . . – the other Lenin,* edited and introduced by Tamara Deutscher, London, Allen & Unwin, 1973

Documents on British Foreign Policy, 1919–1969, see Woodward, E. L. and Butler, Rohan (eds.)

Donath, Friedrich. *Auf Lenins Spuren in Deutschland,* unter Mitarbeit von Jutta Frommelt und Rolf Gelve, Berlin, VEB Deutscher Verlag der Wissenschaften, 1970

Dukes, Paul. *A History of Russia Medieval, Modern, Contemporary,* London, Macmillan, 1974

Duranty, Walter. I *Write As I Please,* New York, Simon & Schuster, 1935

Eastman, Max. *Artists in Uniform. A Study of Literature and Bureaucratism,* London, Allen & Unwin, 1934

Edwards, Paul (ed.). *The Encyclopedia of Philosophy,* 8 vols., New York, Macmillan Publishing Co., Inc.; London, Collier Macmillan, 1967

Erenburg, Ilya Gregorevich. *People and Life: Memoirs of 1891– 1917,* vol. 1 of *Men, years – life,* 6-part memoirs, translated by Anna Bostock and Yvonne Kapp, London, MacGibbon and Kee, 1961

Eudin, Xenia Joukoff and Fisher, Harold H. *Soviet Russia and the West,* 1920–1027. *A Documentary Survey,* Stanford, California,

Stanford University Press, 1957

Farbman, Michael S. *Bolshevism in Retreat,* London, Glasgow, Melbourne, Auckland, Collins, 1923

Farnsworth, Beatrice. *William C. Bullitt and the Soviet Union,* Bloomington and London, Indiana University Press, 1967

Fischer, Fritz. *Germany's Aims in the First World War,* London, Chatto & Windus, 1967

Fischer, Louis. *The Life of Lenin,* London, Weidenfeld and Nicolson, 1965

—*Men and Politics. An Autobiography,* London, Jonathan Cape, 1941

—*The Soviets in World Affairs. A History of Relations Between the Soviet Union and the Rest of the World,* 2 vols., London, Jonathan Cape, 1930

Fitzpatrick, Sheila. *The Commissariat of Enlightenment: Soviet Organization of Education and the Arts under Lunacharsky, October, 1917–1921,* Cambridge, Cambridge University Press, 1970

Fotieva, L[ydia]. *Pages from Lenin's Life,* translated from the Russian by Olga Shartse, Moscow, Foreign Languages Publishing House, 1960

Fox, Ralph. *Lenin: A Biography,* London, Victor Gollancz, 1933

Francis, David R[owland]. *Russia from the American Embassy (April, 1916-November, 1918),* New York, Charles Scribner's Sons, 1921

Frankel, Jonathan. 'Martov and Lenin', *Survey: A Journal of Soviet and East European Studies,* no. 70/71, (Winter/Spring 1969), pp. 202–6

Fréville, Jean. *Lénine à Paris,* Paris, Editions Sociales, 1968

Futrell, Michael. 'Alexander Keskuela', *St Antony's Papers,* no. 12, Soviet Affairs no. 3, pp. 23–52, edited by David Footman, London, Chatto & Windus, 1962

—*Northern Underground. Episodes of Russian Revolutionary Transport and Communications through Scandinavia and Finland, 1863–1917,* London, Faber and Faber, 1963

Gapon, Father George. *The Story of My Life,* London, Chapman & Hall, 1905

Gautschi, Willi. *Lenin als Emigrant in der Schweiz,* Zurich, Köln, Benziger Verlag, 1973

George, David Lloyd. *War Memoirs,* 6 vols., London, Ivor Nicholson & Watson, 1933–36

Getzler, Israel. *Martov: A Political Biography of a Russian Social Democrat,* Cambridge, Cambridge University Press, 1967

Goldman, Emma. *Living My Life,* 2 vols., London, Duckworth, 1932

Gollin, A. M. *Proconsul in Politics: A study of Lord Milner in Opposition and in Power,* London, Anthony Blond, 1964

Gorky, Maxim. *Days With Lenin,* London, Martin Lawrence, 1932

—'The Letters of Maksim Gorikij to V. F. Xodasevič', see McLean, Hugh (ed.) Grey, Ian. *The First Fifty Years. Soviet Russia, 1917–67,* London, Hodder and Stoughton, 1967

Haimson, Leopold H[enri]. *The Russian Marxists & The Origins of Bolshevism,* Cambridge, Massachusetts, Harvard University Press, 1955

Hanna, the late George (ed.). *About Lenin,* translated from the Russian by J. Guralsky and O. Shartse, second enlarged edition, Moscow, Progress Publishers, 1969

Hard, William. *Raymond Robins' Own Story,* New York, Harper, 1920

Hardach, Gerd. *The First World War, 1914–1918,* London, Allen Lane, 1977

Hare, Richard. *Maxim Gorky: Romantic Realist and Conservative*

Revolutionary, London, New York, Toronto, Oxford University Press, 1962

Harris, Kenneth. *Attlee,* London, Weidenfeld and Nicolson, 1982

Haupt, Georges and Marie, Jean-Jacques. *Makers of the Russian Revolution: Biographies of Bolshevik leaders,* translated from the Russian by C. I. P. Ferdinand, commentaries translated from the French by D. M. Bellos, London, Allen & Unwin, 1974

Heller, Michael. 'Lenin and the Cheka: the Real Lenin', *Survey. A Journal of East & West Studies,* vol. 24, no. 2 (107) (Spring 1979), pp. 175–92

Hill, Christopher. *Lenin and the Russian Revolution,* London, Hodder and Stoughton, 1947

Hill, Capt. George A., DSO. GO *Spy the Land, Being the Adventures of I.K.8. of the British Secret Service,* London, Cassell, 1932

Hill, Elizabeth and Mudie, Doris (eds.). *The Letters of Lenin,* translated and edited by Elizabeth Hill and Doris Mudie, London, Chapman and Hall, 1937

Hindenburg, Marshal von. *Out of My Life,* translated by F. A. Holt, London, New York, Toronto and Melbourne, Cassell, 1920

Hingley, Ronald. *Russian Revolution,* London, The Bodley Head, 1970

Hoffmann, General Max. *Der Krieg der versäumten Gelegenheiten,* München, Verlag für Kulturpolitik, 1924

— Major-General Max: *War Diaries and Other Papers,* translated from the German by Eric Sutton, 2 vols., London, Martin Secker, 1929

Hollis, Christopher. *Lenin. Portrait of a Professional Revolutionary,* London, New York, Toronto, Longmans, Green, 1938

House, Colonel Edward Mandell. *The Intimate Papers of Colonel House,* see Seymour, Charles

Howard of Penrith, Lord. *Theatre of Life,* 2 vols., London, Hodder and Stoughton, 1935 and 1936

Huskey, Eugene. *Russian Lawyers and the Soviet State: The Origins and Development of the Soviet Bar, 1917–1939,* Princeton, New Jersey, Princeton University Press, 1986

Israel, Gérard. *The Jews in Russia,* translated by Sanford L. Chernoff, London and Tonbridge, Charles Knight, 1975

Kamenev, L. B. *Lenins literarisches Erbe,* Hamburg 8, Verlag Carl Hoym Machf. Louis Cahnbley, 1924

Katkov, George. 'The Assassination of Count Mirbach', *St Antony's Papers,* no. 12, Soviet Affairs no. 3, (1962), pp. 53–93

—German Foreign Office Documents on Financial Support to the Bolsheviks in 1917', *International Affairs,* vol. 32, no. 2 (April 1956), pp. 181–9

—The Kronstadt Rising', *St Antony's Papers,* no. 6, Soviet Affairs no. 2, (1959), pp. 9–74

—*Russia 1917: The February Revolution,* London, Longmans, Green, 1967

Katkov, George and Shukman, Harold. *Lenin's Path to Power: Bolshevism and the Destiny of Russia,* London, Macdonald; New York, American Heritage Press, 1971

Kaun, Alexander. *Maxim Gorki and his Russia,* London, Jonathan Cape, 1932

Kenetskaya, L. *Lenin in the Kremlin. His apartment and study. The people he met. The books he read,* Moscow, Novosti Press Agency Publishing House, n.d.

Kennan, George F. *Russia and the West under Lenin and Stalin,* London, Hutchinson, 1961

—'The Sisson Documents', *The Journal of Modern History,* vol. 28, no. 2 (June 1956), pp. 130–54

—Soviet-American Relations, 1917–1920, 2 vols., London, Faber and Faber, 1958

Kerensky, Alexander F. *The Catastrophe. Kerensky's Own Story of the Russian Revolution*, New York, London, D. Appleton and Company, 1927

—*The Kerensky Memoirs: Russia and History's Turning Point*, London, Cassell, 1966

Kettle, Michael. *The Allies and the Russian Collapse, March 1917-March 1918*, London, André Deutsch, 1918

Kline, George L. 'Alexander Aleksandrovich Bogdanov', *The Encyclopedia of Philosophy*, vol. I, p. 331

Kollontay, Alexandra. *The Workers' Opposition in Russia*, London, Dreadnought, 1923

Knox, Major-General Sir Alfred, KCB, CMG. *With the Russian Army, 1914–1917. Being chiefly extracts from the Diary of a Military Attaché, 2* vols., London, Hutchinson, 1921

Krasin, Prof. Y. A. (ed.). *Lenin: His Life and Work. Documents and Photographs*, Moscow, Progress Publishers, 1985

Krassin, Lubov. *Leonid Krassin: His Life and Work, by his wife*, London, Skeffington, 1929

Krupskaya, Nadezhda K. *How Lenin studied Marx*, London, Labour Monthly Pamphlets no. 2, published at 7 John Street, Theobald's Road, London WCI, 1934

—*Memories of Lenin*, translated by E. Verney, 2 vols., London, Martin Lawrence, 1930

—*Reminiscences of Lenin*, Moscow, Foreign Languages Publishing House, 1959; London, Lawrence and Wishart, 1960

Lansbury, George. *What I Saw in Russia*, London, Leonard Parsons, 1920

Lansing, Robert. *War Memoirs of Robert Lansing, Secretary of State*, Indianapolis and New York, The Bobbs-Merrill Company, 1935

Leggett, George H. 'Lenin, Terror, and the Political Police', *Survey. A Journal of East & West Studies*, vol. 21, no. 4 (97)

(Autumn 1975), pp. 157–87

—'Lenin's Reported Destruction of the Cheka Archive', *Survey. A Journal of East & West Studies*, vol. 24, no. 2 (107) (Spring 1979), pp. 193–9.

Lenin. Comrade and Man, translated from the Russian, Moscow, Progress Publishers, n.d.

Lenin Through the Eyes of Lunacharsky, Moscow, Novosti Press Agency Publishing House, 1981

Lenin, Vladimir Ilyich.

The bulk of Lenin's voluminous writings, ranging in length and importance from the few paragraphs of items in *Pravda* to long polemical pamphlets and extensive letters dealing with both personal affairs and Party policy are published in a 47-volume English edition of *Collected Works,* a translation of the fourth enlarged Russian edition prepared by the Institute of Marxism-Leninism, Moscow:

V. I. Lenin, Collected Works, 47 vols., Moscow, Foreign Languages Publishing House, 1960–63, and Progress Publishers, 1964–80, with additional title leaves bearing the imprint 'Lawrence & Wishart, London' inserted in each volume

An earlier English edition, translated from material in the 2nd /3rd Russian editions, is:

The *Collected Works of V. I. Lenin,* 7 vols., numbered IV; XIII; XVIII-XXI; XXIII, London, Martin Lawrence, 1930, 1927–46

A three-volume selection of Lenin's writings contains *What Is To Be Done?; Imperialism, the Highest Stage of Capitalism', The State and Revolution; One Step Forward, Two Steps Back; The Tasks of the Proletariat in our Revolution* and speeches at various Party congresses. A one-volume selection contains, among other works, *Two Tactics of Social Democracy in the Democratic Revolution* and *The Socialist Revolution and the Right of Nations to Self-Determination*

Lenin's other writings available in English include: *Materialism and Empirio-Criticism; On Britain; On the Dictatorship of the Proletariat; On Literature and Art; On the Paris Commune; On Trade Unions; The Development of Capitalism in Russia;* and *Lenin's Economic Writings.*

For a selection of his letters, see Hill, Elizabeth and Mudie, Doris (eds.), *The Letters of Lenin.*

Lenin's 'Testament' is in *Collected Works* and also in *The Suppressed Testament of Lenin,* the complete original text, with two explanatory articles by Leon Trotsky (New York, Pioneer Publishers, n.d. but Introduction signed 'M.S.' is dated February 5, 1935, New York).

Levin, Dan. *Stormy Petrel: The Life and Work of Maxim Gorky,* London, Frederick Muller, 1967

Levytsky, Boris. *The Uses of Terror: The Soviet Secret Service 1917–1970,* translated by H. A. Piehler, London, Sidgwick & Jackson, 1971

Lewin, Moshe. *Lenin's Last Struggle,* translated from the French by A. M. Sheridan Smith, London, Faber and Faber, 1969

Ley, J. 'A Memorable Day in April', *New Statesman,* vol. LV, no. 1414 (19 April 1958), pp. 496–8.

Liberman, Simon. *Building Lenin's Russia,* Chicago, University of Chicago Press, 1945

Lindström, Ludwig. 'På Flykt med Vladimir Uljanov, mera bekant som Lenin', *Allsvensk Samling* (Gothenburg), (December 1946), pp. 14–16 and 44–8

Link, Arthur S. (ed.) *et al. The Papers of Woodrow Wilson,* 57 vols., Princeton, New Jersey, Princeton University Press, 1966–87

Litvinov, Maxim. *Notes for a Journal,* Introduction by E. H. Carr,

London, André Deutsch, 1955

Lockhart, R. H. Bruce. *Memoirs of a British Agent. Being an account of the Author's early life in many lands and of his official mission to Moscow in 1918,* London and New York, Putnam, 1932

—*My Scottish Youth,* London, Putnam, 1937

Lockhart, Sir Robert Bruce. 'The Unanimous Revolution. Russia, February 1917', *Foreign Affairs,* vol. 35, no. 2 (Jan. 1957), pp. 320–33

—*The Diaries of Sir Robert Bruce Lockhart,* edited by Kenneth Young, 2 vols., London, Macmillan, 1973

Ludendorff, Erich. *Meine Kriegserinnerungen 1914–1918,* Berlin, Ernst Siegfried Mittler und Sohn Verlagsbuchhandlung, 1919

Lunacharskii, Anatolii. *The Politics of Soviet Culture,* translated by Timothy Edward O'Connor, Ann Arbor, Michigan, UMI Research Press, 1983

Lunacharsky, Anatoly Vasilievich. *Revolutionary Silhouettes,* translated from the Russian and edited by Michael Glenny, with an Introduction by Isaac Deutscher, London, Allen Lane, The Penguin Press, 1967

MacDonald, J. Ramsay. *Parliament and Revolution,* Manchester, National Labour Press, 1919

McCauley, Martin (ed.). *The Russian Revolution and the Soviet State, 1917–1921. Documents,* selected and edited by Martin McCauley in association with the School of Slavonic and East European Studies, University of London, London and Basingstoke, Macmillan, 1975

McLean, Hugh (ed.). 'The Letters of Maksim Gorikij to V. F. Xodasevič, 1922–1925', with notes by V. F. Xodasevič and an Introduction by Sergius Yakobson, translated and edited by Hugh McLean, *Harvard Slavic Studies,* vol. I (1953), pp. 279–334

McNeal, Robert H. *Bride of the Revolution: Krupskaya and Lenin,*

London, Victor Gollancz, 1973

Magnes, Judah L. *Russia and Germany at Brest-Litovsk. A Documentary History of the Peace Negotiations,* New York, Rand School of Social Science, 1919

Marquand, David. *Ramsay MacDonald,* London, Jonathan Cape, 1977

Maugham, W. Somerset. *The Summing Up,* London, Toronto, William Heinemann, 1938

Mavor, James. *The Russian Revolution,* London, Allen & Unwin, 1928

Max of Baden, Prince. *The Memoirs of Prince Max of Baden,* authorized translation by W. M. Calder and C. W. H. Sutton, 2 vols., London, Constable, 1928

Maxton, James. *Lenin,* Edinburgh, University Press, 1932

Medvedev, Roy. *Let History Judge,* London, Macmillan, 1971

—*The October Revolution,* translated by George Saunders, Foreword by Harrison E. Salisbury, London, Constable 1979; New York, Columbia University Press, 1979

Mee, Charles L., Jr. *The End of Order, Versailles, 1919,* London, Secker & Warburg, 1981

Meijer, Jan M. (ed.). *The Trotsky Papers, 1917–1922* (edited and annotated by Jan M. Meijer), 2 vols., London, The Hague, Paris, Mouton, 1964 and 1971

Miliukov, Paul N. *The Russian Revolution,* 2 vols., vol. I edited by Richard Stites, translated by Tatyana and Richard Stites, vol. II edited, translated and with an Introduction by G. M. Hamburg, Gulf Breeze, Florida, Academic International Press, 1978 and 1984

Mirsky, D. S. *Lenin,* London, The Holme Press, 1931

Mohrenschildt, Dimitri von (ed.). *The Russian Revolution of 1917: Contemporary accounts,* New York, London, Toronto, Oxford University Press, 1971

Moorehead, Alan. *The Russian Revolution,* London, Collins with Hamish Hamilton, 1958

Morgan, M. C. *Lenin,* London, Edward Arnold, 1971

Muravyova, L. and Sivolap-Kaftanova, I. *Lenin in London,* Moscow, Progress Publishers, 1983

Nettl, J. P. *Rosa Luxemburg, 2* vols., London, New York, Toronto, Oxford University Press, 1966

Nicolson, Harold. *Peacemaking 1919,* London, Constable, 1945

Nikolaevsky, Boris I. *Power and the Soviet Elite,* edited by Janet D. Zagoria, New York, Washington, Hoover Institution on War, Revolution and Peace; London, Frederick A. Praeger, 1965

Noulens, Joseph. *Mon Ambassade en Russe Soviétique 1917–1919, 2* vols., Paris, Librairie Plon, 1933

Paléologue, Maurice. *An Ambassador's Memoirs,* translated by F. A. Holt, OBE, 3 vols., London, Hutchinson, 1923, 1924 and 1925

Payne, Robert. *The Life and Death of Trotsky,* London, W. H. Allen, 1978

Pearson, Michael. *The Sealed Train,* London, Macmillan, 1975; New York, G. P. Putnam's Sons, 1975

Pethybridge, Roger. *The Spread of the Russian Revolution. Essays on 1917,* London, Macmillan, 1972

Pethybridge, Roger, (ed.). *Witnesses to the Russian Revolution,* London, Allen & Unwin, 1964

Pianzola, Maurice. *Lénine en Suisse,* Genève, Éditions Librairie Rousseau, 1965

Pipes, Richard. *Social Democracy and the St Petersburg Labor Movement, 1885–1897,* Cambridge, Massachusetts, Harvard University Press, 1963

—*Struve: Liberal of the Right, 1905–1944,* Cambridge, Massachusetts, Harvard University Press, 1980

Platten, Fritz. *Die Reise Lenins durch Deutschland im plombierten Wagen,* Berlin, Neuer Deutscher Verlag, 1924

Pope, Arthur Upham. *Maxim Litvinoff,* London, Martin Secker & Warburg, 1943

Porter, Cathy. *Alexandra Kollontai. A Biography,* London, Virago, 1980

Price, M. Philips. *My Reminiscences of the Russian Revolution,* London, Allen & Unwin, 1921

Rabinowitch, Alexander. *The Bolsheviks Come to Power,* London, NLB, 1979

—*Prelude to Revolution: The Petrograd Bolsheviks and the July 1917 Uprising,* Bloomington, London, Indiana University Press, 1968

Radkey, Oliver Henry. *The Election to the Russian Constituent Assembly of 1917,* Cambridge, Harvard University Press, 1950

Ransome, Arthur. *Six Weeks in Russia in 1919,* London, Allen & Unwin, 1919

Raskolnikov, F. F. *Kronstadt and Petrograd in 1917,* translated and annotated by Brian Pearce, London, New Park Publications, 1982

Reed, John. *Ten Days That Shook the World,* reprinted with an Introduction by A. J. P. Taylor, Harmondsworth, Penguin Books, 1977

Riddell, Lord. *Lord Riddell's Intimate Diary of the Peace Conference and After, 1918–1923,* London, Victor Gollancz, 1933

Rigby, T. H. *Lenin's Government: Sovnarkom 1917–1922,* Cambridge, London, New York, Melbourne, Cambridge University Press, 1979

Rosmer, Alfred. *Moscou sous Lénine. Les Origines du communisme,* Préface by Albert Camus, Paris, Pierre Horay, 1953

Rothstein, Andrew. *A House on Clerkenwell Green,* London, Lawrence & Wishart, 1966 – *Lenin in Britain,* Communist Party Pamphlet, n.d.

Sadoul, Capt. Jacques. *Notes sur la révolution bolshevique,* Paris,

Editions de la Siène, 1919

Scammell, Michael. *Solzhenitsyn: A Biography,* New York, London, W. W. Norton, 1984

Schapiro, Leonard. *The Communist Party of the Soviet Union,* second edition, London, Eyre & Spottiswoode, 1970

Schapiro, Leonard and Reddaway, Peter (eds.). *Lenin, the Man, the Theorist, the Leader. A Reappraisal,* London, Pall Mall Press, 1967

Scott, E. J. 'The Cheka', *St Antony's Papers,* nos. 1–3, Soviet Affairs no. 1 (1956), pp. 1–23.

Seaton, Albert. *Stalin as Warlord,* London, B. T. Batsford, 1976

Senn, Alfred Erich. *The Russian Revolution in Switzerland, 1914–1917,* Madison, Milwaukee and London, University of Wisconsin Press, 1971

Serge, Victor. *Memoirs of a Revolutionary, 1901–1941,* translated and edited by Peter Sedgwick, London, New York, Toronto, Oxford University Press, 1963

—*Year One of the Russian Revolution,* translated and edited by Peter Sedgwick, London, Allen Lane, The Penguin Press, 1972

Serge, Victor and Trotsky, Natalia Sedova. *The Life and Death of Leon Trotsky,* translated by Arnold J. Pomerans, London, Wildwood House, 1975

Seymour, Charles. *The Intimate Papers of Colonel House,* 4 vols., London, Ernest Benn, 1926–8

Shub, David. 'New Light on Lenin', *The Russian Review,* vol. 11, no. 3 (July 1952), pp.131–37

Shukman, Harold. *Lenin and the Russian Revolution,* London, B. T. Batsford, 1966

Sisson, Edgar. *One Hundred Red Days: A Personal Chronicle of The Bolshevik Revolution,* New Haven, Yale University Press, 1931

Snell, John L. 'Wilson on Germany and the Fourteen Points – Document', *The Journal of Modern History,* vol. XXVI, no. 4

(December 1954), pp. 364–9

Solzhenitsyn, Alexander. *Lenin in Zurich*, London, The Bodley Head, 1976

Steffens, Lincoln. *The Autobiography of Lincoln Steffens*, 2 vols., New York, Harcourt Brace, 1931

Steinberg, I. *Spiridonova: Revolutionary Terrorist*, London, Methuen, 1933

Steinberg, I. N. *In the Workshop of the Revolution*, London, Victor Gollancz, 1955

Stevenson, Adlai. 'Putting First Things First', *Foreign Affairs*, vol. 38 (October-July 1959–60), pp. 191–208

Strachey, John. 'The Great Awakening; or: From Imperialism to Freedom', *Encounter*, pamphlet No. 5 (London 1961), pp. 1–35

Struve, Peter. 'My Contacts and Conflicts with Lenin', *The Slavonic and East European Review*, vol. XII, no. 36 (April 1934), pp. 573–95

Sukhanov, N. N. *The Russian Revolution 1917. A Personal Record*, edited, abridged and translated by Joel Carmichael from *Zapiski O Revolution*, London, New York, Toronto, Geoffrey Cumberlege, Oxford University Press, 1955

Summers, Anthony and Mangold, Tom. *The File on the Tsar*, London, Victor Gollancz, 1976

Szamuely, Tibor. *The Russian Tradition*, edited and with an introduction by Robert Conquest, London, Secker & Warburg, 1974

Tait, A. L. *Lunacharsky: Poet of the Revolution. (1875–1907)*, Birmingham Slavonic Monographs no. 15, Birmingham, Department of Russian Language and Literature, University of Birmingham, n.d.

Taylor, A. J. P. *Revolutions and Revolutionaries*, London, Hamish Hamilton, 1980

Taylor, A. J. P. (ed.). *Lloyd George: A Diary by Frances Stevenson*,

London, Hutchinson of London, 1971

Theen, Rolf H. W. *Lenin,* Princeton, New Jersey, Princeton University Press, 1980

—*Lenin. Genesis and Development of a Revolutionary,* Princeton, New Jersey, Princeton University Press, 1979

They Knew Lenin. Reminiscences of Foreign Contemporaries, translated from the Russian by David Myshne, Moscow, Progress Publishers, 1968

Thompson, John M. *Russia, Bolshevism, and the Versailles Peace,* Princeton, New Jersey, Princeton University Press, 1966

Trotsky, Leo N. *Der Krieg and die Internationale,* Munich, Verlag 'Borba', n.d.

Trotsky, Leon. *The History of the Russian Revolution,* translated from the Russian by Max Eastman, 3 vols., London, Victor Gollancz, 1932–3

—*Lenin,* authorized translation, London, Calcutta, Sydney, George G. Harrap, 1925

—*On Lenin: Notes Towards a Biography,* translated and annotated by Tamara Deutscher with an introduction by Lionel Kochan, London, Toronto, Wellington, Sydney, George G. Harrap, 1971

—*The Military Writings and Speeches of Leon Trotsky: How the Revolution Armed,* 5 vols., translated and annotated by Brian Pearce, London, New Park Publications, 1979–81

—*My Life: The Rise and Fall of a Dictator,* London, Thornton Butterworth, 1930

—*The Trotsky Papers.* See Meijer, Jan M. (ed.)

—*Trotsky's Diary in Exile,* 1935, translated from the Russian by Elena Zarudnaya, London, Faber and Faber, 1959

—*The Young Lenin,* translated from the Russian by Max Eastman, edited and annotated by Maurice Friedberg, Newton Abbot,

David and Charles, 1972

Tumarkin, Nina. *Lenin Lives! The Lenin Cult in Soviet Russia*, Cambridge, Massachusetts and London, England, Harvard University Press, 1983

Ulam, Adam B. *The Bolsheviks. The Intellectual and Political History of the Triumph of Communism in Russia*, New York, the Macmillan Company; London, Collier-Macmillan Limited, 1965

—'Lenin: His Legacy', *Foreign Affairs*, vol. 48, no. 3 (April 1970), pp. 460–70

—*Russia's Failed Revolutions. From the Decembrists to the Dissidents*, London, Weidenfeld & Nicolson, 1981

—*Stalin The Man and His Era*, London, Allen Lane, 1973

Ullman, Richard H. *Anglo-Soviet Relations, 1917–1921*, 3 vols., Princeton, New Jersey, Princeton University Press; London, Oxford University Press, 1961, 1968, 1972

The Ulyanov Family. See Baranov, I. (ed.)

United States, The Department of State. *Papers Relating to the Foreign Relations of the United States: The Lansing Papers, 1914–1920*, 2 vols., Washington, US Government Printing Office, 1939–40

—*Papers Relating to the Foreign Relations of the United States: Paris Peace Conference, 1919*, 13 vols., Washington, US Government Printing Office, 1942–7

—*Papers Relating to the Foreign Relations of the United States: 1918, Russia*, 3 vols., Washington, D.C., U.S. Government Printing Office, 1931–2

Papers Relating to the Foreign Relations of the United States: 1919, Russia. Washington D.C., US Government Printing Office, 1937

Valentinov, Nikolai (N. V. Volski). *The Early Years of Lenin*, translated and edited by Rolf H. W. Theen, Introduction by Bertram D. Wolfe, Ann Arbor, The University of Michigan Press, 1969

Valentinov, Nikolay (N. V. Volsky). *Encounters with Lenin*, translated from the Russian by Paul Rosta and Brian Pearce with a Foreword by Leonard Schapiro, London, New York, Toronto, Oxford University Press, 1968

Vernadsky, George. *Lenin: Red Dictator*, translated from the Russian by Malcolm Waters Davis, New Haven, Yale University Press; London, Humphrey Milford; Oxford University Press, 1931

Vulliamy, C. E. (ed.). *The Red Archives*, Russian State Papers and other documents relating to the years 1915–18, translation by A. L. Hynes, with an Introduction by Dr C. T. Hagberg Wright, London, Geoffrey Bles, 1929

Warth, Robert D. *The Allies and the Russian Revolution: From the Fall of the Monarchy to the Peace of Brest-Litovsk*, Durham, North Carolina, Duke University Press, 1954

Weber, Gerda and Hermann. *Lenin: Life and Works*, edited and translated by Martin McCauley, London, Macmillan Chronology Series, 1980

Wells, H. G. *Russia in the Shadows*, London, Hodder and Stoughton, 1920

Wheatcroft, S. G. and Davies, R. W. (eds.). *Materials for a Balance of the Soviet National Economy 1928—1930*, Cambridge, London, New York, New Rochelle and Melbourne, Sydney, Cambridge University Press, 1985

Wheeler-Bennett, John W. *Brest-Litovsk: The Forgotten Peace, March 1918*, London, Macmillan, 1938

White, Stephen. *Britain and the Bolshevik Revolution. A Study in the Politics of Diplomacy, 1920–1924*, London and Basingstoke, Macmillan, 1979

Williams, Edward V. *The Bells of Russia: History and Technology'*, Princeton, New Jersey, Princeton University Press, 1985

Williams, Harold Whitmore, Ph.D. *Russia of the Russians,* London, Pitman, 1914

Wilson, Woodrow. *The Papers of Woodrow Wilson,* See Link, Arthur S. (ed.)

Wolfe, Bertram D. 'Krupskaya purges the People's Libraries', *Survey. A Journal of Soviet and East European Studies,* no. 72 (Summer 1969), pp. 141–55

—'Lenin and Inessa Armand', *Slavic Review. American Quarterly of Soviet and East European Studies,* vol. XXII, no. 1 (March 1963), pp. 96–114

—*Three Who Made a Revolution. A Biographical History,* Boston, Beacon Press, 1955

Wollenberg, Erich. *The Red Army,* London, Secker & Warburg, 1938

Woodward, David. *The Russians at Sea,* London, William Kimber, 1965

Woodward, E. L. and Butler, Rohan, (eds.). *Documents on British Foreign Policy, 1919–1939,* first series, vol. III, 1919. 6 vols., London, HMSO, 1947–56

Zeman, Z. A. B. *A Diplomatic History of the First World War,* London, Weidenfeld & Nicolson, 1971

—*Germany and the Revolution in Russia, 1915–1918. Documents from the Archives of the German Foreign Ministry,* London, New York, Toronto, Oxford University Press, 1958

Zeman, Z. A. B. and Scharlau, W. B. *The Merchant of Revolution: The Life of Alexander Israel Helphand (Parvus), 1867–1924,* London, New York, Toronto, Oxford University Press, 1965

Zetkin, Clara. *Reminiscences of Lenin,* London, Modern Books, 1929

Zinoviev, G. *N. Lénine (Vladimir Hitch Oulianov),* Paris, Librairie de l'Humanité, 1924

Ronald Clark was born in London in 1916 and educated at King's College School. In 1933 he chose journalism as a career; during the Second World War, after being turned down for military duty on medical grounds, he served as a war correspondent. During this time Clark landed on Juno Beach with the Canadians on D-Day and followed the war until its end, then remained in Germany to report on the major War Crimes trials.

Clark returned to Britain in 1948 and wrote extensively on subjects ranging from mountain climbing to the atomic bomb, Balmoral Castle to world explorers. He also wrote a number of biographies on a myriad of figures, such as Charles Darwin, Thomas Edison, Albert Einstein, Benjamin Franklin, Sigmund Freud, and Bertrand Russell. Clark died in 1987.